CASES AND MATERIALS ON

CRIMINAL LAW

Janet Dine, Reader in Law, University of Essex

James Gobert, Professor of Law, University of Essex

BLACKSTONE
PRESS LIMITED

First published in Great Britain 1993 by Blackstone Press Limited,
9–15 Aldine Street, London W12 8AW. Telephone 081-740 1173

© J. Dine and J. Gobert, 1993

ISBN: 1 85431 262 6

British Library Cataloguing in Publication Data
A CIP catalogue record for this book is available from the British Library

Typeset by Style Photosetting Ltd, Mayfield, East Sussex
Printed by Ashford Colour Press, Gosport, Hampshire

CONTENTS

PREFACE

This book is designed for use in a course in criminal law. It contains extracts from leading cases, statutes, and other sources, as well as numerous notes and questions. It is by no means comprehensive, as such a tome would be impractical for teaching purposes. Our goal is not only to impart substantive knowledge but also to teach the skills needed to successfully steer one's way through the landmines of the criminal law, whether one is a barrister, a solicitor, a magistrate or judge, or a legislator.

In particular we believe that a criminal law course should help students to acquire the skills of fact analysis, issue recognition, and statutory interpretation. Taking these in reverse order, most criminal law today (with a few notable exceptions) is contained in statutes. The successful lawyer needs to be able to read statutes critically, to dissect their component elements and to interpret those parts of a statute that are susceptible to more than one possible interpretation. Judges too, are constantly engaged in the task of statutory interpretation. Ambiguities are perhaps inevitable both because of the inherent indeterminacy of language and because it is impossible to envisage the myriad factual guises in which cases arise. If the facts of some of the cases in this book appear a bit bizarre, it is because these are the types of cases that raise the most difficult questions of interpretation and application, and which test the limits of the criminal law. In some instances statutory ambiguity results from Parliament's attempt to steer a middle course between excessive rigidity (which may create unwanted loopholes in the law) and unacceptable vagueness (which may not provide fair notice to the citizenry of what is expected of them).

In addition to general statutory analysis skills, the successful lawyer needs to be able to critically read and understand judicial opinions. One first must identify the issues raised by any given case. This requires a careful sifting through the facts of a case, determining which facts have legal significance and identifying what issues are raised by these facts. For this reason we have tried to include as many of the facts of each case as possible, although we have to confess that space limitations have somewhat impaired our ability to do so. Space limitations have also precluded exploration of the many fascinating questions of procedure and evidence which permeate the criminal law.

The purpose of the Notes and Questions that are liberally sprinkled throughout the book is to raise issues which lay imbedded but unarticulated within a case and to stimulate the reader's thinking about the case. We want students to question judicial assumptions, and to return to first principles. We do not want students simply to accept uncritically whatever a judge says as gospel to be memorised and regurgitated in examinations. In short, our aim is to help students to develop that critical faculty which is the hallmark of all great lawyers. The Notes and Questions are designed with this goal in mind.

A particular word should be said about Chapter 1. It goes beyond materials normally included in most criminal law casebooks and might seem more appropriate to a course in criminology. We believe, however, that an appreciation of such issues as criminalisation, grading of offences, and theories of punishment is not only important in its own right, but facilitates the development of the student's critical faculties. At its roots, criminal law raises fundamental questions about the values of a society, and the choices which a society must make between individual freedom and social control. Such choices raise issues which extend beyond the narrow confines of the criminal law, and we have attempted to integrate where appropriate relevant insights from other academic fields.

Most of the other chapters in the book address areas of substantive criminal law. We do so first through an analysis of the building blocks of a crime (*actus reus, mens rea,* etc.), often referred to as the general part of criminal law, and then through an examination of specific offences and defences, which require the student to reexamine these building blocks in context. Chapter 6 addresses the problems of criminal law in the corporate context, where traditional individualistic notions of criminality break down.

We would like to thank those who gave us permission to reprint copyrighted material. In particular, we wish to acknowledge the permissions received from Oxford University Press, Sweet and Maxwell, Butterworth's and the Incorporated Council for Law Reporting for England and Wales.

Janet Dine
James Gobert
30 September 1993

ACKNOWLEDGMENTS

The authors and publishers would like to thank the following for permission to reproduce copyright material:

Oxford University Press for extracts from N. Walker *Crime and Criminology* (1987); P. Devlin *The Enforcement of Morals* (1965); H. L. A. Hart *Law, Liberty and Morality*; and A. Ashworth *Principles of Criminal Law* (1991).

The Incorporated Council of Law Reporting for England and Wales for extracts from the following reports: King's/Queen's Bench Division, Appeal Cases and the *Weekly Law Reports*.

Butterworth & Co. for extracts from the *All England Law Reports*.

Kenneth Mason Publications for extracts from the *Road Traffic Reports*.

Sweet & Maxwell Ltd for extracts from the *Criminal Law Review* and *Criminal Appeal Reports*.

Times Newspapers Ltd for extracts from the following reports: *R* v *Kingston* (1993) *The Times*, 10 May 1993 and *R* v *Sulman* (1993) *The Times* 21 May 1993.

The Sunday Telegraph for extracts from an article entitled 'Doctor Convicted of Attempted Murder', 20 September 1992.

University of Pennsylvania Law Review for extracts from J. Andenaes 'The General Preventative Effects of Punishment' (1966).

TABLE OF CASES

Cases reported in full are shown in heavy type. The page at which the report is printed is shown in heavy type.

TABLE OF STATUTES

1 INTRODUCTION TO CRIMINAL LAW

I Criminalisation

A The criminalisation decision

We begin by examining one of the most ignored topics in criminal law – criminalisation. The tendency in most criminal law courses is to plunge directly into the substantive subject matter of the course, without ever examining how that behaviour which is classified as criminal came to occupy that status. And yet the most fundamental task in criminal law is to determine what conduct should be made criminal. From this decision all else flows.

Despite the critical nature of the criminalisation decision, relatively little attention has been paid to it. General criteria for determining what to criminalise are rarely set out formally. Often a criminal statute is precipitated by some widely publicised incident, and the statute is enacted with the aim of ensuring that in the future similar conduct will not escape penalty. Sometimes the criminal law is coopted to help solve social problems, such as drug addiction or prostitution.

The development of the criminal law tends to be sporadic and haphazard, with too little thought given to the long-term implications of the criminalisation decision. Some offences – such as murder, rape, and theft – all would agree should be criminal (although the precise boundaries may be a matter of dispute), but what to add to this foundation is often controversial. What actually happens is that Parliament tends to add layer upon layer of crimes to the core. The reverse process of decriminalisation (the removal of existing offences from the rolls of the criminal law) is far more rare. The result may be, in the words of one commentator, a 'crisis of overcriminalisation.' See Kadish, 'The Crisis of Overcriminalisation' (1958) 374 Annals 157.

Notes and questions
1.   Crime is often said to be on the increase, but what does this mean? To some extent an increase in crime merely reflects an increase in criminal law. In theory we could 'solve' the 'crime problem' by doing away with criminal laws. But this is not suggested seriously (although Marxist philosophy did envisage an ultimate utopia in which criminal law would be unnecessary). Why not? What do you think would happen if there were no criminal laws?
2.   Is it better to err on the side of over- or under-inclusiveness when it comes to criminalisation? If too broad a spectrum of human behaviour is made illegal, will not the inevitable result be that many citizens will find themselves ensnared in the net of the criminal law, with the concomitant stigma of a criminal conviction? Is this desirable? Should there be a general principle that criminal law should be a last rather than a first resort, to be employed only when all other means of addressing the social problem at issue have been exhausted?
3.   Is there a practical solution to over-criminalisation, which is to have a large number of criminal offences on the books but to enforce relatively few of them? The statutory law would serve as a statement of the principles and values for which the society stood, and as a safety net to allow prosecutions in egregious cases. The decision not to prosecute would protect citizens who commit technical offences but who are not morally blameworthy. The prosecutor could be given discretion to proceed with formal charges only in those cases where the defendant's blameworthiness was manifest. What are the merits and demerits of such an approach?

If the criminalisation process is to become more rational and less haphazard, the challenge facing the law-maker is to develop general criteria and principles which can be employed in determining whether or not to make conduct criminal. There would need to be principles of inclusion and exclusion, i.e., principles which would advise the law-maker as to what should be made criminal (e.g., actions which cause or threaten physical harm to others should be made criminal) and principles that counsel against criminalisation (e.g. it is inadvisable to criminalise conduct which is approved of and engaged in by the vast majority of the citizenry). The following is an attempt by one noted criminologist to identify such principles:

N. Walker, *Crime and Criminology* (1987)

i.   Objectives of the criminal law
Is it possible to discuss the proper content of the criminal law in general terms? If the contents of criminal codes are examined with a sociological eye, no fewer than fourteen different objectives can be discerned:

   (a)   the protection of human persons (and to some extent animals also) against intentional violence, cruelty, or unwelcome sexual approaches;

(b)   the protection of people against some forms of unintended harm (for example from traffic, poisons, infections, radiation);

(c)   the protection of easily persuadable classes of people (that is, the young or the weak-minded) against the abuse of their persons or property (for example by sexual intercourse or hire-purchase);

(d)   the prevention of acts which, even if the participants are adult and willing, are regarded as 'unnatural' (for example incest, sodomy, bestiality, drug 'trips');

(e)   the prevention of acts which, though not included under any of the previous headings, are performed so publicly as to shock other people (for example public nakedness, obscene language, or heterosexual copulation between consenting adults);

(f)   the discouragement of behaviour which might provoke disorder (such as insulting words at a public meeting);

(g)   the protection of property against theft, fraud, or damage;

(h)   the prevention of inconvenience (for example the obstruction of roads by vehicles);

(i)   the collection of revenue (for example keeping a motor car or television set without a licence);

(j)   the defence of the State (for example espionage or – in some countries – political criticism);

(k)   the enforcement of compulsory benevolence (for example the offence of failing to send one's children to school);

(l)   the protection of social institutions, such as marriage or religious worship (for example by prohibiting bigamy or blasphemy);

(m)   the prevention of unreasonable discrimination (for example against ethnic groups, religions, the female sex);

(n)   the enforcement of the processes regarded as essential to these other purposes (for example offences connected with arrest, assisting offenders to escape conviction, and testimony at trials).

ii.   Moral limits
Now and again there have been attempts to formulate what might be called 'limiting principles', which declare that the criminal law should *not* be used for certain purposes, or in certain circumstances.

The oldest seems to be

(A)   Prohibitions should not be included in the criminal law for the sole purpose of ensuring that breaches of them are visited with retributive punishment.

Some years later, Bentham's *An Introduction to the Principles of Morals and Legislation* (1789) stated three more limiting principles. The first was

(B)   The criminal law should not be used to penalise behaviour which does no harm.

In his phraseology, punishment was groundless when, on the whole, there was no evil in the act. It is a principle to which everyone would give general assent, and would agree that it was the reason why we do not use the law to discourage bad manners or bad art. Nevertheless there would be many disagreements over other sorts of conduct. The idea of prohibiting bad art by law sounds ridiculous, but one of the things which town and country planning legislation tries to control is bad architecture, and anyone who flouts it can suffer heavy penalties.

Another of Bentham's principles was

(C)   The criminal law should not be used to achieve a purpose which can be achieved as effectively at less cost in suffering.

. . . A better formulation of the principle would be

(CC)   The criminal law should not be used where measures involving less suffering are as effective or almost as effective in reducing the frequency of the conduct in question.

Bentham's third principle was

(D)   The criminal law should not be used if the harm done by the penalty is greater than the harm done by the offence.

For in such cases punishment would be 'unprofitable' when the felicific balance sheet was added up. The difficulty about this principle is that it requires us to weigh, let us say, the unhappiness caused by bad architecture against the unhappiness caused by a large fine. Since the two sorts of unhappiness are inflicted on different people we cannot simply leave it to individual choice, as we do when we ask someone whether he would rather be fined or pull his new house down. The difficulty of choosing between incommensurables is one of the weaknesses of Benthamism which have been exploited by its opponents.

(E)   The criminal law should not be used for the purpose of compelling people to act in their own best interests.

Mill himself recognised that there should be exceptions to this rule. 'Despotism', he thought, 'is a legitimate mode of government in dealing with barbarians provided that the end be their improvement'; and he took much the same view of the upbringing of children. So far as children were concerned, therefore, he would not have said that his principle ruled out compulsory benevolence such as enforced attendance at school.

iii.   Pragmatic limits
The principles which Beccaria, Bentham, and Mill formulated were moral prescriptions, which said that the penal system *ought* not to attempt this or that task. Other writers, however, were pursuing a more pragmatic line of thought and asking what the law could reasonably be expected to achieve. This is how Montesquieu approached the subject in *The Spirit of the Laws*. He recognised that prohibition by law can be carried further in some societies than in others, but thought that in any kind of society there were areas of conduct (which he called 'les moeurs et les manières') in which it was most unwise to use the law in the hope of effecting changes.
   [T]his principle might read

(F)   The criminal law should not include prohibitions which do not have strong public support.

The principle has its own weaknesses – such as the difficulty of measuring public opinion in a morally pluralistic society. . . . its justification is not self-evident, and it raises the question 'Why not?' . . .

iv. A positive justification?

The thoroughgoing pragmatist, however, is one who abandons the defensive approach. Instead of merely setting up warning notices in the form of limiting principles which try – not very practically – to indicate to legislators where they should stop, he asks why the onus of proof should not lie on those who want to extend the scope of the criminal law. They should, on this view, be required to show why it is desirable. Shifting the burden of proof in this way has obvious difficulties. The very diversity of functions to which I have already drawn attention makes any attempt to approach the problem in this way sound naïve. Nevertheless, if an institution is as costly – whether in terms of economic resources or of human happiness – as the penal system undoubtedly is, it seems more realistic to ask for positive justifications whenever it is to be used against a given sort of conduct. . . .

Something like a non-moralistic justification was offered by Sir Patrick (now Lord) Devlin, in his well-known lecture on *The Enforcement of Morals,* where he said

> The State must justify in some other way [than by reference to the moral law] the punishment which it imposes on wrongdoers and a function for the criminal law independent of morals must be found. This is not difficult to do. The smooth functioning of society and the preservation of order require that a number of activities should be regulated.

[T]he need to ensure 'the smooth functioning of society' must, after all, be the main justification for the parts of the criminal code which are concerned with the protection of health, the collection of revenue, and the defence of the realm – objectives (b), (i), and (j) in my list. Most, though probably not all, of the other prohibitions can be regarded as necessary for 'the preservation of order', to the extent at least that if they were not enforced on some occasions there would be disorder. Not all thefts or damage would provoke public disturbances; some victims, for example, would be afraid to retaliate. But some would not, and their methods of protecting themselves or avenging their losses would lead to breaches of the peace. The same is true of intentional violence against the person or unwelcome sexual advances. The prohibition of these can be justified because they are classes of actions of which by no means all, but a substantial number, would provoke disorder.

Nevertheless, there are some prohibitions which it is not very plausible to justify in this way. The obvious examples are in my group (d), which consists largely of sexual behaviour that has come to be regarded as 'unnatural', and is prohibited by many criminal codes even if it takes place in private, and between participants who are adult, sane, and under no coercion or inducement other than their own desires. . . .

v. Pragmatism versus morality

One interesting feature distinguishes the pragmatist's approach which I have just been discussing from the moralist's approach. Suppose that both are agreed in disapproving very strongly of some type of conduct. For the pragmatist the question is simply whether on balance anything useful would be achieved by invoking the criminal law against it. The moralist, however, seems to agonise in a special way over this step. He may be willing to see all sorts of other steps taken to reduce the frequency of the conduct – education, propaganda, restriction of opportunities – and yet may consider it morally wrong to use the criminal law in the campaign.

It is hard to see, however, what it is that in the moralist's eyes distinguishes the criminal law. It may of course be simply that he regards its penalties as excessively

severe; but that is not an essential feature of the criminal law. Would he still object if a
fine were the maximum penalty for whatever conduct is in question? He might still
object that the criminal law seeks to *compel* whereas other techniques of social control
work by persuasion or indoctrination. This seems an undeniable distinction, which
appeals to one's instinctive dislike of being ordered to do something, even if it is in one's
interests.

It raises two questions, however. Are all other techniques of social control less
objectionable morally than the compulsion of the criminal law? Is one-sided indoctrination – for example against birth control or abortion – any better? The second question
is whether a strong and sincere belief in the harmfulness – or sinfulness – of the conduct
does or does not create a duty to do what one can to prevent it, short of doing even
greater harm. Whether or not one takes sides on this issue, it is clear that the moralist
has a choice between three positions, two simple and one complex:

(a)   he may hold sincere and well-defined views about the wrongness of conduct and
yet think it wrong to try to influence the behaviour of others by *any* means (a very rare
position);
(b)   he may on the other hand think it justifiable, even obligatory, to seek to
influence the behaviour of others by *any* means (a fairly rare position);
(c)   he may take position (b) by with a difference, regarding *some* means as
unacceptable (the commonest position of the moralist).

Note that (c) involves ruling out certain *means*, not certain types of conduct. The
difficulties for the moralist of drawing distinctions between types of conduct which he
may or must seek to eliminate and those which he should not have already been shown
to be insuperable, if not in theory, at least in practice. It is the techniques about which
he has to worry. So far as the use of the criminal law is concerned, he has to decide
whether, with all its crudities and undesirable side-effects, it is less acceptable than say,
one-sided moral indoctrination.

Notes and questions
1.   Are there other objectives which might be added to Walker's list? Some
that might be deleted? Other 'principles' which should bear on the decision to
criminalise or decriminalise? See also A. Ashworth, *Principles of Criminal Law*
(1991), pp. 19–43.
2.   Having examined general criminalisation principles and criteria, it is
valuable to attempt to apply these to specific examples. Examples often reveal
weak spots in the principles and criteria, and contribute to the task of fine
tuning. By going back and forth between specific examples and generalised
criteria, one eventually will reach a state of 'reflective equilibrium', whereby
both should be in balance, the criteria and principles yielding what seems to be
the 'right' result in respect to the examples.

Should the following conduct be made criminal?

(a)   failure to wear a seat belt while driving an automobile;
(b)   corporal punishment of children/adults;
(c)   cruelty to animals;
(d)   industrial pollution;

(e)   abortion;
(f)   misleading advertising;
(g)   ticket touting (offering to sell a ticket to a theatrical or sporting event at a price above the face value of the ticket);
(h)   public drunkenness;
(i)   racially offensive speech.

Not all criminal offences involve immoral conduct (e.g., illegal parking), and not all immoral conduct is criminal (e.g., lying), but often the two overlap. One of the most controversial of criminalisation issues is whether Parliament may (should?) make illegal conduct which is immoral but not directly harmful to the participants or third parties. The topic gave rise to a famous debate between Lord Devlin, one of the most prominent and well-respected judges of his time, and Professor H.L.A. Hart, whom many would regard as the foremost legal jurisprudent in England in the twentieth century. Consider their respective positions:

P. Devlin, *The Enforcement of Morals* (1965)

. . . I have framed three interrogatories addressed to myself to answer:

1.   Has society the right to pass judgement at all on matters of morals? Ought there, in other words, to be a public morality, or are morals always a matter for private judgement?
2.   If society has the right to pass judgement, has it also the right to use the weapon of the law to enforce it?
3.   If so, ought it to use that weapon in all cases or only in some; and if only in some, on what principles should it distinguish?

I shall begin with the first interrogatory and consider what is meant by the right of society to pass a moral judgement, that is, a judgement about what is good and what is evil. The fact that a majority of people may disapprove of a practice does not of itself make it a matter for society as a whole. Nine men out of ten may disapprove of what the tenth man is doing and still say that it is not their business. There is a case for a collective judgement (as distinct from a large number of individual opinions which sensible people may even refrain from pronouncing at all if it is upon somebody else's private affairs) only if society is affected. Without a collective judgement there can be no case at all for intervention. . . .

This view – that there is such a thing as public morality – can . . . be justified by *a priori* argument. What makes a society of any sort is community of ideas, not only political ideas but also ideas about the way its members should behave and govern their lives; these latter ideas are its morals. Every society has a moral structure as well as a political one: or rather, since that might suggest two independent systems, I should say that the structure of every society is made up both of politics and morals. . . .

The institution of marriage is a good example for my purpose because it bridges the division, if there is one, between politics and morals. Marriage is part of the structure of our society and it is also the basis of a moral code which condemns fornication and adultery. The institution of marriage would be gravely threatened if individual judgements were permitted about the morality of adultery; on these points there must be a public morality. But public morality is not to be confined to those moral principles which support institutions such as marriage. People do not think of monogamy as something which has to be supported because our society has chosen to organise itself upon it; they think of it as something that is good in itself and offering a good way of life and that it is for that reason that our society has adopted it. I return to the statement that I have already made, that society means a community of ideas; without shared ideas on politics, morals, and ethics no society can exist. Each one of us has ideas about what is good and what is evil; they cannot be kept private from the society in which we live. If men and women try to create a society in which there is no fundamental agreement about good and evil they will fail; if, having based it on common agreement, the agreement goes, the society will disintegrate. For society is not something that is kept together physically; it is held by the invisible bonds of common thought. If the bonds were too far relaxed the members would drift apart. A common morality is part of the bondage. The bondage is part of the price of society; and mankind, which needs society, must pay its price.

. . . I believe that the answer to the first question determines the way in which the second should be approached and may indeed very nearly dictate the answer to the second question. If society has no right to make judgements on morals, the law must find some special justification for entering the field of morality: if homosexuality and prostitution are not in themselves wrong, then the onus is very clearly on the lawgiver who wants to frame a law against certain aspects of them to justify the exceptional treatment. But if society has the right to make a judgement and has it on the basis that a recognised morality is as necessary to society as, say, a recognised government, then society may use the law to preserve morality in the same way as it uses it to safeguard anything else that is essential to its existence. If therefore the first proposition is securely established with all its implications, society has a prima facie right to legislate against immorality as such.

. . . Society is entitled by means of its laws to protect itself from dangers, whether from within or without. Here again I think that the political parallel is legitimate. The law of treason is directed against aiding the king's enemies and against sedition from within. The justification for this is that established government is necessary for the existence of society and therefore its safety against violent overthrow must be secured. But an established morality is as necessary as good government to the welfare of society. Societies disintegrate from within more frequently than they are broken up by external pressures. There is disintegration when no common morality is observed and history shows that the loosening of moral bonds is often the first stage of disintegration, so that society is justified in taking the same steps to preserve its moral code as it does to preserve its government and other essential institutions. . . . There are no theoretical limits to the power of the State to legislate against treason and sedition, and likewise I think there can be no theoretical limits to legislation against immorality. . . .

. . . [T]his brings me to the third question – the individual has a *locus standi* too; he cannot be expected to surrender to the judgement of society the whole conduct of his life. It is the old and familiar question of striking a balance between the rights and interests of society and those of the individual. . . . While every decision which a court of law makes when it balances the public against the private interest is an *ad hoc* decision, the cases contain statements of principle to which the court should have regard when it reaches its decision. In the same way it is possible to make general statements of principle which it may be thought the legislature should bear in mind when it is considering the enactment of laws enforcing morals.

I believe that most people would agree upon the chief of these elastic principles. There must be toleration of the maximum individual freedom that is consistent with the integrity of society. . . . The principle appears to me to be peculiarly appropriate to all questions of morals. Nothing should be punished by the law that does not lie beyond the limits of tolerance. It is not nearly enough to say that a majority dislike a practice; there must be a real feeling of reprobation. Those who are dissatisfied with the present law on homosexuality often say that the opponents of reform are swayed simply by disgust. If that were so it would be wrong, but I do not think one can ignore disgust if it is deeply felt and not manufactured. Its presence is a good indication that the bounds of toleration are being reached. Not everything is to be tolerated. No society can do without intolerance, indignation, and disgust; they are the forces behind the moral law, and indeed it can be argued that if they or something like them are not present, the feelings of society cannot be weighty enough to deprive the individual of freedom of choice. . . .

. . . [M]atters of this sort are not determined by rational argument. Every moral judgement, unless it claims a divine source, is simply a feeling that no right-minded man could behave in any other way without admitting that he was doing wrong. It is the power of a common sense and not the power of reason that is behind the judgements of society. . . .

The limits of tolerance shift. This is supplementary to what I have been saying but of sufficient importance in itself to deserve statement as a separate principle which law-makers have to bear in mind. . . .

The last and the biggest thing to be remembered is that the law is concerned with the minimum and not with the maximum; there is much in the Sermon on the Mount that would be out of place in the Ten Commandments. We all recognise the gap between the moral law and the law of the land. No man is worth much who regulates his conduct with the sole object of escaping punishment, and every worthy society sets for its members standards which are above those of the law. We recognise the existence of such higher standards when we use expressions such as 'moral obligation' and 'morally bound'. The distinction was well put in the judgement of African elders in a family dispute: 'We have power to make you divide the crops, for this is our law, and we will see this is done. But we have not power to make you behave like an upright man.'

. . . The criminal law is not a statement of how people ought to behave; it is a statement of what will happen to them if they do not behave; good citizens are not expected to come within reach of it or to set their sights by it, and every enactment should be framed accordingly.

The arm of the law is an instrument to be used by society, and the decision about what particular cases it should be used in is essentially a practical one. . . .

The part that the jury plays in the enforcement of the criminal law, the fact that no grave offence against morals is punishable without their verdict, these are of great importance in relation to the statements of principle that I have been making. They turn what might otherwise be pure exhortation to the legislature into something like rules that the law-makers cannot safely ignore. The man in the jury box is not just an expression; he is an active reality. It will not in the long run work to make laws about morality that are not acceptable to him.

This then is how I believe my third interrogatory should be answered – not by the formulation of hard and fast rules, but by a judgement in each case taking into account the sort of factors I have been mentioning. The line that divides the criminal law from the moral is not determinable by the application of any clear-cut principle. It is like a line that divides land and sea, a coastline of irregularities and indentations. There are gaps and promontories, such as adultery and fornication, which the law has for centuries left substantially untouched. Adultery of the sort that breaks up marriage seems to me to be just as harmful to the social fabric as homosexuality or bigamy. The only ground for putting it outside the criminal law is that a law which made it a crime would be too difficult to enforce; it is too generally regarded as a human weakness not suitably punished by imprisonment. All that the law can do with fornication is to act against its worst manifestations; there is a general abhorrence of the commercialisation of vice, and that sentiment gives strength to the law against brothels and immoral earnings. There is no logic to be found in this. The boundary between the criminal law and the moral law is fixed by balancing in the case of each particular crime the pros and cons of legal enforcement in accordance with the sort of considerations I have been outlining. The fact that adultery, fornication, and lesbianism are untouched by the criminal law does not prove that homosexuality ought not to be touched. The error of jurisprudence in the Wolfenden Report is caused by the search for some single principle to explain the division between crime and sin. The Report finds it in the principle that the criminal law exists for the protection of individuals; on this principle fornication in private between consenting adults is outside the law and thus it becomes logically indefensible to bring homosexuality between consenting adults in private within it. But the true principle is that the law exists for the protection of society. It does not discharge its function by protecting the individual from injury, annoyance, corruption, and exploitation; the law must protect also the institutions and the community of ideas, political and moral, without which people cannot live together. Society cannot ignore the morality of the individual any more than it can his loyalty; it flourishes on both and without either it dies. . . .

I return now to the main thread of my argument and summarise it. Society cannot live without morals. Its morals are those standards of conduct which the reasonable man approves. A rational man, who is also a good man, may have other standards. If he has no standards at all he is not a good man and need not be further considered. If he has standards, they may be very different; he may, for example, not disapprove of homosexuality or abortion. In that case he will not share in the common morality; but that should not make him deny that it is a social necessity. A rebel may be rational in thinking that he is right but he is irrational if he thinks that society can leave him free to rebel.

A man who concedes that morality is necessary to society must support the use of those instruments without which morality cannot be maintained. The two instruments are those of teaching, which is doctrine, and of enforcement, which is the law. If morals could be taught simply on the basis that they are necessary to society, there would be no social need for religion; it could be left as a purely personal affair. But morality cannot be taught in that way. Loyalty is not taught in that way either. No society has yet solved the problem of how to teach morality without religion. So the law must base itself on Christian morals and to the limit of its ability enforce them, not simply because they are the morals of most of us, nor simply because they are the morals which are taught by the established Church – on these points the law recognises the right to dissent – but for the compelling reason that without the help of Christian teaching the law will fail.

H.L.A. Hart, *Law, Liberty, and Morality* (1963)

Both in England and in America the criminal law still contains rules which can only be explained as attempts to enforce morality as such: to suppress practices condemned as immoral by positive morality though they involve nothing that would ordinarily be thought of as harm to other persons. . . .

I shall start with an example stressed by Lord Devlin. He points out that, subject to certain exceptions such as rape, the criminal law has never admitted the consent of the victim as a defence. It is not a defence to a charge of murder or a deliberate assault, and this is why euthanasia or mercy killing terminating a man's life at his own request is still murder. This is a rule of criminal law which many now would wish to retain, though they would also wish to object to the legal punishment of offences against positive morality which harm no one. Lord Devlin thinks that these attitudes are inconsistent, for he asserts of the rule under discussion, 'There is only one explanation,' and this is that 'there are certain standards of behaviour or moral principles which society requires to be observed'. . . .

But this argument is not really cogent, for Lord Devlin's statement that 'there is only one explanation' is simply not true. The rules excluding the victim's consent as a defence to charges of murder or assault may perfectly well be explained as a piece of paternalism, designed to protect individuals against themselves. . . . [P]aternalism – the protection of people against themselves – is a perfectly coherent policy. Indeed, it seems very strange in mid-twentieth century to insist upon this, for the wane of laissez faire since Mill's day is one of the commonplaces of social history, and instances of paternalism now abound in our law, criminal and civil. The supply of drugs or narcotics, even to adults, except under medical prescription is punishable by the criminal law, and it would seem very dogmatic to say of the law creating this offence that 'there is only one explanation,' namely, that the law was concerned not with the protection of the would-be purchasers against themselves, but only with the punishment of the seller for his immorality. If, as seems obvious, paternalism is a possible explanation of such laws, it is also possible in the case of the rule excluding the consent of the victim as a defence to a charge of assault. In neither case are we forced to conclude with Lord Devlin that the law's 'function' is 'to enforce a moral principle and nothing else'. . . .

According to the moderate thesis, a shared morality is the cement of society; without it there would be aggregates of individuals but no society. 'A recognised morality' is, in Lord Devlin's words, 'as necessary to society's existence as a recognised government,' and though a particular act of immorality may not harm or endanger or corrupt others nor, when done in private, either shock or give offence to others, this does not conclude the matter. For we must not view conduct in isolation from its effect on the moral code: if we remember this, we can see that one who is 'no menace to others' nonetheless may by his immoral conduct 'threaten one of the great moral principles on which society is based.' In this sense the breach of moral principle is an offence 'against society as a whole,' and society may use the law to preserve its morality as it uses it to safeguard anything else essential to its existence. This is why 'the suppression of vice is as much the law's business as the suppression of subversive activities'. . . .

Lord Devlin appears to defend the moderate thesis. I say 'appears' because, though he says that society has the right to enforce a morality as such on the ground that a shared morality is essential to society's existence, it is not at all clear that for him the statement that immorality jeopardises or weakens society is a statement of empirical fact. It seems sometimes to be an *a priori* assumption, and sometimes a necessary truth and a very odd one. The most important indication that this is so is that, apart from one vague reference to 'history' showing that 'the loosening of moral bonds is often the first stage of disintegration,' no evidence is produced to show that deviation from accepted sexual morality, even by adults in private, is something which, like treason, threatens the existence of society. No reputable historian has maintained this thesis, and there is indeed much evidence against it. As a proposition of fact it is entitled to no more respect than the Emperor Justinian's statement that homosexuality was the cause of earthquakes. Lord Devlin's belief in it, and his apparent indifference to the question of evidence, are at points traceable to an undiscussed assumption. This is that all morality – sexual morality together with the morality that forbids acts injurious to others such as killing, stealing, and dishonesty – forms a single seamless web, so that those who deviate from any part are likely or perhaps bound to deviate from the whole. It is of course clear (and one of the oldest insights of political theory) that society could not exist without a morality which mirrored and supplemented the law's proscription of conduct injurious to others. But there is again no evidence to support, and much to refute, the theory that those who deviate from conventional sexual morality are in other ways hostile to society.

There seems, however, to be central to Lord Devlin's thought something more interesting, though no more convincing, than the conception of social morality as a seamless web. For he appears to move from the acceptable proposition that *some* shared morality is essential to the existence of any society to the unacceptable proposition that a society is identical with its morality as that is at any given moment of its history, so that a change in its morality is tantamount to the destruction of a society. The former proposition might be even accepted as a necessary rather than an empirical truth depending on a quite plausible definition of society as a body of men who hold certain moral views in common. But the latter proposition is absurd. Taken strictly, it would prevent us saying that the morality of a given society had changed, and would compel us instead to say that one society had disappeared and another one taken its place. But it is only on this absurd criterion of what it is for the same society to continue to exist that it could be asserted without evidence that any deviation from a society's shared morality threatens its existence.

It is clear that only this tacit identification of a society with its shared morality supports Lord Devlin's denial that there could be such a thing as private immorality and his comparison of sexual immorality, even when it takes place 'in private,' with treason. No doubt it is true that if deviations from conventional sexual morality are tolerated by the law and come to be known, the conventional morality might change in a permissive direction, though this does not seem to be the case with homosexuality in those European countries where it is not punishable by law. But even if the conventional morality did so change, the society in question would not have been destroyed or 'subverted.' We should compare such a development not to the violent overthrow of government but to a peaceful constitutional change in its form, consistent not only with the preservation of a society but with its advance.

. . . A very great difference is apparent between inducing persons through fear of punishment to abstain from actions which are harmful to others, and inducing them to abstain from actions which deviate from accepted morality but harm no one. The value attached to the first is easy to understand; for the protection of human beings from murder or violence or others forms of injury remains a good whatever the motives are by which others are induced to abstain from these crimes. But where there is no harm to be prevented and no potential victim to be protected, as is often the case where conventional sexual morality is disregarded, it is difficult to understand the assertion that conformity, even if motivated merely by fear of the law's punishment, is a value worth pursuing, notwithstanding the misery and sacrifice of freedom which it involves . . . Lord Devlin, assumes that the society to which his doctrine is to apply is marked by a considerable degree of moral solidarity, and is deeply disturbed by infringements of its moral code. Just as for Lord Devlin the morality to be enforced by law must be 'public,' in the sense that it is generally shared and identifiable by the triple marks of 'intolerance, indignation, and disgust,' so for Stephen 'you cannot punish anything which public opinion as expressed in the common practice of society does not strenuously and unequivocally condemn . . . To be able to punish a moral majority must be overwhelming.' It is possible that in mid-Victorian England these conditions were satisfied in relation to 'that considerable number of acts' which according to Stephen were treated as crimes merely because they were regarded as grossly immoral. Perhaps an 'overwhelming moral majority' then actually did harbour the healthy desire for revenge of which he speaks and which is to be gratified by the punishment of the guilty. But it would be sociologically naïve to assume that these conditions obtain in contemporary England at least as far as sexual morality is concerned. The fact that there is lip service to an official sexual morality should not lead us to neglect the possibility that in sexual, as in other matters, there may be a number of mutually tolerant moralities, and that even where there is some homogeneity of practice and belief, offenders may be viewed not with hatred or resentment but with amused contempt or pity.

In a sense, therefore, Stephen's doctrine, and much of Lord Devlin's, may seem to hover in the air above the *terra firma* of contemporary social reality; it may be a well-articulated construction, interesting because it reveals the outlook characteristic of the English judiciary but lacking application to contemporary society. . . .

Notes and questions
1.   The specific issue which triggered the Hart/Devlin debate was whether to decriminalise homosexual conduct between consenting adults, as was recommended in 1957 by the Wolfenden Committee Report on Homosexual Offences and Prostitution (Cmnd. 247) and implemented in the Sexual Offences Act 1967. Which theorist has the better of the arguments on this issue? What if the homosexual conduct is between minors? Between an adult and a minor? What if it takes place in public?
2.   Is Hart correct when he asserts that there is no such thing as a moral consensus? Are moral judgments like tastes in food, there being no right or wrong but only personal preferences? If there is a popular morality, how can it be ascertained?
3.   Should popular morality be enforced if it is based on stereotypes? Can (should?) the law distinguish between morality based on prejudice and morality based on virtue?
4.   As a practical matter, is not the law powerless to enforce a prohibition against homosexual conduct? The crime typically occurs in private, the participants are unlikely to report their own criminal activity, and both police and prosecutors have more pressing business on their plate than to pursue homosexuals. Should these facts be relevant to the criminalisation decision? If the Government decides to prohibit an activity, does it thereby commit itself to those resources necessary to enforce that prohibition?

B   The grading of offences

Once the decision to criminalise has been made, there is a still a grading issue to be considered. Not all crimes engender the same degree of concern, or cause the same amount of harm. Few would disagree that murder and rape are more

serious offences than criminal damage and tax evasion. All may need to be
made criminal, but the same penalty should not be attached to each. The
penalty that is attached reflects the grading of the offence by Parliament.

Both inter- and intra-crime grading issues arise. Inter-crime grading relates
to offences which are not in any way comparable. As a practical exercise, on a
scale of seriousness of from 1 to 10, where would you place each of the
following crimes (currently arranged in alphabetical order): assault, burglary,
dangerous driving, murder, rape, theft? There are issues of both absolute
ranking (which is the most serious crime, the second most serious, etc.) and
relative ranking (*how much* more serious is one crime than another).

A. Ashworth, *Principles of Criminal Law* (1991)

. . . To assess the relative seriousness of harms on a single scale is not only a matter of
identifying the values behind each class of offence and then ranking those values in
order of priority. The issues revolve not around this single axis but around several axes,
of which the most important are:

high culpability > low culpability;
virtual certainty of harm > remote risk of harm;
actual occurrence of harm > non-occurrence of harm;
widespread effects > effects confined to small area;
significant psychological trauma for victim > no psychological trauma for victim;
no social justification for activity involved > some social justification for activity
  involved.

Only by reference to these other axes can one find a principled answer to the
comparison between, say, a negligent homicide and an intentional robbery involving
only slight injury; or between, say, reckless driving and intentional pollution of clean
waters. Many other complexities will also be apparent. The seriousness of an offence
may be greatly affected by the position of the offender (for example, breach of a position
of trust in relation to the victim must aggravate the offence) and of the victim (for
example, theft from a person living on social-security payments must be more serious
than theft of an equivalent amount from a wealthy person or company, at least if the
offenders know of the relative wealth of their victims). But, beneath all these
complexities of detail, are there any general principles which can serve to point the way
to meaningful comparisons?

. . . One proposal, by Andrew von Hirsch and Nils Jareborg, is aimed specifically at
assessing offence-seriousness. The first question to be asked, following their approach,
is what interests are violated or threatened by the standard case of this crime. Their
analysis, which is confined to crimes with individual victims, identifies four generic
interests:

(i)   physical integrity: health, safety, and the avoidance of physical pain;
(ii)   material support and amenity: includes nutrition, shelter, and other basic
amenities, various material comforts, and luxuries as well;
(iii)   freedom from humiliation or degrading treatment;
(iv)   privacy and autonomy.

Their approach would be to ask which of these interests are affected by a standard house burglary, rape or shop theft.

The four types of interest listed are intended to be illustrative and not exhaustive: the authors' method could accommodate more such interests. Once the nature of the violated interests has been determined, the second stage is to apply a scale of seriousness to each one affected. The scale which they put forward has five bands of effect on the 'living standards' of victims:

(1)   subsistence: survival with maintenance of elementary human functions – no satisfactions presupposed at this level;

(2)   minimum well-being: maintenance of a minimum level of comfort and human dignity;

(3)   adequate well-being: maintenance of an 'adequate' level (but no more) of comfort and dignity.

(4)   significant enhancement: significant enhancement in quality of life above the merely 'adequate' level;

(5)   marginal impact: living standards not significantly affected.

Once again, the differences between the levels are couched in fairly vague terms, such as 'adequate' and 'significant', but that is surely inevitable if one is seeking general principles, and it is also appropriate in view of the cultural relativity of offence-seriousness: what is crucial in a cold country or a poor country might be peripheral in a hot country or an affluent country . . . the key issue becomes the effect of the offence (which violates certain types of individual interest) upon the conditions for enjoying some 'quality of life'. But whose view of these conditions should be treated as determinative? The value-preferences of each individual victim should not usually be allowed to determine offence-seriousness, but where the offender knows of the special situation of the victim, it is right to take this into account. For the general run of cases, however, the criterion should be the typical impact on victims of this kind of offence. This allows monetary value to be a primary determinant of seriousness in property and drug offences, and it also allows the psychological impact of residential burglary to be given some weight in assessing the seriousness of this crime . . .

Assessments of offence-seriousness should therefore be concerned with the standard impact and effects of the type of offence. On this approach, offences involving death would be ranked at the top level, 'subsistence', on the 'living standards' scale proposed by Von Hirsch and Jareborg. Serious offences against the person, such as grievous bodily harm, would be ranked at the first or second level. Rape unaccompanied by serious physical injury might be ranked at the second level, 'minimum well-being', taking account both of the physical threat and of the extreme humiliation and degradation. Offences such as reckless driving, drunken driving, and unsafe working conditions may well be placed at the first or second level, though undoubtedly some of the offences towards the lower end of each scale would rank at the third level or below. . . . there is no doubt that the higher offences in each of these categories is properly placed at the second level of seriousness of harm. Property offences, likewise, straddle the third, fourth, and fifth levels, according to the value of what is taken or damaged and the effect it has upon the victim. Most shop thefts will be in the fifth category, whereas some larger offences of theft and deception involving elderly victims would be at the third level or even higher. Thus one strength of the 'living standards' framework is that it enables one to rank offences in a more sophisticated way than the legal categories themselves would allow: an offence falling within the legal category of theft might be ranked at a different level of seriousness, depending on the impact of a standard case of that kind. Moreover, the living standards' approach can be adapted to take account of such other variables as high or low culpability, high or low risk of harm, occurrence or non-occurrence of harm, high or low psychological effects, and low or moderate social justification for the offence. It would take a complex mathematical model to show how these could be brought into the calculation, but it is relatively straightforward to take account of one variable, such as the degree of risk inherent in the offence. Figure 2.2 is a two-dimensional grid which, having plotted harm against risk of harm, is able to yield some assessment of the seriousness of an offence.

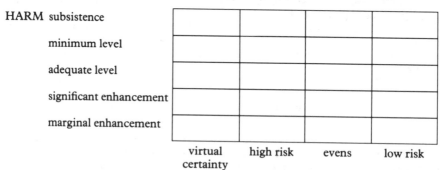

HARM subsistence

minimum level

adequate level

significant enhancement

marginal enhancement

virtual certainty   high risk   evens   low risk

Figure 2.2   The von Hirsch–Jareborg scale for ranking harms

The complexity of judgments of offence-seriousness, however, makes it necessary to search for a model which takes account not merely of two dimensions but of several. That requires a considerable degree of mathematical sophistication, which will not be attempted here, but it is evident that the conscientious judge and legislator already performs this kind of exercise in a rough and ready form. Many assessments of offence-seriousness do attempt to take proper account of various factors which are, in reality, operating on different scales. To take even three major factors – intrinsic gravity of harm, culpability, and degree of risk of harm – and to produce an intelligible joint scale is not easy. If the calculation is not accomplished mathematically, then there is inevitably room for error or for the infiltration of extraneous opinions and factors.

Notes and questions

Intra-crime grading involves offences that are loosely related to each other in that they involve similar kinds of activities, but some in more aggravated form. How would you grade the following array of driving offences contained in the Dangerous Driving Act 1991 and the Aggravated Vehicle Taking Act 1992?

Dangerous Driving Act 1991

1. Causing death by dangerous driving
A person who causes the death of another person by driving a mechanically propelled vehicle dangerously on a road or other public place is guilty of an offence.

2. Dangerous driving
A person who drives a mechanically propelled vehicle dangerously on a road or other public place is guilty of an offence.

3. Careless, and inconsiderate, driving

If a person drives a mechanically propelled vehicle on a road or other public place without due care and attention, or without reasonable consideration for other persons using the road or place, he is guilty of an offence.

3A. Causing death by careless driving when under influence of drink or drugs

(1) If a person causes the death of another person by driving a mechanically propelled vehicle on a road or other public place without due care and attention, or without reasonable consideration for other persons using the road or place, and —

(a) he is, at the time when he is driving, unfit to drive through drink or drugs, or

(b) he has consumed so much alcohol that the proportion of it in his breath, blood or urine at that time exceeds the prescribed limit, or

(c) he is, within 18 hours after that time, required to provide a specimen in pursuance of section 7 of this Act, but without reasonable excuse fails to provide it, he is guilty of an offence.

22A. Causing danger to road-users

(1) A person is guilty of an offence if he intentionally and without lawful authority or reasonable cause —

(a) causes anything to be on or over a road, or

(b) interferes with a motor vehicle, trailer or cycle, or

(c) interferes (directly or indirectly) with traffic equipment, in such circumstances that it would be obvious to a reasonable person that to do so would be dangerous.

28. Dangerous cycling

(1) A person who rides a cycle on a road dangerously is guilty of an offence.

Aggravated Vehicle Taking Act 1992

12A. Aggravated vehicle-taking

(1) Subject to subsection (3) below, a person is guilty of aggravated taking of a vehicle if —

(a) he commits an offence under section 12(1) above (in this section referred to as a 'basic offence') in relation to a mechanically propelled vehicle; and

(b) it is proved that, at any time after the vehicle was unlawfully taken (whether by him or another) and before it was recovered, the vehicle was driven, or injury or damage was caused, in one or more of the circumstances set out in paragraphs (a) to (d) of subsection (2) below.

(2) The circumstances referred to in subsection (1)(b) above are —

(a) that the vehicle was driven dangerously on a road or other public place;

(b) that, owing to the driving of the vehicle, an accident occurred by which injury was caused to any person;

(c) that, owing to the driving of the vehicle, an accident occurred by which damage was caused to any property, other than the vehicle;

(d) that damage was caused to the vehicle.

Notes and questions

1. The penalties under the Dangerous Driving Act 1991 can be found in the schedules attached to the statute. The penalty for violation of the Aggravated Vehicle Taking Act 1992 is contained in s. 4 of the statute. What criteria account for the heavier penalisation of some offences than others? Are these criteria rational? What others might be used?

2.   One apparent critical difference is whether or not the defendant's offence results in death. Is the difference between one who causes death by dangerous driving and one who commits only the offence of dangerous driving more a matter of luck than anything else? The latter may not have been so unlucky as to have a child dart into the street at the fatal moment. If so, should the penalty for the two offences be the same? Should there be only one crime, dangerous driving, with the range of penalties expanded to take into account the risk of death posed by the dangerous driver, but with the actual result being deemed irrelevant?

3.   Should it matter whether a particular kind of activity is very prevalent? The perception that 'joyriding' had become rampant was a major factor in the passage of the 1992 Act.

C   The definition of a crime

What is a crime? How do we know when a statute creates a criminal offence? Those who have sought to provide a definition of the term 'crime' have found themselves challenged by the elusiveness of the concept. Blackstone, for example, offered the following: 'A crime . . . is an act committed or omitted, in violation of a public law either forbidding or commanding it' (4 Bl. Comm. 5).

Blackstone's definition was criticised for its failure to recognise the role of punishment in criminal law. A statute which simply stated that one shall or shall not do something but which provides no sanction for non-compliance would not be a criminal statute.

There may well not be any single, all-inclusive definition of a crime – it is hard to come up with a definition that encompasses all crimes – but there may be certain questions we might ask, the answers to which will help us to determine whether or not a statute creates a crime:

(a)   Is the behaviour being condemned regarded as a moral wrong? It may not be the case that all crimes involve immoral conduct, and it may not be the case that we should criminalise all immoral conduct but if a statute is aimed at controlling conduct generally regarded as immoral, it is in all likelihood a criminal statute.

(b)   Does the behaviour in question harm the public? The victim in a criminal trial is said to be the state. Indeed, in some instances, it may be impossible to identify an individual who has been injured by the defendant's conduct.

(c)   May the behaviour lead to the punishment of the offender? As was mentioned previously, punishment is a key feature of criminal law, although what constitutes punishment may be unclear. What is the difference, for example, between civil damages and a criminal fine? Civil damages, you might answer, go to the plaintiff, while a fine goes to the state. Civil damages are also based on the actual injury to the plaintiff, which may not be the case in respect of a criminal fine. But from the perspective of the defendant, he may be out of pocket the same amount in both instances.

(d)   Is a criminal or civil procedure used in respect of the conduct in question? In an influential article, 'The Definition of Crime' [1955] *Current Legal Problems* 107, Glanville Williams argued that a crime is an act capable of being followed by criminal proceedings. The problem with this definition is that it is circular. In order to determine whether an act should be followed by criminal proceedings, either Parliament or the court has to determine whether the act is criminal in nature.

See also J. Dine, 'Wrongful Trading – Quasi-Criminal Law', in H. Rajak (ed.), *Insolvency Law and Practice* (1993).

D   Criminal and civil law

One of the reasons why it is important to know whether or not a statute creates a criminal offence is to identify the procedures which will govern a legal proceeding. More generally we might ask what are the differences between civil and criminal cases. Let us examine this issue by looking at a hypothetical fact situation which could give rise to either criminal liability, civil liability or both:

Example
An absent-minded professor, while driving his automobile out of the university parking lot, hits a student. The student suffers serious injuries. There is, however, some question whether either the student or the professor was paying close attention to what the other was doing.

Let us compare the differences depending upon whether a civil or criminal action is brought:

	Civil	*Criminal*
Initiator of suit	student	DPP, CPS
Victim	student	state
Title of case	Student v Professor	R v Professor
Fault standard	negligence	recklessness
Damage	harm to plaintiff	harm to state
Burden of proof	balance of probabilities	beyond reasonable doubt
Procedures	no jury; differing rules of evidence	jury possibility in serious cases
Remedies/sanctions	damages	fine/imprisonment community service
Goal	compensate victim	punish offender

(i)   Generally

Civil law is concerned with private rights; criminal law is concerned with public wrongs. Civil law is also primarily concerned with compensating the injured victim; criminal law is concerned with condemning and punishing the guilty offender. Both may aim to redress past harms and deter future harm.

(ii)   Who decides to bring the action?

In civil cases, it is for the victim to decide whether or not to bring suit. No state authority can force the victim to do so. In our example, if Student decided that he would try to curry favour with Professor by not suing, that would be legally permissible even if ethically questionable. In criminal law, on the other hand, the decision to proceed is made by the state in its various guises. The police will decide whether to arrest or caution the offender, or to take no action. The prosecutor (Director of Public Prosecutions or Crown Prosecution Service) will determine whether formal charges will be brought. Technically, the desires of the victim are irrelevant, although often they will be taken into account.

(iii)   Title of case

A criminal case is brought in the name of the Crown (*R* v *Defendant*), while a civil case is brought in the name of the injured party (*Plaintiff* v *Defendant*). The title of the case illustrates an important theoretical point about who is considered to be the aggrieved party. In both of our suits, the person physically injured is Student, but the titular victim in a criminal case is the state. Because the victim in the civil suit is the plaintiff, his negligence may be a relevant legal consideration. But in the criminal case the victim is the state; the contributory negligence of the person injured is irrelevant (although where the victim is largely at fault, the defendant may be able to argue that the victim's negligence was the cause of the injury).

(iv)   Fault

Criminal law is concerned with moral fault and blameworthiness. Civil law is more concerned with victim compensation. One consequence is that the legal system makes it easier for a civil plaintiff to recover than it does for the Crown to obtain a criminal conviction. In our example, Student will succeed in his civil suit if he can establish that Professor was negligent. To secure a conviction in criminal court, the Crown will have to establish more than mere negligence, probably recklessness or intention.

(v)   Damage

The goal of civil law is to provide compensation to an injured victim; in our example, Student. If Student had not been injured, either physically or psychologically, there would be no basis for a civil suit. In criminal law, however, it is not necessary that any person be injured. In our example Professor could be prosecuted for dangerous or careless driving even if he was fortunate enough to avoid hitting anybody. If he had intentionally tried to run down Student but failed, he could be charged with attempted murder.

(vi) Burden of proof

Another manifestation of the greater rigour demanded in criminal law is the higher burden of proof placed on the Crown. In order to secure a criminal conviction, the prosecution must establish its case by proof beyond a reasonable doubt. In order to prevail in his civil case, Student would need only to establish his case on a balance of probabilities. Thus if a court or jury were to conclude that a defendant had probably committed the wrongful act alleged, but still had some reasonable doubts, it could return a verdict for a plaintiff in the civil case but would have to acquit in the criminal prosecution. Before imposing the stigma and sanctions (including possible imprisonment) of a criminal conviction, society wants to be sure that it is doing the right thing.

(vii) Difference in procedures

Beside the burden of proof, procedures are generally stricter in criminal cases than in civil cases. Again, the concern with the consequences of getting it wrong inclines the law to err on the side of caution in criminal cases. Rules of evidence differ, with the rules in criminal trials on the whole being more stringent. Furthermore, the defendant facing a serious criminal charge has the right to a jury trial. Jury trials are permitted in only a small category of civil cases, and as a practical matter are very rare. Lastly, the right of the state to appeal against a jury acquittal in a criminal case is severely restricted; not so the right of a civil plaintiff to appeal.

(viii) Remedies and sanctions

One of the key features which distinguishes criminal from civil law is the penalty attached to a verdict against the defendant. The criminal defendant can sometimes be sent to jail. In a civil case the worst that can happen to the defendant is to be required to pay money damages. The defendant's liberty is not in jeopardy. The amount of damages in a particular case is determined by the extent of the harm to the victim; this is not necessarily the most critical variable in determining the length of sentence imposed on the convicted criminal defendant. Note that while one of the primary goals of both systems is to deter future would-be wrongdoers, civil damages may not be a sufficient deterrent to wealthy defendants. In these cases criminal sanctions may have greater effect. Conversely, for many crimes the penalty is a relatively minor fine, but civil damages can be very expensive. In cases where corporate fault has resulted in, for example, an aeroplane crash, the civil penalty may be far in excess of the criminal fine. The two sets of remedies, in any event, are not mutually exclusive. In our example Professor can be made to pay damages in civil court and be sent to prison as a result of the criminal trial.

II Punishment

A Theories of punishment

If punishment is a key distinguishing feature of criminal law, as we have suggested, it is fair to ask what function punishment serves. Over the years many answers have been given to this question. The four most cited justifications for punishment are retribution, restraint (incapacitation), rehabilitation, and deterrence (general prevention).

(i) Retribution

Retribution is the oldest of the rationales for punishment, tracing its roots to the Bible:

Leviticus 24:17–22, The New English Bible

When one man strikes another and kills him, he shall be put to death. Whoever strikes a beast and kills it shall make restitution, life for life. When one man injures and disfigures his fellow-countryman, it shall be done to him as he has done; fracture for fracture, eye for eye, tooth for tooth; the injury and disfigurement that he has inflicted upon another shall in turn be inflicted upon him.

Retribution is often assimilated to revenge, but a public rather than a private revenge. Sir James Stephen put it this way: 'The sentence of the law is to the moral sentiment of the public in relation to any offence what a seal is to wax' (Stephen, *A History of the Criminal Law in England*, II (1883), p. 81). Indeed, one of the arguments for a retributive theory of punishment is that it forestalls the need for private revenge. Retribution theory punishes offenders because they are deserving of punishment. It says to the offender: 'You have caused harm to society; now you must pay back society for that harm. You must atone for your misdeeds.' Implicit in retribution is the condemnation or denunciation of both the offender and the offending behaviour. Retribution, however, is not in kind – society does not rape rapists or steal from thieves (although in some countries the death penalty is exacted for murder). Instead, the law attempts to convert the offence into a common currency, and to impose a sentence which is proportional to the harm caused. In this regard it might be observed that retribution, with its emphasis on proportional punishment, provides a basis for the grading of offences.

(ii) Restraint

Restraint theory has a more pragmatic focus. Offenders need to be separated from the rest of society in order to protect ordinary citizens from their committing other offences. The implicit premise is that, if not incarcerated, offenders will continue in their criminal ways. Whether this is true as an empirical proposition is not entirely clear; certainly one can envisage criminals who may never err again, in which case restraint is not needed. Even if an offender needs to be restrained, the question arises for how long. A plausible answer is until the offender is no longer a threat to society. This answer is troublesome, however, for it can lead to lengthy imprisonment for minor offences.

(iii)   Rehabilitation

The other side of the restraint coin is rehabilitation. If a dangerous offender needs to be isolated until he or she is no longer dangerous, it behoves the state to rehabilitate offenders so that they can be released. This makes sense both from the altruistic perspective of helping the offender and from the pragmatic perspective of not burdening the state with the costs of maintaining an offender in prison any longer than is necessary. But being in favour of rehabilitation is one thing and knowing how to rehabilitate criminals is quite another. Innumerable rehabilitation programmes have been essayed over the years with marginal success and unpredictable results. It may well be that our hopes for rehabilitation exceed our knowledge of why people commit crimes. Despite what seemed at one time to be promising advances in the fields of psychology and sociology, we still find the scientific control of criminal behaviour to be beyond our capability.

(iv)   Deterrence

Restraint and rehabilitation theory focus on the individual offender. General deterrence is concerned with other would-be offenders. The idea is to make an example of the actual offenders so that others will learn from their experience and not be tempted into criminal activity. In like vein, the offenders themselves should also be deterred from future criminal activities as a result of the punishment. Society will be protected if deterrence works as envisaged. Whether or not it in fact does is difficult to prove, for success can only be measured by the incidence of those who do not commit crimes. And how is one to measure this negative? Moreover, the process by which deterrence works, assuming it does, is not at all clear. Consider the views of the respected criminologist Johannes Andenaes:

Johannes Andenaes, 'The General Preventive Effects of Punishment' (1966) 114 University of Pennsylvania Law Review 949

In continental theories of criminal law, a basic distinction is made between the effects of punishment on the man being punished – individual prevention or special prevention – and the effects of punishment upon the members of society in general – general prevention. The characteristics of special prevention are termed 'deterrence,' 'reformation' and 'incapacitation,' and these terms have meanings similar to their meanings in the English speaking world. General prevention, on the other hand, may be described as the *restraining influences emanating from the criminal law and the legal machinery.*

By means of the criminal law, and by means of specific applications of this law, 'messages' are sent to members of a society. The criminal law lists those actions which are liable to prosecution, and it specifies the penalties involved. The decisions of the courts and actions by the police and prison officials transmit knowledge about the law, underlining the fact that criminal laws are not mere empty threats, and providing detailed information as to what kind of penalty might be expected for violations of specific laws. To the extent that these stimuli restrain citizens from socially undesired actions which they might otherwise have committed, a general preventive effect is secured.

. . . While the effects of special prevention depend upon how the law is implemented in each individual case, general prevention occurs as a result of an interplay between the provisions of the law and its enforcement in specific cases. In former times, emphasis was often placed on the physical exhibition of punishment as a deterrent influence, for example, by performing executions in public. Today it is customary to emphasize the *threat* of punishment as such. From this point of view the significance of the individual sentence and the execution of it lies in the support that these actions give to the law. . . .

The effect of the criminal law and its enforcement may be *mere deterrence*. Because of the hazards involved, a person who contemplates a punishable offense might not act. But it is not correct to regard general prevention and deterrence as one and the same thing. The concept of general prevention also includes the *moral* or *socio-pedagogical* influence of punishment. The 'messages' sent by law and the legal processes contain factual information about what would be risked by disobedience, but they also contain proclamations specifying that it is *wrong* to disobey. . . .

The moral influence of the criminal law may take various forms. It seems to be quite generally accepted among the members of society that the law should be obeyed even though one is dissatisfied with it and wants it changed. If this is true, we may conclude that the law as an institution itself to some extent creates conformity. But more important than this formal respect for the law is respect for the values which the law seeks to protect. It may be said that from law and the legal machinery there emanates a flow of propaganda which favors such respect. Punishment is a means of expressing social disapproval. In this way the criminal law and its enforcement supplement and enhance the moral influence acquired through education and other non-legal processes. Stated negatively, the penalty neutralizes the demoralizing consequences that arise when people witness crimes being perpetrated.

Deterrence and moral influence may both operate on the conscious level. The potential criminal may deliberate about the hazards involved, or he may be influenced by a conscious desire to behave lawfully. However, with fear or moral influence as an intermediate link, it is possible to create unconscious inhibitions against crime, and perhaps to establish a condition of habitual lawfulness. In this case, illegal actions will not present themselves consciously as real alternatives to conformity, even in situations where the potential criminal would run no risk whatsoever of being caught.

General preventive effects do not occur only among those who have been informed about penal provisions and their applications. Through a process of learning and social imitation, norms and taboos may be transmitted to persons who have no idea about their origins – in much the way that innovations in Parisian fashions appear in the clothing of country girls who have never heard of Dior or Lanvin.

There is an interesting interplay between moral reprobation and legal implementation. At least three conditions combine to prevent an individual from perpetrating a punishable act he is tempted to perform: his moral inhibitions, his fear of the censure of his associates and his fear of punishment. The latter two elements are interwoven in many ways. A law violation may become known to the criminal's family, friends and neighbors even if there is no arrest or prosecution. However, it is frequently the process of arrest, prosecution and trial which brings the affair into the open and exposes the criminal to the censure of his associates. If the criminal can be sure that there will be no police action, he can generally rest assured that there will be no social reprobation. The legal machinery, therefore, is in itself the most effective means of mobilizing that kind of social control which emanates from community condemnation.

Note

The theories of punishment are not mutually exclusive. Imprisoning an offender may serve both retributive and deterrent functions, while at the same time restraining the offender for the duration of the sentence. While in prison, rehabilitative services may be provided.

Questions
1.   To what extent under each theory will punishment fit (a) the crime, (b) the criminal?
2.   Consider the task of a Parliament which has decided to make careless driving a criminal offence. What penalties should be imposed if the goal is (a) restraint, (b) rehabilitation, (c) deterrence, (d) retribution?
3.   To what extent are the various theories based on different theories of human nature? Which of the theories is premised on an assumption of 'free will'? What would be the implications if one were to accept a determinist philosophy that events are predetermined by forces beyond the control of individuals?
4.   Are there some persons, such as children and the mentally ill, who are not deterrable? Does it logically follow that the criminal law is useless in such cases? What of criminals who assume that they will never be caught (is it not the exceptional and masochistic criminal who proceeds on the opposite assumption)? For these individuals, is not the potential penalty little more than a matter of academic interest?

B   Sentencing

Sentencing represents the application of the theories of punishment in the 'real world'. There are three stages. In the first, Parliament sets the maximum (very rarely the minimum) sentence which can be imposed for each offence. In the second, the trial judge determines the appropriate sentence for the individual offender convicted of a particular crime. In the third, the Court of Appeal may review the sentence imposed by the trial judge.

Underlying each of the stages may be a philosophy of the appropriate function of punishment which is being served by the sentencing decision. This philosophical base may be expressly articulated or simply implied. Consider in this regard the Criminal Justice Act 1991, which had a short and stormy existence.

Criminal Justice Act 1991

1.   Restrictions on imposing custodial sentences
(1)   This section applies where a person is convicted of an offence punishable with a custodial sentence other than one fixed by law.
(2)   Subject to subsection (3) below, the court shall not pass a custodial sentence on the offender unless it is of the opinion —
(a)   that the offence, or the combination of the offence and one other offence associated with it, was so serious that only such a sentence can be justified for the offence; or
(b)   where the offence is a violent or sexual offence, that only such a sentence would be adequate to protect the public from serious harm from him.

(3)   Nothing in subsection (2) above shall prevent the court from passing a custodial sentence on the offender if he refuses to give his consent to a community sentence which is proposed by the court and requires that consent.

(4)   Where a court passes a custodial sentence, it shall be its duty —

(a)   in a case not falling within subsection (3) above, to state in open court that it is of the opinion that either or both of paragraphs (a) and (b) of subsection (2) above apply and why it is of that opinion; and

(b)   in any case, to explain to the offender in open court and in ordinary language why it is passing a custodial sentence on him.

(5)   A magistrates' court shall cause a reason stated by it under subsection (4) above to be specified in the warrant of commitment and to be entered in the register.

2.   Length of custodial sentences

(1)   This section applies where a court passes a custodial sentence other than one fixed by law.

(2)   The custodial sentence shall be —

(a)   for such term (not exceeding the permitted maximum) as in the opinion of the court is commensurate with the seriousness of the offence, or the combination of the offence and other offences associated with it; or

(b)   where the offence is a violent or sexual offence, for such longer term (not exceeding that maximum) as in the opinion of the court is necessary to protect the public from serious harm from the offender.

(3)   Where the court passes a custodial sentence for a term longer than is commensurate with the seriousness of the offence, or the combination of the offence and other offences associated with it, the court shall —

(a)   state in open court that it is of the opinion that subsection (2)(b) above applies and why it is of that opinion; and

(b)   explain to the offender in open court and in ordinary language why the sentence is for such a term.

(4)   A custodial sentence for an indeterminate period shall be regarded for the purposes of subsections (2) and (3) above as a custodial sentence for a term longer than any actual term.

29.   Effect of previous convictions etc.

(1)   An offence shall not be regarded as more serious for the purposes of any provision of this Part by reason of any previous convictions of the offender or any failure of his to respond to previous sentences.

(2)   Where any aggravating factors of an offence are disclosed by the circumstances of other offences committed by the offender, nothing in this Part shall prevent the court from taking those factors into account for the purpose of forming an opinion as to the seriousness of the offence.

Questions

1.   What theory of punishment underlay ss. 1(2)(a) and 2(2)(a) of the 1991 Act? Sections 1(2)(b) and 2(2)(b)? Section 29?

2.   The Act and the White Paper preceding it (*Crime, Justice, and Protecting the Public* (Cmd. 965, 1990)) specifically rejected the value of deterrence:

[M]uch crime is committed on impulse, given the opportunity presented by an open window or unlocked door, and it is committed by offenders who live from moment to moment; their crimes are as impulsive as the rest of their feckless, sad or pathetic lives. It is unrealistic to construct sentencing arrangements on the assumption that most offenders will weigh up the possibilities in advance and base their conduct on rational calculation. Often they do not.

Assuming the Committee was correct, did it follow that the deterrent effect of sentences should be ignored?

Note
The Act favoured a policy of community sentences. Community sentences have traditionally been associated with a philosophy of rehabilitation. The emphasis on community sentences in the 1991 Act, however, seemed to be inspired more by the lesser costs of such sentences compared to imprisonment than by any genuine commitment to the rehabilitative idea.

Sentences can be appealed by either the defendant or the prosecution, although an appeal by the latter is rare. The rationale for allowing an appeal is to provide consistency of treatment for comparably situated defendants who commit similar crimes. In the exercise of the judge's initial discretion, as well as in the review of that sentence, the court often took into account the theoretical justifications for punishment:

R v Sargeant
(1974) 60 Cr App R 74
Court of Appeal

LAWTON LJ: On May 20, 1974, at the Central Criminal Court, the appellant pleaded guilty to a charge of affray at the end of the prosecution's case. On May 24, 1974, he was sentenced by His Honour Judge Argyle to two years' imprisonment. He now appeals against that sentence.

During the evening of October 26, 1973, the appellant was on duty at a discotheque at Crown Hill at Croydon, together with three other doormen. Their job in colloquial language was to act as 'bouncers.' The appellant had no criminal record. The other bouncers had. One of them had a bad criminal record. There was another man on the staff of this discotheque who was taking part in what the prosecution alleged was the affray. He too had a bad criminal record.

. . . [The] appellant has had no previous convictions. He is 26 years of age, and a skilled green-keeper in the golfing world. He started acting as an assistant green-keeper in his adolescence. He has acquired a good deal of expertise. He has had jobs as green-keeper with a number of distinguished and well-known golf clubs. The tragedy of his case is that the very day on which he appeared at the Central Criminal Court he should have been starting work as head green-keeper with one of the best known golf clubs in the south of England. His conviction has inevitably meant that that job is no longer available to him, and it also means that there is a strong possibility that no golf club will ever employ him again. By his stupidity on this occasion he has deprived himself of a career in the golfing world, and all because he lost his temper when trouble started. The very fact that he has lost his career is of course a severe penalty for him.

The problem for this Court is whether the sentence was wrong in principle. It is necessary for this Court to analyse the facts of this case. We have come to the conclusion that, if the trial judge did analyse them, he analysed them incorrectly. What really was the case against this appellant? His job was to help to keep order. He was inexperienced in that job. It is clear from his record that he is inclined to be headstrong. I say that, because despite his skill as a green-keeper, he has had some difficulty in keeping jobs, because he cannot always see eye to eye with golf clubs' secretaries. He had had something to drink whilst he was on duty that night, though there was nothing to suggest that he had had too much to drink. If he had followed the instructions of his employers, he would not have had anything to drink. He was faced with a situation in which a young man had been misbehaving. He took the view, wrongly with hindsight, that the best way of dealing with the potential difficulties which that young man might cause, if he resumed misbehaving, was to use some force on him. He used no weapon. What he did do was to butt the young man, which can be very painful for the victim. If he had thought for a moment, he would have appreciated the nature and extent of the chain of events which he was starting. It is almost certain that he did not think. Young men who act in this kind of physical way seldom do think of which the consequences are going to be. The evidence establishes that very soon after he did what he did he was put out of action and took no further part in the appalling violence which followed.

What ought the proper penalty to be? We have thought it necessary not only to analyse the facts, but to apply to those facts the classical principles of sentencing. Those classical principles are summed up in four words: retribution, deterrence, prevention and rehabilitation. Any judge who comes to sentence ought always to have those four classical principles in mind and to apply them to the facts of the case to see which of them has the greatest importance in the case with which he is dealing.

I will start with retribution. The Old Testament concept of an eye for an eye and tooth for tooth no longer plays any part in our criminal law. There is, however, another aspect of retribution which is frequently overlooked; it is that society, through the courts, must show its abhorrence of particular types of crime, and the only way in which the courts can show this is by the sentences they pass. The courts do not have to reflect public opinion. On the other hand courts must not disregard it. Perhaps the main duty of the court is to lead public opinion. Anyone who surveys the criminal scene at the present time must be alive to the appalling problem of violence. Society, we are satisfied, expects the courts to deal with violence. The weapons which the courts have at their disposal for doing so are few. We are satisfied that in most cases fines are not sufficient punishment for senseless violence. The time has come, in the opinion of this Court, when those who indulge in the kind of violence with which we are concerned in this case must expect custodial sentences.

But we are also satisfied that, although society expects the courts to impose punishment for violence which really hurts, it does not expect the courts to go on hurting for a long time, which is what this sentence is likely to do. We agree with the trial judge that the kind of violence which occurred in this case called for a custodial sentence. This young man has had a custodial sentence. Despite his good character, despite the excellent background from which he comes, very deservedly he has had the humiliation of hearing prison gates closing behind him. We take the view that for men of good character the very fact that prison gates have closed is the main punishment. It does not necessarily follow that they should remain closed for a long time.

I turn now to the element of deterrence, because it seems to us the trial judge probably passed this sentence as a deterrent one. There are two aspects of deterrence: deterrence of the offender and deterrence of likely offenders. Experience has shown over the years that deterrence of the offender is not a very useful approach, because those who have their wits about them usually find the closing of prison gates an experience which they do not want again. If they do not learn that lesson, there is likely to be a high degree of recidivism anyway. So far as deterrence of others is concerned, it is the experience of the courts that deterrent sentences are of little value in respect of offences which are committed on the spur of the moment, either in hot blood or in drink or both. Deterrent sentences may very well be of considerable value where crime is premeditated. Burglars, robbers and users of firearms and weapons may very well be put off by deterrent sentences. We think it unlikely that deterrence would be of any value in this case.

We come now to the element of prevention. Unfortunately it is one of the facts of life that there are some offenders for whom neither deterrence nor rehabilitation works. They will go on committing crimes as long as they are able to do so. In those cases the only protection which the public has is that such persons should be locked up for a long period. This case does not call for a preventive sentence.

Finally, there is the principle of rehabilitation. Some 20 to 25 years ago there was a view abroad, held by many people in executive authority, that short sentences were of little value, because there was not enough time to give in prison the benefit of training. That view is no longer held as firmly as it was. This young man does not want prison training. It is not going to do him any good. It is his memory of the clanging of prison gates which is likely to keep him from crime in the future.

In the light of that analysis of the classical principles to be applied in sentencing, what is the result on the facts of this case? The answer is that this sentence is much too long. It was submitted that a suspended sentence should have been passed. For the reasons I have already given, we do not agree. But we are satisfied, having regard to the facts of this case and the social inquiry and prison reports which the Court has been given that we can deal with this case by substituting for the sentence which was passed such a sentence as will enable him to be discharged today. To that extent the appeal is allowed.

Consider the following case which raises many of the criminological issues discussed to this point:

R v Brown
[1993] 2 WLR 556
House of Lords

LORD TEMPLEMAN: . . . The question whether the defence of consent should be extended to the consequences of sado-masochistic encounters can only be decided by consideration of policy and public interest. Parliament can call on the advice of doctors, psychiatrists, criminologists, sociologists and other experts and can also sound and take into account public opinion. But the question must at this stage be decided by this House in its judicial capacity in order to determine whether the convictions of the appellants should be upheld or quashed.

The assertion was made on behalf of the appellants that the sexual appetites of sadists and masochists can only be satisfied by the infliction of bodily harm and that the law should not punish the consensual achievement of sexual satisfaction. There was no evidence to support the assertion that sado-masochist activities are essential to the happiness of the appellants or any other participants but the argument would be acceptable if sado-masochism were only concerned with sex, as the appellants contend. In my opinion sado-masochism is not only concerned with sex. Sado-masochism is also concerned with violence. The evidence discloses that the practices of the appellants were unpredictably dangerous and degrading to body and mind and were developed with increasing barbarity and taught to persons whose consents were dubious or worthless.

A sadist draws pleasure from inflicting or watching cruelty. A masochist derives pleasure from his own pain or humiliation. The appellants are middle-aged men. The victims were youths some of whom were introduced to sado-masochism before they attained the age of 21. . . .

The evidence disclosed that drink and drugs were employed to obtain consent and increase enthusiasm. The victim was usually manacled so that the sadist could enjoy the thrill of power and the victim could enjoy the thrill of helplessness. The victim had no control over the harm which the sadist, also stimulated by drink and drugs might inflict. In one case a victim was branded twice on the thigh and there was some doubt as to whether he consented to or protested against the second branding. The dangers involved in administering violence must have been appreciated by the appellants because, so it was said by their counsel, each victim was given a code word which he could pronounce when excessive harm or pain was caused. The efficiency of this precaution, when taken, depends on the circumstances and on the personalities involved. No one can feel the pain of another. The charges against the appellants were based on genital torture and violence to the buttocks, anus, penis, testicles and nipples. The victims were degraded and humiliated sometimes beaten, sometimes wounded with instruments and sometimes branded. Bloodletting and the smearing of human blood produced excitement. There were obvious dangers of serious personal injury and blood infection. Prosecuting counsel informed the trial judge against the protests of defence counsel, that although the appellants had not contracted Aids, two members of the group had died from Aids and one other had contracted an H.I.V. infection although not necessarily from the practices of the group. Some activities involved excrement. The assertion that the instruments employed by the sadists were clean and sterilised could not have removed the danger of infection, and the assertion that care was taken demonstrates the possibility of infection. Cruelty to human beings was on occasions supplemented by cruelty to animals in the form of bestiality. It is fortunate that there were no permanent injuries to a victim though no one knows the extent of harm inflicted in other cases. It is not surprising that a victim does not complain to the police when the complaint would involve him in giving details of acts in which he participated. Doctors of course are subject to a code of confidentiality.

In principle there is a difference between violence which is incidental and violence which is inflicted for the indulgence of cruelty. The violence of sado-masochistic encounters involves the indulgence of cruelty by sadists and the degradation of victims. Such violence is injurious to the participants and unpredictably dangerous. I am not prepared to invent a defence of consent for sado-masochistic encounters which breed and glorify cruelty and result in offences under sections 47 and 20 of the Act of 1861.

. . . Charges under the Act of 1861 are concerned with violence. The violence of sadists and the degradation of their victims have sexual motivations but sex is no excuse for violence.

Society is entitled and bound to protect itself against a cult of violence. Pleasure derived from the infliction of pain is an evil thing. Cruelty is uncivilised. I would answer the certified question in the negative and dismiss the appeals of the appellants against conviction.

LORD MUSTILL (dissenting): My Lords, this is a case about the criminal law of violence. In my opinion it should be a case about the criminal law of private sexual relations, if about anything at all. Whatever the outsider might feel about the subject matter of the prosecutions – perhaps horror, amazement or incomprehension, perhaps sadness – very few could read even a summary of the other activities without disgust. The House has been spared the video tapes, which must have been horrible. If the criminality of sexual deviation is the true ground of these proceedings, one would have expected that these above all would have been the subject of attack. Yet the picture is quite different.

The issue before the House is not whether the appellants' conduct is morally right, but whether it is properly charged under the Act of 1861. When proposing that the conduct is not rightly so charged I do not invite your Lordships' House to endorse it as morally acceptable. Nor do I pronounce in favour of a libertarian doctrine specifically related to sexual matters. Nor in the least do I suggest that ethical pronouncements are meaningless, that there is no difference between right and wrong, that sadism is praiseworthy, or that new opinions on sexual morality are necessarily superior to the old, or anything else of the same kind. What I do say is that these are questions of private morality; that the standards by which they fall to be judged are not those of the criminal law; and that if these standards are to be upheld the individual must enforce them upon himself according to his own moral standards, or have them enforced against him by moral pressures exerted by whatever religious or other community to whose ethical ideals he responds. The point from which I invite your Lordships to depart is simply this, that the state should interfere with the rights of an individual to live his or her life as he or she may choose no more than is necessary to ensure a proper balance between the special interests of the individual and the general interests of the individuals who together comprise the populace at large. Thus, whilst acknowledging that very many people, if asked whether the appellants' conduct was wrong, would reply 'Yes, repulsively wrong,' I would at the same time assert that this does not in itself mean that the prosecution of the appellants under sections 20 and 47 of the Offences against the Person Act 1861 is well founded.

This point leads directly to the second. As I have ventured to formulate the crucial question, it asks whether there is good reason to impress upon section 47 an interpretation which penalises the relevant level of harm irrespective of consent, i.e., to recognise sado-masochistic activities as falling into a special category of acts, such as duelling and prize-fighting, which 'the law says shall not be done.' This is very important, for if the question were differently stated it might well yield a different answer. In particular, if it were to be held that as a matter of law all infliction of bodily harm above the level of common assault is incapable of being legitimated by consent, except in special circumstances, then we would have to consider whether the public interest required the recognition of private sexual activities as being in a specially exempt category. This would be an altogether more difficult question and one which I would not be prepared to answer in favour of the appellants, not because I do not have my own opinions upon it but because I regard the task as one which the courts are not suited to perform, and which should be carried out, if at all, by Parliament after a thorough review of all the medical, social, moral and political issues, such as was performed by the Wolfenden Committee. Thus, if I had begun from the same point of departure as my noble and learned friend, Lord Jauncey of Tullichettle, I would have arrived at a similar conclusion; but differing from him on the present state of the law, I venture to differ.

Let it be assumed however that we should embark upon this question. I ask myself, not whether as a result of the decision in this appeal, activities such as those of the appellants should *cease* to be criminal, but rather whether the Act of 1861 (a statute which I venture to repeat once again was clearly intended to penalise conduct of a quite different nature) should in this new situation be interpreted so as to *make* it criminal. Why should this step be taken? Leaving aside repugnance and moral objection, both of

which are entirely natural but neither of which are in my opinion grounds upon which the court could properly create a new crime, I can visualise only the following reasons.
(1) Some of the practices obviously created a risk of genito-urinary infection, and others of septicaemia. These might indeed have been grave in former times, but the risk of serious harm must surely have been greatly reduced by modern medical science.
(2) The possibility that matters might get out of hand, with grave results. It has been acknowledged throughout the present proceedings that the appellants' activities were performed as a pre-arranged ritual, which at the same time enhanced their excitement and minimised the risk that the infliction of injury would go too far. Of course things might go wrong and really serious injury or death might ensue. If this happened, those responsible would be punished according to the ordinary law, in the same way as those who kill or injure in the course of more ordinary sexual activities are regularly punished. But to penalise the appellants' conduct even if the extreme consequences do not ensue, just because they might have done so would require an assessment of the degree of risk, and the balancing of this risk against the interests of individual freedom. Such a balancing is in my opinion for Parliament, not the courts; and even if your Lordships' House were to embark upon it the attempt must in my opinion fail at the outset for there is no evidence at all of the seriousness of the hazards to which sado-masochistic conduct of this kind gives rise. This is not surprising, since the impressive argument of Mr Purnell for the respondents did not seek to persuade your Lordships' to bring the matter within the Act of 1861 on the ground of special risks, but rather to establish that the appellants are liable *under the general law* because the level of harm exceeded the critical level marking off criminal from non-criminal consensual violence which he invited your Lordships to endorse.
(3) I would give the same answer to the suggestion that these activities involved a risk of accelerating the spread of auto-immune deficiency syndrome, and that they should be brought within the Act of 1861 in the interests of public health. The consequence would be strange, since what is currently the principal cause for the transmission of this scourge, namely consenting buggery between males, is now legal. Nevertheless, I would have been compelled to give this proposition the most anxious consideration if there had been any evidence to support it. But there is none, since the case for the respondent was advanced on an entirely different ground.
(4) There remains an argument to which I have given much greater weight. As the evidence in the present case has shown, there is a risk that strangers (and especially young strangers) may be drawn into these activities at an early age and will then become established in them for life. This is indeed a disturbing prospect, but I have come to the conclusion that it is not a sufficient ground for declaring these activities to be criminal under the Act of 1861. The element of the corruption of youth is already catered for by the existing legislation; and if there is a gap in it which needs to be filled the remedy surely lies in the hands of Parliament, not in the application of a statute which is aimed at other forms of wrongdoing. As regards proselytisation for adult sado-masochism the argument appears to me circular. For if the activity is not itself so much against the public interest that it ought to be declared criminal under the Act of 1861 then the risk that others will be induced to join in cannot be a ground for making it criminal.

Leaving aside the logic of this answer, which seems to me impregnable, plain humanity demands that a court addressing the criminality of conduct such as that of the present should recognise and respond to the profound dismay which all members of the community share about the apparent increase of cruel and senseless crimes against the defenceless. Whilst doing so I must repeat for the last time that in the answer which I propose I do not advocate the decriminalisation of conduct which has hitherto been a crime; nor do I rebut a submission that a new crime should be created, penalising this conduct, for Mr Purnell has rightly not invited the House to take this course. The only question is whether these consensual private acts are offences against the existing law of violence. To this question I return a negative response.

Questions
1.   Should the conduct in question in *Brown* have been prosecuted in the first place? What factors should enter into this decision? Who is the victim when sado-masochistic sexual activity occurs between consenting adults in private?
2.   What does *Brown* reveal about the relationship between law and morality? About judges and their moral values?
3.   What functions of punishment were served by the sentences imposed on the defendants in *Brown*?

III   The sources of the criminal law

A   Common law crimes

Originally criminal law was the primary responsibility of the judiciary. The courts laid down general principles of criminal liability, established the elements of specific crimes, and determined what defences to a criminal charge should be permitted. This so-called common law was not contained in any code or statute book but could be distilled from the opinions of the judges.

Over the years, the responsibility for determining what to make criminal and for defining crimes has shifted from the judiciary to the legislature. There are many reasons for and advantages to this shift. Unlike a court, Parliament is not limited by the facts of a particular case and can consider the global dimensions of a problem. Courts are also restricted to the evidence presented by the lawyers in the case, while Parliament can hold hearings, receive opinions of expert authorities and commission studies. Parliamentary debates may clarify the issues, and any resulting law represents a consensus judgment. The trial judge is more of a solitary figure, deciding cases with little input from others. Appellate courts will usually not consist of more than a panel of five. Finally, members of Parliament are democratically accountable for their decisions – they must periodically face the electorate, which can vote them out of office if dissatisfied with their performance. Judges are appointed rather than elected, and are not directly accountable to the public.

Today the common law of crimes has been largely, but not completely, displaced by statute. *But*:

(a)   Some crimes, such as murder and manslaughter, have never been defined in statute. We need to look at common law decisions to determine the elements of these crimes. Likewise, many defences to crime have never been reduced to statute and retain their common law definition.

(b)   Often Parliament will use a term in a statute without defining it formally. There is no statutory definition of even such basic criminal law terms as 'intention' or 'recklessness'. There may, however, be a well settled meaning of the term in the law. It may be Parliament's intent to preserve that meaning, in which case judicial decisions will need to be consulted in order to determine that meaning. In the case of terms that are not given specific definition by Parliament, judges may resort to common law cases for guidance or may utilise techniques of interpretation embodied in common law decisions.

(c)   Common law crimes may still be in force:

Shaw v *Director of Public Prosecutions*
[1962] AC 220
House of Lords

The appellant published a booklet, the Ladies' Directory, of some 28 pages, most of which were taken up with the names and addresses of prostitutes; the matter published left no doubt that the advertisers could be got in touch with at the telephone numbers given and were offering their services for sexual intercourse and, in some cases, for the practice of sexual perversions. The appellant's avowed purpose in publication was to assist prostitutes to ply their trade when, as a result of the Street Offences Act 1959, they were no longer able to solicit in the street. The prostitutes paid for the advertisements and the appellant derived a profit from the publication. The appellant pleaded not guilty to an indictment charging him with (1) conspiracy to corrupt public morals in that he conspired with the advertisers and other persons by means of the Ladies' Directory and the advertisements to debauch and corrupt the morals of youth and other subjects of the Queen; (2) living on the earnings of prostitution contrary to s. 30 of the Sexual Offences Act 1956; and (3) publishing an obscene article contrary to s. 2 of the Obscene Publications Act 1959.

At the trial evidence was given by prostitutes that they had paid for the advertisements out of their earnings, that the advertisements were good at bringing clients in, and as to the ages of the persons resorting to them and the meaning of abbreviations and expressions in the advertisements; they also gave evidence of the practices in which they indulged and there was evidence by the police as to objects found at their addresses. The summing-up gave no direction to the jury as to the relevance of the appellant's honesty of purpose. The jury convicted the appellant. He appealed, on the ground, *inter alia*, that there was no such offence at common law as the conspiracy alleged.

VISCOUNT SIMONDS: My Lords, . . . the first count in the indictment is 'Conspiracy to corrupt public morals,' and the particulars of offence will have sufficiently appeared. I am concerned only to assert what was vigorously denied by counsel for the appellant, that such an offence is known to the common law, and that it was open to the jury to find on the facts of this case that the appellant was guilty of such an offence. I must say categorically that, if it were not so, Her Majesty's courts would strangely have failed in their duty as servants and guardians of the common law. Need I say, my Lords, that I am no advocate of the right of the judges to create new criminal offences? I will repeat well-known words:

Amongst many other points of happiness and freedom which your Majesty's subjects have enjoyed there is none which they have accounted more dear and precious than this, to be guided and governed by certain rules of law which giveth both to the head and members that which of right belongeth to them and not by any arbitrary or uncertain form of government.

These words are as true today as they were in the seventeenth century and command the allegiance of us all. But I am at a loss to understand how it can be said either that the law does not recognise a conspiracy to corrupt public morals or that, though there may not be an exact precedent for such a conspiracy as this case reveals, it does not fall fairly within the general words by which it is described. . . . The fallacy in the argument that was addressed to us lay in the attempt to exclude from the scope of general words acts well calculated to corrupt public morals just because they had not been committed or had not been brought to the notice of the court before. It is not thus that the common law has developed. We are perhaps more accustomed to hear this matter discussed upon the question whether such and such a transaction is contrary to public policy. At once the controversy arises. On the one hand it is said that it is not possible in the twentieth century for the court to create a new head of public policy, on the other it is said that this is but a new example of a well-established head. In the sphere of criminal law I entertain no doubt that there remains in the courts of law a residual power to enforce the supreme and fundamental purpose of the law, to conserve not only the safety and order but also the moral welfare of the State and that it is their duty to guard it against attacks which may be the more insidious because they are novel and unprepared for. . . .

Note
The question after *Shaw* was whether courts were limited to discovering existing common law crimes, or whether they could create new common law crimes. The issue was addressed in *Knuller* v *Director of Public Prosecutions* [1973] AC 435, where the House of Lords purported to limit the judiciary's power to create new common law crimes. One might question whether it really matters, however, given the breadth of many common law crimes. Take, for instance, the common law crime of outraging public decency:

R v *Gibson and Another*
[1991] 1 All ER 439
Court of Appeal

The first defendant exhibited at an exhibition in a commercial art gallery run by the second defendant a model's head to which were attached earrings made out of freeze-dried human foetuses. The exhibit was entitled 'Human Earrings'. The gallery was open to, and was visited by, members of the public. The defendants were charged with, and convicted of, outraging public decency contrary to common law.

LORD LANE CJ: The article in question was one of 41 items which had been selected for display out of a much larger number by Sylveire. It was exhibit number 9, and was described in the catalogue as 'Human Earrings'.
    Although it was not suggested that Sylveire had taken active steps to publicise this particular exhibit, there was no doubt that the more people who attended the gallery,

the better pleased Sylveire would be, and the greater would be the likelihood of selling exhibits.

Now by leave of this court these two men appeal against their convictions.

. . .

The first ground is that the prosecution were precluded from proceeding on count 1, on which the appellants were eventually convicted, by s. 2(4) of the Obscene Publications Act 1959. That subsection reads as follows:

A person publishing an article shall not be proceeded against for an offence at common law consisting of the publication of any matter contained or embodied in the article where it is of the essence of the offence that the matter is obscene.

The first question to decide then is whether there is an offence at common law of outraging public decency. The answer to that question is to be found in the speech of Lord Simon of Glaisdale in the well-known case of *Knuller (Publishing Printing and Promotions) Ltd* v *DPP* [1972] 2 All ER 898 at 935, [1973] AC 435 at 493:

Fourthly, my noble and learned friend, Lord Morris of Borth-y-Gest, in [*Shaw* v *DPP*] [1961] 2 All ER 446 at 467, [1962] AC 220 at 292, where, though there was no count of conspiracy to outrage public decency, most of the cases were reviewed, said: 'The cases afford examples of the conduct of individuals which has been punished because it outraged public decency . . . ' And my noble and learned friend, Lord Reid, though dissenting on the main issue, said ([1961] 2 All ER 446 at 460, [1962] AC 220 at 281): 'I think that they [the authorities] establish that it is an indictable offence to say or do or exhibit anything in public which outrages public decency, whether or not it also tends to corrupt and deprave those who see or hear it.'

. . . Mr Worsley points out, and points out correctly, that the object of the common law offence is to protect the public from suffering feelings of outrage by such exhibition. Thus, if a defendant intentionally does an act which in fact outrages public decency, the public will suffer outrage whatever the defendant's state of mind may be. If the defendant's state of mind is a critical factor, then, he submits, a man could escape liability by the very baseness of his own standards.

. . . The authorities on the question of exhibition outraging public decency are few and far between. One of the very few which it has been possible to trace is *R* v *Crumden* (1809) 2 Camp 89, 170 ER 1091. That was a case where a gentleman was bathing in the nude at Brighton. It is a brief report, and M'Donald CB said (2 Camp 89 at 90, 170 ER 1091 at 1091–1092):

I can entertain no doubt that the defendant, by exposing his naked person on the occasion alluded to, was guilty of a misdemeanour. The law will not tolerate such an exhibition. Whatever his intention might be, the necessary tendency of his conduct was to outrage decency, and to corrupt the public morals. Nor is it any justification that bathing at this spot might a few years ago be innocent. For any thing that I know, a man might a few years ago have harmlessly danced naked in the fields beyond Montague house; but it will scarcely be said by the learned counsel for the defendant, that any one might now do so with impunity in Russell Square. Whatever place becomes the habitation of civilized men, there the laws of decency must be enforced. The defendant was found guilty; and when he was brought up for judgment, the Court of KB expressed a clear opinion, that the offence imputed to him was a misdemeanour, and that he had been properly convicted.

The result, in our judgment, seems to be this. First of all the requirements with regard to mens rea should be the same in this offence as they are in the cognate offence of obscene libel. That is borne out by what Lord Scarman said in *R v Lemon* [1979] 1 All ER 898, [1979] AC 617. If that is so, then the decision of the House of Lords in *R v Lemon*, albeit by a majority, indicates that the submissions of the prosecution in this case are to be preferred to those of the appellants'.

One turns then to examine in a little more detail the speeches of their Lordships in that case. They are most conveniently summarised by Lord Russell of Killowen, where he said, in his usual trenchant and felicitous language ([1979] 1 All ER 898 at 921, [1979] AC 617 at 657–658):

> So I return to the question of intent. The authorities embrace an abundance of apparently contradictory or ambivalent comments. There is no authority in your Lordships' House on the point. The question is open for decision. I do not, with all respect to the speech of my noble and learned friend, Lord Diplock, consider that the question is whether this is an offence of strict liability. It is necessary that the editor or publisher should be aware of that which he publishes. Indeed that was the function of Lord Campbell's Act (Libel Act 1843), which assumed the law to be that an intention in the accused to blaspheme was not an ingredient of the offence, since it removed by statute a vicarious liability for an act of publication done by another without authority. Why then should this House, faced with a deliberate publication of that which a jury with every justification has held to be a blasphemous libel, consider that it should be for the prosecution to prove, presumably beyond reasonable doubt, that the accused recognised and intended it to be such or regarded it as immaterial whether it was? I see no ground for that. It does not to my mind make sense: and I consider that sense should retain a function in our criminal law. The reason why the law considers that the publication of a blasphemous libel is an offence is that the law considers that such publication should not take place. And if it takes place, and the publication is deliberate, I see no justification for holding that there is no offence when the publisher is incapable for some reason particular to himself of agreeing with a jury on the true nature of the publication.

Moreover, *R v Lemon*, as will have been clear from the passages which we have cited, was an allegation of an outrage on the public on a religious basis rather than a general basis, which is the case in the instant appeal. But outrage it certainly was, and the same considerations in logic should apply to this case as applied to the religious outrage in *R v Lemon*. That is the submission to us this morning of Mr Worsley, and we find that a cogent argument.

The result is this. Those passages, and the argument of Mr Worsley to which I have just made reference, lead us to the conclusion that, where the charge is one of outraging public decency, there is no requirement that the prosecution should prove an intention to outrage or such recklessness as is submitted by Mr Robertson. If the publication takes place, and if it is deliberate, there is, in the words of Lord Russell —

> no justification for holding that there is no offence when the publisher is incapable for some reason particular to himself of agreeing with the jury on the true nature of the publication.

. . .

Questions
1. It is said that hard cases make bad law. Do *Shaw* and *Gibson* illustrate the point? Do common law crimes simply provide judges (who have been characterised as middle-aged, middle class, and middle-minded males) with a way to punish conduct of which they personally disapprove? What problems are posed by common law crimes in terms of a citizen's ability to discover and know the law?
2. Some would argue that common law crimes serve as a safety net in which to catch those individuals who violate society's norms but not its statutory criminal law. Which functions of punishment are served by having this residual catch-all category of crime? Which are not?

Notes
1. In most of Europe there are neither common law crimes nor statutes but written codes. Unlike statutes, which are adopted piecemeal over time, a code constitutes a comprehensive and integrated expression of the whole of a country's criminal law. Greater consistency in terminology can be achieved than in statutes passed by different Parliaments at different times. Often the code will go beyond a simple listing of crimes and defences to include a statement of general criminal law principles. Examples and commentary may also be included.
2. The Law Commission has proposed a draft criminal code for the UK. Its provisions will on occasion be referred to in this book, not because they are the current law (to this date Parliament has not enacted the code into law), but because they represent the well thought out views of those who have given the matter serious consideration.

B   Statutory interpretation

To say that the common law has largely been replaced by statute is not to say that judges no longer have a role in the development of the law. It remains the judge's responsibility

(a)   to interpret the meaning of the terms of the statute
(b)   to determine what conduct falls within the ambit of the statute and what defences may be raised by way of excuse, justification, or mitigation
(c)   to provide guidance to juries, and, in the case of appellate courts, to trial judges and
(d)   to determine the appropriate sentence, within limits set by legislature, for those convicted of violating the statute.

Of the above tasks, perhaps the most challenging, as well as far-reaching, is that of statutory interpretation. Statutory interpretation is a complicated subject and books have been written on the topic (see, e.g., J. Bell and G. Engle (eds), *Cross on Statutory Interpretation* (2nd ed.) (1987); F. Bennion, *Statutory Interpretation* (1984)). It would be impossible to do justice to the complexity of the subject here, and we will simply present one case which illustrates some of the types of problems which can arise:

R v *Bloxham*
[1982] 1 All ER 582
House of Lords

LORD BRIDGE OF HARWICH: My Lords, in January 1977 the appellant purchased a motor car for £1,300. He paid the seller £500 in cash and was to pay the balance when the seller produced the car's registration document, but in the event this never happened. The car had in fact been stolen. It is accepted by the Crown that the appellant did not know or believe this when he acquired the car. In December 1977 he sold the car for £200 to an unidentified third party who was prepared to take the car without any registration document.

The appellant was charged under s. 22(1) of the Theft Act 1968 with handling stolen goods, the particulars of the relevant count in the indictment alleging that he —

> dishonestly undertook or assisted in the disposal or realization of certain stolen goods, namely a Ford Cortina motor car registered number SJH 606M, by or for the benefit of another, namely the unknown purchaser knowing or believing the same to be stolen goods.

At the trial it was submitted that the count disclosed no offence in that the disposal or realisation of the car had been for the appellant's own benefit, not for the benefit of the unknown purchaser, and that in any event the purchaser was not within the ambit of the categories of 'other person' contemplated by s. 22(1). The judge ruled that the purchaser derived a benefit from the transaction, in that, although he got no title, he had the use of the car, that there was no reason to give any restricted construction to the words 'another person' in the subsection, and that, accordingly, on the undisputed facts, the appellant had undertaken the disposal or realisation of the car for the benefit of another person within the meaning of s. 22(1). In face of this ruling the appellant entered a plea of guilty, thereby, it may be noted, confessing both his guilty knowledge and his dishonesty in relation to the December transaction.

On appeal against conviction to the Court of Appeal, the court affirmed the trial judge's ruling and dismissed the appeal (see [1981] 2 All ER 647, [1981] 1 WLR 859). The court certified the following point of law of general public importance as involved in their decision:

> Does a bona fide purchaser for value commit an offence of dishonestly undertaking the disposal or realisation of stolen property for the benefit of another if when he sells the goods on he knows or believes them to be stolen?'

The present appeal is brought by leave of your Lordships' House.

The full text of s. 22(1) of the Theft Act 1968 reads:

> A person handles stolen goods if (otherwise than in the course of the stealing) knowing or believing them to be stolen goods he dishonestly receives the goods, or dishonestly undertakes or assists in their retention, removal, disposal or realisation by or for the benefit of another person, or if he arranges to do so.

. . .

The critical words to be construed are 'undertakes . . . their . . . disposal or realisation . . . for the benefit of another person'. Considering these words first in isolation, it seems to me that, if A sells his own goods to B, it is a somewhat strained use of language to describe this as a disposal or realisation of the goods for the benefit of B. True it is that B obtains a benefit from the transaction, but it is surely more natural to say that the disposal or realisation is for A's benefit than for B's. It is the purchase, not the sale, that is for the benefit of B. It is only when A is selling as agent for a third party C that it would be entirely natural to describe the sale as a disposal or realisation for the benefit of another person.

But the words cannot, of course, be construed in isolation. They must be construed in their context, bearing in mind, as I have pointed out, that the second half of the section creates a single offence which can be committed in various ways. I can ignore for present purposes the concluding words 'or if he arranges to do so', which throw no light on the point at issue. The preceding words contemplate four activities (retention, removal, disposal, realisation). The offence can be committed in relation to any one of these activities in one or other of two ways. First, the offender may himself undertake the activity *for the benefit* of another person. Second, the activity may be undertaken by another person and the offender may assist him. Of course, if the thief or an original receiver and his friend act together in, say, removing the stolen goods, the friend may be committing the offence in both ways. But this does not invalidate the analysis, and if the analysis holds good it must follow, I think, that the category of other persons contemplated by the subsection is subject to the same limitations in whichever way the offence is committed. Accordingly, a purchaser, as such, of stolen goods cannot, in my opinion, be 'another person' within the subsection, since his act of purchase could not sensibly be described as a disposal or realisation of the stolen goods by him. Equally, therefore, even if the sale to him could be described as a disposal or realisation for his benefit, the transaction is not, in my view, within the ambit of the subsection. In forming this opinion I have not overlooked that in *R v Deakin* [1972] 3 All ER 803 at 808, [1972] I WLR 1618 at 1624 Phillimore LJ said of the appellant, a purchaser of stolen goods who was clearly guilty of an offence under the first half of s. 22(1) but had only been charged under the second half, that he was 'involved in the realisation'. If he meant to say that a purchase of goods is a realisation of those goods by the purchaser, I must express my respectful disagreement.

If the foregoing considerations do not resolve the issue of construction in favour of the appellant, at least they are, I believe, sufficient to demonstrate that there is an ambiguity. Conversely, it is no doubt right to recognise that the words to be construed are capable of the meaning which commended itself to the learned trial judge and to the Court of Appeal. In these circumstances, it is proper to test the question whether the opinion I have expressed in favour of a limited construction of the phrase 'for the benefit of another person' is to be preferred to the broader meaning adopted by the courts below, by any available aids to construction apt for the resolution of statutory ambiguities.

As a general rule, ambiguities in a criminal statute are to be resolved in favour of the subject, [sic] in favour of the narrower rather than the wider operation of an ambiguous penal provision. But here there are, in my opinion, more specific and weightier indications which point in the same direction as the general rule.

First, it is significant that the Theft Act 1968, notwithstanding the wide ambit of the definition of theft provided by ss. 1 and 3(1), specifically protects the innocent purchaser of goods who subsequently discovers that they were stolen, by s. 3(2) which provides:

Where property or a right or interest in property is or purports to be transferred for value to a person acting in good faith, no later assumption by him of rights which he believes himself to be acquiring shall, by reason of any defect in the transferor's title, amount to theft of the property.

It follows that, though some might think that in this situation honesty would require the purchaser, once he knew the goods were stolen, to seek out the true owner and return them, the criminal law allows him to retain them with impunity for his own benefit. It hardly seems consistent with this that, if he deals with them for the benefit of a third party in some way that falls within the ambit of the activities referred to in the second half of s. 22(1), he risks prosecution for handling which carries a heavier maximum penalty (14 years) than theft (10 years). The force of this consideration is not, in my view, significantly weakened by the possibility that the innocent purchaser of stolen goods who sells them after learning they were stolen may commit the quite distinct offences of obtaining by deception (if he represents that he has a good title) or, conceivably, of aiding and abetting the commission by the purchaser of the offence of handling by receiving (if both know the goods were stolen).

Second, it is clear that the words in parenthesis in s. 22(1) ('otherwise than in the course of the stealing') were designed to avoid subjecting thieves, in the ordinary course, to the heavier penalty provided for handlers. But most thieves realise the goods they have stolen by disposing of them to third parties. If the judge and the Court of Appeal were right, all such thieves are liable to prosecution as principals both for theft and for handling under the second half of s. 22(1).

Finally, we have the benefit of the Eighth Report of the Criminal Law Revision Committee (Cmnd 2977), which led to the passing of the Theft Act 1968 including the provisions presently under consideration in the same form as they appeared in the draft Bill annexed to the report, to assist us in ascertaining what was the mischief which the Act, and in particular the new offence created by s. 22(1), was intended to cure. We are entitled to consider the report for this purpose to assist us in resolving any ambiguity, though we are not, of course, entitled to take account of what the committee thought their draft Bill meant: see *Black-Clawson International Ltd* v *Papierwerke Waldhof-Aschaffenburg AG* [1975] 1 All ER 810, [1975] AC 951.

There is a long section in the report headed 'Handling Stolen Goods etc' from paras 126 to 144. The committee, after drawing attention to the limitations of the existing offence of receiving, say in para 127:

. . . we are in favour of extending the scope of the offence to certain other kinds of meddling with stolen property. This is because the object should be to combat theft by making it more difficult and less profitable to dispose of stolen property. Since thieves may be helped not only by buying the property but also in other ways such as facilitating its disposal, it seems right that the offence should extend to these kinds of assistance.

This gives a general indication of the mischief aimed at. The ensuing paragraphs, after setting out the proposed new provision in the terms which now appear in s. 22(1) of the Act, give numerous illustrations of the activities contemplated as proper to attract the same criminal sanction as that previously attaching to the old offence of receiving. Throughout these paragraphs there is no hint that a situation in any way approximating to the circumstances of the instant case lay within the target area of the mischief which the committee intended their new provision to hit.

For these reasons I have reached the conclusion that any ambiguity in the relevant language of s. 22(1) should be resolved in favour of the narrower meaning suggested earlier in this opinion. . . .

Notes and questions

1. Statutory interpretation problems often arise because language has an indeterminate quality to it. A word may have multiple dictionary meanings, and in common usage (not to mention technical usage) more meanings still. Indeterminacy of language is a two-edged sword. While such language broadens the sweep of the law and helps to ensure that wrongdoers do not escape the law's net, it can also lead to situations where conduct which Parliament may not have intended to be made criminal falls within the literal wording of the statute. Was *Bloxham* such a case? Why might Parliament deliberately choose to use broad and somewhat general language, and to leave key terms undefined?

2. Lord Bridge states in *Bloxham* that the words of a statute should be read in context. Why? Why should they not simply be given their literal, or dictionary or, as used to be asserted, their 'plain meaning'? How does a court determine 'context'?

3. In his opinion in *Bloxham*, Lord Bridge examined the Report of the Criminal Law Revision Committee, on which the Theft Act was based, but added this cryptic comment:

> We are entitled to consider the report [to assist us in ascertaining what was the mischief which the Act, and in particular the new offence created by s. 22(1), was intended to cure], though we are not, of course, entitled to take account of what the committee thought their draft Bill meant.

Why the latter limitation? Why look to the Committee report at all, since the concern surely must be with *Parliament's* goals and purposes rather than with those of the *Committee*?

The doctrine of Parliamentary sovereignty requires a court to defer to the will of Parliament as expressed in its statutory enactments. Courts are not free to substitute their views as to the proper scope of a criminal law statute for those of Parliament. The problem lies in determining Parliament's purpose. Parliament may not expressly disclose its purpose and the members of Parliament do not speak with one voice. Parliamentary debates might seem a useful source to consult, but until recently the declared position of the House of Lords was that it would be improper for a judge to do so. See *Davis v Johnson* [1979] AC 264. This position has to some extent now been modified in *Pepper v Hart* [1992] WLR 1032, where the House of Lords held that a court could refer to *Hansard* if a statute is ambiguous, or obscure or leads to an absurdity and the reference is to a statement by a minister or other promoter of the Bill. This does not, however, mean that a court *must* look to either legislative debates or background reports if the judges do not believe that such reports would be helpful. See *R v Gomez* [1992] 3 WLR 1067 (infra, p. 473).

Questions

1. If words in a statute are ambiguous, should the statute be strictly construed in favour of the defendant? Is it not better, as the courts commonly maintain, that a guilty defendant go free than that an innocent defendant be sent to prison?

2.   How important is it that citizens should be given 'fair warning' of what is prohibited? Is the more appropriate approach along the lines suggested by Lord Morris in *Knuller* v *DPP* [1973] AC 435, to the effect that 'those who skate on thin ice can hardly expect to find a sign which will denote the precise spot where they will fall in'?

IV   Generalised elements of a crime

Are there certain generic elements of a crime which can be identified? An attempt will be made here to do so, but the reader should be cautioned that there is no rule that every element must appear in every crime. The elements are a means of advancing your conceptual understanding of criminal law, rather than some form of absolute checklist. With that caveat, it is possible to identify six elements. Of these a further subdivision can be made – two of the elements might be better regarded as preconditions to criminal liability; two are elements strictly speaking; and two establish critical relationships between the elements.

(i)   Preconditions to criminal liability

(a)   *Law*. The existence of a law forbidding the conduct in question is an absolute prerequisite to the imposition of criminal liability (*nullum crimen sine lege*). One cannot be prosecuted for an offence that was not in existence at the time it was committed. The law need not necessarily be written in a statute book, as we saw in the case of common law crimes, but it must exist. Those subject to the law have a right to know what it proscribes, in order that they may conform their conduct to the law's requirements.

(b)   *Punishment*. A second prerequisite is that the law in question must prescribe punishment for its violation. Without prescribed punishment the law does not create a crime. We noted previously that punishment was one of the key distinguishing features of a crime. The punishment is inflicted in the name of the state for the violation of its law, and exists separate and independent of whether the defendant is required to pay damages in a civil suit.

(ii)   Elements strictly speaking

(a)   *Actus reus*. A general principle of criminal law holds that one cannot be punished for bad thoughts alone. The term *actus reus* refers to the conduct or behaviour prohibited by the law. It may have three dimensions. First is the act which must be perpetrated before one can be held criminally liable. In some instances, however, an omission or failure to act may satisfy the *actus reus* element. The second dimension is a specified result in relation to crimes defined in terms of result. No crime of murder or manslaughter, for example, takes place unless a person is killed. The final dimension of *actus reus* consists of the attendant circumstances that lend character to what would otherwise be a neutral act. The attendant circumstance that converts sexual relations with an adult woman into rape is the absence of consent on the part of the woman, and that which converts an ordinary marriage into bigamy is the fact that the defendant is already married to another at the time.

(b) *Mens rea.* Just as one cannot be punished for bad thoughts alone, one usually cannot be punished for acts which are not accompanied by a guilty mind. The term *mens rea* refers to the wrongful state of mind required to be proven by the prosecutor in order to secure a conviction. Usually the type of *mens rea* which will suffice for a conviction will be specified by statute or case law. In some instances the prosecutor will have to prove that the defendant acted intentionally; in others only that the defendant acted recklessly; and in still others simply that the defendant acted negligently or carelessly. A sliding scale of mental fault exists which varies depending on the crime charged. At the far end of this scale can be found statutes which do away with *mens rea* altogether and impose strict liability.

(iii) Critical relationships

(a) *Concurrence.* Concurrence (an inapt term) refers to the temporal relationship between *mens rea* and *actus reus*. Usually they will coincide at the point of the *actus reus*, but in crimes of intention it may be a more accurate description of the relationship to say that the *mens rea* was the precipitating factor in the defendant's decision to commit the crime.

(b) *Causation.* Some crimes are defined in terms of the occurrence of a particular result. In regard to these crimes, of which murder is the clearest example, the defendant's acts must be the cause of that result. As we will see, problems arise when the results are other than those intended or occur in a way other than intended.

The elements of *actus reus, mens rea,* concurrence, and causation will be examined more closely in the following chapters. At this juncture the point should be emphasised that the elements do not exist in a vacuum but only in relation to a specific crime. One might refer to the *actus reus* of murder, or the *actus reus* of theft, but it would be inappropriate to refer to an *actus reus* in the abstract divorced from a specified crime. Each crime has its own *actus reus*, which can only be determined by looking at the definition of the crime. The same is true for all of the elements.

The student of criminal law must learn to dissect a statute in the same way as a student of English might be taught to identify the subject, verb, object, etc. of a sentence. In criminal law it is necessary to identify each element of the crime. In a criminal case a prosecutor will go through this exercise in order to ensure that no element is overlooked (the Crown must prove each and every element of the offence beyond a reasonable doubt or its case fails); and a defence lawyer will go through the same exercise in order to hold the prosecution to its legal burden of proof. It is helpful at this stage of your career to get into the habit of identifying the elements of a crime and determining how each of the elements is satisfied in a particular case.

Question

Consider the following statutes and determine the component elements of each. Are there interpretation issues which are not resolved by the bare words of the statute that will need to be addressed by the courts? See if you can identify such issues.

Criminal Damage Act 1971

1. Destroying or damaging property

(1) A person who without lawful excuse destroys or damages any property belonging to another intending to destroy or damage any such property or being reckless as to whether any such property would be destroyed or damaged shall be guilty of an offence.

Sexual Offences Act 1956

1. Rape

(1) It is felony for a man to rape a woman.

Sexual Offences Act 1976

1. Meaning of 'rape' etc

(1) For the purposes of section 1 of the Sexual Offences Act 1956 (which relates to rape) a man commits rape if —

(a) he has unlawful sexual intercourse with a woman who at the time of the intercourse does not consent to it; and

(b) at the time he knows that she does not consent to the intercourse or he is reckless as to whether she consents to it;

and references to rape in other enactments (including the following provisions of this Act) shall be construed accordingly.

(2) It is hereby declared that if at a trial for a rape offence the jury has to consider whether a man believed that a woman was consenting to sexual intercourse, the presence or aobsence of reasonable grounds for such a belief is a matter to which the jury is to have regard, in conjunction with any other relevant matters, in considering whether he so believed.

Firearms Act 1968

18. Carrying firearm with criminal intent

(1) It is an offence for a person to have with him a firearm or imitation firearm with intent to commit an indictable offence, or to resist arrest or prevent the arrest of another, in either case while he has the firearm or imitation firearm with him.

Public Order Act 1986

1. Riot

(1) Where 12 or more persons who are present together use or threaten unlawful violence for a common purpose and the conduct of them (taken together) is such as would cause a person of reasonable firmness present at the scene to fear for his personal

safety, each of the persons using unlawful violence for the common purpose is guilty of riot.

(2)   It is immaterial whether or not the 12 or more use or threaten unlawful violence simultaneously.

(3)   The common purpose may be inferred from conduct.

(4)   No person of reasonable firmness need actually be, or be likely to be, present at the scene.

(5)   Riot may be committed in private as well as in public places.

(6)   A person guilty of riot is liable on conviction on indictment to imprisonment for a term not exceeding ten years or a fine or both.

2.   Violent disorder

(1)   Where 3 or more persons who are present together use or threaten unlawful violence and the conduct of them (taken together) is such as would cause a person of reasonable firmness present at the scene to fear for his personal safety, each of the persons using or threatening unlawful violence is guilty of violent disorder.

(2)   It is immaterial whether or not the 3 or more use or threaten unlawful violence simultaneously.

(3)   No person of reasonable firmness need actually be, or be likely to be, present at the scene.

(4)   Violent disorder may be committed in private as well as in public places.

(5)   A person guilty of violent disorder is liable on conviction on indictment to imprisonment for a term not exceeding 5 years or a fine or both, or on summary conviction to imprisonment for a term not exceeding 6 months or a fine not exceeding the statutory maximum or both.

V   A methodology for approaching the study of criminal law

It is possible to construct a general methodology which might prove helpful in your study of criminal law. In respect of each case you should ask yourself:

(a)   What crime has been charged? What are its elements? How are these elements defined by the statute (or by the court in the case of a common law crime)? How have they interpreted by the court?

(b)   At trial, on the basis of what facts did the Crown establish each of the elements of the crime? Were there other legally relevant facts of note? Often the decision of the appellate court will address a narrow issue, but that should not stop you from asking the more general question. As a lawyer preparing for an appeal, you will not know in advance on which issue the appellate court will focus. Sometimes the answer will be obvious, but one should get in the habit of this element-by-element analysis in order that no potential issue is overlooked. What is obvious to the lawyer is not necessarily obvious to the court.

(c)   Who has brought the appeal (usually the defendant, but sometimes the Crown)? What is the basis of the appeal? What issue is the court being asked to address? What issue does it address? What relief is sought and what relief, if any, is granted?

(d)   What is the decision of court? (Often there is more than one opinion, so one must begin by counting noses.) Who prevailed and why? What was the rationale for the decision? For what proposition of law does the case stand? (You need to learn to distinguish between statements of law necessary for the decision, and general comments on the law not essential to the decision, which are known as *obiter dicta*.)

(e)   Did the court reach the 'right' result? In one sense an appellate court's decision is 'right' because it has the authority to decide the issue in the case, and whatever it decides is 'right'. But on a less formalistic level, one is entitled to question the result. Does it make good sense? Is it just? Is it consistent with general principles of criminal law? Other cases? If not, are these other cases distinguishable in such a way that we can state that both cases make sense? Is the court's reasoning persuasive? Judges are not gods, and judicial decisions are not above criticism. The student of criminal law should inculcate the habit of thinking critically about judicial decisions.

(f)   How does the decision contribute to an overall understanding of criminal law? It is seductive, the way criminal law texts are perforce organised, to focus on the issue with which a particular case is concerned (generally identifiable by the chapter and section in which the case appears) and to see that issue in isolation. But one should not lose sight of the 'big picture'. Each case is part of a complex puzzle, and the interrelationship between the pieces of that puzzle needs to be understood.

2 *ACTUS REUS*

I Introduction

A common law maxim held that *actus non facit reum nisi mens sit rea*. The maxim served to draw attention to the two most critical elements of criminal liability: *actus reus* and *mens rea*. Literally it meant that an act was not wrongful unless accompanied by a wrongful state of mind. It was generally interpreted, however, to require the prosecutor to prove both a wrongful act *and* a wrongful state of mind on the part of the accused. As it related to *actus reus*, the maxim was correct in this sense: as a general proposition, one cannot be convicted for mere criminal thoughts; one must normally do something towards bringing those thoughts to fruition. This approach to criminal liability is justified by three primary considerations:

(a) the difficulty in proving what a person is thinking;
(b) the difficulty in distinguishing between those with a genuine criminal purpose and those who are simply fantasising or letting off steam; and
(c) perhaps most importantly, to exclude from criminal liability those whose adventures do not extend beyond the thought stage. Such individuals are neither dangerous nor in need of restraint or rehabilitation. They do no harm nor pose a threat to the public.

To the extent that the maxim seems to imply that in regard to every crime the offender must have committed a personal positive act, it is incorrect. Some crimes are defined in such a way that the failure to act constitutes the *actus reus* of the offence; in others an omission to act when there is a legal duty to act is treated as the equivalent of a positive act. Further, in some offences the *actus reus* is a state of affairs, with no requirement of an 'act' as such on the part of the accused. There are, for example, crimes in which the *actus reus* is possession of an illegal or dangerous item. Lastly, there are situations in which it is not necessary for the offender to have acted personally: the act of another will satisfy the requirement of *actus reus*.

The student should be advised that *actus reus* is an artificial creation which has no significance in and of itself. It provides a shorthand way of referring to that part of the crime concerned with the conduct prohibited by the law. The term is used by lawyers, judges and teachers of criminal law because they believe that it provides a useful framework for analysis. This opinion, however, is not universally shared:

R v Miller
[1983] 1 All ER 978
House of Lords

LORD DIPLOCK: . . . My Lords, it would I think be conducive to clarity of analysis of the ingredients of a crime that is created by statute, as are the great majority of criminal offences today, if we were to avoid bad Latin and instead to think and speak . . . about the conduct of the accused and his state of mind at the time of that conduct, instead of speaking of actus reus and mens rea.

Note
Whether or not Lord Diplock is correct, he draws our attention to two important points. First, a coherent criminal law code could easily be constructed without using the terms *actus reus* or *mens rea*. Parliament does not use these terms in its criminal law codifications. Nor are they used in the Draft Criminal Code Bill (1989), the drafters preferring 'fault' to *mens rea* and 'act' to *actus reus*. Secondly, the concepts of *actus reus* and *mens rea* are intended to aid analysis. If they have the opposite effect, then there is little point in stubbornly pursuing the search for them as such. It is sufficient to be clear about the elements of the crime as spelled out in the relevant statute. The law of crime is to be found in statutes and judicial decisions, not in the artificial constructs of *actus reus* and *mens rea*.

To the extent that it remains useful to speak of an *actus reus*, and courts and commentators alike do continue to use the term, it is best understood to refer to the prohibited conduct component, as opposed to the mental component, of the crime. This approach to *actus reus* may include either the results of the defendants conduct or the attendant circumstances which convert what might otherwise be an innocent or neutral act into one that is criminal. While it may be no crime to fire a gun in a deserted area, it is attempted murder if the gun is aimed at another human being, and if the bullet finds the human mark, the defendant may be guilty of either murder of manslaughter.

Some respected theorists, such as Glanville Williams, have suggested that *actus reus* should be conceived of as including the absence of excuse or justification. It may promote clarity of analysis, however, to discuss excuse and justification in the context of defences rather than as part of *actus reus*. This is the usual approach adopted and that taken in this book (see Chapter 8).

A somewhat different merger of elements may, on the other hand, be warranted. Literally translated, *actus reus* seems to refer to a physical act. There is, however, a mental component to most physical acts, in that they are the product of the will, and the courts have long accepted that a defendant whose acts are not the product of the defendant's will has not committed an *actus reus*. While if starting afresh one might include this so-called requirement of voluntariness within the rubric of *mens rea*, the judicial tradition is to view it as part of the *actus reus*. Keeping with this tradition, the issue of voluntariness and its somewhat esoteric limb known as automatism are examined in the present chapter.

Actus reus and *mens rea* are linked in a different way. Some acts are ambiguous, and *mens rea* can help determine whether the act is wrongful (*reus*). In *R v Court* [1988] 2 All ER 221, for example, a defendant who smacked a 12-year-old girl on her buttocks was charged with indecent assault. To determine whether the assault was indecent, the court looked at the defendant's state of mind. See also *R v Marcus* [1981] 2 All ER 833 (whether sleeping pills are a 'noxious thing' within the meaning of a statute depends in part on the intent with which they are administered).

Conversely, a defendant's acts can assist the jury in determining whether the defendant had the *mens rea* required for a crime. If an accused has shot her victim in the heart from close range, the jury may infer an intent to kill. This, however, must be understood only as a *logical inference* for a jury to draw; it is not a conclusion that they can be required to reach.

II   Liability for failure to act

A   Crimes defined in terms of a failure to act

Some statutory offences are defined in terms of a failure to act. The statute imposes a duty to act and the failure to act is itself the *actus reus*. The failure to pay one's taxes or to honour the rules of the road are examples.

In regard to other crimes, the statute may be less clear, and the court may be called upon to determine whether liability may be imposed for a failure to act. This is what occurred in the following case:

R v Mavji
[1987] 2 All ER 758
Court of Appeal

MICHAEL DAVIES J: . . . [I]t was alleged by the prosecution that . . . the appellant was trading in gold on a large scale at prices which would have inevitably produced a loss but for the fact that the appellant pocketed value added tax moneys which he charged but for which he did not account. The appellant was a director of a company called Princeve Ltd which traded from a shop with workshop and flat attached in North Wembley. . . .

'Cheating' is, as counsel for the appellant correctly submitted, a common law offence. As such, it was abolished by s. 32(1)(a) of the Theft Act 1968 'except as regards offences relating to the public revenue'. Punishment for cheating the revenue at common law remains at large . . . To establish cheating, so it was submitted, there must be an actual deceit, a positive act such as a false representation and not merely an omission such as a failure to make a value added tax return, even if the purpose of the omission is to avoid the payment of value added tax lawfully due. No such deceit or misrepresentation or other positive act was alleged in this indictment or in the prosecution's evidence or argument at the trials.

. . . In our judgment, 'cheating the revenue' can take place without any positive act of deceit or, to adopt and respectfully indorse the words of Drake J when ruling on this matter in the appellant's first trial:

> The common law offence of cheating does not necessarily require a false representation, either by words or conduct. Cheating can include any form of fraudulent conduct which results in diverting money from the revenue and in depriving the revenue of money to which it is entitled.

The appellant was in circumstances in which he had a statutory duty to make value added tax returns and to pay over to the Crown the value added tax due. He dishonestly failed to do either. Accordingly, he was guilty of cheating HM The Queen and the public revenue. No further act or omission required to be alleged or proved.

Appeal dismissed.

Although most of the crimes in which a failure to act will satisfy the *actus reus* requirement are creatures of Parliament, the issue may arise in respect to common law crimes.

R v Dytham
[1979] 3 All ER 641
Court of Appeal

LORD WIDGERY CJ: The appellant was a police constable in Lancashire. On 17th March 1977 at about one o'clock in the morning he was on duty in uniform and was standing by a hot dog stall in Duke Street, St Helens. A Mr Wincke was inside the stall and a Mr Sothern was by it. Some thirty yards away was the entrance to Cindy's Club. A man named Stubbs was ejected from the club by a bouncer. A fight ensued in which a number of men joined. There arose cries and screams and other indications of great violence. Mr Stubbs became the object of a murderous assault. He was beaten and kicked to death in the gutter outside the club. All this was audible and visible to the three men at the hot dog stall. At no stage did the appellant make any move to intervene or any attempt to quell the disturbance or to stop the attack on the victim. When the hubbub had died down he adjusted his helmet and drove away. . . .

His conduct was brought to the notice of the police authority. As a result he appeared on 10th October 1978 in the Crown Court at Liverpool to answer an indictment which was in these terms:

> . . . the charge against you is one of misconduct of an officer of justice, in that you . . . misconducted yourself whilst acting as an officer of justice in that you being present and a witness to a criminal offence namely a violent assault upon one . . . Stubbs by three others deliberately failed to carry out your duty as a police constable by wilfully omitting to take any steps to preserve the Queen's Peace or to protect the person of the said . . . Stubbs or to arrest or otherwise bring to justice [his] assailants.

[After conceding that a police constable was a public officer and that there did exist at common law an offence of misconduct in office, counsel for the appellant argued] that not every failure to discharge a duty which devolved on a person as the holder of a public office gave rise to the common law offence of misconduct in that office. As counsel for the appellant put it, non-feasance was not enough. There must be a malfeasance or at least a misfeasance involving an element of corruption. In support of this contention a number of cases were cited from 18th and 19th century reports. It is the fact that in nearly all of them the misconduct asserted involved some corrupt taint; but this appears to have been an accident of circumstance and not a necessary incident of the offence. . . .

In the present case it was not suggested that the appellant could not have summoned or sought assistance to help the victim or to arrest his assailants. The charge as framed left this answer open to him. Not surprisingly he did not seek to avail himself of it, for the facts spoke strongly against any such answer. The allegation made was not of mere non-feasance but of deliberate failure and wilful neglect. This involves an element of culpability which is not restricted to corruption or dishonesty but which must be of such a degree that the misconduct impugned is calculated to injure the public interest so as to call for condemnation and punishment. Whether such a situation is revealed by the evidence is a matter that a jury has to decide . . .

. . . The appeal is dismissed. . . .

Questions

1.   The court in *Dytham* distinguishes between failing to do what one ought to do (nonfeasance) and deliberate and wilful neglect (often referred to as misfeasance). Is this distinction a meaningful one in practice, or simply a way of characterising those cases where the accused's inaction has deviated so far from what would generally deemed to be acceptable that a court has no compunctions about imposing criminal liability?

2.   To anticipate an issue which will be addressed in a subsequent chapter, is there a problem in saying that in crimes such as Dytham's, the defendant's inaction, rather than the assailant's actions, caused the victim's death? If Dytham had not been present, the victim would still have died.

3.   Is there a difference in *moral* culpability between the infliction of harm and the failure to prevent harm; between one whose inaction causes death and one whose actions cause death? If so, should this difference be reflected in the criminal law?

B   *Crimes of commission by omission*

In the preceding section we saw instances where the failure to act was itself criminal. These cases pose little problem other than semantic – is the absence of an act an act? The problem is created by the tradition of using the term *actus reus* to include inaction. Once it is recognised that the illegality is itself the failure to act, the problem disappears.

A somewhat different situation occurs where the definition of the crime appears to require affirmative conduct leading to a particular result, but the defendant is tried for a failure to act that would have prevented that result. The issue has arisen most often in cases of homicide, where the victim would have lived if the defendant had taken appropriate action. When should such a failure warrant criminal liability?

There is in the UK no general legal, as opposed to moral, duty to help others. There is, for example, no legal obligation to shout a warning to a blind man about to walk off a cliff or to summon aid when he in fact falls over the cliff. Whether such duties should be imposed by law is an issue for Parliament. In many European countries there is a statutory duty to help a person in peril if the actor can do so without personal risk or risk to others. For example, Article 63(2) of the French Penal Code provides:

Any person who voluntarily fails to render assistance to a person in peril, which he or she could have given either personally or by calling for help, without personal danger or danger to others, is guilty of an offence and may be punished by imprisonment from three months to five years or by a fine of 360 francs to 20,000 francs or both.

Question
What are the arguments for and against a general duty to help others in distress? Should a duty to help others be deemed part of the obligation of citizenship? See generally E.J. Weinrib, 'The Case for a Duty to Rescue' (1980) *Yale Law Journal* 247.

In some instances, however, one may be under a legal, not simply a moral, duty to help another.

(i) Duties created by contract or office
A professional swimmer who happens to be standing by the pool in which a child is drowning has no legal duty to rescue the child. But is the same true for the lifeguard employed to watch the children in the pool? The lifeguard is under a contractual duty to prevent harms of precisely this type. The lifeguard who sits idly by while a child drowns is in breach of contract, but should criminal liability also attach for the child's death?

R v Pittwood
(1902) 19 TLR 37
Taunton Assizes

Philip Pittwood was charged with the manslaughter. It appeared that the prisoner occupied a hut as a gate-keeper on the Somerset and Dorset Railway near Glastonbury. His duties were to keep the gate shut whenever a train was passing along the line, which was a single line, and not many trains used to pass during the day. His hours of duty were from 7 in the morning till 7 p.m. On 18 July, at about 2.45 in the afternoon, White was in a hay cart crossing the line with several others, when a train came up and hit the cart, White being, struck and killed. Another man was also seriously injured, while the three remaining men by jumping out of the cart saved their lives.

MR JUSTICE WRIGHT: without calling upon the prosecution, gave judgment. He said he was clearly of opinion that in this case there was gross and criminal negligence, as the man was paid to keep the gate shut and protect the public. In his opinion: – (1) There might be cases of misfeasance and cases of mere non-feasance. Here it was quite clear there was evidence of misfeasance as the prisoner directly contributed to the accident. (2) A man might incur criminal liability from a duty arising out of contract.

Notes and questions

1. Compare *Pittwood* with *Dytham*, above. Dytham was convicted of misconduct in office; Pittwood of manslaughter. Is it more appropriate to charge defendants such as Pittwood and Dytham with crimes based on their failure to act, without regard to the consequences of their inaction, or crimes reflecting the resulting harm? Often the result is fortuitous. If it were not for Pittwood's inaction the death would not have occurred, but if no person were crossing the tracks, or if the conductor of the train had been able to bring it to a timely stop, there also would have been no death. Yet Pittwood's *actus reus* would be the same in all cases.

2. Pittwood's liability would seem to turn on the fact that there was a clause in his contract that could be made the basis for imposing liability. Yet the contract was between Pittwood and his employer, and the contractual duty was owed to the employer, not to members of the general public. Is it possible (desirable) to find an implied contractual duty to the public in regard to all occupations where the failure to perform competently can give rise to injury? Consider the situation of prison officials or warders in an institution for the criminally insane. Should they be held criminally responsible if, due to their incompetence, one of their charges were to escape and commit murder? Reconsider *Dytham*.

(ii)   Duties arising from the voluntary assumption of care
Similar and yet distinguishable from cases of duties arising out of the obligation of office (e.g., *Dytham*) and duties arising out of the obligation of contract (e.g., *Pittwood*) are cases where a duty of care has been voluntarily undertaken. In these cases the person has undertaken a duty but, unlike in the other two categories, there is no legal consideration for the undertaking. Can there nonetheless be criminal liability?

R v Instan
[1893] 1 QB 450
Queen's Bench Division

DAY J: Kate Instan . . . who is between thirty and forty years of age and unmarried, had no occupation and no means of her own of living. She was a niece of the deceased.

At the time of the committal of the alleged offence, and for some time previous thereto, she had been living with and had been maintained by the deceased. Deceased was a woman of some seventy-three years of age, and until a few weeks before her death was healthy and able to take care of herself. . . .

The deceased shortly before her death suffered from gangrene in the leg, which rendered her during the last ten days of her life quite unable to attend to herself or to move about or to do anything to procure assistance. No one but the prisoner had previous to the death any knowledge of the condition in which her aunt thus was. The prisoner continued to live in the house at the cost of the deceased, and took in the food supplied by the tradespeople; but does not appear to have given any to the deceased, and she certainly did not give or procure any medical or nursing attendance to or for her, or give notice to any neighbour of her condition or wants, although she had abundant opportunity and occasion to do so.

The body of the deceased was on August 2, while the prisoner was still living in the house, found much decomposed, partially dressed in her day clothes, and lying partly on the ground and partly prone upon the bed. The death probably occurred from four to seven days before August 3, the date of the post-mortem examination of the body. The cause of death was exhaustion caused by the gangrene, but substantially accelerated by neglect, want of food, of nursing, and of medical attendance during several days previous to the death. . . .

LORD COLERIDGE CJ: We are all of opinion that this conviction must be affirmed. It would not be correct to say that every moral obligation involves a legal duty; but every legal duty is founded on a moral obligation. A legal common law duty is nothing else than the enforcing by law of that which is a moral obligation without legal enforcement. There can be no question in this case that it was the clear duty of the prisoner to impart to the deceased so much as was necessary to sustain life of the food which she from time to time took in, and which was paid for by the deceased's own money for the purpose of the maintenance of herself and the prisoner; it was only through the instrumentality of the prisoner that the deceased could get the food. There was, therefore, a common law duty imposed upon the prisoner which she did not discharge.

Nor can there be any question that the failure of the prisoner to discharge her legal duty at least accelerated the death of the deceased, if it did not actually cause it. There is no case directly in point; but it would be a slur upon and a discredit to the administration of justice in this country if there were any doubt as to the legal principle, or as to the present case being within it. The prisoner was under a moral obligation to the deceased from which arose a legal duty towards her; that legal duty the prisoner has wilfully and deliberately left unperformed, with the consequence that there has been an acceleration of the death of the deceased owing to the non-performance of that legal duty. It is unnecessary to say more than that upon the evidence this conviction was most properly arrived at.

Question
Is the decision in the following case a logical extension of *Instan*?

R v *Stone; R* v *Dobinson*
[1977] 2 All ER 341
Court of Appeal

GEOFFREY LANE LJ: . . . In 1972, at 75 Broadwater, Bolton-on-Dearne in Yorkshire, there lived three people. Stone, an ex-miner now aged 67, widowed for ten years, who is partially deaf, almost totally blind and has no appreciable sense of smell; Gwendoline Dobinson, now aged 43, who had been his housekeeper and mistress for some eight years, and Stone's son called Cyril, aged 34, who is mentally subnormal. Stone is of low average intelligence. Dobinson is described as ineffectual and somewhat inadequate.

. . . Stone had a younger sister called Fanny, about 61 at the date of her death. She had been living with another sister called Rosy. For some reason, probably because Rosy could not tolerate her any longer, she had decided to leave. She came to live at no. 75, where she occupied a small front room. She was in receipt of a pension of £11.60 per week and gave her brother £1.50 towards the rent. She was eccentric in many ways. She was morbidly and unnecessarily anxious about putting on weight and so denied herself proper meals. She would take to her room for days. She would often stay in her room all day until the two appellants went to the public house in the evening, when she would creep down and make herself a meal.

In early spring 1975 the police called at the house. Fanny had been found wandering about in the street by herself without apparently knowing where she was. This caused the appellants to try and find Fanny's doctor. They tried to trace him through Rosy, but having walked a very considerable distance in their search they failed. . . . Fanny herself refused to tell them the doctor's name. She thought she would be 'put away' if she did. Nothing more was done to enlist outside professional aid.

In the light of what happened subsequently there can be no doubt that Fanny's condition over the succeeding weeks and months must have deteriorated rapidly. By July 1975 she was, it seems, unable or unwilling to leave her bed . . .

. . . It seems that some efforts were made to get a local doctor, but the neighbour who volunteered to do the telephoning (the appellants being incapable of managing the instrument themselves) was unsuccessful.

On 2nd August 1975 Fanny was found by Dobinson to be dead in her bed. . . .

[The] contention was advanced by counsel . . . that the evidence which the judge had suggested to the jury might support the assumption of a duty by the appellants did not, when examined, succeed in doing so. He suggested that the situation here was unlike any reported case. Fanny came to this house as a lodger. Largely, if not entirely due to her own eccentricity and failure to look after herself or feed herself properly, she became increasingly infirm and immobile and eventually unable to look after herself. Is it to be said, asks counsel for the appellants rhetorically, that by the mere fact of becoming infirm and helpless in these circumstances, she casts a duty on her brother and Mrs Dobinson to take steps to have her looked after or taken to hospital? The suggestion is that, heartless though it may seem, this is one of those situations where the appellants were entitled to do nothing; where no duty was cast on them to help, any more than it is cast on a man to rescue a stranger from drowning, however easy such a rescue might be.

This court rejects that proposition. Whether Fanny was a lodger or not she was a blood relation of the appellant Stone; she was occupying a room in his house; Mrs Dobinson had undertaken the duty of trying to wash her, of taking such food to her as she required. There was ample evidence that each appellant was aware of the poor condition she was in by mid-July. It was not disputed that no effort was made to summon an ambulance or the social services or the police despite the entreaties of Mrs Wilson and Mrs West. A social worker used to visit Cyril. No word was spoken to him. All these were matters which the jury were entitled to take into account when considering whether the necessary assumption of a duty to care for Fanny had been proved.

This was *not* a situation analagous to the drowning stranger. They *did* make efforts to care. They tried to get a doctor; they tried to discover the previous doctor. Mrs Dobinson helped with the washing and the provision of food. All these matters were put before the jury in terms which we find it impossible to fault. The jury were entitled to find that the duty had been assumed. They were entitled to conclude that once Fanny became helplessly infirm, as she had by 19th July, the appellants were, in the circumstances, obliged either to summon help or else to care for Fanny themselves. . . .

The duty which a defendant has undertaken is a duty of caring for the health and welfare of the infirm person. What the Crown has to prove is a breach of that duty in such circumstances that the jury feel convinced that the defendant's conduct can properly be described as reckless. That is to say a reckless disregard of danger to the health and welfare of the infirm person. Mere inadvertence is not enough. The defendant must be proved to have been indifferent to an obvious risk of injury to health, or actually to have foreseen the risk but to have determined nevertheless to run it.

The direction given by the judge was wholly in accord with these principles. If any criticism is to be made it would be that the direction was unduly favourable to the defence. The appeals against conviction therefore fail.

Appeals against conviction dismissed.

Notes and questions

1. Both Stone and Dobinson left something to be desired in terms of competence – Stone was described as deaf, blind, and of low intelligence; his mistress Dobinson as ineffectual and inadequate. Was it just to impose a duty on them to care for Fanny when they could barely care for themselves? The Court of Appeal did not seem at all troubled by their general inadequacy, let alone their inability to cope with the extraordinary situation in which they found themselves, one which would have taxed persons of far greater competence.

2. What was the legal basis for imposing a duty on Stone and Dobinson? Of what relevance was:

(a) The fact that Fanny was a blood relation? (In the case, Stone, the blood relative, initially received almost twice the sentence of Dobinson, who was not a blood relative. The sentence, however, was modified on appeal because of Stone's handicapped condition.)

(b) The fact that Fanny paid £1.50 per week towards the rent? Did this create a contractual obligation? Are landlords generally responsible for the welfare of their tenants?

(c) The fact that Stone and Dobinson had taken Fanny into their home and provided her with shelter? From a legal point of view, would they have been better advised to have been more cold-hearted and turned Fanny away at the door? What if she had refused to leave?

(d) The fact that if Stone and Dobinson had not undertaken the care of Fanny, some social agency might have discovered her plight and provided the necessary care? Indeed, a social worker regularly visited Stone and Dobinson because of their disabled child, yet they failed to take advantage of the opportunity to alert the social worker of Fanny's condition. In a sense, Stone and Dobinson isolated Fanny and prevented her from receiving help from others.

(e) The fact that at the end Fanny was totally helpless. See *R v Smith* [1979] Crim LR 251.

3. What of the responsibility of Fanny, an adult, to help herself? She refused to cooperate in the search for a doctor and also refused to eat properly. Did Stone and Dobinson have an obligation to force feed her? Note the legal dilemma in which Stone and Dobinson found themselves – the law says that a competent adult cannot be compelled to accept unwanted medical treatment, which suggests that Stone and Dobinson might have been guilty of an assault

if they had forced Fanny to eat. On the other hand, they were convicted of manslaughter when they failed to do so and she died. Is there a way to avoid this dilemma? See *R* v *Smith* [1979] Crim LR 251.

4.   How does one ever terminate a duty of the sort imposed by the Court of Appeal?

(iii)   Duties arising from a close familial relationship
We said previously that an experienced swimmer would not be criminally liable for failing to rescue a drowning child in a pool, but that a lifeguard under a contractual duty to safeguard the welfare of those in the pool would be liable. What of the parents of the child? Are they under a legal duty to save their drowning child?

R v *Gibbins and Proctor*
(1919) 13 Cr App R 134
Court of Criminal Appeal

DARLING J: The two appellants were indicted and tried together for the wilful murder of Nelly Gibbins, the daughter of Gibbins. The facts were that Gibbins's wife had left him, and he was living in adultery with Proctor. There were several children, one of whom was the child of Proctor, in the house. He earned good wages, which he brought home and gave to Proctor to maintain the house and those in it. There is no evidence that there was not enough to keep them all in health. And all were looked after except one, namely Nelly, who was starved to death. Her organs were healthy, and there was no reason why she should have died if she had been supplied with food. . . .
    . . . It is sufficient to refer to *Bubb and Hook* [(1850) 4 Cox CC 457], where Williams J said:

> It remains for me to explain to what extent she is responsible. If the omission or neglect to perform the duty was malicious, then the indictment would be supported, and the crime of murder would be made out against the prisoner; but if the omission or neglect were simply culpable, but not arising from a malicious motive on the part of the prisoner, then, though it would be your duty to find her guilty, it should be of manslaughter only. And here it becomes necessary to explain what is meant by the expression malicious, which is thus used. If the omission to provide necessary food or raiment was accompanied with an intention to cause the death of the child, or to cause some serious bodily injury to it, then it would be malicious in the sense imputed by this indictment, and in a case of this kind it is difficult, if not impossible, to understand how a person who contemplated doing serious bodily injury to the child by the deprivation of food, could have meditated anything else than causing its death.

The word used is 'contemplated,' but what has to be proved is an intention to do grievous bodily injury. In our opinion the judge left the question correctly to the jury, and there is no ground for interfering with the convictions for those reasons.
    It has been said that there ought not to have been a finding of guilty of murder against Gibbins. The Court agrees that the evidence was less against Gibbins than Proctor, Gibbins gave her money, and as far as we can see it was sufficient to provide for the wants of themselves and all the children. But he lived in the house and the child was his own, a little girl of seven, and he grossly neglected the child. . . .

The case of Proctor is plainer. She had charge of the child. She was under no obligation to do so or to live with Gibbins, but she did so, and receiving money, as it is admitted she did, for the purpose of supplying food, her duty was to see that the child was properly fed and looked after, and to see that she had medical attention if necessary. We agree with what Lord Coleridge CJ said in *Instan* [1893] 1 QB 450. 'There is no case directly in point, but it would be a slur upon, and a discredit to the administration of, justice in this country if there were any doubt as to the legal principle, or as to the present case being within it. The prisoner was under a moral obligation to the deceased from which arose a legal duty towards her; that legal duty the prisoner has wilfully and deliberately left unperformed, with the consequence that there has been an acceleration of the death of the deceased owing to the non-performance of that legal duty.' Here Proctor took upon herself the moral obligation of looking after the children; she was *de facto*, though not *de jure*, the wife of Gibbins and had excluded the child's own mother. She neglected the child undoubtedly, and the evidence shews that as a result the child died. So a verdict of manslaughter at least was inevitable.

Appeals dismissed.

Question
Is the decision in the following case at all reconcilable with *Gibbins and Proctor*?

R v Lowe
[1973] 1 QB 702
Court of Appeal

On 20 July 1972, at Nottingham Crown Court (May J), the defendant, Robert Lowe, was charged jointly with Patricia Marshall, with whom he was living, on two counts in an indictment. The first count charged him with manslaughter, in that between 4 October 1971, and 5 November 1971, he unlawfully caused the death of Amanda Marshall. The second count charged him with cruelty to a child, contrary to s. 1(1) of the Children and Young Persons Act 1933, in that he, being a person who had attained the age of 16 years and who had the custody, charge or care of Amanda Marshall, a child under the age of 16 years, wilfully neglected Amanda Marshall in a manner likely to cause her unnecessary suffering or injury to health. The defendant submitted that he had done all that he could have been expected to do and that it was possible that the child's critical condition had arisen only in the last few days prior to 5 November 1971, when he assumed that Patricia Marshall had taken the child to the doctor. By their verdict the jury exonerated the defendant of gross negligence or recklessness but found him guilty of wilful neglect.

PHILLIMORE LJ: . . . In the present case the jury negatived recklessnes. How then can mere neglect, albeit wilful, amount to manslaughter? This court feels that there is something inherently unattractive in a theory of constructive manslaughter. It seems strange that an omission which is wilful solely in the sense that it is not inadvertent and the consequences of which are not in fact foreseen by the person who is neglectful should, if death results, automatically give rise to an indeterminate sentence instead of the maximum of two years which would otherwise be the limit imposed.

We think that there is a clear distinction between an act of omission and an act of commission likely to cause harm. Whatever may be the position with regard to the latter it does not follow that the same is true of the former. In other words, if I strike a child in a manner likely to cause harm it is right that, if the child dies, I may be charged with manslaughter. If, however, I omit to do something with the result that it suffers injury to health which results in its death, we think that a charge of manslaughter should not be an inevitable consequence, even if the omission is deliberate.

Notes and questions

1. A baby is born with severe handicaps. The parents instruct the doctor not to provide treatment. If the doctor complies and the child dies, are the parents criminally liable? See *Re B (a minor)* [1981] 1 WLR 1421. Is the doctor criminally liable? See *Arthur* (1981), *The Times*, 6 November 1981, discussed in Helen Benyon, 'Doctors as murderers' [1982] Crim LR 17. Is there a difference between withholding food and withholding life-saving treatment? Between withholding life-saving treatment and suffocating the child to death?

2. Where a legal duty is imposed as a result of contract or voluntary agreement, the scope and extent of the duty are determined by the terms of the contract or agreement. Where a legal duty arises as a result of a relationship, however, no such terms exist. Are there logical limits on the scope and extent of the duty?

3. In our drowning child hypothetical, would a parent who could not swim be liable for failing to jump into the water to attempt to save his or her child? A parent who was a weak swimmer? A pregnant mother who was at the same time watching over an infant?

4. What if the parents are unaware of the plight of their child? They do not appreciate that their child is slowly starving to death, or do not know that the child has jumped into the neighbour's swimming pool. Is there a duty to be aware of what is happening to one's child? In this context one must carefully distinguish between unawareness of a legal duty, which is generally not a defence (ignorance of the law will not excuse), and unawareness of facts which give rise to a legal duty, which may be a defence.

5. Is there a geographical limitation on liability? Is a parent responsible for his or her child when the child is visiting a friend? When the child is living with one's ex-spouse in another country? Does the duty extend only to members of one's household?

6. Can duties arise by virtue of relationships other than parent-child? Does 'parent' include a step-parent or the unmarried live-in partner of a parent? The unmarried occasional partner of a parent?

7. If a parent has a duty to his or her child, does an adult child have a duty to his or her parents? Do spouses have duties to one another? See *R v Smith* [1979] Crim LR 251. Do siblings? Reconsider *Stone and Dobinson*, above.

(iv) Duties arising by virtue of the creation of danger

Consider the person whose actions or inactions are responsible for creating a peril. By virtue of those actions or inactions, does a legal duty arise which did not previously exist?

R v *Miller*
[1983] 1 All ER 978
House of Lords

LORD DIPLOCK: My Lords, the facts which give rise to this appeal are sufficiently narrated in the written statement made to the police by the appellant Miller. That statement, subject to two minor orthographical corrections, reads:

> Last night I went out for a few drinks and at closing time I went back to the house where I have been kipping for a couple of weeks. I went upstairs into the back bedroom where I've been sleeping. I lay on my mattress and lit a cigarette. I must have fell to sleep because I woke up to find the mattress on fire. I just got up and went into the next room and went back to sleep. Then the next thing I remember was the police and fire people arriving. I hadn't got anything to put the fire out with so I just left it.

He was charged on indictment with the offence of 'arson contrary to section 1(1) and (3) of the Criminal Damage Act, 1971'. . . .

Since arson is a result-crime the period may be considerable, and during it the conduct of the accused that is causative of the result may consist not only of his doing physical acts which cause the fire to start or spread but also of his failing to take measures that lie within his power to counteract the danger that he has himself created. And if his conduct, active or passive, varies in the course of the period, so may his state of mind at the time of each piece of conduct. If, at the time of any particular piece of conduct by the accused that is causative of the result, the state of mind that actuates his conduct falls within the description of one or other of the states of mind that are made a necessary ingredient of the offence of arson by s. 1(1) of the Criminal Damage Act 1971 (i.e. intending to damage property belonging to another or being reckless whether such property would be damaged), I know of no principle of English criminal law that would prevent his being guilty of the offence created by that subsection. Likewise I see no rational ground for excluding from conduct capable of giving rise to criminal liability conduct which consists of failing to take measures that lie within one's power to counteract a danger that one has oneself created, if at the time of such conduct one's state of mind is such as constitutes a necessary ingredient of the offence. I venture to think that the habit of lawyers to talk of 'actus reus', suggestive as it is of action rather than inaction, is responsible for any erroneous notion that failure to act cannot give rise to criminal liability in English law.

No one has been bold enough to suggest that if, in the instant case, the accused had been aware at the time that he dropped the cigarette that it would probably set fire to his mattress and yet had taken no steps to extinguish it he would not have been guilty of the offence of arson, since he would have damaged property of another being reckless whether any such property would be damaged.

I cannot see any good reason why, so far as liability under criminal law is concerned, it should matter at what point of time before the resultant damage is complete a person becomes aware that he has done a physical act which, whether or not he appreciated that it would at the time when he did it, does in fact create a risk that property of another will be damaged, provided that, at the moment of awareness, it lies within his power to take steps, either himself or by calling for the assistance of the fire brigade if this be necessary, to prevent or minimise the damage to the property at risk.

. . .

My Lords, in the instant case the prosecution did not rely on the state of mind of the accused as being reckless during that part of his conduct that consisted of his lighting and smoking a cigarette while lying on his mattress and falling asleep without extinguishing it. So the jury were not invited to make any finding as to this. What the prosecution did rely on as being reckless was his state of mind during that part of his conduct after he awoke to find that he had set his mattress on fire and that it was smouldering, but did not then take any steps either to try to extinguish it himself or to send for the fire brigade, but simply went into the other room to resume his slumbers, leaving the fire from the already smouldering mattress to spread and to damage that part of the house in which the mattress was.

The recorder, in his lucid summing up to the jury (they took 22 minutes only to reach their verdict), told them that the accused, having by his own act started a fire in the mattress which, when he became aware of its existence, presented an obvious risk of damaging the house, became under a duty to take some action to put it out. The Court of Appeal upheld the conviction, but its ratio decidendi appears to be somewhat different from that of the recorder. As I understand the judgment, in effect it treats the whole course of conduct of the accused, from the moment at which he fell asleep and dropped the cigarette onto the mattress until the time the damage to the house by fire was complete, as a continuous act of the accused, and holds that it is sufficient to constitute the statutory offence of arson if at any stage in that course of conduct the state of mind of the accused, when he fails to try to prevent or minimise the damage which will result from his initial act, although it lies within his power to do so, is that of being reckless whether property belonging to another would be damaged.

My Lords, these alternative ways of analysing the legal theory that justifies a decision which has received nothing but commendation for its accord with common sense and justice have, since the publication of the judgment of the Court of Appeal in the instant case, provoked academic controversy. Each theory has distinguished support. Professor J C Smith espouses the 'duty theory' (see [1982] Crim LR 526 at 528); Professor Glanville Williams who, after the decision of the Divisional Court in *Fagan v Metropolitan Police Comr* [1968] 3 All ER 442, [1969] 1 QB 439 appears to have been attracted by the duty theory, now prefers that of the continuous act (see [1982] Crim LR 773). When applied to cases where a person has unknowingly done an act which sets in train events that, when he becomes aware of them, present an obvious risk that property belonging to another will be damaged, both theories lead to an identical result and, since what your Lordships are concerned with is to give guidance to trial judges in their task of summing up to juries, I would for this purpose adopt the duty theory as being the easier to explain to a jury; though I would commend the use of the word 'responsibility', rather than 'duty' which is more appropriate to civil than to criminal law since it suggests an obligation owed to another person, ie the person to whom the endangered property belongs, whereas a criminal statute defines combinations of conduct and state of mind which render a person liable to punishment by the state itself.

While, in the general run of cases of destruction or damage to property belonging to another by fire (or other means) where the prosecution relies on the recklessness of the accused, the direction recommended by this House in *R v Caldwell* [1982] AC 341 is appropriate, in the exceptional case (which is most likely to be one of arson and of which the instant appeal affords a striking example), where the accused is initially unaware that he has done an act that in fact sets in train events which, by the time the accused becomes aware of them, would make it obvious to anyone who troubled to give his mind to them that they present a risk that property belonging to another would be damaged, a suitable direction to the jury would be that the accused is guilty of the offence under s. 1(1) of the 1971 Act if, when he does become aware that the events in question have happened as a result of his own act, he does not try to prevent or reduce the risk of damage by his own efforts or if necessary by sending for help from the fire brigade and the reason why he does not is either because he has not given any thought to the possibility of there being any such risk or because having recognised that there was some risk involved he has decided not to try to prevent or reduce it.

Appeal dismissed. Certified question answered in the affirmative.

Notes and questions
1. What was Miller's *actus reus* – the setting of the fire, or the failure to take steps to extinguish it after he became aware of it? The problem with finding the *actus reus* in the former is that at that time Miller did not have the mental state required by the statute; indeed, at that time he was asleep. There may have been an *actus reus* but there was no *mens rea*. After awakening and discovering the fire, however, Miller took no steps to cause it to be extinguished. Now there was a *mens rea* (recklessness) but no act. The problem is one of 'concurrence' – the requirement that the *actus reus* and the *mens rea* concur, or, stated perhaps more accurately, that the *actus reus* be the product of the *mens rea*. Lord Diplock resolved the problem by finding that Miller's failure to act when he had a duty to do so constituted the *actus reus*. An alternative approach would have been to regard the entire series of events as one transaction, with the concurrence element satisfied if there was the requisite *mens rea* at any time during the course of the transaction. See, e.g., *Attorney-General's Reference (No. 4 of 1980)* [1981] 1 WLR 705; *Fagan* v *Metropolitan Police Commissioner* [1968] 3 All ER 442; *R* v *Thabo Meli* [1954] 1 WLR 228. Issues of concurrence will be discussed in greater depth in Chapter 4.
2. What if the fire had been accidentally set by a visiting friend who had since departed? Would Miller still be liable for failing to take steps to extinguish it? If so, on what basis could a duty to act be said to arise?

(v) Duties arising by virtue of a duty to control
In some instances persons who have the power to control other persons or animals can be held criminally responsible for harm caused by those other entities. An owner of a dangerous animal, for example, may be liable if the animal escapes and attacks another. Sometimes this duty is imposed by statute:

Dangerous Dogs Act 1991

3. Keeping dogs under proper control
(1) If a dog is dangerously out of control in a public place —
    (a) the owner; and
    (b) if different, the person for the time being in charge of the dog,
is guilty of an offence, or, if the dog while so out of control injures any person, an aggravated offence, under this subsection.
   . . .
(3) If the owner or, if different, the person for the time being in charge of a dog allows it to enter a place which is not a public place but where it is not permitted to be and while it is there —

(a)   it injures any person; or
(b)   there are grounds for reasonable apprehension that it will do so,
he is guilty of an offence, or, if the dog injures any person, an aggravated offence, under
this subsection.

Note
Where one's power to control relates to another person, liability may also be
imposed. Often the crime charged will be one of aiding and abetting, the aiding
consisting of the failure to prevent or discourage the other's actions.

Du Cros v Lambourne
[1907] 1 KB 40
King's Bench Division

LORD ALVERSTONE CJ: . . . We have to consider the facts found in this case. The case
states that the appellant must have known that the speed of the car was dangerous; that if
Miss Godwin was driving, she was doing so with the consent and approval of the appellant,
who was in control of the car, and that he could, and ought to, have prevented her from
driving at this excessive and dangerous speed, but that he allowed her to do so and did not
interfere in any way. I will not attempt to lay down any general rule or principle, but having
regard to these findings of fact, it is, in my opinion, impossible to say that there was in this
case no evidence of aiding and abetting on the part of the appellant. . . .

DARLING J: I am of the same opinion. I think that there was ample evidence on
which the appellant could be convicted of aiding and abetting Miss Godwin in driving
the car at a speed dangerous to the public. The appellant was the owner of the car and
in control of it, and he was therefore the person to say who should drive it. The case
finds that he *allowed* (I emphasise that) Miss Godwin to do so; that he knew that the
speed was dangerous, and that he could and ought to have prevented it. Now, does it
affect the validity of the conviction that the appellant was not charged with aiding and
abetting but with having driven the car himself? I do not think that it does. . . .

Appeal dismissed.

C   Vicarious liability

Similar to cases involving a duty to control are those in which there is the
authority to supervise the actions of others. Does one then become liable for the
criminal acts of those others? In such cases there has been an *actus reus*
committed, but not by the accused. The cases generally arise in the
employment context, and the defendant's liability is said to be 'vicarious'. Such
liability has long been recognised in tort law, where the concern is to provide
compensation for the injured party. However, in criminal law vicarious liability
is more controversial. Where it does occur, it is often the product of statute.

Road Traffic Regulation Act 1984

107.   Liability of vehicle owner in respect of excess parking charge
   (1)   This section applies where —

(a)   an excess charge has been incurred in pursuance of an order under sections 45 and 46 of this Act;

(b)   notice of the incurring of the excess charge has been given or affixed as provided in the order; and

(c)   the excess charge has not been duly paid in accordance with the order;
and in the following provisions of this Part of this Act 'the excess charge offence' means the offence under section 47 of this Act of failing duly to pay the excess charge.

(2)   Subject to the following provisions of this section —

(a)   for the purposes of the institution of proceedings in respect of the excess charge offence against any person as being the owner of the vehicle at the relevant time, and

(b)   in any proceedings in respect of the excess charge offence brought against any person as being the owner of the vehicle at the relevant time,
it shall be conclusively presumed (notwithstanding that that person may not be an individual) that he was the driver of the vehicle at that time and, accordingly, that acts or omissions of the driver of the vehicle at that time were his acts or omissions.

Licensing Act 1964

59.   Prohibition of sale, etc. of intoxicating liquor outside permitted hours

(1)   Subject to the provisions of this Act, no person shall, except during the permitted hours —

(a)   himself or by his servant or agent sell or supply to any person in licensed premises or in premises in respect of which a club is registered any intoxicating liquor, whether to be consumed on or off the premises;

. . .

Questions

1.   What considerations might prompt Parliament to enact a statute imposing vicarious liability? What are the pros and cons of such liability?

2.   A publican instructs her employees that under no circumstances is any of them to sell liquor to customers outside permitted hours. The publican maintains a constant supervision of the employees. When the publican is ill, however, she remains at home so as not to infect her customers. On one such occasion her employee sells liquor during a time when such sales are prohibited. Is the publican liable under s. 59(1) of the Licensing Act 1964 above? See *Lindsay* v *Vickers Ltd* [1978] Crim LR 55; *Anderton* v *Rodgers and Others* [1981] Crim LR 404.

3.   What if the publican's employee, unbeknownst to her, sells stolen radios to customers in the pub? Assume that the employee is guilty of handling stolen goods. Would the publican also be vicariously liable? Is this situation different from the previous hypothetical? How so?

Note

In some situations vicarious liability is quite clearly contemplated by Parliament and the statute in question is clear. In others, the statute does not on its face impose vicarious liability. If vicarious liability is to be imposed, it will be as a result of judicial interpretation.

Mousell Brothers Ltd v London and North-Western Railway Company
[1917] 2 KB 836
King's Bench Division

VISCOUNT READING CJ: In this case Foss, whose duty it was as manager to fill up or direct the filling up of the consignment notes from his principals, the appellants, to the respondents, wrongly described the goods with intent to avoid the payment of the rate payable in respect of the right classification of the goods. The question of law is whether the appellants, a limited liability company, can be convicted for this offence. It was not suggested that the directors of the appellant company were themselves parties to this false description. But it is suggested that they can be made criminally responsible for the act of their servant entrusted with the performance of this class of acts, and therefore acting within the scope of his employment. The magistrate convicted the appellants and stated a case for this Court. . . .

The first thing to consider is the language of the statute. Section 98 imposes upon every person being the owner or having the care of goods the obligation to give an exact account in writing of the number or quantity of goods liable to each of the tolls. Then by s. 99: 'If any such owner or other such person fail to give such account, or to produce his way-bill or bill of lading to such . . . servant of the company demanding the same' – then comes these important words – 'or if he give a false account . . . with intent to avoid the payment of any tolls payable in respect thereof, he shall for every such offence forfeit to the company a sum not exceeding ten pounds for every ton of goods, . . . and such penalty shall be in addition to the toll to which such goods may be liable.' By s. 2 of the Interpretation Act 1899, it is provided that 'In the construction of every enactment relating to an offence punishable on indictment or on summary conviction, whether contained in an Act passed before or after the commencement of this Act, the expression "person" shall, unless the contrary intention appears, include a body corporate.' In order to determine whether or not the contrary intention does appear, we must consider the broad question under what circumstances can a principal be made criminally responsible for the act of his servant. And then the narrower question, does this section, which imposes the penalty upon the owner, make the principal liable for the act of his servant done within the scope of his employment, but without the knowledge or the instructions of the principal?

The true principle of law is laid down in the case of *Pearks, Gunston & Tee* v *Ward* [[1902] 2 KB 1]. The passage to which I particularly wish to refer is in the judgment of Channell J:

> By the general principles of the criminal law, if a matter is made a criminal offence, it is essential that there should be something in the nature of mens rea, and, therefore, in ordinary cases a corporation cannot be guilty of a criminal offence, nor can a master be liable criminally for an offence committed by his servant. But there are exceptions to this rule in the case of quasi-criminal offences, as they may be termed, that is to say, where certain acts are forbidden by law under a penalty, possibly even under a personal penalty, such as imprisonment, at any rate in default of payment of a fine.

. . .

Prima facie, then, a master is not to be made criminally responsible for the acts of his servant to which the master is not a party. But it may be the intention of the Legislature, in order to guard against the happening of the forbidden thing, to impose a liability upon a principal even though he does not know of, and is not party to, the forbidden act done by his servant. Many statutes are passed with this object. Acts done by the servant of the licensed holder of licensed premises render the licensed holder in some instances liable, even though the act was done by his servant without the knowledge of the master. Under the Food and Drugs Acts there are again instances well known in these Courts where the master is made responsible, even though he knows nothing of the act done by his servant, and he may be fined or rendered amenable to the penalty enjoined by the law. In those cases the Legislature absolutely forbids the act and makes the principal liable without a mens rea.

. . .

Coming now to the present case, in my view the Legislature must be taken to have known that the forbidden acts were of a kind which, even in the year 1845, would in most cases be done by servants; and yet the penalty is imposed upon 'every person being the owner or having the care of any carriage or goods passing or being upon the railway.' It may be that the words 'person having the care of any carriage or goods,' etc., are wide enough to cover a person who occupied the position of Foss. I am by no means convinced of it. I am inclined to think they mean the bailee who is entrusted with the goods for carriage and who is not the owner. They would clearly not include a servant merely entrusted with the duty of filling up a consignment note. But the forbidden acts are such as would be performed by a servant. The object of the statute was, in my opinion, to forbid the giving of a false description of goods carried by the railway and so protect the railway company from being cheated into carrying goods at less than the due rate. I think, looking at the language and the purpose of this Act, that the Legislature intended to fix responsibility for this quasi-criminal act upon the principal if the forbidden acts were done by his servant within the scope of his employment. If that is the true view, there is nothing to distinguish a limited company from any other principal, and the defendants are properly made liable for the acts of Foss. The magistrate was right and this appeal fails.

ATKIN J: I agree, but I should like to add a few words in view of the argument of Mr Atkinson. I think that the authorities cited by my Lord make it plain that while prima facie a principal is not to be made criminally responsible for the acts of his servants, yet the Legislature may prohibit an act or enforce a duty in such words as to make the prohibition or the duty absolute; in which case the principal is liable if the act is in fact done by his servants. To ascertain whether a particular Act of Parliament has that effect or not regard must be had to the object of the statute, the words used, the nature of the duty laid down, the person upon whom it is imposed, the person by whom it would in ordinary circumstances be performed, and the person upon whom the penalty is imposed. . . .

Notes
1. Vicarious liability is not limited to the employer-employee context. See, e.g., *Quality Dairies (York) Ltd* v *Pedley* [1952] 1 KB 275 (liability for acts of sub-contractor); *Linnet* v *Metropolitan Police Commissioner* [1946] 1 All ER 380 (liability for acts of co-licensee); *Clode* v *Barnes* [1974] 1 All ER 1166 (liability for acts of partner); *Anderton* v *Rodgers* [1981] Crim LR 404 (committee members of club liable for illegal sales of barman). Is there a common nexus among the cases that allows a lawyer to predict when a relationship can lead to vicarious liability? See M. Allen, *Textbook on Criminal Law* (2nd ed.) (1991), p. 189.

2.   Crimes imposing vicarious liability need to be distinguished from those imposing strict liability. In regard to the latter, Parliament has dispensed with the need for the Crown to prove *mens rea*; in regard to the former, it is the requirement of a personal *actus reus* which has been dispensed with. Often crimes which impose strict liability are construed to allow vicarious liability as well. This coupling is not mere coincidence. *Mens rea* cannot as easily be attributed to another as *actus reus*, so if strict liability could not be imposed, there would be no vicarious liability where such was intended by Parliament. The courts have been willing to impute *mens rea* to an employer who has delegated responsibility to an employee:

Allen v *Whitehead*
[1930] 1 KB 211
House of Lords

   (a)   The respondent was the occupier and licensee of premises at 16 Norton Folgate, Stepney, which he used as a licensed refreshment house open day and night.
   (b)   The respondent, although he received the profits of the business, did not himself manage the refreshment house but employed a manager for the purpose.
   (c)   On February 26, 1929, and on each of the seven days following, a number of women known to the respondent's manager to be prostitutes resorted to the said refreshment house, meeting there together and with a number of men, and remaining therein between the hours of 8 p.m. and 4 a.m. and indulging in obscene language. From time to time men and women were seen to leave the premises in couples and to return within a few minutes. This conduct took place frequently in the presence of the manager, and on one occasion disorderly conduct took place on the part of those resorting to the café.
   (d)   On September 1, 1928, the respondent was warned by the police about harbouring prostitutes at the said refreshment house, and he thereupon gave instructions to his manager that no prostitutes were to be allowed to congregate in the premises, and a notice was displayed forbidding women to enter the refreshment house after midnight.
   (e)   The respondent visited the premises about once or twice a week. There was no evidence that misconduct occurred on any occasion in his presence or to his knowledge, but there was evidence that he had given general instructions to his manager to prevent the assembling of prostitutes on the premises, and had caused a notice to this effect to be displayed on the walls.
   On behalf of the respondent it was contended that as the respondent did not himself manage the refreshment house, and had no personal knowledge that prostitutes met together and remained therein, and had not been negligent in failing to notice these facts, and had not wilfully closed his eyes to the said facts, he could not in law be held responsible for the acts of his manager in his absence acting in direct contravention to his instructions.

On behalf of the appellant it was contended that the position of the respondent was analogous to that of a licensee under the Licensing Acts, and that he was responsible for the acts of his manager within the scope of his employment.

LORD HEWART CJ: This is a case stated by one of the Metropolitan Police magistrates and it raises a question under s. 44 of the Metropolitan Police Act, 1839. The respondent was summoned to answer an information, laid by the appellant, which charged that the respondent on a day in February, 1929, being the keeper of certain premises where refreshments were sold or consumed, did knowingly suffer prostitutes to meet together and remain therein contrary to s. 44 of the statute. [His Lordship having read the material words of the section, continued:] The magistrate, having heard the evidence, came to the conclusion that the charge was not proved, and the question for this Court is whether he came to a correct determination in point of law in dismissing the case.
. . .
Now what is the fair meaning of [the] facts, if it be not this, that the respondent was to all intents and purposes an absentee who had told his manager to use the discretion which, if he had been upon the premises, he must have used himself? . . . Now here, upon the facts of the case, it is abundantly plain that there was knowledge on the part of the manager. The question is whether upon the proper construction of s. 44 of the Metropolitan Police Act, 1839, that knowledge in the servant is to be imputed to the employer so as to make the employer liable. In my opinion, the answer to that question is in the affirmative. The principle seems to me to be that which was explained, for example, in *Mousell Brothers* v *London and North Western Ry* [see Atkin J's judgment above]. Applying that canon to the present case, I think that this provision in this statute would be rendered nugatory if the contention raised on behalf of this respondent were held to prevail. That contention was this, that as the respondent did not himself manage the refreshment house and had no personal knowledge that prostitutes met together and remained therein, and had not been negligent in failing to notice these facts, and had not wilfully closed his eyes to them, he could not in law be held responsible. This seems to me to be a case where the proprietor, the keeper of the house, had delegated his duty to a manager, so far as the conduct of the house was concerned. He had transferred to the manager the exercise of discretion in the conduct of the business, and it seems to me that the only reasonable conclusion is, regard being had to the purposes of this Act, that the knowledge of the manager was the knowledge of the keeper of the house.

BRANSON J: I agree. The essence of the respondent's case was that he had no personal knowledge of the fact that prostitutes were meeting and remaining upon these premises. It is found that his manager knew, and Lord Coleridge CJ said in *Somerset* v *Hart* (1884) 12 QBD 360 'that a man may put another in his position so as to represent him for the purpose of knowledge.' I think that is what the respondent has done here and that, consequently, the contention set up by the respondent fails.

Questions
1. The problem in *Allen* v *Whitehead* was that the defendant 'knew' that prostitutes were using his premises but was powerless to prevent it. He specifically told his manager not to allow prostitutes on the premises, he posted signs to the same effect, and he periodically checked the premises for violations. What more could (should) he have done? Except by taking personal

responsibility for every phase of the operation of a business, how can an owner of a business avoid 'delegating' authority?
2.   What purpose is served by holding a defendant such as Whitehead liable?
3.   Is the court in *Allen* v *Whitehead* compensating for poor draftsmanship on the part of Parliament, or creating a new crime on its own? See also *Vane* v *Yiannopoullos* [1965] AC 486.

D   State of affairs crimes

Occasionally a state of affairs can satisfy the *actus reus* requirement of a crime. As in cases of a failure to act, the defendant has not performed any affirmative act. In the failure to act cases, however, the defendant has omitted to do something which he or she should have done. In the state of affairs cases, it is often not clear what, if anything, the defendant should or could have done.

R v Larsonneur
(1933) 149 LT 542
Court of Criminal Appeal

The appellant who was a French subject, landed in the United Kingdom on the 14 March 1933 with a French passport, which was endorsed with conditions prohibiting her employment in the United Kingdom. On the 22 March 1933 these conditions were varied by a condition requiring her to leave the United Kingdom on that date. She went . . . to the Irish Free State, and an order for her deportation therefrom was subsequently made by the executive of that country. On the 20 April she was brought to Holyhead in the custody of the Irish Free State police, who there handed her over to the police of the United Kingdom, and she was kept in custody until her trial. She was convicted of a charge that she 'being an alien to whom leave to land in the United Kingdom had been refused was found in the United Kingdom' contrary to acts 1(3) and 18(1)(b) of the Aliens Order 1920, as amended.

LORD HEWART C J: . . . The fact is, as the evidence shows, that the appellant is an alien. She has a French passport, which bears this statement under the date the 14th March 1933, 'Leave to land granted at Folkestone this day on condition that the holder does not enter any employment, paid or unpaid, while in the United Kingdom,' but on the 22nd March that condition was varied and one finds these words: 'The condition attached to the grant of leave to land is hereby varied so as to require departure from the United Kingdom not later than the 22nd March 1933.' Then follows the signature of an Under-Secretary of State. In fact, the appellant went to the Irish Free State and afterwards, in circumstances which are perfectly immaterial, so far as this appeal is concerned, came back to Holyhead. She was at Holyhead on the 21st April 1933, a day after the day limited by the condition on her passport.
    In these circumstances, it seems to be quite clear that art. 1(4) of the Aliens Order 1920 (as varied by the Orders of the 12th March 1923 and the 11th Aug. 1931) applies. The article is in the following terms:

    An immigration officer, in accordance with general or special directions of the Secretary of State, may, by general order or notice or otherwise, attach such conditions as he may think fit to the grant of leave to land, and the Secretary of State may at any time vary such conditions in such manner as he thinks fit, and the alien shall comply with the conditions so attached or varied. An alien who fails to comply with any conditions so attached or varied, and an alien who is found in the United Kingdom at any time after the expiration of the period limited by any such condition, shall for the purposes of this Order be deemed to be an alien to whom leave to land has been refused.

The appellant was, therefore, on the 21st April 1933, in the position in which she would have been if she had been prohibited from landing by the Secretary of State and, that being so, there is no reason to interfere with the finding of the jury. She was found here and was, therefore, deemed to be in the class of persons whose landing had been prohibited by the Secretary of State, by reason of the fact that she had violated the condition on her passport. The appeal, therefore, is dismissed and the recommendation for deportation remains.

Appeal dismissed.

Notes and questions
1.   Lord Hewart CJ, says that the circumstances by which Madame Larsonneur found herself in England were 'perfectly immaterial'. Is he correct? Is not the fact that she was returned involuntarily by the police entitled to no weight? See generally D.J. Lanham, 'Larsonneur Revisited' [1976] Crim LR 276. In *Winzar* v *Chief Constable of Kent*, (1983) *The Times*, 28 March 1983, the defendant was brought to a hospital in a state of intoxication. He was subsequently removed by the police to a public highway, where he was arrested and charged with being found drunk in the highway. His conviction was affirmed on appeal.
   A contrary result to *Winzar* was reached in an American case, *Martin* v *State* (1944) 31 Ala App 334, 17 So 2d 427, where the court said that 'an accusation of drunkenness in a designated public place cannot be established by proof that the accused, while in an intoxicated condition, was involuntarily and forcibly carried to that place by the arresting officer'. Which result makes better sense – *Martin* or *Winzar*? Would your answer change if the defendant had been evicted from the pub by the owner rather than by the police?
2.   As advocated in Chapter 1, one must always carefully examine a criminal statute to determine the precise elements of the crime. Part of the reason for the result in *Larsonneur* lay in how the offence was defined – 'being found' in England. The *actus reus* was physical presence in a particular place.

The potentially harsh results which can flow from 'state of affairs' crimes which, as in *Larsonneur*, also purport to impose strict liability, can sometimes be avoided by resourceful statutory interpretation:

Lim Chin Aik v *R*
[1963] 1 All ER 224
Judicial Committee of the Privy Council

LORD EVERSHED: The appellant Lim Chin Aik (who appears to have been known by several other names but to whom their Lordships will hereafter refer as 'the

appellant') has appealed to the Board by special leave from the dismissal on Feb. 24, 1960, by the High Court of Singapore of his appeal against conviction by a magistrate on Aug. 27, 1959, for an offence under s. 6 of the Immigration Ordinance, (1), of the State of Singapore (as later amended) and the sentence then imposed of a fine of $1,250 or three months' imprisonment. The relevant facts fall within a small compass but the point involved in the appeal is one, their Lordships think, of no little importance.
    . . . This charge was in the following terms:

> . . . you . . . having entered Singapore from the Federation of Malaya in May, 1959, did remain therein whilst prohibited by an order made by the minister under s. 9 prohibiting you from entering Singapore and have thereby contravened s. 6(2) of the Immigration Ordinance, an offence under s. 6(3) punishable under s. 57 thereof.

It is not in dispute that . . . the Minister of Labour and Welfare did make, on May 28, 1959, an order prohibiting the appellant from entering Singapore.
    At the trial (which as already stated took place on Aug. 17, 1959) it was proved by the Deputy Assistant Controller of Immigration that the minister's order was received by him on the day on which it was made; but there was no evidence of what was done with the order thereafter and no evidence of any step having been taken by way of publication or otherwise so as to bring the order to the attention of the appellant – or indeed of anyone else. The appellant at his trial did not personally give any evidence at all.
    It follows from the foregoing recital of facts that there was at the trial no evidence at all from which it could be properly inferred that the order had in fact come to the notice or attention of the appellant. It was therefore said on the appellant's behalf before the magistrate that, since there was no evidence of guilty intent on his part and that since such a guilty intent on general principles must be an ingredient of any criminal offence, it therefore followed that no offence had been proved against the appellant under the ordinance. This plea was rejected by the magistrate who, basing himself on the terms of the relevant section of the ordinance, held that there was in this case no need for any evidence of mens rea. The appellant then appealed to the High Court of Singapore but that court dismissed his appeal without stating any reasons for the dismissal . . ..
    Where the subject-matter of the statute is the regulation for the public welfare of a particular activity – statutes regulating the sale of food and drink are to be found among the earliest examples – it can be and frequently has been inferred that the legislature intended that such activities should be carried out under conditions of strict liability. The presumption is that the statute or statutory instrument can be effectively enforced only if those in charge of the relevant activities are made responsible for seeing that they are complied with. When such a presumption is to be inferred, it displaces the ordinary presumption of mens rea. . . .
    But it is not enough in their Lordships' opinion merely to label the statute as one dealing with a grave social evil and from that to infer that strict liability was intended. It is pertinent also to inquire whether putting the defendant under strict liability will assist in the enforcement of the regulations. That means that there must be something he can do, directly or indirectly, by supervision or inspection, by improvement of his business methods or by exhorting those whom he may be expected to influence or control, which will promote the observance of the regulations. Unless this is so, there is no reason in penalising him, and it cannot be inferred that the legislature imposed strict liability merely in order to find a luckless victim. . . .

. . . Counsel for the respondent was unable to point to anything that the appellant could possibly have done so as to ensure that he complied with the regulations. It was not, for example, suggested that it would be practicable for him to make continuous inquiry to see whether an order had been made against him. Clearly one of the objects of the ordinance is the expulsion of prohibited persons from Singapore, but there is nothing that a man can do about it if, before the commission of the offence, there is no practical or sensible way in which he can ascertain whether he is a prohibited person or not.

Counsel for the respondent, therefore, relied chiefly on the text of the ordinance and their Lordships return, accordingly, to the language of the two material sections. It is to be observed that the Board is here concerned with one who is said (within the terms of s. 6(3)) to have 'contravened' the subsection by 'remaining' in Singapore (after having entered) when he had been 'prohibited' from entering by an 'order' made by the ministry containing such prohibition. It seems to their Lordships that, where a man is said to have contravened an order or an order of prohibition, the common sense of the language presumes that he was aware of the order before he can be said to have contravened it. Their Lordships realise that this statement is something of an oversimplification when applied to the present case: for the 'contravention' alleged is of the unlawful act, prescribed by sub-s. (2) of the section, of remaining in Singapore after the date of the order of prohibition. None the less it is their Lordships' view that, applying the test of ordinary sense to the language used, the notion of contravention here alleged is more consistent with the assumption that the person charged had knowledge of the order than the converse. But such a conclusion is in their Lordships' view much reinforced by the use of the word 'remains' in its context. It is to be observed that if the respondent is right a man could lawfully enter Singapore and could thereafter lawfully remain in Singapore until the moment when an order of prohibition against his entering was made; that then, instanter, his purely passive conduct in remaining – that is, the mere continuance, quite unchanged, of his previous behaviour, hitherto perfectly lawful – would become criminal. These considerations bring their Lordships clearly to the conclusion that the sense of the language here in question requires for the commission of a crime thereunder mens rea as a constituent of such crime; or at least that there is nothing in the language used which suffices to exclude the ordinary presumption. Their Lordships do not forget the emphasis placed by counsel for the respondent on the fact that the word 'knowingly' or the phrases 'without reasonable cause' or 'without reasonable excuse' are found in various sections of the ordinance (as amended) but find no place in the section now under consideration – see for example s. 16(4), s. 18(4), s. 19(2), s. 29, s. 31(2), s. 41(2) and s. 56(d) and (e) of the ordinance. In their Lordships' view the absence of such a word or phrase in the relevant section is not sufficient in the present case to prevail against the conclusion which the language as a whole suggests. In the first place, it is to be noted that to have inserted such words as 'knowingly' or 'without lawful excuse' in the relevant part of s. 6(3) of the Immigration Ordinance would in any case not have been sensible. Further, in all the various instances where the word or phrase is used in the other sections of the ordinance before-mentioned the use is with reference to the doing of some specific act or the failure to do some specific act as distinct from the more passive continuance of behaviour theretofore perfectly lawful. . . .

Question
Which result, that in *Larsonneur* or *Lim Chin Aik*, is more just? In which case was the court more faithful to the legislature's intent?

Note
Crimes of 'possession' can similarly be interpreted to require 'knowing' possession. See, e.g., *Lockyer* v *Gibb* [1967] 2 QB 243. Problems can be avoided if more care is taken in drafting the statute in the first place. In *Warner* v *Metropolitan Police Commissioner* [1969] 2 AC 256 Lord Pearce suggested:

> It would, I think, be an improvement of a difficult position if Parliament were to enact that when a person has ownership or physical possession of drugs he shall be guilty unless he proves on a balance of probabilities that he was unaware of their nature or had reasonable excuse for their possession.

III Voluntary acts

A Rationale

In most criminal cases the accused has committed an affirmative act, thus satisfying the *actus reus* requirement. This does not necessarily mean that the accused has caused any harm to any individual. A witness, for example, is guilty of perjury for lying under oath even if nobody believes the witness and the jury's verdict is unaffected by the witness's testimony.

Nonetheless, not every affirmative act which on its face violates the law will result in criminal liability. The act has to be voluntary, i.e., an act of the will; or, stated perhaps more accurately, an act that one had, by the exercise of one's will, the power to refrain from doing. The justification for the voluntariness requirement is that an actor cannot be said to be responsible (in the moral sense of the term) for a truly involuntary act. Punishment is also pointless from a deterrence perspective, as involuntary acts cannot be deterred.

It may seem that characterising an act as involuntary is simply another way of saying that the defendant did not act with *mens rea*. In most instances the result of either line of analysis will be the same. However, in the case of strict liability crimes, where no *mens rea* need be proved and there is consequently no *mens rea* element which can be negated, only an involuntary act defence will be available to an accused.

B Involuntary acts

(i) Acts which are the product of an external force
There are two distinct types of involuntary act cases. One involves the situation where the defendant's act is the product of an external force. Say X pushes Y into Z, who falls into the path of an oncoming lorry. Y's acts are not voluntary, and she is not responsible for the injuries to Z. Indeed, if the push was deliberate, X may well be liable; Y is nothing more than X's innocent agent, even though her acts are the direct cause of the resulting harm.

The same basic principle may also apply where the defendant's acts, although not caused by an external force, are the product of external circumstances beyond the defendant's control. Is the following case an appropriate example?

Burns v *Bidder*
[1966] 3 All ER 29
Queen's Bench Division

The appellant was driving a motor car at a speed which was not high towards a pedestrian crossing. The road surface was good, although slightly wet. He passed the offside of a bus which had stopped at the crossing and which had been stationary there for several seconds. Several persons were using the crossing. The appellant failed to stop his car, at no time did he apply his hand-brake, and the car continued over the crossing and struck a pedestrian who was on the crossing some five or six feet from the centre of the road. The car came to a halt some distance beyond the crossing. Immediately afterwards the appellant complained that his footbrake had failed and, at the request of a police officer, took the car to a police station, where it was tested by an experienced traffic patrol officer who found that the footbrake worked correctly. On an information charging the appellant with unlawfully failing to accord precedence to a foot-passenger who was on the carriageway within the limits of an uncontrolled crossing, contrary to reg. 4 of the Pedestrian Crossings Regulations 1954, the stipendiary magistrate was not satisfied on a balance of probabilities that the brakes of the car had failed, nor was he satisfied that they had not failed and, as he considered that the offence was an absolute offence, he convicted the appellant.

JAMES J: . . . Counsel for the appellant contended that the learned stipendiary magistrate was wrong in his construction of that regulation as imposing an absolute obligation, and urges that to accord precedence involves a positive act such as 'a granting' or 'a bestowing' of something, and that, where the driver of a vehicle is precluded from doing a positive act, then he cannot be said to be failing to accord. Counsel for the appellant further points out that the magistrate was not satisfied that there was not a sudden failure of the brakes, and that there therefore remained a possibility that, due to a latent defect in the braking system, the appellant had been prevented through no fault of his own from according precedence to the pedestrian; this, he contends, being a regulation not imposing absolute obligations there was on that basis a complete defence to the information laid. . . . Some circumstances over which the driver had no reasonable or possible control brought about the collision. The basis is the same as that referred to by Nield J, in *Levy v Hockey* [(1961)] 105 SJ 157]. Regulation 4 must be read 'subject to the principle of impossibility', as he put it in that case. In my judgment, the regulation does not impose an absolute duty come what may, and there is no breach of the obligation under the regulation in circumstances where the driver fails to afford precedence to a foot-passenger solely because his control of the vehicle is taken from him by the occurrence of an event which is outside his possible or reasonable control and in respect of which he is in no way at fault.

The cases of the driver suddenly stunned by a swarm of bees or suffering a sudden epileptiform disabling attack, or of a vehicle being propelled forward by reason of another vehicle hitting it from behind are illustrations of where no offence may be shown, because control over the vehicle is taken completely out of the hands of the driver, and his failure to accord precedence on that account would be no offence. Likewise, in my view, a sudden removal of control over the vehicle occasioned by a latent defect of which the driver did not know, and could not reasonably be expected to know, would render the resulting failure to accord precedence no offence, provided that he is in no way at fault himself. Beyond that limited sphere, however, the obligation of the driver under the regulations can properly be described, as it has been described, as an absolute one. . . .

(ii)   Automatism

The second type of involuntary act case travels under the name of automatism. There are two subcategories of automatism cases. One involves the situation where the defendant is conscious, but his acts are the product of a spasm, reflex, or convulsion. For example, a doctor hits a patient in the knee with a rubber hammer to test the patient's reflexes. The patient's reflexes are extraordinary and his leg flies forward, striking the doctor's assistant. There is little doubt that, if charged with assault, the patient would have a defence based on the fact that his act was a reflex action and involuntary.

The second subcategory of automatism involves the situation where the defendant commits an act in an unconscious or semi-conscious state, or in a state of impaired consciousness. This type of automatism case has proved quite resistant to reasoned analysis. While there is agreement that the automatism negates an element of the crime, there is disagreement as to whether the element negated is the *actus reus* or the *mens rea*, or both.

When the automatism is due to a disease of the mind, the confusion seems to be compounded. Is the appropriate defence in such a case insanity or automatism? If insanity, the burden of proof rests on the defendant, who must establish insanity on the balance of probabilities. If the appropriate defence is automatism, the burden of negating automatism rests on the prosecution, because it is required to establish both *actus reus* and *mens rea* by proof beyond a reasonable doubt. Thus, regardless of whether automatism is seen as negating the *actus reus* or the *mens rea* of the offence, the burden of negating automatism is on the prosecution. The defendant does, however, bear the initial burden of introducing evidence (medical evidence will almost always be necessary) to show automatism, for until he does, the Crown is entitled to rely on the presumption that a defendant has the capacity to commit the crime. The issues were examined in the following case:

Bratty v *Attorney-General For Northern Ireland*
[1961] 3 All ER 523
House of Lords

The accused killed a girl, with whom he was driving in his car on an errand. He took off her stocking and strangled her with it. He gave evidence that a 'blackness' came over him and that 'I didn't know what I was doing. I didn't realise anything.' He also said that previously he had had 'feelings of blackness' and headaches, and there was evidence of his odd behaviour at times, of his mental backwardness and his religious leanings. There was medical evidence that the accused might have been suffering from an attack of psychomotor epilepsy, which was a disease of the mind affecting the reason and which could cause ignorance of the nature and quality of acts done. No other pathological cause for the accused's acts, or a state of automatism on his part was assigned by medical evidence at the trial. The defences of automatism (i.e., unconscious involuntary action) and of insanity within the M'Naghten rules were raised at the trial. The trial judge refused to leave the defence of automatism to the jury, but left to them the defence of insanity, which the jury rejected. The accused was convicted of murder.

VISCOUNT KILMUIR LC: My Lords, this is an appeal from the Court of Criminal Appeal in Northern Ireland. . . . The court certified that the decision involved two points of law of general public importance, namely:

(i)   Whether, his plea of insanity having been rejected by the jury, it was open to the accused to rely on a defence of automatism; and
(ii) If the answer to (i) be in the affirmative, whether, on the evidence, the defence of automatism should have been left to the jury.

. . . The Court of Criminal Appeal [agreed] that the learned judge was right in not leaving to the jury the defence of automatism in so far as it purported to be founded on a defect of reason from disease of the mind within the M'Naghten rules. In this I think that they were right. To establish the defence of insanity within the M'Naghten rules the accused must prove on the preponderance of probabilities first a defect of reason from a disease of the mind, and, secondly, as a consequence of such a defect, ignorance of the nature and quality (or the wrongfulness) of the acts. We have to consider a case in which it is sought to do so by medical evidence to the effect that the conduct of the accused might be compatible with psychomotor epilepsy, which is a disease of the mind affecting the reason, and that psychomotor epilepsy could cause ignorance of the nature and quality of the acts done, but in which the medical witness can assign no other cause for that ignorance. Where the possibility of an unconscious act depends on, and only on, the existence of a defect of reason from disease of the mind within the M'Naghten rules, a rejection by the jury of this defence of insanity necessarily implies that they reject the possibility.

The Court of Criminal Appeal also took the view that where the alleged automatism is based solely on a disease of the mind within the M'Naghten rules, the same burden of proof rests on the defence whether the 'plea' is given the name of insanity or automatism. I do not think that statement goes further than saying that when one relies on insanity as defined by the M'Naghten rules one cannot by a difference of nomenclature avoid the road so often and authoritatively laid down by the courts.

What I have said does not mean that, if a defence of insanity is raised unsuccessfully, there can never, in any conceivable circumstances, be room for an alternative defence based on automatism. For example, it may be alleged that the accused had a blow on the head after which he acted without being conscious of what he was doing or was a sleep-walker. There might be a divergence of view whether there was a defect of reason from disease of the mind (compare the curious position which arose in *R* v *Kemp* [1957] 1 QB 399). The jury might not accept the evidence of a defect of reason from disease of the mind, but at the same time accept the evidence that the prisoner did not know what he was doing. If the jury should take that view of the facts they would find him not guilty. But it should be noted that the defence would only have succeeded because the necessary foundation had been laid by positive evidence which, properly considered, was evidence of something other than a defect of reason from disease of the mind. In my opinion, this analysis of the two defences (insanity and automatism) shows that where the only cause alleged for the unconsciousness is a defect of reason from disease of the mind, and that cause is rejected by the jury, there can be no room for the alternative defence of automatism. . . . It is necessary that a proper foundation be laid before a judge can leave 'automatism' to the jury. That foundation, in my view, is not forthcoming merely from unaccepted evidence of a defect of reason from disease of the mind. . . .

Nevertheless, one must not lose sight of the overriding principle, laid down by this House in *Woolmington's* case [1935] AC 462, that it is for the prosecution to prove every element of the offence charged. One of these elements is the accused's state of mind; normally the presumption of mental capacity is sufficient to prove that he acted consciously and voluntarily and the prosecution need go no further. But, if, after considering evidence properly left to them by the judge, the jury are left in real doubt whether or not the accused acted in a state of automatism, it seems to me that on principle they should acquit because the necessary mens rea – if indeed the actus reus – has not been proved beyond reasonable doubt. . . .

LORD DENNING: My Lords, in *Woolmington* v *Director of Public Prosecutions* [1935] AC 462 Viscount Sankey LC, said: 'When dealing with a murder case the Crown must prove (a) death as the result of a voluntary act of the accused and (b) malice of the accused.' The requirement that it should be a voluntary act is essential, not only in a murder case, but also in every criminal case. No act is punishable if it is done involuntarily: and an involuntary act in this context – some people nowadays prefer to speak of it as 'automatism' – means an act which is done by the muscles without any control by the mind such as a spasm, a reflex action or a convulsion; or an act done by a person who is not conscious of what he is doing such as an act done whilst suffering from concussion or whilst sleepwalking. . . . The term 'involuntary act' is, however, capable of wider connotations: and to prevent confusion it is to be observed that in the criminal law an act is not to be regarded as an involuntary act simply because the doer does not remember it. When a man is charged with dangerous driving, it is no defence for him to say 'I don't know what happened. I cannot remember a thing': see *Hill* v *Baxter* [1958] 1 All ER 193. Loss of memory afterwards is never a defence in itself, so long as he was conscious at the time; see *Russell* v *H. M. Advocate* [1946] SC (J) 37]; *R* v *Podola* [[1959] 3 All ER 418]. Nor is an act to be regarded as an involuntary act simply because the doer could not control his impulse to do it. . . .

My Lords, I think that Devlin J, was quite right in *R* v *Kemp* [1957] 1 QB 399 in putting the question of insanity to the jury, even though it had not been raised by the defence. When it is asserted that the accused did an involuntary act in a state of automatism, the defence necessarily puts in issue the state of mind of the accused man: and thereupon it is open to the prosecution to show what his true state of mind was. The old notion that only the defence can raise a defence of insanity is now gone. The prosecution are entitled to raise it and it is their duty to do so rather than allow a dangerous person to be at large. . . .

On the other point discussed by Devlin J, namely, what is a 'disease of the mind' within the M'Naghten rules, I would agree with him that this is a question for the judge. The major mental diseases, which the doctors call psychoses, such as schizophrenia, are clearly diseases of the mind. But in *R* v *Charlson* [1955] 1 WLR 317, Barry J, seems to have assumed that other diseases such as epilepsy or cerebral tumour are not diseases of the mind, even when they are such as to manifest themselves in violence. I do not agree with this. It seems to me that any mental disorder which has manifested itself in violence and is prone to recur is a disease of the mind. At any rate it is the sort of disease for which a person should be detained in hospital rather than be given an unqualified acquittal.

. . . [W]hilst the *ultimate* burden rests on the Crown of proving every element essential in the crime, nevertheless in order to prove that the act was a voluntary act, the Crown is entitled to rely on the *presumption* that every man has sufficient mental capacity to be responsible for his crimes: and that if the defence wish to displace that presumption they must give some evidence from which the contrary may reasonably be inferred. . . .

The presumption of mental capacity of which I have spoken is a provisional presumption only. It does not put the legal burden on the defence in the same way as the presumption of sanity does. It leaves the legal burden on the prosecution, but nevertheless, until it is displaced, it enables the prosecution to discharge the ultimate burden of proving that the act was voluntary. Not because the presumption is evidence itself, but because it takes the place of evidence. In order to displace the presumption of mental capacity, the defence must give sufficient evidence from which it may reasonably be inferred that the act was involuntary. The evidence of the man himself will rarely be sufficient unless it is supported by medical evidence which points to the cause of the mental incapacity. . . . When the only cause that is assigned for an involuntary act is drunkenness, then it is only necessary to leave drunkenness to the jury, with the consequential directions, and not to leave automatism at all. When the only cause that is assigned for it is a disease of the mind, then it is only necessary to leave insanity to the jury, and not automatism. When the cause assigned is concussion or sleepwalking, there should be some evidence from which it can reasonably be inferred before it should be left to the jury. If it is said to be due to concussion, there should be evidence of a severe blow shortly beforehand. If it is said to be sleepwalking, there should be some credible support for it. His mere assertion that he was asleep will not suffice. Once a proper foundation is thus laid for automatism, the matter becomes at large and must be left to the jury. . . .

This brings me to the root question in the present case: Was a proper foundation laid here for the defence of automatism apart from the plea of insanity? There was the evidence of the appellant himself that he could not remember anything because 'this blackness was over me'. He said 'I did not realise exactly what I was doing', and added afterwards 'I didn't know what I was doing. I didn't realise anything'. He said he had four or five times previously had 'feelings of blackness' and frequently headaches. There was evidence, too, of his odd behaviour at times, his mental backwardness and his religious leanings. Added to this there was the medical evidence. Dr Sax, who was called on his behalf, said there was a possibility that he was suffering from psychomotor epilepsy. It was, he said, practically the only possibility that occurred to him. Dr Walker, his general practitioner, said you could not leave the possibility out of account. Dr Robinson, a specialist, who gave evidence on behalf of the Crown, said he thought it was extremely unlikely that it was an epileptic attack, but one could not rule it out. All the doctors agreed that psychomotor epilepsy, if it exists, is a defect of reason due to disease of the mind: and the judge accepted this view. No other cause was canvassed.

In those circumstances, I am clearly of opinion that, if the act of the appellant was an involuntary act, as the defence suggested, the evidence attributed it solely to a disease of the mind and the only defence open was the defence of insanity. There was no evidence of automatism apart from insanity. There was, therefore, no need for the judge to put it to the jury. And when the jury rejected the defence of insanity, they rejected the only defence disclosed by the evidence. . . .

Notes and questions

1. Is it appropriate to characterise epilepsy as a mental disorder? Is this a medical opinion? The view of the ordinary person? Or a definition adopted by the judges for legal purposes?

2. For an automatism claim to succeed, there must be a total loss of voluntary control; impaired or reduced control is not enough. *Attorney-General's Reference (No. 2 of 1992)*, Independent 31 May 1993.

3. Why should the defence of insanity trump the defence of automatism? Is it a matter of legal principle, or because judges do not want persons who cannot control their actions running around loose, which would be the case if they could successfully claim automatism? Until recently, a person acquitted by reason of insanity was automatically committed to a mental institution 'at Her Majesty's pleasure'. Thus, an accused found not guilty by reason of insanity would be locked away in a mental institution, and the community would be safe; while an accused who raised a successful automatism defence would be released back into the community.

Under the Criminal Procedure (Insanity and Unfitness to Plead) Act 1991 (discussed also in Chapter 8), commitment no longer automatically follows from a verdict of not guilty by reason of insanity. The decision lies within the discretion of the judge.

When a defendant raises a defence of automatism, the prosecution is allowed to introduce evidence of insanity and to argue that the appropriate verdict should be not guilty by reason of insanity. Prior to the 1991 Act, the defendant who wished to raise a defence of automatism had to take the not inconsiderable risk that the prosecution would argue insanity, and that the jury would agree, with the result that the defendant would be confined to a mental institution, possibly for life. It is possible that some defendants made a strategic decision not to risk this eventuality and consequently not to raise a possible automatism defence. The 1991 Act to a large extent removes this deterrent. It is still too early, however, to tell what effect this statute will have.

The issues raised in *Bratty* were further explored in the next case:

R v Quick; R v Paddison
[1973] QB 910
Court of Appeal

LAWTON LJ: In its broadest aspects these appeals raise the question what is meant by the phrase a defect of reason from disease of the mind' within the meaning of the M'Naghten Rules. More particularly the question is whether a person who commits a criminal act whilst under the effects of hypoglycaemia can raise a defence of automatism, as the appellants submitted was possible, or whether such a person must rely on a defence of insanity if he wishes to relieve himself of responsibility for his acts, as Bridge J ruled.

The appellants were both employed at Farleigh Mental Hospital, Flax Bourton, Somerset. Quick was a charge nurse, Paddison a state enrolled nurse. At the trial it was not disputed that, at about 4 p.m. on 27th December 1971, one Green, a paraplegic spastic patient, unable to walk, was sitting in Rosemount Ward at the hospital, watching television. Quick was on duty; Paddison had gone off duty at 2 p.m. but was still present in the ward. Half an hour later, Green had sustained two black eyes, a fractured nose, a split lip which required three stitches, and bruising of his arm and shoulders. There was undisputed medical evidence that these injuries could not have been self-inflicted.

The Crown's case was that Quick had inflicted the injuries on Green and that Paddison had been present aiding and abetting him, not by actual physical participation, but by encouragement. On arraignment Quick pleaded not guilty. At the close of the evidence, following a ruling by the judge as to the effect in law of the evidence relied on by Quick to support a defence of automatism, he pleaded guilty to count 2 of the indictment. The judge's ruling was to the effect that this evidence could only be relied on to support a defence of insanity.

. . . Quick said that he could not remember assaulting Green. He admitted that he had been drinking and that his drinks had included whisky and a quarter of a bottle of rum. He also said that he was, and had been since the age of seven, a diabetic and that that morning he had taken insulin as prescribed by his doctor. After taking the insulin he had had a very small breakfast and no lunch. Dr Cates said that on 12 or more occasions Quick had been admitted to hospital either unconscious or semi-conscious due to hypoglycaemia, which is a condition brought about when there is more insulin in the bloodstream than the amount of sugar there can cope with. When this imbalance occurs, the insulin has much the same effect as an excess of alcohol in the human body. At the onset of the imbalance the higher functions of the mind are affected. As the effects of the imbalance become more marked, more and more mental functions are upset; and unless an antidote is given (and a lump of sugar is an effective one) the sufferer can relapse into coma. In the later stages of mental impairment a sufferer may become aggressive and violent without being able to control himself or without knowing at the time what he was doing or having any recollection afterwards of what he had done. . . .

At the trial and before this court it was accepted by the Crown that the evidence to which we have referred was enough to justify an issue being left to the jury whether Quick could be held responsible for what he had done to Green. If the jury were to accept the evidence relied on by Quick what should the verdict be? Quick's counsel submitted 'not guilty'; counsel for the Crown submitted that it should be 'not guilty by reason of insanity'. The judge ruled in favour of the Crown. As Quick did not want to put forward a defence of insanity, after consulting with his counsel, he pleaded guilty to count 2.

. . . In this case, if Quick's alleged condition could have been caused by hypoglycaemia and that condition, like psychomotor epilepsy, was a disease of the mind, then Bridge J's ruling was right. The question remains, however, whether a mental condition arising from hypoglycaemia does amount to a disease of the mind. . . .

. . . Quick was setting up a defence of insanity. He may have been at the material time in a condition of mental disorder manifesting itself in violence. Such manifestations had occurred before and might recur. The difficulty arises as soon as the question is asked whether he should be detained in a mental hospital? No mental hospital would admit a diabetic merely because he had a low blood sugar reaction; and common sense is affronted by the prospect of a diabetic being sent to such a hospital when in most cases the disordered mental condition can be rectified quickly by pushing a lump of sugar or a teaspoonful of glucose into the patient's mouth.

The 'affront to common sense' argument, however, has its own inherent weakness, as counsel for the Crown pointed out. If an accused is shown to have done a criminal act whilst suffering from a 'defect of reason from disease of the mind', it matters not 'whether the disease is curable or incurable . . . temporary or permanent' (see *R v Kemp* [1957] 1 QB 399, per Devlin J). If the condition is temporary, the Secretary of State may have a difficult problem of disposal; but what happens to those found not guilty by reason of insanity is not a matter for the courts.

In *Hill* v *Baxter* [1958] 1 All ER 193, Lord Goddard CJ did not equate unconsciousness due to a sudden illness, which must entail the malfunctioning of the mental processes of the sufferer, with disease of the mind, and in our judgment no one outside a court of law would . . . It seems to us that the law should not give the words 'defect of reason from disease of the mind' a meaning which would be regarded with incredulity outside a court . . .

In this quagmire of law seldom entered nowadays save by those in desperate need of some kind of a defence, *Bratty* v *Attorney-General for Northern Ireland* [1963] AC 386; [1961] 3 All ER 523 provides the only firm ground. Is there any discernible path? We think there is – judges should follow in a common sense way their sense of fairness. . . . In our judgement no help can be obtained by speculating (because that is what we would have to do) as to what the judges who answered the House of Lords' questions in 1843 meant by disease of the mind, still less what Sir Matthew Hale meant in the second half of the 17th century. A quick backward look at the state of medicine in 1843 will suffice to show how unreal it would be to apply the concepts of that age to the present time. Dr Simpson had not yet started his experiments with chloroform, the future Lord Lister was only 16 and laundanum was used and prescribed like aspirins are today. Our task had been to decide what the law means now by the words 'disease of the mind'. In our judgment the fundamental concept is of a malfunctioning of the mind caused by disease. A malfunctioning of the mind of transitory effect caused by the application to the body of some external factor such as violence, drugs, including anaesthetics, alcohol and hypnotic influences cannot fairly be said to be due to disease. Such malfunctioning, unlike an accused from criminal responsibility. A self-induced incapacity will not excuse . . . nor will one which could have been reasonably foreseen as a result of either doing, or omitting to do something, as, for example, taking alcohol against medical advice after using certain prescribed drugs, or failing to have regular meals whilst taking insulin. From to time to time difficult borderline cases are likely to arise. When they do, the test suggested by the New Zealand Court of Appeal . . . is likely to give the correct result, viz can this mental condition be fairly regarded as amounting to or producing a defect of reason from disease of the mind?

In this case Quick's alleged mental condition, if it ever existed, was not caused by his diabetes but by his use of the insulin prescribed by his doctor. Such malfunctioning of his mind as there was, was caused by an external factor and not by a bodily disorder in the nature of a disease which disturbed the working of his mind. It follows in our judgment that Quick was entitled to have his defence of automatism left to the jury and that Bridge J's ruling as to the effect of the medical evidence called by him was wrong. Had the defence of automatism been left to the jury, a number of questions of fact would have had to be answered. If he was in a confused mental condition, was it due to a hypoglycaemic episode or to too much alcohol? If the former, to what extent had he brought about his condition by not following his doctor's instructions about taking regular meals? Did he know that he was getting into a hypoglycaemic episode? If Yes, why did he not use the antidote of eating a lump of sugar as he had been advised to do? On the evidence which was before the jury Quick might have had difficulty in answering these questions in a manner which would have relieved him of responsibility for his acts. We cannot say, however, with the requisite degree of confidence, that the jury would have convicted him. It follows that his conviction must be quashed on the ground that the verdict was unsatisfactory.

Appeals allowed.

Questions

1. The Court of Appeal in *Quick* drew a distinction between those acts of a diabetic which may be attributable to insulin, an external source, and those which may be attributable to the diabetes, an internal source. What if a patient who is prescribed medication to control a mental illness suffers an adverse reaction from the medication which causes the patient to go out of control? Are acts done in this state attributable to the disease or to the medication? Are not the two inextricably linked.

2. What if the external source is psychological rather than physical? Compare *R v Rabey* (1978) 79 DLR 3d 435 (automatism defence rejected where defendant claimed his crime was committed while in a disassociative state brought on by his rejection by a girl with whom he was infatuated) with *R v T* [1990] Crim LR 256 (automatism defence available where defendant was suffering from Post Traumatic Stress Disorder brought on as a result of having been raped).

Note

1. The relationship between automatism and insanity is also examined in the section on the latter defence. See Chapter 8.

In *Quick* there was evidence that the defendant, contrary to his doctor's instructions, may have been drinking alcohol and not eating food. If so, indicated the court, such evidence may have defeated his automatism claim. The issue of self-induced automatism was re-examined in the following case:

R v Bailey
[1983] 1 WLR 760
Court of Appeal

GRIFFITHS LJ: At the Crown Court at Bolton on October 14, 1982, the appellant was convicted of wounding with intent to cause grievous bodily harm, contrary to section 18 of the Offences against the Person Act 1861 (24 & 25 Vict. c. 100). The jury were not required to give a verdict on an alternative count of unlawful wounding contrary to section 20 of that Act. He now appeals against this conviction.

The appellant is a diabetic and has been so for some 30 years. He requires to take insulin to control his condition. His defence at the trial was that he was acting in a state of automatism caused by hypoglycaemia.

In early January 1982, the woman with whom the appellant had been living for the previous two years left him and formed an association with the victim, Mr Harrison. At about 7 p.m. on January 20, 1982, the appellant, seeming upset, visited Mr Harrison at his home. They had a cup of tea and discussed the matter. After 10 or 15 minutes the appellant said that he felt unwell and asked Mr Harrison to make him some sugar and water, which the appellant drank. About 10 minutes later the appellant started to leave. He then said that he had lost his glove and that it might be down the side of the chair on which he had been sitting. Mr Harrison bent down to look and the appellant struck him on the back of the head with an iron bar, which was a case opener about 18″ long. The appellant remained there holding the iron bar. Mr Harrison ran from the house. His wound required 10 stitches.

The Crown's case was that although it was theoretically possible, from a medical point of view, for there to have been a temporary loss of awareness due to hypoglycaemia, as the appellant claimed, this was not what had happened. On the contrary, it was contended that the appellant, upset and jealous about Mr Harrison's relationship with his girlfriend, had armed himself with the iron bar and gone to Mr Harrison's house with the intention of injuring him. . . .

When he gave evidence, the appellant, who was a man of good character, maintained he had no intention of harming Mr Harrison and he had acted in a state of automatism. He said that he had to take two doses of insulin a day and was under his general practitioner and a special clinic. He had arrived home at 5.30 p.m. and had his insulin and a cup of tea. At 7 p.m. he decided to go and see Harrison and his account of what took place accorded with that of Mr Harrison up to the point where he asked Mr Harrison to look for his glove. The next thing he could remember was standing with the bar in his hand. He saw that Mr Harrison was injured and he said: 'What the hell am I doing?' He then described how he went home and later to the public house where he was arrested.

The appellant's general practitioner gave evidence. He confirmed that the appellant was a diabetic and received insulin treatment, after which he had to take food within a short period. If he failed to do so it could produce symptoms of weakness, palpitations, tremor and sweating. He might develop more aggressive tendencies than normal and this could be accompanied by loss of memory. After describing what the appellant had said he had had to eat he said that the appellant had not had sufficient to counteract and balance the dose of insulin. So far as he was aware the appellant in 30 years had never developed a condition of coma due to hypoglycaemia. He said that the effect of taking sugar and water in Mr Harrison's house would be to help bring back the sugar level within five or ten minutes. When he was cross-examined he said he thought it unlikely that there could have been the sudden switch-off effect alleged by the appellant and he regarded the likelihood of such a thing happening as being remote if sugar and water had been taken five minutes before it happened.

It was therefore the appellant's case that the attack had taken place during a period of loss of consciousness occurring due to hypoglycaemia caused by his failure to take sufficient food following his last dose of insulin. Accordingly it was submitted that he had neither the specific intent to cause grievous bodily harm for the purpose of section 18 nor the appropriate mens rea or basic intent for the purpose of the section 20 offence.

But the recorder, in effect, told the jury that this defence was not available to the appellant. . . . The recorder appears to have derived this proposition, which he applied to both counts of the indictment, from *R* v *Quick* [1973] QB 910. . . .

But in that case, the offence, assault occasioning actual bodily harm, was an offence of basic intent. No specific intent was required. It is now quite clear that even if the incapacity of mind is self-induced by the voluntary taking of drugs or alcohol, the specific intent to kill or cause grievous bodily harm may be negatived: see *R* v *Majewski* [1977] AC 443. This being so, as it is conceded on behalf of the Crown, the direction to which we have referred cannot be correct so far as the offence under section 18 is concerned.

But it is also submitted that the direction is wrong or at least in too broad and general terms, so far as the section 20 offence is concerned. If . . . *R* v *Quick* correctly represents the law, then the direction given by the recorder was correct so far as the second count was concerned even though the appellant may have had no appreciation of the consequences of his failure to take food and even though such failure may not have been due to deliberate abstention but because of his generally distressed condition. In our judgment the passage from Lawton LJ's judgment was obiter and we are free to re-examine it.

Automatism resulting from intoxication as a result of a voluntary ingestion of alcohol or dangerous drugs does not negative the mens rea necessary for crimes of basic intent, because the conduct of the accused is reckless and recklessness is enough to constitute the necessary mens rea in assault cases where no specific intent forms part of the charge: see *R v Majewski* [1977] AC 443, 476 . . . But it seems to us that there may be material distinctions between a man who consumes alcohol or takes dangerous drugs and one who fails to take sufficient food after insulin to avert hypoglycaemia.

It is common knowledge that those who take alcohol to excess or certain sorts of drugs may become aggressive or do dangerous or unpredictable things, they may be able to foresee the risks of causing harm to others but nevertheless persist in their conduct. But the same cannot be said without more of a man who fails to take food after an insulin injection. If he does appreciate the risk that such a failure may lead to aggressive, unpredictable and uncontrollable conduct and he nevertheless deliberately runs the risk or otherwise disregards it, this will amount to recklessness. But we certainly do not think that it is common knowledge, even among diabetics, that such is a consequence of a failure to take food and there is no evidence that it was known to this appellant. Doubtless he knew that if he failed to take his insulin or proper food after it, he might lose consciousness, but as such he would only be a danger to himself unless he put himself in charge of some machine such as a motor car, which required his continued conscious control.

In our judgment, self-induced automatism, other than that due to intoxication from alcohol or drugs, may provide a defence to crimes of basic intent. The question in each case will be whether the prosecution have proved the necessary element of recklessness. In cases of assault, if the accused knows that his actions or inaction are likely to make him aggressive, unpredictable or uncontrolled with the result that he may cause some injury to others and he persists in the action or takes no remedial action when he knows it is required, it will be open to the jury to find that he was reckless. . . .

But we have to consider whether, notwithstanding these misdirections, there has been any miscarriage of justice and whether the jury properly directed could have failed to come to the same conclusion. As Lawton LJ said in *Quick's* case at p. 922, referring to the defence of automatism, it is a 'quagmire of law seldom entered nowadays save by those in desperate need of some kind of a defence . . . ' This case is no exception. We think it very doubtful whether the appellant laid a sufficient basis for the defence to be considered by the jury at all. But even if he did we are in no doubt that the jury properly directed must have rejected it. Although an episode of sudden transient loss of consciousness or awareness was theoretically possible it was quite inconsistent with the graphic description that the appellant gave to the police both orally and in his written statement. There was abundant evidence that he had armed himself with the iron bar and gone to Mr Harrison house for the purpose of attacking him because he wanted to teach him a lesson and because he was in the way.

Moreover the doctor's evidence to which we have referred showed it was extremely unlikely that such an episode could follow some five minutes after taking sugar and water. For these reasons we are satisfied that no miscarriage of justice occurred and the appeal will be dismissed.

Appeal dismissed.

In the early cases the courts often cited the sleepwalker as the prototype example of automatism. When the actual fact situation finally came before the courts, however, it turned out to be more complicated.

R v Burgess
[1991] 2 QB 92
Court of Appeal

LORD LANE CJ: On 20 July 1989 in the Crown Court at Bristol before Judge Sir Ian Lewis and a jury, the appellant was found not guilty by reason of insanity on a charge of wounding with intent. He was ordered to be admitted and detained in such hospital as the Secretary of State should direct. He now appeals against that verdict by certificate of the trial judge under section 12 of the Criminal Appeal Act 1968.

The appellant did not dispute the fact that in the early hours of 2 June 1988 he had attacked Katrina Curtis by hitting her on the head first with a bottle when she was asleep, then with a video recorder and finally grasping her round the throat. She suffered a gaping three centimetre laceration to her scalp requiring sutures.

His case was that he lacked the mens rea necessary to make him guilty of the offence, because he was 'sleep walking' when he attacked Miss Curtis. He was, it was alleged, suffering from 'non-insane' automatism and he called medical evidence, in particular from Dr d'Orban and Dr Eames to support that contention.

Where the defence of automatism is raised by a defendant, two questions fall to be decided by the judge before the defence can be left to the jury. The first is whether a proper evidential foundation for the defence of automatism has been laid. The second is whether the evidence shows the case to be one of insane automatism, that is to say, a case which falls within the M'Naghten Rules, or one of non-insane automatism.

The judge in the present case undertook that task and on the second question came to the conclusion that – assuming the appellant was not conscious at the time of what he was doing – on any view of the medical evidence so far as automatism was concerned, it amounted to evidence of insanity within the M'Naghten Rules and not merely to evidence of non-insane automatism. The sole ground of appeal is that that ruling was wrong.

There can be no doubt but that the appellant, on the basis of the jury's verdict, was labouring under such a defect of reason as not to know what he was doing when he wounded Miss Curtis. The question is whether that was from 'disease of the mind'. The first point that has to be understood is that the phrase is 'disease of the mind' and not 'disease of the brain'. . . .

The appellant plainly suffered from a defect of reason from some sort of failure (for lack of a better term) of the mind causing him to act as he did without conscious motivation. His mind was to some extent controlling his actions which were purposive rather than the result simply of muscular spasm, but without his being consciously aware of what he was doing. Can it be said that that 'failure' was a *disease* of the mind rather than a defect or failure of the mind not due to disease? That is the distinction, by no means always easy to draw, upon which this case depends, as others have depended in the past.

What help does one derive from the authorities as to the meaning of 'disease' in this context? Lord Denning in *Bratty v Attorney-General for Northern Ireland* [1963] AC 386, 412 said:

Upon the other point discussed by Devlin J, namely, what is a 'disease of the mind' within the M'Naghten Rules, I would agree with him that this is a question for the judge. The major mental diseases, which the doctors call psychoses, such as schizophrenia, are clearly diseases of the mind. But in *Charlson's* case [1955] 1 WLR 317, Barry J seems to have assumed that other diseases such as epilepsy or cerebral tumour are not diseases of the mind, even when they are such as to manifest themselves in violence. I do not agree with this. It seems to me that any mental disorder which has manifested itself in violence and is prone to recur is a disease of the mind. At any rate it is the sort of disease for which a person should be detained in hospital rather than be given an unqualified acquittal.

It seems to us that if there is a danger of recurrence that may be an added reason for categorising the condition as a disease of the mind. On the other hand, the absence of the danger of recurrence is not a reason for saying that it cannot be a disease of the mind. Subject to that possible qualification, we respectfully adopt Lord Denning's suggested definition.

It seems to us that on [the] evidence the judge was right to conclude that this was an abnormality or disorder, albeit transitory, due to an internal factor, whether functional or organic, which had manifested itself in violence. It was a disorder or abnormality which might recur, though the possibility of it recurring in the form of serious violence was unlikely. Therefore since this was a legal problem to be decided on legal principles, it seems to us that on those principles the answer was as the judge found it to be. . . .

The judge was alive to the apparent incongruity of labelling this sort of disability as insanity. He drew attention, as we would also wish to do, to the passage of the speech of Lord Diplock in *R* v *Sullivan* [1984] AC 156, where he said, at p. 173:

it is natural to feel reluctant to attach the label of insanity to a sufferer from psychomotor epilepsy of the kind to which Mr Sullivan was subject, even though the expression in the context of a special verdict of 'not guilty by reason of insanity' is a technical one which includes a purely temporary and intermittent suspension of the mental faculties of reason, memory and understanding resulting from the occurrence of an epileptic fit. But the label is contained in the current statute, it has appeared in this statute's predecessors ever since 1800. It does not lie within the power of the courts to alter it. Only Parliament can do that. It has done so twice; it could do so once again.

This appeal must accordingly be dismissed.

Appeal dismissed.

Notes and questions
1.   Sleepwalkers seem to fall somewhere between a state of consciousness and unconsciousness. They are able to manoeuvre their way about, opening doors and walking down steps, for example, without injuring themselves. Yet they seem to have no conscious awareness or subsequent recollection of their actions. Is it appropriate (just?) to characterise the sleepwalker as insane? Why does the law do so?
2.   What disposition should be made in the case of the sleepwalkers who commit serious violent crimes such as murder? Should they be sent to prison? To a mental institution? Or should they be allowed to return to the community?
3.   Suppose that James begins to drive home from work in a state of extreme drowsiness. He subsequently falls asleep at the wheel and is involved in an accident. If charged with dangerous driving, should he be able to assert a defence of automatism? Is *Burgess* distinguishable? See *Hill* v *Baxter* [1958] 1 All ER 193. Sometimes the issue of automatism can be avoided by finding an

antecedent act on which to premise criminal liability, such as the fact that defendant began driving knowing that he was sleepy. The decision to drive under such circumstances may itself be a reckless act satisfying the *actus reus* (as well as the *mens rea*) elements of the crime.

4.   There are some mental health experts who believe that what one does while sleepwalking reflects what one subconsciously wants to do but cannot bring oneself to do while in a conscious state. Should this fact affect the sleepwalker's criminal liability?

3   *MENS REA*

I   Introduction

Traditionally, academics and judges alike have seemed to agree that there were two indispensable elements – *actus reus* and *mens rea* – which the Crown had to establish before criminal liability could be imposed. As we have already noted, a common law maxim held that '*actus non facit reum nisi mens sit rea*' – an act is not wrongful unless there is a wrongful state of mind. In the last chapter we examined *actus reus*; now we turn our attention to *mens rea*.

Mens rea is the generic term which refers to the mental element of a crime. It is misleading, however, to talk of *mens rea* in the abstract. In regard to any specific crime, the statutory or common law definition of the crime must be consulted in order to determine the *mens rea* of the crime in question. One's search does not end with the identification of *a mens rea*. Many crimes have more than one mental element, and different types of *mens rea* may be applicable to different elements of the crime.

Mens rea is a far more elusive creature than *actus reus*. An act is observable, and provable through objective evidence. Witnesses can and will testify to what a defendant did. They cannot testify as accurately to what the defendant was thinking. State of mind often can only be inferred from actions. If X stands immediately in front of Y with a loaded gun and shoots Y, a jury might infer that X intended to kill Y. But what if X testifies that she was aiming at an area to the left of Y, or was only intending to scare Y? Or what if X says that she did not know that the gun was loaded, or that she thought Y was a dummy (cardboard) or that she thought that Y was about to shoot her and fired in self-defence? Implausible, perhaps; but how does one know for sure? Unless a defendant confesses (and sometimes not even then: there are many documented cases of false confessions, for reasons ranging from improper police pressure to guilt on the part of the confessor for some unrelated childhood incident), there will always remain doubt about what was going on in the defendant's mind at the time of the offence.

Notwithstanding the problems relating to proof, *mens rea* is perhaps the most critical concept in criminal law. Mental state will often be the determining factor as to whether one who causes another's death will receive a life sentence, a term of years in prison short of life, or no legal sanction whatsoever. For example, driving through the High Street Zachary hits and kills a pedestrian: if Zachary intended to run over the pedestrian, he is guilty of murder; if he was driving recklessly, he is guilty of manslaughter or causing death by dangerous driving; and if the victim jumped in front of his car and the accident was unavoidable, he is guilty of no crime. The same act, the same result, but entirely different legal consequences because of Zachary's state of mind.

A   Motive and intent

Before examining specific cases, there are several preliminary distinctions worth making, for they arise again and again in different guises. The first relates to the difference between motive and intent. Intent refers to the idea that the defendant's act was not involuntary or accidental but purposive; and that the result which was brought about was one that the defendant wanted to bring about. Motive refers to the reasons why the defendant wanted to bring about that result.

Motive is generally said to be irrelevant to guilt. A praiseworthy motive will not alter what would otherwise be a crime, and a blameworthy motive will not justify the conviction of a defendant who lacks *mens rea*. For example, if Marshall robs Barclay's Bank, it does not matter, for legal purposes, whether Marshall planned to give the money to charity or to spend it on himself. The reason motive is said to be irrelevant is not only that motive is so difficult to prove (so is intent), nor that it is so easy to fabricate (of course I was going to give the proceeds from the bank robbery to charity), but that we do not want to get into the messy business of evaluating individual motives and saying whether or not they justify criminal conduct. What if our bank robber wanted to give the money to the Labour Party? The leader of the Labour Party might find this an honourable motive, but would jurors who belonged to the Conservative or Liberal Parties?

While motive is not relevant to guilt, it may be relevant at other stages of the criminal process. First, it may affect the prosecutor's decision to bring formal charges. Prosecutors often have considerable discretion in this matter, both so that the state's limited resources are not wasted in frivolous prosecutions, and so that defendants who are not truly blameworthy are not subjected to the emotional trauma and legal expense of a criminal prosecution, despite a technical violation of the law. The defendant's motive may have some bearing at this point. Secondly, at trial the prosecution may want to introduce evidence of motive, although it is not required to do so, because it provides logical support to the state's assertion that the defendant was the one who committed the crime (the fact that the defendant was the sole beneficiary under the terms of the will of the wealthy victim provides a motive for the killing; if nobody else had a motive, it makes it more likely that the defendant was the murderer). Motive may also influence a jury's uncontrollable discretion to acquit – either the absence of motive may lead them to conclude that the defendant did not commit the crime; or an honourable motive, as in the case of a mercy killing, may lead them to acquit despite the belief that defendant was technically guilty. Lastly, a judge may take into account motive in sentencing.

To say that motive is legally irrelevant may also be a bit misleading. Motive may have legal significance in some instances. If Beatrice's motive in striking Elvin is to prevent him from attacking her, that motive will lead to a viable claim of self-defence. Similarly, if Beatrice's motive for driving the car of the bank robbers was that they had kidnapped her children and were threatening to kill them if she did not cooperate, that motive may lead to a successful defence of duress. Whether it is semantically correct to use motive in the context of defences is debatable, but clearly we are talking about the reasons why the defendant acted as he or she did.

Consider the following account of a recent case which received widespread publicity and which raises legal, medical, and ethical issues:

Robert Porter, 'Doctor convicted of attempted murder'
Sunday Telegraph, 20 September, 1992

AMID emotional scenes, the hospital consultant Dr Nigel Cox was convicted at Winchester Crown Court yesterday of attempting to murder a patient dying of rheumatoid arthritis.

The jury, many weeping, reached a majority verdict of 11–1 after more than eight hours of deliberations spread over two days.

The verdict was greeted with gasps of surprise and the judge, Mr Justice Ognall, said at once that he was not proposing to send the 47-year-old consultant to prison.

Sentence will be pronounced tomorrow in a case which has aroused the interest and compassion of the nation. At its heart lay the dilemma over how far a doctor can go to ease suffering of a dying patient. Reaction came swiftly. Frank Field, the Labour MP, said: 'In terms of law the decision of the jury may be correct but in terms of compassions both to the patient and the doctor it is totally lacking.'

Dr Fleur Fisher, head of the ethics, science and information division of the BMA said active euthanasia should remain illegal. But there could be occasions where a doctor might feel compelled by conscience to end a life and to justify that decision in a court of law.

'All doctors have the clinical responsibility to ensure that patients nearing the end of life have access to the pain control techniques available,' she said.

Mrs Lillian Boyes's sons were shocked by the verdict. John Boyes, 44, said: 'I am so devastated. I feel so betrayed.' He and his brother Patrick, 42, had never complained about Dr Cox and the court was told of their relief when their mother died.

But Paddy Ross, a leading consultant and colleague at the Royal Hampshire County Hospital, insisted that the jury had no option but to convict Dr Cox.

The judge told jurors: 'There are times, speaking for myself, and I strongly suspect speaking for all of you as well as counsel, when a criminal trial is an almost overwhelming burden.'

As the judge was speaking many friends and relatives of Dr Cox broke down in tears.

Dr Cox left the court arm-in-arm with his girlfriend Jennifer Green a 45-year-old local government officer. He appealed to journalists: 'Respect my privacy.'

He has been found guilty of administering a lethal injection of potassium chloride to Mrs Boyes, of Bishopstoke, Hampshire, who died in August last year within minutes of the injection.

Her agony had become so appalling that not even near-lethal doses of heroin could keep the pain at bay.

Dr Cox, who had treated Mrs Boyes for 13 years and was said to have developed a special bond with her, never denied administering the injection but said it had been to relieve pain not to kill.

Dr Cox will remain suspended on full pay, Dr Graham Winyard, medical director of Wessex Regional Health Authority, said yesterday. He added that the case 'will undoubtedly stimulate demands for a review in the law'.

Questions

1. What was Doctor Cox's motive? His intent?
2. If you were on Doctor Cox's jury, what verdict would you have favoured? Why?
3. What would be an appropriate sentence in the case?

B   *Subjective and objective mens rea*

A second preliminary distinction that is worth noting is that between subjective and objective states of mind. Subjective states of mind are concerned with what the actor was actually thinking; objective states of mind refer to what a reasonable person in the position of the actor would have been thinking. In such a case the defendant will be liable even though the actor may have been thinking no such thing. Where *mens rea* is objective, a defendant's fault consists of failing to appreciate a risk that would have been appreciated by a reasonable person. Crimes which involve subjective fault require that the prosecution prove that the defendent actually had the state of mind required for the crime. Crimes that involve objective fault do not require that the prosecution prove that the defendant actually had a particular state of mind but only that defendant failed to meet a certain standard of conduct, usually determined by what would have been expected of a reasonable person. For example, if Edward drives his car on the High Street at a pedestrian, intending to run him over, his subjective state of mind is to kill the pedestrian. But when Edward is not paying sufficient attention to what he is doing, his subjective state of mind is not to run anybody over, although a reasonable person would have seen that there was a clear risk that this might occur. As a general proposition (although it is not always true), persons who commit crimes with subjective *mens rea* are considered to be more morally blameworthy, and therefore deserving of greater punishment, than persons whose *mens rea* is objective.

To determine whether a statute requires proof of objective or subjective *mens rea* one needs to look at the statute, the words it uses, and how those words have been interpreted by the courts. Listed below are examples of words which are generally held to connote subjective or objective fault.

Subjective Fault	*Objective Fault*
purposely	
recklessly	recklessly
knowingly	negligently
intentionally	carelessly
wilfully	
deliberately	
with intent to . . .	without due care and attention

Note that in the above list 'recklessly' appears in both columns. The courts have recognised both a subjective and an objective strain of this type of *mens rea*. See section IIC below

In addition to objective and subjective *mens rea*, sometimes statutes appear to contain no *mens rea*. The statute defines the crime only in terms of the *actus reus* without any express reference to mental state, imposing what is known as strict liability. This category of strict liability crimes is obviously an exception to the Latin maxim *actus non facit reum mens sit rea*. Problems arise, however, because Parliament does not always say what it means, or so the courts think. Thus statutes which contain no mental element on their face may be interpreted by a court so as to require proof of some sort of *mens rea*. Cases of this type are examined in section IIE on strict liability, below.

In creating a new offence, Parliament can draft the statute to require proof of either subjective or objective *mens rea*, or can make the offence one of strict liability. Which path it chooses will be reflected in the wording of the statute. Say, for instance, Parliament decides to make the handling of stolen goods a crime. It can make an element of the offence 'knowing the goods to be stolen', thus requiring subjective *mens rea* in the form of proof that the defendant actually knew the goods were stolen. Or it can write the statute in terms of 'having reason to know' the goods are stolen, thus requiring only objective *mens rea* and proof that a reasonable person would have realised that the goods were stolen. Or it can make the crime into one of strict liability, mentioning nothing about knowing or having reason to know the goods are stolen, but simply making criminal the handling of goods that are in fact stolen. Now a court might nonetheless read into such a statute a *mens rea* element but if Parliament really wanted to, it could expressly declare that proof that a defendant knew or had reason to know that the goods were stolen is not required for conviction.

Whenever you analyse the *mens rea* of a statute, you should ask yourself whether the statute requires it to be subjective, objective, or no fault. If *mens rea* is an element of a crime and the prosecution do not prove it, or the defence raise a reasonable doubt about that element in the jury's mind, the defendant cannot be convicted, even though he may have committed the *actus reus* of the crime and even brought about the proscribed consequences.

While courts will often draw a sharp distinction in theory between objective and subjective states of mind, in practice the distinction is often blurred. The reason is this: The question of whether the defendant possessed the subjective *mens rea* required for a particular crime is a question of fact for the jury. Suppose that after pumping six bullets into her victim's heart from close range, a defendant claims that she did not intend to kill but simply intended to frighten the victim. The jury is likely to decide that the defendant's denial is not credible. Why? – because it makes no sense to them. If they were in the defendant's shoes they would have realised that the bullets would kill the victim. They would have realised it because they are reasonable persons, and any reasonable person would have so realised. By projecting on to the defendant the thought process which they themselves would have gone through the jurors reason that the defendant's version of events is not credible, that the defendant lied, and that the defendant in fact had the requisite subjective *mens rea*. Thus they convict. As a result of an objective exercise in logical reasoning they will have *inferred* a subjective state of mind on the part of the defendant.

C   *Mens rea in respect of what?*

Often a crime will contain more than one *mens rea* element. Different elements of a crime may have attached to them different *mens rea* requirements. In rape, for example, the Crown must prove that the accused had the intent to have sexual intercourse with the victim, but need only prove that he was reckless in respect to whether the victim was consenting. Thus it is always important to ask what it is that the *mens rea* element or elements refer to:

Mens rea can refer to:

(a)   acts (but where the act is not the product of defendant's will the practice of the courts is to speak of an involuntary *actus reus* rather than a lack of *mens rea*);

(b)   circumstances (as, in theft, the defendant's knowledge that the property he is taking belongs to another);

(c)   results (as, in homicide, the death of the victim).

Criminal Damage Act 1971

1. Destroying or damaging property

(1)   A person who without lawful excuse destroys or damages any property belonging to another intending to destroy or damage any such property or being reckless as to whether any such property would be destroyed or damaged shall be guilty of an offence.

(2)   A person who without lawful excuse destroys or damages any property, whether belonging to himself or another —

(a)   intending to destroy or damage any property or being reckless as to whether any property would be destroyed or damaged; and

(b)   intending by the destruction or damage to endanger the life of another or being reckless as to whether the life of another would be thereby endangered; shall be guilty of an offence.

(3) An offence committed under this section by destroying or damaging property by fire shall be charged as arson.

Notes and questions
1. What are the *mens rea* elements of s. 1(2)? To what does each of the elements refer? Which of the *mens rea* elements are subjective and which are objective?
2. Note in s. 1(2) the conjunction 'and' between paras (a) and (b). The appropriate *mens rea* elements in each part must be proved. Where the conjunction instead is '*or*' (as it is in s.1 (1) and in each of the paragraphs of s. 1 (2), the prosecution can satisfy their burden by proof of either *mens rea*.
3. Sometimes a *mens rea* may be implicit rather than explicit, although litigants may have to await a judicial interpretation to this effect. Is part of the *mens rea* of criminal damage in s. 1(1) a requirement that the defendant must *know* or have reason to know that the property which is damaged 'belongs to another'? The issue might arise where defendant claimed that he thought that it was his own property that he was destroying.

D Proof of mens rea

We noted previously the difficulty of establishing what is going on in a defendant's mind at the time of the crime. How does the Crown prove *mens rea*? The issue came to the fore in the following, instructive case:

R v *Steane*
[1947] KB 997
Court of Criminal Appeal

The appellant, a British subject, entered the service of the German broadcasting system, and on several occasions broadcast through that system. The evidence called by the prosecution was that of one witness who proved that the appellant did, in fact, so broadcast and said that he had seen a telegram, in the appellant's possession, signed Emmie Goering, which stated that he could expect to be released and be home very shortly. The principal evidence against him was a statement taken from him by an officer of the British Intelligence Service in October, 1945, purporting to give an account of his activities in the German broadcasting service, concluding with the words: 'I have read this statement over and to the best of my knowledge and belief it is all true, and must request it to be used in conjunction with my written report dated July 5, 1945 to the American C.I.C. in Augsburg.' This earlier report was not produced in evidence. Before the war, the appellant was employed in Germany as a film actor and was so engaged when the war broke out. His wife and two sons were living in Germany. On the outbreak of war the appellant was at once arrested, but his wife and two sons remained in Oberammergau.

The only other evidence was that of the appellant. He said that on his arrest he was questioned and that the interview ended with the order: 'Say

Heil Hitler, you dirty swine.' He refused and was thereupon knocked down losing several teeth, and he was interned on September 11, 1939. Just before Christmas of that year he was sent for by Goebbels, who asked him to broadcast. He refused. He was thereupon warned that he was in an enemy country and that they had methods of making people do things. A week later an official named von Bockman saw him and dropped hints as to German methods of persuasion. A professor named Kossuth also warned him that these people could be dangerous to those who gave trouble. In consequence he submitted to a voice test, trying to perform as badly as he could. The next day he was ordered to read news three times a day, and did so until April, 1940. In that month he refused to do any more broadcasting. Two Gestapo men called on him. They said: 'If you don't obey, your wife and children will be put in a concentration camp.' In May three Gestapo men saw him and he was badly beaten up, one ear being partly torn off. He agreed to work for his old employers, helping to produce films. There was no evidence that the films he helped to produce were or could be of any assistance to the Germans or at all harmful to this country. He swore that he was in continual fear for his wife and children. He asserted, and said he had asserted, in his report of July 5, 1945, that he never had the slightest idea or intention of assisting the enemy, and that what he did was done to save his wife and children and that what he did could not have assisted the enemy except in a very technical sense. There was no record of the actual broadcasts made by the appellant.

LORD GODDARD: . . . In the opinion of the court, there was undoubtedly evidence from which a jury could infer that the acts done by the appellant were acts likely to assist the enemy.

The far more difficult question that arises, however, is in connexion with the direction to the jury with regard to whether these acts were done with the intention of assisting the enemy. The case as opened, and indeed, as put by the learned judge appears to this court to be this: A man is taken to intend the natural consequences of his acts; if, therefore, he does an act which is likely to assist the enemy, it must be assumed that he did it with the intention of assisting the enemy. Now, the first thing which the court would observe is that, where the essence of an offence or a necessary constituent of an offence is a particular intent, that intent must be proved by the Crown just as much as any other fact necessary to constitute the offence.

The wording of the regulation itself shows that it is not enough merely to charge a prisoner with doing an act likely to assist the enemy; he must do it with the particular intent specified in the regulation. While no doubt the motive of a man's act and his intention in doing the act are, in law, different things, it is, none the less, true that in many offences a specific intention is a necessary ingredient and the jury have to be satisfied that a particular act was done with that specific intent, although the natural consequences of the act might, if nothing else were proved, be said to show the intent for which it was done. . . .

. . . No doubt, if the prosecution prove an act the natural consequence of which would be a certain result and no evidence or explanation is given, then a jury may, on a proper direction, find that the prisoner is guilty of doing the act with the intent alleged, but if on the totality of the evidence there is room for more than one view as to the intent of the prisoner, the jury should be directed that it is for the prosecution to prove the intent to the jury's satisfaction, and if, on a review of the whole evidence, they either think that the intent did not exist or they are left in doubt as to the intent, the prisoner is entitled to be acquitted. . . .

Now, another matter which is of considerable importance in the case, but does not seem to have been brought directly to the attention of the jury, is that very different considerations may apply where the accused at the time he did the acts is in subjection to an enemy power and where he is not. British soldiers who were set to work on the Burma road or, if invasion had unhappily taken place, British subjects who might have been set to work by the enemy digging trenches would undoubtedly be doing acts likely to assist the enemy. It would be unnecessary surely in their cases to consider, any of the niceties of the law relating to duress, because no jury would find that merely by doing this work they were intending to assist the enemy. In our opinion it is impossible to say that where an act was done by a person in subjection to the power of others, especially if that other be a brutal enemy, an inference that he intended the natural consequences of his act must be drawn merely from the fact that he did it. The guilty intent cannot be presumed and must be proved. The proper direction to the jury in this case would have been that it was for the prosecution to prove the criminal intent, and that while the jury would be entitled to presume that intent if they thought that the act was done as the result of the free uncontrolled action of the accused, they would not be entitled to presume it, if the circumstances showed that the act was done in subjection to the power of the enemy, or was as consistent with an innocent intent as with a criminal intent, for example, the innocent intent of a desire to save his wife and children from a concentration camp. They should only convict if satisfied by the evidence that the act complained of was in fact done to assist the enemy, and if there was doubt about the matter, the prisoner was entitled to be acquitted.

Notes and questions

1. What was Steane's intent? His motive? Does the court confuse the two?

2. Given its logical force, why does the court reject the position that a defendant should be held to have intended the natural and probable consequences of his acts?

3. Probably it would be fair to say that Steane intended to do acts which he knew (or should have known) would assist the enemy. Notice how crucial is the answer to the question of what it is that the *mens rea* refers to:

(a) if it is acts which Steane knows will help the enemy, he is probably guilty;

(b) if it is the provision of actual assistance to the enemy, he is probably not.

The actual statutory language was '*with intent to assist the enemy*'. Does this statutory language answer our question?

4. What if Steane did his broadcasts in order to establish his reputation as an announcer but without any thought as to whether his announcing would help the enemy? Or what if he cooperated in order to avoid latrine duty? Would the result have been the same? In these cases, as in the original, there may be no intent to assist the cause of the enemy, but would you, as a juror, not somehow feel differently about them? If *Steane* had been analysed in terms of whether he had a valid defence of duress (he committed the crime in order to avoid the greater evil of death to his family), as perhaps it should have been, there would have been a sound basis for distinguishing the original case from our examples.

One of the key issues raised in *Steane* has now been addressed by Parliament.

Criminal Justice Act 1967

8.   A court or jury, in determining whether a person has committed an offence —
   (a)   shall not be bound in law to infer that he intended or foresaw a result of his actions by reason only of its being a natural and probable consequence of those actions; but
   (b)   shall decide whether he did intend or foresee that result by reference to all the evidence, drawing such inferences from the evidence as appear proper in the circumstances.

II   Varieties of *mens rea*

If the types of *mens rea* which the courts have recognised were to be placed on a ladder of culpability, it might look something like this:

> intention
>
> knowledge
>
> recklessness (subjective)
>
> recklessness (objective)
>
> gross negligence
>
> negligence
>
> strict liability

As one moves down the ladder, the degree of moral culpability which attaches to the offender tends to diminish, as does the penalty for the relevant crime. There is not a strict linear correlation, however, and there may be crimes of negligence or strict liability which are considered more morally blameworthy and deserving of punishment than crimes where the defendant acted intentionally. Other factors, such as the harm threatened or caused, come into play. Nor is the line between categories as clear as the ladder might seem to suggest.

A   Intention

(i)   Foresight of consequences
What does it mean to say that a defendant acted intentionally? We might take as our example the defendant whose deliberate actions bring about results which it was the defendant's purpose to bring about. More troublesome has been the situation where results are virtually certain to follow from the defendant's acts and which the defendant knew (or should have known?)

would follow from his acts as a virtual certainty. Is it fair to say under those circumstances that the defendant intended the consequences? This was one of the issues raised by *Steane* (above): If Steane knew that his acts would help the enemy, can it be said that he intended to help the enemy?

In an incident that attracted considerable international attention and condemnation, a bomb was placed on Pan Am flight 103 in Germany. The bomb exploded over Scotland, killing the passengers and crew. Assume that the bomber was intending only to make a political statement but 'knew' that the aircraft would blow up in mid-air, in all probability killing everybody aboard. Assume further that the bomber could not have cared one way or the other if there were survivors, or, alternatively, hoped that no deaths would result. Did the bomber 'intend' the resulting deaths?

Perhaps the more important point for criminalisation purposes is: Should it matter? If your not unreasonable conclusion is no, then you could draft your statute accordingly. A murder statute, for example, could be written so that the mental element was either intending to cause death or engaging in conduct which the actor knows is virtually certain to cause death. This is in fact the approach taken by the drafters of the Model Penal Code in America. In England, however, murder retains its common law definition, which requires proof of malice aforethought, which the courts define as either an intent to kill or an intent to inflict grievous bodily harm (GBH), death resulting. Because the past and present state of English law requires proof of an intent to kill or cause grievous bodily harm, the courts have had to wrestle with the question of whether engaging in acts 'knowing' that death or GBH is virtually certain to follow amounts to an intent to kill.

R v Moloney
[1985] 1 AC 905
House of Lords

LORD BRIDGE OF HARWICH: . . . [T]he appellant was interviewed by the acting detective chief superintendent, Superintendent Cole, and Detective Sergeant Fletcher. Sergeant Fletcher made a full written record of this interview which the appellant in due course signed as correct. It is in the course of this record that one reads the appellant's full account of the tragic events at his family home on the morning of 22 November. He has, in all essentials, adhered to that account ever since. The material part of the statement reads as follows:

> It started with a dinner party which was thrown for my grandparents' fortieth wedding anniversary. Towards the end, we all had a lot to drink and our guests had left and I told me Dad I wanted to leave the army. He disagreed with me and started to outline his reasons for disagreeing with me. It was obviously set for being a long discussion so my mother, my sister and grandparents went to bed. We had a couple more drinks while the discussion went on and I was very drunk, and I suspect he was as well. At this point I have to become vague because the conversation came round to personal prowess and in particular with a shotgun. Me Dad claimed that he could not only outshoot me but outload me, outdraw me, i.e. he was faster than me, and claimed even with a crippled left arm he was still faster than me. I disagreed with him

and said: 'Don't be silly' or words to that effect. In fact we were swearing at each other at this time. So he said: 'We'll prove it. Go and get two of the shotguns.' He has four, I have one. So I went upstairs and got my shotgun and I got his shotgun. I gave him his shotgun and he told me to get two cartridges out of a box in the cupboard. I gave him one and took the other myself. He opened his gun and started to remove his snap caps. I opened my gun and removed two empty cartridges which I use as snap caps as I don't have any. I inserted the cartridge in the right hand barrel, closed the gun, took off the safety catch and pulled the trigger of the left hand barrel, and told him he'd lost. By this time I don't think he'd even cleared his barrel of the snap caps. He looked at me and said: 'I didn't think you'd got the guts, but if you have pull the trigger.' I didn't aim the gun. I just pulled the trigger and he was dead. I then went and called the police and told the operator I had just murdered my father, and that's the story.

. . .

The golden rule should be that, when directing a jury on the mental element necessary in a crime of specific intent, the judge should avoid any elaboration or paraphrase of what is meant by intent, and leave it to the jury's good sense to decide whether the accused acted with the necessary intent, unless the judge is convinced that, on the facts and having regard to the way the case has been presented to the jury in evidence and argument, some further explanation or elaboration is strictly necessary to avoid misunderstanding. In trials for murder or wounding with intent, I find it very difficult to visualise a case where any such explanation or elaboration could be required, if the offence consisted of a direct attack on the victim with a weapon, except possibly the case where the accused shot at A and killed B, which any first year law student could explain to a jury in the simplest of terms. Even where the death results indirectly from the act of the accused, I believe the cases that will call for a direction by reference to foresight of consequences will be of extremely rare occurrence.

I do not, of course mean to question the necessity, which frequently arises, to explain to a jury that intention is something quite distinct from motive or desire. But this can normally be quite simply explained by reference to the case before the court or, if necessary, by some homely example. A man who, at London Airport, boards a plane which he knows to be bound for Manchester, clearly intends to travel to Manchester, even though Manchester is the last place he wants to be and his motive for boarding the plane is simply to escape pursuit. The possibility that the plane may have engine trouble and be diverted to Luton does not affect the matter. By boarding the Manchester plane, the man conclusively demonstrates his intention to go there, because it is a moral certainty that that is where he will arrive.

In the rare cases in which it is necessary to direct a jury by reference to foresight of consequences, I do not believe it is necessary for the judge to do more than invite the jury to consider two questions. First, was death or really serious injury in a murder case (or whatever relevant consequence must be proved to have been intended in any other case) a natural consequence of the defendant's voluntary act? Secondly, did the defendant foresee that consequence as being a natural consequence of his act? The jury should then be told that if they answer yes to both questions it is a proper inference for them to draw that he intended that consequence.

Questions

1. The trial judge in *Moloney* had instructed the jury that it could convict if it concluded that the accused had foreseen the consequences, even though he did not desire them. In what respect, according to the House of Lords, was this instruction incorrect?

2. Of what relevance, according to Lord Bridge, is foresight of consequences? What, according to Lord Bridge, should a jury be told:

(a) in the ordinary case?
(b) in a case requiring instruction regarding foresight of consequence?

Lord Bridge's proposed guidelines for instructing the jury in the rare cases involving foresight of consequences were reconsidered by the House of Lords one year later in the following case.

R v Hancock and Shankland
[1986] 1 AC 455
House of Lords

LORD SCARMAN: ... On 16 May 1985 at the Crown Court, Cardiff, Reginald Dean Hancock and Russell Shankland were convicted of the murder of Mr Wilkie. In the dark hours of the early morning of 30 November 1984 Mr David Wilkie was driving his taxi along the Heads of the Valley Road. As he approached the bridge over the road at Rhymney he was killed when two lumps of concrete hit the car. The two lumps, a block and a post, had been dropped from the bridge as he approached it.

Mr Wilkie's passenger was a miner going to work. Mr Hancock and Mr Shankland were miners on strike, and strongly objected to Mr Wilkie's passenger going to work. That morning they had collected the block and the post from nearby, had brought them to the bridge under which the Heads of the Valley Road runs through a cutting, and had placed them on the parapet on the side facing towards the Rhymney roundabout. They then awaited the arrival of a convoy escorting the miner on his way to work. The convoy approached the bridge at about 5.15 a.m.: it consisted of a police motor-cycle, a police Land Rover, the taxi driven by Mr Wilkie, and a police Sherpa van. The convoy was travelling from the Rhymney roundabout towards the bridge in the nearside lane of the carriageway. Estimates of its speed varied: it was put somewhere between 30 and 40 mph. As the convoy neared the bridge, the concrete block struck the taxi's windscreen. The post struck the carriageway some 4ft. 8in. from the nearside verge. Before, however, the post subsided on the ground, it was hit by the taxi. The taxi skidded out of control, coming to rest on the embankment. Mr Wilkie died from the injuries he received in the wrecking of the taxi by the two lumps of concrete.

The case for the prosecution was that the two concrete objects were either thrown from the bridge or pushed over its parapet in the path of the taxi at a time when the taxi could not avoid being struck by one or both of them. And, as the trial judge told the jury, the prosecution case could be compressed into one question and answer, the question being 'what else could a person who pushed or threw such objects have intended but to cause really serious bodily harm to the occupants of the car?' The answer in the prosecution's submission was that a person acting in that way could in the circumstances have intended nothing less.

The defence was simple enough: that the two men intended to block the road, to stop the miner going to work, but not to kill or to do serious bodily harm to anyone. Hancock told Detective Chief Superintendent Caisley that he did not throw the two pieces of 'masonry' over the bridge but merely 'dropped' them. He told him that he dropped them on the side of the bridge 'nearest to the roundabout where I could see them coming.' At a later interview Hancock admitted 'shoving' the block of concrete over the parapet of the bridge, but declared that he believed when he did so that he was standing 'over the *middle* lane,' i.e. not over the nearside lane, along which the convoy was moving. He said that he did not mean to do anyone damage – 'just to frighten him [i.e. the miner going to work] more than anything.' Shankland admitted that he was party to the plan to obstruct the road but denied that they intended to hurt anyone. Like Hancock, he emphasised that their plan was to drop the objects in the middle lane of the carriageway, i.e. clear of the lane along which the convoy was travelling, and that they believed that this was what they did.

Hancock and Shankland were prepared to plead guilty to manslaughter but the Crown decided to pursue the charge of murder. The issue was ultimately one of intention. Did they (or either of them) intend to kill or to cause anyone serious bodily harm?

The case called for a careful direction by judge to jury as to the state of mind required by law to be proved to their satisfaction before they could return a verdict of murder. The jury would also want his help in weighing up the evidence. The judge's direction as to the intention required by law was impeccable. He said:

> If the prosecution has made you satisfied so as to be sure that Dean Hancock and Russell Shankland agreed that they would, in concert, push or throw missiles from the bridge, each having the intention either to kill or to cause really serious injury, then you will find each of them guilty of murder as the block was thrown or pushed by Dean Hancock in pursuance of the agreement.

When he came to help them on the facts, he offered guidance along the *Moloney* lines:

> You may think that critical to the resolution of this case is the question of intent. In determining whether a person intended to kill or to cause really serious injury, you must have regard to all of the evidence which has been put before you, and draw from it such inferences as to you seem proper and appropriate. You may or may not, for the purpose of considering what inferences to draw, find it helpful to ask: Was death or serious injury a natural consequence of what was done? Did a defendant foresee that consequence as a natural consequence? That is a possible question which you may care to ask yourselves. If you find yourselves not satisfied so as to be sure that there was an intent to kill or to cause really serious injury, then it is open to you to return a verdict of not guilty of murder, but guilty of manslaughter.

The question for the House is, therefore, whether the *Moloney* guidelines are sound. In *Moloney's* case the ratio decidendi was that the judge never properly put to the jury the defence, namely that the accused was unaware that the gun was pointing at his stepfather. The House, however, held it necessary in view of the history of confusion in this branch of the law to attempt to clarify the law relating to the establishment of the mental element necessary to constitute the crime of murder and to lay down guidelines for assisting juries to determine in what circumstances it is proper to infer intent from foresight. The House certainly clarified the law. First, the House cleared away the confusions which had obscured the law during the last 25 years laying down authoritatively that the mental element in murder is a specific intent, the intent to kill or to inflict serious bodily harm. Nothing less suffices: and the jury must be sure that the intent existed when the act was done which resulted in death before they can return a verdict of murder.

Secondly, the House made it absolutely clear that foresight of consequences is no more than evidence of the existence of the intent; it must be considered, and its weight assessed, together with all the evidence in the case.

. . .

Thirdly, the House emphasised that the probability of the result of an act is an important matter for the jury to consider and can be critical in their determining whether the result was intended.

These three propositions were made abundantly clear by Lord Bridge of Harwich. His was the leading speech and received the assent of their other Lordships, Lord Hailsham of St. Marylebone LC, Lord Fraser of Tullybelton, Lord Edmund-Davies, and Lord Keith of Kinkel. His speech has laid to rest ghosts which had haunted the case law ever since the unhappy decision of your Lordships' House in *R v Smith* [1961] AC 290 and which were given fresh vigour by the interpretation put by some upon the speeches of members of this House in *R v Hyam* [1975] AC 55.

It is only when Lord Bridge of Harwich turned to the task of formulating guidelines that difficulty arises. It is said by the Court of Appeal that the guidelines by omitting any express reference to probability are ambiguous and may well lead a jury to a wrong conclusion. The omission was deliberate. Lord Bridge omitted the adjective 'probable' from the time-honoured formula 'foresight of the natural and probable consequences of his acts' because he thought that 'if a consequence is natural, it is really otiose to speak of it as also being probable' [1985] AC 905, 929B. But is it?

Lord Bridge of Harwich did not deny the importance of probability. He put it thus, at p. 925:

> But looking on their facts at the decided cases where a crime of specific intent was under consideration, including *R v Hyam* [1975] AC 55 itself, they suggest to me that the probability of the consequence taken to have been foreseen must be little short of overwhelming before it will suffice to establish the necessary intent.

In his discussion of the relationship between foresight and intention, Lord Bridge of Harwich reviewed the case law since the passing of the Homicide Act 1957 and concluded, at p. 928:

> foresight of the consequences, as an element bearing on the issue of intention in murder, or indeed any other crime of specific intent, belongs, not to the substantive law, but to the law of evidence.

He referred to the rule of evidence that a man is presumed to intend the natural and probable consequences of his acts, and went on to observe that the House of Lords in *Smith's* case [1961] AC 290 had treated the presumption as irrebuttable, but that Parliament intervened by section 8 of the Criminal Justice Act 1967 to return the law to the path from which it had been diverted, leaving the presumption as no more than an inference open to the jury to draw if in all the circumstances it appears to them proper to draw it.

Yet he omitted any reference in his guidelines to probability. He did so because he included probability in the meaning which he attributed to 'natural.' My Lords, I very much doubt whether a jury without further explanation would think that 'probable' added nothing to 'natural.' I agree with the Court of Appeal that the probability of a consequence is a factor of sufficient importance to be drawn specifically to the attention of the jury and to be explained. In a murder case where it is necessary to direct a jury on the issue of intent by reference to foresight of consequences the probability of death or serious injury resulting from the act done may be critically important. Its importance will depend on the degree of probability: if the likelihood that death or serious injury will result is high, the probability of that result may, as Lord Bridge of Harwich noted and the Lord Chief Justice emphasised, be seen as overwhelming evidence of the existence of the intent to kill or injure. Failure to explain the relevance of probability may, therefore, mislead a jury into thinking that it is of little or no importance and into concentrating exclusively on the causal link between the act and its consequence. In framing his guidelines Lord Bridge of Harwich [1985] AC 1905, 929G, emphasised that he did not believe it necessary to do more than to invite the jury to consider his two questions. Neither question makes any reference (beyond the use of the word 'natural') to probability. I am not surprised that when in this case the judge faithfully followed this guidance the jury found themselves perplexed and unsure. In my judgment, therefore, the *Moloney* guidelines as they stand are unsafe and misleading. They require a reference to probability. They also require an explanation that the greater the probability of a consequence the more likely it is that the consequence was foreseen and that if that consequence was foreseen the greater the probability is that that consequence was also intended. But juries also require to be reminded that the decision is theirs to be reached upon a consideration of all the evidence.

Accordingly, I accept the view of the Court of Appeal that the *Moloney* guidelines are defective. I am, however, not persuaded that guidelines of general application, albeit within a limited class of case, are wise or desirable. Lord Lane CJ formulated in this case ante, p. 461D-G guidelines for the assistance of juries but for the reason which follows, I would not advise their use by trial judges when summing up to a jury.

I fear that their elaborate structure may well create difficulty. Juries are not chosen for their understanding of a logical and phased process leading by question and answer to a conclusion but are expected to exercise practical common sense. They want help on the practical problems encountered in evaluating the evidence of a particular case and reaching a conclusion. It is better, I suggest, notwithstanding my respect for the comprehensive formulation of the Court of Appeal's guidelines, that the trial judge should follow the traditional course of a summing up. He must explain the nature of the offence charged, give directions as to the law applicable to the particular facts of the case, explain the incidence and burden of proof, put both sides' cases making especially sure that the defence is put; he should offer help in understanding and weighing up all the evidence and should make certain that the jury understand that whereas the law is for him the facts are for them to decide. Guidelines, if given, are not to be treated as rules of law but as a guide indicating the sort of approach the jury may properly adopt to the evidence when coming to their decision on the facts.

In a case where foresight of a consequence is part of the evidence supporting a prosecution submission that the accused intended the consequence, the judge, if he thinks some general observations would help the jury, could well, having in mind section 8 of the Criminal Justice Act 1967, emphasise that the probability, however high, of a consequence is only a factor, though it may in some cases be a very significant factor, to be considered with all the other evidence in determining whether the accused intended to bring it about. The distinction between the offence and the evidence relied on to prove it is vital. Lord Bridge's speech in *Moloney* made the distinction crystal clear: it would be a disservice to the law to allow his guidelines to mislead a jury into overlooking it.

For these reasons I would hold that the *Moloney* guidelines are defective and should not be used as they stand without further explanation. The laying down of guidelines for use in directing juries in cases of complexity is a function which can be usefully exercised by the Court of Appeal. But it should be done sparingly, and limited to cases of real difficulty. If it is done, the guidelines should avoid generalisation so far as is possible and encourage the jury to exercise their common sense in reaching what is their decision on the facts. Guidelines are not rules of law: judges should not think that they must use them. A judge's duty is to direct the jury in law and to help them upon the particular facts of the case.

Questions
1. What was the accuseds' intent? Their motive?
2. In what respects does Lord Scarman find the *Moloney* guidelines deficient? Are his suggestions any more helpful? In the final analysis, does not Lord Scarman simply dump into the laps of the jurors an issue which their lordships had been unable to resolve, hoping that the jury would do a better job of it in practice than they had been able to do in theory?
3. What according to Lord Scarman, is the proper relationship between probability, foresight, and intention?

The Court of Appeal has attempted to provide further clarification in:

R v Nedrick
[1986] 3 All ER 1
Court of Appeal

LORD LANE CJ: . . . The case for the Crown was that the appellant had a grudge against a woman called Viola Foreshaw, as a result of which, after threats that he would 'burn her out', he went to her house in the early hours of 15 July 1984, poured paraffin through the letter box and onto the front door and set it alight. He gave no warning. The house was burnt down and one of Viola Foreshaw's children, a boy aged 12 called Lloyd, died of asphyxiation and burns.

After a number of interviews during which he denied any responsibility, the appellant eventually confessed to the police that he had started the fire in the manner described, adding, 'I didn't want anyone to die, I am not a murderer; please tell the judge; God knows I am not a murderer.' When asked why he did it, he replied. 'Just to wake her up and frighten her.'

We have endeavoured to crystallise the effect of their Lordships' speeches in *R v Moloney* and *R v Hancock* in a way which we hope may be helpful to judges who have to handle this type of case.

It may be advisable first of all to explain to the jury that a man may intend to a certain result whilst at the same time not desiring it to come about. In *R v Moloney* [1985] 1 All ER 1025 at 1037, [1985] AC 905 at 926 Lord Bridge gave an illustration of the distinction:

A man who, at London Airport, boards a plane which he knows to be bound for Manchester, clearly intends to travel to Manchester, even though Manchester is the last place he wants to be and his motive for boarding the plane is simply to escape pursuit.

The man who knowingly boards the Manchester aircraft wants to go there in the sense that boarding it is a voluntary act. His desire to leave London predominates over his desire not to go to Manchester. When he decides to board the aircraft, if not before, he forms the intention to travel to Manchester.

In *R v Hancock* the House decided that the *R v Moloney* guidelines require a reference to probability. Lord Scarman said ([1986] 1 All ER 641 at 651, [1986] AC 455 at 473):

They also require an explanation that the greater the probability of a consequence the more likely it is that the consequence was foreseen and that if that consequence was foreseen the greater the probability is that that consequence was also intended.

When determining whether the defendant had the necessary intent, it may therefore be helpful for a jury to ask themselves two questions. (1) How probable was the consequence which resulted from the defendant's voluntary act? (2) Did he foresee that consequence?

If he did not appreciate that death or serious harm was likely to result from his act, he cannot have intended to bring it about. If he did, but thought that the risk to which he was exposing the person killed was only slight, then it may be easy for the jury to conclude that he did not intend to bring about that result. On the other hand, if the jury are satisfied that at the material time the defendant recognised that death or serious harm would be virtually certain (barring some unforeseen intervention) to result from his voluntary act, then that is a fact from which they may find it easy to infer that he intended to kill or do serious bodily harm, even though he may not have had any desire to achieve that result.

As Lord Bridge said in *R* v *Moloney* [1985] 1 All ER 1025 at 1036, [1985] AC 905 at 925:

> . . . the probability of the consequence taken to have been foreseen must be little short of overwhelming before it will suffice to establish the necessary intent.

Later he uses the expression 'moral certainty' (see [1985] 1 All ER 1025 at 1037, [1985] AC 905 at 926) and says, 'will lead to a certain consequence unless something unexpected supervenes to prevent it' (see [1985] 1 All ER 1025 at 1039, [1985] AC 905 at 929).

Where the charge is murder and in the rare cases where the simple direction is not enough, the jury should be directed that they are not entitled to infer the necessary intention unless they feel sure that death or serious bodily harm was a virtual certainty (barring some unforeseen intervention) as a result of the defendant's actions and that the defendant appreciated that such was the case.

Where a man realises that it is for all practical purposes inevitable that his actions will result in death or serious harm, the inference may be irresistible that he intended that result, however little he may have desired or wished it to happen. The decision is one for the jury to be reached on a consideration of all the evidence.

Notes
1.   When a defendant acts with the intent to achieve a particular result (A), knowing that that result cannot be brought about without causing result (B), he will be held to have intended result B as well as result A. If Claude shoots at Abigail, who is standing behind a closed plate glass window, Claude will be taken to have intended the criminal damage which occurs when the window is shattered by the force of the bullet. This is sometimes referred to as 'oblique intention'. See G. Williams, 'Oblique intention' [1987] CLJ 417.
2.   The general topic of intention has proved fertile territory for academic minds. See, e.g., A. Norrie, 'Oblique intention and legal politics' [1989] Crim LR 793; R. Duff, 'The politics of intention: a response to Norrie' [1990] Crim LR 637; J.C. Smith, 'A note on intention' [1990] Crim LR 85.

(ii)   Transferred intent
X shoots at Y, intending to kill him. His aim is off, and the bullet hits Z with fatal results. Alternatively, Y moves at the critical moment and the bullet hits Z, who is directly behind him, again with fatal results. Is X, who had no intent to kill Z, guilty of Z's murder?

R v Saunders and Archer
(1573) 2 Plowden 473

John Saunders had a wife whom he intended to kill, in order that he might marry another woman with whom he was in love, and he opened his design to the said Alexander Archer, and desired his assistance and advice in the execution of it, who advised him to put an end to her life by poison. With this intent the said Archer bought the poison, viz. arsenick and roseacre, and delivered it to the said John Saunders to give it to his wife, who accordingly gave it to her, being sick, in a roasted apple, and she eat a small part of it, and gave the rest to the said Eleanor Saunders, an infant, about three years of age, who was the daughter of her and the said John Saunders her husband. And the said John Saunders seeing it, blamed his wife for it, and said that apples were not good for such infants; to which his wife replied that they were better for such infants than for herself: and the daughter eat the poisoned apple, and the said John Saunders, her father, saw her eat it, and did not offer to take it from her lest he should be suspected, and afterwards the wife recovered, and the daughter died of the said poison.

And whether or no this was murder in John Saunders, the father, was somewhat doubted, for he had no intent to poison his daughter, nor had he any malice against her, but on the contrary he had a great affection for her, and he did not give her the poison, but his wife ignorantly gave it her, and although he might have taken it from the daughter, and so have preserved her life, yet the not taking it from her did not make it felony, for it was all one whether he had been present or absent, as to this point, inasmuch as he had no malice against the daughter, nor any inclination to do her any harm. But at last the said justices, upon consideration of the matter, and with the assent of Saunders, Chief Baron, who had the examination of the said John Saunders before, and who had signified his opinion to the said justices (as he afterwards said to me) were of opinion that the said offence was murder in the said John Saunders. And the reason thereof (as the said justices and the Chief Baron told me) was, because the said John Saunders gave the poison with an intent to kill a person, and in the giving of it he intended that death should follow. And when death followed from his act, although it happened in another person than her whose death he directly meditated, yet it shall be murder in him, for he was the original cause of the death, and if such death should not be punished in him, it would go unpunished; for here the wife, who gave the poisoned apple to her daughter, cannot be guilty of any offence, because she was ignorant of any poison contained in it, and she innocently gave it to the infant by way of necessary food, and therefore it is reasonable to adjudge her innocent in this case, and to charge the death of the infant, by which the Queen has lost a subject, upon him who was the cause of it, and who intended death in the act which occasioned the death here. (a) But if a man prepares poison, and lays it in several parts of his house, with an intent to kill rats and such sort of vermin, and a person comes and eats it, and dies of it, this is not felony in him who prepared and laid it there, because he had no intent to kill any reasonable creature. (b) But when he lays the poison with an intent to kill some reasonable creature, and another reasonable creature, whom he does not intend to kill, is poisoned by it, such death shall not be dispunishable, but he who prepared the poison shall be punished for it, because his intent was evil. And therefore it is every man's business to foresee what wrong or mischief may happen from that which he does with an ill intention, and it shall be no excuse for him to say that he intended to kill another, and not the person killed. (c) For if a man of malice prepense shoots an arrow at another with an intent to kill him, and a person to whom he bore no malice is killed by it, this shall be murder in him, for when he shot the arrow he intended to kill, and inasmuch as he directed his instrument of death at one, and thereby has killed another, it shall be the same offence in him as if he had killed the person he aimed at, for the end of the act shall be construed by the beginning of it, and the last part shall taste of the first, and as the beginning of the act had malice prepense in it, and consequently imported murder, so the end of the act, viz. the killing of another, shall be in the same degree, and therefore it shall be murder, and not homicide only. (d) For if one lies in wait in a certain place to kill a person, and another comes by the place, and he who lies in wait kills him out of mistake, thinking that he is the very person whom he waited for, this offence is murder in him, and not homicide only, for the killing was founded upon malice prepense. So in the principal case, when John Saunders of malice prepense gave to his wife the instrument of death, viz. the poisoned apple, and this upon a subsequent accident killed his daughter, whom he had no intention to kill, this is the same offence in him as if his act had met with the intended effect, and his intention in doing the act was to commit murder, wherefore the event of it shall be murder. And so the justices declared their opinion, to the jurors, whereupon they found both the prisoners guilty, and John Saunders had his judgment, and was hanged.

Question

Why charge Saunders with a crime that he did not intend to commit (murder of the child) rather than the crime that he did intend to commit (attempt to murder his wife)? Would it have made more sense to say that Saunders acted recklessly in ignoring the known risk of death to the child, and to charge him with a crime (manslaughter) whose *mens rea* was recklessness?

Note

In *Saunders and Archer* the crime charged was of the same type (homicide) as was intended. All that changed was the victim. Under such circumstances the courts have had little difficulty concluding that an accused who has the intent to kill, who acts pursuant to that intent and whose acts result in death, is liable for that death. The identity of the victim is not relevant for legal purposes. An even clearer example would occur where P, intending to kill Q, mistook T for Q and killed T. P would still be liable for murder. These are cases of what we might call intra-crime transferred intent. More troublesome analytically are cases of inter-crime transferred intent.

R v Pembliton
[1874–80] All ER 1163
Court for Consideration of Crown Cases Reserved

At the quarter sessions of the peace held at Wolverhampton on Jan. 8, 1874. Henry Pembliton was indicted for that he 'unlawfully and maliciously did commit damage, injury, and spoil upon a window in the house of Henry Kirkham,' contrary to s. 51 of the Malicious Damage Act 1861.

On the night of Dec. 6, 1873, the prisoner was drinking with others at a public house called 'The Grand Turk' kept by the prosecutor. At about eleven o'clock p.m. the whole party were turned out of the house for being disorderly, and they then began to fight in the street and near the prosecutor's window, where a crowd of from 40 to 50 persons collected. The prisoner, after fighting some time with persons in the crowd, separated himself from them, and removed to the other side of the street, where he picked up a large stone, and threw it at the persons he had been fighting with. The stone passed over the heads of those persons, and struck a large plate glass window in the prosecutor's house, and broke it, thereby doing damage to the extent of £7 12s. 9d. The jury, after hearing evidence on both sides, found that the prisoner threw the stone which broke the window, but that he threw it at the people he had been fighting with, intending to strike one or more of them with it, but not intending to break the window. They returned a verdict of 'guilty.' The recorder respited the sentence, and admitted the prisoner to bail, and prayed the judgment of the Court for Crown Cases Reserved, whether, on the facts stated, and the finding of the jury, the prisoner was rightly convicted or not.

LORD COLERIDGE CJ: I am of opinion that this conviction must be quashed. [His Lordship stated the facts, and continued:] The question is whether, under an indictment for unlawfully and maliciously committing an injury to the window in the house of the prosecutor, the proof of these facts alone coupled with the finding of the jury will do. I think that is not enough. The indictment is framed under the Malicious Damage Act 1861, s. 51, which relates to malicious injuries to property, and the section enacts that whosoever shall unlawfully and maliciously commit any damage, etc., to or upon any real or personal property whatsoever either of a public or a private nature shall be guilty of a misdemeanour. Section 58 also deserves attention. That enacts:

Every punishment and forfeiture by this Act imposed on any person maliciously committing any offence, whether the same be punishable upon indictment or upon summary conviction, shall equally apply and be enforced, whether the offence shall be committed from malice conceived against the owner of the property in respect of which it shall be committed, or otherwise.

It seems to me that, in both these sections, what was intended to be provided against by the Act is the wilfully doing an unlawful act, and that that act must be wilfully and intentionally done on the part of the person doing it to render him liable to be convicted. Without saying that, on these facts, if the jury had found that the prisoner had been guilty of throwing the stone recklessly, knowing that there was a window near which it might probably hit. I should have been disposed to interfere with the conviction, yet, as they have found that he threw the stone at the people he had been fighting with intending to strike them and not intending to break the window, I think that the conviction must be quashed. I do not intend to throw any doubt on the cases which have been cited and which show what is sufficient to constitute malice in the case of murder. They rest on the principles of the common law, and have no application to a statutory offence.

Conviction quashed.

Questions
In principle, what is wrong with mixing and matching the *actus reus* of one crime with the *mens rea* of another, particularly when the defendant might otherwise escape liability for both crimes? At a minimum, why not permit

inter-crime transferred intent when the crime actually committed is less
serious than the crime intended?

Note
Usually there is little difficulty in holding an accused such as Pembliton
criminally liable. Either the accused can be charged with an attempt to commit
the crime intended, or, alternatively, he can be charged with a crime of
recklessness if that would be appropriate. Under modern law, Pembliton could
have been charged with criminal damage, since his arguably reckless acts
caused the damage and recklessness is, as we have seen, a sufficient *mens rea* for
criminal damage.

B   Knowledge

We have seen that where a result is virtually certain to follow, 'knowingly' can
become tantamount to 'intentionally'. Does the term have meaning in other
contexts?

Roper v Taylor's Central Garage (Exeter) Ltd
[1951] 2 TLR 284
King's Bench Division

DEVLIN J.: . . . All that the word 'knowingly' does is to say expressly what is normally
implied, and if the presumption that the statute requires *mens rea* is not rebutted I find
difficulty in seeing how it can be said that the omission of the word 'knowingly' has, as
a matter of construction the effect of shifting the burden of proof from the prosecution
to the defence . . . it seems to me to be very important, in cases of this sort, that the
prosecution, where the burden lies on the prosecution, should explain to lay justices,
who are not necessarily very skilled in the handling of evidence and in the drawing of
distinctions which the law requires to be drawn, exactly what sort of knowledge the
prosecution desires to be found. There are, I think, three degrees of knowledge which
it may be relevant to consider in cases of this kind. The first is actual knowledge, which
the justices may find because they infer it from the nature of the act done, for no man
can prove the state of another man's mind; and they may find it even if the defendant
gives evidence to the contrary. They may say, 'We do not believe him; we think that that
was his state of mind.' They may feel that the evidence falls short of that, and if they do
they have then to consider what might be described as knowledge of the second degree;
whether the defendant was, as it has been called, shutting his eyes to an obvious means
of knowledge. Various expressions have been used to describe that state of mind. I do
not think it necessary to look further, certainly not in cases of this type, than the phrase
which Lord Hewart, CJ, used in a case under this section, *Evans v Dell* ((1937) 53 *The
Times* LR 310), where he said (at p. 313): ' . . . the respondent deliberately refrained
from making inquiries the results of which he might not care to have.'. . .
   The third kind of knowledge is what is generally known in the law as constructive
knowledge: it is what is encompassed by the words 'ought to have known' in the phrase
'knew or ought to have known.' It does not mean actual knowledge at all; it means that
the defendant had in effect the means of knowledge. When, therefore, the case of the
prosecution is that the defendant fails to make what they think were reasonable
inquiries it is, I think, incumbent on them to make it plain which of the two things they

are saying. There is a vast distinction between a state of mind which consists of deliberately refraining from making inquiries, the result of which the person does not care to have, and a state of mind which is merely neglecting to make such inquiries as a reasonable and prudent person would make. If that distinction is kept well in mind I think that justices will have less difficulty than this case appears to show they have had in determining what is the true position. The case of shutting the eyes is actual knowledge in the eyes of the law; the case of merely neglecting to make inquiries is not knowledge at all – it comes within the legal conception of constructive knowledge, a conception which, generally speaking, has no place in the criminal law.

Notes and questions
1.   What does it mean to 'know' something? If an individual believes that a particular result is 70 per cent likely to follow from her acts, does she 'know' that the result will follow? What if the result is 90 per cent likely? Must she be 100 per cent certain? Is there such a thing as 100 per cent certainty?
2.   Is Devlin J correct in stating that 'knowingly' only says expressly what is implied? If so, why would Parliament include 'knowingly' as part of the definition of the crime?
3.   Does 'knowingly' imply a subjective or objective standard? If a reasonable person, albeit not the defendant, 'knows' what results will occur as a result of particular acts, should the defendant be deemed to have this knowledge?
4.   Devlin J's second category of knowledge is sometimes referred to as 'wilful blindness'. It occurs where the reason why a defendant does not have the requisite knowledge of consequences is because he chooses to turn a blind eye to them. Is it appropriate to equate wilful blindness and knowledge?
5.   Why does Devlin J say that, generally speaking 'constructive knowledge' has no place in the criminal law?

Knowingly' often is used in connection with the existence of circumstances, and knowledge thereof.

R v Taaffe
[1984] AC 530
House of Lords

On his arraignment on a charge of having been knowingly concerned in the fraudulent evasion of the prohibition on the importation of cannabis resin, contrary to section 170(2) of the Customs and Excise Management Act 1979 and the Misuse of Drugs Act 1971, the defendant pleaded not guilty. No evidence having been called, the recorder was asked to rule on the question whether the defendant's version of events, if accepted by the jury, would entitle him to be acquitted. That version was: (a) the defendant had been enlisted by a third party in Holland to import a substance from that country into England in fraudulent evasion of the prohibition on its importation and had so imported it; (b) that substance had in fact been cannabis, importation of which was prohibited by the Act of 1971; (c) the defendant had mistakenly believed the substance to be currency; (d) currency was not subject to any such prohibition; (e) the defendant had believed that it was. The recorder ruled that he would be obliged, even on the defendant's version of events, to direct the jury to convict. Thereupon, the defendant pleaded guilty and was sentenced. The Court of Appeal (Criminal Division) allowed his appeal against conviction.

LORD SCARMAN: . . . Lord Lane CJ construed the subsection under which the respondent was charged as creating not an offence of absolute liability but an offence of which an essential ingredient is a guilty mind. To be 'knowingly concerned' meant, in his judgment, knowledge not only of the existence of a smuggling operation but also that the substance being smuggled into the country was one the importation of which was prohibited by statute. The respondent thought he was concerned in a smuggling operation but believed that the substance was currency. The importation of currency is not subject to any prohibition. Lord Lane CJ concluded, at p. 631:

[The respondent] is to be judged against the facts that he believed them to be. Had this indeed been currency and not cannabis, no offence would have been committed.

Lord Lane CJ went on to ask this question:

Does it make any difference that the [respondent] thought wrongly that by clandestinely importing currency he was committing an offence?

The Crown submitted that it does. The court rejected the submission: the respondent's mistake of law could not convert the importation of currency into a criminal offence: and importing currency is what it had to be assumed that the respondent believed he was doing.

My Lords, I find the reasoning of the Lord Chief Justice compelling. I agree with his construction of section 170(2) of the Act of 1979: and the principle that a man must be judged upon the facts as he believes them to be is an accepted principle of the criminal law when the state of a man's mind and his knowledge are ingredients of the offence with which he is charged.

Note
The Draft Criminal Code Bill 1989 provides as follows:

Draft Criminal Code Bill 1989

18.   For the purposes of this Act and of any offence other than a pre-Code offence as defined in section 6 (to which section 2(3) applies) a person acts —
     (a) 'Knowingly' with respect to a circumstance not only when he is aware that it exists or will exist, but also when he avoids taking steps that might confirm his belief that it exists or will exist;
     . . .

Question
Does the draft bill adopt a subjective or an objective test of 'knowingly'?

C   *Recklessness*

When the law speaks of intent in relation to result it is concerned with results which it was the actor's purpose to bring about. When it speaks of recklessness in relation to result-orientated crimes, on the other hand, it is not concerned with results which the defendant wished to bring about, but rather results to which he or she was ambivalent or ignorant of. The actor's fault lies in not taking into account or failing sufficiently to take into account the relevant risks.

Recklessness may exist in respect of:

(a)   acts;
(b)   circumstances; or
(c)   consequences.

A driver who fails to observe the speedometer of the car as it creeps over 100 mph may be reckless in respect of the act of driving; if he ignores the pedestrians crossing the road, he may be reckless as to the consequences of his speeding. If a would-be seducer pays insufficient attention to whether his companion's protests to his sexual advances are perfunctory or real, he is reckless as to circumstances.

In the introductory section of this chapter, we drew a distinction between *mens rea* that was measured by a subjective standard and *mens rea* that was measured by an objective standard. The subjective-objective distinction also rears its head in the context of recklessness. Subjective recklessness refers to a risk that the actor appreciated might be brought about by his conduct, but to which he was indifferent. The reckless driver who proceeds at 100 mph may well be aware that his driving may result in his being unable to stop if a pedestrian should step into the roadway, but he proceeds in conscious disregard of that risk. Objective recklessness, in contrast, refers to risks that the actor was not aware of but which a reasonable person would have been aware of – the possibility that by driving 100 mph he was creating risks to pedestrians may not have occurred to our driver, but would have occurred to a reasonable person. The critical difference between objective and subjective recklessness is this: in subjective recklessness the actor is aware of the risk that is created; in objective recklessness he is not, but a reasonable person would be. Neither the subjectively nor objectively reckless actor desires the harmful result to occur.

At common law, most crimes required proof of subjective intent. Today, for many crimes proof of recklessness will be an alternative basis for the imposition of criminal sanctions. Often new statutory crimes (or codifications of common law crimes by Parliament) allow for proof of either intent or recklessness (see, e.g., the Criminal Damage Act 1971, above). Unfortunately the term 'recklessness' is not always defined. When this occurs, the courts must determine whether subjective or objective recklessness will be sufficient for liability.

(i)   Subjective recklessness
That subjective recklessness should satisfy the mental element of a crime whose *mens rea* is recklessness is relatively uncontroversial. The leading case is *R* v *Cunningham*.

R v *Cunningham*
[1957] 2 QB 396
Court of Appeal

BYRNE J: . . . The facts were that the appellant was engaged to be married and his prospective mother-in-law was the tenant of a house, No. 7A, Bakes Street, Bradford, which was unoccupied, but which was to be occupied by the appellant after his marriage. Mrs Wade and her husband, an elderly couple, lived in the house next door. At one time the two houses had been one, but when the building was converted into two houses a wall had been erected to divide the cellars of the two houses, and that wall was composed of rubble loosely cemented.

On the evening of January 17, 1957, the appellant went to the cellar of No. 7A, Bakes Street, wrenched the gas meter from the gas pipes and stole it, together with its contents, and in a second indictment he was charged with the larceny of the gas meter and its contents. To that indictment he pleaded guilty and was sentenced to six months' imprisonment. In respect of that matter he does not appeal.

The facts were not really in dispute, and in a statement to a police officer the appellant said: 'All right, I will tell you. I was short of money, I had been off work for three days, I got eight shillings from the gas meter. I tore it off the wall and threw it away.' Although there was a stop tap within two feet of the meter the appellant did not turn off the gas, with the result that a very considerable volume of gas escaped, some of which seeped through the wall of the cellar and partially asphyxiated Mrs Wade, who was asleep in her bedroom next door, with the result that her life was endangered.
. . .

The act of the appellant was clearly unlawful and therefore the real question for the jury was whether it was also malicious within the meaning of section 23 of the Offences against the Person Act, 1861.

Before this court Mr Brodie has taken three points, all dependent upon the construction of that section. Section 23 provides: 'Whosoever shall unlawfully and maliciously administer to or cause to be administered to or taken by any other person any poison or other destructive or noxious thing, so as thereby to endanger the life of such person, or so as thereby to inflict upon such person any grievous bodily harm, shall be guilty of felony . . . '

Mr Brodie argued, first, that mens rea of some kind is necessary. Secondly, that the nature of the mens rea required is that the appellant must intend to do the particular kind of harm that was done, or, alternatively, that he must foresee that that harm may occur yet nevertheless continue recklessly to do the act. . . .

. . . [W]e have . . . considered, . . . , the following principle which was propounded by the late Professor C. S. Kenny in the first edition of his Outlines of Criminal Law published in 1902 and repeated at p. 186 of the 16th edition edited by Mr J. W. Cecil Turner and published in 1952:

In any statutory definition of a crime, malice must be taken not in the old vague sense of wickedness in general but as requiring either (1) An actual intention to do the particular kind of harm that in fact was done; or (2) recklessness as to whether such harm should occur or not (i.e., the accused has foreseen that the particular kind of harm might be done and yet has gone on to take the risk of it). It is neither limited to nor does it indeed require any ill will towards the person injured.

The same principle is repeated by Mr Turner in his 10th edition of Russell on Crime at p. 1592.

We think that this is an accurate statement of the law. It derives some support from the judgments of Lord Coleridge CJ and Blackburn J in *Pembliton's* case [1874–80] All ER 1163. In our opinion the word 'maliciously' in a statutory crime postulates foresight of consequence.

Questions

1. What was the *mens rea* of the crime charged?

2. The trial judge had instructed the jury that maliciously could be equated with wickedly, and this was clearly an error. The Court of Appeal did not have to go any further to decide the case, but nonetheless chose to seize the occasion to explain what it deemed to constitute recklessness. How did it define this term?

3. If there had been a retrial, which of the following facts would the prosecution have had to have established in order to prove that Cunningham was reckless?

    (a)   that he knew that coal gas could cause asphyxiation;

    (b)   that he foresaw that coal gas would escape as a result of his removal of the meter;

    (c)   that he knew that coal gas would remain in its lethal form after being exposed to air;

    (d)   that he foresaw that the coal gas could and would seep through the wall connecting the basements of two houses;

    (e)   that he foresaw that the coal gas could and would seriously harm the occupant of the house next door;

    (f)   that a reasonable person would have foreseen or known all of the above.

How would the Crown go about satisfying a jury of each of the above elements that needed to be proved?

Note

In determining whether Cunningham was aware of the risk that he was creating, doubtless jurors would ask themselves whether they themselves would have realised the risk. If the answer is yes, the jurors are likely to project this appreciation of the danger on to Cunningham, at least if they do not consider him to be qualitatively different from themselves. Thus if the risks fell into the category of common knowledge, the kind of thing that most reasonable people would know, the jury would be likely to conclude that Cunningham too was aware of the risks. But recall that what is not permissible is for a court to instruct the jury that they *must* conclude that defendant did in fact realise the danger if the jurors believe that a reasonable person would have realised the danger. The difference is illustrated in the case where it can be shown that the defendant is not a reasonable person.

R v *Stephenson*
[1979] 1 QB 695
Court of Appeal

GEOFFREY LANE LJ: . . . The facts giving rise to the charge of arson were as follows. On November 28, 1977, the appellant went to a large straw stack in a field near Ampleforth, made a hollow in the side of the stack, crept into the hollow and tried to go to sleep. He felt cold, so he lit a fire of twigs and straw inside the hollow. The stack caught fire and damage of some £3,500 in all resulted. The appellant was stopped by the police soon afterwards. He first of all maintained that the fire had been caused by his smoking a cigarette. However, the next day he admitted what he had done. He said: 'I kept putting bits of straw on the fire. Then the lot went up. As I ran away I looked back and saw the fire. Then getting bigger. I ran off down the road, that's when I was picked up. I'm sorry about it, it was an accident.'

On those facts without more no jury would have had any difficulty in coming to the certain conclusion that the appellant had damaged the straw stack and had done so being reckless as to whether the stack would be damaged or not, whatever the true definition may be of the word 'reckless.'

However, the appellant did not give evidence, and the only witness called on behalf of the defence was Dr Hawkings, a very experienced consultant psychiatrist. His evidence was to the effect that the appellant had a long history of schizophrenia. This, he said, would have the effect of making the appellant quite capable of lighting a fire to keep himself warm in dangerous proximity to a straw stack without having taken the danger into account. In other words he was saying that the appellant may not have had the same ability to foresee or appreciate risk as the mentally normal person.

. . . The appellant, through no fault of his own, was in a mental condition which might have prevented him from appreciating the risk which would have been obvious to any normal person. When the judge said to the jury 'there may be . . . all kinds of reasons which make a man close his mind to the obvious fact – among them may be schizophrenia – ' we think he was guilty of a misapprehension, albeit possibly an understandable misapprehension. The schizophrenia was on the evidence something which might have prevented the idea of danger entering the appellant's mind at all. If that was the truth of the matter, then the appellant was entitled to be acquitted. That was something which was never left clearly to the jury to decide.

We should add this. The mere fact that a defendant is suffering from some mental abnormality which may affect his ability to foresee consequences or may cloud his appreciation of risk does not necessarily mean that on a particular occasion his foresight or appreciation of risk was in fact absent. In the present case, for example, if the matter had been left to the jury for them to decide in the light of all the evidence, including that of the psychiatrist, whether the appellant must have appreciated the risk, it would have been open to them to decide that issue against him and to have convicted. As it is, we are of the view that, for the reasons indicated, the conviction for arson was unsafe and must be quashed.

Question
In light of *Stephenson*, is it in the interest of a defendant who is charged under a statute which requires proof of subjective recklessness to argue his lack of intelligence? How can the Crown rebut a claim of stupidity?

(ii)   Objective recklessness

The possibility that a defendant might lie about his lack of awareness of a risk (and in so doing fool the jury) may have been part of the impetus behind the search for a more objective standard of recklessness. The leading cases are *Caldwell* and *Lawrence*.

R v Caldwell
[1982] AC 341
House of Lords

By section 1 of the Criminal Damage Act 1971:

> (1)   A person who ... destroys or damages any property belonging to another intending to destroy or damage any such property or being reckless as to whether any such property would be destroyed or damaged shall be guilty of an offence. (2) A person who ... destroys or damages any property ... (a) intending to destroy or damage any property or being reckless as to whether any property would be destroyed or damaged; and (b) intending by the destruction or damage to endanger the life of another or being reckless as to whether the life of another would be thereby endangered; shall be guilty of an offence. ...

The defendant set fire by night to a residential hotel where he had been employed and against the proprietor of which he bore a grudge. According to his evidence he was so drunk at the time that it did not occur to him that there might be people there whose lives might be endangered. He pleaded guilty to a charge under section 1(1) of the Act of 1971 but not guilty to a charge under section 1(2) of intending to damage property intending to endanger life or being reckless as to whether life was endangered.

LORD DIPLOCK: ... My Lords, the restricted meaning that the Court of Appeal in *R v Cunningham* had placed upon the adverb 'maliciously' in the Malicious Damage Act 1861 in cases where the prosecution did not rely upon an actual intention of the accused to cause the damage that was in fact done, called for a meticulous analysis by the jury of the thoughts that passed through the mind of the accused at or before the time he did the act that caused the damage, in order to see on which side of a narrow dividing line they fell. If it had crossed his mind that there was a risk that someone's property might be damaged but, because his mind was affected by rage or excitement or confused by drink, he did not appreciate the seriousness of the risk or trusted that good luck would prevent its happening, this state of mind would amount to malice in the restricted meaning placed upon that term by the Court of Appeal; whereas if, for any of these reasons, he did not even trouble to give his mind to the question whether there was any risk of damaging the property, this state of mind would not suffice to make him guilty of an offence under the Malicious Damage Act 1861.

Neither state of mind seems to me to be less blameworthy than the other; but if the difference between the two constituted the distinction between what does and what does not in legal theory amount to a guilty state of mind for the purposes of a statutory offence of damage to property, it would not be a practicable distinction for use in a trial by jury. The only person who knows what the accused's mental processes were is the accused himself – and probably not even he can recall them accurately when the rage or excitement under which he acted has passed, or he has sobered up if he were under the influence of drink at the relevant time. If the accused gives evidence that because of his rage, excitement or drunkenness the risk of particular harmful consequences of his acts simply did not occur to him, a jury would find it hard to be satisfied beyond reasonable doubt that his true mental process was not that, but was the slightly different mental process required if one applies the restricted meaning of 'being reckless as to whether' something would happen, adopted by the Court of Appeal in *R v Cunningham*.

My Lords, I can see no reason why Parliament when it decided to revise the law as to offences of damage to property should go out of its way to perpetuate fine and impracticable distinctions such as these, between one mental state and another. One would think that the sooner they were got rid of, the better.

. . . 'Reckless' as used in the new statutory definition of the mens rea of these offences is an ordinary English word. It had not by 1971 become a term of legal art with some more limited esoteric meaning than that which it bore in ordinary speech – a meaning which surely includes not only deciding to ignore a risk of harmful consequences resulting from one's acts that one has recognised as existing, but also failing to give any thought to whether or not there is any such risk in circumstances where, if any thought were given to the matter, it would be obvious that there was.

In my opinion, a person charged with an offence under section 1(1) of the Criminal Damage Act 1971 is 'reckless as to whether any such property would be destroyed or damaged' if (1) he does an act which in fact creates an obvious risk that property will be destroyed or damaged and (2) when he does the act he either has not given any thought to the possibility of there being any such risk or has recognised that there was some risk involved and has nonetheless gone on to do it. That would be a proper direction to the jury; cases in the Court of Appeal which held otherwise should be regarded as overruled.

Where the charge is under section 1(2) the question of the state of mind of the accused must be approached in stages, corresponding to paragraphs (a) and (b). The jury must be satisfied that what the accused did amounted to an offence under section 1(1), either because he actually intended to destroy or damage the property or because he was reckless (in the sense that I have described) as to whether it might be destroyed or damaged. Only if they are so satisfied must the jury go on to consider whether the accused also either actually intended that the destruction or damage of the property should endanger someone's life or was reckless (in a similar sense) as to whether a human life might be endangered.

. . .

So, in the instant case, the fact that the respondent was unaware of the risk of endangering lives of residents in the hotel owing to his self-induced intoxication, would be no defence if that risk would have been obvious to him had he been sober.

Questions

1. What is the test of recklessness adopted in *Caldwell*? In what respects does it differ from that of *Cunningham*? Is *Cunningham* in effect overruled? Is *Stephenson*?

2. Lord Diplock observes that there is little difference in terms of blameworthiness between the defendant who ignores a risk of which he is conscious and the defendant who gives no thought to the potential risk. Do you agree?

3. Lord Diplock also observes that the distinction between the defendant who ignores a risk of which he is conscious and the defendant who gives no thought to the potential risk is not a practicable one. Why?

4. Lord Diplock notes that *Cunningham* was based on an interpretation of the term 'maliciously', which has been replaced by the term 'recklessly' in the Criminal Damage Act 1971 which was at issue in *Caldwell*. Of what significance is this fact?

R v Lawrence
[1982] AC 510
House of Lords

LORD DIPLOCK: My Lords, on Good Friday, April 13, 1979, after night had fallen, the respondent ('the driver') was riding his motor cycle along an urban street in Lowestoft. The street was subject to a 30 mph speed limit and there was a good deal of other traffic using it at the time. The driver ran into and killed a pedestrian who was crossing the road to return from an off-licence shop to her car which was parked on the opposite side of the street. The driver was in due course tried upon indictment for the offence of causing her death by driving a motor vehicle on a road recklessly, contrary to section 1 of the Road Traffic Act 1972.

. . .

My Lords, this House has very recently had occasion in *R* v *Caldwell* [1982] AC 341 to give close consideration to the concept of recklessness as constituting mens rea in criminal law. The conclusion reached by the majority was that the adjective 'reckless' when used in a criminal statute, i.e. the Criminal Damage Act 1971, had not acquired a special meaning as a term of legal art, but bore its popular or dictionary meaning of careless, regardless, or heedless of the possible harmful consequences of one's acts. The same must be true of the adverbial derivative 'recklessly.'

The context in which the word 'reckless' appears in section 1 of the Criminal Damage Act 1971 differs in two respects from the context in which the word 'recklessly' appears in sections 1 and 2 of the Road Traffic Act 1972, as now amended. In the Criminal Damage Act 1971 the actus reus, the physical act of destroying or damaging property belonging to another, is in itself a tort. It is not something that one does regularly as part of the ordinary routine of daily life, such as driving a car or a motor cycle. So there is something out of the ordinary to call the doer's attention to what he is doing and its possible consequences, which is absent in road traffic offences. The other difference in context is that in section 1 of the Criminal Damage Act 1971 the mens rea of the offences is defined as being reckless as to whether particular harmful consequences would occur, whereas in sections 1 and 2 of the Road Traffic Act 1972, as now amended, the possible harmful consequences of which the driver must be shown to have been heedless are left to be implied from the use of the word 'recklessly' itself. In ordinary usage 'recklessly' as descriptive of a physical act such as driving a motor vehicle which can be performed in a variety of different ways, some of them entailing danger and some of them not, refers not only to the state of mind of the doer of the act when he decides to do it but also qualifies the manner in which the act itself is performed. One does not speak of a person acting 'recklessly,' even though he has given no thought at all to the consequences of his act, unless the act is one that presents a real risk of harmful consequences which anyone acting with reasonable prudence would recognise and give heed to. So the actus reus of the offence under sections 1 and 2 is not simply driving a motor vehicle on a road, but driving it in a manner which in fact creates a real risk of harmful consequences resulting from it. Since driving in such a manner as to do no worse than create a risk of causing inconvenience or annoyance to other road users constitutes the lesser offence under section 3, the manner of driving that constitutes the actus reus of an offence under sections 1 and 2 must be worse than that; it must be such as to create a real risk of causing physical injury to someone else who happens to be using the road or damage to property more substantial than the kind of minor damage that may be caused by an error of judgment in the course of parking one's car.

. . .

I turn now to the mens rea. My task is greatly simplified by what has already been said about the concept of recklessness in criminal law in *R v Caldwell* [1982] AC 341. Warning was there given against adopting the simplistic approach of treating all problems of criminal liability as soluble by classifying the test of liability as being either 'subjective' or 'objective.' Recklessness on the part of the doer of an act does presuppose that there is something in the circumstances that would have drawn the attention of an ordinary prudent individual to the possibility that his act was capable of causing the kind of serious harmful consequences that the section which creates the offence was intended to prevent, and that the risk of those harmful consequences occurring was not so slight that an ordinary prudent individual would feel justified in treating them as negligible. It is only when this is so that the doer of the act is acting 'recklessly' if before doing the act, he either fails to give any thought to the possibility of there being any such risk or, having recognised that there was such risk, he nevertheless goes on to do it.

In my view, an appropriate instruction to the jury on what is meant by driving recklessly would be that they must be satisfied of two things:

First, that the defendant was in fact driving the vehicle in such a manner as to create an obvious and serious risk of causing physical injury to some other person who might happen to be using the road or of doing substantial damage to property; and

Second, that in driving in that manner the defendant did so without having given any thought to the possibility of there being any such risk or, having recognised that there was some risk involved, had nonetheless gone on to take it.

It is for the jury to decide whether the risk created by the manner in which the vehicle was being driven was both obvious and serious and, in deciding this, they may apply the standard of the ordinary prudent motorist as represented by themselves.

If satisfied that an obvious and serious risk was created by the manner of the defendant's driving, the jury are entitled to infer that he was in one or other of the states of mind required to constitute the offence and will probably do so; but regard must be given to any explanation he gives as to his state of mind which may displace the inference.

Questions

1. Are there differences between recklessness in the reckless driving context and recklessness in the criminal damage context? Do (should) these differences change the analysis? See also *R v Seymour* [1983] 2 AC 493.
2. In *Lawrence*, Lord Diplock adopts the standard not simply of the ordinary prudent person, but of the ordinary prudent motorist. How does one determine the standards of the ordinary prudent motorist? What if the jury consists of persons who have failed their driving licence tests?
3. Where Lord Diplock in *Caldwell* spoke in terms of an 'obvious' risk, in *Lawrence* he described a risk that is 'obvious and serious'. Of what significance, if any, is this change of language? See *R v Reid* [1992] 1 WLR 793.

In *Caldwell* and *Lawrence* Lord Diplock expanded recklessness beyond the defendant who is aware of the risk to the defendant who, had he stopped to think, would have been aware of the risk. But what if the defendant did stop to think and concluded incorrectly that there was no risk? At one point in *Caldwell* Lord Diplock spoke of circumstances where, if any thought were given to the matter, it would be obvious that there was a risk. This seemed to suggest a risk that would be obvious to a reasonable person, and that the defendant who stopped to think but arrived at the wrong conclusion would be deemed reckless. But in *Lawrence* Lord Diplock clouded the issue by referring to the doer of the act not giving any thought to the risk, and throughout both opinions his concern seemed more with those who cannot be bothered to think than with those who stop to think but come to the wrong conclusions. Is there, as some commentators have maintained, a lacuna in the law? Consider the following two cases:

Chief Constable of Avon and Somerset Constabulary v *Shimmen*
(1986) 84 Cr App R 7
Queen's Bench Division

TAYLOR J: . . . The charge against the defendant was that on February 15, 1985, in the City of Bristol, without lawful excuse, he destroyed property belonging to Maskreys Ltd, namely a plate glass window of the value of £495, intending to destroy such property or being reckless as to whether such property would be destroyed, contrary to section 1(1) of the Criminal Damage Act 1971. The justices found the following facts, inter alia.

The defendant had, on the relevant evening, been in the company of four friends. They had been in a public-house and later they went to a club. During the evening, the defendant consumed a quantity of alcohol. He and his four friends left the club together and made their way along the road to a position outside Maskrey's shop. There the defendant and one of his friends. David Woodhouse were laughing, joking, and larking around. Woodhouse pushed the defendant who then started flailing his arms and legs, contriving not to make any contact with Mr Woodhouse. Mr Woodhouse issued a warning to the defendant that he might one day hurt someone. The defendant assured Woodhouse that he had everything under control and, to prove it, he made as if to strike the window with his foot. His foot, however, did make contact with the window and broke it. The defendant was the holder of a green-belt and yellow-belt in the Korean art of self-defence. He was a skilled and experienced practitioner of that art.

It was conceded that he had no intent to break the window. But the prosecutor's contention was that his act amounted to recklessness and that he ought to be convicted on that ground. The defendant contended that by reason of the skill which he had, he had satisfied himself that the window would not break and that he was, in those circumstances, not reckless. The court was, as one would expect, referred to the leading authorities on the nature of recklessness. They are two decisions of the House of Lords. The first is *R* v *Caldwell* (1981) 73 Cr App R 13; [1982] AC 341. The second is *R* v *Lawrence* (1981) 73 Cr App R 1; [1982] AC 510. The defendant relied particularly on a passage in the speech of Lord Diplock in *R* v *Lawrence* at p. 11 and p. 527 respectively. The passage reads as follows:

> If satisfied that an obvious and serious risk was created by the manner of the defendant's driving, the jury are entitled to infer that he was in one or other of the states of mind required to constitute the offence and will probably do so; but regard

must be given to any explanation he gives as to his state of mind which may displace the inference.

Relying upon that passage, it was suggested that the explanation which had been given by the defendant in this case, that he had taken what he considered to be the necessary steps to avoid any risk of damage, entitled him to be acquitted. The two states of mind which were referred to by Lord Diplock were those which he himself described in the earlier case of *Caldwell* . . .

In my opinion, a person charged with an offence under section 1(1) of the Criminal Damage Act 1971 is 'reckless as to whether any such property would be destroyed or damaged' if (1) he does an act which in fact creates an obvious risk that property will be destroyed or damaged and (2) when he does the act he either has not given any thought to the possibility of there being any such risk or has recognised that there was some risk involved and has nonetheless gone on to do it.

The two decisions in *R v Caldwell (supra)* and *R v Lawrence (supra)* have been followed by a considerable volume of academic writing. It was conceded on behalf of the prosecutor here that a number of the writers have expressed the view that between the two possible states of mind constituting recklessness as defined in *R v Caldwell*, there exists or could exist a lacuna, that is a state of mind which fell into neither of the two alternative categories posed by Lord Diplock. The way in which the matter is put is perhaps most helpfully, in the circumstances of this case, illustrated by an article 'Reckless Damage and Reckless Driving: Living with Caldwell and Lawrence' in the Criminal Law Review of 1981 at p. 743 by Professor Griew. At p. 748, he cited two hypothetical cases under the heading 'The conscientious but inefficient actor.' The Professor said:

The following cases are outside the terms of the model direction in *Caldwell*. (a) M does give thought to whether there is a risk of damage to another's property attending his proposed act. He mistakenly concludes that there is no risk; or he perceives only a risk such as would in the circumstances be treated as negligible by the ordinary prudent individual. He missed the obvious and substantial risk. (b) N's case is a more likely one. He is indeed aware of the kind of risk that will attend his act if he does not take adequate precautions. He takes precautions that are intended and expected to eliminate the risk (or to reduce it to negligible proportions). But the precautions are plainly, though not plainly to him, inadequate for this purpose. These appear not to be cases of recklessness. Evidence of conscientiousness displaces what would otherwise be an available inference of recklessness, (to use the language of Lord Diplock in *Lawrence*, . . . The position of the person doing his best is further considered in the special context of reckless driving . . . ')

He then went on to refer to *R v Lawrence (supra)*.

Those two examples which were given by Professor Griew seem to me not to be 'on all fours.' In the first example, it may well be arguable that the lacuna exists because it is not a case where M failed to give any consideration to the possibility of a risk. It is a case where he did give consideration to the possibility of the risk and concluded, albeit mistakenly, that there was no risk. In terms, therefore, of Lord Diplock's definition, he has not recognised that there was some risk involved. He therefore is outside the second possible state of mind referred to in *R v Caldwell (supra)*.

A different situation, however, seems to me to apply in the case of N posed by Professor Griew. He was aware of the kind of risk which would attend his act if he did not take adequate precautions. He seeks to rely upon the fact that he did take precautions which were intended, and by him expected, to eliminate the risk. He was wrong, but the fact that he was conscientious to the degree of trying to minimise the risk does not mean that he falls outside the second limb of Lord Diplock's test. Lord Diplock's second limb is simply whether or not he has recognised that there was some risk. It seems clear to me that in the case of N, as posed by Professor Griew, N certainly did recognise that there was some risk and went on to do the act.

In my judgment, therefore, the second example given by Professor Griew does not constitute any lacuna in the definition given by Lord Diplock. Applying those examples to the present case, it seems to me that on the findings of the justices and more particularly, as I shall indicate in a moment, on the evidence which they exhibited to their case, this defendant did recognise the risk. It was not a case of his considering the possibility and coming to the conclusion that there was no risk. What he said to the justices in cross-examination should be quoted. He said: 'I thought I might break the window but then I thought I will not break the window . . . I thought to myself, the window is not going to break.' A little later on he said: 'I weighed up the odds and thought I had eliminated as much risk as possible by missing by two inches instead of two millimetres.'

The specific finding of the justices, at para. 5(c) of the case, was as follows: ' . . . the defendant perceived there could be a risk of damage but after considering such risk concluded that no damage would result.' It seems to me that what this case amounts to is as follows; that this defendant did perceive, which is the same as Lord Diplock's word 'recognise.' that there could be a risk, but by aiming off rather more than he normally would in this sort of display, he thought he had minimised it and therefore no damage would result. In my judgment, that is far from saying that he falls outside the state of mind described by Lord Diplock in these terms, ' . . . has recognised that there was some risk involved and has nonetheless gone on to do it.'

In my judgment, therefore, whatever may be the situation in a hypothetical case such as that of M as detailed by Professor Griew, which may need to be considered on another occasion, so far as this case is concerned, the justices were wrong in coming to the conclusion that this was not recklessness by reason of what the defendant had put forward. I should say that I have considerable sympathy with the justices when there is so much academic discussion of this particular test and where, as I have indicated, some of that discussion does not seem to result in accurate conclusions. However that may be, I, for my part, would allow this appeal and send the case back to the justices and require them to convict.

R v Crossman
[1986] RTR 49
Court of Appeal

LORD LANE CJ: . . . The facts of the case are not in dispute and they are these. At about 1.30 p.m. on 26 September 1984 the appellant was driving a large articulated lorry with a tractor unit and a trailer unit. The circumstances in which he was driving it were these. He had collected the trailer unit from the compound of Caterpillar Tractors in Birtley. The trailer unit had been loaded with a very large and weighty piece of machinery called a welding positioner. It seems that that piece of machinery weighed between 3 and 5 tons. There were other extensive pieces of metal on the back of the lorry together with the welding positioner making the load which was to be transported.

Mr Richardson was the loader and, according to him, and for purposes of argument it can be taken as correct, it is the driver's responsibility to secure the load. Mr

Richardson told the appellant that in his, Mr Richardson's, view this load was unsafe and that it should be chained down and sheeted before the lorry was taken on to the road. The appellant disregarded that advice. In his view, he said, it was 'as safe as houses', and in any event he was just going round the corner in order to chain the load down at the depot. There was evidence of two other employees of the firm who were likewise of the view that this load was unsafe.

So, without the load having been chained down or sheeted, the lorry was driven by the appellant on to the public road and along a highway called Station Lane. As the vehicle went over some depression or pot-hole in the road the welding positioner, which in any event was top heavy quite apart from being not secure, fell off on to the near side footpath, and unhappily on to a pedestrian, Mrs Fenton, who was killed almost instantly. The lorry then continued on for 40 yards and the appellant drove on without ascertaining what had happened, but that does not form part of this case.

At the close of the prosecution case, a summary of which I have just given, counsel for the appellant submitted that the appellant had been charged with the wrong offence, and that there was no evidence capable of justifying the jury in coming to the conclusion that there had been what amounted to reckless driving. . . .

. . . Mr Gatland on behalf of the appellant suggests that where something in the nature of a load falls off a lorry and kills someone, the driver of the lorry cannot properly be charged with or convicted of causing death by reckless driving. His suggestion is that 'reckless driving' must be something to do with the handling or control of the vehicle itself. If a person is driving along the road gingerly and with great care, as no doubt the appellant was, the mere fact that something falls off that lorry cannot be the basis of a charge of reckless driving, even though the driver may have known that the load was unsafe, or likely to fall off, and nevertheless determined to run the risk that it might.

. . . Counsel for the appellant submits in effect that there is a distinction between deciding to drive recklessly and recklessly deciding to drive. The latter does not come within the mischief of the Act, he contends. What has to be considered, in his submission, is the actual care and control of the vehicle and, if no criticism can be made of the way the vehicle was driven, steered or braked, or if no criticism can be made of the constituent parts of the vehicle, what may happen to the load being carried on the vehicle is not relevant to the offence.

We respectfully disagree with those contentions.

The jury could, and no doubt would, have found that the appellant foresaw the high degree of risk that the load would fall off and if it did might injure someone, but nevertheless decided to run that risk. He caused that risk, or put it into operation by driving the vehicle on to the road. He was driving with the knowledge that by doing so, however slowly, however gingerly, however carefully he drove, he was putting other road users at risk of serious injury or death. This seems to us to fall quite clearly as a matter of simple wording under the expression 'reckless driving', driving with the knowledge that by moving the vehicle along the road at all, he was running the serious risk of injuring someone. That, in our view, was reckless driving and in consequence we are of the view that the judge was correct in the conclusion which he reached. Accordingly this appeal must be dismissed.

Notes and questions

1. Do *Shimmen* and *Crossman* confirm or refute the lacuna thesis? In what other way could it be said that the defendants were reckless?

2. An alternative, and perhaps more straightforward, way of analysing *Shimmen* would be to say that where the risk created is high and the social

utility of the conduct in question low, a defendant will be judged to have acted unreasonably in taking the risk. From this perspective the critical question becomes not whether a reasonable person would have foreseen the risk, but whether a reasonable person would have taken the risk.

3. In which of the following situations would a defendant be held to have acted recklessly, assuming the proscribed harm resulted? Which type of recklessness (subjective or objective) is involved?

(a) defendant thinks about the risk, recognises its seriousness, but decides to proceed in disregard of it;

(b) defendant thinks about the risk but incorrectly and unreasonably concludes that it is negligible or non-existent;

(c) defendant thinks about the risk, recognises its seriousness, but takes inadequate precautions to avoid the risk;

(d) defendant fails to think about a risk that a reasonable person would have recognised as serious;

(e) defendant fails to consider a risk that the reasonable person would have thought about but would have concluded was not serious.

It may make sense to hold criminally liable a defendant who is aware of a danger and disregards it. That defendant consciously chooses to risk causing harm. It may also make sense to hold criminally liable a defendant who is indifferent to a danger that he should have appreciated, but which he did not because, as in *Caldwell*, he drank himself to a point where he was unable to think critically about the risk. That defendant consciously chooses to put himself in a state where he is unable to exercise rational choice. It may even make sense to hold criminally liable a defendant who is shown to be a reasonable person and who is indifferent to an obvious risk that a reasonable person would have appreciated. Indeed, in this situation it may well be that the court does not really believe the defendant's denial but is unwilling to run the risk of a jury being taken in by perjurious testimony. In any event, in all these cases the defendant is in some respect morally blameworthy. But what of the defendant who is incapable, through no fault of his own, of appreciating the risk in the first place?

Elliott v C
[1983] 1 WLR 939
Queen's Bench Division

ROBERT GOFF LJ: . . . I start of course with the facts of the case, which have been set out with clarity by the justices. For present purposes, the salient features are these. (1) The defendant, 14-year-old schoolgirl, set fire to a shed by pouring white spirit onto a carpet on the floor of the shed and throwing two lighted matches onto the spirit, the second of which ignited it. (2) While she realised that the contents of the bottle which contained the white spirit was possibly inflammable, she had not handled it before and had not appreciated how explosively it would burn and immediately become out of control, thereby destroying both the shed and its contents. (3) She gave no thought at the time when she started the fire to the possibility of there being a risk that the shed and its contents would be destroyed. (4) This risk would not have been obvious to her or have been appreciated by her if she had given thought to the matter. I add that these conclusions were reached by the justices, having regard to the age and understanding of the defendant, her lack of experience of dealing with inflammable spirit, and the fact that she must have been tired and exhausted at the time.

I turn next to the crime with which she was charged, viz. that she without lawful excuse destroyed by fire the shed and contents, intending to destroy such property or being reckless as to whether such property would be destroyed, contrary to section 1(1) of the Criminal Damage Act 1971. The case advanced against her was not that she intended to destroy the property, but that she was reckless as to whether the property would be destroyed.

Plainly, she did destroy the shed and its contents by fire; plainly, too, she did so without lawful excuse. But was she reckless as to whether the shed and its contents would be destroyed? Here I turn, as Glidewell J, has done, to authority; and in the decision of the House of Lords in *R v Caldwell* [1982] AC 341, I find an authority, binding upon this court, which was concerned with the interpretation of the word 'recklessness' as used in the very subsection under which the defendant was charged. In that case, although the House was divided, the ratio decidendi of the decision of the House is to be found in the speech of Lord Diplock, with which both Lord Keith and Lord Roskill agreed. Lord Diplock analysed the word 'reckless' as used in this subsection, and his analysis culminated in the conclusion, expressed, at p. 354:

> In my opinion, a person charged with an offence under section 1(1) of the Criminal Damage Act 1971 is 'reckless as to whether any such property would be destroyed or damaged' if (1) he does an act which in fact creates an obvious risk that property will be destroyed or damaged and (2) when he does the act he either has not given any thought to the possibility of there being any such risk or has recognised that there was some risk involved and has nonetheless gone on to do it. That would be a proper direction to the jury; cases in the Court of Appeal which held otherwise should be regarded as overruled.

Now, if that test is applied literally in the present case, the conclusion appears inevitable that, on the facts found by the justices, the defendant was reckless whether the shed and contents would be destroyed; because first she did an act which carried an obvious risk that the property would be destroyed, and second she had not given any thought to the possibility of there being such risk.

Yet, if I next pause (as I have done, in accordance with what I consider to be my proper function) and ask myself the question – would I, having regard only to the ordinary meaning of the word, consider this girl to have been, on the facts found, *reckless* whether the shed and contents would be destroyed, my answer would, I confess, be in the negative. This is not a case where there was a deliberate disregard of a known risk of damage or injury of a certain type or degree; nor is it a case where there was mindless indifference to a risk of such damage or injury, as is expressed in common speech in the context of motoring offences (though not, I think, of arson) as 'blazing on regardless'; nor is it even a case where failure to give thought to the possibility of the risk was due to some blameworthy cause, such as intoxication. This is a case where it appears that the only basis upon which the accused might be held to have been reckless would be if the appropriate test to be applied was purely objective – a test which might in some circumstances be thought justifiable in relation to certain conduct (e.g. reckless driving), particularly where the word 'reckless' is used simply to characterise the relevant conduct. But such a test does not appear at first sight to be appropriate to a crime such as that under consideration in the present case, especially as recklessness in that crime has to be related to a particular consequence. I therefore next ask myself the question whether I can, consistently with the doctrine of precedent, sensibly interpreted, legitimately construe or qualify the principle stated by Lord Diplock in *R* v *Caldwell* [1982] AC 341 so as to accommodate what I conceive to be the appropriate result on the facts of the present case, bearing in mind that those facts are very different from the facts under consideration by the House of Lords in *R* v *Caldwell*, where the defendant had set fire to a hotel when in a state of intoxication.

Here again, it would be unrealistic if I were to disguise the fact that I am well aware that the statement of principle by Lord Diplock in *R* v *Caldwell* has been the subject of comment, much of it critical, in articles written by jurists; and that I have studied certain of these articles with interest. I find it striking that the justices, in reaching their conclusion in the present case, have done so (no doubt in response to an argument advanced on the defendant's behalf) by imposing upon Lord Diplock's statement of principle a qualification similar to one considered by Professor Glanville Williams in his article 'Recklessness Redefined' in (1981) 40 CLJ 252, 270–271. This is that a defendant should only be regarded as having acted recklessly by virtue of his failure to give any thought to an obvious *to him* if he had given any thought to the matter. However, having studied Lord Diplock's speech, I do not think it would be consistent with his reasoning to impose any such qualification. . . .

Questions
What purpose is served by holding Elliott liable? Is she deserving of punishment? Will her punishment serve to deter others of her age and experience? What type of rehabilitation can be offered to her?

Note
The Draft Criminal Code Bill 1989 defines recklessness in the following terms:

Draft Criminal Code 1989

18. For the purposes of this Act and of any offence other than a pre-Code offence as defined in section 6 (to which section 2(3) applies) a person acts —
. . .
   (c) 'recklessly' with respect to —
     (i) a circumstance when he is aware of a risk that it exists or will exist;
     (ii) a result when he is aware of a risk that it will occur; and it is, in the circumstances known to him, unreasonable to take the risk;
. . .

Question
Is this an objective or a subjective standard? How can you tell?

One possible way to avoid the result in *Elliott* while remaining true to the test of *Caldwell* would be to imbue the reasonable person with the characteristics of the accused. As we shall see later, this is an approach which has appealed to the judges in the context of manslaughter. It represents a half-way house between a pure subjective and a pure objective standard. The possibility of imbuing the reasonable person with relevant characteristics of the accused was considered by the Court of Appeal in the next case:

R v *Stephen Malcolm R*
(1984) 79 Cr App R 334
Court of Appeal

The appellant, when aged 15, committed a series of burglaries, other youths being involved in two of them. A few days after the last burglary, after receiving an anonymous telephone call, police went to a ground floor flat occupied by a mother and daughter and found the appellant there and the other youths and the stolen property. Four days later, at 11.30 p.m., when the mother was in the sitting room and the daughter in her bedroom, they heard three loud bangs and the daughter saw sheets of flame at her bedroom window, caused by three separate fires coming from three milk bottles. She ran screaming from her room. The police found blackened areas on the wall in the close proximity of the daughter's bedroom. They went straight to the appellant's house. It smelt of petrol and a pair of gloves soaked in petrol belonging to the appellant were found there. The next day when seen by the police the appellant said that he and one of the aforesaid youths had formed the opinion that the daughter had 'grassed' upon them, giving information leading to their arrests for the burglaries. They made and used the petrol bombs, intending, he said, not to injure the girl but only to frighten her. He did not realise that if the petrol bomb had gone through her window it might have killed her.

ACKNER L J: . . . When the matter came on for trial the appellant admitted the facts which were the basis of count 6, which did not charge with intent to endanger human life, but he pleaded not guilty to count 5 on the ground that he did not have the requisite intent and had not acted recklessly. That question – 'had he acted recklessly?' – was the real issue. Mr Timms at the beginning of the trial sought a ruling from the trial judge as to the direction which the learned judge would give on the subject of recklessness. He submitted that when considering recklessness, the jury could only convict the appellant if he did an act which created a risk to life obvious to someone of his age and with such of his characteristics as would affect his appreciation of the risk. He should not in law be capable of being convicted if the act created a risk which was obvious to an ordinary prudent person of mature years and understanding, but was not obvious to him at his age and with his characteristics. The learned judge ruled against that submission and accordingly, Mr Timms, with characteristic good sense, advised his client to alter his plea. The appellant then pleaded guilty and was sentenced as we have indicated.

The point of law which is raised before us is the point which Mr Timms took before Judge Abdela. It is said that the learned judge erred in law in deciding that the test of recklessness as to whether life was endangered was as follows: A person is guilty of the offence if (i) he does an act which in fact creates a risk to the ordinary prudent man, i.e. one of mature years and understanding, that life will be endangered; (ii) he did the act not having given thought to the possibility of such a risk; or (iii) recognising that there was some risk, he nonetheless continued the act.

The learned judge, it is urged, was wrong in law because he failed to apply the law in relation to what constitutes the 'ordinary prudent man' and failed adequately to consider *Director of Public Prosecutions* v *Camplin* (1978) 67 Cr App R 14; [1978] AC 705. He should have found that the ordinary prudent man is synonymous with the reasonable man and therefore the jury should have had regard to the particular situation of the appellant, namely his age, and any other characteristics which would affect his appreciation of the risk.

... Mr Timms sought to induce us to adopt a *via media*. He said he accepted it would be wrong to ask the question whether the defendant himself was aware of the risk, but it would be right to inquire whether a person of the age of the defendant and with his characteristics which might be relevant to his ability to foresee the risk, would have appreciated it. He drew our attention in particular to the submission made by the prosecution before the justices in *Elliott's* case (1983) 77 Cr App R 103; [1983] 1 WLR 939 (see p. 110 and p. 940 respectively) 'that in relation to the defendant aged 14 years, the proper approach was whether such risk would have been obvious to a normal 14 year old child.' Therefore he said he was not seeking to relate the test to the particular defendant, but merely, so to speak, to a class of which he is a member. This, he says, provides him with the same logical basis of approach to the reasonable man or the reasonably prudent person as *DPP* v *Camplin* (*supra*) had suggested. We do not think that that *via media* was for one moment in the mind of Lord Diplock. The opportunity so to ingraft this important modification on the principle which he had enunciated had arisen in the subsequent cases and would have been just the sort of point (if it was a valid one) which we would have expected the House of Lords to have desired to have dealt with, thus clearing up the position, when they had the opportunity to do so when considering whether or not to give leave in *Elliott's* case (*supra*). If they had desired to say, for instance, that the age of the defendant was a factor to which particular regard must be had in applying the test, then *Elliott* was just the sort of case to do that, excising, if appropriate, any reference to any other ephemeral characteristics such as exhaustion from which the girl was said to be suffering. But they did not take that opportunity. We do not think that we should seek by this subtlety to avoid applying principles which we also have difficulty in accepting. We respectfully share the regrets voiced by Robert Goff LJ that in essence 'recklessness' has now been construed synonymously with 'carelessness.'

... Although we would have preferred that the judge should have at least been entitled in law to have left to the jury the question, would a boy of the defendant's age have appreciated that to have thrown petrol bombs very close to the windows of this dwelling house was a danger to the life of the occupants of that house, we have little doubt that on the facts of this case the answer would have been clearly in the affirmative. As we have already stressed, this was a ground floor flat and the petrol bombs were thrown so close to the window where the girl whom it was sought, so it was said, to frighten, had her bedroom, that one landed within 18 inches of that window.

Questions
1. How far are does the logic of *Stephen Malcolm R* extend? Janet hands Gerry, who is blind, a loaded pistol, telling him that it is unloaded. He pulls the trigger to experience the sensation, and an innocent bystander is killed. Should Gerry's blindness be taken into account in determining whether he acted recklessly?
2. Consider the case where it is shown that the defendant possesses more knowledge than the ordinary person. A chemistry professor knows that agents

X and Y when left together for more than an hour will cause an explosion. She leaves her laboratory at night, forgetting that she has mixed X and Y in a beaker. The laboratory explodes. Has our professor acted recklessly if an ordinary person would not have appreciated the danger?

3.   Consider the converse case. The chemistry professor knows that the mixing of agents C and D is extremely unlikely to cause an explosion. The ordinary person, however, seeing the smoke and hearing the crackling noises when the chemicals are mixed, might reasonably believe that an explosion was imminent. If in fact a fluke explosion occurs, would the chemistry professor be liable?

Note

To what offences does *Caldwell* apply? The courts have approached this issue on a case by case basis. The logic of *Caldwell* seems to suggest that the decision should apply wherever recklessness, or some variant thereof, is required to be proved. But the courts have not disturbed precedents where recklessness has been defined in terms of subjective fault. Thus where 'maliciously' constitutes the *mens rea* the courts have adhered to the strict letter of *Cunningham*. (See *W (a minor)* v *Dolbey* [1983] Crim LR 691.)

D   Negligence and gross negligence

The courts have recognised degrees of negligence. Primarily in the context of homicide, there is a category of gross negligence.

R v Sulman
(1993) *The Times*, 21 May 1993
Court of Appeal

The Lord Chief Justice, giving the judgment of the court, said that essentially the question was that posed in *Archbold Criminal Pleading Evidence and Practice* (1992 edition, paragraph 19-92): whether gross negligence manslaughter had survived *R v Caldwell* ([1982] AC 341) and *R v Lawrence* ([1982] AC 510).

Their Lordships had been referred to a plethora of legal authority, going as far back as Bracton and Coke and as far abroad as the Commonwealth jurisdictions.

In their Lordships' view, however, it was necessary to cite only two authorites before the leading case, *Andrews* v *DPP* ([1937] AC 576): *R v Doherty* ((1887) 16 Cox CC 306, 309) and *R v Bateman* (1925) 19 Cr App R 8, 11). In *Andrews*, a case of motor manslaughter, Lord Atkin had quoted the passage from *Bateman* and (at p. 583) introduced the word 'reckless' to denote the degree of negligence required.

Further, while he thought that 'reckless' most nearly covered the case, he recognised it was not exhaustive; there was still scope for manslaughter by a high degree of negligence, even in the absence of indifference. He excluded 'mere inadvertence' (p. 582) but he was not saying that all inadvertence fell short of creating criminal liability. On the contrary, he indicated that to establish guilt of manslaughter, the accused must be proved to have had 'criminal disregard' for the safety of other (p. 582) and he gave as examples 'the grossest ignorance or the most criminal inattention'.

Where a duty of care was owed, the inattentive would often be negligence so as to be civilly liable even though, as a result of their inattention, they might not have adverted to the risk. But negligent inattention characterised as mere inadvertence did not create criminal liability. To do so, the inattention or inadvertence had to be, in the jury's view, grossly negligent.

In *R v Stone* ([1977] QB 354, 362) Lord Justice Lane made clear that proof of foresight of the consequences was not necessary. What was necessary was proof of a high degree of negligence reflecting the *Andrews* approach. He said specifically (p. 363C) that it was to *Andrews* that one had to turn to discover the definition of the requisite degree of negligence.

After quoting from *Andrews* (p. 583) Lord Justice Lane went on: 'It is clear from that passage that indifference to an obvious risk and appreciation of such risk, coupled with a determination nevertheless to run it, are both examples of recklessness . . . Mere inadvertence is not enough. The defendant must be proved to have been indifferent to an obvious risk of injury to health, or actually to have foreseen the risk but to have determined nevertheless to run it.'

The definition of recklessness by Lord Diplock in *Caldwell* and *Lawrence* involved two stages: the *actus reus* consisted of the defendant creating an obvious and serious risk. The *mens rea* was defined in the alternative as 'without having given any thought to the possibility of there being any such risk or, having recognised that there was some risk involved, had nevertheless gone on to take it.'

The wide Diplock meaning of recklessness had survived all attacks on it, most recently in *R v Reid* ([1992] 1 WLR 793).

It was beyond doubt that, at least since 1982, the word 'reckless' had caused the courts problems in regard to involuntary manslaughter which would not have occurred had the focus been on gross negligence rather than on recklessness.

His Lordship cited from *R v Seymour (Edward)* ([1983] 2 AC 493) and *Kong Cheuk Kwan v The Queen* ((1985) 82 Cr App R 18) and stated that their Lordships accepted the submission that Lord Roskill's sentence in *Seymour*, that 'reckless' was to be given the same meaning in relation to all offences which involved recklessness as one of the elements unless Parliament had otherwise ordained, was *obiter* and should not be followed in regard to the class of manslaughter involved in the cases under appeal.

All counsel had submitted that the effect of the history which their Lordships had briefly outlined had been to create conflicting approaches and uncertainty about the appropriate tests and the proper jury direction in cases of involuntary manslaughter involving breach of duty.

The diversity of views was illustrated by the stances adopted in the appeals which had not been consistent even among counsel for the Crown on the one hand and those for the defence on the other.

Andrews had not been disapproved in any case their Lordships had seen, and it had been applied in *Stone*. There was no reason to doubt that *Andrews* was still good law and *Stone* had been referred to in argument and not disapproved in *Seymour*.

Leaving motor manslaughter aside, however, in their Lordships' judgment the proper test in manslaughter cases based on breach of duty was the gross negligence test established in *Andrews* and *Stone*. Their Lordships reached that conclusion principally because the line of cases from *Doherty* through *Bateman* to *Andrews* and *Stone* was, they believed, binding authority.

Second, they considered that the *Lawrence/Caldwell* recklessness approach was for reasons, some of which had been given, inappropriate in the present class of case.

Accordingly, except in motor manslaughter, the ingredients of involuntary manslaughter by breach of duty which needed to be proved were: (1) the existence of the duty; (2) a breach of the duty causing death; (3) gross negligence which the jury considered justified a criminal conviction.

The range of possible duties, breaches and surrounding circumstances was so varied that it was not possible to prescribe a standard jury direction appropriate in all cases. The judge should tailor his summing up to the specific circumstances of the particular case.

However, in accordance with the authorities reviewed and without purporting to give an exhaustive definition, their Lordships considered proof of any of the following states of mind in the defendant might properly lead a jury to make a finding of gross negligence.

(a) indifference to an obvious risk of injury to health; (b) actual foresight of the risk coupled with the determination nevertheless to run it; (c) an appreciation of the risk coupled with an intention to avoid it but also coupled with such a high degree of negligence in the attempted avoidance as the jury considered justified the conviction; (d) inattention or failure to advert to a serious risk which went beyond 'mere inadvertence' in respect of an obvious and important matter which the defendant's duty demanded he should address.

Their Lordships had borne in mind the *dicta* in *Seymour* (p. 216) and in *Kong Cheuk Kwan* (p. 26). They were to the effect that the word 'reckless' was to be preferred to the word 'negligence' with whatever epithet. However, in view of the different tests and meanings which had in various contexts been attached to reckless and recklessness their Lordships thought it preferable to avoid those words when directing juries as to involuntary manslaughter by breach of duty.

In each of the three appeals, criticism had been made in argument of the directions given by the judge. Before proceeding to the specific issues raised in each appeal, their Lordships wished to say that they had the greatest sympathy with the judges in having to decide how to direct the jury as to the true ingredients of involuntary manslaughter. It had been difficult for judges to know which line of authority to follow.

Their Lordships considered each appeal in detail and concluded that for reasons which they had set out, the appeals of Dr Prentice and Dr Sulman would be allowed, the appeal of Dr Adomako would be dismissed and the appeal of Mr Holloway would be allowed.

His Lordship, in concluding, said that, before parting with the cases, the state of the law of manslaughter prompted their Lordships to urge that the Law Commission take the opportunity to examine the subject in all its aspects as a matter of urgency. The appeals had exemplified the problems in the particular type of manslaughter.
© Times Newspapers Limited 1993

Questions
1. How does gross negligence differ from recklessness? Which is the better defined concept?
2. In the course of his opinion Lord Taylor gives several examples of gross negligence. Are they all of the same order? Are there degrees of gross negligence? Is there in fact a spectrum, with due care at one end and gross negligence at the other, with an infinite number of points in-between? Even if the idea of a spectrum is sound in theory, is it a concept which is of little use in practice?

Less culpable than gross negligence (though how much so may be unclear) is ordinary negligence. One of the problems with *Caldwell* recklessness is that it seems to eliminate the traditional distinction between recklessness and ordinary negligence. Nonetheless, there continue to be crimes of negligence, such driving without due care and attention (see Road Traffic Act 1991, s. 2);

dangerous driving)? One possible distinction may lie in the nature of the risk, 'recklessness' referring to risks that are obvious and serious (*Lawrence*) and 'negligence' to risks that are of a lesser order; or perhaps the difference lies in the degree of departure from the standard of a reasonable person, recklessness requiring a greater departure from this standard. In support of the latter distinction, the Road Traffic Act 1991, defines driving dangerously as driving that falls *far below* what would be expected of a competent and careful driver (see Road Traffic Act 1991, s. 2A(1)(a)); there is a lesser form of culpability which consists of careless and inconsiderate driving. A further possibility is that negligence fills in the so-called lacuna in *Caldwell*, where the defendant considered the risk but incorrectly concluded that it was negligible or non-existent.

Negligence is measured by an objective standard, the failure to measure up to what the reasonable person would have done under the circumstances. It is a standard that does not vary with the individual qualities of the defendant.

McCrone v *Riding*
[1938] 1 All ER 157
King's Bench Division

The respondent was charged with driving a private motor vehicle without due care and attention contrary to the Road Traffic Act 1930, s. 12. The justices dismissed the charge, on the ground that the respondent 'was exercising all the skill and attention to be expected from a person with his short experience'.

LORD HEWART LCJ: . . . That standard is an objective standard, impersonal and universal, fixed in relation to the safety of other users of the highway. It is in no way related to the degree of proficiency or degree of experience attained by the individual driver. I think that it is made quite plain that the justices held the notion that two standards could be entertained, because they say in their findings ultimately that they were of opinion that, 'had the respondent been an ordinary driver, we would have convicted him on the information.' They add, however:

Though he failed to display such skill as would be expected from an ordinary driver under the circumstances and drove into the said pedestrian, such failure being due to his inexperience and lack of skill did not constitute such want of care and attention [as amounted to an offence].

I think, therefore, that the proper course is that the appeal should be allowed, and that the case should go back to the justices with the direction that regard must be had to the words of this statute 'without due care and attention,' and that it is wrong to assume that the word 'skill' is synonymous with the word 'care,' and that it is wrong to assume that there can be one standard for an ordinary driver and another standard for somebody else. . . .

Question
The court in *McCrone* does not ask whether the defendant exercised the due care and caution that it would be reasonable to expect from a learner driver.

Why is this not relevant? What purposes are served by applying an objective standard to all?

E Strict liability

The final group of crimes which needs to be examined consists of those which, at least on their face, appear to have no *mens rea*. These are referred to as offences of strict or (less accurately) absolute liability. Looks can be deceiving, however. While the crimes in question may appear on their face to have no *mens rea* requirement, courts have been known to interpret the statute in a way which introduces a *mens rea* requirement.

Questions
1. What policy considerations support the establishment of strict liability crimes? Are there risks to innocent individuals in such crimes? What mechanisms might be used to prevent injustice?
2. Corporate criminality is examined in Chapter 6, but anticipating an issue that arises in this context, do crimes of strict liability make more sense when the defendant is a company than they do when the defendant is an individual?

(i) Common law crimes
Strict liability offences are generally the product of statute, but there have been some common law offences that have been construed to impose strict liability. The clear implication of the common law maxim '*actus non facit reum nisi mens sit rea*' is that *mens rea* is required for all crimes. The law, however, was never this stringent, and the most that could be said is that crimes without *mens rea* were the exception (with libel and public nuisance being the most prominent examples).

Curiously, in recent years, there seems to have been a revival of prosecutions for common law crimes, in regard to which the courts have found no *mens rea* requirement.

R v Lemon; R v Gay News Ltd
[1979] 1 All ER 898
House of Lords

LORD DIPLOCK (dissenting): My Lords, the appellants are the editor and publishers of a newpaper called Gay News. As its name suggests its readership consists mainly of homosexuals though it is on sale to the general public at some bookstalls. In an issue of Gay News published in June 1976 there appeared a poem by a Professor James Kirkup entitled 'The Love that Dares to Speak its Name' and accompanied by a drawing illustrating its subject-matter. The poem purports to describe in explicit detail acts of sodomy and fellatio with the body of Christ immediately after His death and to ascribe to Him during His lifetime promiscuous homosexual practices with the Apostles and with other men.

The issue in this appeal is not whether the words and drawing are blasphemous. The jury, though only by a majority of ten to two, have found them to be so. As expressed in the charge against them they 'vilify Christ in His life and His crucifixion', and do so in terms that are likely to arouse a sense of outrage among those who believe in or respect the Christian faith and are not homosexuals and probably among many of them that are. The only question in this appeal is whether in 1976 the mental element or mens rea in the common law offence of blasphemy is satisfied by proof only of an intention to publish material which in the opinion of the jury is likely to shock and arouse resentment among believing Christians or whether the prosecution must go further and prove that the accused in publishing the material in fact intended to produce that effect on believers, or (what comes to the same thing in criminal law) although aware of the likelihood that such effect might be produced, did not care whether it was or not, so long as the publication achieved some other purpose that constituted his motive for publishing it. Wherever I speak hereafter of 'intention' I use the expression as a term of art in that extended sense. . . .

My Lords, if your Lordships were to hold that Lord Coleridge CJ and those judges who preceded and followed him in directing juries that the accused's intention to shock and arouse resentment among believing Christians was a necessary element in the offence of blasphemous libel were wrong in doing so, this would effectively exclude that particular offence from the benefit of Parliament's general substitution of the subjective for the objective test in applying the presumption that a man intends the natural consequences of his acts; and blasphemous libel would revert to the exceptional category of crimes of strict liability from which, on what is, to say the least, a plausible analysis of the contemporaneous authorities, it appeared to have escaped nearly a century ago. This would, in my view, be a retrograde step which could not be justified by any considerations of public policy.

The usual justification for creating by statute a criminal offence of strict liability, in which the prosecution need not prove mens rea as to one of the elements of the actus reus, is the threat that the actus reus of the offence poses to public health, public safety, public morals or public order. The very fact that there have been no prosecutions for blasphemous libel for more than fifty years is sufficient to dispose of any suggestion that in modern times a judicial decision to include this common law offence in this exceptional class of offences of strict liability could be justified on grounds of public morals or public order. . . .

VISCOUNT DILHORNE: In the light of the authorities to which I have referred and for the reasons I have stated, I am unable to reach the conclusion that the ingredients of the offence of publishing a blasphemous libel have changed since 1792. Indeed, it would, I think, be surprising if they had. If it be accepted, as I think it must, that that which is sought to prevent is the publication of blasphemous libels, the harm is done by their intentional publication, whether or not the publisher intended to blaspheme. To hold that it must be proved that he had that intent appears to me to be going some way to making the accused judge in his own cause. If Mr Lemon had testified that he did not regard the poem and drawing as blasphemous, that he had no intention to blaspheme, and it might be, that his intention was to promote the love and affection of some homosexuals for Our Lord, the jury properly directed would surely have been told that unless satisfied beyond reasonable doubt that he intended to blaspheme they should acquit, no matter how blasphemous they thought the publication. Whether or not they would have done so on such evidence is a matter of speculation on which views may differ.

The question we have to decide is a pure question of law and my conclusions thereon do not, I hope, evince any distrust of juries. The question here is what is the proper direction to give to them, not how they might act on such a direction; and distrust, which I do not have, of the way a jury might act, does not enter into it.

My Lords, for the reasons I have stated in my opinion the question certified should be answered in the affirmative. Guilt of the offence of publishing a blasphemous libel does not depend on the accused having an intent to blaspheme but on proof that the publication was intentional (or, in the case of a bookseller, negligent (Lord Campbell's Libel Act 1843)) and that the matter published was blasphemous.

I would dismiss these appeals.

Appeals dismissed.

Note

Note that in *Lemon* the jury still had to find that the defendants' acts were intentional – what we have termed a voluntary *actus reus*. For this reason, that the prosecution must still prove an intentional *actus reus*, it is sometimes said that strict liability is not absolute liability. But note carefully what their lordships have done. In construing the intent to shock or outrage Christians or outrage public decency in the way that they did, the court in effect reduced the Crown's burden to proof that the defendants' acts were not involuntary. But the Crown was already under the burden of proving a voluntary *actus reus*. Thus the court's decision removed the *mens rea* element from the respective crimes. See also *R v Gibson and Another* [1991] 1 All ER 439 (supra, p. 35).

(ii) Statutory offences

The common law crimes cited in the previous section notwithstanding, the overwhelming bulk of modern crimes which purport to eliminate *mens rea* are the creation of statute. The issue which has confronted the courts is one of statutory interpretation – whether to read into a statute as a matter of interpretation a *mens rea* element that does not appear on the face of the statute.

The hallmark of the decisions does not appear to be consistency. Sometimes the judicial analysis begins and ends with the words of the statute; but at other times the courts take a less literal and more functional approach, looking at the purpose to be served by the statute. It is also not uncommon to find courts proclaiming that they are merely implementing Parliamentary intent, but until quite recently the courts would not allow themselves to look at Parliamentary debates, white papers or other official reports to determine Parliamentary intent. (See Chapter 1.)

As well as the general conflict between a literal and a functional approach to statutory interpretation, one can identify conflicts relating to specific interpretative guides. The evil to be eradicated is often cited as a factor in imposing strict liability, with the implication that the greater the evil, the more likely the statute will be found to impose strict liability. This rationale was used to justify strict liability for offences involving drugs (see *Yeandel v Fisher* [1966] 1 QB 440). But in other cases the courts reason that because strict liability offences are not true crimes and carry little stigma, it is not necessary to put the Crown to the inconvenience and expense of proving *mens rea*. In construing a statute to require *mens rea*, the courts may point to the fact that there was nothing more that the defendant could have done to avoid liability; but when they want liability to be strict they say that such considerations are irrelevant. Sometimes the courts will compare the wording of a specific provision of a statute with other parts of the same statute or comparable statutes; but at other times they will simply brush aside any striking change of expression as being entitled to no weight.

'If a statute contains words expressive of a *mens rea* element – such as 'intentionally', 'recklessly', or 'knowingly' – the courts will not construe the statute to be one of strict liability. To do so would be in clear contradiction of Parliamentary intent. Sometimes, however, whether a verb or adverb carries connotations of *mens rea* is not all that clear.

James & Son Ltd v *Smee*; *Green* v *Burnett*
[1955] 1 QB 78
Court of Appeal

By regulation 101 of the Motor Vehicles (Construction and Use) Regulations 1951, 'If any person uses or causes or permits to be used on any road a motor vehicle or trailer in contravention of or fails to comply with any of the preceding regulations . . . he shall for each offence be liable to a fine . . . '

The prohibition in regulation 101 of user in contravention of regulation 75 is an absolute one in the sense that no mens rea, apart from user, need be shown to constitute the offence; but to 'permit' the use in contravention of the regulation imports a state of mind.

Where, therefore, in one case a limited company was charged with 'using' a motor-vehicle with a defective braking system contrary to regulations 75 and 101 when the defect in the brakes arose from circumstances over which they had no control; and in another case a limited company were charged with 'permitting' a motor-vehicle and trailer to be used with a defective braking system contrary to regulations 75 and 101 when the defect was solely due to the fault of their servants:-

Held that, since a master used his vehicle if it was used by his servant, the company charged with 'using' a vehicle in contravention of regulation 75 was guilty of the offence charged; but that (Slade J dissenting) before a company could be held guilty of permitting a user in contravention of the regulation it must be proved that some person 'permitted' as opposed to 'committed' the offence, and, there being no evidence of any such permission by a responsible officer of the company, the company charged with 'permitting' the use was not guilty of an offence.

Note
Even if a court construes a statute to require proof of *mens rea*, it may limit the requirement of proof of *mens rea* to a particular element of the offence, and hold that in regard to some other element there is strict liability.

Cotterill v *Penn*
[1936] 1 KB 53
King's Bench Division

LORD HEWART CJ: This is a case stated by justices for the county of Worcester arising out of an information preferred by the appellant against the respondent under the Larceny Act 1861, s. 23, for unlawfully and wilfully killing a pigeon in such circumstances as did not amount to larceny at common law. . . .

Section 23 of the Larceny Act 1861, which is a compendious section, provides that: 'Whosoever shall unlawfully and wilfully kill, wound, or take any house dove or pigeon under such circumstances as shall not amount to larceny at common law, shall, on conviction,' pay a penalty.

One contention on behalf of the respondent was that to sustain a change under the section it is necessary to prove that the pigeon was killed or taken with felonious intent. In my opinion, although the section says 'unlawfully and wilfully,' it does not require the element of mens rea beyond the point that the facts must show an intention on the part of the person accused to do the act forbidden, which was here that of shooting. It seems to me to be immaterial that the bird which the respondent shot was of a different kind from that which he thought that he was shooting. If the section had used the word 'maliciously,' the state of mind of the person charged would have been relevant. But using the terms 'unlawfully and wilfully' the section seems to me only to mean that the person accused intended to shoot and that the shooting was without a lawful excuse.

Another contention for the respondent was that he was entitled to kill the pigeon if he thought that it was a wood pigeon which might damage his crops, and the justices, adopting that contention, were of opinion that he was not liable, inasmuch as he shot the pigeon honestly believing it to be a wood pigeon about to feed off his crops. He shot the pigeon not because it was actually damaging his crops, but because he thought that it might or would do so – an event which was purely hypothetical. It seems to me to be an undue straining of the authorities to say that an apprehension of danger which may or may not turn out to be real is a lawful excuse. If such an extension of the principle were to be permitted one wonders where the process would end.

Notes and questions

1.   Cotterill's belief that the bird in question was a wild pigeon was held to be irrelevant. The approach is similar to that which we saw in *Lemon*. What the court has done is to limit the *mens rea* so that it applies only to the *actus reus* and not to the critical circumstances of the offence. But in that sense does *mens rea* add anything to the requirement of a voluntary *actus reus*, which the Crown is already under a duty to prove?

2.   While courts will not abrogate a *mens rea* element where Parliament has clearly included one, the converse is not true. The courts may read in a mental element although the wording of the statute contains none on its face. But when will (should) they do so? Compare the following factually similar cases:

Cundy v *Le Cocq*
(1884) 13 QBD 207
Queen's Bench Division

The Licensing Act, 1872, s. 13, makes it an offence for any licensed person to sell any intoxicating liquor to any drunken person. A publican sold intoxicating liquor to a drunken person who had given no indication of intoxication, and without being aware that the person so served was drunk.

STEPHEN J: I am of opinion that this conviction should be affirmed. Our answer to the question put to us turns upon this, whether the words of the section under which the conviction took place, taken in connection with the general scheme of the Act, should be read as constituting an offence only where the licensed person knows or has means of knowing that the person served with intoxicating liquor is drunk, or whether the offence is complete where no such knowledge is shewn. I am of opinion that the words of the section amount to an absolute prohibition of the sale of liquor to a drunken person, and that the existence of a bonâ fide mistake as to the condition of the person served is not an answer to the charge, but is a matter only for mitigation of the penalties that may be imposed. I am led to that conclusion both by the general scope of the Act, which is for the repression of drunkenness, and from a comparison of the various sections under the head 'offences against public order.' Some of these contain the word 'knowingly,' as for instance s. 14, which deals with keeping a disorderly house, and s. 16, which deals with the penalty for harbouring a constable. Knowledge in these and other cases is an element in the offence; but the clause we are considering says nothing about the knowledge of the state of the person served. I believe the reason for making this prohibition absolute was that there must be a great temptation to a publican to sell liquor without regard to the sobriety of the customer, and it was thought right to put upon the publican the responsibility of determining whether his customer is sober. Against this view we have had quoted the maxim that in every criminal offence there must be a guilty mind; but I do not think that maxim has so wide an application as it is sometimes considered to have. In old time, and as applicable to the common law or to earlier statutes, the maxim may have been of general application; but a difference has arisen owing to the greater precision of modern statutes.

Sherras v *De Rutzen*
[1895] 1 QB 918
Queen's Bench Division

Section 16(2), of the Licensing Act 1872, which prohibits a licensed victualler from supplying liquor to a police constable while on duty, does not apply where the licensed victualler bonâ fide believes that the police constable is off duty.

DAY J: I am clearly of opinion that this conviction ought to be quashed. This police constable comes into the appellant's house without his armlet, and with every appearance of being off duty. The house was in the immediate neighbourhood of the police-station, and the appellant believed, and he had very natural grounds for believing, that the constable was off duty. In that belief he accordingly served him with liquor. As a matter of fact, the constable was on duty; but does that fact make the innocent act of the appellant an offence? I do not think it does. He had no intention to do a wrongful act and acted in the bonâ fide belief that the constable was off duty. It seems to me that the contention that he committed an offence is utterly erroneous. An argument has been based on the appearance of the word 'knowingly' in sub-s. 1 of s. 16, and its omission in sub-s. 2. In my opinion the only effect of this is to shift the burden of proof. In cases under sub-s. 1 it is for the prosecution to prove the knowledge, while in cases under sub-s. 2 the defendant has to prove that he did not know. That is the only inference I draw from the insertion of the word 'knowingly' in the one sub-section and its omission in the other.

It appears to me that it would be straining the law to say that this publican, acting as he did in the bonâ fide belief that the constable was off duty, and having reasonable grounds for that belief, was nevertheless guilty of an offence against the section, for which he was liable both to a penalty and to have his licence indorsed.

Notes and questions
1.   Notice the similarities between these two cases – both involved publicans; both defendants served liquor to persons whom they were forbidden to serve by statute; both profited from the sales; and both pleaded mistake in defence. It is further not in society's interest that either officers of the law or those already in a state of inebriation should be served alcoholic drinks. Yet Sherras was successful in his defence where Le Cocq was not. Why? What is the difference between the two cases which justifies a difference in result?
2.   If an offence is truly one of strict liability, the defendant will be liable despite having done everything and more that a reasonable person would have done under the circumstances. Thus if serving an on-duty constable was a strict liability crime, the publican would be guilty even if he enquired whether the constable was on duty and received a negative reply. He would also be liable if a stranger entered the pub and ordered a drink, if it should turn out that the stranger was an on-duty constable.

Sometimes courts will ask what, if any, purpose would be served by imposing strict liability.

Lim Chin Aik v R
[1963] 1 All ER 224
Judicial Committee of the Privy Council

For the facts and holding, see p. 71.

Questions
1.   Did the defendant in *Lim Chin Aik* break the law intentionally, recklessly, or negligently? Should this matter if the statute is one of strict liability?
2.   The court in *Lim Chin Aik* had to deal with the statutory argument which we have seen previously – that other sections of the relevant ordinance spoke of knowing violations and this one did not. What does the court have to say on this issue?

Probably the most important decision to date on strict liability is *Sweet* v *Parsley*:

Sweet v Parsley
[1970] AC 133
House of Lords

By section 5 of the Dangerous Drugs Act, 1965:

If a person – (a) being the occupier of any premises, permits those premises to be used for the purpose of smoking . . . cannabis resin . . . or

(b) is concerned in the management of any premises used for any such purpose as aforesaid; he shall be guilty of an offence against this Act.

The appellant, the sub-tenant of a farmhouse, let out several rooms to tenants who shared the use of the kitchen. She herself retained and occupied a bedroom. Later she gave up living there, though she came occasionally to collect letters and rent. On June 11, 1967, quantities of drugs, including cannabis resin, were found in the farmhouse and the appellant was charged with being concerned in the management of premises used for the purpose of smoking cannabis resin, contrary to section 5(b) of this Act. The appellant conceded that the premises had been so used. The prosecutor conceded that she did not know this. She was convicted of the offence.

LORD REID: . . . My Lords, a Divisional Court dismissed her appeal, holding that she had been concerned in the management of those premises. The reasons given for holding that she was managing the property were that she was in a position to choose her tenants: that she could put them under as long or as short a tenancy as she desired: and that she could make it a term of any letting that smoking of cannabis was not to take place. All these reasons would apply to every occupier who lets out parts of his house or takes in lodgers or paying guests. But this was held to be an absolute offence, following the earlier decision in *Yeandel* v *Fisher* [1966] 1 QB 440.

How has it come about that the Divisional Court has felt bound to reach such an obviously unjust result? It has in effect held that it was carrying out the will of Parliament because Parliament has chosen to make this an absolute offence. And, of course, if Parliament has so chosen the courts must carry out its will, and they cannot be blamed for any unjust consequences. But has Parliament so chosen?

. . .

Our first duty is to consider the words of the Act: if they show a clear intention to create an absolute offence that is an end of the matter. But such cases are very rare. Sometimes the words of the section which creates a particular offence make it clear that mens rea is required in one form or another. Such cases are quite frequent. But in a very large number of cases there is no clear indication either way. In such cases there has for centuries been a presumption that Parliament did not intend to make criminals of persons who were in no way blameworthy in what they did. That means that whenever a section is silent as to mens rea there is a presumption that, in order to give effect to the will of Parliament, we must read in words appropriate to require mens rea.

. . .

It is also firmly established that the fact that other sections of the Act expressly require mens rea, for example because they contain the word 'knowingly,' is not in itself sufficient to justify a decision that a section which is silent as to mens rea creates an absolute offence. In the absence of a clear indication in the Act that an offence is intended to be an absolute offence, it is necessary to go outside the Act and examine all relevant circumstances in order to establish that this must have been the intention of Parliament. I say 'must have been' because it is a universal principle that if a penal provision is reasonably capable of two interpretations, that interpretation which is most favourable to the accused must be adopted.

What, then, are the circumstances which it is proper to take into account? In the well known case of *Sherras* v *De Rutzen* [1895] 1 QB 918 Wright J only mentioned the subject matter with which the Act deals. But he was there dealing with something which was one of a class of acts which 'are not criminal in any real sense, but are acts which in the public interest are prohibited under a penalty' (p. 922). It does not in the least follow that when one is dealing with a truly criminal act it is sufficient merely to have regard to the subject matter of the enactment. One must put oneself in the position of a legislator. It has long been the practice to recognise absolute offences in this class of quasi-criminal acts, and one can safely assume that, when Parliament is passing new legislation dealing with this class of offences, its silence as to mens rea means that the old practice is to apply. But when one comes to acts of a truly criminal character, it appears to me that there are at least two other factors which any reasonable legislator would have in mind. In the first place a stigma still attaches to any person convicted of a truly criminal offence, and the more serious or more disgraceful the offence the greater the stigma. So he would have to consider whether, in a case of this gravity, the public interest really requires that an innocent person should be prevented from proving his innocence in order that fewer guilty men may escape. And equally important is the fact that fortunately the Press in this country are vigilant to expose injustice and every manifestly unjust conviction made known to the public tends to injure the body politic by undermining public confidence in the justice of the law and of its administration. But I regret to observe that, in some recent cases where serious offences have been held to be absolute offences, the court has taken into account no more than the wording of the Act and the character and seriousness of the mischief which constitutes the offence.

The choice would be much more difficult if there were no other way open than either mens rea in the full sense or an absolute offence; for there are many kinds of case where putting on the prosecutor the full burden of proving mens rea creates great difficulties and may lead to many unjust acquittals. But there are at least two other possibilities. Parliament has not infrequently transferred the onus as regards mens rea to the accused, so that, once the necessary facts are proved, he must convince the jury that on balance of probabilities he is innocent of any criminal intention. I find it a little surprising that more use has not been made of this method: but one of the bad effects of the decision of this House in *Woolmington* v *Director of Public Prosecutions* [1935] AC 462 may have been to discourage its use. The other method would be in effect to substitute in appropriate classes of cases gross negligence for mens rea in the full sense as the mental element necessary to constitute the crime. It would often be much easier to infer that Parliament must have meant that gross negligence should be the necessary mental element than to infer that Parliament intended to create an absolute offence. A variant of this would be to accept the view of Cave J in *R* v *Tolson* (1889) 23 QBD 168, 181. This appears to have been done in Australia where authority appears to support what Dixon J said in *Proudman* v *Dayman* (1941) 67 CLR 536, 540:

> As a general rule an honest and reasonable belief in a state of facts which, if they existed, would make the defendant's act innocent affords an excuse for doing what would otherwise be an offence.

It may be that none of these methods is wholly satisfactory but at least the public scandal of convicting on a serious charge persons who are in no way blameworthy would be avoided.

If this section means what the Divisional Court have held that it means, then hundreds of thousands of people who sublet part of their premises or take in lodgers or are concerned in the management of residential premises or institutions are daily incurring a risk of being convicted of a serious offence in circumstances where they are in no way to blame. For the greatest vigilance cannot prevent tenants, lodgers or inmates or guests whom they bring in from smoking cannabis cigarettes in their own rooms. It was suggested in argument that this appellant brought this conviction on herself because it is found as a fact that when the police searched the premises there were people there of the 'beatnik fraternity.' But surely it would be going a very long way to say that persons managing premises of any kind ought to safeguard themselves by refusing accommodation to all who are of slovenly or exotic appearance, or who bring in guests of that kind. And unfortunately drug taking is by no means confined to those of unusual appearance.

Notes and questions

1. Lord Reid says that if a statute contains no *mens rea* on its face, the presumption should be that proof of *mens rea* is intended. Why should a court engage in this presumption rather than the opposite one – that Parliament meant what it said and did not intend to require the Crown to be put to the proof of *mens rea*? Is not the latter presumption more logical? Is not the absence of words of *mens rea* themselves a *clear indication*, in Lord Reid's words, of the intent to omit *mens rea*?

2. If a court is to presume *mens rea* when a statute is silent, what *mens rea* should it presume – intent, knowledge of circumstances, recklessness, negligence? Since the statute is silent, how is the court to choose? Interestingly, the House of Lords in *Sweet* was not prepared to adopt a negligence standard, deeming the choice to lie between no *mens rea* or some form of traditional *mens rea*. Is the court's reasoning on this point persuasive?

3. The reluctance of the court to adopt a negligence standard makes even less sense when placed against the assertions of several of their Lordships that Ms Sweet had taken appropriate steps to inform herself of the true state of affairs, and that it would be unfair to punish her when there had been no showing that she had been anything but diligent. Is this not in effect saying that she was not negligent? Had it been proved that she had been negligent, on the other hand, in, say, turning a blind eye to the strange and sweet-smelling aroma which was emanating from the farmhouse and which was making her giddy, would their Lordships have strained so to avoid holding her liable?

4. Lord Reid draws a distinction between truly criminal acts and those which are illegal only because the public welfare so demands. Is this distinction a viable one? How does a court determine whether an offence falls into the true crime or the public welfare category? Into which camp did Ms Sweet's offence fall?

5. Taking a functional approach to the issue of strict liability, what sense would strict liability make in a case like Sweet's? What is a landlord to do to prevent violations?

6. In *Sweet* several of their lordships suggested a middle position between traditional *mens rea* and strict liability, which would be to allow the Crown to establish its case without proof of *mens rea*, but to permit the defendant to have a defence of due diligence or reasonable care. What are the relative merits of such an approach? Note that, unlike in the case of offences, most defences are created by the courts. Their lordships, had they wanted, could have created a defence of due diligence without infringing on Parliamentary sovereignty. Such a defence of due diligence was adopted by the Canadian Supreme Court

in *R* v *City of Sault Ste Marie* (1978) 85 DLR (3d) 161. Furthermore, some statutes, such as the Trade Descriptions Act 1968, s 24(1), the Weights and Measures Act 1985, s. 34, and the Food Safety Act 1991, s. 21, incorporate a due diligence defence.

For those who feared that *Sweet* represented a step on the road to abolition of all strict liability offences, reassurance came in *Pharmaceutical Society of Great Britain* v *Storkwain Ltd:*

Pharmaceutical Society of Great Britain v *Storkwain*
[1986] 2 All ER 635
House of Lords

LORD GOFF OF CHIEVELEY: My Lords, this appeal is concerned with a question of construction of s. 58 of the Medicines Act 1968. Section 58(2)(a) of that Act provides as follows:

> Subject to the following provisions of this section – (a) no person shall sell by retail, or supply in circumstances corresponding to retail sale, a medicinal product of a description, or falling within a class, specified in an order under this section except in accordance with a prescription given by an appropriate practitioner . . .

By s. 67(2) of the 1968 Act it is provided that any person who contravenes, inter alia, s. 58 shall be guilty of an offence. The question which has arisen for decision in the present case is whether, in accordance with the well-recognised presumption, there are to be read into s. 58(2)(a) words appropriate to require mens rea, on the principle stated in *R* v *Tolson* (1889) 23 QBD 168, [1886–90] All ER Rep 26 and *Sweet* v *Parsley* [1969] 1 All ER 347, [1970] AC 132.

The matter has arisen in the following way. On 2 February 1984 informations were preferred by the respondents, the Pharmaceutical Society of Great Britain, against the appellants, Storkwain Ltd, alleging that the appellants had on 14 December 1982 unlawfully sold by retail certain medicines. It was alleged that they unlawfully sold by retail, to a person purporting to be Linda Largey, 200 Physeptone tablets and 50 Ritalin tablets, and further that they unlawfully sold by retail, to a person purporting to be Thomas J. Paterson, 50 ampoules of Physeptone and 30 Valium tablets. All these medicines are substances controlled under art. 3(1)(b) of the Medicines (Prescription Only) Order 1980, SI 1980/1921; and the informations alleged in each case that the sale was not in accordance with a prescription issued by an appropriate practitioner, contrary to ss. 58(2) and 67(2) of the 1968 Act. Before the magistrate, the evidence (which was all agreed) was to the effect that the medicines were supplied under documents which purported to be prescriptions signed by a doctor, Dr Irani, of Queensdale Road, London, but that subsequent inquiries revealed that the prescriptions were both forgeries. It was submitted on behalf of the appellants that the presumption of mens rea applied to the prohibition in s. 58(2)(a) of the 1968 Act and that, the medicines having been supplied by the appellants on the basis of prescriptions which they believed in good faith and on reasonable grounds to be valid prescriptions, the informations should be dismissed. The magistrate accepted that submission and accordingly dismissed the informations: but he stated a case for the opinion of the High Court, the question for the opinion of the court being whether or not mens rea was required in the case of a prosecution under ss. 58(2) and 67(2) of the 1968 Act. On 2

May 1985 a Divisional Court (Farquharson and Tudor Price JJ) ([1985] 3 All ER 4 answered the question in the negative, and accordingly allowed the appeal of the respondents and directed that the case should be remitted to the magistrate with a direction to convict. The Divisional Court certified the following point of law as being of general public importance:

> Whether the prosecution have to prove mens rea where an information is laid under Section 58(2)(a) of the Medicines Act 1968 where the allegation is that the supply of 'prescription only' drugs was made by the [defendant] in accordance with a forged prescription and without fault on [his] part.

From that decision, the appellants now appeal with leave of your Lordships' House, the Divisional Court having refused leave.

For the appellants, counsel submitted that there must, in accordance with the well-recognised presumption, be read into s. 58(2)(a) words appropriate to require mens rea in accordance with *R v Tolson* (1889) 23 QBD 168, [1886–90] All ER Rep 26; in other words, to adopt the language of Lord Diplock in *Sweet v Parsley* [1969] 1 All ER 347 at 361, [1970] AC 132 at 163, the subsection must be read subject to the implication that a necessary element in the prohibition (and hence in the offence created by the subsection together with s. 67(2) of the 1968 Act) is the absence of belief, held honestly and on reasonable grounds, in the existence of facts which, if true, would make the act innocent. He further submitted, with reference to the speech of Lord Reid in *Sweet v Parsley* [1969] 1 All ER 347 at 350, [1970] AC 132 at 149, that the offence created by ss. 58(2(a) and 67(2) of the 1968 Act was not to be classified as merely an offence of a quasi-criminal character in which the presumption of mens rea might more readily be rebutted, because in his submission the offence was one which would result in a stigma attaching to a person who was convicted of it, especially as Parliament had regarded it as sufficiently serious to provide that it should be triable on indictment, and that the maximum penalty should be two years' imprisonment. He also submitted that, if Parliament had considered that a pharmacist who dispensed under a forged prescription in good faith and without fault should be convicted of the offence, it would surely have made express provision to that effect: and that the imposition of so strict a liability could not be justified on the basis that it would tend towards greater efficiency on the part of pharmacists in detecting forged prescriptions. Finally, he referred your Lordships to the Misuse of Drugs Act 1971. Under s. 4(1) and (3) of that Act it is an offence to supply a controlled drug to another: but it is provided in s. 28 that subject to an immaterial exception) it shall be a defence for the accused to prove that he neither knew of nor suspected nor had reason to suspect the existence of some fact alleged by the prosecution which it is necessary for the prosecution to prove if he is to be convicted of the offence charged. Counsel for the appellants submitted that it would be anomalous if such a defence were available in the case of the more serious offence of supplying a controlled drug to another, but that the presumption of mens rea should be held inapplicable in the case of the offence created by ss. 58(2)(a) and 67(2) of the 1968 Act.

I am unable to accept counsel's submission, for the simple reason that it is, in my opinion, clear from the 1968 Act that Parliament must have intended that the presumption of mens rea should be inapplicable to s. 58(2)(a). First of all, it appears from the 1968 Act that, where Parliament wished to recognise that mens rea should be an ingredient of an offence created by the Act, it has expressly so provided. Thus, taking first of all offences created under provisions of Pt II of the 1968 Act, express requirements of mens rea are to be found both in s. 45(2) and in s. 46(1), (2) and (3) of the Act. More particularly, in relation to offences created by Pt III and Pts V and VI of the 1968 Act, s. 121 makes detailed provision for a requirement of mens rea in respect of certain specified sections of the act, including ss. 63 to 65 (which are contained in Pt III), but significantly not s. 58, nor indeed ss. 52 and 53. I have already set out the full text of s. 121 and need not repeat it. It is very difficult to avoid the conclusion that, by omitting s. 58 from those sections to which s. 121 is expressly made applicable, Parliament intended that there should be no implication of a requirement of mens rea in s. 58(2)(a). This view is fortified by sub-ss. (4) and (5) of s. 58 itself. Subsection (4)(a) provides that any order made by the appropriate ministers for the purposes of s. 58 may provide that s. 58(2)(a) or (b), or both, shall have effect subject to such exemptions as may be specified in the order. From this subsection alone it follows that the ministers, if they think it right, can provide for exemption where there is no mens rea on the part of the accused. Subsection (5) provides that any exemption conferred by an order in accordance with sub-s(4)(a) may be conferred subject to such conditions or limitations as may be specified in the order. From this it follows that, if the ministers, acting under sub-s. (4), were to confer an exemption relating to sales where the vendor lacked the requisite mens rea, they may nevertheless circumscribe their exemption with conditions and limitations which render the exemption far narrower than the implication for which counsel for the appellants contends should be read into the statute itself. I find this to be very difficult to reconcile with the proposed implication.

It comes as no surprise to me, therefore, to discover that the relevant order in force at that time, the Medicines (Prescriptions Only) Order 1980, is drawn entirely in conformity with the construction of the statute which I favour. It is unnecessary, in the present case, to consider whether the relevant articles of the order may be taken into account in construing s. 58 of the 1968 Act; it is enough, for present purposes, that I am able to draw support from the fact that the ministers, in making the order, plainly did not read s. 58 as subject to the implication proposed by counsel for the appellants. . . .

Question
Did the court reach a just result? Are there considerations of public policy present in the context of the case which might incline a court towards strict liability?

Notes
1.   There is an additional aspect of *Storkwain* worth noting. When a statute is aimed at those in a particular trade, business or profession, there is a greater willingness to construe a regulatory provision to require strict liability. Those in the trade can be presumed to have made a conscious choice to enter it. If they do not like the idea of strict liability, they can earn their living in some other way. Those who choose to continue in the trade, business or profession are expected to be aware of and fully conversant with the statutes which affect them, and how those statutes are interpreted by the courts.
2.   Under the Draft Criminal Code Bill 1989, *mens rea* is presumed and strict liability can be imposed only if Parliament expressly or impliedly so provides. See Commentary on Draft Criminal Code Bill, Clause 20. Many would have preferred it if the drafters had stopped after 'expressly'.

4 CAUSATION AND CONCURRENCE

I Causation

A Introduction

Some crimes are defined such that the offence consists of wrongful conduct accompanied by a wrongful state of mind. No harmful result need occur. Examples include perjury (neither the judge nor the jury need believe the perjurer's lies) and dangerous driving (no accident need result from defendant's driving). Other crimes, however, have as a requirement that a certain result occur. Examples include homicide, where a human being must be killed, and arson, where there must be some damage to property. In crimes defined in terms of results, the prosecution must prove beyond a reasonable doubt that the defendant's acts caused the harmful result.

The term 'causation' is an unfortunate one. The criminal law is not really concerned with causation at all but with whether it is fair and just to hold a particular defendant responsible for a particular result. Sometimes the answer to this question is 'yes' because the defendant caused the result. But sometimes the answer is 'yes' although we cannot really say in any strictly logical sense that the defendant caused the result.

The issue most commonly arises in homicide. A person has set out to cause death, and the intended victim has died. The issue may at first blush seem straightforward but often it is complicated by intervening events. For example, X shoots Y. An ambulance is summoned and Y is rushed to a hospital. On the way to the hospital, the ambulance is struck by a car which is being recklessly driven by Z. All in the ambulance, including Y, are killed. Who caused Y's death – X, but for whose assault Y would not have been in the ambulance, or Z? Or what if the ambulance arrives safely at the hospital, but an incompetent doctor botches a simple operation which would have saved Y's life? Who caused Y's death – X or the doctor? Or what if the operation is successful, but Y subsequently contracts pneumonia due to a combination of his weakened condition and his own failure to take adequate care of himself? Or what if the hospital is struck by lightning and Y dies in the ensuing blaze?

The question of causation becomes even more complex when the *actus reus* is an omission. We looked at this type of case in Chapter 2. Say that a lifeguard fails to rescue a child in waters which were under the lifeguard's control. Because he was under a legal, and not just a moral, duty to save the child, the lifeguard has committed an *actus reus*. But in what sense can it be said that the lifeguard caused the child's death? Let us examine this hypothetical more closely, for it points out several features of causation:

(a) The coroner's report will read 'death by drowning'. The doctor who performs an autopsy will not be able to say whose acts caused that death. The point is that medical cause should not be confused with legal cause. Medical cause is concerned with *what* caused the death; legal cause is concerned with *who* caused the death.

(b) There are often multiple causes of a result. One cause of the child's death was the child's inability to swim. Another was the lifeguard's failure to rescue the child. If others were present who could have saved the child, must they too be considered as part of the cause of the child's death? The death may further be traced back to the parent's decision to send the child to the pool unaccompanied. As a practical matter the legal system will sift through these various contributors to the child's death, and will single out one to hold criminally responsible for the death.

(c) To hold a defendant criminally liable for a death one must at a minimum be able to say that 'but for' that person's action or inaction, the death would not have resulted. However, 'but for' or *sine qua non* causation, while *necessary* to justify criminal liability, is not *sufficient* to justify criminal liability. There may be, as we have just seen, an infinite number of 'but for' causes – but for the lifeguard's inaction, the child would not have drowned; but for the parents' decision to send the child to the pool, the child would be alive; but for an earlier decision not to provide the child with swimming lessons, the child would have been capable of staying afloat; but for the parents' decision to conceive the child, etc., etc. Obviously a line must be drawn somewhere, and equally obviously most of the 'but for' causes will be legally irrelevant. *Sine qua non* or 'but for' causation is a *necessary but not a sufficient condition* of criminal liability. It would be improper to convict somebody of a result crime if we cannot say that but for that person's actions the result would have occurred; but the fact that we can say that but for defendant's actions the result would not have occurred is not enough to justify a conviction.

The cause beyond 'but for' cause that is necessary for criminal liability is sometimes called legal or proximate cause. The term 'legal', however, seems tautologous, and the term 'proximate' is positively misleading. If A sends a letter bomb through the post to B, the fact that it does not arrive until two months later will not break the chain of causation. Nor will the postman who delivers the letter be liable, even though his acts are most proximate to the victim's death. The real issue is one of imputability or attribution – is it fair and just to attribute the bad result to a particular defendant's act or failure to act, as the case may be? Recognition that this is the real issue in one sense advances our enquiry and in one sense does not. It advances our enquiry in that it directs our attention to questions other than the narrow one of simply whether the defendant's acts caused the result in question. It does not, however, tell us when it would be fair and just to attribute the bad result to the defendant. The student should be aware that a statement that a defendant caused a harmful result is often a shorthand way of stating a conclusion rather than providing an explanation.

There are therefore two questions which must be answered in the affirmative before a defendant can be said to have caused a harmful result:

(a)   But for the defendant's action or inaction, would the harmful result have occurred?

(b)   Should the defendant's action be deemed the legal cause of the harmful result?

A classic work on the subject is H.L.A. Hart and Tony Honore, *Causation in the Law* (2nd edn) (1985).

B   *'But for' causation*

'But for' or *sine qua non* cause (sometimes also referred to as cause in fact) is, as we have said, a necessary but not sufficient condition of liability. Consider, for example, the case of theft by deception, where it must be shown that it was the defendant's deception which caused the victim to part with his property.

R v Hensler
[1861–73] All ER Rep Ext 1806

The attempt to obtain money by false pretences was made by the writing and sending of a letter to John Hutton, Esq., M.P., for Northallerton.

This letter dated 23 October 1869, is as follows: —

Southampton, 23 October, 1869.

Honered Sir, – I humbly hope you will pardon the liberty a poor ship-wrecked widow, the native of Northallerton, as taking, in thus addressing you, I beg to state I was proceeding to Sydney, New South Wales, with my husband and four children, thinking of bettering my condition, but fortune proved unkind, and cast me with my poor orphans ashore in France, and my husband to the boundless deep.

Sir, I have no friends at Northallerton to appeal to, as they all emigrated some years ago, and sir, it is useless me returning home as the workhouse would be my doom, all I want is a outfit, my passage being secured, and to effect that purpose the British Consul at Boulogne as most kindly granted me the enclosed certificate to appeal to the humane and benevolent, one of my children is lying in a dying state owing to the injuries it received at the time of the melancholy catastrophe. Sir, if your late much respected father was living, he would know me, and knowing your family's humane and tender feelings to the truly unfortunate, humbly do I trust you will be so kind as to take my distressed case into your kind consideration, and sir, you will have the prayers of a poor shipwrecked widow and orphans when far away on the ocean. Sir, I have part towards accomplishing my wishes. I will not take up your time with a further detail of my distresses, but will not forget to acknowledge your kindness when I reach my destination. – I am, Honered Sir, your humble and obedient servant,

ELLEN HOLMES

P.S., – Honered sir, I am waiting your kind and benevolent answer by return of post, as I cannot appeal to any person without my certificate. Sir, please to address to 'ELLEN HOLMES, 12 Simbol Street, Southampton.'

This letter was addressed for, 'John Hutton, Esq., M.P., Sowler Hill, Northallerton, Yorks.'

With it was enclosed a certificate purporting to be a confirmation of the facts contained in this letter, and to be signed by the English Consul at Boulogne.

Mr Hutton in answer to this letter sent a post office order for 5s., he also received two other letters dated 30 October, which are as follows:

12 Simbol Street, Southampton.
30 October, 1869.

Honered Sir, – The poor shipwrecked family of the name of Ellen Holmes, that enclosed the British Consuls certificate to your honour and did not receive it back, being in a most destitute state not having sufficient to obtain a outfit and, Sir, I cannot make application without my certificate humbly do I trust you will be so kind as to return it, and your kind answer, as it is useless me returning home to Northallerton, to which place I am a native, one of my children is lying very ill owing to the injuries it received at the time of the melancholy catastrophe. I am, honered sir, your humble and obedient servant,

ELLEN HOLMES.

12, Simbol Street, Southampton, Hants.
Southampton, 30 October, 1869.

Honered Sir, – Thinking you had mislaid my certificate, I wrote to you this morning, since which time I received your letter together with my certificate and a post office order for 5s., and with heartfelt gratitude I return my sincere thanks, and, sir, you will have the prayers of the widow and orphans when far away on the ocean. I am honered sir, your humble and obedient servant,

ELLEN HOLMES.

To J. Hutton, Esq., M.P.

Both these letters were addressed, 'John Hutton, Esq., M.P., Sowler Hill, Northallerton, Yorks.'

Mr Hutton on his examination, stated that he knew that the statements contained in the letter of 23 October were untrue.

The counsel for the prisoner objected, on the authority of *R* v *Mills* (1857) 26 LJ MC 79, that inasmuch as Mr Hutton knew the falsehood of the pretences made in the letter of 23 October, the prisoner could not be convicted for attempting to obtain money from Mr Hutton by false pretences.

. . .

Notes

1. If counsel's assertions were correct, i.e., the victim knew that the defendant was not telling the truth, then it could not be said that her deceptions were the cause of his parting with his money. Perhaps for this reason the defendant was convicted of an attempt to obtain money by false pretences. Would the result have been the same if the victim suspected, but did not know, that the defendant was lying?

2. In a case of a homicide, if it can be shown that the defendant's acts were not the cause of the death, then the defendant cannot be convicted of murder, even where he had the intent to kill. See *R v White* [1910] 2 KB 124. He can, on the other hand, be guilty of attempted murder. It is only the result crime which is affected by the failure of proof of causation.

Even if a result would not have occurred but for a defendant's acts, it is appropriate to ask to what extent the defendant's acts contributed to the result. An old Latin maxim holds that *de minimis non curat lex* (the law does not care about trifles). The critical question then is, how much must a defendant's acts have contributed to the harmful result before the law will take notice? Compare the following cases:

R v Cato and Others
[1976] 1 All ER 260
Court of Appeal

LORD WIDGERY CJ: . . . The victim was a young man called Anthony Farmer. The events leading up to his death occurred on 25th July 1974. On that day Cato and Farmer had been in each other's company for most of the day. The evidence suggests certain intervals when they were apart, but by and large they seem to have been together all that day, and they spent much of the day with Morris and Dudley as well. All four of them at that time were living at a house called 34 Russell Street, and on 25th July their activities brought them to the Crown public house where they were until closing time, and after closing time they went back to 34 Russell Street.

There were others living in the house. They went to bed, and the four (that is to say, Cato, Morris, Dudley and the deceased Farmer) remained downstairs for a time. The moment came when Farmer produced a bag of white powder and some syringes and invited the others to have a 'fix' with him; and so they did. The white powder was put in its bag on the mantelpiece, the syringes were distributed amongst the four who were to participate, and the procedure which they adopted (which may or may not be a common one) was to pair off so that each could do the actual act of injection into the other half of his pair. Following this procedure Morris and Dudley paired off together and so did Cato and Farmer (the deceased). All four had a number of injections following this procedure, but the time came when Dudley and Morris went to bed, leaving Cato and Farmer downstairs in the sitting room. Cato and Farmer continued to give each other these injections from time to time right through the night.

. . . The method, as I have already indicated, was that each would take his own syringe. He would fill it to his own taste with whatever mixture of powder and water he thought proper. He would then give his syringe to the other half of his pair – in this case Farmer would give his syringe to Cato – and the other half of the pair would conduct the actual act of injection. It is important to notice that the strength of the mixture to be used was entirely dictated by the person who was to receive it because he prepared his own syringe; but it is also to be noticed that the actual act of injection was done by the other half of the pair, which of course has a very important influence on this case when one comes to causation.

. . . The first question was: was there sufficient evidence on which the jury could conclude, as they must have concluded, that adequate causation was present?

When one looks at the evidence it is important to realise that no other cause of Farmer's death was supplied. Dr Robinson thought that there might have been another drug, and she said at one stage it might have been cocaine, but there was never any cocaine found in the body. The only cause of death actually supplied by the evidence was morphine. No natural disease was present and no other drug was identified. Furthermore, the symptoms of the external appearance of the body, and the nature of the final terminal cause, were consistent with poison by the administration of heroin in the way which was described.

Further, when the people who lived in the house were giving their evidence about the death of Farmer, it was, as the judge pointed out, quite clear that they thought there was no doubt about what the cause had been. It may be of course that young people living in those circumstances know a great deal about the symptoms of heroin poisoning; I know not.

The judge said:

Members of the jury, it seems to me that that evidence about the condition of Cato when he was senseless on the floor and was put to bed, what he looked like and so forth is quite material in regard to the cause of Tony Farmer's death because Cato and he had both been dosing themselves with the same sort of thing, in the same sort of way, in the same sort of number of times, and that is clear evidence in this particular case. The opinions of the people in the house is of course not medical opinion but everybody there seemed to draw the conclusion that probably the heroin injections had caused both of them to be in the condition they were in.

That is an important and proper conclusion, if the jury thought fit to adopt it, because the fact that Cato very nearly suffered the same fate as Farmer, and showed the same kind of symptoms following the same kind of injections, is a pointer to indicate that the cause of Farmer's condition was the heroin which he had taken; and, furthermore, the jury were entitled, if they thought fit, to be influenced by the fact that the non-medical evidence from the residents was of the kind which the judge related.

Of course behind this whole question of the sufficiency of evidence of causation is the fact that it was not necessary for the prosecution to prove that the heroin was the only cause. As a matter of law, it was sufficient if the prosecution could establish that it was a cause, provided it was a cause outside the de minimis range, and effectively bearing on the acceleration of the moment of the victim's death.

When one has that in mind it is, we think, really possible to say that if the jury had been directed to look for heroin as a cause, not de minimis but a cause of substance, and they came back with a verdict of not guilty, the verdict could really be described as a perverse one. The whole background of the evidence was the other way and there certainly was ample evidence, given a proper direction, on which a charge of manslaughter could be supported.

But what about the proper direction? It will be noted that in none of the versions which I have quoted of the judge's direction on this point, nor in any of those which I have not quoted which appear in the summing-up, is there any reference to it being necessary for the cause to be a substantial one. It is said in clear terms in one of the six questions that the jury can consider whether the administration of the heroin was a cause or contributed to or accelerated the death, and in precise terms the word 'contributed' is not qualified to show that a substantial contribution is required.

Counsel for Cato, whose eagle eye misses nothing, sees here, and seeks to exploit here, what is a misdirection on the part of the trial judge. In other words, taking the judge's words literally, it would be possible for the jury to bring in a verdict of guilty of manslaughter even though the contribution was not of substance.

Before pursuing that, it is worth reminding oneself that some of the more recent dicta in the textbooks about this point do not support as strongly as was once the case the theory that the contribution must be substantial.

In Smith and Hogan there is this rather interesting extract:

It is commonly said by judges and writers that, while the accused's act need not be the sole cause of the death, it must be a substantial cause. This appears to mean only that a minute contribution to the cause of death will not entail responsibility. It may therefore be misleading to direct a jury that D is not liable unless his conduct was a 'substantial' cause. Killing is merely an acceleration of death and factors which produce a very trivial acceleration will be ignored.

Whether that be so or not, and we do not propose to give that passage the court's blessing today at all events, if one looks at the circumstances of the present case with any real sense of reality, we think there can be no doubt that when the judge was talking about contribution the jury knew perfectly well that he was talking about something more than the mere de minimis contribution. We have given this point particular care in our consideration of the case because it worried us to some extent originally, but we do feel in the end, having looked at all the circumstances, that there could not have been any question in this case of the jury making the mistake of thinking that the contribution would suffice if it were de minimis. Therefore in our judgment there is no substance in the attack of counsel for Cato on the basis of causation, whether it be an attack on the available evidence or on the trial judge's treatment of that evidence.

R v *Armstrong*
[1989] Crim LR 149
St Albans Crown Court

OWEN J: The defendant, a drug addict, supplied to C, who had already consumed a potentially lethal quantity of alcohol, heroin and the means by which to mix and inject the heroin. There was no evidence that D had injected the heroin into C. The case proceeded upon the assumption that C injected himself. Shortly after injecting himself, C died.

D was charged *inter alia* with manslaughter. At the trial the Crown called a pathologist and a toxicologist: the former opined that death was caused primarily by the deceased's alcohol intake and said that it was 'possible' that heroin had been a contributory cause; the latter initially expressed a different view but deferred to the pathologist's opinion.

It was submitted at the close of the Crown's case (1) that there was no or insufficient evidence that heroin had been a substantial cause of death, alternatively (2) that if heroin did cause death, C injecting himself was a *novus actus interveniens* breaking the chain of causation flowing from D's acts. *Held*, upholding the submissions, (1) that if the experts could not be sure that heroin caused C's death, the jury could not be and (2) that the alternative submission was well-founded. Regard was held to *Cato* 62 Cr App R 41 and *Dalby* 74 Cr App R 348: the facts proved were closest to *Dalby*.

Notes and questions

1.   Is the *Cato* court concerned with who caused death or with what caused death? What is the test that it uses to determine whether the defendant caused the victim's death? Why does the court in *Armstrong* reach a different result?

2.   *Armstrong* supplied the heroin which proved fatal to the victim. In *Cato* the heroin appears to have been supplied by the victim and, in any event, the victim mixed the fatal dose. Are these facts relevant? If so, should they not have led to the opposite result in the two cases?

3.   Of what relevance is the identity of the person who injects the heroin? In *Armstrong* the court seems prepared to hold that the victim's injection of himself would preclude the defendant's conviction. Is the fortuity of who administers the fatal injection a satisfactory basis for distinguishing *Armstrong* from *Cato*?

4.   Note that under the test used by the courts, it is possible that a defendant can be held to have caused a death even though the defendant was not the primary causer of death. Why should not a result be attributed to the person who can be said to be most responsible for bringing it about?

5.   It is inappropriate for a judge to attempt to quantify the degree to which the defendant's conduct contributed to the harmful result. In *Hennigan* [1971] 3 All ER 133, it was held to be error for the trial court to instruct the jury that the defendant could not be held liable if he was less than one-fifth to blame for the result.

6.   The Draft Criminal Code Bill 1989 requires an act which makes more than a negligible contribution to the result. Is this simply a restatement of the *Cato* test, or does it impose a more demanding standard?

Draft Criminal Code Bill 1989

17.—(1)   Subject to subsections (2) and (3), a person causes a result which is an element of an offence when —

(a)   he does an act which makes a more than negligible contribution to its occurrence; or

(b)   he omits to do an act which might prevent its occurrence and which he is under a duty to do according to the law relating to the offence.

(2)   A person does not cause a result where, after he does such an act or makes such an omission, an act or event occurs —

(a)   which is the immediate and sufficient cause of the result;

(b)   which he did not foresee, and

(c)   which could not in the circumstances reasonably have been foreseen.

(3)   A person who procures, assists or encourages another to cause a result that is an element of an offence does not himself cause that result so as to be guilty of the offence as a principal except when—

(a)   section 26(1)(c) applies; or

(b)   the offence itself consists in the procuring, assisting or encouraging another to cause the result.

Note

The commentary to the Bill states that a substantial or significant contribution is envisaged. Is this a more demanding standard than that contained in the actual language of the Bill? Some courts in fact use the term 'substantial' in their instructions, although this may be more favourable to a defendant than the letter of the law requires.

The fact that a victim was near death will not affect the defendant's liability if the defendant's acts hastened the death. All homicide is but a hastening of the inevitable. Thus a mercy killing may still constitute murder or manslaughter. The legal position was set out by Devlin J in the trial of Dr Adams for murder:

Henry Palmer, 'Dr Adams' Trial for Murder'
[1957] Crim LR 365

Devlin J, summing-up to the jury, said murder was an act or series of acts, done by the prisoner, which were intended to kill, and did in fact kill. It did not matter whether Mrs Morrell's death was inevitable and that her days were numbered. If her life were cut short by weeks or months it was just as much murder as if it was cut short by years. There had been a good deal of discussion as to the circumstances in which doctors might be justified in administering drugs which would shorten life. Cases of severe pain were suggested and also cases of helpless misery. The law knew of no special defence in this category, but that did not mean that a doctor who was aiding the sick and dying had to calculate in minutes or even hours, perhaps not in days or weeks, the effect on a patient's life of the medicines which he would administer. If the first purpose of medicine – the restoration of health – could no longer be achieved, there was still much for the doctor to do, and he was entitled to do all that was proper and necessary to relieve pain and suffering even if the measures he took might incidentally shorten life by hours or perhaps even longer. The doctor who decided whether or not to administer the drug could not do his job if he were thinking in terms of hours or months of life. The defence in the present case was that the treatment given by Dr Adams was designed to promote comfort, and if it was the right and proper treatment, the fact that it shortened life did not convict him of murder.

Note
The case of Dr Adams is further discussed in Chapter 9 (Homicide).

C   Legal or proximate cause

Once the Crown has established 'but for' cause, the issue becomes whether the defendant's acts were the legal or proximate cause of the result. The real question is whether it is fair and just to impute or attribute the resulting harm to the defendant's conduct. The answer to this question to a large extent turns on the defendant's moral culpability. The most difficult cases involve intervening acts by the victim or a third party.

(i)   Intervening acts of the victim
We can start with the general proposition that the contributory negligence
of the victim will usually not relieve a defendant of criminal liability. For
example, Anthony, not paying attention to whether there is any traffic,
stumbles into the middle of the street, where he is fatally struck by a car driven
by Debra. If Debra is driving dangerously, she will be liable for causing death
by dangerous driving (see *Swindall and Osborn* (1846) 2 Car & Kir 230).
However, there is authority to the effect that if the injuries could not have been
avoided even if Debra were driving safely, she would not be liable for the harm
caused (see *R* v *Dalloway* (1847) 2 Cox CC 273).
    A different type of negligence case involves the victim of a serious but not
fatal wound. If the victim is negligent in treating the wound, such that it
becomes infected and the victim dies, is the person who inflicted the wound
liable for the death?

R v Holland
(1841) 2 Mood & R 351
King's Bench

It appeared by the evidence that the deceased had been waylaid and assaulted by the
prisoner, and that, amongst other wounds, he was severely cut across one of his fingers
by an iron instrument. On being brought to the infirmary, the surgeon urged him to
submit to the amputation of the finger, telling him, unless it were amputated, he
considered that his life would be in great hazard. The deceased refused to allow the
finger to be amputated. It was thereupon dressed by the surgeon, and the deceased
attended at the infirmary from day to day to have his wounds dressed; at the end of a
fortnight, however, lock-jaw came on, induced by the wound on the finger; the finger
was then amputated, but too late, and the lockjaw ultimately caused death. The surgeon
deposed, that if the finger had been amputated in the first instance, he thought it most
probable that the life of the deceased would have been preserved.
    For the prisoner, it was contended that the cause of death was not the wound inflicted
by the prisoner, but the obstinate refusal of the deceased to submit to proper surgical
treatment, by which the fatal result would, according to the evidence, have been
prevented.
    Maule J, however, was clearly of opinion that this was no defence, and told the jury
that if the prisoner wilfully, and without any justifiable cause, inflicted the wound on
the party, which wound was ultimately the cause of death, the prisoner was guilty of
murder; that for this purpose it made no difference whether the wound was in its own
nature instantly mortal, or whether it became the cause of death by reason of the
deceased not having adopted the best mode of treatment; the real question is, whether
in the end the wound inflicted by the prisoner was the cause of death?

Guilty.

Questions
1.   What were the 'but for' causes of death in *Holland*? The proximate cause
of death?
2.   Would the result in the case have been the same if the Draft Criminal Code
provision on causation (above) had been in force?

3. What is the justification for treating differently two similarly situated defendants both of whom have inflicted a wound of similar gravity on their victim, but one of whose victim takes proper care of himself and recovers while the other does not and dies?

If the negligence of the victim is legally irrelevant, what of attempts by the victim to escape an unlawful attack?

R v Roberts
(1971) 56 Cr App Rep 95
Court of Appeal

The girl's story was that on the evening of May 1 she went to a base camp for troops in Lancashire, being at that time engaged to be married to an American serviceman who had gone to Vietnam. She was friendly with many of the people at that base, and from there she went on to a party where she met the appellant, for the first time. She left that party at about 3 a.m., having agreed to travel with the appellant in his car to what he said was another party in Warrington. After they had driven out of Warrington in the direction of Liverpool, she asked the appellant where the party was, and he said that they were going to Runcorn. They took a curious route to Runcorn, and eventually, she said, they stopped on what seemed like a big cinder-track. The time by then was apparently about 4 a.m. Then, she said, 'He just jumped on me. He put his hands up my clothes and tried to take my tights off. I started to fight him off, but the door of the car was locked and I could not find the catch. Suddenly he grabbed me and then he drove off and I started to cry and asked him to take me home. He told me to take my clothes off and, if I did not take my clothes off, he would let me walk home, so I asked him to let me do that. He said, if he did, he would beat me up before he let me go. He said that he had done this before and had got away with it and he started to pull my coat off. He was using foul language.' And then she said that she told him, 'I am not like this,' and he said something like, 'You are all like that.' Then he drove on. 'Again,' said the girl, 'he tried to get my coat off, so I got hold of my handbag and I jumped out of the car. When I opened the door he said something and revved the car up and I jumped out. . . . '

STEPHENSON LJ: We have been helpfully referred to a number of reported cases, some well over a century old, of women jumping out of windows, or jumping or throwing themselves into a river, as a consequence of threats of violence or actual violence. The most recent case is the case of *Lewis* [1970] Crim LR 647. An earlier case is that of *Beech* (1912) 7 Cr App R 197, which was a case of a woman jumping out of a window and injuring herself, and of a man who had friendly relations with her, whom she knew and might have had reason to be afraid of, being prosecuted for inflicting grievous bodily harm upon her, contrary to section 20 of the Offences against the Person Act. In that case the Court of Criminal Appeal (at p. 200) approved the direction given by the trial judge in these terms: 'Will you say whether the conduct of the prisoner amounted to a threat of causing injury to this young woman, was the act of jumping the natural consequence of the conduct of the prisoner, and was the grievous bodily harm the result of the conduct of the prisoner?' That, said the Court, was a proper direction as far as the law went, and they were satisfied that there was evidence before the jury of the prisoner causing actual bodily harm to the woman. 'No-one could say,' said Darling J when giving the judgment of the Court, 'that if she jumped from the window it was not a natural consequence of the prisoner's conduct. It was a very likely thing for a woman to do as the result of the threats of a man who was conducting himself as this man indisputably was.'

This Court thinks that that correctly states the law, and that Mr Carus was wrong in submitting to this Court that the jury must be sure that a defendant, who is charged either with inflicting grievous bodily harm or assault occasioning actual bodily harm, must foresee the actions of the victim which result in the grievous bodily harm, or the actual bodily harm. That, in the view of this Court, is not the test. The test is: Was it the natural result of what the alleged assailant said and did, in the sense that it was something that could reasonably have been foreseen as the consequence of what he was saying or doing? As it was put in one of the old cases, it had got to be shown to be his act, and if of course the victim does something so 'daft,' in the words of the appellant in this case, or so unexpected, not that this particular assailant did not actually foresee it but that no reasonable man could be expected to foresee it, then it is only in a very remote and unreal sense a consequence of his assault, it is really occasioned by a voluntary act on the part of the victim which could not reasonably be foreseen and which breaks the chain of causation between the assault and the harm or injury.

Questions
1. Were the victim's actions in *Roberts* reasonable, or rash and precipitous? When the court speaks of an action being reasonably foreseeable, is it saying that a reasonable person in Roberts's position would have judged that his passenger was, under the circumstances, likely to jump from the moving vehicle, or that this was simply a possibility? Or is the court rather saying that in retrospect the victim's actions were not unreasonable?
2. Would the result in *Roberts* have been the same if the victim had jumped from the car because Roberts had threatened to kiss her? Would it matter whether the victim had warned Roberts that she would jump out of the car if he tried to kiss her?
3. What of the jilted lover who threatens suicide if his beloved will not marry him? If she declines and he carries through with his threat, has she caused the death?

There is a general rule in criminal law that you must take your victim as you find him. It would be unseemly if criminal trials were to become bogged down in medical debate as to whether a healthier victim would have survived the injuries inflicted by the defendant. In theory, the rule strengthens the deterrent effect of the law, since potential lawbreakers are aware that they must accept not only the risks that they intend to incur, but also the risk of an infirm victim. Although there are few real life cases, a favourite example of text writers of the rule's application is the haemophiliac who bleeds to death from cuts which in an ordinary person would have rapidly clotted. Another often cited example is the victim with the eggshell skull, whose skull is fractured by a blow which would have given an ordinary person nothing but a headache. Beyond these cases of physical frailties, how much further does the rule extend?

R v Blaue
[1975] 1 WLR 1411
Court of Appeal

LAWTON LJ: . . . The victim was aged 18. She was a Jehovah's Witness. She professed the tenets of that sect and lived her life by them. During the late afternoon of May 3, 1974, the defendant came into her house and asked her for sexual intercourse. She refused. He then attacked her with a knife inflicting four serious wounds. One pierced her lung. The defendant ran away. She staggered out into the road. She collapsed outside a neighbour's house. An ambulance took her to hospital, where she arrived at about 7.30 p.m. Soon after she was admitted to the intensive care ward. At about 8.30 p.m. she was examined by the surgical registrar who quickly decided that serious injury had been caused which would require surgery. As she had lost a lot of blood, before there could be an operation there would have to be a blood transfusion. As soon as the girl appreciated that the surgeon was thinking of organising a blood transfusion for her, she said that she should not be given one and that she would not have one. To have one, she said, would be contrary to her religious beliefs as a Jehovah's Witness. She was told that if she did not have a blood transfusion she would die. She said that she did not care if she did die. She was asked to acknowledge in writing that she had refused to have a blood transfusion under any circumstances. She did so. The prosecution admitted at the trial that had she had a blood transfusion when advised to have one she would not have died. She did so at 12.45 a.m. the next day. The evidence called by the prosecution proved that at all relevant times she was conscious and decided as she did deliberately, and knowing what the consequences of her decision would be. In his final speech to the jury, Mr Herrod for the prosecution accepted that her refusal to have a blood transfusion was *a* cause of her death. . . .

As was pointed out to Mr Comyn in the course of argument, two cases, each raising the same issue of reasonableness because of religious beliefs, could produce different verdicts depending on where the cases were tried. A jury drawn from Preston, sometimes said to be the most Catholic town in England, might have different views about martyrdom to one drawn from the inner suburbs of London. Mr Comyn accepted that this might be so: it was, he said, inherent in trial by jury. It is not inherent in the common law as expounded by Sir Matthew Hale and Maule J. It has long been the policy of the law that those who use violence on other people must take their victims as they find them. This in our judgment means the whole man, not just the physical man. It does not lie in the mouth of the assailant to say that his victim's religious beliefs which inhibited him from accepting certain kinds of treatment were unreasonable. The question for decision is what caused her death. The answer is the stab wound. The fact that the victim refused to stop this end coming about did not break the casual connection between the act and death.

If a victim's personal representatives claim compensation for his death the concept of foreseeability can operate in favour of the wrong-doer in the assessment of such compensation: the wrongdoer is entitled to expect his victim to mitigate his damage by accepting treatment of a normal kind: see *Steele* v *R. George & Co. (1937) Ltd* [1942] AC 497. As Mr Herrod pointed out, the criminal law is concerned with the maintenance of law and order and the protection of the public generally. A policy of the common law applicable to the settlement of tortious liability between subjects may not be, and in our judgment is not, appropriate for the criminal law.

The issue of the cause of death in a trial for either murder or manslaughter is one of fact for the jury to decide. But if, as in this case, there is no conflict of evidence and all the jury has to do is to apply the law to the admitted facts, the judge is entitled to tell the jury what the result of that application will be. In this case the judge would have been entitled to have told the jury that the defendant's stab wound was an operative cause of death. The appeal fails.

Questions
1.   Is *Blaue* distinguishable from the eggshell skull cases, or must he too take his victim as he finds her, replete with her religious convictions? Does the decision turn on the foreseeability of the victim of a stab wound refusing life saving treatment, the reasonableness of the refusal, or the court's belief that Blaue was a totally unsavoury character deserving of a manslaughter conviction? Would the result have been the same if the victim had claimed to have had a vision in which Jesus told her that she was the Virgin Mary incarnate and she should refuse life-saving treatment so that they could be reunited? What if the victim had refused treatment, not out of any religious conviction but because she wanted to see Blaue convicted of murder?
2.   Is *Blaue* analogous to the contributory negligence cases where the victim fails to take care of a wound which becomes infected with fatal results? Is it analogous to or in conflict with *Roberts* (above)?
3.   Would Blaue have been liable if the wounds which he inflicted were non-fatal but the victim had subsequently committed suicide in a state of severe depression brought on by the incident?
4.   What if the doctors had administered a transfusion to the victim over her objection? Subsequently, unable to live with this perceived insult to her religion, she committed suicide. Who would be legally liable for the death – the victim by her own hand, Blaue, or the doctors?

Note
Consider the case where the response to an attack places the victim in a certain place at a certain point in time. The victim attempts to hide from her assailant behind a tree. The tree is struck by lightning and the victim dies. Or the victim ducks into a building which explodes because of a terrorist bomb which had been placed in the building. In these cases the courts find that there is a break in the chain of causation. Why? Sometimes one runs across statements to the effect that an intended result is never too remote, but the lightning and the terrorist bomb examples should illustrate that that is an overstatement.

(ii)   Intervening acts of third parties
As a general proposition, one is legally responsible only for one's own acts or inactions. But who is responsible when one person's acts set the stage for the acts of another that lead to the result proscribed by the law? For example, Smith invites Jones to a party at her house. On route, Jones is assaulted and robbed. Smith is not legally responsible, even if she knew that she lived in a

high crime area where an assault was foreseeable. The fact that Smith's act of inviting Jones to her house provided the setting for the robbery is mere coincidence. On the other hand, clearly Smith would be liable if the robber acted on her directions, she having set up Jones for the robbery. In this case the intervening acts of the third party were an integral part of Smith's criminal plan.

Between the case of the innocent act which sets the stage for the commission of a crime and the not-so-innocent act which is part and parcel of the criminal scheme, lie the more troublesome cases where the initial act is wrongful but a subsequent act neither intended nor foreseen by the original actor causes fatal results. If the cause of death is clearly foreseeable, such as the victim who is left unconscious by the ocean's edge and is drowned when the tide comes in, the defendant will be held liable. When the act is less clearly foreseeable, however, the courts have experienced difficulties. The situation most often arises in cases of medical malpractice. For example, Frank inflicts a non-fatal wound on Guy. Guy is rushed to the hospital, where a doctor botches an operation that would have saved his life. Is it Frank's wound or the doctor's negligence, or both, which has caused Guy's death? (Frank would still be liable, of course, for assault, but the question is whether he is liable for manslaughter.)

These cases have proved troublesome both in theory and practice. In part the problem is that, perhaps more clearly than in other causation cases, the actions of several individuals have contributed to the resulting death, yet the Crown has chosen to single out one (usually the most morally culpable of the actors) for prosecution. The confusion is in no way lessened by the invocation of the Latin phrase *novus actus interveniens* to describe the case where the second act prevents the defendant's conviction. Compare the following cases:

R v Jordan
(1956) 40 Cr App R 152
Court of Appeal

HALLETT J: The facts of the case, so far as I need refer to them, are as follows. The appellant, together with three other men, all serving airmen of the United States Forces, were charged with the murder of a man named Beaumont as the result of a disturbance which arose in a café at Hull. Beaumont was stabbed with a knife. There was no evidence that any one of the other three men used a knife on Beaumont or was acting in concert with the man who did use the knife, and accordingly Byrne J, who tried the case, directed the acquittal of those three men. With regard to the appellant it was ultimately conceded by Mr Veale, who appeared for him in the court below and in this court, that he did use the knife and stab Beaumont. Beaumont was admitted to hospital very promptly and the wound was stitched up, but none the less he died not many days after. In those circumstances the appellant was tried for murder. Various defences were raised, accident, self-defence, provocation and stabbing in the course of a quarrel. On all of those defences the direction of the learned judge is not in any way challenged and the jury rejected them.

. . . The further evidence is said to show that death was not, to use the words of Byrne J, 'consequent upon the wound inflicted.' On the contrary, both the doctors called are of opinion that, from the medical point of view, it cannot be described as caused by the wound at all. Whether from the legal point of view it could be described as caused by the wound is a more doubtful question. . . . First, as to the requirements allowing fresh evidence to be called; in the present case it seems clear to us that the fresh evidence was not in any true sense available at the trial. It did not occur to the prosecution, the defence, the judge, or the jury that there could be any doubt but that the stab caused death. The trial proceeded upon that basis. In those circumstances we thought it right to take the view that this was a case where the evidence sought to be given had not been in any true sense available at the trial. . . .

As to the second requisite, namely, that the evidence proposed to be tendered is such that, if the jury had heard that evidence, they might very likely, and indeed probably would, have come to a different verdict, we feel that, if the jury had heard two doctors of the standing of Dr Keith Simpson and Mr Blackburn give evidence that in their judgment death was not due to the stab wound but to something else, the jury might certainly have hesitated very long before saying that they were satisfied that death was due to the stab wound. The jury, of course, would not be bound by medical opinion, but flying in the face of it, particularly in a capital case, is a thing any jury would hesitate to do. . . . There were two things other than the wound which were stated by these two medical witnesses to have brought about death. The stab wound had penetrated the intestine in two places, but it was mainly healed at the time of death. With a view to preventing infection it was thought right to administer an antibiotic, terramycin.

It was agreed by the two additional witnesses that that was the proper course to take, and a proper dose was administered. Some people, however, are intolerant to terramycin, and Beaumont was one of those people. After the initial doses he developed diarrhoea, which was only properly attributable, in the opinion of those doctors, to the fact that the patient was intolerant to terramycin. Thereupon the administration of terramycin was stopped, but unfortunately the very next day the resumption of such administration was ordered by another doctor and it was recommenced the following day. The two doctors both take the same view about it. Dr Simpson said that to introduce a poisonous substance after the intolerance of the patient was shown was palpably wrong. Mr Blackburn agreed.

Other steps were taken which were also regarded by the doctors as wrong – namely, the intravenous introduction of wholly abnormal quantities of liquid far exceeding the output. As a result the lungs became waterlogged and pulmonary oedema was discovered. Mr Blackburn said that he was not surprised to see that condition after the introduction of so much liquid, and that pulmonary oedema leads to broncho-pneumonia as an inevitable sequel, and it was from broncho-pneumonia that Beaumont died.

We are disposed to accept it as the law that death resulting from any normal treatment employed to deal with a felonious injury may be regarded as caused by the felonious injury, but we do not think it necessary to examine the cases in detail or to formulate for the assistance of those who have to deal with such matters in the future the correct test which ought to be laid down with regard to what is necessary to be proved in order to establish causal connection between the death and the felonious injury. It is sufficient to point out here that this was not normal treatment. Not only one feature, but two separate and independent features, of treatment were, in the opinion of the doctors, palpably wrong and these produced the symptoms discovered at the post-mortem examination which were the direct and immediate cause of death, namely, the pneumonia resulting from the condition of oedema which was found.

The question then is whether it can be said that, if that evidence had been before the jury, it ought not to have, and in all probability would not have, affected their decision.

We recognise that the learned judge, if this matter had been before him, would have had to direct the jury correctly on how far such supervening matters could be regarded as interrupting the chain of causation; but we feel that in the end it would have been a question of fact for the jury depending on what evidence they accepted as correct and the view they took on that evidence. We feel no uncertainty at all that, whatever direction had been given to the jury and however correct it had been, the jury would have felt precluded from saying that they were satisfied that death was caused by the stab wound.

For these reasons we come to the conclusion that the appeal must be allowed and the conviction set aside.

R v *Smith*
[1959] 2 QB 35
Courts-Martial Appeal Court

LORD PARKER CJ: . . . The deceased man in fact received two bayonet wounds, one in the arm and one in the back. The one in the back, unknown to anybody, had pierced the lung and caused haemorrhage. There followed a series of unfortunate occurrences. A fellow-member of his company tried to carry him to the medical reception station. On the way he tripped over a wire and dropped the deceased man. He picked him up again, went a little farther, and fell apparently a second time, causing the deceased man to be dropped onto the ground. Thereafter he did not try a third time but went for help, and ultimately the deceased man was brought into the reception station. There, the medical officer, Captain Millward, and his orderly were trying to cope with a number of other cases, two serious stabbings and some minor injuries, and it is clear that they did not appreciate the seriousness of the deceased man's condition or exactly what had happened. A transfusion of saline solution was attempted and failed. When his breathing seemed impaired he was given oxygen and artificial respiration was applied, and in fact he died after he had been in the station about an hour, which was about two hours after the original stabbing. It is now known that having regard to the injuries which the man had in fact suffered, his lung being pierced, the treatment that he was given was thoroughly bad and might well have affected his chances of recovery. There was evidence that there is a tendency for a wound of this sort to heal and for the haemorrhage to stop. No doubt his being dropped on the ground and having artificial respiration applied would halt or at any rate impede the chances of healing. Further, there were no facilities whatsoever for blood transfusion, which would have been the best possible treatment. There was evidence that if he had received immediate and different treatment, he might not have died. Indeed, had facilities for blood transfusion been available and been administered, Dr Camps, who gave evidence for the defence, said that his chances of recovery were as high as 75 per cent.

In these circumstances Mr Bowen urges that not only was a careful summing-up required but that a correct direction to the court would have been that they must be satisfied that the death of Private Creed was a natural consequence and the sole consequence of the wound sustained by him and flowed directly from it. If there was, says Mr Bowen, any other cause, whether resulting from negligence or not, if, as he contends here, something happened which impeded the chance of the deceased recovering, then the death did not result from the wound. The court is quite unable to accept that contention. It seems to the court that if at the time of death the original wound is still an operating cause and a substantial cause, then the death can properly be said to be the result of the wound, albeit that some other cause of death is also operating. Only if it can be said that the original wounding is merely the setting in which another cause operates can it be said that the death does not result from the wound. Putting it in another way, only if the second cause is so overwhelming as to make the original wound merely part of the history can it be said that the death does not flow from the wound.

. . .

In the present case it is true that the judge-advocate did not in his summing-up go into the refinements of causation. Indeed, in the opinion of this court he was probably wise to refrain from doing so. He did leave the broad question to the court whether they were satisfied that the wound had caused the death in the sense that the death flowed from the wound, albeit that the treatment he received was in the light of after-knowledge a bad thing. In the opinion of this court that was on the facts of the case a perfectly adequate summing-up on causation; I say 'on the facts of the case' because, in the opinion of the court, they can only lead to one conclusion: a man is stabbed in the back, his lung is pierced and haemorrhage results; two hours later he dies of haemorrhage from that wound; in the interval there is no time for a careful examination, and the treatment given turns out in the light of subsequent knowledge to have been inappropriate and, indeed, harmful. In those circumstances no reasonable jury or court could, properly directed, in our view possibly come to any other conclusion than that the death resulted from the original wound. Accordingly, the court dismisses this appeal.

R v *Cheshire*
[1991] 3 All ER 670
Court of Appeal

In the course of an argument in a fish and chip shop the appellant shot the deceased in the leg and stomach seriously wounding him. The deceased was taken to hospital where he was operated on and placed in intensive care. While in hospital he developed respiratory problems and a tracheotomy tube was placed in his windpipe to assist his breathing. The tube remained in place for four weeks. The deceased suffered further chest infections and other complications and complained of difficulty in breathing. More than two months after the shooting, while still in hospital, the deceased died of cardio-respiratory arrest because his windpipe had become obstructed due to narrowing where the tracheotomy had been performed, such a condition being a rare but not unknown complication arising out of a tracheotomy. The appellant was charged with murder. At his trial evidence for the defence was given by a consultant surgeon that the deceased's leg and stomach wounds no longer threatened his life at the time of his death and that his death was caused by the negligent failure of the medical staff at the hospital to diagnose and treat the deceased's respiratory condition. The trial judge directed the jury that the appellant was responsible for the deceased's death even if the treatment given by the hospital medical staff was incompetent and negligent and it was only if they had been reckless in their treatment of the deceased that he was entitled to be acquitted. The appellant was convicted. He appealed.

BELDAM LJ: . . . [W]hat we think does emerge from . . . the . . . cases is that when the victim of a criminal attack is treated for wounds or injuries by doctors or other medical staff attempting to repair the harm done, it will only be in the most extraordinary and unusual case that such treatment can be said to be so independent of the acts of the accused that it could be regarded in law as the cause of the victim's death to the exclusion of the accused's acts.

Where the law requires proof of the relationship between an act and its consequences as an element of responsibility, a simple and sufficient explanation of the basis of such relationship has proved notoriously elusive.

In a case in which the jury have to consider whether negligence in the treatment of injuries inflicted by the accused was the cause of death we think it is sufficient for the judge to tell the jury that they must be satisfied that the Crown have proved that the acts of the accused caused the death of the deceased, adding that the accused's acts need not be the sole cause or even the main cause of his death, it being sufficient that his acts contributed significantly to that result. Even though negligence in the treatment of the victim was the immediate cause of his death, the jury should not regard it as excluding the responsibility of the accused unless the negligent treatment was so independent of his acts, and in itself so potent in causing death, that they regard the contribution made by his acts as insignificant.

It is not the function of the jury to evaluate competing causes or to choose which is dominant provided they are satisfied that the accused's acts can fairly be said to have made a significant contribution to the victim's death. We think the word 'significant' conveys the necessary substance of a contribution made to the death which is more than negligible.

In the present case the passage in the summing up complained of has to be set in the context of the remainder of the direction given by the judge on the issue of causation. He directed the jury that they had to decide whether the two bullets fired into the deceased on 10 December caused his death on 15 February following. Or, he said, put in another way, did the injuries caused cease to operate as a cause of death because something else intervened? He told them that the prosecution did not have to prove that the bullets were the only cause of death but they had to prove that they were one operative and substantial cause of death. He was thus following the words used in *R v Smith*.

The judge then gave several examples for the jury to consider before reverting to a paraphrase of the alternative formulation used by Lord Parker CJ in *R v Smith*. Finally, he reminded the jury of the evidence which they had heard on this issue. We would remark that on several occasions during this evidence the jury had passed notes to the judge asking for clarification of expressions used by the medical witnesses, which showed that they were following closely the factual issues they had to consider. If the passage to which exception has been taken had not been included, no possible criticism could have been levelled at the summing up. Although for reasons we have stated we think that the judge erred when he invited the jury to consider the degree of fault in the medical treatment rather than its consequences, we consider that no miscarriage of justice has actually occurred. Even if more experienced doctors than those who attended the deceased would have recognised the rare complication in time to have prevented the deceased's death, that complication was a direct consequence of the appellant's acts, which remained a significant cause of his death. We cannot conceive that, on the evidence given, any jury would have found otherwise.

According, we dismiss the appeal.

Questions

1. Are the three cases reconcilable? If not, which opinion is the more persuasive? How would you characterise the degree of medical ineptitude that is capable of breaking the chain of causation? Is this a test that will be capable of ease of application by a jury?

2.   Why should a defendant's criminal liability turn on the competence of the doctor who treats the victim, given that the defendant has no control over the doctor's performance? Would it make more sense to ask whether the victim was on the way to recovery at the time of the medical intervention, or would have survived but for the medical intervention? Is it in fact fatuous to try to determine whether it was defendant's wound or the medical intervention which was the cause of death, since the latter would not have been necessary except for the former? Is the risk of medical incompetence simply one that a defendant should have to absorb, just as the defendant must take the victim as he finds him? Why should medical mistreatment be regarded differently from the negligent failure of a victim to tend to his own wounds (see *Holland*, above).

Note

In *R v Malcherek and Steel* [1981] 2 All ER 422, the doctors were alleged to have switched off life support machines prematurely, thereby causing the victim's death. At the time there was a legitimate medical debate as to when a person should be deemed to have died. The court held that the fact that the doctors in the case had adopted a definition of death with which other doctors might disagree would not break the chain of causation. Whatever might be said about the doctors' treatment, the wound inflicted by the accused was one of the operative causes of death. Stepping back from a strict legal perspective, courts may well be reluctant to expose doctors, trying to do their best in an often difficult situation, to either criminal liability or the civil liability which might follow if any responsibility were to be attributed to their actions.

Fascinating causation questions are raised by the human shield cases:

R v Pagett
(1983) 76 Cr App R 279
Court of Appeal

The defendant, who was armed with a shotgun, used his pregnant girlfriend (Ms Kinchen) as a shield to prevent his arrest by armed police. He fired at the police, who returned his shots. One of the bullets fired by the police killed the girlfriend.

ROBERT GOFF LJ: . . . [I]t was pressed upon us by Lord Gifford that there either was, or should be, a . . . rule of English law, whereby, as a matter of policy, no man should be convicted of homicide (or, we imagine, any crime of violence to another person) unless he himself, or another person acting in concert with him, fired the shot (or, we imagine, struck the blow) which was the immediate cause of the victim's death (or injury).

No English authority was cited to us in support of any such proposition, and we know of none. So far as we are aware, there is no such rule in English law; and, in the absence of any doctrine of constructive malice, we can see no basis in principle for any such rule in English law. Lord Gifford urged upon us that, in a case where the accused did not, for example, fire the shot which was the immediate cause of the victim's death, he will inevitably have committed some lesser crime, and that it would be sufficient that he should be convicted of that lesser crime. So, on the facts of the present case, it would be enough that the appellant was convicted of the crime of attempted murder of the two police officers, D.S. Sartain and D.C. Richards. We see no force in this submission. In point of fact, it is not difficult to imagine circumstances in which it would manifestly be inadequate for the accused merely to be convicted of a lesser offence; for example, a man besieged by armed terrorists in a house might attempt to make his escape by forcing some other person to act as a shield, knowing full well that that person would in all probability be shot, and possibly killed, in consequence. For that man merely to be convicted of an assault would, if the person he used as a shield were to be shot and killed, surely be inadequate in the circumstances; we can see no reason why he should not be convicted at least of manslaughter. But in any event there is, so far as we can discern, no basis of legal principle for Lord Gifford's submission. We are therefore unable to accept it.

In our judgment, the question whether an accused person can be held guilty of homicide, either murder or manslaughter, of a victim the immediate cause of whose death is the act of another person must be determined on the ordinary principles of causation, uninhibited by any such rule of policy as that for which Lord Gifford has contended. We therefore reject the second ground of appeal.

We turn to the first ground of appeal, which is that the learned judge erred in directing the jury that it was for him to decide *as a matter of law* whether by his unlawful and deliberate acts the appellant caused or was a cause of Gail Kinchen's death. . . .

In cases of homicide, it is rarely necessary to give the jury any direction on causation as such. Of course, a necessary ingredient of the crimes of murder and manslaughter is that the accused has by his act caused the victim's death. But how the victim came by his death is usually not in dispute. What is in dispute is more likely to be some other matter: for example, the identity of the person who committed the act which indisputably caused the victim's death; or whether the accused had the necessary intent; or whether the accused acted in self-defence, or was provoked. Even where it is necessary to direct the jury's minds to the question of causation, it is usually enough to direct them simply that in law the accused's act need not be the sole cause, or even the main cause, of the victim's death, it being enough that his act contributed significantly to that result. It is right to observe in passing, however, that even this simple direction is a direction of law relating to causation, on the basis of which the jury are bound to act in concluding whether the prosecution has established, as a matter of fact, that the accused's act did in this sense cause the victim's death. Occasionally, however, a specific issue of causation may arise. One such case is where, although an act of the accused constitutes a *causa sine qua non* of (or necessary condition for) the death of the victim, nevertheless the intervention of a third person may be regarded as the sole cause of the victim's death, thereby relieving the accused of criminal responsibility. Such intervention, if it has such an effect, has often been described by lawyers as a *novus actus interveniens*. We are aware that this time-honoured Latin term has been the subject of criticism. We are also aware that attempts have been made to translate it into English; though no simple translation has proved satisfactory, really because the Latin term has become a term of art which conveys to lawyers the crucial feature that there has not merely been an intervening act of another person, but that that act was so independent of the act of the accused that it should be regarded in law as the cause of the victim's death, to the exclusion of the act of the accused. At the risk of scholarly criticism, we shall for the purposes of this judgment continue to use the Latin term.

Now the whole subject of causation in the law has been the subject of a well-known and most distinguished treatise by Professors Hart and Honoré, *Causation in the Law*. Passages from this book were cited to the learned judge, and were plainly relied upon by him; we, too, wish to express our indebtedness to it. It would be quite wrong for us to consider in this judgment the wider issues discussed in that work. But, for present purposes, the passage which is of most immediate relevance is to be found in Chapter XII, in which the learned authors consider the circumstances in which the intervention of a third person, not acting in concert with the accused, may have the effect of relieving the accused of criminal responsibility. The criterion which they suggest should be applied in such circumstances is whether the intervention is voluntary i.e. whether it is 'free, deliberate and informed.' We resist the temptation of expressing the judicial opinion whether we find ourselves in complete agreement with that definition; though we certainly consider it to be broadly correct and supported by authority. Among the examples which the authors give of non-voluntary conduct, which is not effective to relieve the accused of responsibility, are two which are germane to the present case, *viz*, a reasonable act performed for the purpose of self-preservation, and an act done in performance of a legal duty.

There can, we consider, be no doubt that a reasonable act performed for the purpose of self-preservation, being of course itself an act caused by the accused's own act, does not operate as a *novus actus interveniens*. . . . if a reasonable act of self-defence against the act of the accused causes the death of a third party, we can see no reason in principle why the act of self-defence, being an involuntary act caused by the act of the accused, should relieve the accused from criminal responsibility for the death of the third party. Of course, it does not necessarily follow that the accused will be guilty of the murder, or even of the manslaughter, of the third party; though in the majority of cases he is likely to be guilty at least of manslaughter. Whether he is guilty of murder or manslaughter will depend upon the question whether all the ingredients of the relevant offence have been proved; in particular, on a charge of murder, it will be necessary that the accused had the necessary intent . . . .

No English authority was cited to us, nor we think to the learned judge, in support of the proposition that an act done in the execution of a legal duty, again of course being an act itself caused by the act of the accused, does not operate as a *novus actus interveniens*. . . . We agree with the learned judge that the proposition is sound in law, because as a matter of principle such an act cannot be regarded as a voluntary act independent of the wrongful act of the accused. A parallel may be drawn with the so-called 'rescue' cases in the law of negligence, where a wrongdoer may be held liable in negligence to a third party who suffers injury in going to the rescue of a person who has been put in danger by the defendant's negligent act. Where, for example, a police officer in the execution of his duty acts to prevent a crime, or to apprehend a person suspected of a crime, the case is surely *a fortiori*. Of course, it is inherent in the requirement that the police officer, or other person, must be acting in the execution of his duty that his act should be reasonable in all the circumstances: see section 3 of the Criminal Law Act 1967. Furthermore, once again we are only considering the issue of causation. If intervention by a third party in the execution of a legal duty, caused by the act of the accused, results in the death of the victim, the question whether the accused is guilty of the murder or manslaughter of the victim must depend on whether the necessary ingredients of the relevant offence have been proved against the accused, including in particular, in the case of murder, whether the accused had the necessary intent.

The principles which we have stated are principles of law. This is plain from, for example, the case of *Pitts* (1842) C & M 284, to which we have already referred. It follows that where, in any particular case, there is an issue concerned with what we have for convenience called *novus actus interveniens*, it will be appropriate for the judge to direct the jury in accordance with these principles. It does not however follow that it is accurate to state broadly that causation is a question of law. On the contrary, generally speaking causation is a question of fact for the jury. . . . But that does not mean that there are no principles of law relating to causation, so that no directions on law are ever to be given to a jury on the question of causation. On the contrary, we have already pointed out one familiar direction which is given on causation, which is that the accused's act need not be the sole, or even the main, cause of the victim's death for his act to be held to have caused the death. . . . [I]n cases where there is an issue whether the act of the victim or of a third party constituted a *novus actus interveniens*, breaking the causal connection between the act of the accused and the death of the victim, it would be appropriate for the judge to direct the jury, of course in the most simple terms, in accordance with the legal principles which they have to apply. It would then fall to the jury to decide the relevant factual issues which, identified with reference to those legal principles, will lead to the conclusion whether or not the prosecution have established the guilt of the accused of the crime of which he is charged.

. . .

There is however one further aspect of the present case to which we must advert. On the evidence, Gail Kinchen was not just an innocent bystander killed by a shot fired from the gun of a police officer who, acting in reasonable self-defence, fired his gun in response to a lethal attack by the appellant: though on those facts alone it would, in our opinion, have been open to the jury to convict the appellant of murder or manslaughter. But if, as the jury must have found to have occurred in the present case, the appellant used Gail Kinchen by force and against her will as a shield to protect him from any shots fired by the police, the effect is that he committed not one but two unlawful acts, both of which were dangerous – the act of firing at the police, and the act of holding Gail Kinchen as a shield in front of him when the police might well fire shots in his direction in self-defence. Either act could in our judgment, if on the principles we have stated it was held to cause the death of Gail Kinchen, constitute the *actus reus* of the manslaughter or, if the necessary intent were established, murder of Gail Kinchen by the appellant, even though the shot was fired not by the appellant but by a police officer.

Questions
1. On what basis can it be said that Pagett's acts killed the victim when the fatal shots were fired by the police? What was Pagett's *actus reus*? His *mens rea*?
2. Was the result foreseeable? Does it matter?
3. Would Pagett have been liable if a third party had been killed as a result of an errant shot by the police? Would this be a stronger or weaker case for liability?
4. Did the decision turn on the fact that the shots fired by the police were justifiable? If the judge had ruled at the trial that the police should have held their fire and were wrong not to do so, would (should) it have made any difference to Pagett's liability?
5. In April 1993, in Waco, Texas, a religious sect known as the Branch Davidians set their compound on fire rather than submit to arrest by federal officers. The latter had laid siege to the compound for 51 days following the killing of several of their number in the initial attempt to arrest the Branch Davidians for firearms violations. Eighty-six members of the cult were killed in the blaze. Did the FBI 'cause' the deaths?

II Concurrence

The coincidence of *actus reus* and *mens rea* will not necessarily lead to criminal liability. There is the additional requirement that there be a concurrence between the *actus reus* and *mens rea*. What this means is that the two must be related in a particular way. It is not simply enough that a disgruntled spouse is speeding home, thinking about killing her husband, when he suddenly leaps in front of her car, bent on committing suicide. The speeding may be the cause of the resulting death, and the wife's mind may have been full of homicidal thoughts at the critical moment, but all that is matter of coincidence. What the law requires is that the evil thoughts be the activating cause of the evil deeds. This is what the law means when it speaks of concurrence. The problem cases involve situations where the defendant's *mens rea* occurs after the *actus reus* is completed, and cases where the defendant's *mens rea* is claimed to have been abandoned before the *actus reus* was complete.

If a defendant has *mens rea*, but never takes any steps to actuate that *mens rea*, there is no crime; evil thoughts by themselves do not a criminal make. Conversely, once the crime is complete, a subsequent change of heart is irrelevant. Courts are no doubt suspicious when a putative criminal who has been apprehended says, 'Well, the fact is that I had already changed my mind'. Illustrative is *Jakeman*:

R v *Jakeman*
(1982) 76 Cr App R 223
Court of Appeal

The applicant travelled by air to Accra in Ghana. She took with her two suitcases. There she booked a return flight to Rome two days later and a day after that a further flight from there to London. When she checked in at Accra for the return flight with her two suitcases, she booked them through to London. They contained 21.44 kilogrammes of cannabis, a controlled drug pursuant to section 2(1) of, and Part II of Schedule 2 to, the Misuse of Drugs Act 1971, and the importation of which to the United Kingdom was prohibited by section 3(1) of that Act. The flight to Rome was cancelled and the next day the passengers, including the applicant, were flown to Paris, where she took a flight to Rome, leaving her luggage in Paris, and then on to London. The customs officials in Paris assumed that the applicant's luggage there had been mis-routed and sent it on to London where customs officers on examination found the aforesaid amount of cannabis. They interviewed the applicant who eventually admitted that the two suitcases were hers and that she knew they contained cannabis. She was charged with being knowingly concerned in the fraudulent evasion of a prohibition in relation to goods contrary to section 170(2) of the Customs and Excise Management Act 1979, 'goods' in that subsection under paragraphs 1 and 3 of Schedule 1 to that Act including cannabis. At her trial she contended that she had been persuaded by two unknown men to take the drugs to London for £500; but that upon leaving Accra she had decided to have nothing further to do with the fraudulent enterprise and so had not collected the suitcases in Paris and had torn up her baggage tags. Her counsel then asked the trial judge whether in his view the intention to abandon her part in the importation, if accepted by the jury, provided a defence. The judge indicated that he thought that it did not and that he would so direct the jury. The applicant thereupon changed her plea to one of guilty. On an application for leave to appeal against conviction on the ground that the judge's ruling was wrong since for the offence under section 170(2) the participation of the applicant and her *mens rea* must continue throughout the offence, i.e. until the aircraft touched down at London Airport.

WOOD J: . . . We will deal first with the application for leave to appeal against conviction. Mr Mansfield first submits that the learned judge was wrong in the ruling which he gave. He submits that for the offence under section 170(2) of the 1979 Act, the participation of the applicant and her *mens rea* must continue throughout the offence – in this case at least until the wheels of the aircraft touched down at Heathrow Airport.
. . .

In developing his submission on the first ground of appeal, Mr Mansfield relied upon the applicant's assertion that she had changed her mind immediately on leaving Accra and on the facts that she did not collect her suitcases in Paris, that she tore up the baggage tags on arrival at Heathrow and that she did not seek to claim her suitcases. He submitted that whether one referred to 'withdrawal' or 'abandonment' or 'lack of *mens rea*' as the necessary ingredient of the defence, assistance was to be obtained from such cases as *Croft* (1944) 29 Cr App R 169; [1944] KB 295 and *Becerra and Cooper* (1975) 62 Cr App R 212. These cases are concerned with accomplices and secondary parties to crime, not to the principal offender, and in the view of this court are not of assistance to test the submission which is made. It is our view that the correct approach is to analyse the offence itself, but before turning to consider the wording of the section as a whole, it is valuable to look at decided cases and to see what assistance can be derived from them.

The following propositions are supported by decisions of this court. First, that the importation takes place when the aircraft bringing the goods lands at an airport in this country, see *Smith (Donald)* (1973) 57 Cr App R 737, 748; [1973] QB 924, 935G. Secondly, acts done abroad in order to further the fraudulent evasion of a restriction on importation into this country are punishable under this section, see *Wall (Geoffrey)* (1974) 59 Cr App R 58, 61; [1974] 1 WLR 930, 934C.

For guilt to be established the importation must, of course, result as a consequence, if only in part, of the activity of the accused. If, for example, in the present case the applicant had taken her two suitcases off the carousel at Charles de Gaulle airport in Paris, removed all the luggage tags, placed the suitcases in a left luggage compartment and thrown the key of that compartment into the Seine, and then subsequently, in a general emergency, all left luggage compartments had been opened, a well-known English travel label had been found on her suitcase and those suitcases had been sent to the Travel Agents' agency, care of Customs and Excise at Heathrow, then that undoubted importation would not be the relevant one for the purposes of a charge against the applicant.

We have already set out the wording of the relevant section and where the allegation concerns cannabis, the offence is, to be knowingly concerned in the fraudulent evasion (or attempt at evasion) of the prohibition on the importation of cannabis. Put more shortly, it is to be knowingly concerned in the fraudulent importation (or attempt at importation) of cannabis.

Although the importation takes place at one precise moment – when the aircraft lands – a person who is concerned in the importation may play his part before or after that moment. Commonly, the person responsible for despatching the prohibited drugs to England acts fraudulently and so does the person who removes them from the airport at which they have arrived. Each is guilty. *Wall (supra)* is an example of the former and *Green* (1975) 62 Cr App R 74; [1976] QB 985 of the latter.

There is no doubt, that, putting aside the question of duress, as we have done, the applicant had a guilty mind when at Accra she booked her luggage to London. By that act, she brought about the importation through the instrumentation of innocent agents. In this way, she caused the airline to label it to London, and the labels were responsible for the authorities in Paris sending it on to London.

What is suggested is that she should not be convicted unless her guilty state of mind subsisted at the time of importation. We see no reason to construe the Act in this way. If a guilty mind at the time of importation is an essential, the man recruited to collect the package which has already arrived and which he knows contains prohibited drugs commits no offence. What matters is the state of mind at the time the relevant acts are done, i.e. at the time the defendant is concerned in bringing about the importation. This accords with the general principles of common law. To stab a victim in a rage with the necessary intent for murder or manslaughter leads to criminal responsibility for the resulting death regardless of any repentance between the act of stabbing and the time of death, which may be hours or days later. This is so even if, within seconds of the stabbing, the criminal comes to his senses and does everything possible to assist his victim. Only the victim's survival will save him from conviction for murder or manslaughter.

The applicant alleged that she repented as soon as she boarded the aircraft; that she deliberately failed to claim her luggage in Paris, that she tore up the baggage tags attached to her ticket and so on, but none of this could have saved her from being held criminally responsible for the importation which she had brought about by deliberate actions committed with guilty intent. Thus, the learned judge was right in the ruling he made.

Appeal dismissed.

The more troublesome cases, at least intellectually, involve the defendant who commits a series of acts: the original acts are done with intent to bring about a result but are ineffectual; the subsequent acts are not done with any criminal intent but bring about the originally desired result:

Thabo Meli and Others v *R*
[1954] 1 WLR 228
Privy Council

LORD REID: The four appellants in this case were convicted of murder after a trial before Sir Walter Harragin, judge of the High Court of Basutoland, in March, 1953. The appeal which has been heard by this Board dealt with two matters: first, whether the conclusions of the learned judge on questions of fact were warranted: and, secondly, whether, on a point of law, the accused are entitled to have the verdict quashed.

On the first matter, there really is no ground for criticising the learned judge's treatment of the facts. It is established by evidence, which was believed and which is apparently credible, that there was a preconceived plot on the part of the four accused to bring the deceased man to a hut and there to kill him, and then to fake an accident, so that the accused should escape the penalty for their act. The deceased man was brought to the hut. He was there treated to beer and was at least partially intoxicated; and he was then struck over the head in accordance with the plan of the accused. Witnesses say that while the deceased was seated and bending forward he was struck a heavy blow on the back of the head with a piece of iron like the instrument produced at the trial. But a post-mortem examination showed that his skull had not been fractured and medical evidence was to the effect that a blow such as the witnesses described would have produced more severe injuries than those found at the post-mortem examination. There is at least doubt whether the weapon which was produced as being like the weapon which was used could have produced the injuries that were found, but it may be that this weapon is not exactly similar to the one which was used, or it may be that the blow was a glancing blow and produced less severe injuries than those which one might expect. In any event, the man was unconscious after receiving the blow, but he was not then dead. There is no evidence that the accused then believed that he was dead, but their Lordships are prepared to assume from their subsequent conduct that they did so believe; and it is only on that assumption that any statable case can be made for this appeal. The accused took out the body, rolled it over a low krantz or cliff, and dressed up the scene to make it look like an accident. Obviously, they believed at that time that the man was dead, but it appears from the medical evidence that the injuries which he received in the hut were not sufficient to cause the death and that the final cause of his death was exposure when he was left unconscious at the foot of the krantz.

The point of law which was raised in this case can be simply stated. It is said that two acts were done: – first, the attack in the hut; and, secondly, the placing of the body outside afterwards – and that they were separate acts. It is said that, while the first act was accompanied by mens rea, it was not the cause of death; but that the second act, while it was the cause of death, was not accompanied by mens rea; and on that ground, it is said that the accused are not guilty of murder, though they may have been guilty of culpable homicide. It is said that the mens rea necessary to establish murder is an intention to kill, and that there could be no intention to kill when the accused thought that the man was already dead, so their original intention to kill had ceased before they did the act which caused the man's death. It appears to their Lordships impossible to divide up what was really one series of acts in this way. There is no doubt that the accused set out to do all these acts in order to achieve their plan, and as parts of their plan; and it is much too refined a ground of judgment to say that, because they were under a misapprehension at one stage and thought that their guilty purpose had been achieved before, in fact, it was achieved, therefore they are to escape the penalties of the law. Their Lordships do not think that this is a matter which is susceptible of elaboration. There appears to be no case, either in South Africa or England, or for that matter elsewhere, which resembles the present. Their Lordships can find no difference relevant to the present case between the law of South Africa and the law of England; and they are of opinion that by both laws there can be no separation such as that for which the accused contend. Their crime is not reduced from murder to a lesser crime merely because the accused were under some misapprehension for a time during the completion of their criminal plot.

Their Lordships must, therefore, humbly advise Her Majesty that this appeal should be dismissed.

Note

Glanville Williams suggests that the more straightforward way of dealing with cases such as *Thabo Meli* is to hold that if the first act would have constituted manslaughter if the victim died, death which occurs during a subsequent attempt to dispose of the body should not affect liability. Another approach is presented in the following case:

Attorney-General's Reference (No. 4 of 1980)
[1981] 1 WLR 705
Court of Appeal

ACKNER LJ: This is a reference to the court by the Attorney-General of a point of law seeking the opinion of the court pursuant to s. 36 of the Criminal Justice Act 1972. It raises yet again the problem of the supposed corpse, and the facts, which I take from the terms of the reference itself, are inevitably macabre.

The deceased was the fiancée of the accused and for some months before her death they had lived together in a maisonette consisting of two floors of a house connected by two short flights of carpeted wooden stairs. The deceased was employed locally and was last seen at work on 17th January 1979 at about 5 p.m. Thereafter no one, other than the accused, ever saw her alive again.

The deceased met her death on 18th January 1979, although this fact was not known until over three weeks later when the defendant so informed a friend. His account, the first of a number, was that in the course of an argument on the evening of 17th January he had slapped her on the face causing her to fall downstairs and bang her head. He said that he had then put her to bed but discovered next morning that she was dead. He then took her body to his home town and buried her.

On the following day, 14th February, he gave his second account, telling the same friend that after the deceased had 'fallen downstairs' he had dragged her upstairs by a piece of rope tied round her neck. He subsequently cut up her body with a saw before burying it. The next day, on the advice of his friend, the accused went to see a superior and gave an account similar to the one he had given his friend.

We now come to the statements which he made to the police. On 27th February, having consulted solicitors, the accused was interviewed by the police at his solicitors' office. He began by giving the police substantially the same account that he had given to his friend and his superior but added that instead of burying the deceased he had 'dumped' the various parts of her body on a tip. At the police station later that day he amplified his statement by saying that the incident when the deceased 'fell downstairs' occurred at about 7 p.m. on 17th January and that it was the following day, when he found her motionless, that he pulled her upstairs by a rope around her neck and then cut up her body in the bathroom. On the following day after much questioning by the police he changed his account stating that everything had happened on Thursday, 18th January at about 7 a.m. This is what he then said happened. (i) He and the deceased had an argument on the landing in the course of which each slapped the other; he seized the deceased and shook her hard; she dug her nails into him and he pushed her away instinctively, causing her to fall backwards over the handrail, down the stairs head first onto the floor. (ii) He went downstairs immediately to find her motionless and on a very cursory examination discovered no pulse, and no sign of breath but frothy blood coming from her mouth. (iii) Almost immediately thereafter he dragged her upstairs by a rope tied around her neck, placed her in the bath and cut her neck with a penknife to let out her blood, having already decided to cut up her body and dispose of the pieces.

He agreed that his previous account was untrue and he made a detailed voluntary statement along the lines set out in (i), (ii) and (iii) above describing how subsequently he had cut up and disposed of her body.

Subsequently the police discovered evidence which corroborated the accused's account of how, where and when he had cut up the body. They also found the saw he had used and the shopkeeper who sold it to him. However, the body of the deceased was never found, only some minute fragments of bone, which were discovered in the maisonette. There was thus no expert evidence as to the cause of death. The deceased died either as a result of being pushed and thus caused to fall backwards over the handrail and backwards down the stairs head first onto the floor, or by being strangled with the rope, or having her throat cut. The Crown conceded that it was not possible for them to prove whether the deceased died as the result of the 'fall' downstairs or from what the accused did to the deceased thereafter.

The indictment charged the accused with (i) manslaughter, (ii) obstructing the coroner in the execution of his duty, and (iii) preventing the burial of a corpse.

The accused pleaded guilty to the third count, the Crown offered no evidence on the second and the trial proceeded on the count of manslaughter.

At the close of the Crown's case counsel for the accused stated that he proposed to submit that on the facts proved there was no case of manslaughter capable of going to the jury. It is not easy to follow from the transcript the exact basis of his submissions, but what he appears to have been contending was that (a) it was not possible for the jury to be sure what caused the deceased's death and (b) whether the death was caused as a result of her 'fall' down the stairs or from what the accused subsequently did, believing her to be dead, in neither event was there a prima facie case of manslaughter.

The judge, although expressing his reluctance to accept that the accused could be in a better position as a result of his dismembering the body of the deceased, appeared to have been very concerned at what he described as 'an insuperable problem of sentencing', were the accused to be convicted of manslaughter. He expressed the view that the real criminality of the accused's behaviour was in disposing of the body, a view which this court is unable to accept. These views appear to have influenced his decision, which was to withdraw the case from the jury and to direct an acquittal on the ground that the Crown had failed to prove the cause of the death of the deceased.

On the above facts this reference raises a single and simple question, *viz*, if an accused kills another by one or other of two or more different acts each of which, if it caused the death, is a sufficient act to establish manslaughter, is it necessary in order to found a conviction to prove which act caused the death? The answer to that question is No, it is is not necessary to found a conviction to prove which act caused the death. No authority is required to justify this answer, which is clear beyond argument, as was indeed immediately conceded by counsel on behalf of the accused.

What went wrong in this case was that counsel made jury points to the judge and not submissions of law. He was in effect contending that the jury should not convict of manslaughter if the death had resulted from the 'fall', because the push which had projected the deceased over the handrail was a reflex and not a voluntary action, as a result of her digging her nails into him. If, however, the deceased was still alive when he cut her throat, since he then genuinely believed her to be dead, having discovered neither pulse nor sign of breath, but frothy blood coming from her mouth, he could not be guilty of manslaughter because he had not behaved with gross criminal negligence. What counsel and the judge unfortunately overlooked was that there was material available to the jury which would have entitled them to have convicted the accused of manslaughter, whichever of the two sets of acts caused her death. It being common ground that the deceased was killed by an act done to her by the accused and it being conceded that the jury could not be satisfied which was the act which caused the death, they should have been directed in due course in the summing up, to ask themselves the following questions: (i) 'Are we satisfied beyond reasonable doubt that the deceased's "fall" downstairs was the result of an intentional act by the accused which was unlawful and dangerous?' If the answer was No, then they would acquit. If the answer was Yes, then they would need to ask themselves a second question, namely: (ii) 'Are we satisfied beyond reasonable doubt that the act of cutting the girl's throat was an act of gross criminal negligence?' If the answer to that question was No, then they would acquit, but if the answer was Yes, then the verdict would be guilty of manslaughter. The jury would thus have been satisfied that, whichever act had killed the deceased, each was a sufficient act to establish the offence of manslaughter.

Questions
1.   According to the Court of Appeal, what would the jury need to have found to justify a conviction? Is the Court's position still unduly favourable to the defendant?
2.   Which approach, that taken in *Thabo Meli* or that taken in *Attorney-General's Reference (No. 4)* is preferable? Why? Reconsider *R v Miller* (supra, p. 61).

III   The fortuity of consequence

Causation and concurrence are difficult issues. Perhaps fortunately for the courts, as well as law students, they are not issues which arise frequently. When they do, however, they expose a certain fortuity inherent in the criminal law – two offenders who do the same act with the same *mens rea* may wind up with quite different punishments because of the results that their actions produce. Fair enough, one might say – offenders should have to bear the risk of the consequences of their evil acts – but is it really fair to treat as a murderer the defendant whose victim neglects his wound with the result that gangrene sets in with fatal effect, while the defendant whose victim takes proper care of himself is convicted only of assault? Is it fair that whether a defendant receives a mandatory life sentence turns on whether, unbeknownst to the defendant, the victim is a religious zealot who refuses all medical treatment, preferring to place her faith in God? Granted that if convicted of attempted murder, the defendant may receive the same life sentence as a murderer, but this does not automatically follow as it does after a conviction for murder. In practice the attempted murderer is likely to receive a significantly lesser sentence. In some instances focusing on results allows an offender to receive less in the way of punishment than one would have predicted if one had looked at the situation as of the time the defendant committed the *actus reus*; while in other instances it leads to an offender facing charges far more serious than would have been predicted as of the same time.

Faced with the sometimes almost random results of legal principles of causation and concurrence, and understandably reluctant to allow malefactors to escape their just deserts because of the intervening acts of a victim, a third party or simply fate, courts stretch legal principle to reach equitable results.

They are not content with simply finding a defendant liable for the way he has behaved, but strive to hold him liable for all the results which follow from his actions. To a large extent this desire to hold a defendant liable for the full effects of his conduct is traceable to the retributive philosophy that a defendant's punishment should be in proportion to the harm which the defendant's acts have produced.

The problem in part is that the perspective of a criminal trial is always backwards-looking. The jurors know what results have occurred, and they ask themselves whether such results were foreseeable. The fact that they have occurred skews the enquiry, while casting the defendant's character in a more sinister light than it might otherwise have appeared had the results of the defendant's conduct been more benign. The proper focal point, it could be argued, is the time of the defendant's acts: What results were foreseeable as of that moment? But once we accept this proposition, a short further step seems logical. That would be to make actual results irrelevant. If the defendant's acts could have produced the harmful results, it should not matter, from a point of view of moral blameworthiness, whether they in fact did. Crimes should be defined in terms of *actus reus*, *mens rea* and the results that a type of conduct *threatens* to produce, as opposed to the results the conduct in fact produces, which may be completely fortuitous. A defendant should be punished not for the harm that he or she actually causes, but for the harm that he or she sets out to cause or recklessly risks causing, at least in the absence of excuse or justification. In this connection, consider the merits of the proposed New Zealand legislation:

Endangering

130. Endangering with intent to cause serious bodily harm
(1) Every person is liable to imprisonment for 14 years who—

(a) Does any act, or omits without lawful excuse to perform or observe any legal duty, with intent to cause serious bodily harm to any other person; or

(b) With reckless disregard for the safety of others, does any act or omits without lawful excuse to perform or observe any legal duty, knowing that the act or omission is likely to cause serious bodily harm to any other person.

(2) This section applies whether or not the act or omission results in death or bodily harm to any other person.

. . .

132. Endangering with intent to injure, etc.
(1) Every person is liable to imprisonment for five years who—

(a) Does any act, or omits without lawful excuse to perform or observe any legal duty, with intent to injure any other person; or

(b) With reckless disregard for the safety of others, or heedlessly, does any act or omits without lawful excuse to perform or observe any legal duty, the act or omission being likely to cause injury to any other person or to endanger the safety or health of any other person.

(2) Every person is liable to imprisonment for two years who negligently does any or omits without lawful excuse to perform or observe any legal duty, the act or omission being likely to cause injury.

Questions
1.   Does the proposed New Zealand legislation go too far? Should negligent endangerment be criminal? What constitutes heedlessness?
2.   Late to catch her train, Maria dashes down the street. Rounding the corner, she collides with Golding, who is knocked over and injured. Has Maria violated the New Zealand statute? Should such conduct be criminal?

Note
The issues raised by the fortuity of consequences have been well explored in the legal literature. See, e.g., A. Ashworth, 'Criminal attempts and the role of resulting harm under the Code and in the common law' 19 Rutgers LJ 725 (1988); A. Ashworth, 'Belief, Intent, and Criminal Liability' in J. Eekelar and J. Bell (eds) *Oxford Essays in Jurisprudence* 1 (1987); J. Gobert, 'The Fortuity of Consequence' [1993] 4 Crim Law Forum 1; J.C. Smith, 'The element of chance in criminal liability' [1971] Crim LR 63.

5 PARTIES TO CRIME

I Introduction

Often more than one person is involved in the commission of a criminal offence. On a conceptual level, we can identify four general classes of individuals who might be so involved. First, there are those who solicit or encourage others to commit a crime. Such persons are guilty of the independent offence of incitement (discussed in Chapter 7), but they may also be liable as an accessory to the substantive crime committed by the person whom they incite. Secondly, there are those who actually commit the crime, whose acts and mental state render them liable for the substantive offence itself. These persons are known in law as principals. Thirdly, there are those who assist or in some other way help the principal to commit the crime. The term 'accessory' is used to refer to these individuals. Lastly, there are those who help the perpetrator to escape capture and prosecution after the crime has been committed. The last group of post-crime assisters are not generally treated within the law of complicity; that is, they are not liable for the substantive offence, but may be guilty of separate statutory offences (see Criminal Law Act 1967, s. 4). This is a recognition of the fact that their crime is more appropriately characterised as one of obstructing the course of justice, rather than one of furthering the substantive offence which has already occurred.

This chapter focuses on the law as it relates to principals and accessories. Which category the offender falls into is usually clear, but, in any event, is often not of legal significance. Accessories and Abettors Act 1861 s. 8, provides that one can be charged as an accessory and convicted as a principal, and vice versa. Further, accessories and perpetrators are subject to the same maximum penalty. There do remain, however, evidentiary distinctions which can affect liability: the *actus reus* and *mens rea* elements which must be proved may differ depending on whether one is charged as a principal or an accessory; and some defences may be available to an accessory that are not available to a principal.

One can also be convicted as an accessory to a crime for which the principal himself cannot be convicted, as illustrated in the following case:

R v *Austin and Others*
[1981] 1 All ER 374
Court of Appeal

A husband, who was living apart from his wife, employed a firm of enquiry agents, of which W was a member, to find his wife and their three-year-old child. After the firm had done so, the husband instructed W to recover the child, who was in the lawful possession of the wife. W enlisted the services of A, T and F, and the four of them lay in wait, with the husband, for the wife and child. The husband forcibly snatched the child from the wife and then he and the others made off. W, A, T and F were charged with, and convicted of, child stealing, contrary to s. 56 of the Offences against the Person Act 1861. They appealed, contending that although they had deliberately aided and abetted the husband, they were not guilty of the offence charged because the husband had not been acting 'unlawfully' within the meaning of s. 56 and had committed no offence, or, alternatively, even if he had been acting unlawfully, they were entitled to immunity from prosecution under the proviso to s. 56 since they were the agents of a 'person who . . . claimed [a] right to the possession of such child'.

WATKINS LJ: . . . At the close of the case for the Crown in the Crown Court at Winchester counsel for the appellants, to whom we are extremely indebted for his restrained, able and frank submissions to us, made a number of concessions on behalf of the appellants. He has repeated them to this court. They are: (1) that each of these appellants aided and abetted King in taking Lara away from the possession of her mother; and (2) that the child was taken by King by the use of force on the mother and on the child. It was also conceded that they all knew the child was in the lawful possession of the mother, since there was no order in this country which affected her right to that at the material time and the order of the American court could not affect it in any practical way. It was also admitted that they had the intention to deprive the mother of possession of the child.

Having regard to those admissions and the background of this affair, one looks at s. 56 of the 1861 Act which provides:

Whosoever shall unlawfully . . . by force . . . take away . . . any child under the age of fourteen years, with intent to deprive any parent . . . of the possession of such child . . . shall be liable, at the discretion of the court . . . to be imprisoned: Provided, that no person who shall have claimed any right to the possession of such child, or shall be the mother or shall have claimed to be the father of an illegitimate child, shall be liable to be prosecuted by virtue hereof on account of the getting possession of such child . . .

It is submitted that there are two questions relevant to the issue of whether the appellants were rightly convicted: (1) did King commit an offence under s. 56, bearing in mind that he assaulted his wife and when taking the child away the child too, and (2) if King committed an offence under s. 56, does it follow that the appellants are also guilty of that offence? Furthermore, suppose King had been indicted and found not guilty by reason only of being able to take advantage of the proviso, could the appellants have escaped conviction in that way too?

. . .

Undoubtedly King could properly have claimed a right of possession to the child and so have gained the protection of the proviso. What would have been the effect of that? The effect would have been that, although he had committed the offence of child stealing, because he was the child's father and could claim a right to possession of the child he would not have been prosecuted. It is submitted on the appellants' behalf that the proviso also protects a class of persons wide enough to include those who aid a person such as the father of the child in gaining possession of his child by force. They become his agents for the purpose. Many persons have from time to time the temporary possession of a child as agents of parents. Why are they not protected to the same extent as parents when regaining possession as agents of parents?

In our view the only sensible construction of the proviso allows of its protection being granted to a small class of persons only, which includes the father and the mother of the child, whether the child be legitimate or illegitimate, or a guardian appointed by a testamentary document, or by an order conferring the status of guardianship, or a person to whom is granted an order conferring some form of care, control, custody or access. We can think of no other who could claim exemption from prosecution by reason of the proviso.

What of these appellants? They had no good reason for doing what they did. They had no right to assert, and no interest in, the possession of the child. They were the paid hirelings of King to aid him in the commission of a criminal offence, namely stealing a child, and with him they committed it as aiders and abettors. While King may shelter behind the proviso, there is no room there for them. Parliament in its wisdom undoubtedly decided that the mischiefs of matrimonial discord which are unhappily so widespread should not give rise to wholesale criminal prosecutions arising out of disputes about children, about who should have possession and control of them. That and that alone is the reason for the existence of the proviso to s. 56. Thus, as we have said, its application is confined to the select class of persons we have endeavoured to define.

It should be clearly understood that those such as these appellants who aid a father or a mother to take possession of a child from the other parent, and who do so by the use of force as aiders and abettors to it, commit the offence of child stealing, and that they are not immune from prosecution.

This was a wicked example of aiding and abetting the commission of the offence, child stealing. In the judgment of this court, the appellants are extremely fortunate that the trial judge treated them so mercifully by the sentences he imposed. This kind of activity must be condemned and those who are tempted to engage in it should be deterred from doing so.

Appeals dimissed.

Notes and questions

1. Does it seem odd that the defendants in *Austin* could be guilty of an offence for helping another person to do something which would not have been an offence if that other person had acted alone? Has the court created a crime where none was intended by Parliament?

2. Sometimes Parliament addresses the issue more directly. For example, although it is no longer criminal to commit suicide, it is an offence to be an accessory to a suicide. See Suicide Act 1961.

3. The courts have sometimes seemed to apply a 'derivative' theory of accessorial liability; that is, a theory that views the accessory's liability as deriving from that of the principal. The strict logic of this theory would lead one to the conclusion that there could not be a guilty accessory unless there was a guilty principal. However, there are numerous cases, many of which will be examined in this chapter, that suggest that the courts' adherence to this theory is not as rigorous as it is sometimes represented to be. Confronting the basic thesis head-on, however, why should an accessory's liability depend on whether the principal is either guilty of or can be convicted of (the two are not necessarily the same) an independent crime? Why should not the accessory be judged on the basis of his or her own acts, and the mental state with which those acts were performed?

II Liability as a principal

The person who acts with the requisite intent and whose acts cause the prohibited harm is in law deemed to be the principal. It is not necessary, however, that the principal personally commits the act which causes the harmful result. A principal may act through an 'innocent agent', as in the case where a person sends a letter bomb through the post – the principal is the sender of the letter and not the postal employee who delivers it. Sometimes the innocent agent is a person who, had he or she been charged with the substantive offence, would have had a defence such as infancy or insanity.

There can be more than one principal to a crime.

Mohan v *R*
[1967] 2 AC 187
Privy Council

The appellants, father and son, were convicted at Port of Spain Assizes of the murder of M., who received several wounds in an encounter with the appellants and died from his injuries. He had received, together with minor wounds, a very severe wound on the right leg and a very severe wound in the back. On the evidence there was a possibility that the death might have been caused solely by the leg wound, and the case was considered on that hypothesis.

LORD PEARSON: . . . The question . . . arises whether each of the appellants can be held responsible for the leg wound, when it may have been inflicted by the other of them. There is conflicting evidence as to which of them struck the blow on Mootoo's leg, the evidence for the prosecution tending to show that the appellant Deonath struck it and the evidence for the defence tending to show that the appellant Ramnath struck it. There is uncertainty on that point.

Also it cannot be inferred with any certainty from the evidence that the appellants had a pre-arranged plan for their attack on Mootoo.

It is, however, clear from the evidence for the defence, as well as from the evidence for the prosecution, that at the material time both the appellants were armed with cutlasses, both were attacking Mootoo, and both struck him. It is impossible on the facts of this case to contend that the fatal blow was outside the scope of the common intention. The two appellants were attacking the same man at the same time with similar weapons and with the common intention that he should suffer grievous bodily harm. Each of the appellants was present, and aiding and abetting the other of them in the wounding of Mootoo.

That is the feature which distinguishes this case from cases in which one of the accused was not present or not participating in the attack or not using any dangerous weapon, but may be held liable as a conspirator or an accessory before the fact or by virtue of a common design if it can be shown that he was party to a pre-arranged plan in pursuance of which the fatal blow was struck. In this case one of the appellants struck the fatal blow, and the other of them was present aiding and abetting him. In such a case the prosecution do not have to prove that the accused were acting in pursuance of a pre-arranged plan.

Questions

Why is the court in *Mohan* not more concerned with which of the defendants struck the fatal blow? With both defendants attacking the victim, was it little more than chance whose blow was fatal? The case would presumably have been analysed differently if one defendant had attacked the victim with his fists and the other with a knife, the victim dying from a knife wound – or would it?

Note

There is a somewhat similar situation which needs to be distinguished, where the two defendants cannot be shown to be acting in concert. Say that the leaders of the Conservative, Labour, and Liberal Democrat parties closet themselves in a locked room to settle their political differences. Only two walk out alive. The third has been strangled to death. Both of the survivors claim that the other was the strangler. If the prosecution are unable to prove which of the two survivors was the murderer, even though they know for certain it was one of them, there cannot be a criminal conviction in the absence of a showing, as in *Mohan*, of a joint enterprise or concert of action. It may seem strange that one of our two surviving politicians will be literally getting away with murder but the burden of proof is upon the prosecution to establish guilt beyond a reasonable doubt, and all we really have is a fifty-fifty probability that each of the potential defendants is guilty (assuming the evidence against each is equal). The philosophy embodied in the requirement of proof beyond reasonable doubt is that it is preferable that a guilty person go free, which is what will happen, than that an innocent person go to jail, which is what would happen if both were to be convicted.

R v Lane
(1986) 82 Cr App R 5
Court of Appeal

CROOM-JOHNSON LJ: . . . The medical evidence went no further than to prove that the injuries from which Sara died had been caused at some time between 12.30 and 8.30 p.m. During that time each of the appellants, as has been said, had been alone for some time with the child. When the Crown opened the case on count 1, manslaughter, it was said that the child's injuries had been caused by one or other or both of the appellants, but that it could not be established which of them had done so. Analysing it further, there was no evidence of the time when the blow was struck, who did it, or even who was present when it happened.

. . .

At the close of the prosecution case it was submitted on behalf of both appellants that there was no case to answer. The learned judge rejected that submission. Neither appellant gave evidence. They both appeal to this Court on the ground that the judge erred in law in rejecting their submission, that he erred in law in his directions to the jury, and that the convictions are unsafe and unsatisfactory. The appeal raises again the problem where the evidence available to the prosecution goes to prove that someone caused the injury to the baby but there is no admissible evidence implicating one defendant rather than the other.

What is the law? The starting-point is *Abbott* (1955) 39 Cr App R 141; [1955] 2 QB 497. The headnote in 39 Cr App R 141 reads:

> The appellant was indicted and tried with one W for forgery. By the close of the case for the prosecution the case against the appellant had collapsed and a submission was made on his behalf that there was no case to go to the jury. The judge, however, allowed the case against the appellant to proceed, because he took the view that the jury could not acquit both prisoners and that the co-prisoner's case which sought to throw the whole blame on the appellant might be prejudiced if the case against the appellant were withdrawn from the jury. The jury convicted both prisoners.
>
> *Held*, that, there being no evidence against the appellant at the close of the case for the prosecution, it was the duty of the judge to withdraw the case against him from the jury and that the conviction of the appellant must be quashed.

The classic passage in the judgment of Lord Goddard CJ is at p. 148 and p. 503, *viz.*:

> I think what possibly led the learned judge to act as he did when he was of opinion that there was no evidence against this appellant was that he had got into his mind that the jury could not say in this particular case: 'We find a verdict of Not Guilty in the case of both, because we are not satisfied which was guilty, if one of them was.' With great respect to the learned judge, that is not the law. If two people are jointly indicted for the commission of a crime and the evidence does not point to one rather than the other, and there is no evidence that they were acting in concert, the jury ought to return a verdict of Not Guilty in the case of both because the prosecution have not proved the case. If, in those circumstances, it is left to the defendants to get out of the difficulty if they can, that would put the onus on the defendants to prove themselves not guilty. . . .

The evidence against each appellant, taken separately, at the end of the prosecution's case did not establish his or her presence at the time when the child was injured, whenever that was, or any participation. Neither had made any admission; both had denied taking part in any injury; both had told lies but lies which did not lead to the inference of that defendant's presence.

The conclusion therefore is that the learned judge ought to have ruled in favour of the appellants on their submission of no case to answer.

Question

Could a conviction against both parents have been obtained on the theory that one was guilty for having inflicted the fatal blow and the other for failing to obtain medical assistance, there being a legal duty to do so because of the parent-child relationship? See *Russell and Russell* (1987) 85 Cr App R 388, below. See also *R* v *Forman and Ford* [1988] Crim LR 677.

Note
One must distinguish the situation where the principal acts through an innocent agent from that where a defendant is vicariously liable for the acts of some other person. The topic of vicarious liability has been examined in Chapter 2 (*Actus Reus*). Vicarious liability usually arises in the context of an employer-employee relationship, the employer being held vicariously liable for the crimes of the employee who has acted within the scope or authority of his employment. Liability is most often imposed by statute (or a court's interpretation of a statute). The employer can be vicariously liable not only for acts which he did not authorise (if he did authorise the acts, he would be liable on normal principal/accessory principles), but even for acts which he may have expressly forbidden. One cannot, however, be vicariously liable as an accessory, for, as will be discussed, proof of *mens rea* is required for accessorial liability. See *Ferguson* v *Weaving* [1951] 1 All ER 412. Curiously, where an employer is vicariously liable for the acts of an employee, the courts have held that the employee can be liable as an accessory. See *Griffiths* v *Studebakers* [1924] 1 KB 102.

III Liability as an accessory

An accessory is one who aids, abets, counsels or procures the commission of a crime but who is not the principal. The controlling statute is the Accessories and Abettors Act 1861, as amended by the Criminal Law Act 1977:

Accessories and Abettors Act 1861

8. Whosoever shall aid, abet, counsel, or procure the commission of any indictable offence, whether the same be an offence at common law, or by virtue of any Act passed or to be passed, shall be liable to be tried, indicted, and punished as a principal offender.

Note
See also the Magistrates' Courts Act 1980, s. 44.

A Elements of the offence

In order to convict a defendant as an accessory, the prosecution must prove that:

(a) an offence was committed;
(b) the defendant aided, abetted, counselled or procured the offence (the *actus reus*); and
(c) the defendant had the intent to further the commission of the offence or knew that his assistance would have this effect (the *mens rea*). This intent must be proven even though the offence aided may be one of strict liability.

(i)   An offence was committed
The prosecution must prove that an offence (or at least the *actus reus* of an offence) has been committed.

Thornton v *Mitchell*
[1940] 1 All ER 339
King's Bench

Appeal by the conductor by way of case stated from a decision of a court of summary jurisdiction sitting at Rochdale, whereby the conductor of an omnibus was convicted of having aided and abetted the driver of the omnibus in driving without due care and attention and without using reasonable consideration for others using the road. The charges against the driver were dismissed. On the hearing of the information, the following facts were proved or admitted. On 18 March 1939, the omnibus arrived at a road junction where all the passengers disembarked. Before the omnibus reversed, the conductor looked out of the back to see if the road was clear. Then he rang the bell three times as a signal to the driver to reverse. At the time when he gave the signal, the conductor, following his usual practice, was standing on the platform at the back of the omnibus. The time was about 7.45 p.m., and the visibility was poor. After giving the signal, the conductor jumped off the omnibus, which was reversed slowly. Two persons who had just disembarked were knocked down by the back of the omnibus as it was reversing, and one of them received fatal injuries. The driver could not see any person immediately behind the omnibus while he was reversing, owing to the obstruction caused by the steps to the upper deck, and owing to the height of the window at the back, and he had, therefore, to rely upon the conductor's signal.

LORD HEWART LCJ: In my opinion, it is quite clear that this appeal must be allowed.

... [t]his case is *a fortiori* upon *Morris* v *Tolman* [1923] 1 KB 166, to which our attention has been directed. I will read one sentence from the judgment of Avory J, at p. 171:

> ... in order to convict, it would be necessary to show that the respondent was aiding the principal, but a person cannot aid another in doing something which that other has not done.

That, I think, is the very thing which these justices have decided that this bus conductor did. In one breath they say that the principal did nothing which he should not have done, and in the next breath they hold that the bus conductor aided and abetted the driver in doing something which had not been done or in not doing something which he ought to have done. I really think that, with all respect to the ingenuity of counsel for the respondent, the case is too plain for argument, and this appeal must be allowed and the conviction quashed.

Questions
1.   Why, once the case against the driver was dismissed, should the conductor have escaped all liability? After all, harm did occur and arguably would not

have were it not for his reckless conduct. Are there other possible bases on which to premise a case against the conductor? Should accessorial liability be dependent on principal liability?

2.   Is *Thornton* v *Mitchell* reconciliable with *Austin* (supra, p. 180)?

Note
One must be careful to distinguish between the case where no crime has occurred and the case where a crime has occurred but the principal cannot be convicted.

R v *Bourne*
(1952) 36 Cr App R 125
Court of Appeal

The appellant was convicted at Worcestershire Assizes on 21 May 1952, on two counts of an indictment charging him with aiding and abetting his wife to commit buggery with a dog, and was sentenced by Hallett J to eight years' imprisonment. He was also convicted on two counts charging incitement to commit buggery, and on two counts charging indecent assault on his wife, and in respect of these he received concurrent sentences.

The indictment alleged an offence to have been committed on two separate occasions. The evidence showed that the appellant had on each occasion sexually excited the animal, and then caused his wife to submit to its having connection with her *per vaginam*. The wife stated in her evidence that she had been terrorised into submission and that the acts were entirely against her will. The judge left questions to the jury as follows:- (1) 'Did the prisoner on a day in or about the month of September 1949, in the county of Stafford cause his wife, Adelaide Bourne, to have carnal knowledge of a dog?' to which the jury replied: 'Yes.' (2) 'Are you satisfied that she did not consent to having such carnal knowledge?' to which the jury replied: 'Yes, we are satisfied she did not consent,' and he also left two similar questions with regard to the second offence, and the jury returned similar answers.

THE LORD CHIEF JUSTICE: The case against the appellant was that he was a principal in the second degree to the crime of buggery which was committed by his wife, because if a woman has connection with a dog, or allows a dog to have connection with her, that is the full offence of buggery. She may be able to show that she was forced to commit the offence. I will assume that the plea of duress could have been set up by her on the evidence, and in fact we have allowed Mr Green to argue this case on the footing that the wife would have been entitled to be acquitted on the ground of duress. The learned judge left no question to the jury on duress, but the jury have found that she did not consent. Assuming that she could have set up duress, what does that mean? It means that she admits that she has committed the crime but prays to be excused from punishment for the consequences of the crime by reason of the duress, and no doubt in those circumstances the law would allow a verdict of Not Guilty to be entered. . . .

There may be certain doctrines with regard to murder which do not apply to other cases, but I am willing to assume for the purpose of this case, and I think my brethren are too, that if this woman had been charged herself with committing the offence, she

could have set up the plea of duress, not as showing that no offence had been committed, but as showing that she had no *mens rea* because her will was overborne by threats of imprisonment or violence so that she would be excused from punishment. But the offence of buggery whether with man or beast does not depend upon consent; it depends on the act, and if an act of buggery is committed, the felony is committed.
. . .

In the opinion of the court, there is no doubt that the appellant was properly indicted for being a principal in the second degree to the commission of the crime of buggery. That is all that it is necessary to show. The evidence was, and the jury by their verdict have shown they accepted it, that he caused his wife to have connection with a dog, and if he caused his wife to have connection with a dog he is guilty, whether you call him an aider and abettor or an accessory, as a principal in the second degree. For that reason, this appeal fails and is dismissed.

Appeal dismissed

Notes
1.   Note the critical distinction between an affirmative defence and a defence which negates an element of the crime. Duress is an affirmative defence; if the defence were one that negated an element of the crime there would be no crime to which the defendant could have been an accessory.
2.   While the requirement of an offence having been committed seems to be logically inherent in the definition of accessorial liability, the courts at times seem prepared to hold a defendant liable as an accessory as long as the principal has committed the *actus reus* of the offence, even if the alleged principal cannot be convicted of the offence because he did not have the requisite *mens rea*. In these situations, ironically, it is *the accessory* who has the requisite *mens rea* for the substantive offence.

R v *Cogan and Leak*
[1976] 1 QB 217
Court of Appeal

The defendant L took the defendant C back to his home and told his wife that C wanted to have sexual intercourse with her and that he was going to see that she did. L's wife was not willing to have intercourse with C but she was frightened of L who made her go to the bedroom where C had sexual intercourse with her. The wife was sobbing throughout the intercourse. She did not struggle with C but she did try to turn away from him. C was charged with rape and L was charged with 'being aider and abettor to' that rape: the particulars of the offence being that he 'at the same time and place did abet counsel and procure [C] to commit the said offence.' At the trial, C's defence was that he believed that L's wife had consented to the intercourse. In a written statement he made to the police, L, who did not give evidence at the trial, confessed that he had procured C to have sexual intercourse with his wife, that she had not consented to that intercourse and that he had intended her to be raped by C. The jury found both defendants guilty and returned a special verdict that C had believed the wife was consenting but

that he had no reasonable grounds for such belief. Both defendants appealed
against conviction and C's appeal was allowed.

LAWTON LJ: . . . At the trial Cogan gave evidence that he thought Mrs Leak had
consented. The basis for his belief was what he had heard from her husband about her.
The drink he had had seems to have been a reason, if not the only one, for mistaking
her sobs and distress for consent.

The trial started on October 23, 1974. A few days before, namely, on October 14,
press publicity had been given to the fact that the Court of Appeal in *R v Morgan* [1976]
AC 182 had certified a point of law of general public importance as to whether in rape
the defendant can properly be convicted notwithstanding that he in fact believed that
the woman consented if such belief was not based on reasonable grounds and had given
leave to appeal to the House of Lords. In the course of his summing up the trial judge
stressed the need for the jury to be sure before convicting either of the defendants that
the wife had not consented to sexual intercourse. He then went on to direct them in
relation to Cogan's case in accordance with the decision of the Court of Appeal in *R v
Morgan*. He prudently decided to ask the jury to make a finding as to whether any belief
in consent which Cogan may have had was based upon reasonable grounds. The jury
returned a verdict of guilty against Cogan thereby showing that they were sure the wife
had not consented. They went on to say that Cogan had believed she was consenting
but that he had had no reasonable grounds for such belief.

As to Leak he directed the jury that even if Cogan believed that the wife was
consenting and had reasonable grounds for such a belief they would still be entitled to
find Leak guilty as charged.

Cogan's appeal against conviction was based on the ground that the decision of the
House of Lords in *R v Morgan* [1976] AC 182 applied. It did. There is nothing more
to be said. It was for this reason that we allowed the appeal and quashed his conviction.

Leak's appeal against conviction was based on the proposition that he could not be
found guilty of aiding and abetting Cogan to rape his wife if Cogan was acquitted of that
offence as he was deemed in law to have been when his conviction was quashed.

. . . [O]ne fact is clear – the wife had been raped. Cogan had had sexual intercourse
with her without her consent. The fact that Cogan was innocent of rape because he
believed that she was consenting does not affect the position that she was raped.

Her ravishment had come about because Leak had wanted it to happen and had taken
action to see that it did by persuading Cogan to use his body as the instrument for the
necessary physical act. In the language of the law the act of sexual intercourse without
the wife's consent was the actus reus: it had been procured by Leak who had the
appropriate mens rea, namely, his intention that Cogan should have sexual intercourse
with her without her consent. In our judgment it is irrelevant that the man whom Leak
had procured to do the physical act himself did not intend to have sexual intercourse
with the wife without her consent. Leak was using him as a means to procure a criminal
purpose.

Before 1861 a case such as this, pleaded as it was in the indictment, might have
presented a court with problems arising from the old distinctions between principals
and accessories in felony. Most of the old law was swept away by section 8 of the
Accessories and Abettors Act 1861 and what remained by section 1 of the Criminal Law
Act 1967. The modern law allowed Leak to be tried and punished as a principal
offender. In our judgment he could have been indicted as a principal offender. It would
have been no defence for him to submit that if Cogan was an 'innocent' agent, he was
necessarily in the old terminology of the law a principal in the first degree, which was a
legal impossibility as a man cannot rape his own wife during cohabitation. The law no

longer concerns itself with niceties of degrees in participation in crime; but even if it did Leak would still be guilty. The reason a man cannot by his own physical act rape his wife during cohabitation is because the law presumes consent from the marriage ceremony: see *Hale, Pleas of the Crown* (1778), vol. 1, p. 629. There is no such presumption when a man procures a drunken friend to do the physical act for him. Hale CJ put this case in one sentence, at p. 629:

> . . . tho in marriage she hath given up her body to her husband, she is not to be by him prostituted to another: see loc. cit.

Had Leak been indicted as a principal offender, the case against him would have been clear beyond argument. Should he be allowed to go free because he was charged with 'being aider and abettor to the same offence'? If we are right in our opinion that the wife had been raped (and no one outside a court of law would say that she had not been), then the particulars of offence accurately stated what Leak had done, namely, he had procured Cogan to commit the offence. This would suffice to uphold the conviction. We would prefer, however, to uphold it on a wider basis. In our judgment convictions should not be upset because of mere technicalities of pleading in an indictment. Leak knew what the case against him was and the facts in support of that case were proved. But for the fact that the jury thought that Cogan in his intoxicated condition might have mistaken the wife's sobs and distress for expressions of her consent, no question of any kind would have arisen about the form of pleading. By his written statement Leak virtually admitted what he had done. As Judge Chapman said in *R v Humphreys* [1965] 3 All ER 689, 692:

> It would be anomalous if a person who admitted to a substantial part in the perpetration of a misdemeanour as aider and abettor could not be convicted on his own admission merely because the person alleged to have been aided and abetted was not or could not be convicted.

In the circumstances of this case it would be more than anomalous: it would be an affront to justice and to the common sense of ordinary folk. It was for these reasons that we dismissed the appeal against conviction.

Questions
1. Is it logical to say, as does the court, that a rape took place but that Cogan could not be convicted of it because he lacked the requisite *mens rea*? Is not *mens rea* a defining element of the crime?
2. Is it correct to suggest that Cogan was Leak's agent? At the time of the decision the law, now changed, was that a husband could not be convicted of raping his wife. If so, how could he be convicted of raping her through an agent?
3. If Cogan could not be convicted of raping Leak's wife because he lacked the *mens rea* for that crime, and Leak could not commit a rape upon his own wife because of spousal immunity, what sense does it make to say that Leak is guilty because of the sexual relations between Cogan and Leak's wife? Is the key to understanding the court's decision the recognition that whatever illogicality there is in holding Leak liable is outweighed by the undesirability of allowing him to escape punishment for his morally reprehensible conduct? Does the court's problem in explaining its holding stem from its assumption of a derivative theory of accessorial liability; that is, one where the accessory's liability flows from that of the principal?

Notes
1.   If an accessory can be convicted of a crime committed by a principal even though the principal himself cannot be convicted of the crime, it would seem to follow that an accessory can be convicted of a more serious crime than the principal. For example, Alicia informs Benjamin that his wife is having an affair with Chatsworth. In the heat of passion Benjamin kills Chatsworth, as Alicia intended. Benjamin will most probably have his crime reduced to manslaughter because of the provocation, but Alicia may be convicted as an accessory to murder. See *R* v *Howe* [1987] 1 AC 417.
2.   Sometimes the alleged principal is acquitted for lack of evidence. In this situation the jury have not found that no offence has occurred, only that there was insufficient evidence to convict the person charged. Thus an accomplice might still be convicted of aiding and abetting. See, e.g., *Hughes* (1860) Bell CC 242.

(ii)   Actus reus
In order to secure a conviction as an accessory, the prosecutor must show that the defendant either aided, abetted, counselled or procured the offence. In theory each of these terms describes conceptually distinct behaviour. 'Aid' means to help or assist, 'abet' involves instigation or encouragement, 'counsel' implies advising or urging, and 'procure' has been defined as 'causing to be committed'. The line between the categories is often blurred, however, and the Crown is permitted to list all of these acts in the same charge. This is in part no doubt to avoid the absurdity of a defendant, charged with aiding, arguing that he is not guilty because he procured the offence, and then on a subsequent charge of procuring that he really was guilty of abetting, and then on a charge of abetting . . . .
    The range of activity which will render one liable as an accessory is as diverse as the human imagination. While aiding, abetting, and counselling are fairly straightforward concepts, this is not true of procuring.

Attorney-General's Reference (No. 1 of 1975)
[1975] QB 773
Court of Appeal

LORD WIDGERY CJ: This case comes before the court on a reference from the Attorney-General under s. 36 of the Criminal Justice Act 1972, and by his reference he asks the following question:

    Whether an accused who surreptitiously laced a friend's drinks with double measures of spirits when he knew that his friend would shortly be driving his car home, and in consequence his friend drove with an excess quantity of alcohol in his body and was convicted of the offence under the Road Traffic Act 1972, s. 6(1) is entitled to a ruling of no case to answer on being later charged as an aider and abetter, counsellor and procurer, on the ground that there was no shared intention between the two, that the accused did not by accompanying him or otherwise positively encourage the friend to drive, or on any other ground. . . .

The present question has no doubt arisen because in recent years there have been a number of instances where men charged with driving their motor cars with an excess quantity of alcohol in the blood have sought to excuse their conduct by saying that their drinks were 'laced', as the jargon has it; that is to say some strong spirit was put into an otherwise innocuous drink and as a result the driver consumed more alcohol than he had either intended to consume or had the desire to consume. The relevance of all that is not that it entitles the driver to an acquittal, because such driving is an absolute offence, but that it can be relied on as a special reason for not disqualifying the driver from driving. Hence no doubt the importance which has been attached in recent months to the possibility of this argument being raised in a normal charge of driving with excess alcohol.

The question requires us to say whether on the facts posed there is a case to answer, and needless to say in the trial from which this reference is derived the judge was of the opinion that there was no case to answer and so ruled. We have to say in effect whether he is right.

The language in the section which determines whether a 'secondary party', as he is sometimes called, is guilty of a criminal offence committed by another embraces the four words 'aid, abet, counsel or procure'. The origin of those words is to be found in s. 8 of the Accessories and Abettors Act 1861 which provides:

Whosoever shall aid, abet, counsel, or procure the commission of any misdemeanor, whether the same be a misdemeanor at common law or by virtue of any Act passed or to be passed, shall be liable to be tried, indicted, and punished as a principal offender.

Thus, in the past, when the distinction was still drawn between felony and misdemeanor, it was sufficient to make a person guilty of a misdemeanor if he aided, abetted, counselled or procured the offence of another. When the difference between felonies and misdemeanors was abolished in 1967, s. 1 of the Criminal Law Act 1967 in effect provided that the same test should apply to make a secondary party guilty either of treason or felony.

Of course it is the fact that in the great majority of instances where a secondary party is sought to be convicted of an offence there has been a contact between the principal offender and the secondary party. Aiding and abetting almost inevitably involves a situation in which the secondary party and the main offender are together at some stage discussing the plans which they may be making in respect of the alleged offence, and are in contact so that each knows what is passing through the mind of the other.

In the same way it seems to us that a person who counsels the commission of a crime by another, almost inevitably comes to a moment when he is in contact with that other, when he is discussing the offence with that other and when, to use the words of the statute, he counsels the other to commit the offence.

The fact that so often the relationship between the secondary party and the principal will be such that there is a meeting of minds between them caused the trial judge in the case from which this reference is derived to think that this was really an essential feature of proving or establishing the guilt of the secondary party and, as we understand his judgment, he took the view that in the absence of some sort of meeting of minds, some sort of mental link between the secondary party and the principal, there could be no aiding, abetting or counselling of the offence within the meaning of the section.

So far as aiding, abetting and counselling is concerned we would go a long way with that conclusion. It may very well be, as I said a moment ago, difficult to think of a case of aiding, abetting or counselling when the parties have not met and have not discussed in some respects the terms of the offence which they have in mind. But we do not see why a similar principle should apply to procuring. We approach s. 8 of the 1861 Act on the basis that the words should be given their ordinary meaning, if possible. We approach the section on the basis also that if four words are employed here, 'aid, abet, counsel or procure', the probability is that there is a difference between each of those four words and the other three, because, if there were no such difference, then Parliament would be wasting time in using four words where two or three would do. Thus, in deciding whether that which is assumed to be done under our reference was a criminal offence we approach the section on the footing that each word must be given its ordinary meaning.

To procure means to produce by endeavour. You procure a thing by setting out to see that it happens and taking the appropriate steps to produce that happening. We think that there are plenty of instances in which a person may be said to procure the commission of a crime by another even though there is no sort of conspiracy between the two, even though there is no attempt at agreement or discussion as to the form which the offence should take. In our judgment the offence described in this reference is such a case.

If one looks back at the facts of the reference: the accused surreptitiously laced his friend's drink. This is an important element and, although we are not going to decide today anything other than the problem posed to us, it may well be that in similar cases where the lacing of the drink or the introduction of the extra alcohol is known to the driver quite different considerations may apply. We say that because where the driver has no knowledge of what is happening, in most instances he would have no means of preventing the offence from being committed. If the driver is unaware of what has happened, he will not be taking precautions. He will get into his car seat, switch on the ignition and drive home and, consequently, the conception of another procuring the commission of the offence by the driver is very much stronger where the driver is innocent of all knowledge of what is happening, as in the present case where the lacing of the drink was surreptitious.

The second thing which is important in the facts set out in our reference is that following and in consequence of the introduction of the extra alcohol, the friend drove with an excess quantity of alcohol in his blood. Causation here is important. You cannot procure an offence unless there is a causal link between what you do and the commission of the offence, and here we are told that in consequence of the addition of this alcohol the driver, when he drove home, drove with an excess quantity of alcohol in his body.

Giving the words their ordinary meaning in English, and asking oneself whether in those circumstances the offence has been procured, we are in no doubt that the answer is that it has. It has been procured because, unknown to the driver and without his collaboration, he has been put in a position in which in fact he has committed an offence which he never would have committed otherwise. We think that there was a case to answer and that the trial judge should have directed the jury that an offence is committed if it is shown beyond reasonable doubt that the accused knew that his friend was going to drive, and also knew that the ordinary and natural result of the additional alcohol added to the friend's drink would be to bring him above the recognised limit of 80 milligrammes per 100 millilitres of blood.

Question

Consider the case of the social host who encourages his guests to imbibe of a punch liberally laced with alcohol. The guests know that the punch contains alcohol but not the percentage amount. Is the host liable as an accessory to drunk driving in the case of those guests who drive home? Under these circumstances what should the host do?

Note
Under the approach of the court in *A-G's Reference (No. 1 of 1975)* there need be no agreement between principal and accessory, the two do not ever have to have met, and the principal does not have to know of the accessory's assistance or existence. If there is an agreement, on the other hand, the two may also be guilty of conspiracy (see Chapter 7).

Can one be an accessory by omission, by doing nothing?

R v Clarkson and Others
[1971] 3 All ER 344
Courts-Martial Appeal Court

MEGAW LJ: . . . The relevant facts will be recited as briefly as possible. The victim of the offences was an 18 year old girl named Elke von Groen. On 9th May 1970 she, having recently come out of hospital where she had undergone an operation to her womb, went to a party at the barracks at Menden. At about midnight she left the party to go to see a soldier with whom she had in the past been familiar. She went to his room. He was not there but other soldiers were there. Eventually she went to another room, room 64, where the rapes occurred. There she was raped at least by Newton, by Holloway and by Marshall at one time or another between midnight and about 3.15 a.m. She was physically injured and her clothes were torn to shreds. To say that those who attacked her behaved like animals would be unjust to animals. At some time after the raping began and when she had been screaming and moaning, there were clustered outside the door of room 64 a number of men, including the three appellants, no doubt listening to what was going on inside. The only thing to be said in their favour is that they may have been in a drunken condition when their moral sense and sense of the requirements of human decency had left them. The door of room 64 opened and they, including the three appellants, in the words of a witness 'piled in' to the room. There is no doubt that they remained there for a considerable time and there is no doubt that during that time the unfortunate girl was raped. . . . there was no evidence on which the prosecution sought to rely that either the appellant Clarkson or the appellant Carroll had done any physical act or uttered any word which involved direct physical participation or verbal encouragement. There was no evidence that they had touched the girl, helped to hold her down, done anything to her, done anything to prevent others from assisting her or to prevent her from escaping, or from trying to ward off her attackers, or that they had said anything which gave encouragement to the others to commit crime or to participate in committing crime. Therefore, if there was here aiding and abetting by the appellants Clarkson or Carroll it could only have been on the basis of inferences to be drawn that by their very presence they, each of them separately as concerns himself, encouraged those who were committing rape. Let it be accepted, and there was evidence to justify this assumption, that the presence of those two appellants in the room where the offence was taking place was not accidental in any sense and that it was not by chance, unconnected with the crime, that they were there. Let it be accepted that they entered the room when the crime was committed because of what they had heard, which indicated that a woman was being raped, and they remained there.

    R v *Coney* (1882) 8 QBD 534 decided that non-accidental presence at the scene of the crime is not conclusive of aiding and abetting. The jury has to be told by the judge, or as in this case the court-martial has to be told by the judge-advocate, in clear terms what it is that has to be proved before they can convict of aiding and abetting; what it is of which the jury or the court-martial, as the case may be, must be sure as matters of inference before they can convict of aiding and abetting in such a case where the evidence adduced by the prosecution is limited to non-accidental presence. What has to be proved is stated by Hawkins J in a well-known passage in his judgment in *R* v *Coney* where he said:

> In my opinion, to constitute an aider and abettor some active steps must be taken by word, or action, with the intent to instigate the principal, or principals. Encouragement does not of necessity amount to aiding and abetting, it may be intentional or unintentional, a man may unwittingly encourage another in fact by his presence, by misinterpreted words, or gestures, or by his silence, or non-interference, or he may encourage intentionally by expressions, gestures, or actions intended to signify approval. In the latter case he aids and abets, in the former he does not. It is no criminal offence to stand by, a mere passive spectator of a crime, even of a murder. Non-interference to prevent a crime is not itself a crime. But the fact that a person was voluntarily and purposely present witnessing the commission of a crime, and offered no opposition to it, though he might reasonably be expected to prevent and had the power so to do, or at least to express his dissent, might under some circumstances, afford cogent evidence upon which a jury would be justified in finding that he wilfully encouraged and so aided and abetted. But it would be purely a question for the jury whether he did so or not.
>
> . . .

It is not enough, then, that the presence of the accused has, in fact, given encouragement. It must be proved that the accused intended to give encouragement; that he *wilfully* encouraged. In a case such as the present, more than in many other cases where aiding and abetting is alleged, it was essential that that element should be stressed; for there was here at least the possibility that a drunken man with his self-discipline loosened by drink, being aware that a woman was being raped, might be attracted to the scene and might stay on the scene in the capacity of what is known as a voyeur; and, while his presence and the presence of others might in fact encourage the rapers or discourage the victim, he himself, enjoying the scene or at least standing by assenting, might not intend that his presence should offer encouragement to rapers and would-be rapers or discouragement to the victim; he might not realise that he was giving encouragement; so that, while encouragement there might be, it would not be a case in which, to use the words of Hawkins J, the accused person 'wilfully encouraged'.

Notes and questions

1.   What more would the defendants in *Clarkson* have had to have done to be deemed accessories? What if they had shouted encouragement to the rapists? Would (should) it matter whether the rapists heard their shouts? Whether they were spurred on by them?

2.   Should the defendants in *Clarkson* have been liable for failing to summon the police? Should failure to report a crime itself be a crime, perhaps on the theory that one has a social responsibility and duty as a citizen to do so? At one

point in English history, such an offence (misprision of felony) existed (see *Sykes* v *Director of Public Prosecutions* [1961] 3 All ER 33), but it was abolished by the Criminal Law Act 1967. Now it is only a crime to accept consideration for not disclosing an arrestable offence (Criminal Law Act 1967, s. 5(1)). Should the law have gone in the opposite direction? If assistance to a victim of a crime can be provided at no risk to the actor, why should such assistance not be legally required, and why should one not be criminally liable for failing to provide such assistance?

3.   Assume that the spectators in *Clarkson* had made a mental resolve to prevent the interruption of the rape, without communicating this resolve to the rapists. Would this be sufficient to hold them liable as accessories, even if it should turn out that their assistance was not required? How does this hypothetical situation differ from that where a defendant has agreed to serve as lookout for a principal but no third parties intervene, and therefore no need arises for a warning to the principal? Can a principal draw support from an uncommunicated resolve to help, or is this the wrong question to be asking? Consider *Allan*.

R v *Allan and Others*
[1965] 1 QB 130
Court of Appeal

EDMUND DAVIES J: . . . [T]he judge [in effect] directed the jury that they were duty bound to convict an accused who was proved to have been present and witnessing an affray if it was also proved that he nursed an intention to join in if help was needed by the side he favoured and this notwithstanding that he did nothing by words or deeds to evince his intention and outwardly played the role of a purely passive spectator. It was said that, if that direction is right, where A and B behave themselves to all outward appearances in an exactly similar manner, but it be proved that A had the intention to participate if needs be, whereas B had no such intention, then A must be convicted of being a principal in the second degree to the affray, whereas B should be acquitted. To do that, it is objected, would be to convict A on his thoughts, even though they found no reflection in his actions. For the Crown, on the other hand, it is contended that the direction was unimpeachable, and that in the given circumstances a jury doing its duty would be bound to convict A of aiding and abetting in an affray even though he uttered no word of encouragement and acted throughout in exactly the same manner as all the other spectators of what was happening.

. . . [W]e have come to the conclusion that, in effect, the trial judge here dealt with facts which, at most, might provide some evidence of encouragement as amounting to conclusive proof of guilt. The jury were in terms told that a man who chooses to remain at a fight, nursing the secret intention to help if the need arose, but doing nothing to evince that intention, *must* in law be held to be principal in the second degree and that, on these facts being proved, the jury would have no alternative but to convict him. In our judgment that was a misdirection. . . . In our judgment, before a jury can properly convict an accused person of being a principal in the second degree to an affray, they must be convinced by the evidence that, at the very least, he by some means or other encouraged the participants. To hold otherwise would be, in effect, as the appellants' counsel rightly expressed it, to convict a man on his thoughts, unaccompanied by any physical act other than the fact of his mere presence.

Questions
1.   A is aware that B and C plan to kill D. A is also aware that E has sent a telegram warning D of the danger. A orders the telegraph operator not to deliver the warning, which directive is obeyed. Is A, whose actions are not known to B or C, an accessory to the murder of D? See *State ex rel Attorney-General* v *Tally*, 102 Ala 25, 15 So 722 (1894).
2.   Compare *Clarkson* with *Wilcox* v *Jeffery*.

Wilcox v *Jeffery*
[1951] 1 All ER 464
King's Bench Division

LORD GODDARD CJ: This is a Case stated by the metropolitan magistrate at Bow Street Magistrate's Court before whom the appellant, Herbert William Wilcox, the proprietor of a periodical called 'Jazz Illustrated,' was charged on an information that 'on Dec. 11, 1949, he did unlawfully aid and abet one Coleman Hawkins in contravening art. 1(4) of the Aliens Order, 1920, by failing to comply with a condition attached to a grant of leave to land, to wit, that the said Coleman Hawkins should take no employment paid or unpaid while in the United Kingdom, contrary to art. 18(2) of the Aliens Order, 1920.' Under the Aliens Order, art. 1(1), it is provided that

> ... an alien coming ... by sea to a place in the United Kingdom – (a) shall not land in the United Kingdom without the leave of an immigration officer ... '

It is provided by art. 1(4) that:

> An immigration officer, in accordance with general or special direction of the Secretary of State, may, by general order or notice or otherwise, attach such conditions as he may think fit to the grant of leave to land, and the Secretary of State may at any time vary such conditions in such manner as he thinks fit, and the alien shall comply with the conditions so attached or varied ...

If the alien fails to comply, he is to be in the same position as if he has landed without permission, i.e., he commits an offence.

The case is concerned with the visit of a celebrated professor of the saxophone, a gentleman by the name of Hawkins who was a citizen of the United States. He came here at the invitation of two gentlemen of the name of Curtis and Hughes, connected with a jazz club which enlivens the neighbourhood of Willesden. They, apparently, had applied for permission for Mr Hawkins to land and it was refused, but, nevertheless, this professor of the saxophone arrived with four French musicians. When they came to the airport, among the people who were there to greet them was the appellant. He had not arranged their visit, but he knew they were coming and he was there to report the arrival of these important musicians for his magazine. So, evidently, he was regarding the visit of Mr Hawkins as a matter which would be of interest to himself and the magazine which he was editing and selling for profit. Messrs Curtis and Hughes arranged a concert at the Princes Theatre, London. The appellant attended that concert as a spectator. He paid for his ticket. Mr Hawkins went on the stage and delighted the audience by playing the saxophone. The appellant did not get up and protest in the name of the musicians of England that Mr Hawkins ought not to be here competing with them and taking the bread out of their mouths or the wind out of their instruments. It is not found that he actually applauded, but he was there having paid to

go in, and, no doubt, enjoying the performance, and then, lo and behold, out comes his magazine with a most laudatory description, fully illustrated, of this concert. On those facts the magistrate has found that he aided and abetted.
. . .

There was not accidental presence in this case. The appellant paid to go to the concert and he went there because he wanted to report it. He must, therefore, be held to have been present, taking part, concurring, or encouraging, whichever word you like to use for expressing this conception. It was an illegal act on the part of Hawkins to play the saxophone or any other instrument at this concert. The appellant clearly knew that it was an unlawful act for him to play. He had gone there to hear him, and his presence and his payment to go there was an encouragement. He went there to make use of the performance, because he went there, as the magistrate finds was justified in finding, to get 'copy' for his newspaper. It might have been entirely different, as I say, if he had gone there and protested, saying: 'The musicians' union do not like you foreigners coming here and playing and you ought to get off the stage.' If he had booed, it might have been some evidence that he was not aiding and abetting. If he had gone as a member of a *claque* to try to drown the noise of the saxophone, he might very likely be found not guilty of aiding and abetting. In this case it seems clear that he was there, not only to approve and encourage what was done, but to take advantage of it by getting 'copy' for his paper. In those circumstances there was evidence on which the magistrate could find that the appellant aided and abetted, and for these reasons I am of opinion that the appeal fails.

Notes and questions
1. Would the defendant have been liable if he had written an unfavourable review? What about the members of the audience – did they also commit an offence? Did it matter whether or not they protested? Whether or not they applauded? Whether or not they had paid admission to the concert? The key to answering these questions lies in determining what constituted the aiding and abetting and at what point in time this occurred.
2. What is the difference between *Wilcox* v *Jeffrey* and *Clarkson*? Is it the fact that in *Clarkson* the rape was already underway when the alleged aiding occurred, while in *Wilcox* v *Jeffrey* there would have been no crime if there had been no audience? Did the audience in *Wilcox* v *Jeffrey* provide more in the way of positive encouragement than the audience in *Clarkson*? See also *Coney* (1882) 8 QBD 534.
3. Must there be a causal relationship between the acts of the accessory and the offence of the principal? It is often the case that while the accessory's assistance facilitates the commission of the offence, the principal would have in any event committed it. Does it depend on the form that the accessory's participation takes? Smith and Hogan, *Criminal Law* (7th ed) (1992), pp. 128–9, suggest:

(a) 'procuring' implies causation but not consensus;
(b) 'abetting' and 'counselling' imply consensus but not causation;
(c) 'aiding' requires actual assistance but neither consensus nor causation.

See also H.L.A. Hart and H. Honore, *Causation and the Law* (2nd ed.) (1985, ch. XIII).

In the context of liability for inaction you should recall (see Chapter 2) that in some instances one has a legal duty to act and the failure to act can give rise to criminal liability. Often the liability takes the form of a conviction for being an accessory. The following cases are illustrative:

R v *Russell and Russell*
(1987) 85 Cr App R 388
Court of Appeal

The appellants A and M were registered drug addicts, in receipt of daily prescriptions of methadone, which they obtained in liquid form. They were living with their 15-month-old daughter. One day the child died from a massive overdose of methadone. When interviewed separately by the police the appellants both denied giving methadone to the child save that they had on occasion dipped her dummy into the liquid methadone to placate her while she was teething. The appellants were charged with the child's manslaughter (count 1) and with cruelty to a person under 16, contrary to s.1(1) of the Children and Young Persons Act 1933 (count 2). The evidence at their trial was that, as to count 1, the amount of the drug in the child's body was such that it could not have been ingested solely by the dipping of the dummy into the mixture. Forensic evidence was given on the likely effect upon a baby of the administration of methadone on a dummy. At the close of the prosecution case a submission of no case to answer on behalf of A was overruled by the trial judge. The jury convicted A and M on both counts, as to count 1, indicating that they did so on the basis of deliberate administration.

THE LORD CHIEF JUSTICE: . . . Generally speaking, parents of a child are in no different position from any other defendants jointly charged with a crime. To establish guilt against either, the Crown must prove at the least that that defendant aided, abetted, counselled or procured the commission of the crime by the other. The only difference in the position of parents, as opposed to others jointly indicted, is that one parent may have a duty to intervene in the ill-treatment of their child by the other where a stranger would have no such duty. . . .

Appeals against conviction dismissed.

Rubie v *Faulkner*
[1940] 1 KB 571
King's Bench Division

The appellant, while in a motor vehicle driven by the holder of a provisional licence (a 'learner-driver') who was driving under his supervision in accordance with reg. 16(3)(a) of the Motor Vehicles (Driving Licences) Regulations 1937, was in a position to see that the driver was about to overtake another vehicle by pulling considerably to the offside at a pronounced bend of the road, but he neither said nor did anything to prevent it. An accident having occurred and the driver having been convicted of driving without due care and attention:—

Held, that the appellant was rightly convicted of aiding and abetting the driver in the commission of the offence.

LORD HEWART CJ: . . . [T]he condition on which the holder of a provisional licence is allowed to drive a motor-vehicle on a highway is that he is under the supervision of an experienced driver. The very essence of the matter is that there should be a supervisor competent to supervise. The duty being clear on the face of the regulation, it was a pure question of fact for the justices to decide whether that duty had been performed.

It seems to me that it was open to the justices to find that the appellant, by his passive conduct in circumstances which required him to be active, if only by exclaiming: 'Keep in!', failed to discharge the duty which he had undertaken, and thus was guilty of the offence with which he was charged. In my opinion, therefore, this appeal should be dismissed.

HILBERY J: I agree. The regulation is framed to make some provision for the protection of the public against the dangers to which they are exposed through a car being driven on the road by a driver who is still a learner and therefore assumed to be not fully competent. It is, I can only suppose, because a learner-driver is assumed to be not fully competent that the regulation provides that a supervisor shall accompany him. This being so, the supervisor must be intended by the regulation to have the duty, by supervision, of making up as far as possible for the driver's incompetence. In other words, it is the supervisor's duty, when necessary, to do whatever can reasonably be expected to be done by a person supervising the acts of another to prevent that other from acting unskilfully or carelessly or in a manner likely to cause danger to others, and to this extent to participate in the driving.

In this case it was found that the supervisor could see the driver was about to do the unlawful act of which he was convicted and the magistrates found that the supervisor remained passive. There is no hint in the case that the supervisor in evidence ever asserted that he did anything. For him to refrain from doing anything when he could see that an unlawful act was about to be done, and his duty was to prevent an unlawful act if he could, was for him to aid and abet.

(iii)   Mens rea
The *mens rea* of accessorial liability is an intent to do acts which the actor intends will assist the commission of the crime or which the actor knows will have this effect. Several points follow:

(a)   It is not enough simply to do acts which have the effect of furthering the commission of the crime – they must be done with the intent to further the commission of the crime or with the knowledge that they will have this effect. If, for example, Donald were to help Penny to move premises, not knowing that Penny's possessions were stolen, Donald would not be guilty of aiding in the transportation of stolen goods, although his acts would have had this effect. Even more compelling is the case where a bystander shouts at a youth to discontinue his assault on an old man but the youth misinterprets the shouting as encouragement.

(b)   It is the state of mind of the accessory and not that of the principal which is determinative of liability. As discussed previously, an accessory can be convicted of a more serious offence than the principal; the accessory who intentionally provides a gun to the excited husband who has just discovered his wife's adultery may be an accessory to murder even though the husband may only be guilty of manslaughter.

Can one, through recklessness, become an accessory?

Blakely and Sutton v *Director of Public Prosecutions*
[1991] Crim LR 764
Queen's Bench Division

T was an associate of B's. On the nights when he intended to stay with B, he would leave his car at the meeting place, but if he intended to go home, he would drink no more than two pints, thereafter drinking tonic water. On the night in question, he told B that he intended to go home to his wife. She discussed this with S, who suggested that if T had alcohol he might be unwilling to drive. Unknown to T, they added vodka to his tonic water. B intended to tell him later believing that he would not be prepared to drive. However, at closing time, T left before B had told him. He was arrested, and charged with a drink-driving offence. He advanced special reasons for not being disqualified. B and S testified with the result that T was given an absolute discharge. They were charged with 'aiding, abetting, counselling, procuring and commanding' T to drive when his blood-alcohol level exceeded that prescribed. It was contended that they did not intend T to drive; contrariwise, they intended that he should not drive. Following dismissal of their appeal to the Crown Court, they appealed by case stated, the questions being (i) whether the offence of procuring could be committed by someone who brought it about, not intending that the offence should be committed but reckless as to whether it be committed or not; (ii) if so, whether the meaning of recklessness in such a case was that given to it by Lord Diplock in *Lawrence* [1981] 2 WLR 524, 535.

Held, allowing the appeal, recklessness had two limbs: (a) pursuing a course of conduct and giving no thought to the possibility that it involved a risk when there was an obvious risk (inadvertent); (b) recognising that the conduct involved a risk but going on nevertheless to run it (advertent). Although the charge was framed compendiously only procuring was alleged, so only the *mens rea* of procuring the commission of an offence by another need be considered. The relevant issue was what must be proved to have been the state of the accused's mind in relation to the offence which the principal offender went on to commit? Counsel for the appellants submitted that the accused must not only have done his own act intentionally but must also have intended thereby to bring about the principal offence. Alternatively, he must have been aware that his intentional act might bring about the principal offence and have been prepared to do it nevertheless. Counsel for the DPP contended that an accused might be convicted of procuring an offence of strict liability if he intentionally did an act, or brought about a state of affairs, without which the offence would not have been committed and, at the time, he either intended that offence to occur or was reckless, in either of the *Caldwell* and *Lawrence* senses, as to whether the other essential acts or states constituting that offence would occur.

In *Carter* v *Richardson* [1974] RTR 314, the supervising driver was charged with aiding and abetting the learner driver's drink-driving offence. There was only one reference (317H) to recklessness which was not part of the *ratio*. Elsewhere in his judgment, Lord Widgery referred to the supervisor's knowledge or awareness, and there was nothing to suppose that, in approving the justices' opinion containing the word 'reckless,' he was thinking of anything other than advertent recklessness. In *Att.-Gen.'s Reference (No. 1)* [1975] 2 All ER 684, Lord Widgery said that to procure meant 'to produce by endeavour. You procure a thing by setting out to see that it happens and taking the appropriate steps to produce that happening.' That strongly suggested that the procurer must be shown to have intended to bring about the commission of the principal offence, and that mere awareness that it might result would not suffice. The language throughout the judgment was of knowledge of the offence the driver went on to commit: there was no hint that recklessness, let alone inadvertent recklessness, might suffice to convict the procurer.

There was no warrant for the suggestion that an accessory before the fact, whether aider and abettor, counsellor, commander or procurer, might be convicted on what might be called a less strict *mens rea* than would suffice to convict a principal in the second degree. Indeed, in *Ferguson v Weaving* [1951] 1 KB 814, it was suggested that something more might be required to convict one who 'counsels and procures.' That case would also appear to negate the submission for the DPP that it might be the case that the *mens rea* for procuring an absolute offence was less strict than that required of a person accused of procuring an offence which itself required *mens rea* (see also *Thomas v Lindop* [1950] 1 All ER 966). The conclusions on the question of the *mens rea* of an accessory before the fact were as follows. While it might now be the law that advertent recklessness to the consequences of his deliberate act of assistance might suffice to convict some, if not all, of those accused of being an accessory before the fact, it was clear that inadvertent recklessness did not. It must, at least, be shown that the accused contemplated that his act would or might bring about or assist the commission of the principal offence: he must have been prepared nevertheless to do his own act, and he must have done that act intentionally. Those requirements matched those needed to convict principals in the second degree, and they fitted well with the liability of the parties to a joint enterprise. In relation to those accused only of procuring and perhaps also those accused only of counselling and commanding, it might be, as Lord Goddard's judgment in *Ferguson v Weaving* would permit and as Lord Widgery's judgment in *Att. Gen.'s Reference (No. 1 of 1975)* strongly suggested, that it was necessary to prove that the accused intended to bring about the principal offence. The present case did not require that to be decided. The stated question would be answered: (1) the use of the word 'recklessness' was best avoided when considering the *mens rea* of a person accused of procuring the commission of a substantive offence; (ii) in so far as the correct approach to that *mens rea* accorded with the concept of 'recklessness,' 'No.'

Questions

1.   In *Blakely* the defendants did not wish the crime of drunk driving to take place – indeed, they spiked the victim's drink in order to induce him not to drive. Would the result in the case have been the same if they did not care whether or not he drove?

2.   Would Blakely and Sutton have been convicted under the Draft Criminal Code Bill?

Draft Criminal Code Bill 1989

27. – (1)   A person is guilty of an offence as an accessory if —

(a)   he intentionally procures, assists or encourages the act which constitutes or results in the commission of the offence by the principal; and

(b)   he knows of, or (where recklessness suffices in the case of the principal) is reckless with respect to, any circumstance that is an element of the offence; and

(c)   he intends that the principal shall act, or is aware that he is or may be acting, or that he may act, with the fault (if any) required for the offence.

(2)   In determining whether a person is guilty of an offence as an accessory it is immaterial that the principal is unaware of that person's act of procurement or assistance.

Notes and questions

1.   If recklessness were to be deemed a sufficient *mens rea* to convict one of being an accessory, should *Caldwell* (objective) recklessness suffice, or should liability be limited to *Cunningham* (subjective) recklessness?

2.   The accessory does not have to desire that the crime be committed – he may be ambivalent about it, or may prefer that it not to be committed. For example, if X sells a gun to Y, which Y tells X that she is going to use to kill her husband, X may be an accessory even though he does not care whether Y actually goes through with the killing. His sole motivation is to make a profit from the sale of the gun. The seller's liability rests on his providing assistance to the crime, knowing that the assistance will facilitate the commission of the crime. While the seriousness of murder may argue for the law to be structured so as to maximise prevention of its occurrence, should this analysis be extended to less serious crimes?

National Coal Board v *Gamble*
[1959] 1 QB 11
Queen's Bench Division

On 3 October 1957, M, the servant of a firm of hauliers, took his lorry to a colliery of the National Coal Board where it was filled with coal from a hopper and was then taken to a weighbridge, where the weighbridge operator H, who was employed by the board, weighed the lorry and its load and told M that the load was nearly 4 tons overweight. M., saying that he would risk taking the over-load, took the weighbridge ticket from H and left the colliery premises. He was subsequently stopped by the police and his firm were later convicted of contravening the Motor Vehicles (Construction and Use) Regulations 1955. It appeared that the hauliers were collecting the coal for carriage to a power station of an electricity authority, to whom the Coal Board were bound by contract to supply a bulk quantity of coal. The board were charged with aiding and abetting the firm in the commission of an offence.

LORD GODDARD CJ: . . . As soon as Haslam weighed the coal he knew it was overweight and called Mallender's attention to that fact. From Mallender's answer he knew that Mallender intended to drive the overweighted lorry on the highway and with that knowledge he completed the sale and handed the weight ticket to Mallender whose duty then was to give it to the purchasers, namely, the Central Electricity Authority. Haslam could, in my opinion, have refused to allow the overweight amount of 3 tons 18 cwts. to leave the colliery. No specific amount had been asked for. The board were no doubt bound to deliver coal to the electricity authority under their contract, but were not bound to deliver any particular amount of coal at any particular moment.

The justices drew the inference, and it was not disputed, that the board were bound by contract to supply a bulk quantity of coal to the authority. It was urged on behalf of the board that they had no right to require Mallender to unload the coal or rather the excess, but with this I cannot agree. For the reasons I have already given the property had not passed until the delivery was completed, and it could only be completed by the weighing and the delivery and acceptance of the ticket.

. . . Here no specific amount was asked for, but the board, by their servant, knew that more had been put into the lorry than could be lawfully carried on the road and with that knowledge completed the sale. In my opinion that amounted to an aiding and abetting of the offence, as Haslam knew Mallender was going there and then to drive the lorry on the highway, in other words, a specific offence was contemplated. . . .

DEVLIN J: . . . It was contended on behalf of the board that Haslam had no option after weighing but to issue the ticket for the amount then in the lorry. I think that this contention is unsound. In the circumstances of this case the loading must be taken as subject to adjustment; otherwise, if the contract were for a limited amount, the seller might make an over-delivery or an under-delivery which could not thereafter be rectified and the carrier might be contractually compelled to carry away a load in excess of that legally permitted. I think that the delivery of the coal was not completed until after the ascertained weight had been assented to and some act was done signifying assent and passing the property. The property passed when Haslam asked Mallender whether he intended to take the load and Mallender said he would risk it and when the mutual assent was, as it were, sealed by the delivery and acceptance of the weighbridge ticket. Haslam could therefore after he knew of the overload have refused to transfer the property in the coal.

. . . [A] man is presumed to intend the natural and probable consequences of his acts, and the consequence of supplying essential material is that assistance is given to the criminal. It is always open to the defendant, as in *R v Steane* [1947] KB 997, to give evidence of his real intention. But in this case the defence called no evidence. The prima facie presumption is therefore enough to justify the verdict, unless it is the law that some other mental element besides intent is necessary to the offence.

This is what Mr Thompson argues, and he describes the additional element as the purpose or motive of encouraging the crime. No doubt evidence of an interest in the crime or of an express purpose to assist it will greatly strengthen the case for the prosecution. But an indifference to the result of the crime does not of itself negative abetting. If one man deliberately sells to another a gun to be used for murdering a third, he may be indifferent about whether the third man lives or dies and interested only in the cash profit to be made out of the sale, but he can still be an aider and abettor. To hold otherwise would be to negative the rule that mens rea is a matter of intent only and does not depend on desire or motive.

. . . [T]he facts show an act of assent made by Haslam after knowledge of the proposed illegality and without which the property would not have passed. If some positive act to complete delivery is committed after knowledge of the illegality, the position in law must, I think, be just the same as if the knowledge had been obtained before the delivery had been begun. Of course, it is quite likely that Haslam was confused about the legal position and thought that he was not entitled to withhold the weighbridge ticket. There is no mens rea if the defendant is shown to have a genuine belief in the existence of circumstances which, if true, would negative an intention to aid. . . . But this argument, which might have been the most cogent available to the defence, cannot now be relied upon, because Haslam was not called to give evidence about what he thought or believed. . . .

Notes and Questions

1. What constituted the *actus reus* of the crime? The *mens rea*? The defendants had little interest in whether the lorry driver proceeded with his overweight load. They stood to gain neither financially nor in any other way.

2. What should the weighbridge operator have done? Is the effect of the decision to create a private police force – must citizens prevent crimes from being committed or risk being deemed accessories? Or is *Gamble* distinguishable because the weighbridge operator *knew* that with the ticket he provided the lorry driver would commit a crime? Where should the law draw the line of liability as we move away from 'knowledge' to some lesser state of awareness? What about criminal consequences which are foreseen to a high degree of probability? Foreseen as more probable than not? Foreseen as a possibility but not a probability? See also *Carter* v *Richardson* [1974] RTR 314.

3. Should the nature of the aid provided be relevant? What if the aid consists of an item of ordinary commerce, purchasable anywhere? Arlene walks into Brian's cutlery shop and asks for a knife sharp enough to kill a human being. Brian, having read *Gamble* and suspecting that the knife may be used for a criminal purpose, refuses to sell. Will not Arlene now simply purchase the knife at another store, being less indiscreet about her intended use of it? Such was not the case with the weighbridge ticket.

A not uncontroversial civil case, *Gillick* v *West Norfolk & Wisbech Area Health Authority* [1986] AC 112, raises questions about the continuing force of *Gamble*. The issue in the case was whether a doctor could give contraceptive advice to a female under the age of 16 without parental consent. Among the arguments raised by the girl's mother was that by giving such advice the doctor was aiding and abetting a criminal offence, it being illegal to have sexual intercourse with a girl under the age of 16. In a passage approved by the majority of the House of Lords, Woolf J addressed this argument:

Gillick v West Norfolk and Wisbech Area Health Authority
[1984] 1 QB 581
Queen's Bench Division

The Department of Health and Social Security issued to area health authorities a notice dealing with the organisation and development of a family planning service in which it was stated that family planning clinic sessions should be available to people irrespective of their age. It emphasised that attempts should always be made to persuade children under 16 who attended clinics to involve parents or guardians and said that it would be most unusual to provide contraceptive advice and treatment without parental consent, but that in exceptional cases it was for a doctor, exercising his clinical judgment, to decide whether contraceptive advice or treatment should be provided. The plaintiff, who was the mother of five girls under the age of 16, wrote to her local area health authority seeking an assurance from them that no contraceptive advice or treatment would be given to any of her children while under 16 without her knowledge and consent. The area health authority refused to give such an assurance, expressing their intention of abiding by the advice contained in the notice.

WOOLF J: . . . *Does the prescribing of contraceptives to a girl under 16 amount to criminal conduct on the part of a doctor?*
Section 28(1) of the Sexual Offences Act 1956 makes it

an offence for a person to cause or encourage . . . the commission of unlawful sexual intercourse with . . . a girl under the age of 16 for whom he is responsible.

Subsection (3) provides:

The persons who are to be treated for the purposes of this section as responsible for a girl are . . . (c) any other person who has the custody, charge or care of her.

Putting aside the question of whether or not the doctor's conduct could be said to amount to encouraging unlawful sexual intercourse, I cannot accept Mr Wright's submission that when a girl goes to a clinic for advice and/or treatment, she is in the ad hoc care of the doctor or the clinic. The words should not be narrowly construed but, in my view, they are inappropriate to cover a situation where a girl attends a clinic to seek help.
So far as the offence against section 6 of the Sexual Offences Act 1956, is concerned, I accept that a doctor who is misguided enough to provide a girl who is under the age of 16, or a man, with advice and assistance with regard to contraceptive measures with the intention thereby of encouraging them to have sexual intercourse, is an accessory before the fact to an offence contrary to section 6. I stress the words 'with the intention thereby of encouraging them to have sexual intercourse.' However, this, I assume, will not usually be the attitude of a doctor.
There will certainly be some cases, and I hope the majority of cases, where the doctor decides to give the advice and prescribe contraceptives despite the fact he was firmly against unlawful sexual intercourse taking place but felt, nevertheless, that he had to prescribe the contraceptives because, whether or not he did so, intercourse would in fact take place and the provision of contraceptives would, in his view, be in the best interests of the girl in protecting her from an unwanted pregnancy and the risk of a sexually transmitted disease. It is as to whether or not in such a situation the doctor is to be treated as being an accessory, that I have found the greatest difficulty in applying the law.
Mr Wright submits, and I accept that he is right in this submission, that it is necessary to distinguish between motive and intent. Even if your motives are unimpeachable, if you in fact assist in the commission of an offence, Mr Wright submits you are an accessory. He relies on the judgment of Devlin J in *National Coal Board* v *Gamble* [1959] 1 QB 11. In that case, Devlin J said, at p. 20:

A person who supplies the instrument for a crime or anything essential to its commission aids in the commission of it; and if he does so knowingly and with intent to aid, he abets it as well and is therefore guilty of aiding and abetting. . . . Another way of putting the point is to say that aiding and abetting is a crime that requires proof of mens rea, that is to say, of intention to aid as well as of knowledge of the circumstances, and that proof of the intent involves proof of a positive act of assistance voluntarily done.

Devlin J's judgment in that case was considered by Lord Simon of Glaisdale in *Director of Public Prosecutions for Northern Ireland* v *Lynch* [1975] AC 653, 698–699:

> As regards the actus reus, 'aiding' and 'abetting' are, as *Smith and Hogan* notes (p. 93), synonymous. But the phrase is not a pleonasm; because 'abet' clearly imports mens rea, which 'aid' might not. As Devlin J said in *National Coal Board* v *Gamble* . . . – and he quotes the passage I have just quoted – The actus reus is the supplying of an instrument for a crime or anything essential for its commission. On Devlin J's analysis the mens rea does not go beyond this. The act of supply must be voluntary (in the sense I tried to define earlier in this speech), and it must be foreseen that the instrument or other object or service supplied will probably (or possibly and desiredly) be used for the commission of a crime. The definition of the crime does not in itself suggest any ulterior intent; and whether anything further in the way of mens rea was required was precisely the point at issue in *Gamble's* case. Slade J thought the very concept of aiding and abetting imported the concept of motive. But Lord Goddard CJ and Devlin J disagreed with this. So do I. Slade J thought that abetting involved assistance or encouragement, and that both implied motive. So far as assistance is concerned, this is clearly not so. One may lend assistance without any motive, or even with the motive of bringing about a result directly contrary to that in fact assisted by one's effort.

However, in applying those statements of the law, three matters have to be borne in mind. First of all, contraceptives do not in themselves directly assist in the commission of the crime of unlawful sexual intercourse. The analogy of providing the motor car for a burglary or providing poison to the murderer, relied on in argument, are not true comparisons. While if the man wears a sheath, there may be said to be a physical difference as to the quality of intercourse, the distinction that I am seeking to draw is clearer where the woman takes the pill or is fitted with an internal device, when the unlawful act will not be affected in any way. The only effect of the provision of the means of contraception is that in some cases it is likely to increase the likelihood of a crime being committed by reducing the inhibitions of the persons concerned to having sexual intercourse because of their fear of conception or the contraction of disease. I therefore see a distinction between the assistance or aiding referred to by Lord Simon of Glaisdale and Devlin J and the act of the doctor in prescribing contraceptives. I would regard the pill prescribed to the woman as not so much 'the instrument for a crime or anything essential to its commission' but a palliative against the consequences of the crime.

The second factor that has to be borne in mind is that the girl herself commits no offence under section 6 since the section is designed to protect her from herself: see *R* v *Tyrrell* [1894] 1 QB 710. This creates problems with regard to relying upon any encouragement by the doctor as making him the accessory to the offence where the girl alone attends the clinic. The well-known case, *R* v *Bourne* (1952) 36 Cr App R 125, has to be distinguished because there, the woman can be said to have committed the offence although she was not criminally responsible because of duress. The doctor, if he is to be an accessory where the woman alone consults him, will only be an accessory if it can be shown that he acted through the innocent agency of the woman, the situation dealt with in *R* v *Cooper* (1833) 5 C & P 535.

The final point that has to be borne in mind is that there will be situations where long-term contraceptive measures are taken to protect girls who, sadly, will strike up promiscuous relationships whatever the supervision of those who are responsible for their well-being, the sort of situation that Butler-Sloss J had to deal with in *In re P. (A Minor)* (1981) 80 LGR 301. In such a situation the doctor will prescribe the measures to be taken purely as a safeguard against the risk that at some time in the future, the girl will form a casual relationship with a man when sexual intercourse will take place. In order to be an accessory, you normally have to know the material circumstances. In such a situation the doctor would know no more than that there was a risk of sexual intercourse taking place at an unidentified place with an unidentified man on an unidentified date – hardly the state of knowledge which is normally associated with an accessory before the fact.

Under this limb of the argument, the conclusion which I have therefore come to is, that while a doctor could, in following the guidance, so encourage unlawful sexual intercourse as to render this conduct criminal, in the majority of situations the probabilities are that a doctor will be able to follow the advice without rendering himself liable to criminal proceedings. Before leaving this limb of the argument, I should make it absolutely clear that the absence of consent of the parents makes no difference to the criminal responsibility of the doctor. If his conduct would be criminal without the parents' consent, it would be equally criminal with their consent.

Notes and questions
1.   Are *Gillick* and *National Coal Board* v *Gamble* reconcilable? For all intents and purposes, did not the doctor in *Gillick* know as surely as the weighbridge operator in *National Coal Board* v *Gamble* that the assistance which he provided would lead to the commission of a crime? At the very least, was not the doctor guilty of 'wilful blindness'?
2.   In his opinion in the House of Lords, Lord Scarman spoke of cases where '[t]he bona fide exercise by a doctor of his clinical judgment must be a complete negation of the guilty mind which is an essential ingredient of the criminal offence of aiding and abetting the commission of unlawful sexual intercourse'. Why should this be so? Is Lord Scarman confusing motive and intent? What is the difference between such a case and that of the seller who supplies a gun to a buyer whom the seller knows will use it for an illegal purpose, but who is ambivalent about that purpose? Assuming its validity, should the principle espoused by Lord Scarman be limited to doctors? Consider the case of prison officials who distribute condoms to prisoners to prevent AIDS, knowing that this will encourage the offence of buggery.

B   Scope of liability

Sometimes one who provides aid knows that a crime will be committed but does not know what crime. Is the aider then liable for whatever crime is committed?

R v *Bainbridge*
[1959] 1 QB 129
Court of Appeal

On the night of 30 October 1958, the Stoke Newington branch of the Midland Bank was broken into by cutting the bars of a window, the doors of the strong room and of a safe inside the strong room. They were opened by means of oxygen cutting equipment and nearly £18,000 was stolen. The cutting equipment was left behind and it was later found that that cutting equipment so left behind by the thieves had been purchased by the appellant, Alan Bainbridge, some six weeks earlier. He appealed against his conviction of being accessory before the fact to office-breaking.

LORD PARKER CJ: ... The case against him [the appellant] was that he had bought this cutting equipment on behalf of one or more of the thieves with the full knowledge that it was going to be used, if not against the Stoke Newington branch of the Midland Bank, at any rate for the purposes of breaking and entering premises.

The appellant's case, as given in his evidence, was this:

> True, I had bought this equipment from two different firms. I had gone there with a man called Shakeshaft to buy it for him. As a result of conversation which I had with him I was suspicious that he wanted it for something illegal, I thought it was for breaking up stolen goods which Shakeshaft had received, and as the result in those purchases I gave false names and addresses, but I had no knowledge that the equipment was going to be used for any such purpose as it was used.

. . .

Mr Simpson, who has argued this case very well, contends that ... in order that a man should be convicted of being accessory before the fact, it must be shown that at the time he bought the equipment in a case such as this he knew that a particular crime was going to be committed, and by a particular crime Mr Simpson means that the premises in this case which were going to be broken into were known to the appellant and contemplated by him, and not only the premises in question but the date when the breaking was going to occur; in other words, that he must know that on a particular date the Stoke Newington branch of the Midland Bank is intended to be broken into.

The court fully appreciates that it is not enough that it should be shown that a man knows that some illegal venture is intended. To take this case, it would not be enough if he knew – he says he only suspected – that the equipment was going to be used to dispose of stolen property. That would not be enough. Equally, this court is quite satisfied that it is unnecesssry that knowledge of the particular crime which was in fact committed should be shown to his knowledge to have been intended, and by 'particular crime' I am using the words in the same way in which Mr Simpson used them, namely, on a particular date and particular premises.

It is not altogether easy to lay down a precise form of words which will cover every case that can be contemplated but, having considered the cases and the law this court is quite clear that the direction of Judge Aarvold in this case cannot be criticised.

Judge Aarvold in this case ... makes it clear that there must be not merely suspicion but knowledge that a crime of the type in question was intended, and that the equipment was bought with that in view. In his reference to the felony of the type intended it was, as he stated, the felony of breaking and entering premises and the stealing of property from those premises. The court can see nothing wrong in that direction.

Director of Public Prosecutions for Northern Ireland v *Maxwell*
[1978] 3 All ER 1140
House of Lords

The appellant was a member of an illegal organisation in Northern Ireland which had been responsible for sectarian murders and bombings. On the night of 3 January 1976 the appellant was told by a member of the organisation to guide a car at night to a public house in a remote country area. The appellant knew that he was being sent on a terrorist attack but did not know what form it would take. Driving his own car he led another car containing three or four men to the public house. When he arrived there the appellant drove slowly past and then drove home. The other car stopped opposite the public house, one of the occupants got out, ran across to the public house and threw a pipe bomb containing 5 lbs of explosive into the hallway. The attack failed due to action taken by the licensee's son. The appellant was charged with doing an act with intent to cause an explosion by a bomb, contrary to s. 3(a) of the Explosive Substances Act 1883 and with possession of a bomb contrary to s. 3(b) of that Act. The appellant was convicted of both offences as principal in the second degree (i.e. as an accomplice). He appealed contending that since he did not know what form the attack would take or of the presence of the bomb in the other car he could not properly be convicted of aiding and abetting in the commission of crimes of which he was ignorant. The Court of Criminal Appeal in Northern Ireland dismissed his appeal. The appellant appealed to the House of Lords.

VISCOUNT DILHORNE: . . . At the trial, counsel for the appellant submitted that there was no evidence that the appellant knew the nature of the job that was to be done or that he knew of the presence of the bomb in the Cortina and that he could not be convicted of aiding and abetting in the commission of crimes of which he was ignorant. In the course of a careful and thorough judgment this submission was rejected by MacDermott J. It was repeated before the Court of Criminal Appeal in Northern Ireland and rejected by them. They, however, certified that the following point of law of general public importance was involved, namely:

> If the crime committed by the principal, and actually assisted by the accused, was one of a number of offences, one of which the accused knew the principal would probably commit, is the guilty mind which must be proved against an accomplice thereby proved against the accused?

. . . When the appellant was told at Dunadry what he was required to do, he must have known that he was required to take part in UVF 'military' operation. He cannot have thought that at that time of the evening welfare was involved. MacDermott J inferred that the preparation for timing and route of the journey indicated that the job was to be an attack on the Crosskeys bar. Even if the appellant did not appreciate that, which is most unlikely, he must have known that the 'military' operation was to take place at or near the Crosskeys Inn. Knowing that, he led the way and so played an important part in the operation. Counsel for the appellant however contended that he could not properly be convicted unless he knew either as a moral certainty or possibly beyond reasonable doubt or arguably on a balance of probabilities that a bomb was to be placed in the bar (count 1) and that the Cortina was carrying it (count 2).

I do not agree. In *R v Bainbridge* [1959] 1 QB 129 Bainbridge was convicted of being an accessory before the fact to office breaking. A bank had been broken into and oxygen cutting equipment left there. It was found to have been bought by Bainbridge some six weeks earlier. On appeal it was contended that he should not have been convicted unless it was shown that when he bought the equipment he knew it was to be used for breaking into that bank. Lord Parker CJ, delivering the judgment of the Court of Criminal Appeal, while recognising that it was not enough to show that a man knows that some illegal venture is intended, said that it was unnecessary that 'knowledge of the particular crime which was in fact committed should be shown to his knowledge to have been intended'. He approved of the direction given by Judge Aarvold who had told the jury that it must be proved that Bainbridge knew the type of crime which was in fact committed was intended

That case establishes that a person can be convicted of aiding and abetting the commission of an offence without his having knowledge of the actual crime intended. I do not think that any useful purpose will be served by considering whether the offences committed by the UVF can or cannot be regarded as the same type of crime. Liability of an aider and abettor should not depend on categorisation. The question to be decided appears to me to be what conduct on the part of those in the Cortina was the appellant aiding and abetting when he led them to the Crosskeys Inn. He knew that a 'military' operation was to take place. With his knowledge of the UVF's activities, he must have known that it would involve the use of a bomb or shooting or the use of incendiary devices. Knowing that he led them there and so he aided and abetted whichever of these forms the attack took. It took the form of placing a bomb. To my mind the conclusion is inescapable that he was rightly convicted on count 1.

I would dismiss the appeal.

LORD HAILSHAM OF ST MARYLEBONE: My Lords, in my opinion this appeal should be dismissed. The appellant was the owner and driver of the guide car in what subsequently turned out to be a terrorist attack by members of the criminal and illegal organisation known as the Ulster Volunteer Force ('UVF') on a public house owned by a Roman Catholic licensee at 40 Grange Road, Toomebridge, and known as the Crosskeys Inn. The attack was carried out on the night of 3rd January 1976 by the occupants of a Cortina car and took the form of throwing a pipe bomb containing about five pounds of explosive into the hallway of the public house. The attack failed because the son of the proprietor had the presence of mind to pull out the burning fuse and detonator and throw it outside the premises where the detonator exploded either because the fuse had reached the detonator or on contact with the ground. . . .

The only substantial matter to be discussed in the appeal is the degree of knowledge required before an accused can be found guilty of aiding, abetting, counselling or procuring. To what extent must the accused be proved to have particular knowledge of the crime in contemplation at the time of his participation and which was ultimately committed by its principal perpetrators? For myself I am content for this purpose to adopt the words of Lord Parker CJ in *R v Bainbridge* [1959] 1 QB 129 when, after saying that it is not easy to lay down a precise form of words which will cover every case, he observed that 'there must not be merely suspicion but knowledge that a crime of the type in question was intended', and the words of Lord Goddard CJ in *Johnson v Youden* [1950] 1 KB 544, endorsed by this House in *Churchill v Walton* [1967] 1 All ER 497 at 502–503, that 'Before a person can be convicted of aiding and abetting the commission of an offence he must at least know the essential matters which constitute that offence'. The only question in debate in the present appeal is whether the degree of knowledge possessed by the appellant was of the 'essential matters constituting' the offence in fact committed, or, to put what in the context of the instant case is exactly the same question in another form, whether the appellant knew that the offence in which he participated was 'a crime of the type' described in the charge.

For that purpose I turn to two passages in the findings of fact of the learned judge. The first is as follows:

In my judgment, the facts of this case make it clear to me that the accused knew the men in the Cortina car were going to attack the inn and had the means of attacking the inn with them in their car. The accused may not, as he says, have known what form the attack was going to take, but in my judgment he knew the means of the attack, be they bomb, bullet or incendiary device, were present in that car.

In the second passage MacDermott J said:

In my judgment, the accused knew that he was participating in an attack on the inn. He performed an important role in the execution of that attack. He knew that the attack was one which would involve the use of means which would result in danger to life or damage to property. In such circumstances, where an admitted terrorist participates actively in a terrorist attack, having knowledge of the type of attack intended, if not of the weapon chosen by his colleagues, he can in my view be properly charged with possession of the weapon with which it is intended that life should be endangered or premises seriously damaged.

The learned judge also found, *inter alia* that the word 'job' (as used in the appellant's statements) is 'synonymous with military action which raises, having regard to the proven activities of the UVF, the irresistible inference [that] the attack would be one of violence in which people would be endangered or premises seriously damaged'.

Questions
1.   If a dealer sells a gun to a person who is widely reputed to be a hit man for the mob, is the dealer an accessory to every murder which the buyer commits with the gun?
2.   Cecil enters Margaret's house with the intent to steal a painting, having gained access by using a key supplied by the gardener. The gardener knew that Cecil's intention was not honourable, but did not know what specific crime he contemplated. While in the house, Cecil decided to rape Margaret. Is the gardener liable for rape? Burglary? Consider in this regard Lord Scarman's observation in *Maxwell* that 'An accessory who leaves it to his principal to choose is liable, provided always the choice is made from the range of offences from which the accessory contemplates the choice will be made'.
3.   Is an accessory liable for the acts of a principal which are within the scope of their agreement, but which result in unintended consequences?

R v Creamer
[1965] 3 All ER 257
Court of Appeal

LORD PARKER CJ: In March, 1965, at the Central Criminal Court the appellant, together with a Mrs Harris, were jointly indicted with unlawfully killing one Angela Price, and both were convicted of manslaughter. Mrs Harris was sentenced to three years' imprisonment and the appellant was fined £150, and in default six months' imprisonment. The appellant now appeals by certificate of the learned common serjeant, the ground of appeal being whether being an accessory before the fact to manslaughter, i.e., involuntary manslaughter resulting from criminal abortion, is an offence known to the law. It was the case for the prosecution that the deceased died in the course of an abortion performed solely by Mrs Harris, and that the appellant, who was not present at the time, had arranged for the abortion to be performed, and indeed had introduced the parties, and was, accordingly, an accessory before the fact. Having regard to the point raised by the certificate, which is the only point with which we are concerned in this appeal, it is unnecessary to recite the facts. Suffice it to say that there was ample evidence that the appellant had counselled or procured the abortion; the sole question is whether, that being so, he could be found guilty of being an accessory before the fact to manslaughter, and, therefore, found guilty of the charge as laid against him. In dealing with the appellant, the common serjeant in his direction to the jury, said this:

If [the appellant] intended that that woman should do an unlawful and dangerous act on the girl, and took the steps to procure the doing of that act, and if the girl died as a result of that act, then, members of the jury, this case is proved against him, and your verdict against him would be guilty.

It is that direction which is attacked in that, so it is said, there is no offence known to the law of being an accessory before the fact to manslaughter.

. . . [C]ounsel for the appellant – and I may add that the court is very indebted to counsel's argument – submits that there is no case binding on this court which compels this court to hold that there is an offence known to the law of being an accessory before the fact to manslaughter. In his clear argument he takes a number of points. In the first instance, he points out that it is of the essence of counselling and procuring that you intend the result which you counsel or procure. A man cannot procure what he cannot intend, and he cannot intend an accidental killing. He supports that argument by saying, what is undoubtedly true, that attempted manslaughter and conspiracy to commit manslaughter are clearly offences unknown to the law. In passing, however, it has to be observed that, so far as an attempt is concerned, it clearly presupposes that death has not resulted and that, so far as conspiracy is concerned, it is the agreement to do the illegal act which constitutes the offence, and death, if it occurs, is due to some overt act. He secondly invokes the principle referred to by this court in *R v Bainbridge* [1959] 1 QB 129, that a man cannot be guilty of being an accessory before the fact to a felony different from that which he counselled and procured. Here counsel for the appellant contends that the appellant only counselled and procured the felony of abortion, whereas manslaughter is a separate felony. Thirdly, he contends that, in any event, the death is too remote to constitute the appellant an accessory to the causing of that death. He points out that the principal himself who commits the act from which death results is anyhow one stage removed from the death. Accordingly, a person who counsels and procures the act is two stages removed from the death. Bearing in mind that the appellant in the present case could have been charged as accessory before the fact to the abortion, he invites the court to say that the consequences here are too remote.

In the opinion of this court, the conclusion reached by Edmund Davies J, is correct. A man is guilty of involuntary manslaughter when he intends an unlawful act and one likely to do harm to the person and death results which was neither foreseen nor intended. It is the accident of death resulting which makes him guilty of manslaughter as opposed to some lesser offence, such as assault or, in the present case, abortion. This can no doubt be said to be illogical, since the culpability is the same, but, nevertheless, it is an illogicality which runs throughout the whole of our law, both the common law and the statute law. A comparatively recent example is clearly that of dangerous driving and causing death by dangerous driving. Bearing that in mind, it is quite consistent that a man who has counselled and procured such an illegal and dangerous act from which death, unintended, results should be guilty of being accessory before the fact to manslaughter. Nor can it be validly said that, when death results, a different felony has been committed within the principle referred to in *R v Bainbridge* [1959] 1 QB 129. The act intended is the same whether or not death results, and it is merely the accident of death which gives that act a different label. This court is quite satisfied that the law is as stated in 4 *Blackstone's Commentaries* (23rd Edn.), p. 38, . . .

> It is likewise a rule, that he who in any wise commands or counsels another to commit an unlawful act, is accessory to all that ensues upon that unlawful act; but is not accessory to any act distinct from the other.

It is worth observing that the next passage in *Blackstone* refers to the case of a man who has procured another to commit grievous bodily harm, and it is clear there that, because death results, he can be found guilty of being an accessory before the fact to murder. If that is so in the case of murder, then clearly it is also the case in the case of manslaughter.

For these reasons, this court is of opinion that this appeal fails and must be dismissed.

Appeal dismissed.

Also to be considered are cases where it is alleged that one of the principals went beyond the scope of the agreement:

R v Anderson and Morris
[1966] 2 QB 110
Court of Appeal

On an indictment of A and M for the murder of W the evidence was, *inter alia*, that A and M went from a flat in search of W, A being armed with a knife (which M denied knowing A had), and W died from stab wounds consequent on a fight in which A was seen punching W, with M standing at W's back apparently not taking any definite part in the fight.

A was convicted of murder, and M of manslaughter. M appealed on the ground of misdirection.

LORD PARKER CJ: . . . What is complained of is a passage of the summing-up. It is unnecessary to read the direction on law in full. The material direction is:

> If you think there was a common design to attack Welch but it is not proved, in the case of Morris, that he had any intention to kill or cause grievous bodily harm, but that Anderson, without the knowledge of Morris, had a knife, took it from the flat and at some time formed the intention to kill or cause grievous bodily harm to Welch and did kill him – an act outside the common design to which Morris is proved to have been a party – then you would or could on the evidence find it proved that Anderson committed murder and Morris would be liable to be convicted of manslaughter provided you are satisfied that he took part in the attack or fight with Welch.

Mr Lane submits that that was a clear misdirection. He would put the principle of law to be invoked in this form: that where two persons embark on a joint enterprise, each is liable for the acts done in pursuance of that joint enterprise, that that includes liability for unusual consequences if they arise from the execution of the agreed joint enterprise but (and this is the crux of the matter) that, if one of the adventurers goes beyond what has been tacitly agreed as part of the common enterprise, his co-adventurer is not liable for the consequences of that unauthorised act. Finally, he says it is for the jury in every case to decide whether what was done was part of the joint enterprise, or went beyond it and was in fact an act unauthorised by that joint enterprise.

In support of that, he refers to a number of authorities to which this court finds it unnecessary to refer in detail, which in the opinion of this court shows that at any rate for the last 130 or 140 years that has been the true position. . . .

Mr Caulfield, on the other hand, while recognising that he cannot go beyond this long string of decided cases, has said really that they are all part and parcel of a much wider principle which he would put in this form, that if two or more persons engaged in an unlawful act and one suddenly develops an intention to kill whereby death results, not only is he guilty of murder, but all those who have engaged in the unlawful act are guilty of manslaughter. He recognises that the present trend of authority is against that proposition, but he goes back to *Salisbury's* case [(1553) 1 Plow 100] in 1553. In that case a master had laid in wait to attack a man, and his servants, who had no idea of what his, the master's, idea was, joined in the attack, whereby the man was killed. It was held there that those servants were themselves guilty of manslaughter.

The court is by no means clear on the facts as reported that *Salisbury's* case is really on all fours, but it is in the opinion of the court quite clear that the principle is wholly out of touch with the position today. It seems to this court that to say that adventurers are guilty of manslaughter when one of them has departed completely from the concerted action of the common design and has suddenly formed an intent to kill and has used a weapon and acted in a way which no party to that common design could suspect is something which would revolt the conscience of people today.

Chan Wing-siu and Others v *R*
[1984] 3 All ER 878
Privy Council

The three accused, armed with knives, entered the deceased's flat, and while one guarded the deceased's wife, the other two stabbed the deceased. They then slashed the deceased's wife. The deceased died as a result of his wounds. The accused were charged with murder contrary to common law and with wounding with intent contrary to s. 17(a) of the Hong Kong Offences against the Person Ordinance, in that they had unlawfully and maliciously wounded the deceased's wife with intent to do her grievous bodily harm. The jury unanimously found all three accused guilty on both counts. The accused appealed to the Hong Kong Court of Appeal, which dismissed their appeal. They appealed to the Privy Council, contending that the judge had misdirected the jury by stating that they could convict each of the accused on both counts if he was proved to have had in contemplation that a knife might be used by one of his co-adventurers with the intention of inflicting serious bodily injury.

SIR ROBIN COOKE: . . . The present appeal involves solely an attack on the summing up, albeit in relation to both counts. As in the Court of Appeal, it is submitted for the appellants that it was not enough if an accused foresaw death or grievous bodily harm as a *possible* consequence of the joint enterprise, that the jury ought to have been directed that it must be proved that he foresaw that one of those consequences would *probably* result. Refining the argument somewhat, counsel for the appellants conceded before their Lordships that a person who is charged with murder on the basis of having been a party to an unlawful enterprise, and who was aware that weapons were being carried, need not have foreseen as more probable than not a contingency in which a weapon might be used by one of his companions (for example resistance by the victim of an intended robbery). The main proposition submitted for the appellants remained, however, that such an accused does at least have to be proved to have foreseen that, if such a contingency eventuated, it was more probable than not that one of his companions would use a weapon with intent to kill or cause grievous bodily harm.

In considering that argument it should first be recalled that a person acting in concert with the primary offender may become a party to the crime, whether or not present at the time of its commission, by activities variously described as aiding, abetting, counselling, inciting or procuring it. In the typical case in that class, the same or the same type of offence is actually intended by all the parties acting in concert. In view of the terms of the directions to the jury here, the Crown does not seek to support the present convictions on that ground. The case must depend rather on the wider principle whereby a secondary party is criminally liable for acts by the primary offender of a type which the former foresees but does not necessarily intend.

That there is such a principle is not in doubt. It turns on contemplation or, putting the same idea in other words, authorisation, which may be express but is more usually implied. It meets the case of a crime foreseen as a possible incident of the common unlawful enterprise. The criminal culpability lies in participating in the venture with that foresight.

A line of relevant English authorities from 1830 onwards was considered by the Court of Criminal Appeal in *R v Anderson and Morris* [1966] 2 All ER 644, [1966] 2 QB 110. Delivering the judgment of a court of five, Lord Parker CJ accepted a submission by Geoffrey Lane QC, and stated the law as follows, in terms very close to those reported ([1966]) QB 110 at 114) to have been formulated by counsel:

> . . . where two persons embark on a joint enterprise, each is liable for the acts done in pursuance of that joint enterprise, and that includes liability for unusual consequences if they arise from the execution of the agreed joint enterprise but (and this is the crux of the matter) . . . if one of the adventurers goes beyond what has been tacitly agreed as part of the common enterprise, his co-adventurer is not liable for the consequences of that unauthorised act. Finally . . . it is for the jury in every case to decide whether what was done was part of the joint enterprise, or went beyond it and was in fact an act unauthorised by that joint enterprise.

(See [1966] 2 All ER 644 at 647, [1966] 2 QB 110 at 118–119.)

. . . In agreement with the courts in Hong Kong, Australia and New Zealand, their Lordships regard as wholly unacceptable any argument that would propose, as any part of the criteria of the guilt of an accomplice, whether on considering in advance the possibility of a crime of the kind in the event actually committed by his co-adventurers he thought that it was more than an even risk. The concession that the contingency in which the crime is committed need not itself be foreseen as more probable than not, while virtually inevitable in the light of the reasoning in *Johns* v *R* (1980 143 CLR 108 (Aus) and the other cases, complicates the argument without improving it. What public policy requires was rightly identified in the submissions of the Crown. Where a man lends himself to a criminal enterprise knowing that potentially murderous weapons are to be carried, and in the event they are in fact used by his partner with an intent sufficient for murder, he should not escape the consequences by reliance on a nuance of prior assessment, only too likely to have been optimistic.

On the other hand, if it was not even contemplated by the particular accused that serious bodily harm would be intentionally inflicted, he is not a party to murder. . . .

The test of mens rea here is subjective. It is what the individual accused in fact contemplated that matters. As in other cases where the state of a person's mind has to be ascertained, this may be inferred from his conduct and any other evidence throwing light on what he foresaw at the material time, including of course any explanation that he gives in evidence or in a statement put in evidence by the prosecution. It is no less elementary that all questions of weight are for the jury. The prosecution must prove the necessary contemplation beyond reasonable doubt, although that may be done by inference as just mentioned. If, at the end of the day and whether as a result of hearing evidence from the accused or for some other reason, the jury conclude that there is a reasonable possibility that the accused did not even contemplate the risk, he is in this type of case not guilty of murder or wounding with intent to cause serious bodily harm.

In some cases in this field it is enough to direct the jury by adapting to the circumstances the simple formula common in a number of jurisdictions. For instance, did the particular accused contemplate that in carrying out a common unlawful purpose one of his partners in the enterprise might use a knife or a loaded gun with the intention of causing really serious bodily harm?

The present was such a case. It was not necessary for the trial judge to say more on the subject than he did . . ..

Where there is an evidential foundation for a remoteness issue, it may be necessary for the judge to give the jury more help. Although a risk of a killing or serious bodily harm has crossed the mind of a party to an unlawful enterprise, it is right to allow for a class of case in which the risk was so remote as not to make that party guilty of a murder or intentional causing of grievous bodily harm committed by a co-adventurer in the circumstances that in the event confronted the latter. But if the party accused knew that lethal weapons, such as a knife or a loaded gun, were to be carried on a criminal expedition, the defence should succeed only very rarely.

In cases where an issue of remoteness does arise it is for the jury (or other tribunal of fact) to decide whether the risk *as recognised by the accused* was sufficient to make him a party to the crime committed by the principal. Various formulae have been suggested, including a substantial risk, a real risk, a risk that something might well happen. No one formula is exclusively preferable; indeed it may be advantageous in a summing up to use more than one. For the question is not one of semantics. What has to be brought home to the jury is that occasionally a risk may have occurred to an accused's mind, fleetingly or even causing him some deliberation, but may genuinely have been dismissed by him as altogether negligible. If they think there is a reasonable possibility that the case is in that class, taking the risk should not make that accused a party to such a crime of intention as murder or wounding with intent to cause grievous bodily harm. The judge is entitled to warn the jury to be cautious before reaching that conclusion; but the law can do no more by way of definition; it can only be for the jury to determine any issue of that kind on the facts of the particular case.

. . .

Appeals dismissed.

Question
Is the key to the court's decision in *Chan Wing-siu* an implied (or tacit) agreement, or a contemplation on the part of the defendant that the crime might occur? At different points in its opinion the court seemed to embrace each of these rationales. Does the following case settle the controversy?

R v Hyde and Others
[1990] 3 All ER 892
Court of Appeal

LORD LANE CJ: . . . The incident resulting in the death of Gallagher took place outside the Merlin Public House, Andover, at about 10.25 p.m. on 3 June 1988. There was no dispute that Gallagher sustained a violent blow to the forehead, consistent with a heavy kick from a shod foot, which crushed the front of his skull. He died 73 days later, having never regained consciousness.

The prosecution case was that the three appellants carried out a joint attack on the victim and were all equally responsible for his death, even though it was not possible to say who had actually struck the fatal blow or blows; furthermore, that their intention had been to cause serious injury, or that each knew that such was the intention of the others when he took part.

. . .

All three gave evidence before the jury denying that there was any joint enterprise or any intent to do serious harm to Gallagher. Hyde and Sussex said each had acted on his own with no intention beyond a simple assault. Collins, according to them, was responsible for the fatal blow. His actions and intention were nothing to do with them, nor did they foresee what he might intend or do. Collins for his part maintained that there was no joint attack or, if there was, it involved only Hyde and Sussex.

The jury, it was submitted, could not be sure whose act caused the death, and that therefore no one should be convicted as the killer.

. . .

There are, broadly speaking, two main types of joint enterprise cases where death results to the victim. The first is where the primary object of the participants is to do some kind of physical injury to the victim. The second is where the primary object is not to cause physical injury to any victim but, for example, to commit burglary. The victim is assaulted and killed as a (possibly unwelcome) incident of the burglary. The latter type of case may pose more complicated questions than the former, but the principle in each is the same. A must be proved to have intended to kill or to do serious bodily harm at the time he killed. As was pointed out in R v Slack [1989] 3 All ER 90 at 94, [1989] QB 775 at 781, B, to be guilty, must be proved to have lent himself to a criminal enterprise involving the infliction of serious harm or death, or to have had an express or tacit understanding with A that such harm or death should, if necessary, be inflicted.

We were there endeavouring, respectfully, to follow the principles enunciated by Sir Robin Cooke in Chan Wing-siu v R [1984] 3 All ER 877 at 880–881 [1985] AC 168 at 175:

> The case must depend rather on the wider principle whereby a secondary party is criminally liable for acts by the primary offender of a type which the former foresees but does not necessarily intend. That there is such a principle is not in doubt. It turns on contemplation or, putting the same idea in other words, authorisation, which may be express but is more usually implied. It meets the case of a crime foreseen as a possible incident of the common unlawful enterprise. The criminal culpability lies in participating in the venture with that foresight.

It has been pointed out by Professor Smith, in his commentary on R v Wakely [1990] Crim LR 119 at 120–121, that in the judgments in R v Slack [1989] 3 All ER 90, [1989]

QB 775 and also in *R v Wakely* itself, to both of which I was a party, insufficient attention was paid by the court to the distinction between on the one hand tacit agreement by B that A should use violence, and on the other hand a realisation by B that A, the principal party, may use violence despite B's refusal to authorise or agree to its use. Indeed in *R v Wakely* we went so far as to say:

> The suggestion that a mere foresight of the real or definite possibility of violence being used is sufficient to constitute the mental element of murder is prima facie, academically speaking at least, not sufficient.

On reconsideration, that passage is not in accordance with the principles set out by Sir Robin Cooke which we were endeavouring to follow and was wrong, or at least misleading. If B realises (without agreeing to such conduct being used) that A may kill or intentionally inflict serious injury, but nevertheless continues to participate with A in the venture, that will amount to a sufficient mental element for B to be guilty of murder if A, with the requisite intent, kills in the course of the venture. As Professor Smith points out, B has in those circumstances lent himself to the enterprise and by so doing he has given assistance and encouragement to A in carrying out an enterprise which B realises may involve murder.

Questions
Consider the following cases:

(a)   A supplies B with a gun to kill C; B instead kills D. Is A liable as an accessory to D's death? Here the crime contemplated has not changed but the victim has. See *Saunders and Archer* (1573) 2 Plowden 473. Note that if B, shooting at C, had missed and hit D, it would be a case of transferred intent and neither B's nor A's liability would be affected. Should the result be different because B on his own initiative decided to kill D instead of C?

(b)   F supplies G with a gun to kill H but the gun malfunctions. Unwilling to be defeated, G strangles H to death. Is F liable? What aid or assistance has F supplied?

(c)   P and Q agree to rob V. P stands lookout while Q approaches V in a dark alley. Q not only robs V, but kills him as well. This was not part of their plan, but P knew that Q always went armed. Would P be guilty as an accessory to murder? See *Lovesey v Pearson* [1970] 1 QB 352; *Davies v Director of Public Prosecutions* [1954] 1 All ER 507. Compare *Betty* (1963) 48 Cr App R 6. What if P did not know that Q was carrying a deadly weapon?

(d)   During the course of a robbery, X tells Y to fetch a knife to threaten the victim if she should start to scream. Y cuts the victim's throat. Is X an accessory to murder? See *R v Slack* [1989] Crim LR 903.

C   Defences

(i)   Protected individuals
Where the law exists to protect a category of potential victims, it makes little sense to charge the victim as an accessory.

R v Tyrrell
[1894] 1 QB 710
Court for Crown Cases Reserved

The defendant, Jane Tyrrell, was on 15 September 1893, tried and convicted at the Central Criminal Court on an indictment charging her, in the first count, with having unlawfully aided and abetted, counselled, and procured the commission by one Thomas Ford of the misdemeanor of having unlawful carnal knowledge of her whilst she was between the ages of thirteen and sixteen, against the form of the statute, etc.; and, in the second count, with having falsely, wickedly, and unlawfully solicited and incited Thomas Ford to commit the same offence.

It was proved at the trial that the defendant did aid, abet, solicited and incited Thomas Ford to commit the misdemeanor made punishable by s. 5 of the Criminal Law Amendment Act 1885.

The question for the opinion of the Court was, 'Whether it is an offence for a girl between the ages of thirteen and sixteen to aid and abet a male person in the commission of the misdemeanor of having unlawful carnal connection with her, or to solicit and incite a male person to commit that misdemeanor.'

LORD COLERIDGE CJ: The Criminal Law Amendment Act 1885, was passed for the purpose of protecting women and girls against themselves. At the time it was passed there was a discussion as to what point should be fixed as the age of consent. That discussion ended in a compromise, and the age of consent was fixed at sixteen. With the object of protecting women and girls against themselves the Act of Parliament has made illicit connection with a girl under that age unlawful; if a man wishes to have such illicit connection he must wait until the girl is sixteen, otherwise he breaks the law; but it is impossible to say that the Act, which is absolutely silent about aiding or abetting, or soliciting or inciting, can have intended that the girls for whose protection it was passed should be punishable under it for the offences committed upon themselves. I am of opinion that this conviction ought to be quashed.

MATHEW J: I am of the same opinion. I do not see how it would be possible to obtain convictions under the statute if the contention for the Crown were adopted, because nearly every section which deals with offences in respect of women and girls would create an offence in the woman or girl. Such a result cannot have been intended by the legislature. There is no trace in the statute of any intention to treat the woman or girl as criminal.

Conviction quashed.

Questions
1. Is the result in *Tyrrell* justified on the theoretical basis that, since the purpose of the statute was in part to protect emotionally immature girls from themselves, it would be perverse to punish them for that same immaturity; or the practical basis that it would be counterproductive to prosecute the victim, for it would discourage victims from reporting crimes?

2. Of what relevance is Parliamentary intent? Is it possible in *Tyrrell* to determine what Parliament intended?

3. What if another girl of the victim's age assisted Tyrrell by arranging the rendezvous – could she be convicted as an accessory? Is the decision of the court helpful in answering this question?

4. Does the reasoning of *Tyrrell* apply to:

    (a)   the woman who voluntarily subjects herself to an illegal abortion;

    (b)   the previously unmarried partner in a bigamous marriage?

Is the common thread in these cases the fact that two persons are inevitably necessary to the commission of the crime, but the relevant statute punishes only one? How, then, does one explain the following decision?

Sayce* v *Coupe
[1953] 1 QB 1
Queen's Bench Division

Two informations were preferred by the appellant, George Sayce, an officer of the Customs and Excise, against the respondent, Wilson Coupe, the licensee of the Plough Inn, Manchester Street, Oldham, alleging (1) that on 4 December 1951, he knowingly kept uncustomed goods, namely, 3,580 American cigarettes, with intent to defraud His Majesty of the duty thereon contrary to s. 186 of the Customs Consolidation Act 1876, and (2) that on 24 November 1951, he did aid, abet, counsel and procure a person unknown to sell certain tobacco, to wit 5,600 cigarettes, otherwise than as a licensed manufacturer of or dealer in or retailer of tobacco selling tobacco in his entered premises or on premises wherein he carried on the business of a licensed dealer in or retailer of tobacco contrary to s. 13 of the Tobacco Act 1842, as amended by s. 8 of the Revenue Act. 1867.

LORD GODDARD CJ: [In the first part of its opinion the court found that the respondent had committed the offence of keeping uncustomed goods with intent to defraud the Revenue of the duties thereon.]

The second summons charged the respondent with aiding and abetting Wood – it says a person unknown but it must have been Wood – to commit an offence under section 13 of the Tobacco Act, 1842, by buying the cigarettes from a person who to his knowledge was not a licensed dealer in tobacco, and it is quite clear that the offence charged in the second information was committed.

Mr Hinchliffe has argued that because the statute does not make it an offence to buy, but only makes it an offence to sell, we ought to hold that the offence of aiding and abetting the sale ought not to be preferred or could not be preferred. It is obvious that it can be preferred. The statute does not make it an offence to buy, but obviously, on ordinary general principles of criminal law, if in such a case a person knows the circumstances and knows, therefore, that an offence is being committed and takes part in, or facilitates the commission of the offence, he is guilty as a principal in the second degree, for it is impossible to say that a person who buys does not aid and abet a sale.

For these reasons the justices ought also to have convicted on the second information.

Questions
1. On what basis is *Sayce* v *Coupe* distinguishable from *Tyrrell*?
2. Is the holding in *Sayce* v *Coupe* consistent with Parliamentary intent?
Presumably Parliament must have appreciated that in every sale there would
be both a buyer and a seller, and, in making only the seller liable, made a
conscious decision not to penalise the buyer.
3. A child is kidnapped. The parents, without informing the police, pay the
ransom. Are they accessories to kidnapping?

(ii) Withdrawal
Is it the rule that once an accomplice, always an accomplice? A thief who steals
another's property cannot escape liability if she has a subsequent change of
heart and returns the stolen goods; the crime is already complete. Should the
same be true in cases of an accessory?

R v Becerra
(1975) 62 Cr App R 212
Court of Appeal

The appellant, B, broke into the house with two other men C and one G.
Their intention was to steal from the householder. While in the house, the
tenant of a flat on the first floor surprised them and B calling 'let's go'
climbed out of a window followed by G and ran away. C, meanwhile, who
had been handed a knife by B, stabbed and killed the tenant. B and C were
charged, *inter alia*, with the tenant's murder, and at their trial the
prosecution case was that B and C were acting in concert in pursuance of a
common agreement to kill or inflict bodily harm should the need arise. B
contended that he had withdrawn from the joint adventure before the attack
on the tenant and, therefore, was not liable to be convicted of murder. The
jury were directed that the words 'let's go' and the appellant B's departure
through the window were insufficient to constitute a withdrawal. Both B and
C were convicted of murder.

ROSKILL LJ: . . . The basic prosecution case against Becerra and Cooper was that
they had entered into a common agreement to use such force as was necessary against
anyone in the house to get the money or to avoid identification or arrest. It was urged
that this common agreement included the use, if necessary, of the knife to inflict serious
bodily injury, if not death, and it was alleged that Cooper, in furtherance of that
common agreement, murdered Lewis with the knife in his left hand while he pinioned
Lewis from behind with his right arm around Lewis's shoulder.
    . . . It was argued . . . on behalf . . . of Becerra, that even if there were this common
design, . . . whatever Cooper did immediately before and at the time of the killing of
Lewis, Becerra had by then withdrawn from that common design and so should not be
convicted of the murder of Lewis . . . .
    It is necessary, before dealing with that argument in more detail, to say a word or two
about the relevant law. It is a curious fact, considering the number of times in which

this point arises where two or more people are charged with criminal offences, particularly murder or manslaughter, how relatively little authority there is in this country upon the point. But the principle is undoubtedly of long standing.

Perhaps it is best first stated in *Saunders and Archer* (1577) 2 Plowden 473 (in the eighteenth year of the first Queen Elizabeth) at p. 476, in a note by *Plowden*, thus:

> . . . for if I command one to kill J. S. and before the Fact done I go to him and tell him that I have repented, and expressly charge him not to kill J. S. and he afterwards kills him, there I shall not be Accessory to this Murder, because I have counter-manded my first Command, which in all Reason shall discharge me, for the malicious Mind of the Accessory ought to continue to do ill until the Time of the Act done, or else he shall not be charged; but if he had killed J. S. before the Time of my Discharge or Countermand given, I should have been Accessory to the Death, notwithstanding my private Repentance.

The next case to which I may usefully refer is some 250 years later, but over 150 years ago: *Edmeads and Others* (1828) 3 C & P 390, where there is a ruling of Vaughan B at a trial at Berkshire Assizes, upon an indictment charging Edmeads and others with unlawfully shooting at game keepers. At the end of his ruling the learned Baron said on the question of common intent, at p. 392,

> that is rather a question for the jury; but still, on this evidence, it is quite clear what the common purpose was. They all draw up in lines, and point their guns at the game-keepers, and they are all giving their countenance and assistance to the one of them who actually fires the gun. If it could be shewn that either of them separated himself from the rest, and showed distinctly that he would have no hand in what they were doing, the objection would have much weight in it.

I can go forward over 100 years. Mr Owen (to whose juniors we are indebted for their research into the relevant Canadian and United States cases) referred us to several Canadian cases, to only one of which is it necessary to refer in detail, a decision of the Court of Appeal of British Columbia in *Whitehouse (alias Savage)* (1941) 1 WWR 112. I need not read the headnote. The Court of Appeal held that the trial judge concerned in that case, which was one of murder, had been guilty of misdirection in his direction to the jury on this question of 'withdrawal.' The matter is, if I may most respectfully say so, so well put in the leading judgment of Sloan J.A., that I read the whole of the passage at pp. 115 and 116:

> Can it be said on the facts of this case that a mere change of mental intention and a quitting of the scene of the crime just immediately prior to the striking of the fatal blow will absolve those who participate in the commission of the crime by overt acts up to that moment from all the consequences of its accomplishment by the one who strikes in ignorance of his companions' change of heart? I think not. After a crime has been committed and before a prior abandonment of the common enterprise may be found by a jury there must be, in my view, in the absence of exceptional circumstances, something more than a mere mental change of intention and physical change of place by those associates who wish to dissociate themselves from the consequences attendant upon their willing assistance up to the moment of the actual commission of that crime. I would not attempt to define too closely what must be done in criminal matters involving participation in a common unlawful purpose to break the chain of causation and responsibility. That must depend upon the

circumstances of each case but it seems to me that one essential element ought to be established in a case of this kind: Where practicable and reasonable there must be timely communication of the intention to abandon the common purpose from those who wish to dissociate themselves from the contemplated crime to those who desire to continue in it. What is 'timely communication' must be determined by the facts of each case but where practicable and reasonable it ought to be such communication, verbal or otherwise, that will serve unequivocal notice upon the other party to the common unlawful cause that if he proceeds upon it he does so without the further aid and assistance of those who withdraw. The unlawful purpose of him who continues alone is then his own and not one in common with those who are no longer parties to it nor liable to its full and final consequences.

The learned judge then went on to cite a passage from 1 Hale's *Pleas of the Crown* 618 and the passage from *Saunders and Archer* (*supra*) to which I have already referred.

In the view of each member of this Court, that passage, if we may respectfully say so, could not be improved upon and we venture to adopt it in its entirety as a correct statement of the law which is to be applied in this case.

. . .

We therefore turn back to consider the direction which the learned judge gave in the present case to the jury and what was the suggested evidence that Becerra had withdrawn from the common agreement. The suggested evidence is the use by Becerra of the words 'Come on let's go,' coupled, as I said a few moments ago, with his act in going out through the window. The evidence, as the judge pointed out, was that Cooper never heard that nor did the third man. But let it be supposed that that was said and the jury took the view that it was said.

On the facts of this case, in the circumstances then prevailing, the knife having already been used and being contemplated for further use when it was handed over by Becerra to Cooper for the purpose of avoiding (if necessary) by violent means the hazards of identification, if Becerra wanted to withdraw at that stage, he would have to 'countermand,' to use the word that is used in some of the cases or 'repent' to use another word so used, in some manner vastly different and vastly more effective than merely to say 'Come on, let's go' and go out through the window.

It is not necessary, on this application, to decide whether the point of time had arrived at which the only way in which he could effectively withdraw, so as to free himself from joint responsibility for any act Cooper thereafter did in furtherance of the common design, would be physically to intervene so as to stop Cooper attacking Lewis, as the judge suggested, by interposing his own body between them or somehow getting in between them or whether some other action might suffice. That does not arise for decision here. Nor is it necessary to decide whether or not the learned judge was right or wrong, on the facts of this case, in that passage which appears at the bottom of p. 206, which Mr Owen criticised: 'and at least take all reasonable steps to prevent the commission of the crime which he had agreed the others should commit.' It is enough for the purposes of deciding this application to say that under the law of this country as it stands, and on the facts (taking them at their highest in favour of Becerra), that which was urged as amounting to withdrawal from the common design was not capable of amounting to such withdrawal. Accordingly Becerra remains responsible, in the eyes of the law, for everything that Cooper did and continued to do after Becerra's disappearance through the window as much as if he had done them himself.

Cooper being unquestionably guilty of murder, Becerra is equally guilty of murder. Mr Owen's careful argument must therefore be rejected and the application by Becerra for leave to appeal against conviction fails.

Notes and questions
1.   As a matter of social policy, should the law allow a defence of withdrawal?
What are the arguments for and against?
2.   Should the reason for the withdrawal be relevant? Compare the case of the
accessory who experiences a genuine change of heart because he appreciates
the moral wrongfulness of his conduct with that of the accessory who
experiences a change of mind because he encounters police at the scene of
the crime.
3.   What more would Beccara have had to have done for his defence to
succeed? Does there come a point where it is too late to withdraw? Had Beccara
reached that point? Consider the case where G provides information to
burglars regarding the premises to be burgled, including the location of alarms
and what must be done to neutralise them. Before the burglary the accessory
has a change of heart, and announces that he no longer wishes to be involved.
Is this sufficient to constitute a withdrawal? The rub is that by this point the
accessory has provided all the help that the burglars need to succeed. See
Grundy [1977] Crim LR 543.
4.   If the law is to recognise a defence of withdrawal, what must an accessory
do in order to be able to lay claim to it? Is it enough for the accessory to refrain
from any further involvement in the criminal enterprise, or should he have to
report the principal to the police or otherwise frustrate the accomplishment of
the crime? The answer may depend on how far the criminal enterprise has
progressed:

   (a)   If all that the accessory has done is to encourage a crime, a verbal
countermand of the former encouragement or instructions, or otherwise
making clear that there has been a change of mind may be enough (although
the accessory may still be guilty of incitement).
   (b)   If the crime is already well under way, then arguably the accessory
should have to take steps, such as notifying the victim, or perhaps even the
police, to prevent the crime's commission. At a minimum, there must be a
timely communication of an intention to withdraw; after the crime has been
committed or just as the police arrive on the scene, is too late.

5.   Withdrawal, while it may affect one's liability as an accessory, will not
affect one's liability for conspiracy or attempt (if the enterprise has gone
beyond the stage of mere preparation). See Chapter 7.

(iii)   Entrapment
What of the person who inveigles another into committing a crime for the
purpose of seeing that other person arrested? A 'friend' tells you that there is
a valuable painting inside a home and that the owners are away. The friend
offers to stand guard while you enter the home and take the painting, if you will
agree to split the proceeds of the sale with him. As soon as you are inside the
home, however, the friend telephones the police, who arrive and arrest you.

Under these circumstances, should you be entitled to a defence of entrapment?
Is the fact that the defendant has been entrapped at all relevant?

R v Birtles
(1969) 53 Cr App R 469
Court of Appeal

The appellant pleaded guilty at West Riding Quarter Sessions in March
1969 to burglary and to carrying an imitation firearm with intent to commit
burglary and was sentenced by the Chairman to consecutive terms of three
years' and two years' imprisonment.

THE LORD CHIEF JUSTICE: . . . As I have said, no one will perhaps ever know the
exact truth, but it certainly seems to this Court, doing the best that they can in the
matter, that there is a real possibility here that the appellant was encouraged by the
informer and indeed by the police officer concerned to carry out this raid on the post
office. Whether or not he would have done it without that, again no one can say, but
there is, as it seems to this Court, a real likelihood that he was encouraged to commit an
offence which otherwise he would not have committed.

It is in those circumstances that this Court is asked to review this sentence. On that
assumption, that he was so encouraged, the Court is quite satisfied that some reduction
in sentence is required. Doing the best they can, bearing in mind not only this possible
encouragement but at the same time the fact that the appellant had been minded to use
a real firearm, this Court feels that the greatest reduction that they can make is to make
these two sentences concurrent instead of consecutive, in other words, that the
appellant in the circumstances shall serve three years' imprisonment.

Before leaving this case, the Court would like to say a word about the use which, as
the cases coming before the Court reveal, is being made of informers. The Court of
course recognises that, disagreeable as it may seem to some people, the police must be
able in certain cases to make use of informers, and further – and this is really a corollary
– that within certain limits such informers should be protected. At the same time,
unless the use made of informers is kept within strict limits, grave injustice may result.
In the first place, it is important that the Court of trial should not be misled. A good
example of that occurred in the case of *Macro and Others*, again a raid on a sub-post
office, which came before this Court on February 10 ([1969]] Crim LR 205; *The Times*,
February 11, 1969). There the charge was one of robbery with aggravation, with a man
'unknown.' In fact, the man 'unknown' was an informer who, together with the police,
had warned the victim of what was going to take place, and had in fact gone through the
pretence of tying up the victim while the police were concealed upon the premises. Now
there the effect was that the appellant in that case pleaded Guilty to an offence which
had never been committed. If the facts had been known, there could not have been a
robbery at all, and accordingly it was for that reason that the Court substituted the only
verdict apt on the facts which was open to it, namely, a verdict of larceny. There is, of
course, no harm in not revealing the fact that there is an informer, but it is quite another
thing to conceal facts which go to the quality of the offence.

Secondly, it is vitally important to ensure so far as possible that the informer does not
create an offence, that is to say, incite others to commit an offence which those others
would not otherwise have committed. It is one thing for the police to make use of
information concerning an offence that is already laid on. In such a case the police are
clearly entitled, indeed it is their duty, to mitigate the consequences of the proposed

offence, for example, to protect the proposed victim, and to that end it may be perfectly proper for them to encourage the informer to take part in the offence or indeed for a police officer himself to do so. But it is quite another thing, and something of which this Court thoroughly disapproves, to use an informer to encourage another to commit an offence or indeed an offence of a more serious character, which he would not otherwise commit, still more so if the police themselves take part in carrying it out.

In the result, this appeal is allowed and the sentence reduced to one of three years.

Sentence reduced.

Questions
1. Should it matter whether the entrapper is a 'friend' or a police officer? Why? From the entrapped individual's perspective, is it not a matter of fortuity?
2. Should it matter whether the entrapper plants the idea for the crime in the principal's head, or whether the principal conceives of the plan on his own, with the entrapper simply encouraging the principal to carry through with it? Where the police create, rather than simply encourage, the commission of the offence, is there a stronger case for allowing a defence? Why? What purpose is served by freeing a defendant who has demonstrated a disposition to break the law when given the opportunity?

What of the entrapper? Is he guilty as an accessory?

R v *Clarke*
(1984) 80 Cr App R 344
Court of Appeal

MACPHERSON J: . . . On November 22, 1983, before Judge Gerber, Dennis Geoffrey Clarke was convicted by a jury of an offence of aiding and abetting burglary. He was absolutely discharged. He appeals against conviction by certificate of the trial judge who certified the case as fit for appeal on the ground that: 'I directed the jury with regard to count 2 as follows. The prosecution have to prove that: (a) Clarke knew the burglary was to be committed. (b) With that knowledge he volunteered and deliberately assisted Larch and Emery to carry it out. I further directed the jury that the fact that Clarke had prior to the date of the burglary given full information about it to a police officer was no defence to the charge set out in count 2.'

As we can see from the judgment upon counsels' submissions and the summing-up, the learned judge did in fact direct the jury to convict upon count 2 should they acquit (as they did) on count 1 of the indictment which the appellant faced. . . .

Before the trial began it was known to all, because of what the appellant had said to the policeman who arrested him on June 3, 1984, that he, Clarke, would accept that he did indeed participate in the burglary. But he asserted that he took part solely in order to give information to a police sergeant named Eastwood with whom he had made contact, and with whom he had been involved since 1982 both as an accused man in another matter and as an informer. The appellant said that he had told Sergeant Eastwood about the proposed Muswell Hill burglary two or three weeks before it took place, and he said that not only had he kept Eastwood informed but that Eastwood knew that the appellant was going to take part in the burglary, and told the appellant to try to find out the full identity of Ross, the inside man. The appellant said that he had arranged a place for the storage of the stolen goods, but that this also was done so that he could tell Sergeant Eastwood where the goods were so that they would be recovered almost at once. The appellant was saying that he did not act 'in a criminal sense' (as the judge put it in his summing-up) but was involved solely to assist the police and to give Eastwood information. And he was saying that his intention was that the others should not get away with their crime, and that the stolen goods would be recovered so that their owner would not be deprived permanently of them.

. . . [T]he judge directed the jury to convict on count 2 even if they accepted the appellant's evidence that he was acting honestly and solely in order to betray his associates and ensure the recovery of the goods.

In the result the jury acquitted the appellant on count 1 [burglary] and convicted on count 2. The basis upon which the jury acquitted him on count 1 must have been that they were not sure that the appellant was acting dishonestly (because he intended to bring his confederates to justice), and/or that they were not sure that he intended permanently to deprive the owner of his goods.

Counsel for the Crown accepted in argument in this Court that it is a necessary consequence of his submissions that any person acting as the appellant did, whether he was a police officer or someone acting as an informer or on his behalf, is necessarily and in all circumstances guilty of aiding and abetting provided only that (a) the offence is complete (as of course the burglary was upon the instant facts) before steps are taken to bring those involved to justice, and (b) the accused aider and abettor in some way positively assisted in the carrying out of the offence, knowing all the circumstances. . . .

When a man says (as did the appellant) that he joined the team solely to betray the others involved and to defeat the long term retention by the team of the owner's goods, the question whether he did so and joined thus honestly into a 'laid on' offence or crime ought in our judgment to be at least a matter for the jury's decision in a case where it is appropriate for an aiding and abetting allegation or count to be considered at all.

Normally in an entrapment case the encouraging or entrapping policeman or informer will not have a defence, since they counsel or procure the commission of the offence by their encouragement. 'The fact that the counsellor and procurer is a policeman or police informer, although it may be of relevance in mitigation of penalty for the offence, cannot affect the guilt of the principal offender; both the physical element (*actus reus*) and the mental element (*mens rea*) of the offence with which he is charged are present in his case' (*R* v *Sang* (1979) 69 Cr App R 282, 286). Such cases, it should be noted, are properly cases of incitement or procurement to offend, and would properly be charged as such or as cases of counselling or procuring rather than aiding and abetting in any event.

The present case falls in our judgment within the compass of the *dicta* of Lord Parker CJ in the case of *Birtles* (1969) 53 Cr App R 469, 472–473; [1969] 1 WLR 1047, 1049. . . .

In using the expression 'it may be perfectly proper' the Lord Chief Justice was, in our judgment, contemplating that in such exceptional cases where an informer (and/or a policeman) took part in a 'laid on' case there should be no finding that it was unlawful so to do. It would indeed be a rare case in which the facts would allow such a defence and in which a jury would say that a man might have been thus acting lawfully. But that there are such cases and that the jury should decide whether or not a case is within that exceptional and rare category is in our judgment both right and just. The learned judge should (if this had been a case in which the count of aiding and abetting remained alive at all) at least have left the matter to the jury . . . .

Further, however, we are convinced that this was a case in which the alternative count should not have been added or finally pursued. As a matter of exact analysis the appellant could of course have been said to have aided and abetted the others involved, but in reality he was either a burglar and guilty as such as a primary offender or, in our judgment, he was to be acquitted. Doubtless the appellant Clarke was exceedingly fortunate to be acquitted on count 1 upon the evidence . . . . But the jury did acquit him, and it must have been upon the basis that his evidence may have been true. It would in our judgment be illogical that the appellant should be not guilty of count 1 (in which he accepted that he was fully involved but said that he acted honestly and lawfully within the confines of the Lord Chief Justice's statement in *Birtles'* case), but guilty upon count 2 of aiding and abetting. In our judgment he should be guilty or not guilty of count 1, the full offence, and should not have been made guilty by the artificial addition of count 2.

Questions
1.   Does the entrapper have the *mens rea* of an accessory? On the one hand, the entrapper's objective is not to see a crime successfully committed but precisely the opposite. On the other hand, the entrapper has encouraged or counselled, and in some cases aided, the commission of a crime that might not otherwise have taken place. Has the entrapper performed a public service, or is he a public nuisance?
2.   Is the court in *Clarke* correct that it is illogical to acquit an entrapper of the substantive offence while convicting him of aiding and abetting? Do not the crimes require proof of different *mens rea*?
3.   Should motive be relevant? What if the entrapper's motive is not to expose a would-be criminal but to gain private revenge? See *Wilson* v *People*, 103 Colo 441, 87 P 2d 5 (1939).

Note
The Draft Criminal Code Bill 1989 would allow a defence for *agents provocateurs* who actually prevent the commission of a crime.

6 CORPORATE CRIMINALITY

I Introduction

The idea of holding a company liable for violations of the criminal law tests many of the elements and concepts which we have examined in previous chapters. Criminal law was designed with individuals in mind. The common law judges, whose task it was to shape the development of the criminal law, did so working with a model of the individual offender. The criminal law rests on assumptions of personal responsibility and moral blameworthiness. It is within this context that its doctrines of culpability and limiting principles make most sense and are best understood. Their application to corporations was inevitably bound to be problematic.

A company differs in fundamental respects from a person. It has no hands, heart, or a mind. How does it act, and how does it think? How does it cause results? In what sense can it be said to be morally blameworthy?

If the criminal law was to be applied to companies, there had to be found a counterpart within the corporate structure to these elements of conventional criminal law analysis. Also to be solved was the problem of how to 'punish' a company, as obviously the company itself could not be put in jail. Of course, an alternative approach would be not to try to squeeze companies into the conventional strictures of the criminal law but to start afresh and develop a new body of criminal law designed specifically with the company in mind.

In point of fact, both strategies were pursued. There are statutory enactments which are custom tailored to apply to businesses, and to businesses alone. To the extent that these statutes are backed up by a system of fines to be paid to the state (a traditional criminal sanction), they create what might be considered to be a body of corporate criminal law. At the same time there have been some less successful attempts to apply conventional criminal laws to companies. There are thus two branches of corporate crime – conventional criminal liability and regulatory offences – which need to be examined. We turn our attention first to the former.

II   Conventional criminal law as applied to the company

A   Actus reus

The initial hurdle in attributing an *actus reus* to a company is that many criminal statutes are written in terms of proscribing a particular act by a 'person'. A company of course is not a living person; it does not have the traditional attributes of personhood. Yet it is eminently capable of producing the same types of harmful results against which criminal laws are directed.

The technical problem that a company was not a person was solved by Parliament. Statutes were passed which stated that when the term 'person' appeared it should be construed to include a company. Likewise, procedural roadblocks to the prosecution of a company were removed by legislative fiat.

Interpretation Act 1889

2.—(1)   In the construction of every enactment relating to an offence punishable on indictment or on summary conviction whether contained in an Act passed before or after the commencement of this Act, the expression 'person' shall, unless the contrary intention appears, include a body corporate.

Criminal Justice Act 1925

33.—(1)   Where a corporation is charged, whether alone or jointly with some other person, with an indictable offence, the examining justices may, if they are of opinion that the evidence offered on the part of the prosecution is sufficient to put the accused corporation upon trial, make an order empowering the prosecutor to present . . . at assizes or quarter sessions, as the case may be, a bill in respect of the offence named in the order, and for the purpose of any enactments referring to committal for trial (including this Act) any such order shall be deemed to be a committal for trial:

Evans & Co., Limited v *London County Council*
[1914] 3 KB 315
King's Bench Division

AVORY J: The question whether a company incorporated under the Companies Acts may be made liable under the provisions of a penal statute has been the subject of discussion in many cases in recent years, and the decision on that question turns in my opinion upon the application of s. 2 of the Interpretation Act 1889, to the particular case. That section says that 'In the construction of every enactment relating to an offence punishable on indictment or on summary conviction, whether contained in an Act passed before or after the commencement of this Act, the expression "person" shall unless the contrary intention appears include a body corporate,' and in every case which comes before the Court the question has to be determined whether the contrary intention appears in the statute under which the proceedings are taken. In this case the proceedings are taken under s. 4 of the Shops Act 1912, which provides by sub-s. 1 that 'Every shop shall, save as otherwise provided by this Act, be closed for the serving of customers not later than one o'clock in the afternoon on one weekday in every week,' and by sub-s. 7 that 'In the case of any contravention of or failure to comply with any of the provisions of this section, the occupier of the shop shall be guilty of an offence against this Act and shall be liable to a fine' of the amount therein specified. And by s. 14 'All offences against this Act shall be prosecuted and all fines under this Act shall be recovered in like manner as offences and fines are prosecuted and recovered under the Factory and Workshop Act 1901,' which is in effect saying that they are to be prosecuted and recovered under the Summary Jurisdiction Acts. The first contention of the appellants was that they did not come within s. 4 because they were not 'occupiers' within the meaning of that section. It was not disputed that they were on the rate-book as the occupiers of the shop, and therefore prima facie they were within the section. But it was said that sub-s. 4 of that section shews that the term 'occupier' is used in a restricted sense, for it provides that where the local authority have reason to believe that a majority of the occupiers of shops of any particular class are in favour of being exempted from the provisions of the section they are to take steps to ascertain the wishes of the occupiers, and if satisfied that a majority are in favour of the exemption, or, in case of a vote being taken, at least one half of the votes recorded by the occupiers are in favour of it, they shall make an order exempting the shops of that class. It was said that a limited company cannot vote under that section. I am by no means satisfied that it cannot. There is nothing in the section which renders it impracticable for a company to exercise the right of voting. It does not say that the occupiers must be personally present when recording their vote. There is certainly nothing which prevents a limited company from expressing their wishes as occupiers. They can do so in the ordinary way, either by a resolution of the directors, or by the directors authorising the manager to express their views on their behalf. But even if that were not the case a difficulty in the way of exercising a right of voting would not in my opinion justify the contention that this section cannot be applied in the case of a company occupying a shop which is admittedly kept open in breach of its provisions. Secondly, Mr Turner has argued, apart from the provisions of the Shops Act, that as the fine has to be recovered under the Summary Jurisdiction Acts, and as the Summary Jurisdiction Act 1848, contains certain provisions which are applicable to '*persons*' but inapplicable to an incorporated company, proceedings cannot be taken against such a company for the recovery of a fine, and consequently the proceedings cannot be maintained in the present case. It is quite true that there are certain provisions in that Act which contemplate imprisonment of the defendant in certain events and which are not applicable to a company, but this Court has for many years past had to consider this question in connection with a variety of statutes under which fines are directed to be recovered under the Summary Jurisdiction Acts. For instance it has been held in cases under the Sale of Food and Drugs Act and under the Merchandise Marks Act that there is nothing in the provisions of those Acts or of the Summary Jurisdiction Acts to prevent the summary recovery of a fine from an incorporated company. The fact that some of the provisions of the Summary Jurisdiction Act 1848, are inapplicable to a company does not shew that all its provisions are inapplicable, and does not afford any evidence of that contrary intention which under the provisions of the Interpretation Act is necessary to prevent the term 'person' including a corporation. For these reasons I think the appeal must be dismissed.

Questions

1. The Shops Act 1912 envisaged an 'occupier' capable of exercising the vote. How does a corporation vote? What is the response of the court on this issue? Is it an intellectually satisfying response? Compare *Thornton* v *Mitchell* [1940] 1 All ER 339 (only the actual driver of a vehicle is capable of committing the act of 'driving').

2. Is the decision of the court in *Evans* v *LCC* based on principle or policy? If the latter, what policies?

(i)   Vicarious liability
To declare by legislative decree that a company shall be treated as a person does not cause the conceptual issues thereby raised automatically to disappear. Most crimes have an *actus reus* component. What constitutes an *actus reus* by a corporation? How can an inert entity such as a company 'act'? One possible answer is that a company acts through its employees. It then follows that for legal purposes the acts of the employee should be attributed to the company. This is, of course, a species of vicarious liability.

Mousell Bros Ltd v London and North-Western Railway Company
[1917] 2 KB 836
King's Bench Division

For the facts and holding, see p. 66.

Questions
1. If the act of the employee is unauthorised, is the company liable? Should it matter whether the employee is seeking to benefit the company or himself? See also *Director of Public Prosecutions* v *Kent and Sussex Contractors Ltd* [1944] KB 146; *Moore* v *Bresler* [1944] 2 All ER 515.
2. Is the company liable for acts of employees which have been specifically forbidden? What if the company knows that the act in question is being committed but fails to stop it?

(ii)   The identification principle
Vicarious liability is a useful analytic tool when small companies are involved. In such cases it can be expected that there will be tight control and supervision of the company's employees. Even if there were not the envisaged level of control and supervision, holding the company legally liable serves to exert pressure on the company to put in place policies which will require those in a supervisory capacity to exercise the desired level of supervision. Vicarious liability may make less sense in the case of large companies, which are likely to have hundreds (if not thousands) of employees. Can such a company be responsible for each and every act of each and every employee? Should it have to be?

An alternative to vicarious liability is to identify those persons at the nerve-centre of a company who wield such power and responsibility that for all practical purposes their commands are the commands of the company. Their acts and decisions can then be attributed to the company, not because they are the servants of the company, but because *for legal purposes they are the company*. The following case, one of the leading on point, asks whether a branch manager of a store which is part of a supermarket chain is such a person. There is an interesting twist to the case, however, for the technical issue is whether the branch manager is 'another person' for the purpose of establishing a defence to a violation of the Trade Descriptions Act 1968. To answer this question the House of Lords had to determine whether he was a person who should be identified as the company.

Tesco Supermarkets Ltd v *Nattrass*
[1971] 2 All ER 127
House of Lords

LORD REID: My Lords, the appellants own a large number of supermarkets in which they sell a wide variety of goods. The goods are put out for sale on shelves or stands each article being marked with the price at which it is offered for sale. The customer selects the articles he wants, takes them to the cashier, and pays the price. From time to time the appellants, apparently by way of advertisement, sell 'flash packs' at prices lower than the normal price. In September 1969 they were selling Radiant washing powder in this way. The normal price was 3s 11d but these packs were marked and sold at 2s 11d. Posters were displayed in the shops drawing attention to this reduction in price. . . . Mr Coane, an old age pensioner, saw this and went to buy a pack. He could only find packs marked 3s 11d. He took one to the cashier who told him that there were none in stock for sale at 2s 11d. He paid 3s 11d and complained to an inspector of weights and measures. This resulted in a prosecution under the Trade Descriptions Act 1968 and the appellants were fined £25 and costs. Section 11(2) provides:

> 'If any person offering to supply any goods gives, by whatever means, any indication likely to be taken as an indication that the goods are being offered at a price less than that at which they are in fact being offered he shall, subject to the provisions of this Act, be guilty of an offence.'

It is not disputed that that section applies to this case. The appellants relied on s. 24(1) which provides:

> In any proceedings for an offence under this Act it shall, subject to subsection (2) of this section, be a defence for the person charged to prove – (a) that the commission of the offence was due to a mistake or to reliance on information supplied to him or to the act or default of another person, an accident or some other cause beyond his control; and (b) that he took all reasonable precautions and exercised all due diligence to avoid the commission of such an offence by himself or any person under his control.

The relevant facts as found by the justices were that on the previous evening a shop assistant, Miss Rogers, whose duty it was to put out fresh stock found that there were no more of the specially marked packs in stock. There were a number of packs marked with the ordinary price so she put them out. She ought to have told the shop manager, Mr Clement, about this but she failed to do so. Mr Clement was responsible for seeing that the proper packs were on sale, but he failed to see to this although he marked his daily return 'All special offers OK'. The justice found that if he had known about this he would either have removed the poster advertising the reduced price or given instructions that only 2s 11d was to be charged for the packs marked 3s 11d. Section 24 (2) requires notice to be given to the prosecutor if the accused is blaming another person and such notice was duly given naming Mr Clement. . . .

I must start by considering the nature of the personality which by a fiction the law attributes to a corporation. A living person has a mind which can have knowledge or intention or be negligent and he has hands to carry out his intentions. A corporation has none of these; it must act through living persons, though not always one or the same person. Then the person who acts is not speaking or acting for the company. He is acting as the company and his mind which directs his acts is the mind of the company. There is no question of the company being vicariously liable. He is not acting as a servant, representative, agent or delegate. He is an embodiment of the company or, one could say, he hears and speaks through the persona of the company, within his appropriate sphere, and his mind is the mind of the company. If it is a guilty mind then that guilt is the guilt of the company. It must be a question of law whether, once the facts have been ascertained, a person in doing particular things is to be regarded as the company or merely as the company's servant or agent. In that case any liability of the company can only be a statutory or vicarious liability.

. . . Reference is frequently made to the judgment of Denning LJ in *H L Bolton (Engineering) Co Ltd* v *T J Graham & Sons Ltd* [1957] 1 QB 159. He said:

A company may in many ways be likened to a human body. It has a brain and nerve centre which controls what it does. It also has hands which hold the tools and act in accordance with directions from the centre. Some of the people in the company are mere servants and agents who are nothing more than hands to do the work and cannot be said to represent the mind or will. Others are directors and managers who represent the directing mind and will of the company, and control what it does. The state of mind of these managers is the state of mind of the company and is treated by the law as such.

In that case the directors of the company only met once a year; they left the management of the business to others, and it was the intention of those managers which was imputed to the company. I think that was right. There have been attempts to apply Denning LJ's words to all servants of a company whose work is brain work, or who exercise some managerial discretion under the direction of superior officers of the company. I do not think that Denning LJ intended to refer to them. He only referred to those who 'represent the directing mind and will of the company, and control what it does'.

I think that is right for this reason. Normally the board of directors, the managing director and perhaps other superior officers of a company carry out the functions of management and speak and act as the company. Their subordinates do not. They carry out orders from above and it can make no difference that they are given some measure of discretion. But the board of directors may delegate some part of their functions of management giving to their delegate full discretion to act independently of instructions from them. I see no difficulty in holding that they have thereby put such a delegate in their place so that within the scope of the delegation he can act as the company. It may not always be easy to draw the line but there are cases in which the line must be drawn. . . .

. . . I think that the true view is that the judge must direct the jury that if they find certain facts proved then as a matter of law they must find that the criminal act of the officer, servant or agent including his state of mind, intention, knowledge or belief is the act of the company. I have already dealt with the considerations to be applied in deciding when such a person can and when he cannot be identified with the company. I do not see how the nature of the charge can make any difference. If the guilty man was in law identifiable with the company then whether his offence was serious or venial his act was the act of the company but if he was not so identifiable then no act of his, serious or otherwise, was the act of the company itself.

What good purpose could be served by making an employer criminally responsible for the misdeeds of some of his servants but not for those of others? It is sometimes argued – it was argued in the present case – that making an employer criminally responsible, even when he has done all that he could to prevent an offence, affords some additional protection to the public because this will induce him to do more. But if he has done all he can how can he do more? I think that what lies behind this argument is a suspicion that justices too readily accept evidence that an employer has done all he can to prevent offences. But if justices were to accept as sufficient a paper scheme and perfunctory efforts to enforce it they would not be doing their duty – that would not be 'due diligence' on the part of the employer. Then it is said that this would involve discrimination in favour of a large employer like the appellants against a small shopkeeper. But that is not so. Mr Clement was the 'opposite number' of the small shopkeeper and he was liable to prosecution in this case. The purpose of this Act must have been to penalise those at fault, not those who were in no way to blame.

The Divisional Court decided this case on a theory of delegation. In that they were following some earlier authorities. But they gave far too wide a meaning to delegation. I have said that a board of directors can delegate part of their functions of management so as to make their delegate an embodiment of the company within the sphere of the delegation. But here the board never delegated any part of their functions. They set up a chain of command through regional and district supervisors, but they remained in control. The shop managers had to obey their general directions and also to take orders from their superiors. The acts or omissions of shop managers were not acts of the company itself.

In my judgment the appellants established the statutory defence. I would therefore allow this appeal.

Notes and questions

1. The House of Lords suggests that it would be harsh to hold a company liable when it has exercised due diligence. But is this not one of the dangers inherent in the application of any statute which imposes strict liability? Was the concern of the Lords thus misdirected? Did they in effect resolve one problem (the potential of holding a faultless company liable) by creating another (permitting a company to escape liability for the misdeeds of its employees by taking a narrow view of who can be identified with the company)? In a company as large as Tesco, what percentage of its employees are likely to satisfy the test of identification advanced by the Lords in *Tesco Supermarkets Ltd v Nattrass*?

2. The field of company law recognises 'shadow directors', defined as persons 'in accordance with whose instructions the directors of a company are accustomed to act'. (See Companies Act 1985, s. 741.) Do 'shadow directors' come within the *Tesco Supermarkets Ltd v Nattrass* test?

3. If there had been no statutory defence, would Tesco have been liable for a violation of the Trade Descriptions Act 1968?

4. If Tesco could not have been held liable for the violation of the statute, who could? What about the manager of the store? The assistant who put the wrongly marked packages on the shelf? Would it be fair or just to hold either of these individuals legally liable when the 'profits' of 'the crime' went to Tesco's?

5.   Whether an individual satisfies the identification test is a question of law for the court rather than a question of fact for the jury. Why?

(iii)   Criminal omissions

When we discussed *actus reus*, we discovered that one could be guilty for failing to act when there is a legal duty to act. The legal duty may be imposed by Parliament or may exist independent of statute. Several species of the latter were discussed.

In 1987 the ferry *Herald of Free Enterprise* sunk outside Zeebrugge, causing several hundred deaths, because the bow doors had not been properly closed. The failure was in part attributable to the individual seaman who should have closed the doors but did not, and to the captain who should not have sailed with the bow doors open but did. At another level the company's management had been urged to install a warning system which would have alerted the captain to the danger, but it never got around to doing so. The company was charged with manslaughter.

R v *P & O European Ferries (Dover) Ltd*
(1991) 93 Cr App R 72
Court of Appeal

TURNER J: . . . The main thrust of the argument for the company in support of the submission that the four counts of manslaughter in this indictment should be quashed was not merely that English law does not recognise the offence of corporate manslaughter but that, as a matter of positive English Law, manslaughter can only be committed when one natural person kills another natural person. Hence it was no accident that there is no record of any corporation or non-natural person having been successfully prosecuted for manslaughter in any English Court. It was, however, accepted that there is no conceptual difficulty in attributing a criminal state of mind to a corporation. The broad argument advanced on behalf of the prosecution was that, there being no all embracing statutory definition of murder or manslaughter, there is, in principle, no reason why a corporation, or other non-natural person, cannot be found guilty of most offences in the criminal calendar. The exceptions to such a broad proposition could be found either in the form of punishment, which would be inappropriate for a corporation, or in the very personal nature of individual crimes or categories of crime such as offences under the Sexual Offences Act, bigamy and, arguably, perjury. It was further argued that the definitions of homicide to be found in the works of such as *Coke, Hale, Blackstone* and *Stephen*, and which were strongly relied upon by the company, were and were not intended to be exclusive, but reflected the historical fact that, at the dates when these definitions originated, the concept of criminal liability of a corporation, just as their very existence, was not within the contemplation of the courts or the writers of the legal treatises referred to. Before the days when corporate crime was in contemplation, it can be a matter of no surprise to find that the definition of homicide did not include the possibility of a corporation committing such a crime. . . .

Since the nineteenth century there has been a huge increase in the numbers and activities of corporations whether nationalised, municipal or commercial, which enter the private lives of all or most of 'men and subjects' in a diversity of ways. A clear case can be made for imputing to such corporations social duties including the duty not to offend all relevant parts of the criminal law. By tracing the history of the cases decided by the English Courts over the period of the last 150 years, it can be seen how first tentatively and, finally confidently the Courts have been able to ascribe to corporations a 'mind' which is generally one of the essential ingredients of common law and statutory offences. Indeed, it can be seen that in many Acts of Parliament the same concept has been embraced. The parliamentary approach is, perhaps, exemplified by section 18 of the Theft Act, 1968 which provides for directors and managers of a limited company to be rendered liable to conviction if an offence under section 15, 16 or 17 of the Act are proved to have been committed – and I quote: 'with the consent, connivance of any director, manager, secretary . . . purporting to act in such capacity, then such director, manager or secretary shall be guilty of the offence.' Once a state of mind could be effectively attributed to a corporation, all that remained was to determine the means by which that state of mind could be ascertained and imputed to a non-natural person. That done, the obstacle to the acceptance of general criminal liability of a corporation was overcome. *Cessante ratione legis, cessat ipsa lex.* As some of the decisions in other common law countries indicate, there is nothing essentially incongruous in the notion that a corporation should be guilty of an offence of unlawful killing. I find unpersuasive the argument of the company that the old definitions of homicide positively exclude the liability of a non-natural person to conviction of an offence of manslaughter. Any crime, in order to be justiciable must have been committed by or through the agency of a human being. Consequently, the inclusion in the definition of the expression 'human being' as the author of the killing was either tautologous or, as I think more probable, intended to differentiate those cases of death in which a human being played no direct part and which would have led to forfeiture of the inanimate, or if animate non-human, object which caused the death (*deodand*) from those in which the cause of death was initiated by human activity albeit the instrument of death was inanimate or if animate non-human. I am confident that the expression 'human being' in the definition of homicide was not intended to have the effect of words of limitation as might have been the case had it been found in some Act of Parliament or legal deed. It is not for me to attempt to set the limits of corporate liability for criminal offences in English Law. Examples of other crimes which may or may not be committed by corporations will, no doubt, be decided on a case by case basis in conformity with the manner in which the common law has adapted itself in the past. Suffice it that where a corporation, through the controlling mind of one of its agents, does an act which fulfils the prerequisites of the crime of manslaughter, it is properly indictable for the crime of manslaughter. . . .

Questions

1. Who or what caused the deaths of the passengers? Is the opinion of Turner J helpful in answering these questions? What theory of manslaughter does he advance?

2. Did P & O owe a legal duty to its passengers? Of what relevance is (should be) such a duty?

3. At trial the judge directed the jury to return a verdict of not guilty, in part because of management testimony that the occasional open bow sailings that had previously, albeit inadvertently occurred had not resulted in mishap, and in part because of management's claim not to have been aware of the dangers. Are these reasons persuasive? See generally C. Wells, *Corporations and Criminal Responsibility* (1993).

B   Mens rea

(i)   Intent

It is one thing to attribute to a company the acts of its employees; it is quite another to attribute to it the employee's state of mind. Or is it?

R v ICR Haulage Ltd
[1944] 1 All ER 691
Court of Criminal Appeal

STABLE J: . . . The question before us is whether a limited company can be indicted for a conspiracy to defraud. The Criminal Justice Act 1925, s. 33, removed certain procedural obstacles which had hitherto existed in connection with the trial of criminal offences alleged against corporations, but this section did not enlarge the ambit of a company's criminal responsibility but provided machinery for simplifying its enforcement.

It was conceded by counsel for the appellant that a limited company can be indicted for some criminal offences, while it was conceded by counsel for the respondent that there were some criminal offences for which a limited company cannot be indicted. The controversy centred round the question as to where and on what principle the line must be drawn and on which side of the line an indictment such as the present one falls. Counsel for the appellant contended that the true principle was that an indictment against a limited company for any offence involving as an essential ingredient *mens rea* in the restricted sense of a dishonest or criminal mind must be bad, for the reason that a company not being a natural person cannot have a mind honest or otherwise, and that consequently though under certain circumstances it is civilly liable for the fraud of its officers, agents or servants, it is immune from criminal process.

Counsel for the respondent contended that a limited company, like any other entity recognised by the law, can as a general rule be indicted for its criminal acts, which from the very necessity of the case must be performed by human agency and which in given circumstances become the acts of the company, and that for this purpose there was no distinction between an intention or other function of the mind and any other form of activity.

The offences for which a limited company cannot be indicted are, it was argued, exceptions to the general rule arising from the limitations which must inevitably attach to an artificial entity, such as a company. Included in these exceptions are the cases where, from its very nature, the offence cannot be committed by a corporation, as, for example, perjury, an offence which cannot be vicariously committed, or bigamy, an offence which a limited company, not being a natural person, cannot commit vicariously or otherwise.

A further exception, but for a different reason, comprises offences of which murder is an example, where the only punishment the court can impose is corporal, the basis on which this exception rests being that the court will not stultify itself by embarking on a trial in which, if a verdict of guilty is returned, no effective order by way of sentence can be made. In our judgment these contentions of the respondent are substantially sound, and the existence of these exceptions, and it may be that there are others, is by no means inconsistent with the general rule.

. . .

The latest authority is *Director of Public Prosecutions* v *Kent & Sussex Contractors Ltd* [1944] KB 146. A limited company was charged with offences under the Defence

(General) Regulations, which involved an intent to deceive. The justices dismissed the informations on the ground that a body corporate could not be guilty of the offences charged inasmuch as an act of will or state of mind which could not be imputed to a corporation was implicit in the commission of these offences. On a case stated to a divisional court this conclusion of law on the part of the justices was held to be erroneous and the case was remitted to them to hear and determine. It is clear that the state of mind involved was a dishonest state of mind, namely, an intention to deceive and that the state of mind was an essential element in the offence. There is a distinction between that case and the present, in that there the offences were charged under a regulation having the effect of a statute, whereas here the offence is a common law misdemeanour; but in our judgment this distinction has no material bearing on the question we have to decide.

At p. 151 Viscount Caldecote, LCJ, said:

The real point we have to decide . . . is whether a company is capable of an act of will or of a state of mind, so as to be able to form an intention to deceive or to have knowledge of the truth or falsity of a statement.

And after dealing with a number of authorities, he proceeds at p. 155:

The offences created by the regulation are those of doing something with intent to deceive or of making a statement known to be false in a material particular. There was ample evidence, on the facts as stated in the special case, that the company, by the only people who could act or speak or think for it had done both these things, and I can see nothing in any of the authorities to which we have been referred which requires us to say that a company is incapable of being found guilty of the offences with which the respondent company was charged.

In his judgment in the same case Macnaghten, J, says, at p. 156, as follows:

It is true that a corporation can only have knowledge and form an intention through its human agents, but circumstances may be such that the knowledge and intention of the agent must be imputed to the body corporate . . . If the responsible agent of a company, acting within the scope of his authority, puts forward on its behalf a document which he knows to be false and by which he intends to deceive, I apprehend that according to the authorities that my Lord has cited, his knowledge and intention must be imputed to the company.

With both the decision in that case and the reasoning on which it rests, we agree.

In our judgment, both on principle and in accordance with the balance of authority, the present indictment was properly laid against the appellant company, and the Commissioner rightly refused to quash.

We are not deciding that in every case where an agent of a limited company acting in its business commits a crime the company is automatically to be held criminally responsible. Our decision only goes to the invalidity of the indictment on the face of it, an objection which is taken before any evidence is led and irrespective of the facts of the particular case.

Whether in any particular case there is evidence to go to a jury that the criminal act of an agent, including his state of mind, intention, knowledge or belief is the act of the company, and in cases where the presiding judge so rules whether the jury are satisfied that it has been so proved, must depend on the nature of the charge, the relative position of the officer or agent and the other relevant facts and circumstances of the case.

It was because we were satisfied on the hearing of the appeals in this case that the facts proved were amply sufficient to justify a finding that the acts of Robarts, the managing director, were the acts of the company and the fraud of that person was the fraud of the company, that we upheld the conviction against the company, and, indeed, on the appeal to this court no argument was advanced that the facts proved would not warrant a conviction of the company assuming that the conviction of Robarts was upheld and that the indictment was good in law.

Appeal dismissed.

Questions
1. *ICR Haulage*, like *Evans*, supra, involved a relatively small company. Reconsider *Tesco Supermarkets Ltd* v *Nattrass*. Does the reasoning of the court in *ICR Haulage* make sense when applied to a company like Tesco?
2. The court in *ICR Haulage* indicates in *obiter* a number of offences, such as perjury, for which the company cannot be held liable. Why not? Even if the company cannot be held liable as a principal, should it be subject to liability as an accessory, if, for example, the company management counsels an employee to lie on the witness stand? In many large companies decisions are taken by committees, and ratified by boards of directors. The final decision often represents a compromise of views. Can the final decision be considered to represent the mental state of the company, even if it does not represent the exact position of any particular person in the company?

R v *HM Coroner for East Kent, ex parte Spooner and Others*
(1987) 88 Cr App R 10
Court of Appeal

BINGHAM LJ: A company may be vicariously liable for the negligent acts and omissions of its servants and agents, but for a company to be criminally liable for manslaughter – on the assumption I am making that such a crime exists – it is required that the *mens rea* and the *actus reus* of manslaughter should be established not against those who acted for or in the name of the company but against those who were to be identified as the embodiment of the company itself. The coroner formed the view that there was no such case fit to be left to the jury against this company. I see no reason to disagree. I would add that I see no sustainable case in manslaughter against the directors who are named either.

I do not think the aggregation argument assists the applicants. Whether the defendant is a corporation or a personal defendant, the ingredients of manslaughter must be established by proving the necessary *mens rea* and *actus reus* of manslaughter against it or him by evidence properly to be relied on against it or him. A case against a personal defendant cannot be fortified by evidence against another defendant. The case against a corporation can only be made by evidence properly addressed to showing guilt on the part of the corporation as such. On the main substance of his ruling I am not persuaded that the coroner erred.

Question
Scientists in the laboratory division of a company know that a particular chemical produced in the manufacture of the company's product may be toxic.

Those involved in the actual manufacture know that the chemical is being released into a local stream, but do not know that the chemical is toxic. Neither group is aware that the stream in question is a source of local drinking water. Does the company have the *mens rea* for manslaughter if a local resident dies from drinking the contaminated water? Does the position of the court in *Spooner* help in the analysis? Does it serve to insulate large companies from criminal liability?

(ii)   Recklessness

For some crimes recklessness is a sufficient *mens rea*. Can a company act recklessly? What constitutes recklessness in the corporate context? Consider the following case which arose in the United States:

> In 1973 a manslaughter prosecution was brought against the Ford Motor Company. A van had struck the rear of a Ford Pinto, the petrol tank of the Pinto exploding upon impact. The passengers in the car were killed. Evidence at the trial indicated that the placement of the petrol tank was a major contributing cause of the explosion. The risk was foreseeable, and at minor expense the car could have been redesigned to vitiate the problem. The company was aware of the danger, but took no steps to either redesign the petrol tank or warn owners of the risk.

Questions

1.   Assuming that recklessness will suffice for a manslaughter conviction, was Ford guilty of manslaughter? (In the actual case, the company was acquitted.)
2.   Would Ford have been on stronger grounds if it had warned customers of the danger? Would it matter when Ford became aware of the danger? Can a company be held criminally liable for the creation of a dangerous product if it was not aware of the danger at the time of manufacture? Does the failure to be aware of the danger itself constitute recklessness? Does the answer to the preceding question turn on the state of scientific knowledge at the time?
3.   Is it possible to design an automobile in which the passengers are protected against all harm in the event of a crash? Is this relevant? Would it matter that the cost of designing a safer car would increase the price of the car substantially? That Ford's competitors' cars were comparably designed and equally dangerous?
4.   Cars often have sufficient engine power that they can go far in excess of the speed limit. Marlene is killed in a crash in which the evidence indicates that she was going at 140 mph at the time of the crash. Is the manufacturer of the automobile liable for the death?

(iii)   Strict liability

In part because of the difficulties in attributing *mens rea* to a company, many contemporary statutes impose strict liability. Is this fair to the company? Are there policy justifications for strict liability not present in other areas? The topic of strict liability has been previously examined in Chapter 3.

III   Regulatory offences

The application of conventional criminal laws to companies is not without problem. Whether the courts have adequately addressed these problems is debatable. An alternative strategy would be not to try to fit these square corporate pegs into the round holes of the criminal law, but to enact statutes addressed directly to the crimes likely to be committed by a corporation. In such a statute traditional concepts such as *actus reus*, *mens rea*, and causation could be dispensed with or modified to the extent appropriate. Difficulties can still arise, however, when such a statute comes to be considered by courts and lawyers who think in terms of traditional concepts of criminal liability:

Alphacell Ltd v *Woodward*
[1972] 2 All ER 475
House of Lords

LORD WILBERFORCE: My Lords, the enactment under which the appellants have been convicted is the Rivers (Prevention of Pollution) Act 1951. The relevant words are 'if he causes or knowingly permits to enter a stream any poisonous, noxious or polluting matter'.

The subsection evidently contemplates two things – *causing*, which must involve some active operation or chain of operations involving as the result the pollution of the stream; *knowingly permitting*, which involves a failure to prevent the pollution, which failure, however, must be accompanied by knowledge. I see no reason either for reading back the word 'knowingly' into the first limb, or for reading the first limb as, by deliberate contrast, hitting something which is unaccompanied by knowledge. The first limb involves causing and this is what has to be interpreted.

In my opinion, 'causing' here must be given a common sense meaning and I deprecate the introduction of refinements, such as causa causans, effective cause or novus actus. There may be difficulties where acts of third persons or natural forces are concerned but I find the present case comparatively simple. The appellants abstract water, pass it through their works where it becomes polluted, conduct it to a settling tank communicating directly with the stream, into which the polluted water will inevitably overflow if the level rises over the overflow point. They plan, however, to recycle the water by pumping it back from the settling tank into their works; if the pumps work properly this will happen and the level in the tank will remain below the overflow point. It did not happen on the relevant occasion due to some failure in the pumps.

In my opinion, this is a clear case of causing the polluted water to enter the stream. The whole complex operation which might lead to this result was an operation deliberately conducted by the appellants and I fail to see how a defect in one stage of it, even if we must assume that this happened without their negligence, can enable them to say they did not cause the pollution. In my opinion, complication of this case by infusion of the concept of mens rea, and its exceptions, is unnecessary and undesirable. The section is clear, its application plain. I agree with the majority of the Divisional Court who upheld the conviction, except that rather than say that the actions of the appellants were *a cause* of the pollution I think it more accurate to say that the appellants caused the polluting matter to enter the stream.

LORD SALMON: . . . The appellants contend that even if they caused the pollution still they should succeed since they did not cause it intentionally or knowingly or negligently. Section 2(1)(a) of the Rivers (Prevention of Pollution) Act 1951 is undoubtedly a penal section. It follows that if it is capable of two or more meanings then the meaning most favourable to the subject should be adopted. Accordingly, so the argument runs, the words 'intentionally' or 'knowingly' or 'negligently' should be read into the section immediately before the word 'causes'. I do not agree. It is of the utmost public importance that our rivers should not be polluted. The risk of pollution, particularly from the vast and increasing number of riparian industries, is very great. The offences created by the 1951 Act seem to me to be prototypes of offences which 'are not criminal in any real sense, but are acts which in the public interest are prohibited under a penalty': *Sherras v De Rutzen* [1895] 1 QB 918 per Wright J referred to with approval by my noble and learned friends, Lord Reid and Lord Diplock, in *Sweet v Parsley* [1970] AC 133. I can see no valid reason for reading the word 'intentionally', 'knowingly' or 'negligently' into s. 2(1)(a) and a number of cogent reasons for not doing so. In the case of a minor pollution such as the present, when the justices find that there is no wrongful intention or negligence on the part of the defendant, a comparatively nominal fine will no doubt be imposed. This may be regarded as a not unfair hazard of carrying on a business which may cause pollution on the banks of a river. The present appellants were fined £20 and ordered to pay in all £24 costs. I should be surprised if the costs of pursuing this appeal to this House were incurred to the purpose of saving these appellants £43.

If this appeal succeeded and it were held to be the law that no conviction could be obtained under the 1951 Act unless the prosecution could discharge the often impossible onus of proving that the pollution was caused intentionally or negligently, a great deal of pollution would go unpunished and undeterred to the relief of many riparian factory owners. As a result, many rivers which are now filthy would become filthier still and many rivers which are now clean would lose their cleanliness. The legislature no doubt recognised that as a matter of public policy this would be most unfortunate. Hence s. 2(1)(a) which encourages riparian factory owners not only to take reasonable steps to prevent pollution but to do everything possible to ensure that they do not cause it.

I do not consider that the appellants can derive any comfort (as they seek to do) from the inclusion in s. 2(1)(a) of the words 'knowingly permits' nor from the deeming provision against local authorities in relation to sewage escaping into a river from sewers or sewage disposal units. The creation of an offence in relation to permitting pollution was probably included in the section so as to deal with the type of case in which a man knows that contaminated effluent is escaping over his land into a river and does nothing at all to prevent it. The inclusion of the word 'knowingly' before 'permits' is probably otiose and, if anything, is against the appellants, since it contrasts with the omission of the word 'knowingly' before the word 'causes'. The deeming provision was probably included to meet what local authorities might otherwise have argued was a special case and cannot, in my opinion, affect the plain and unambiguous general meaning of the word 'causes'.

For these reasons I would dismiss the appeal with costs.

Appeal dismissed.

Questions
What if an industrial saboteur had admitted to having placed the debris which caused the violation? Would it have affected the company's liability?

IV Punishment

In *ICR Haulage*, above, the court carved out an exception to the criminal prosecution of companies in cases in which 'if a verdict of guilty is returned, no effective order by way of sentence can be made'. Some would suggest that the dearth of prosecutions against companies is attributable in part to the realisation that, even if a conviction were to be obtained, there would be no appropriate sanction.

Consider the following forms of punishment:

(a) *Capital punishment.* When the death penalty was still in force in England for most felonies, a company could obviously not be put to death. Is closing down the company the corporate counterpart to capital punishment? Is this fair to the company's workforce?

(b) *Imprisonment.* A company cannot be imprisoned, but what about its officers? Often a statute will render individuals as well as the company liable for the same offence. See, e.g., Trade Descriptions Act 1968, s. 20. In addition, an officer of the company may be liable under principles of accomplice liability (examined in Chapter 5). Are there dangers of 'scapegoating' in searching for an individual to hold responsible for the crime? Of what relevance should be proof that it was the company, and not the individual in question, who profited from the wrongdoing?

(c) *Fines.* A fine is generally deemed to be the most appropriate penalty when a crime is committed by a company. But who pays the fine? Often the cost is passed on to the consumers of the company's product. The increase in price may be so small as not to affect sales. If so, what can be done? The Criminal Justice Act 1991, s. 18, introduced the concept of unit fines for individuals. Under the Act, two offenders who committed the identical crime could receive differential fines if each had different 'disposable weekly income'. The idea was to attempt to make the severity of the penalty comparably burdensome for rich and poor. Although this innovation was ultimately removed following a number of highly publicised cases of exorbitant fines for relatively minor offences, might the concept of the unit fine have merit in the corporate context? If unit fines were to be adopted, it could be assumed that any resulting fine would be sufficiently high that it could not be passed on to consumers without the company losing its share of the market. But who then would pay the fine? Arguably the burden would fall upon the company's shareholders in the form of lower dividends. In what sense can they be said to be responsible for the company's criminality?

Where the fine is not for an exorbitant amount it may be cheaper to pay the fine than to institute costly changes in one's way of doing business. In *Alphacell Ltd* v *Woodward* the fine was £20, with an addition of £24 costs. To employ additional personnel to ferret out possible violations would be far more costly than paying the fine, as would the installation of additional pollution control devices. Why then did the company pursue its appeal?

(d) *Community service.* In addition to the unit fine, the Criminal Justice Act 1991 introduced a preference in favour of community service instead of imprisonment, again in respect to individual offenders. Does community service make sense in respect to a company? Of what might it consist?

V Reform of the law

There have been few prosecutions of companies for traditional criminal offences, and therefore the state of the law as it relates to corporate liability has not been well developed by the courts. Because of this, and because the issue is relatively controversial, it might seem that the whole area was ripe for legislative reform. The Law Commission in its draft Bill, however, chose instead to restate the existing law, limiting itself to filling in some of the gaps in that law:

Draft Criminal Code Bill 1989

30.—(1) A corporation may be guilty as a principal of an offence not involving a fault element by reason of —
   (a)   an act done by its employee or agent, as provided by section 29; or
   (b)   an omission, state of affairs or occurrence that is an element of the offence.
   (2)   A corporation may be guilty —
   (a)   as a principal, of an offence involving a fault element; or
   (b)   as an accessory, of any offence,
only if one of its controlling officers, acting within the scope of his office and with the fault required, is concerned in the offence.
   (3)   —
   (a)   'Controlling officer' of a corporation means a person participating in the control of the corporation in the capacity of a director, manager, secretary or other similar officer (whether or not he was, or was validly, appointed to any such office).
   (b)   In this subsection 'director', in relation to a corporation established by or under any enactment for the purpose of carrying on under national ownership any industry or part of an industry or undertaking, being a corporation whose affairs are managed by the members thereof, means a member of the corporation.
   (c)   Whether a person acting in a particular capacity is a controlling officer is a question of law.
   (4)   A controlling officer is concerned in an offence if he does, procures, assists, encourages or fails to prevent the acts specified for the offence.
   (5)   For the purposes of subsection (4), a controlling officer fails to prevent an act when he fails to take steps that he might take —
   (a)   to ensure that the act is not done; or
   (b)   where the offence may be constituted by an omission to do an act or by a state of affairs or occurrence, to ensure that the omission is not made or to prevent or end the state of affairs or occurrence.
   (6)   A controlling officer does not act 'within the scope of his office' if he acts with the intention of doing harm or of concealing harm done by him or another to the corporation.
   (7)   A corporation cannot be guilty of an offence that is not punishable with a fine or other pecuniary penalty.
   (8)   A corporation has a defence consisting of or including —
   (a)   a state of mind only if —

(i)   all controlling officers who are concerned in the offence; or

(ii)   where no controlling officer is so concerned, all other employees or agents who are so concerned,

have that state of mind;

(b)   the absence of a state of mind only if no controlling officer with responsibility for the subject-matter of the offence has that state of mind;

(c)   compliance with a standard of conduct required of the corporation itself only if it is complied with by the controlling officers with responsibility for the subject-matter of the offence.

31.—(1)   Where a corporation is guilty of an offence, other than a pre-Code offence as defined in section 6 (to which section 2(3) applies), a controlling officer of the corporation who is not apart from this section guilty of the offence is guilty of it as an accessory if —

(a)   knowing that or being reckless whether the offence is being or will be committed, he intentionally fails to take steps that he might take to prevent its commission; or

(b)   the offence does not involve a fault element and its commission is attributable to any neglect on his part.

(2)   Subsection (1) applies to a member of a corporation managed by its members as it applies to a controlling officer.

Notes and questions

1.   In what ways would the draft Bill change the existing law? Do the provisions represent helpful reform, or do they simply perpetuate the existing problems?

2.   Approached as a theoretical issue of criminalisation, what are the pros and cons of corporate criminal liability? If the practical problems of enforcement cannot be solved, does this counsel against criminal liability? What alternatives are there to criminal liability? An excellent article exploring many of the relevant issues is Fisse and Braithwaite 'The allocation of responsibility for corporate crime: Individualism, collectivism and accountability' [1988] Sydney L Rev 468.

7   INCHOATE OFFENCES

I   Introduction

The criminalisation of behaviour which results in the commission of one of the inchoate offences of incitement, conspiracy or attempt is primarily justified on the basis that it permits the law to intervene at an early stage, before any actual harm has been done. However, the intervention must not be too soon as evil thoughts alone do not constitute an offence.

R v Higgins
(1801) 2 East 5
King's Bench Division

LE BLANC J: It is contended that the offence charged in the second count, of which the defendant has been convicted, is no misdemeanor, because it amounts only to a bare wish or desire of the mind to do an illegal act. If that were so, I agree that it would not be indictable. But this is charge of an act done; namely, an actual solicitation of a servant to rob his master, and not merely a wish or desire that he should do so. A solicitation or inciting of another, by whatever means it is attempted, is an act done; and that such an act done with a criminal intent is punishable by indictment has been clearly established by the several cases referred to. . . .

Note
According to the *Oxford English Dictionary* 'inchoate' means 'just begun, rudimentary, unformed'. The inchoate offences are committed when steps have been taken to commit a crime. It is not necessary to prove that the crime itself ever happened.

II   Incitement

There are some statutory forms of incitement. Examples include the following:

Offences Against the Person Act 1861

4. Conspiring or soliciting to commit murder

All persons who shall conspire, confederate, and agree to murder any person, whether he be a Subject of Her Majesty or not, and whether he be within the Queen's Dominions or not, and whosoever shall solicit, encourage, persuade, or endeavour to persuade, or shall propose to any person, to murder any other person, whether he be a Subject of Her Majesty or not, and whether he be within the Queen's Dominions or not, shall be guilty of a misdemeanor, and being convicted thereof shall be liable, at the discretion of the court, to be kept in penal servitude for any term not more than ten and not less than three years, – or to be imprisoned for any term not exceeding two years, with or without hard labour.

Incitement to Disaffection Act 1934

1.

If any person maliciously and advisedly endeavours to seduce any member of His Majesty's forces from his duty or allegiance to His Majesty, he shall be guilty of an offence under this Act.

Note

Apart from the specific statutory offences, it is a crime to incite another to commit a criminal offence. When the offence is a summary offence, incitement is triable summarily and the defendant will be liable to the same penalty as if he had been convicted of the full offence (Magistrates' Courts Act 1980, s. 45). Where the full offence is triable either way so too is incitement, with a summary conviction making the offender liable to the same penalty as if he had been summarily convicted of the full offence (Magistrates' Courts Act 1980, s. 32). For a conviction on indictment the penalty is a fine and/or imprisonment at the discretion of the court, whatever the penalty for the full offence.

A   Actus reus

The *actus reus* of incitement usually consists of encouraging or persuading another to commit a crime. However, one can incite by threats and also by putting pressure on someone to commit the crime.

Race Relations Board v *Applin*
[1973] 1 QB 815
Court of Appeal

LORD DENNING MR: Mr and Mrs Watson have for 23 years fostered children in need of a temporary home. They do it from sincere and unselfish motives. They see it as a practical expression of their Christian faith. Normally they take four or five children at a time, but it may rise to seven on occasion. The children only stay for two or three weeks. Quite a number of the children are coloured. Just over half, about 60 per cent.

In January 1970 Mr and Mrs Watson moved to 61 Oakroyd Avenue, Potters Bar, Hertfordshire. There they hoped to extend their good work. At first some of the neighbours objected. They said that the house was under covenant to be used for residential purposes only. But those objections were overcome. Soon afterwards, however, objections were made on another score. An organisation calling itself the National Front complained that most of the children fostered by Mr and Mrs Watson were coloured children. The National Front acted through its branch organiser, Mr Applin, and its area organiser, Mr Taylor, the defendants. These two gentlemen brought pressure on Mr and Mrs Watson to get them to take white children only. These were some of the things they did: on August 5, 1971, Mr Applin sent a circular to the residents of Oakroyd Avenue. It referred to 'the enlargement of premises in Oakroyd Avenue for use as a foster home for largely non-British children.' It accused Mr and Mrs Watson of making 'malicious and disgraceful attacks' on their neighbours. It stated as a fact: 'that immigrant parents, because of their different standards and attitudes are quite prepared to let others take responsibility for their excess offspring.'

In a letter to Mr Watson of August 16, 1971, Mr Taylor said:

> In answer to your question asking me if I am urging you to tell the local authorities that you will only except (sic) white children. Yes I am, as stated in my letter: 'Charity should begin at home.' The number of immigrant parents who are only too ready to dump their unwanted children on to the local ratepayers is a national scandal. Every week one sees advertisements in local papers and in shop windows concerning immigrants who wish to foster out their children. In my opinion, if we the indigenous population did likewise, there would be hell to play.

On August 26, 1971, the National Front organised a public meeting at Potters Bar. Mr Applin read extracts from the circular. Mr Taylor said:

> While you have people such as Mr Watson who delight in putting immigrants' welfare before their own people's, this process of turning more and more of British towns and cities into coloured ghettoes will continue.

On February 9, 1972, the Race Relations Board issued proceedings in the county court claiming that the acts done by Mr Applin and Mr Taylor were unlawful and seeking an injunction.

It is not easy to apply the Act to the situation before us, but I will try and explain it. It is quite clear that Mr and Mrs Watson were acting perfectly lawfully. They were fostering children without making any difference between them on the ground of colour. Mr Applin and Mr Taylor were bringing pressure to bear on Mr and Mrs Watson to get them to take white children only, and not coloured ones. That pressure did not succeed. Mr and Mrs Watson have resisted it. They have continued to take white and coloured children without making any difference. They continue so to take them. But, the point is this: suppose the pressure had succeeded. Suppose that Mr and Mrs Watson had stipulated 'We will only take white children.' Would that conduct of Mr and Mrs Watson have been unlawful? If it would have been unlawful, then it was unlawful of Mr Applin and Mr Taylor to bring pressure to bear on Mr and Mrs Watson to do an unlawful act. This follows from section 12 of the Act of 1968, which says:

> Any person who deliberately aids, induces or incites another person to do an act which is unlawful by virtue of any provision of this Part of this Act shall be treated for the purposes of this Act as doing that act.

If therefore, Mr Applin and Mr Taylor 'incited' Mr and Mrs Watson to do an unlawful act, i.e., to take white children only, they are to be treated as themselves doing that act, even though the incitement did not succeed. Here I may mention a small point. Mr

Vinelott suggested that to 'incite' means to urge or spur on by advice, encouragement, and persuasion, and not otherwise. I do not think the word is so limited, at any rate in this context. A person may 'incite' another to do an act by threatening or by pressure, as well as by persuasion. Mr Applin and Mr Taylor undoubtedly brought pressure to bear on Mr and Mrs Watson to take white children only, and thus 'incited' them to do so.

Note

Notice that, as in *Race Relations Board* v *Applin*, a defendant may be guilty of incitement even though the person incited refuses to succumb to the incitement. The incitement need not be directed to anyone in particular, and may be implied.

R v *Most*
(1881) 7 QBD 244
Queen's Bench Division

M was indicted under 24 & 25 Vict. c. 100, s. 4. The encouragement and endeavour to persuade to murder, proved at the trial, was the publication and circulation by him of an article, written in German in a newspaper published in that language in London, exulting in the recent murder of the Emperor of Russia, and commending it as an example to revolutionists throughout the world.

LORD COLERIDGE CJ: . . . We have to deal here with a publication proved by the evidence at the trial to have been written by the defendant, to have been printed by the defendant, that is, he ordered and paid for the printing of it, sold by the defendant, called by the defendant his article, and intended, as the jury have found, and most reasonably found, to be read by the twelve hundred or more persons who were the subscribers to, or the purchasers of, the *Freiheit* newspaper; and, further, one which the jury have found, and I am of opinion have quite rightly found, to be naturally and reasonably intended to incite and encourage, or to endeavour to persuade persons who should read that article to the murder either of the Emperor Alexander, or the Emperor William, or, in the alternative, the crowned and uncrowned heads of states, as it is expressed in one part of the article, from Constantinople to Washington. . . .

. . . An endeavour to persuade or an encouragement is none the less an endeavour to persuade or an encouragement, because the person who so encourages or endeavours to persuade does not in the particular act of encouragement or persuasion personally address the number of people, the one or more persons, whom the address which contains the encouragement or the endeavour to persuade reaches. The argument has been well put, that an orator who makes a speech to two thousand people, does not address it to any one individual amongst those two thousand; it is addressed to the number. It is endeavouring to persuade the whole number, or large portions of that number, and if a particular individual amongst that number addressed by the orator is persuaded, or listens to it and is encouraged, it is plain that the words of this statute are complied with; because according to well-known principles of law the person who addresses those words to a number of persons must be taken to address them to the persons who, he knows, hear them, who he knows will understand them in a particular way, do understand them in that particular way, and do act upon them. . . .

Invicta Plastics v *Clare*
[1976] RTR 251
Queen's Bench Division

The defendant company manufactured a device called 'Radatec', which emitted a high-pitched whine when within 800 yards of wireless telegraphy transmissions including those used for police radar speed traps. The company advertised the device in a motoring magazine, the advertisement reading: 'You ought to know more about Radatec. Ask at your accessory shop or write for name of nearest stockist to' the company; the advertisement also depicted a view of a road and a speed limit sign through a car windscreen with the device attached.

PARK J: . . . The first question which the justices had to decide was whether a person who used the Radatec in his motor car without a licence from the Secretary of State would be using apparatus for wireless telegraphy contrary to section 1 of the Act of 1949. On the evidence before them they decided that such a person would be committing such an offence. There is no submission to this court that the justices were wrong in coming to that conclusion. So, on the first summons, which concerned the company, the question was whether the company by the advertisement in the magazine incited its readers to commit an offence under the Act.

When summing up to the jury in a case of incitement, judges sometimes use such words as 'incitement involves the suggestion to commit the offence' or 'a proposal to commit the offence' or 'persuasion or inducement to commit the offence' which the defendant is alleged to have incited. But Lord Denning MR considered the meaning of 'incitement' in *Race Relations Board* v *Applin* [1973] QB 815, 825 G, where he said:

> Mr Vinelott suggested that to 'incite' means to urge or spur on by advice encouragement, and persuasion, and not otherwise. I do not think the word is so limited, at any rate in this context. A person may 'incite' another to do an act by threatening or by pressure, as well as persuasion.

Accordingly, the justices had to decide whether, in the context, the advertisement amounted to an incitement to the readers of the magazine to commit the offence.

It is submitted on behalf of the company that, before the offence of incitement could be committed by means of the advertisement, there had to be in it an incitement to use the device which was advertised; that, if not, any matter in the advertisement would not constitute incitement, as it would not be sufficiently proximate to the offence alleged to have been incited; and that, as the advertisement merely encouraged readers to find out more about the device, it did not amount to incitement in fact or in law.

I think that it is necessary to look at the advertisement as a whole. Approaching it in this way, I have come to the conclusion that the company did incite a breach of the Act by means of the advertisement. I think, therefore, that the justices were right to convict the company of this offence.

Notes and questions
1.   In *Invicta Plastics* what constituted the incitement? What crime was incited?
2.   An incitement is normally not committed until the communication reaches the notice of those it is intended to reach. If the communication fails to reach the intended recipient, the defendant may be nonetheless guilty of an attempt to incite.

R v Ransford
(1874) 13 Cox CC 9
Court of Appeal

The prisoner was tried at the September Sessions of the Central Criminal Court, 1874, upon the following indictment:

First count. – That at the time of committing the offence hereinafter in this count mentioned, one William D'Arcy Gardiner O'Halloran was a youth of the age of fourteen years, and was a scholar in the school of Christ's Hospital, and was under the care, custody, and control of the Governors of Christ's Hospital, in the city of London, and was then being educated in the said school in the principles of religion, morality, and virtue, with the object that he might thereafter, when beyond the care and control of the said Governors, enter into the society of his fellow men, and be received by them as a man of honourable, manly, and virtuous habits, and that Edward Ransford, being a person of wicked, immoral, and depraved mind and disposition, with intent to debauch the said William D'Arcy Gardiner O'Halloran, and to vitiate and corrupt his mind, on the 5th of September, 1874, unlawfully and wickedly did write and send, and cause and procure to be written and sent to the said William D'Arcy Gardiner O'Halloran, a certain lewd and indecent letter, in the words and figures following, that is to say:

Henderson's Oakley-square, 5th Sept. 1874.

Dear O'Halloran, – The fates have hitherto prevented us from meeting, owing to my engagements. On Wednesday next, all being well, I shall meet you positively in the South Transept of St Paul's. I shall be there between 2½ o'clock and 2¾: we can then settle where to go. How long can you stay out in the evening? Answer by return. – Yours truly, P. DE LA R. HARRISON.

I shall only be here to-morrow, and therefore a post-office is my safest address.

(The conclusion of the letter is unfit for publication.)

. . .

Seventh count. – That the said Edward Ransford afterwards, to wit, on the same day and in the year aforesaid, unlawfully, wickedly, and indecently did write and send, and cause and procure to be written and sent to the said William D'Arcy Gardiner O'Halloran, a certain letter, to wit, the letter mentioned and set forth in the first count of this indictment, with intent thereby to move and incite the said William D'Arcy Gardiner O'Halloran to attempt and endeavour, feloniously and wickedly, to commit and perpetrate with him the said Edward Ransford, the detestable crime of buggery, and by the means aforesaid with unlawfully and wickedly attempt and endeavour to incite the said William D'Arcy Gardiner O'Halloran to attempt to commit and perpetrate with him the said Edward Ransford, the detestable, horrid, and abominable crime aforesaid.

KELLY CB: I am clearly of opinion, in point of law, that any attempt to commit a misdemeanor is itself a misdemeanor, and I am also of opinion that to incite or even solicit another person to commit a felony, or to do any act with intent to induce another person to commit such offence, is a misdemeanor. The seventh count charges a valid offence, for it alleges that the prisoner did write and send a certain letter with intent to solicit and incite the boy, as to which there might be some doubt, for the letter was not read by the boy, and the boy, therefore, might be said not to have been solicited. But the seventh count is free from any difficulty of that nature, as the charge therein is that the prisoner endeavoured to solicit and incite the boy to the commission of a certain offence. . . .

Question
Given that a defendant will be guilty of incitement if the person incited in a letter declines to commit the crime (see *Race Relations Board* v *Applin* above), why should the defendant not also be guilty of incitement when the letter goes astray? Is the defendant any less culpable?

(i)   Success or failure?
If the incitement has the desired effect and the person incited commits a crime, the incitor becomes an accessory to the crime (see Chapter 5), and both parties may be guilty of conspiracy. If the incitement fails the incitor remains liable for incitement.

(ii)   Where the act incited is not a crime
Three situations can arise:

(a)   Where the act done by the person incited would not amount to a crime.
(b)   Where the person incited is entitled to a defence.
(c)   Where the person incited is a victim intended to be protected by the criminal offence in question.

R v *Whitehouse*
[1977] QB 868
Court of Appeal

SCARMAN LJ: . . . The indictment which the defendant faced in 1976 was an indictment charging him with incitement to commit incest, and the particulars of the offence charged were that he, on a date unknown between December 1, 1975, and February 10, 1976, unlawfully incited a girl then aged 15, who was to his and her knowledge his daughter, to have sexual intercourse with him. To that count he pleaded guilty, as also to a second count charging incitement to commit incest, but on a different occasion, and he pleaded guilty to that as well.

When the court saw those two counts framed in the way I have just described, we queried whether it was an offence known to law and we doubted whether it was because a girl aged 15 is incapable of committing the crime of incest. Later in this judgment it will be necessary to look at the terms of section 11 of the Sexual Offences Act 1956 but that shortly is the effect of the section so far as material to the issue in this case.

. . . It is of course accepted by the Crown that at common law the crime of incitement consists of inciting another person to commit a crime. When one looks at this indictment in the light of the particulars of the offence pleaded, one sees that it is charging the defendant, with inciting a girl to commit a crime which in fact by statute she is incapable of committing. If therefore the girl was incapable of committing the crime alleged, how can the defendant be guilty of the common law crime of incitement? The Crown accepts the logic of that position and does not seek in this court to rely on section 11 of the Act of 1956 or to suggest that this man could be guilty of inciting his daughter to commit incest, to use the old phrase, as a principal in the first degree. But the Crown says that it is open to them upon this indictment to submit that it covers the offence of inciting the girl to aid and abet the man to commit the crime of incest upon her. Section 10 of the Act of 1956 makes it an offence for a man to have sexual intercourse with a woman whom he knows to be his daughter, and the Crown says that upon this indictment it is possible to say that the defendant has committed an offence known to the law, the offence being that of inciting his daughter under the age of 16 to aid and abet him to have sexual intercourse with her.

There is no doubt of the general principle, namely, that a person, provided always he or she is of the age of criminal responsibility, can be guilty of aiding or abetting a crime even though it be a crime which he or she cannot commit as a principal in the first degree. There are two famous illustrations in the books of this principle. A woman can aid and abet a rape so as herself to be guilty of rape, and a boy at an age where he is presumed impotent can nevertheless aid and abet a rape. . . .

The important matters in our judgment are these. First this girl, aged 15, belongs to a class which is protected, but not punished, by sections 10 and 11 of the Sexual Offences Act 1956, and secondly the girl is alleged to be the victim of this notional crime. The whole question has an air of artificiality because nobody is suggesting either that the father has committed incest with her or that she has aided and abetted him to commit incest upon her. What is suggested is that the father has committed the crime of incitement because by his words and conduct he has incited her to do that which, of course, she never has done.

. . . Clearly the relevant provisions of the Sexual Offences Act 1956 are intended to protect women and girls. Most certainly, section 11 is intended to protect girls under the age of 16 from criminal liability, and the Act as a whole exists, in so far as it deals with women and girls exposed to sexual threat, to protect them. The very fact that girls under the age of 16 are protected from criminal liability for what would otherwise be incest demonstrates that this girl who is said to have been the subject of incitement was being incited to do something which, if she did it, could not be a crime by her.

. . .

We have therefore come to the conclusion, with regret, that the indictment does not disclose an offence known to the law because it cannot be a crime on the part of this girl aged 15 to have sexual intercourse with her father, though it is of course a crime, and a very serious crime, on the part of the father. There is here incitement to a course of conduct, but that course of conduct cannot be treated as a crime by the girl. Plainly a gap or lacuna in the protection of girls under the age of 16 is exposed by this decision. It is regrettable indeed that a man who importunes his daughter under the age of 16 to have sexual intercourse with him but does not go beyond incitement cannot be found guilty of a crime. . . .

Notes and questions
1. *Whitehouse* was decided as it was because of a gap in the law. The defendant in *Whitehouse* would now be guilty of an offence under s. 54 of the Criminal Law Act 1977.

2. Generally, if the individual incited lacks the capacity to commit a crime, such as in the case of a child below the age of criminal responsibility, the defendant cannot be convicted of incitement. Why should this be so? If the child commits the *actus reus* of the crime, however, the defendant may be liable as a principal acting through an innocent agent.

3. As we have seen in *Tyrrell* [1894] 1 QB 710 (p. 220), a victim is not liable as an accessory where the action in question was criminalised for her protection. It follows that a defendant cannot be guilty of inciting the victim to commit the crime. Or does it?

B Mens rea

The defendant must intend that the offence incited should be committed. This principle was arguably taken to extremes in the following case:

R v *Curr*
[1968] 2 QB 944
Court of Appeal

FENTON ATKINSON J: . . . The facts shortly were these, that he was in fact a trafficker in family allowance books. His method was to approach some married woman who had a large family of children and lend her money on the security of her family allowance book. A woman would borrow from him, let us say, £6. and would sign three of the vouchers in her family allowance book to the value of, let us say, £9, and hand over the book to him as security. He then had a team of women agents whom he sent out to cash the vouchers, and he would pocket the proceeds in repayment of the loans and thereafter return the books. He admitted quite freely in evidence that he had done, as he put it, 40 to 80 books a week, and he said, in February, 1966, he had between three and five women agents assisting him in this matter, and when he was arrested he had about 80 family allowance books in his possession. He agreed quite frankly that he knew he was not legally entitled to receive these payments, and that it could be risky; in dealing with the husband of one of the women concerned he said: 'When you're doing business like this, you should keep your big mouth shut.' So it is quite plain that the dealings of this man were highly objectionable, and the assistant recorder who tried the case clearly had very strong views about it; on two occasions in his summing-up he spoke of preying on these women with large families, and he finished up his direction to the jury with words to this effect: 'If you are getting interest at 800 per cent per annum it is not bad, is it? That is what the prosecution say here, that the whole system was corrupt,' and the language there used was no whit too strong.

But the very nature of the case being bound to arouse strong prejudice in the mind of any right-thinking juror, for that reason it was all the more important to put the law on each count clearly to the jury, and to make sure that the defence was clearly put before them.

Section 9 is headed 'Penalty for obtaining or receiving payment wrongfully,' and provides:

If any person – . . . (b) obtains or receives any such sum as on account of an allowance, either as in that person's own right or as on behalf of another, knowing that it was not properly payable, or not properly receivable by him or her; that person shall be liable on summary conviction to imprisonment for a term not exceeding three months or to a fine not exceeding fifty pounds or to both such imprisonment and such fine.

Mr Kershaw's argument was that if the woman agent in fact has no guilty knowledge, knowing perhaps nothing of the assignment, or supposing that the defendant was merely collecting for the use and benefit of the woman concerned, then she would be an innocent agent, and by using her services in that way the defendant would be committing the summary offence himself, but would not be inciting her to receive money knowing that it was not receivable by her. He contends that it was essential to prove, to support this charge, that the woman agent in question in this transaction affecting a Mrs Currie knew that the allowances were not properly receivable by her. Mr Hugill's answer to that submission was that the woman agent must be presumed to know the law, and if she knew the law, she must have known, he contends, that the allowance was not receivable by her. . . . in our view the defendant could only be guilty on count 3 if the woman solicited, that is, the woman agent sent to collect the allowance, knew that the action she was asked to carry out amounted to an offence. As has already been said, the defendant himself clearly knew that his conduct in the matter was illegal and contrary to section 9(b), but it was essential in our view for the jury to consider the knowledge, if any, of the woman agent. The assistant recorder dealt with this count by referring to soliciting as follows: 'Solicited means encouraged or incited another person to go and draw that money which should have been paid, you may think, to Mrs Currie.' He later dealt with ignorance of the law being no excuse. He went on to deal with statutory offences, section 4 of the Family Allowances Act, 1945, telling the jury in effect that, apart from the case of sickness, nobody else could legally receive these allowances, and then went on to consider the position of the defendant, asking the rhetorical question whether he could be heard to say with his knowledge of this matter and his trafficking in these books that it was not known to be wrong to employ an agent to go and collect the family allowances. But the assistant recorder never followed that with the question of the knowledge of the women agents, and in the whole of the summing-up dealing with this matter he proceeded on the assumption that either guilty knowledge in the woman agent was irrelevant, or, alternatively, that any woman agent must be taken to have known that she was committing an offence under section 9(b).

Questions
1. Who was right, the Assistant Recorder or the Court of Appeal? Did Curr escape conviction because of a judicial misconception of the *mens rea* of incitement?
2. If incitement can be committed even though the person incited is quite unmoved by the incitement, of what relevance is the state of mind of the person to whom the incitement is directed?

C   Impossibility

The law generally distinguishes between legal and factual impossibility. If the acts incited would not, if committed, constitute a crime, then the defendant is not guilty of incitement. This is a case of legal impossibility. Thus if Harold urges Lloyd to drive at 50 mph thinking that the speed limit on the road is 40 mph when it is in fact 70 mph, he is not guilty of incitement. Similarly, if a woman attempts to persuade a married man to commit adultery in the belief that adultery is a criminal offence (which it is not), she will not be guilty of incitement.

Factual impossibility is another matter. Here there is incitement to commit what is a crime but due to factual circumstances unknown to the incitor, the crime is incapable of being committed. As we shall see, by statute factual impossibility is not a defence to a charge of either attempt or conspiracy. However, in *Fitzmaurice* [1983] QB 1083, the Court of Appeal made *obiter* statements to the effect that if an offence was factually impossible, the defendant could not be liable for incitement. An example would be where A incites B to kill C who is already dead. Difficulties may arise where the incitement to kill C 'next Thursday' takes place on Monday when C is alive, but C dies on Wednesday – is the defendant guilty of incitement? Consider the following case:

R v *Shephard*
(1919) 2 KB 125
Court of Appeal

On 20 September, 1917, the appellant wrote to one Cicely Maria, Shephard, who was then about six weeks gone with child, a letter in which he said: 'When the kiddie is born you must lie on it in the night. Do not let it live.' The child was born alive on 31 May 1918. In March, 1919, the appellant was convicted at the Central Criminal Court on an indictment which charged him with having 'on September 20, 1917, solicited and endeavoured to persuade Cicely Maria Shephard thereafter to murder a newly born child lately before then born of her body.' The indictment was framed under s. 4 of the Offences against the Person Act 1861.

BRAY J: . . . All that is essential to bring a case within the section is that there should be a person capable of being murdered at the time when the act of murder is to be committed. If there is such a person then in existence it is quite immaterial that that person was not in existence at the date of the incitement. . . .

Questions
1.   Ivor incites Dan to steal a diamond ring, telling him that there will be an opportunity to take it in three days' time. Will Ivor be guilty of incitement in each of the following circumstances?

(a)   the ring belongs to Dan;
(b)   before Dan has an opportunity to take the ring the owner loses it down a well;
(c)   the owner of the ring gives it to Dan immediately after the incitement;
(d)   the opportunity to take the ring never arises.

2.   In theory, is there any reason why the law in respect to factual impossibility in regard to incitement should be different than it is in respect to conspiracy and attempt? The Law Commission in its Draft Criminal Code would bring incitement into line with attempt and conspiracy. See Draft Criminal Code 1989, s. 50.

III Conspiracy

Conspiracy at common law was defined as an agreement between two or more persons to do 'an unlawful act or a lawful act by unlawful means'. This included agreements to commit acts which would not of themselves be crimes. The usual justification for this was that a number of people engaged in a harmful enterprise was more menacing to society than one person. (*R* v *Mulcahy* (1868) LR 3 HL 306, *R* v *Kamara* [1974] AC 104). More ambitious, sophisticated and complex crimes become possible, and the likelihood of successful execution increases as more minds and bodies lend themselves to the task at hand. Peer group pressure may also militate against abandonment of the criminal enterprise. (There is also the possibility, of course, that the more people who are involved, the greater the chance of a cock-up). See generally I. Dennis, 'The rationale of criminal conspiracy' (1977) 93 LQR 785.

The law is now in a state of change. The goal of the Law Commission was to confine the offence of conspiracy to agreements to commit acts which would amount to a criminal offence if committed by a single individual. The current legislation does not fully achieve this aim and leaves some grey areas. Further reform awaits the outcome of a review of the law relating to fraud and indecency. The current relevant statutes are the Criminal Law Act 1977, as amended by the Criminal Attempts Act 1981, and the Criminal Justice Act 1987.

It is now an offence to agree:

(a)   to commit any criminal offence triable within the jurisdiction, even an offence triable only summarily (it should be noted that jurisdictional rules will change with the passing of the Criminal Justice Act 1993);

(b)   to defraud, whether or not the fraud amounts to a crime;

(c)   to do an act which tends to corrupt public morals or outrage public decency, whether or not the act amounts to a crime.

Section 1 of the Criminal Law Act 1977 creates the offence of statutory conspiracy.

Criminal Law Act 1977
(is amended by the Criminal Attempts Act 1981)

1.—(1)   Subject to the following provisions of this Part of this Act, if a person agrees with any other person or persons that a course of conduct shall be pursued which, if the agreement is carried out in accordance with their intentions, either —

(a)   will necessarily amount to or involve the commission of any offence or offences by one or more of the parties to the agreement, or

(b)   would do so but for the existence of facts which render the commission of the offence or any of the offences impossible,

he is guilty of conspiracy to commit the offence or offences in question.

Note

In *R* v *Ayres* [1984] AC 447, the House of Lords held that where the carrying out of the conspiracy would necessarily involve a crime, the indictment must allege a statutory conspiracy and not a common law conspiracy. This led to great difficulties, particularly where an offence of conspiracy to defraud was alleged. Defendants argued that the behaviour envisaged would amount to a crime so that the common law conspiracy indictment against them was improper. This rule has now been reversed in respect of conspiracy to defraud by the Criminal Justice Act 1987, s. 12:

Criminal Justice Act 1987

12.—(1) If —
(a) a person agrees with any other person or persons that a course of conduct shall be pursued; and
(b) that course of conduct will necessarily amount to or involve the commission of any offence or offences by one or more of the parties to the agreement if the agreement is carried out in accordance with their intentions,
the fact that it will do so shall not preclude a charge of conspiracy to defraud being brought against any of them in respect of the agreement.

A   Common elements in statutory and common law conspiracies

(i)   Agreement
The essence of conspiracy is an agreement. The agreement need never be put into effect. The offence is complete when the agreement is made but continues as long as the agreement subsists.

Director of Public Prosecutions v *Doot*
[1973] AC 807
House of Lords

The respondents, American citizens, formed a plan abroad to import cannabis into the United States by way of England. In pursuance of the plan, two vans with cannabis concealed in them were shipped from Morocco to Southampton. The cannabis in one of the vans was discovered at Southampton; the other van was traced to Liverpool, from where the vans were to have been shipped to America, and the cannabis in it was found. The respondents were charged with, *inter alia*, conspiracy to import dangerous drugs. At the trial, they contended that the court had no jurisdiction to try them on that count since the conspiracy had been entered into abroad. Lawson J overruled that submission, but the Court of Appeal quashed the respondents' convictions, holding that the offence of conspiracy was completed when the agreement was made.

On appeal by the Director of Public Prosecutions:—

Held, allowing the appeal, that although a conspiracy was complete as a crime when the agreement was made it continued in existence so long as there were two or more parties to it intending to carry out its design; that the English courts had jurisdiction to try the offence if the evidence showed that the conspiracy, whenever or wherever formed, was still in existence when the accused were in England; and that in the present case the acts of the respondents in England sufficed to establish the continuing existence of the conspiracy and their convictions had been right and should be restored.

LORD WILBERFORCE: . . . In my opinion, the key to a decision for or against the offence charged can be found in an answer to the question why the common law treats certain actions as crimes. And one answer must certainly be because the actions in question are a threat to the Queen's peace, or, as we would now perhaps say, to society. Judged by this test, there is every reason for, and none that I can see against, the prosecution. Conspiracies are intended to be carried into effect, and one reason why, in addition to individual prosecution of each participant, conspiracy charges are brought is because criminal action organised, and executed, in concert is more dangerous than an individual breach of the law. Why, then, refrain from prosecution where the relevant concert was, initially, formed outside the United Kingdom?

Often in conspiracy cases the implementing action is itself the only evidence of the conspiracy – this is the doctrine of overt acts. Could it be said, with any plausibility, that if the conclusion or a possible conclusion to be drawn from overt acts in England was that there was a conspiracy, entered into abroad, a charge of conspiracy would not lie? Surely not: yet, if it could, what difference should it make if the conspiracy is directly proved or is admitted to have been made abroad? The truth is that, in the normal case of a conspiracy carried out, or partly carried out, in this country, the location of the formation of the agreement is irrelevant: the attack upon the laws of this country is identical wherever the conspirators happened to meet; the 'conspiracy' is a complex, formed indeed, but not separately completed, at the first meeting of the plotters.

. . .

VISCOUNT DILHORNE: . . . The conclusion to which I have come after consideration of these authorities and of many others to which the House was referred but to which I do not think it is necessary to refer is that though the offence of conspiracy is complete when the agreement to do the unlawful act is made and it is not necessary for the prosecution to do more than prove the making of such an agreement, a conspiracy does not end with the making of the agreement. It continues so long as the parties to the agreement intend to carry it out. It may be joined by others, some may leave it. Proof of acts done by the accused in this country may suffice to prove that there was at the time of those acts a conspiracy in existence in this country to which they were parties and, if that is proved, then the charge of conspiracy is within the jurisdiction of the English courts, even though the initial agreement was made outside the jurisdiction.

Question
Should the result in *DPP* v *Doot* be affected by whether or not the conspirators would be subject to prosecution in the country in which the conspiracy was formed?

Note
Because conspiracy is a continuing offence the conspirators do not need to have joined the conspiracy at the same time. Nor do all need to be in touch with each other, or even have met each other. All that must be shown is that each conspirator agreed with one other to commit the relevant offence. The conspiracy may also extend over a considerable period of time.

R v Ardalan and Others
[1972] 2 All ER 257
Court of Appeal

ROSKILL LJ: . . . The appellants . . . were charged with conspiracy and it is necessary
in order to make clear the point of law which is raised to read the particulars of the
offence charged in count 1 of the indictment. After setting out their names the counts
alleged that between 1st October 1970 and 6th March 1971 in the Middlesex area of
Greater London and elsewhere they conspired together and with Abdul Karim
Chemade and with Omar Badr El Sajadi and other persons unknown to acquire
possession of a quantity of cannabis the importation of which is prohibited with intent
to evade that prohibition. The point of law turns on the true construction of s. 304 of
the Customs and Excise Act 1952. Section 304 provides:

> Without prejudice to any other provision of this Act, if any person – (a) knowingly
> and with intent to defraud Her Majesty of any duty payable thereon, or to evade any
> prohibition or restriction for the time being in force under or by virtue of any
> enactment with respect thereto, acquires possession of, or is in any way concerned in
> carrying, removing, depositing, harbouring, keeping or concealing or in any manner
> dealing with any goods which have been unlawfully removed from a warehouse or
> Queen's warehouse, or which are chargeable with a duty which has not been paid, or
> with respect to the importation or exportation of which any prohibition or restriction
> is for the time being in force as aforesaid; or (b) is, in relation to any goods, in any
> way knowingly concerned in any fraudulent evasion or attempt at evasion of any duty
> chargeable thereon or of any such prohibition or restriction as aforesaid or of any
> provision of this Act applicable to those goods [he is guilty of an offence].

What is said, to put counsel for Ardalan's principal point in a sentence, is that on the
true construction of that section nothing happened sufficiently near to the actual
moment of the importation of the cannabis with which this case is concerned on 6th
February 1971 either in time or in place to render any of these appellants liable to
conviction for an offence against that section, and therefore a fortiori to conviction for
conspiracy to acquire possession of the goods with intent to evade the prohibition on
their importation.

The facts of this case were, as the length of the trial showed, extremely complex, but
in essence those which it is necessary to state in order to deal with this point of law can
be shortly stated. The relevant dates are as follows. On 3rd February 1971 a
consignment 182/11061 consisting of two cases described as containing 'Oriental
goods' was addressed by a Mr Haggi Boukawi from Beirut to a Mr Royed Thompson
at 39A The Broadway, Greenford, Middlesex. That address was the address of
Nicholson. The carriers were a Hungarian airline. The consignment arrived at
Heathrow Airport on 6th February 1971 but the addressee, the so-called Mr Royed
Thompson, was not notified because of the postal strike. On 24th February Nicholson,
using the name of Thompson, made enquiries from the Hungarian Travel Agency
about the consignment bearing the number which I have just mentioned and it was said
by the Crown that Miss Royde helped. On the same day customs officials at Heathrow
examined the consignment and they found in the consignment over 10 kilos, 10,430
grams, of cannabis concealed in the cases. The customs officials repacked the cases and
re-sealed them having carefully first removed the cannabis. It seems plain from what
was related at the trial that thereafter a watch was set to see precisely who became
interested in these two cases of 'Oriental goods', who would appear to claim them, what

steps would be taken to remove them and where they would ultimately then go. To that end a watch was set in more places than one. That all happened on 24 February.

On 4th March at about 4.30 p.m. Nicholson, using the name of Thompson, appears to have telephoned the airport to give directions that these two packages should be sent to a hotel called the Melba House Hotel in Philbeach Gardens near Earls Court. That same evening about five hours later the appellant Babet called at the Melba House Hotel and took a room in that hotel in the name of Thompson, a name which seems to have been remarkably popular in this case. Babet was given a hotel card and a receipt.

At about midday on the next day, 5th March, Babet telephoned the Melba House Hotel and warned them about the delivery of the consignment. At 1.00 p.m. that day a customs officer began a watch on the hotel. At 1.30 p.m. Ardalan called at the hotel with some £27 in order to cover the delivery charge. At 4.20 p.m. the consignment was delivered to the hotel. At about 6.15 p.m. to 6.25 p.m. that same evening Miss Royde drove Sands to Earls Court and at Earls Court Sands spoke to Detective Chief Inspector Kelaher of the New Scotland Yard drugs squad, a senior officer at Scotland Yard. Kelaher, it seems, then went to the Melba House Hotel.

At about 7.00 p.m. a woman telephoned another hotel the other side of London, the Rhine Hotel, and then booked a room, again using the name of Thompson. At 7.20 p.m. a taxi was ordered by a woman to take the consignment from the Melba House Hotel and deliver it to the Rhine Hotel. That woman, whoever she may have been, gave the driver a part of the Melba House Hotel card which had been given to Babet on 4th March. Five minutes later, that is at 7.25 p.m., the taxi collected the consignment from the Melba House Hotel in Philbeach Gardens and as the taxi left the watching customs officers emerged and arrested Nicholson and Babet who were driving along Philbeach Gardens at the time. Kelaher at that moment left the hotel.

It is right to say, and this was accepted at the trial, that the prosecution did not seek to suggest that Nicholson had been a participant in any conspiracy that there may have been at any time before that afternoon of 5th March. Later Nicholson and Babet were both interviewed by customs officers and, as was admitted at the trial, told a number of lies. Later still in the month of March Ardalan, Sands and Miss Royde were severally interviewed by customs officers and also admittedly told a number of lies. Ardalan was arrested on 22nd March, Sands on 7th April and Miss Royde on 13th April.

I have set out those dates and places in some detail because those are the basic facts on which counsel for Ardalan relied in support of his submission that even though the jury did accept the prosecution evidence and rejected the defence evidence, nothing had happened which was capable of amounting to the conspiracy charged in that whatever was done by each of the appellants as part and parcel of the alleged conspiracy, if such it was, was done at a place so physically remote from Heathrow and at a time so long after the importation on 6th February that no offence could possibly be said to be committed contrary to s. 304 of the Customs and Excise Act 1952 (a section which, in effect, re-enacted the earlier corresponding s. 186 of the Customs Consolidation Act 1876. Accordingly there could be no conspiracy to commit such an offence.

It was pointed out to counsel during the argument by MacKenna J that if his suggested construction of the section were right, it produced a very curious result. If nothing that happened after the import of the prohibited goods could ever be an offence, the question naturally arises – what is the point of putting the crucial words into the section and making the acquisition of possession an offence, if acquiring possession at any time after importation cannot on the true construction of the section be an offence? I venture to think that that question has only got to be asked for the answer to become manifest. If once, as counsel was ultimately constrained to accept

under some pressure from the court, there can be an offence committed at some point of time and at some place after importation (for example, acquisition at or near the airport), it is difficult to see why there should be any limit to that point of time or place provided always, of course, that the goods the subject-matter of the charge are goods which are the subject of a prohibition or restriction on importation and the acquisition is done knowingly and with intent to evade that prohibition or restriction. But subject to those two matters, this court sees no reason to think that on the true construction of s. 304 any distinction can be drawn between the case of uncustomed goods on the one hand and goods the importation of which is prohibited or restricted on the other. Therefore, the principal submission, which counsel for Ardalan made and which has been adopted by learned counsel for all the other appellants must, in the view of this court, clearly fail.
. . .

That brings me to the third of counsel's main grounds. He criticised the learned judge by reference to the fact that at two places in the summing-up he is said not to have drawn the jury's attention sufficiently clearly to what it was of which they had to be sure before they could convict any of the appellants of conspiracy. He made particular complaint that the judge talked about 'the cartwheel type of conspiracy'; that he talked about 'sub-conspiracies' and that later on he talked about 'the chain type of conspiracy'. It is said that the learned judge never made plain to the jury to what it was that they had to direct their attention.

It is right to say that these epithets, or labels, such as 'cartwheels' and 'chains' have a certain respectable ancestry and have been used in a number of conspiracy cases that from time to time have come before the courts. Metaphors are invaluable for the purpose of illustrating a particular point or a particular concept to a jury, but there is a limit to the utility of a metaphor and there is sometimes a danger, if metaphors are used excessively, that a point of time arises at which the metaphor tends to obscure rather than to clarify. The essential point in dealing with this type of conspiracy charge, where the prosecution have brought one, and only one, charge against the alleged conspirators, is to bring home to the minds of the jury that before they can convict anybody on that conspiracy charge, they have got to be convinced in relation to each person charged that that person has conspired with another guilty person in relation to that single conspiracy. As has been said again and again, there must not be wrapped up in one conspiracy charge what is, in fact, a charge involving two or more conspiracies.
. . .

R v Scott
(1979) 68 Cr App R 164
Court of Appeal

GEOFFREY LANE LJ: . . . The prosecution put their case in two ways. They suggested that the appellant must have known from the beginning what Jensby and Donovan were up to; having acquired that knowledge she continued to help them, and was therefore proved to have conspired. Had the prosecution left the matter there, no difficulty would have arisen. There was a formidable body of evidence to support the argument; the appellant herself admitted that she knew that Jensby and Donovan were involved in a scheme which was illegal and added 'the only conclusion I could draw since Jan (Jensby) was in Kenya was that I suspected it was drugs. I suppose I closed my mind.'

However, the prosecution, in an endeavour to make assurance double sure, contended that the appellant's admitted knowledge acquired on February 28, 1976, even if that was the first time she had the guilty knowledge, was enough to prove her guilty of conspiracy, despite the fact that thereafter she did no overt act in pursuance of the illegal scheme. She admitted that if she had been asked after that date to help by paying in cheques received from Donovan, she would have done so, but it was plain that she had not been so asked, and that she had not informed either Jensby or Donovan whether or not she was willing to help.

The judge, in directing the jury on the second limb of the prosecution case, used the following words:

> If up to that point she had been an innocent party in doing what she did, she then ceased to be an innocent party [say the prosecution] and became a conspirator so as to render herself liable to conviction in respect of this offence. That is what it comes to, and you have to decide what was meant by it when it was said, if it was . . . that if the cheques had arrived she would have paid them in. Is that, members of the jury, from your point of view, evidence which convinces you that at that stage she was prepared to act in furtherance of her agreement? Is it evidence that the agreement which she was saying that she then had was, whether she liked it or not, to assist in the supplying of drugs by being a person who would, if the cheques had arrived, no doubt as a result of the supply and sale of drugs, she would have then paid them into such accounts as she had been asked to – and thereby assist in the workings of this conspiracy?

What the learned judge was doing there was to put forward to the jury the prosecution's proposition, namely, that even if she was not aware of the illegality of Jensby's activities until February 28, 1976, yet nevertheless she was guilty of conspiracy at that moment by reason of her secret and uncommunicated intention to deal in the way Jensby had requested with any cheques which might arrive from Donovan.

It may be that the jury came to the conclusion (not entirely disavowed by the prosecution) that the appellant was until February 28, 1976, unaware of the true nature of Jensby's activities. On that date she learnt for the first time for certain that he was smuggling drugs. She then determines that she would nevertheless continue to help him in what she then realised for the first time were illegal activities relating to the importation of cannabis. That determination she never communicated to anyone else. It was submitted for the respondent that this was sufficient to make her party to an agreement to assist in the supply of controlled drugs and therefore a conspirator. We do not think it was. It is evidence that she had secretly determined to assist Jensby in his importation and supply of cannabis, should the opportunity arise. It is evidence of what doubtless she would have done, given the chance. But an intent, should the occasion arise, to join in an illegal enterprise, an intent which is never communicated in any way whatsoever to any other person, remains only an intent and cannot at any rate in these circumstances amount to an indictable conspiracy.

The further suggestion put forward is equally untenable, namely that the appellant, by failing to notify Jensby or Donovan after February 28, 1976, that she was no longer prepared to help, notionally or constructively became a party to the illegal enterprise. An intention to enter into an agreement must, to become effective as an agreement, be communicated to the other party by some means or other. It is difficult to see how non-communication can amount to communication. The long and short of this matter is that after February 28 the appellant never went beyond the intention or wish to act illegally. However reprehensible that may be, it was not proof of the conspiracy alleged. To that extent the prosecution's second contention and the judge's direction based upon it were wrong.

. . .

Question
At lunch Ian proposes to Elaine and Eleanor that they spray-paint the university's administrative building that evening at midnight. Neither responds one way or the other. At midnight Elaine, but not Eleanor, shows up outside the administration building, where Ian is waiting. Is there a conspiracy to commit criminal damage? Between whom? When was it formed? Did Eleanor need to inform either Ian or Elaine that she did not wish to participate in order to avoid liability?

Note
If there is an agreement in principle but details remain to be ironed out, the parties can be convicted of conspiracy.

(ii)   Agreement with whom?
There must be another human conspirator, although he/she need not be identified (*R* v *Phillips* (1987) 86 Cr App R 18).

R v *McDonnell*
[1966] 1 QB 233
Queen's Bench Division

At all material times the defendant was a director and the sole person in each of two companies responsible for the acts of the company. He was charged on an indictment containing ten counts: two of the counts (one in respect of each company) charged him with conspiring with the company to defraud, one with conspiring with one of the companies to induce persons to acquire a right or interest in land, four counts charged him with fraudulent conversion of the property of the companies.

NIELD J: . . . [T]hese charges of conspiracy cannot be sustained, upon the footing that in the particular circumstances here, where the sole responsible person in the company is the defendant himself, it would not be right to say that there were two persons or two minds. If it were otherwise, I feel that it would offend against the basic concept of a conspiracy, namely, an agreement of two or more to do an unlawful act, and I think it would be artificial to take the view that the company, although it is clearly a separate legal entity, can be regarded here as a separate person or a separate mind, in view of the admitted fact that this defendant acts alone so far as these companies are concerned.

Notes and questions
1.   For many legal purposes a company is treated as if it were a person (see generally Chapter 6), and in *R* v *ICR Haulage Ltd* [1944] 1 All ER 691 it was held that a company could be guilty of conspiracy. Why, then, the holding in *McDonnell*? What more would a prosecutor need to show in order to secure a conviction?
2.   There is a number of combinations of people whose agreement to commit a crime will not amount to a conspiracy if there are no other parties involved. Thus a husband and wife alone cannot conspire (Criminal Law Act 1977,

s. 2 (2); *Mawji* v *R* [1957] AC 126). The same is true where the only other party to the conspiracy is a child under 10 or the intended victim of the offence (Criminal Law Act 1977, s. 2 (2)). The Draft Criminal Code Bill would remove these exemptions, leaving the various situations to be governed by general principles relating to conspiracy.

Where a person is exempt from liability as a principal, the exemption does not necessarily extend to liability for conspiracy:

R v *Burns (and others)*
(1984) 79 Cr App R 173
Court of Appeal

By s. 56 of the Offences against the Person Act 1861: 'Whosoever shall unlawfully . . . by force . . . take away . . . any child under the age of 14 years, with intent to deprive any parent . . . of the possession of such child . . . shall be . . . liable, at the discretion of the court, to imprisonment for any term not exceeding seven years . . . Provided that no person who shall have claimed any right to the possession of such child, or shall be the mother or shall have claimed to be the father of an illegitimate child, shall be liable to be prosecuted by virtue hereof on account of the getting possession of such child, or taking such child out of the possession of any person having lawful charge thereof.'

The appellant J B married a second time in 1975 and had two children. Between the births of those children he had another child by his second wife's sister who was also living with them. That child became a ward of court and J B divorced his second wife. The children were committed to the care of their mothers, both of whom had returned to their parents' home to live. J B was not allowed access to the children. He decided to seize the children and recruited the three applicants, R, J and S B, for that purpose. One night all four men drove to the house where the women and children were living, forced an entry and took the children, then aged between three and six and a half years, out of the house and into the waiting car. J B then took the children to accommodation he had prepared for them and the three applicants returned to their respective homes. All four men were charged with conspiracy to take the children and substantive counts, again against all four, of child stealing contrary to s. 56 of the Offences against the Person Act 1861. When put to his election, prosecution counsel decided to proceed on the conspiracy count only against J B, and on the child stealing count only against the three applicants. All four were convicted. J B appealed against his conviction on the ground that the judge should not have exercised his discretion in a way that allowed him to be put in jeopardy of being convicted of conspiracy to commit an offence when he could not have been charged with the substantive offence (which he had in fact committed) because of the immunity from prosecution provided by s. 56 of the 1861 Act.

WATKINS LJ: . . . The dangers of permitting a father of children to collect a posse of men and suddenly to launch a seige of the home of his erstwhile wife, to break in and then snatch away sleeping children are surely self-evident. The criminal law does not in our view permit that sort of conduct. When a father who is exempt under section 56 behaves in that way, it is, in our judgment, not only lawful but right and just that the prosecution should be free to bring a charge of conspiracy against him.

Notes
1. Section 56 of the Offences against the Persons Act 1861 was repealed by the Child Abduction Act 1984. On the conspiracy point, see also *R* v *Whitchurch* (1890) 24 QBD 420.
2. Section 5(8) and (9) of the Criminal Law Act 1977 address the situation where some but not all of the conspirators are acquitted. Can the convictions of the others stand?

Criminal Law Act 1977

5.—(8) The fact that the person or persons who, so far as appears from the indictment on which any person has been convicted of conspiracy, were the only other parties to the agreement on which his conviction was based have been acquitted of conspiracy by reference to that agreement (whether after being tried with the person convicted or separately) shall not be a ground for quashing his conviction unless under all the circumstances of the case his conviction is inconsistent with the acquittal of the other person or persons in question.

(9) Any rule of law or practice inconsistent with the provisions of subsection (8) above is hereby abolished.

R v *Longman and Cribben*
(1980) 72 Cr App R 121
Court of Appeal

THE LORD CHIEF JUSTICE: The facts of the case were these. Longman was the proprietor of a garage and car-sales business. Cribben worked for him as a salesman. The prosecution allegation was that they had conspired to defraud an insurance company of £3,323 by making a false claim in respect of the theft of a car; that the purported purchase of the car by Longman from a man called Pentow and the purported sale by Longman to Cribben were shams; that the car was never stolen; that the whole pretended transaction was designed by the two men with a view to perpetrating a fraud on the insurance company.

The evidence adduced by the prosecution was mostly circumstantial evidence of suspicious or highly suspicious actions by the two men. Longman was seen by the police and throughout hotly denied all the allegations made against him. He asserted that the man Pentow had brought the car to his garage, it was apparently in good repair; he bought it and later sold it to Cribben in the ordinary course of business. He denied any fraud.

The case against Cribben was much stronger. In addition to the circumstantial evidence, he made what amounted to a full confession to the police, stating in terms that he had, in fact, conspired with Longman to defraud the insurance company and that the car had never been delivered to the garage at all and had certainly never been bought by him. In short, that confession, if the jury were satisfied as to its truth, was conclusive evidence against Cribben that he had conspired with Longman in the way that the prosecution alleged. Longman gave evidence at the trial. Cribben did not.

... [T]he situation has been changed by the provisions of the Criminal Law Act 1977, s. 5(8) and (9) . . .

In our judgment the effect of those two subsections is to . . . [abolish] the rule of common law that if two persons are accused of conspiring together and one is acquitted and the other convicted, the conviction must be quashed. They also mean that the trial judge is no longer obliged to direct juries that they must convict both conspirators or acquit both conspirators. . . .

We also respectfully adopt the conclusion reached by the Court in that case that the provisions of the Criminal Law Act 1977, s. 5 (8) and (9) do not mean that such a direction may never be given if the circumstances warrant it. When a trial judge is faced with the task of directing a jury in a case of this sort, where the charge is that A and B conspired together but with no one else to commit crime, he will, as in other cases involving two defendants, as a general rule have to tell the jury that they must consider the evidence against each defendant separately. Where the strength of the evidence against each is markedly different, usually (as in the instant case) because A has confessed and B has not, he should then go on to explain that because there is that difference in the evidence against each, the jury may come to the conclusion that the prosecution have proved beyond doubt against A that A conspired with B, but have not proved against B that any such conspiracy existed.

That may appear to be illogical, but it is the necessary result of the rules of evidence which are designed to ensure fairness. If, therefore, the jury are satisfied that A conspired with B but are not satisfied that there is adequate evidence of B's guilt, they should convict A and acquit B. We can see no reason why the jury should not understand such a direction.

Where at the close of the prosecution case the evidence against one of the defendants is such that it would be unsafe to ask any jury to convict, then it goes without saying that the judge should so rule, and the case can then continue against the other defendant.

There will, however, be cases where the evidence against A and B is of equal weight or nearly so. In such a case there may be a risk of inconsistent verdicts, and the judge should direct the jury that because of the similarity of the evidence against each, the only just result would be the same verdict in respect of each: that is to say, both guilty or both not guilty. He must be careful to add, however, that if they are unsure about the guilt of one, then both must be found not guilty.

Whether he gives such a direction will, of course, depend on the way the evidence has emerged. The test is this. Is the evidence such that a verdict of guilty in respect of A and not guilty in respect of B would be, to all intents and purposes, inexplicable and therefore inconsistent? If so, it would be an occasion for the 'both guilty or both not guilty' direction. If not, then the separate verdict direction is required.

B   Statutory conspiracy

The definition of the offence of conspiracy is contained in the Criminal Justice Act 1977, s. 1(1) (see p. 203 above).

(i)   Agreement that a course of conduct shall be pursued

At common law the prosecution had to prove that each conspirator intended the commission of the offence envisaged. Otherwise there would exist the possibility that a conspiracy could exist even though no conspirator actually intended an offence to be committed. The phrase 'course of conduct' within the statute is thus not limited to physical acts but includes intended consequences. The *mens rea* implicit in the requirement of an agreement is an intention that the offence will be committed, even if the offence itself may be committed with a lesser *mens rea* than intent. An example is a conspiracy to murder, which requires an intention to kill on the part of the conspirators. Murder itself can be committed by a defendant who intends only grievous bodily harm, but such an intent is not sufficient to establish a conspiracy to murder. Similarly, even though strict liability or negligence may suffice as to a circumstance of a crime, a conspiracy to commit the crime cannot be established without proof that the conspirators 'intend or know' that the relevant circumstance will exist at the time the offence is to take place. The courts, however, have not always been strictly logical in their approach.

R v Anderson
[1986] AC 27
House of Lords

LORD BRIDGE OF HARWICH: . . . In June 1981 the appellant and Ahmed Andaloussi were both in custody on remand in Lewes prison. Andaloussi was awaiting trial on charges of very serious drug offences and was rightly believed by the appellant to have large sums of money at his disposal. The appellant was on remand in connection with some entirely different matter. He spent one night in the same cell as Andaloussi. The appellant was then confidently expecting that in a short time he would be, as in the event he was, released on bail. During the night they spent together the appellant agreed with Andaloussi to participate in a scheme to effect Andaloussi's escape from prison. Other participants in the scheme were to be Ahmed Andaloussi's brother Mohammed and Mohammed Assou. They were to maintain contact with Ahmed in prison after the appellant's release. The appellant was to be paid £20,000 for his part in the escape scheme. It is not clear, nor is it significant for the purpose of any issue arising in the appeal, how far the details of the escape plan were worked out at the initial meeting in prison between the appellant and Ahmed Andaloussi. What is clear is that either at that meeting or after the appellant's release from prison and after one or more meetings between the appellant and Assou, it was agreed that the appellant would purchase and supply diamond wire, a cutting agent capable of cutting through metal bars, to be smuggled into the prison by Assou or Mohammed Andaloussi to enable Ahmed Andaloussi to escape from his cell. Further steps in the escape plan were to include the provision of rope and a ladder to enable Ahmed Andaloussi to climb on to the roof of an industrial building in the prison and thence over the main wall, transport to drive him away from the prison and safe accommodation where he could hide.

What happened in the event was that the appellant received from Assou a payment of £2,000 on account of the agreed fee of £20,000. Shortly after this the appellant was injured in a road accident and thereafter took no further step in pursuance of the escape plan. His admitted intention, however, was to acquire the diamond wire and give it to Assou. His further intention, according to the version of the facts which we must for present purposes accept, was then to insist that before he would proceed further he should be paid a further £10,000 on account, on receipt of which he would have left the country and gone to live in Spain, taking no further part in the scheme to effect Andaloussi's escape.

On those facts the submission for the appellant which was rejected both by the trial judge and the Court of Appeal was that the appellant lacked the mental element essential to sustain his conviction of a conspiracy to effect Andaloussi's escape, since he never intended that the escape plan, in which, according to what had been agreed, he was to play a major part, should be carried into effect nor, according to some of his statements to the police, which again we must for present purposes accept as indicating his true state of mind, did he believe that, in the circumstances, the plan to enable Andaloussi to escape could possibly succeed.

The Court of Appeal, having dismissed his appeal, certified that their decision involved a point of law of general public importance in terms which can conveniently be divided into two parts, since, in truth, there are two separate questions involved:

(1) Is a person who 'agrees' with two or more others, who themselves intend to pursue a course of conduct which will necessarily involve the commission of an offence, and who has a secret intention himself to participate in part only of that course of conduct, guilty himself of conspiracy to commit that offence under section 1(1) of the Criminal Law Act 1977?

(2) If not, is he liable to be indicted as a principal offender under section 8 of the Accessories and Abettors Act 1861?

... I am clearly driven by consideration of the diversity of roles which parties may agree to play in criminal conspiracies to reject any construction of the statutory language which would require the prosecution to prove an intention on the part of each conspirator that the criminal offence or offences which will necessarily be committed by one or more of the conspirators if the agreed course of conduct is fully carried out should in fact be committed. A simple example will illustrate the absurdity to which this construction would lead. The proprietor of a car hire firm agrees for a substantial payment to make available a hire car to a gang for use in a robbery and to make false entries in his books relating to the hiring to which he can point if the number of the car is traced back to him in connection with the robbery. Being fully aware of the circumstances of the robbery in which the car is proposed to be used he is plainly a party to the conspiracy to rob. Making his car available for use in the robbery is as much a part of the relevant agreed course of conduct as the robbery itself. Yet, once he has been paid, it will be a matter of complete indifference to him whether the robbery is in fact committed or not. In these days of highly organised crime the most serious statutory conspiracies will frequently involve an elaborate and complex agreed course of conduct in which many will consent to play necessary but subordinate roles, not involving them in any direct participation in the commission of the offence or offences at the centre of the conspiracy. Parliament cannot have intended that such parties should escape conviction of conspiracy on the basis that it cannot be proved against them that they intended that the relevant offence or offences should be committed.

There remains the important question whether a person who has agreed that a course of conduct will be pursued which, if pursued as agreed, will necessarily amount to or involve the commission of an offence is guilty of statutory conspiracy irrespective of his intention, and, if not, what is the mens rea of the offence. I have no hesitation in answering the first part of the question in the negative. There may be many situations in which perfectly respectable citizens, more particularly those concerned with law enforcement, may enter into agreements that a course of conduct shall be pursued which will involve commission of a crime without the least intention of playing any part in furtherance of the ostensibly agreed criminal objective, but rather with the purpose of exposing and frustrating the criminal purpose of the other parties to the agreement. To say this is in no way to encourage schemes by which police act, directly or through the agency of informers, as agents provocateurs for the purpose of entrapment. That is conduct of which the courts have always strongly disapproved. But it may sometimes happen, as most of us with experience in criminal trials well know, that a criminal enterprise is well advanced in the course of preparation when it comes to the notice either of the police or of some honest citizen in such circumstances that the only prospect of exposing and frustrating the criminals is that some innocent person should play the part of an intending collaborator in the course of criminal conduct proposed to be pursued. The mens rea implicit in the offence of statutory conspiracy must clearly be such as to recognise the innocence of such a person, notwithstanding that he will, in literal terms, be obliged to agree that a course of conduct be pursued involving the commission of an offence.

I have said already, but I repeat to emphasise its importance, that an essential ingredient in the crime of conspiring to commit a specific offence or offences under section 1(1) of the Act of 1977 is that the accused should agree that a course of conduct be pursued which he knows must involve the commission by one or more of the parties to the agreement of that offence or those offences. But, beyond the mere fact of agreement, the necessary mens rea of the crime is, in my opinion, established if, and only if, it is shown that the accused, when he entered into the agreement, intended to play some part in the agreed course of conduct in furtherance of the criminal purpose which the agreed course of conduct was intended to achieve. Nothing less will suffice; nothing more is required.

Applying this test to the facts which, for the purposes of the appeal, we must assume, the appellant, in agreeing that a course of conduct be pursued that would, if successful, necessarily involve the offence of effecting Andaloussi's escape from lawful custody, clearly intended, by providing diamond wire to be smuggled into the prison, to play a part in the agreed course of conduct in furtherance of that criminal objective. Neither the fact that he intended to play no further part in attempting to effect the escape, nor that he believed the escape to be impossible, would, if the jury had supposed they might be true, have afforded him any defence.

In the result, I would answer the first part of the certified question in the affirmative and dismiss the appeal. Your Lordships did not find it necessary to hear argument directed to the second part of the certified question and it must, therefore, be left unanswered.

Questions

1. Of what offence could Anderson have been convicted without distortion of the law of conspiracy? Could the examples given by Lord Bridge be adequately dealt with by charging aiding and abetting a conspiracy?

2. As a result of Lord Bridge's opinion, what is the position of the police officer who feigns agreement with persons already party to a conspiracy and, further, carries out minor acts towards completion of the offence? Is the officer guilty of conspiracy? Would it make more sense to provide police officers with an affirmative defence in this situation?

Note

Anderson was the object of much criticism. In *R* v *Siracusa* (below), an attempt at damage control was made by the Court of Appeal.

R v *Siracusa (and others)*
(1990) 90 Cr App R 340
Court of Appeal

O'CONNOR LJ: . . . The case arises out of the operations of an organisation of smugglers engaged in moving massive quantities of heroin from Thailand and cannabis from Kashmir to Canada via England. The scheme was simple. The drugs were to be housed in secret compartments in selected items of locally produced furniture, which would be included in substantial shipments of furniture. The object of passing the consignments through England was to support the manifests to be presented to the Canadian customs declaring the country of origin of the goods as England.

. . .

The importation of controlled drugs into this country is prohibited by section 3(1)(a) of the Misuse of Drugs Act 1971. That section does not create any offence. The offence is created by section 170(2)(b) of the Customs and Excise Management Act 1979 which provides:

(2)   . . . if any person is, in relation to any goods, in any way knowingly concerned in any fraudulent evasion or attempt at evasion: . . . (b) of any prohibition or restriction for the time being in force with respect to the goods under or by virtue of any enactment . . . he shall be guilty of an offence. . . .

At the relevant time, the effect of section 170(4) and Schedule 1 of the Act was that importation of drugs of Class A or Class B was punishable with up to 14 years' imprisonment.

In cases where controlled drugs are imported into this country and a substantive offence is charged as a contravention of section 170(2)(b), the particulars of the offence identify the drug and the class to which it belongs so that the appropriate penalty is not in doubt. Case law has established that although separate offences are created as a result of the different penalties authorised, the *mens rea* is the same. The prosecution must prove that the defendant knew that the goods were prohibited goods. They do not have to prove that he knew what the goods in fact were. Thus it is no defence for a man charged with importing a Class A drug to say he believed he was bringing in a Class C drug or indeed any other prohibited goods: *Hussain* (1969) 53 Cr App R 448; *Shivpuri* (1986) 83 Cr App R 178; *Ellis* (1987) 84 Cr App R 235.

The appellants contend that where conspiracy to contravene section 170(2)(b) is charged, the position is different so that in this case the prosecution had to prove against each defendant that he knew that the Kashmir operation involved cannabis and that the Thailand operation involved heroin. If this submission is well-founded, then it is said that the learned judge's direction on conspiracy is flawed and strength is added to the contentions of those appellants who submit that in respect of one, other or both counts, there was no case to go to the jury at the end of the prosecution case.

[In *Anderson* [1986] AC 27, Lord Bridge said: . . .]

I have said already, but I repeat to emphasise its importance, that an essential ingredient in the crime of conspiring to commit a specific offence or offences under section 1(1) of the Act of 1977 is that the accused should agree that a course of conduct be pursued which he knows must involve the commission by one or more of the parties to the agreement of that offence or those offences. But, beyond the mere fact of agreement, the necessary *mens rea* of the crime is, in my opinion, established if, and only if, it is shown that the accused, when he entered into the agreement, intended to play some part in the agreed course of conduct in furtherance of the criminal purpose which the agreed course of conduct was intended to achieve. Nothing less will suffice; nothing more is required.

The last paragraph above cited must be read in the context of that case. We think it obvious that Lord Bridge cannot have been intending that the organiser of a crime who recruited others to carry it out would not himself be guilty of conspiracy unless it could be proved that he intended to play some active part himself thereafter. Lord Bridge had pointed out at p. 259 and p. 38 respectively that

> in these days of highly organised crime the most serious statutory conspiracies will frequently involve an elaborate and complex agreed course of conduct in which many will consent to play necessary but subordinate roles, not involving them in any direct participation in the commission of the offence or offences at the centre of the conspiracy.

The present case is a classic example of such a conspiracy. It is the hallmark of such crimes that the organisers try to remain in the background and more often than not are not apprehended. Secondly, the origins of all conspiracies are concealed and it is usually quite impossible to establish when or where the initial agreement was made, or when or where other conspirators were recruited. The very existence of the agreement can only be inferred from overt acts. Participation in a conspiracy is infinitely variable: it can be active or passive. If the majority shareholder and director of a company consents to the company being used for drug smuggling carried out in the company's name by a fellow director and minority shareholder, he is guilty of conspiracy. Consent, that is the agreement or adherence to the agreement, can be inferred if it is proved that he knew what was going on and the intention to participate in the furtherance of the criminal purpose is also established by his failure to stop the unlawful activity. Lord Bridge's *dictum* does not require anything more.

We return to the first sentence of this paragraph in Lord Bridge's speech. He starts by saying: 'I have said already, but I repeat to emphasise its importance. . . .' We have cited what he had already said when dealing with his clause 2. It is clear that he was not intending to say anything different. So when he goes on to say:

> an essential ingredient in the crime of conspiring to commit a specific offence or offences under section 1(1) of the Act of 1977 is that the accused should agree that a course of conduct be pursued which he knows must involve the commission by one or more of the parties to the agreement of that offence or those offences,

he plainly does not mean that the prosecution have to prove that persons who agree to import prohibited drugs into this country know that the offence which will be committed will be a contravention of section 170(2) of the Customs and Excise Act. He is not to be taken as saying that the prosecution must prove that the accused knew the name of the crime. We are satisfied that Lord Bridge was doing no more than applying the words of section 1 of the Criminal Law Act 1977, namely, that when the accused agreed to the course of conduct, he knew that it involved the commission of an offence.

The *mens rea* sufficient to support the commission of a substantive offence will not necessarily be sufficient to support a charge of conspiracy to commit that offence. An intent to cause grievous bodily harm is sufficient to support the charge of murder, but is not sufficient to support a charge of conspiracy to murder or of attempt to murder.

. . .

Question

A and B add alcohol to C's lemonade, intending him to drive with a higher alcohol level than permitted by law. What must the prosecution show before A and B can be convicted of a conspiracy to commit an offence? What if A but not B believed that the alcohol added was insufficient to cause C to be guilty of an offence?

(ii)   Necessarily involve a crime

Under the Criminal Law Act 1977, s. 5, the agreement that a course of conduct shall be pursued must be such that if carried out in accordance with the conspirators' intention, it would amount to or involve the commission of an offence or offences by one or more parties to the agreement (or would have done so except for facts which made the commission of the offence impossible). Sometimes an agreement may involve a number of alternative courses of action which will be pursued by the conspirators depending on other events. If one course of action is criminal and the other not, is this an agreement to pursue a course of conduct which will necessarily involve a crime? Similarly, if two different crimes are envisaged, which crime have the defendants agreed to?

R v Reed
[1982] Crim LR 819
Court of Appeal

The fourth submission was that the summing up had not adequately conveyed the requirements of the Criminal Law Act 1977, s. 1 (1). These, it was said, clearly indicate that a course of conduct agreed upon must necessarily amount to or involve the commission of an offence if the agreement is carried out in accordance with the parties' intentions. The agreement on the relevant course of conduct must therefore not be capable of a successful conclusion without a crime being committed (*cf.* Smith and Hogan, *Criminal Law* (4th ed.), pp. 226–227). It was argued that the most that could be inferred about the nature of the agreement between L and R was that L would visit individuals and either give them faith healing, consolation and comfort while discouraging suicide or he would actively help them to commit suicide, depending on his assessment of the appropriate course of action. Such an agreement was capable of execution without the law being broken, and therefore should not have attracted the charge of conspiracy. It was argued that the jury should have at least been made aware of such a possible defence in the directions given.

The Court held against the applicant on this point. Donaldson LJ considered two examples:

In the first, A and B agree to drive from London to Edinburgh in a time which can be achieved without exceeding the speed limits, but only if the traffic which they encounter is exceptionally light. Their agreement will not necessarily involve the commission of any offence, even if it is carried out in accordance with their intentions, and they do arrive from London to Edinburgh within the agreed time. Accordingly the agreement does not constitute the offence of statutory conspiracy or indeed of any offence. In the second example, A and B agree to rob a bank, if when they arrive at the bank it seems safe to do so. Their agreement will necessarily involve the commission of the offence of robbery if it is carried out in accordance with their intentions. Accordingly, they are guilty of the statutory offence of conspiracy. The instant case is an example of the latter type of agreement. If circumstances had permitted and the agreement of R and L had been carried out in accordance with their intentions L would have aided, abetted, counselled, and procured a suicide. . . .

. . .

R v Jackson
[1985] Crim LR 442
Court of Appeal

The appellants were convicted of conspiracy to pervert the course of public justice. Their co-defendant, Whitlock, pleaded guilty to inciting a person to have a firearm with criminal intent. All four had discussed Whitlock's plan to have himself shot so as to provide mitigation in the event of being convicted of the burglary offence for which he was being tried. Before the end of that trial Whitlock was shot in the leg and was permanently disabled. The appellants had spent part of the evening in question with Whitlock but lied to the police about their whereabouts. They eventually admitted knowing of the plan. In their defence the appellants denied having any part in the plan and claimed not to have taken Whitlock seriously. The particulars of the offence, charged that the appellants made false statements as to their and Whitlock's whereabouts; that they concealed the identity of the person responsible for the shooting and that they concealed the fact that Whitlock had arranged to be shot to mislead his court of trial. The appellants appealed against conviction on the ground that no offence had been committed since it depended upon a contingency which might not have taken place – the conviction of Whitlock for burglary. Counsel relied upon examples cited in *Reed* (CACD: March 26, 1982) and submitted that the agreement did not 'necessarily' involve the commission of an offence.

Held, dismissing the appeals, planning was taking place for a contingency and if that contingency occurred the conspiracy would necessarily involve the commission of an offence. 'Necessarily' is not to be held to mean that there must inevitably be the carrying out of an offence, it means, if the agreement is carried out in accordance with the plan, there must be the commission of the offence referred to in the conspiracy count. . . .

Questions
1. In the driving example given in *Reed*, why did the court feel there was no conspiracy? Was there not an agreement to commit a crime in the event of heavy traffic being encountered?
2. What would be the result in the following situations?

(a) An agreement to burgle a house, using violence if the occupier returns.
(b) An agreement to steal a car unless police officers are patrolling the street.
(c) An agreement to have intercourse with a woman whether or not she consents.

(iii)   Impossibility
The difference between factual and legal impossibility was outlined in the section on incitement. The issue of impossibility in respect to conspiracy is now dealt with by s. 1(1)(b) of the Criminal Law Act 1977, which was inserted by the Criminal Attempts Act 1981, s. 5 (see above). Whatever ambiguity there may have been in the law before the Act, it is now clear that factual impossibility is not a defence.

(iv) Jurisdiction

Criminal Law Act 1977

1.—(4) In this Part of this Act 'offence' means an offence triable in England and Wales, except that it includes murder notwithstanding that the murder in question would not be so triable if committed in accordance with the intentions of the parties to the agreement.

Note
This means that if the agreement is in England and Wales to commit acts abroad, there will be a criminal conspiracy only if the acts envisaged would amount to an offence triable in England or Wales (except in the case of murder). It should be noted that the rules relating to conspiracy to commit a number of property offences are likely to change when the Criminal Justice Act 1993 becomes law. Any 'relevant event' occurring within the jurisdiction will be sufficient in the case of offences specified in the Bill.

The proposal may not be very different from the law as applied to agreements abroad to commit offences in England or Wales. In *DPP* v *Doot* (above) the House of Lords held that such a conspiracy could be prosecuted in England if the parties acted within the jurisdiction. However, the Privy Council went further in *Somchai Liangsiriprasert* v *United States* [1990] AC 607, not requiring proof of an overt act within the jurisdiction. In *Sansom* (1991) 92 Cr App R 115, the Court of Appeal followed *Somchai*.

C Common law conspiracies

(i) Conspiracy to defraud
The common law offence of conspiracy to defraud was expressly preserved by s. 5(2) of the Criminal Law Act 1977, pending a review of the law relating to fraud by the Law Commission which has yet to be completed. The overlap between conspiracy to defraud and statutory conspiracy is addressed by s. 12 of the Criminal Justice Act 1987:

Criminal Justice Act 1987

12.—(1) If—
(a) a person agrees with any other person or persons that a course of conduct shall be pursued; and
(b) that course of conduct will necessarily amount to or involve the commission of any offence or offences by one or more of the parties to the agreement if the agreement is carried out in accordance with their intentions,
the fact that it will do so shall not preclude a charge of conspiracy to defraud being brought against any of them in respect of the agreement.

Note
1. The choice for the prosecutor of whether to charge statutory or common law conspiracy is governed by guidelines issued by the Director of Public Prosecutions under the Prosecution of Offences Act 1985, s. 10.

The common law crime of conspiracy to defraud will usually take one of three forms:

(a) Where loss is suffered.
(b) Where the victim is deceived into taking an economic risk.
(c) Where a public official is induced by deception to act contrary to his public duty.

(*a*) *Where loss is suffered.* Where actual loss is suffered by the victim, no deceit on the part of the defendant needs to be shown.

Scott v *Metropolitan Police Commissioner*
[1975] AC 819
House of Lords

VISCOUNT DILHORNE: . . . During the course of the opening of the case for the prosecution Mr Blom-Cooper, who represented the appellant, said that the appellant was prepared to admit, and the appellant did admit, the following facts, namely, that he

Agreed with employees of cinema owners temporarily to abstract, without per-mission of such cinema owners, and in return for payments to such employees, cinematograph films, without the knowledge or consent of the owners of the copyright and/or of distribution rights in such films, for the purpose of making infringing copies and distributing the same of a commercial basis.

On these admitted facts Mr Blom-Cooper submitted the appellant could not be convicted on the first count. His contention that there could not be a conspiracy to defraud unless there was deceit was rejected by Judge Hines and the appellant then pleaded guilty to the first and seventh counts and was sentenced to two years' imprisonment on count one and one year's imprisonment on count two.
. . .
The Court of Appeal certified that a point of law of general public importance was involved in the decision to dismiss the appeal against conviction on count one, namely,

Whether, on a charge of conspiracy to defraud, the Crown must establish an agreement to deprive the owners of their property by deception; or whether it is sufficient to prove an agreement to prejudice the rights of another or others without lawful justification and in circumstances of dishonesty.

. . .
In the course of the argument many cases were cited. It is not necessary to refer to all of them. Many were cases in which the conspiracy alleged was to defraud by deceit. Those cases do not establish that there can only be a conspiracy to defraud if deceit is involved and there are a number of cases where that was not the case.
. . .
One must not confuse the object of a conspiracy with the means by which it is intended to be carried out. In the light of the cases to which I have referred, I have come to the conclusion that Mr Blom-Cooper's main contention must be rejected. I have not the temerity to attempt an exhaustive definition of the meaning of 'defraud.' As I have said, words take colour from the context in which they are used, but the words 'fradulently' and 'defraud' must ordinarily have a very similar meaning. If, as I think, and as the Criminal Law Revision Committee appears to have thought, 'fraudulently'

means 'dishonestly,' then 'to defraud' ordinarily means, in my opinion, to deprive a person dishonestly of something which is his or of something to which he is or would or might but for the perpetration of the fraud be entitled.

In *Welham* v *Director of Public Prosecutions* [1961] AC 103, 124 Lord Radcliffe referred to a special line of cases where the person deceived is a person holding public office or a public authority and where the person deceived was not caused any pecuniary or economic loss. Forgery whereby the deceit has been accomplished, had, he pointed out, been in a number of cases treated as having been done with intent to defraud despite the absence of pecuniary or economic loss.

In this case it is not necessary to decide that a conspiracy to defraud may exist even though its object was not to secure a financial advantage by inflicting an economic loss on the person at whom the conspiracy was directed. But for myself I see no reason why what was said by Lord Radcliffe in relation to forgery should not equally apply in relation to conspiracy to defraud.

In this case the accused bribed servants of the cinema owners to secure possession of films in order to copy them and in order to enable them to let the copies out on hire. By so doing Mr Blom-Cooper conceded they inflicted more than nominal damage to the goodwill of the owners of the copyright and distribution rights of the films. By so doing they secured for themselves profits which but for their actions might have been secured by those owners just as in *R* v *Button*, 3 Cox CC 229 the defendants obtained profits which might have been secured by their employer. In the circumstances it is, I think, clear that they inflicted pecuniary loss on those owners.

(*b*)   *Where the victim is deceived into taking an economic risk.*

R v *Allsop*
(1976) 64 Cr App R 29
Court of Appeal

The appellant was a sub-broker for a hire-purchase company. His function as such was to introduce prospective purchasers of cars and to fill in application forms in respect of them. From time to time he put false particulars in the forms so as to induce the hire-purchase company to accept applications which they might otherwise have rejected. When doing this the appellant expected and believed that these transactions would be completed satisfactorily so that the hire-purchase company would profit from them. The appellant was charged with conspiracy to defraud.

SHAW LJ: This appeal raises a short but interesting question in relation to the nature of the intent requisite to constitute the offence of conspiracy to defraud. The argument advanced by Mr Mervyn Heald on behalf of the appellant is that such an intent involves as an essential element the objective of causing actual economic loss to the person alleged to have been defrauded so that it is not sufficient if that person's economic interests are merely threatened incidentally. Miss Goddard, for the Crown, asserts that no more is necessary than the intent to bring about a situation in which the economic interests of the person deceived are threatened or prejudiced, or are likely to be threatened or prejudiced, albeit that such threat or prejudice is undesired or incidental so far as the person responsible for the deceit is concerned.

. . .

It seemed to this Court that Mr Heald's argument traversed the shadowy region between intent and motive. Generally the primary objective of fraudsmen is to advantage themselves. The detriment that results to their victims is secondary to that purpose and incidental. It is 'intended' only in the sense that it is a contemplated outcome of the fraud that is perpetrated. If the deceit which is employed imperils the economic interest of the person deceived, this is sufficient to constitute fraud even though in the event no actual loss is suffered and notwithstanding that the deceiver did not desire to bring about an actual loss.

. . . 'Economic loss' may be ephemeral and not lasting, or potential and not actual; but even a threat of financial prejudice while it exists it may be measured in terms of money.

. . .

In the present case, the part of the history which is common ground reveals that in this sense Prestige did suffer actual loss for they paid too much for cars worth less than their pretended value; and they relied upon the creditworthiness of hire-purchasers as measured by the deposit stated to have been paid when none had been paid.

It matters not that in the end the hire-purchasers concerned paid to Prestige what was due to them. In the interim that corporation suffered economic loss in consequence of the misrepresentation made by the appellant. Mr Heald argues that this is neither here nor there. The essential consideration so his argument ran is what the appellant intended at the outset; he averred that, it is not sufficient if the intention to put Prestige's interests at risk was merely incidental when the ultimate purpose was not to injure them. We do not agree. Interests which are imperilled are less valuable in terms of money than those same interests when they are secure and protected. Where a person intends by deceit to induce a course of conduct in another which puts that other's economic interests in jeopardy he is guilty of fraud even though he does not intend or desire that actual loss should ultimately be suffered by that other in this context.

(c) *Where a public official is induced by deception to act contrary to his public duty.*

Welham v *Director of Public Prosecutions*
[1961] AC 103
House of Lords

The appellant was tried on an indictment which included two counts which charged him with uttering forged documents, contrary to s. 6 of the Forgery Act 1913. The appellant, as sales manager of Motors (Brighton) Ltd, had witnessed forged hire-purchase agreements on the strength of which certain finance companies had advanced large sums of money to Motors (Brighton) Ltd. The appellant's defence was that he had believed that the agreements were brought into being to enable the finance companies to lend money which they could not ordinarily do because of credit restrictions, and because by their memorandum and articles of association they could not act as moneylenders. He claimed that the purpose of the hire-purchase agreements was to make it appear that the finance companies were advancing money in the way of their business as finance companies, and he accordingly contended that he had had no intention to defraud the finance companies but was merely uttering the documents to mislead the relevant authority who might inspect the records to see that the credit restrictions were being observed and whose duty it was to prevent their contravention. The jury were directed that this was a sufficient intention to defraud and the appellant was convicted. He appealed on the ground that his intention was merely an intention to deceive and not an intention to defraud, which involved causing some economic loss to the person deceived.

LORD DENNING: . . . Much valuable guidance is to be obtained from the dictum of Buckley J in the *Whittaker Wright* case, *In re London and Globe Finance Corporation* [1903] 1 Ch 728, but this has been criticised by modern scholars. It has even been hinted that it conceals within it the fallacy of the illegitimate antistrophe, which sounds, I must say, extremely serious. These scholars seem to think they have found the solution. 'To defraud,' they say, involves the idea of economic loss. I cannot agree with them on this. If a drug addict forges a doctor's prescription so as to enable him to get drugs from a chemist, he has, I should have thought, an intent to defraud, even though he intends to pay the chemist the full price and no one is a penny the worse off.

Seeing, therefore, that the words of the statute are of doubtful import, it is, I think, legitimate to turn for guidance to the previous state of the law before the Act. And here I would say at once that the phrase 'with intent to defraud' has been the standard usage of lawyers in defining forgery for over 160 years. In 1796 all the judges of England laid down the definition of forgery as 'the false making of a note or other instrument *with intent to defraud*' (see *R v Parkes and Brown* (1797) 2 Leach 775, 785); and ever since that time it has been held that the very essence of forgery is an *intent to defraud*, and it must be laid in the indictment (see East, Pleas of the Crown (1803), vol. 2, p. 988; Chitty, Criminal Law (1826), vol. 3, pp. 1039, 1042). I cannot help thinking that when Parliament in section 4(1) of the Act of 1913 used a phrase so hallowed by usage, it used it in the sense in which it had been used by generations of lawyers. It was never by them confined to the causing of economic loss. Let me prove this by taking some examples: Take the case where a man forges a reference as to character, intending to get employment by means of it. It is clear forgery: see *R v Sharman* (1854) 1 Dears CC 285; *R v Moah* (1858) 7 Cox CC 503, 504. But there may well be no economic loss intended. The man may intend, if he gets the job, to render full service in return for his wages. Or the post which he seeks may be unpaid, such as a justice of the peace. But he has the intent to defraud all the same.

Take next the case where a servant steals his master's money and afterwards forges a receipt or other document so as to cover up his defalcations. This, too, is forgery: see *R v Martin* (1836) 1 Mood CC 483. He does not intend to deprive his master of anything: for he has already done that. He may not even do it so as to keep his job, because he may be under notice. What he really intends to do is to cover up his tracks so that he should not be found out. But he has the intent to defraud none the less.

Then there are the cases concerned with the release of prisoners. If a man forges an order or letter to the sheriff or to the governor of a prison, intending thereby to secure the release of a prisoner, he is guilty of forgery at common law: see *Fawcett's* case (1793) 2 East PL 862 and *R v Harris* 1 Mood CC 393. There is no idea of economic loss here. He has no intent to deprive the gaoler of any money or valuable thing. But at common law he is held to have an intent to defraud. Mr Gardiner rather suggested that the reason for those decisions was that the documents were documents of a public nature. But I do not so read them. Even if they were public documents it was still essential that there should be an intent to defraud. Ever since *Ward's* case 2 LD Ryam 1461, 3 LD Ryam 358; 2 Str 787 in 1726 public and private documents were at common law on the same footing in this respect: see East's Pleas of the Crown, pp. 859–861. The forgery of any of them was a misdemeanour if done with intent to defraud, but not otherwise: see *R v Hodgson* Dedrs. B. 3, 8 by Jervis CJ.

There remains the case of *R v Toshack* 4 Cox CC 38, 41, which is to my mind decisive. Toshack, a seaman, forged a certificate of good conduct so as to be admitted to sit for an examination for his master's certificate. He had no intention to deprive the examiners or Trinity House of any money or valuable thing. The piece of paper, value one penny, was not mentioned in the counts on which he was convicted. But he was held guilty of forgery. Alderson B said: 'It does amount to a very serious offence if persons do forge certificates of this sort and are found to utter them for the purpose of deceiving the Trinity House.'

What is the common element in all these cases? It is, I think, best expressed in the definition given by East in his Pleas of the Crown, vol. 2, p. 852. He treats the subject, I think, better than any writer before or since:

> *To forge*, (a metaphorical expression borrowed from the occupation of the smith), means, properly speaking, no more than to *make* or *form*: but in our law it is always taken in an evil sense; and therefore Forgery at common law denotes a *false* making (which includes every alteration of or addition to a true instrument), a making malo animo, of any written instrument for the purpose of fraud and deceit. This definition results from all the authorities ancient and modern taken together.

That was written in 1803, but it has been always accepted as authoritative. It seems to me to provide the key to the cases decided since it was written, as well as those before. The important thing about this definition is that it is not limited to the idea of economic loss, nor to the idea of depriving someone of something of value. It extends generally to *the purpose of fraud and deceit*. Put shortly, 'with intent to defraud' means 'with intent to practise a fraud' on someone or other. It need not be anyone in particular. Someone in general will suffice. . . .

At this point it becomes possible to point the contrast in the statute between an 'intent to deceive' and an 'intent to defraud.' 'To deceive' here conveys the element of deceit, which induces a state of mind, without the element of fraud, which induces a course of action or inaction. Take the case of a private document. For instance, where a man fabricates a letter so as to puff himself up in the opinion of others. Bramwell B put the instance: 'If I were to produce a letter purporting to be from the Duke of Wellington inviting me to dine, and say, "See what a respectable person I am"'': *R v Moah*. There would then be an intent to deceive but it would not be punishable at common law or under the statute, because then it would not be done with intent to defraud. Take next the case of a public document. For instance, a parish register. If a man should falsify it so as to make himself appear to be descended of noble family, for the sake of his own glorification, he would not be guilty of an intent to defraud and would therefore not be punishable at common law (see *R v Hodgson*), but he would have an intent to deceive and he would be punishable under the present statute, as indeed he was under its predecessors, such as the Forgery Act 1861, s. 36.

So much for the principal point under discussion. Mr Gerald Gardiner did make a further point. He said that the intent must be to defraud the particular person to whom the document is first presented or his agent, and that it was insufficient if he intended to defraud somebody else. This is not correct. It has long been ruled that it is no answer to a charge of forgery to say that there was no intent to defraud any particular person, because a general intent to defraud is sufficient to constitute the crime. So also it is no answer to say that there was no intent to defraud the recipient, if there was intent to defraud somebody else: see *R v Taylor* (1779) 1 Leach 214.

Notes
1. *Welham* v *DPP* was not a case concerning conspiracy to defraud but it seems to be generally accepted that the same principles are applicable.
2. Note that in the third category of conspiracy to defraud, the possibility or actuality of economic loss is irrelevant. Why should this be so?

(d) Mens rea. There must be dishonesty according to the test set out in *Ghosh* [1982] QB 1053 (see infra. p. 505). Although this case dealt with the *mens rea* of theft, the test of dishonesty which it established has been applied in other contexts, including the present one. The test has two prongs:

(i) was the defendant dishonest as judged by the current standards of reasonable and honest people; and
(ii) did the defendant realise that his acts were contrary to that standard?

There has been confusion in the case law as to whether a defendant has the requisite intent for conspiracy to defraud where there is no clear motive to cause economic loss. This issue was addressed by the Privy Council in *Wai Yu-tsang* v *R*.

Wai Yu-tsang v *R*
[1991] 4 All ER 664
Privy Council

LORD GOFF OF CHIEVELEY: . . . The appellant was the chief accountant of the Hang Lung Bank (the bank). He was charged that, between 7 September and 13 November 1982, he conspired together with Cheng Eng-kuan, Lee Hoi-kwong and others to defraud the bank and its existing and potential shareholders, creditors and depositors, by dishonestly concealing in the accounts of the bank the dishonouring of US dollar cheques in the sum of $US124m, drawn on the account of Overseas Maritime Co. Ltd SA with Citibank International, Chicago, such cheques having been purchased by the bank. Of the other members of the alleged conspiracy, Cheng was the managing director of the bank and Lee was the general manager. Cheng fled the jurisdiction, as did another associate of his, John Mao. Lee originally stood trial with the appellant but, following preliminary argument on the admissibility of certain evidence, the Crown abandoned its case against him. In the result, the appellant stood trial alone.

The events giving rise to the charge against the appellant were as follows. For some years a cheque-kiting cycle, known as the Capri cycle, had been run by John Mao, using a number of companies as its principal vehicle. In May 1982, in order to bring the Capri cycle to an end, a new cheque-kiting cycle (known as the OMC cycle) was set up to create funds for Overseas Maritime Co. Ltd SA (OMC). The object was to transfer the funds into the Capri cycle so that the final cheques in circulation in that cycle could be met. The bank purchased cheques in US currency via a company called Southseas Finance Co. Ltd (SSF). The cheques, drawn on the OMC account, were purchased by the bank from SSF. The proceeds were credited to the account of SSF with the bank, and the cheques were cleared through the bank's foreign exchange with Chemical Bank. Those purchases required the approval of Cheng as the managing director of the bank. However, on 7 September 1982 a rumour started by a taxi-driver caused a run on the bank, and in consequence Cheng gave instructions that no further US dollar cheques or drafts were to be purchased. This had the effect that the second cheque-kiting cycle was brought to a premature end, and that cheques then in circulation could not be met. On 14 September Chemical Bank advised the bank that two or three of the OMC cheques had been returned, and on 18 September another seven. The total face value of those cheques (which had been purchased by the bank from SSF) was $US124m (the equivalent of $HK755m), an amount which exceeded the assets of the bank at that time.

There was no suggestion that the appellant was in any way involved in either of the two cheque-kiting cycles. It was however alleged that he conspired with Cheng and others to defraud the bank and its existing and potential shareholders, creditors and depositors, by dishonestly concealing in the bank's accounts the dishonouring of the US dollar cheques in the sum of $US124m which had been purchased by the bank. During the run on the bank, it had been supported by the Standard Chartered Bank, to which the appellant was under a duty to report, as he was to the Commissioner of Banking. He did not however report the dishonour of the cheques, nor did he cause the dishonour to be recorded in the bank's computerised ledgers. The details of the transactions were recorded only in private ledgers, called 'K' vouchers. Instead there were recorded in the bank's accounts entries purporting to show that the bank had drawn 16 US dollar drafts on Chemical Bank in amounts equivalent to the total amount of the dishonoured cheques, and had sold them to SSF, that short-term loans had been granted to two companies called Thring Trading Ltd (Thring) and Texas Finance Ltd (Texas), and that SSF had paid for the drafts with cheques drawn on its own account and on the accounts of Thring and Texas. The drafts were never presented for payment, although the accounts were debited with the amounts of the cheques. This gave the false picture of balances in the Chemical Bank account and in the SSF account which were approximately the same as they would have been if the dishonoured cheques had been recorded as debits in the SSF account and credits in the Chemical Bank account.

. . .

Before the Court of Appeal, a number of issues were raised by the appellant founded upon criticisms of the summing up of the learned judge. All of those criticisms were rejected by the Court of Appeal. Before their Lordships, however, the appellant's case was directed solely to the judge's direction on the mental element required for a conspiracy to defraud. The judge explained to the jury that the appellant must have been party to an agreement with one or more of the other named conspirators which had a common intention to defraud one or more of the persons or categories of persons named in the indictment. He explained that such an intention must involve dishonesty on the part of the conspirators, and continued as follows:

> It is fraud if it is proved that there was the dishonest taking of a risk which there was no right to take, which – to Mr Wai's knowledge at least – would cause detriment or prejudice to another, detriment or prejudice to the economic or proprietary rights of another. That detriment or prejudice to somebody else is very often incidental to the purpose of the fraudsman himself. The prime objective of fraudsmen is usually to gain some advantage for themselves, any detriment or prejudice to somebody else is often secondary to that objective but nonetheless is a contemplated or predictable outcome of what they do. If the interests of some other person – the economic or proprietary interests of some other person are imperilled, that is sufficient to constitute fraud even though no loss is actually suffered and even though the fraudsman himself did not desire to bring about any loss.

It is plain that that direction was founded upon the judgment of the Court of Appeal in *R* v *Allsop* (1976) 64 Cr App R 29. It was the contention of the appellant that the direction was erroneous in so far as it stated that, for this purpose, the imperilling of an economic interest or the threat of financial prejudice was sufficient to establish fraud, whatever the motive of the accused may have been; and that in so far as *Allsop's* case so decided, it was wrong and should not be followed.

[In *Scott* v *Metropolitan Police Commissioner* [1975] AC 819, Lord Diplock said:]

... (2) Where the intended victim of a 'conspiracy to defraud' is a private individual the purpose of the conspirators must be to cause the victim economic loss by depriving him of some property or right, corporeal or incorporeal, to which he is or would or might become entitled ... (3) Where the intended victim of a 'conspiracy to defraud' is a person performing public duties as distinct from a private individual it is sufficient if the purpose is to cause him to act contrary to his public duty ...

With the greatest respect to Lord Diplock, their Lordships consider this categorisation to be too narrow. In their opinion, in agreement with the approach of Lord Radcliffe in *Welham's* case, the cases concerned with persons performing public duties are not to be regarded as a special category in the manner described by Lord Diplock, but rather as exemplifying the general principle that conspiracies to defraud are not restricted to cases of intention to cause the victim economic loss. On the contrary, they are to be understood in the broad sense described by Lord Radcliffe and Lord Denning in *Welham's* case – the view which Viscount Dilhorne favoured in *Scott's* case, as apparently did the other members of the Appellate Committee who agreed with him in that case (apart, it seems, from Lord Diplock).

... The question whether particular facts reveal a conspiracy to defraud depends upon what the conspirators have dishonestly agreed to do, and in particular whether they have agreed to practise a fraud on somebody. For this purpose it is enough for example that, as in *R* v *Allsop* and in the present case, the conspirators have dishonestly agreed to bring about a state of affairs which they realise will or may deceive the victim into so acting, or failing to act, that he will suffer economic loss or his economic interests will be put at risk. It is however important in such a case, as the Court of Appeal stressed in *Allsop's* case, to distinguish a conspirator's intention (or immediate purpose) dishonestly to bring about such a state of affairs from his motive (or underlying purpose). The latter may be benign to the extent that he does not wish the victim or potential victim to suffer harm; but the mere fact that it is benign will not of itself prevent the agreement from constituting a conspiracy to defraud. Of course, if the conspirators were not acting dishonestly, there will have been no conspiracy to defraud; and in any event their benign purpose (if it be such) is a matter which, if they prove to be guilty, can be taken into account at the stage of sentence.

Questions
1. What was the defendant's motive in *Wai Yu-tsang* v *R*? His intent?
2. Does motive play a different role depending on which category of conspiracy to defraud is at issue? Or does the Privy Council reject the idea of categories completely?
3. If no intention to cause economic loss is required in the case of deceit of private persons, why is it not a crime to pretend to be of noble descent (see Denning in *Welham*)?

(e)   Who is to commit the offence? Unlike statutory conspiracy, it seems that it need not be a conspirator who actually perpetrates the eventual offence:

R v Hollinshead
[1985] AC 975
House of Lords

The defendant G made devices which, if fitted to an electricity meter, reversed the flow of current so that the meter recorded less units of electricity than actually consumed. He and the other two defendants were arrested when they attempted to sell a number of the devices to a third person who unbeknown to them was a police officer. They were charged on indictment which by count 1 alleged conspiracy contrary to s. 1 of the Criminal Law Act 1977 in that they had conspired together to aid, abet, counsel or procure persons unknown by deception dishonestly to induce an electricity board to wait for or forgo payment for electricity supplied. Count 2 alleged a conspiracy to defraud contrary to the common law in that they had conspired together to defraud one or more electricity boards by the manufacture and sale of devices to alter electricity meters. The judge ordered that count 1 should lie on the file and, when he ruled against a defence submission that count 2 did not disclose an offence, the defendants pleaded guilty to conspiracy to defraud contrary to the common law.

On appeals by the Crown by leave of the House of Lords: —

Held, allowing the appeals, that the defendants were liable to be convicted of conspiracy to defraud since they agreed to manufacture and sell and thus put into circulation dishonest devices, the sole purpose of which was to cause loss, and that in order to secure a conviction on count 2 it was not necessary for the prosecution to aver and prove a dishonest agreement by the defendants actually to use the devices themselves . . . .

(ii)   Conspiracy to corrupt public morals or outrage public decency
Section 5(3) of the Criminal Law Act 1977, specifically preserves the common law offence of conspiracy to corrupt public morals or outrage public decency.

Criminal Law Act 1977

5.—(1)   Subject to the following provisions of this section, the offence of conspiracy at common law is hereby abolished.

(2)   . . .

(3)   Subsection (1) above shall not affect the offence of conspiracy at common law if and in so far as it may be committed by entering into an agreement to engage in conduct which —

(a)   tends to corrupt public morals or outrages public decency; but

(b)   would not amount to or involve the commission of an offence if carried out by a single person otherwise than in pursuance of an agreement.

Questions
1.   Is it possible to know from a reading of the statute what behaviour will be caught by these offences? If not, how can people who desire to be law-abiding regulate their conduct to avoid prosecution?

2.   To whom should the decision of determining what behaviour falls within the common law offence be entrusted? Judges? Members of Parliament? The community (as represented by the jury)?

Note
Prosecutions for the common law crime have been few, but the following should give a flavour of the types of cases where it is charged.

Shaw v *Director of Public Prosecutions*
[1962] AC 220
House of Lords

For the facts and holding, see p. 34.

Knuller v *Director of Public Prosecutions*
[1973] AC 435
House of Lords

The appellants were directors of a company which published a fortnightly magazine. On an inside page under a column headed 'Males' advertisements were inserted inviting readers to meet the advertisers for the purpose of homosexual practices. The appellants were convicted on counts of conspiracy to corrupt public morals and conspiracy to outrage public decency.

LORD SIMON OF GLAISDALE: . . . In my view, counsel for the appellants was right to concede that there is a common law offence of conspiring to outrage public decency.
(3) As for whether such an offence is applicable to books and newspapers, the argument based on section 2(4) of the Obscene Publications Act 1959 is concluded against the appellants by the construction put upon that subsection in *Shaw v Director of Public Prosecutions* [1962] AC 220. The passage I have cited from *Mirehouse v Rennell*, (1833) 1 Cl & F 527, 546 indicates that the fact that the authorities show no example of the application of the rule of law in circumstances such as the instant does not mean that it is not applicable, provided that there are circumstances, however novel, which fall fairly within the rule. Counsel for the appellants could not suggest any demarcation in principle. To attempt delimitation would produce absurd anomalies. The newspaper placard would presumably fall within the offence: it would be odd if similar material on the exposed front page of the newspaper did not do so. A picture fly-posted in a small village would fall within the offence; but, on the argument for the appellants, not the same picture contained in a newspaper or book of mass circulation. Safeguards are to be found in the requirement of publicity for the offence to be established, and in the parliamentary undertaking to which my noble and learned friend, Lord Reid, has referred – this must be taken to apply to conspiracy to outrage public decency as much as to conspiracy to corrupt public morals.
(4) I turn, then, to the requirement of publicity. *R v Mayling* [1963] 2 QB 717 shows that the substantive offence (and therefore the conduct the subject of the conspiracy) must be committed in public, in the sense that the circumstances must be such that the alleged outrageously indecent matter could have been seen by more than one person, even though in fact no more than one did see it. If it is capable of being seen by one person only, no offence is committed.
It was at one time argued for the appellants that the matter must have been visible to two or more people simultaneously; and that an article in a newspaper did not fulfil this requirement. But this point was rightly abandoned, and I need not examine it further.
. . .

It was argued for the Crown that it was immaterial whether or not the alleged outrage to decency took place in public, provided that the sense of decency of the public or a substantial section of the public was outraged. But this seems to me to be contrary to many of the authorities which the Crown itself relied on to establish the generic offence. The authorities establish that the word 'public' has a different connotation in the respective offences of conspiracy to corrupt public morals and conduct calculated to, or conspiracy to, outrage public decency. In the first it refers to certain fundamental rules regarded as essential social control which yet lack the force of law: when applicable to individuals, in other words, 'public' refers to persons in society. In the latter offences, however, 'public' refers to the place in which the offence is committed. This is borne out by the way the rule was framed by my noble and learned friend, Lord Reid, in *Shaw v Director of Public Prosecutions* [1962] AC 220 in the passage which I have just cited. It is also borne out by what is presumably the purpose of the legal rule – namely, that reasonable people may venture out in public without the risk of outrage to certain minimum accepted standards of decency.

On the other hand, I do not think that it would necessarily negative the offence that the act or exhibit is superficially hid from view, if the public is expressly or impliedly invited to penetrate the cover. Thus, the public touting for an outrageously indecent exhibition in private would not escape: see *R v Saunders* (1875) 1 QBD 15. Another obvious example is an outrageously indecent exhibit with a cover entitled 'Lift in order to see. . . .' This sort of instance could be applied to a book or newspaper; and I think that a jury should be invited to consider the matter in this way. The conduct must at least in some way be so projected as to have an impact in public: cf. *Smith v Hughes* [1960] 1 WLR 830.

(5)   There are other features of the offence which should, in my view, be brought to the notice of the jury. It should be emphasised that 'outrage,' like 'corrupt,' is a very strong word. 'Outraging public decency' goes considerably beyond offending the susceptibilities of, or even shocking, reasonable people. Moreover the offence is, in my view, concerned with recognised minimum standards of decency, which are likely to vary from time to time. Finally, notwithstanding that 'public' in the offence is used in a locative sense, public decency must be viewed as a whole; and I think the jury should be invited, where appropriate, to remember that they live in a plural society, with a tradition of tolerance towards minorities, and that this atmosphere of toleration is itself part of public decency.

(6)   The Court of Appeal said of the direction on count 2 that it might be that it was not wholly satisfactory. I would myself go further. I regard it as essential that the jury should be carefully directed, on the lines that I have ventured to suggest, on the proper approach to the meaning of 'decency' and 'outrage' and the element of publicity required to constitute the offence. The summing up was generally a careful and fair one, but I think it was defective in these regards; and I therefore do not think it would be safe to allow the conviction on count 2 to stand.

R v Gibson and Another
[1991] 1 All ER 439
Court of Appeal

For the facts and holding, see p. 35.

Notes and questions

1.   Is it possible to know from a reading of the cases what behaviour will be caught by these offences? If not, how can people who desire to be law-abiding regulate their conduct to avoid prosecution?

2. In *Knuller* v *DPP* the House of Lords stated that the courts had no residual discretion to create new criminal offences. Does this signal an awareness of the potential abuses inherent in common law crimes? The topic is discussed in Chapter 1.

3. Are conspiracies to corrupt public morals or outrage public decency common law or statutory conspiracies?

4. The Criminal Law Act 1977, s. 5(3) stipulates that a charge of conspiracy will lie only where there would be an offence if carried out by a single person. While cases such as *Gibson* confirm the existence of a substantive offence of outraging public decency, it is still unclear whether there is behaviour outside the definition of the substantive offence which would not amount to an offence if done by one person, but which might amount to a common law conspiracy to outrage public decency if done by several. Nor is it clear whether there is a substantive offence of corrupting public morals. The House of Lords did not determine the issue in *Shaw* v *DPP* although the Court of Appeal held that there was such a substantive offence. Even if there is such an offence, a similar uncertainty will arise as to the offence of outraging public decency. The fact that the ruling in *Ayres* (above p. 259) still applies to these two conspiracies makes the distinction important, as does the different rules on impossibility (see below). The statute is unhelpful and the whole area ripe for reform.

If the offence charged is a common law conspiracy, impossibility remains a defence.

Director of Public Prosecutions v *Nock*
[1978] AC 979
House of Lords

LORD RUSSELL OF KILLOWEN: My Lords, I have had the advantage of reading in draft the speech in these consolidated appeals of my noble and learned friend, Lord Scarman. I agree with his conclusion that these appeals should be allowed and with the reasons to which he attributes that conclusion.

The important point to note is that the agreement that is said to have been an unlawful conspiracy was not an agreement in general terms to produce cocaine, but an agreement in specific terms to produce cocaine from a particular powder which in fact, however treated, would never yield cocaine. In order to see whether there is a criminal conspiracy it is necessary to consider the whole agreement. The specific limits of the agreement cannot be discarded, leaving a general agreement to produce cocaine, for that would be to find an agreement other than that which was made: and that is not a permissible approach to any agreement, conspiracy or other.

It is, I apprehend, clear on authority that neither appellant, discovered in the act of vainly and optimistically applying sulphuric acid (or any other treatment) to this particular powder, would be guilty of an attempt to produce cocaine. It would appear to me strange that the two should be guilty of a crime if together they bent over the same test tube, having agreed on the joint vain attempt. These appellants thought that they would succeed in their endeavour. But what if they had doubted success, and their agreement had been to 'try it'? That would be an agreement to attempt, and since the attempt would not be unlawful the agreement could not be a criminal conspiracy. But if the conclusion against which these appeals are made were correct, it would mean that those erroneously confident of success would be guilty of the crime of conspiracy, but not those who, unconvinced, agreed to try. The gullible would be guilty, the suspicious stainless. That could not be right.

IV Attempt

Attempting to commit a crime is now a statutory offence defined by the Criminal Attempts Act 1981. The basic definition is contained in s. 1:

Criminal Attempts Act 1981

1—(1)   If, with intent to commit an offence to which this section applies, a person does an act which is more than merely preparatory to the commission of the offence, he is guilty of attempting to commit the offence.

(2)   A person may be guilty of attempting to commit an offence to which this section applies even though the facts are such that the commission of the offence is impossible.

(3)   In any case where —

(a)   apart from this subsection a person's intention would not be regarded as having amounted to an intent to commit an offence; but

(b)   if the facts of the case had been as he believed them to be, his intention would be so regarded, then, for the purposes of subsection (1) above, he shall be regarded as having had an intent to commit that offence.

(4)   This section applies to any offence which, if it were completed, would be triable in England and Wales as an indictable offence, other than —

(a)   conspiracy (at common law or under section 1 of the Criminal Law Act 1977 or any other enactment);

(b)   aiding, abetting, counselling, procuring or suborning the commission of an offence;

(c)   offences under section 4(1) (assisting offenders) or 5(1) (accepting or agreeing to accept consideration for not disclosing information about an arrestable offence) of the Criminal Law Act 1967.

Notes

1.   Because the law of attempt has now been codified by Parliament, cases decided before the Act must be approached with considerable caution.

2.   Under s. 1(4)(b) of the Act it is no longer an offence to attempt to aid and abet the commission of an offence. However, in some instances aiding and abetting is, by statute, itself an offence. Where this is so, there can be a conviction for attempting to commit the statutory crime. An example is assisting suicide contrary to the Suicide Act 1961, s. 2(1).

Questions

Under the Act, can there be an offence of attempting to commit a summary offence? An offence of attempting to commit an offence by omission to act? Attempted voluntary manslaughter?

Jurisdictional issues can sometimes be troublesome. Consider the following case which involved a prominent politician and attracted much media attention at the time.

Director of Public Prosecutions v Stonehouse
[1977] 2 All ER 909
House of Lords

LORD DIPLOCK: My Lords, in 1974, the appellant, John Thomson Stonehouse ('the accused'), was a well-known public figure in this country. A member of Parliament and a Privy Councillor, he had held a number of ministerial posts in the government during the six years up to 1970. Thereafter he became active in business through a company, Export Promotion and Consultancy Services Ltd, which he controlled.

By the summer of 1974, however, his personal finances were in a disastrous state. He decided to fake his death by drowning and to start life afresh under a new identity with money dishonestly obtained and clandestinely transferred to his chosen country of refuge, Australia. He carried out this plan, but was discovered living in Australia under his false identity some five weeks after his pretended death by drowning. He was extradited and stood his trial at the Central Criminal Court on an indictment charging him with 16 complete offences of dishonesty and forgery and five offences of attempting to obtain property by deception (counts 17 to 21).

This House is not concerned in this appeal with any of the charges of complete offences. He was convicted on 13 of these. Your lordships are concerned with those five counts (17 to 21) which charged him with the inchoate crime of attempting to obtain property by deception. The intended victims of the deception charges were five different life insurance companies, which had issued to Mrs Stonehouse, the wife of the accused, policies amounting in all to £125,000 payable on her husband's death within five years.

The facts that gave rise to these charges can be stated briefly. Mrs Stonehouse was not a party to the accused's plan. She was intended to believe that he had died by drowning. The accused intended to transfer to Australia all the money that he could lay his hands on; so on his death being presumed, his estate would be insolvent. To provide for his wife, ostensibly his widow, after his disappearance, there were taken out between July and September 1974, in Mrs Stonehouse's name, the five policies of insurance to a total amount of £125,000 payable to her on the death of her husband within five years. Active steps in arranging for the issue of the policies to his wife were taken by the accused himself in England. On 20th November 1974 the accused faked his death by accidental drowning in the sea off Miami in Florida, USA, to which city he had gone with a business associate. Ostensibly for a business meeting. He had made an appointment for such a meeting later on that day and pending this had told his companion that he was going to the beach to have a swim. When he failed to keep the business appointment, enquiries were set on foot. His clothes, valuables and passport were found to be still in his hotel room and his bath robe was found in a bathing hut on the beach. Of the accused himself there was no trace. In fact he had left Miami secretly by air, wearing a new suit of clothes which he had secreted and equipped with a false passport to conceal his identity. He eventually reached Australia and remained there undetected until 24th December 1974.

As soon as his disappearance at Miami was discovered in the circumstances summarised above, the hue and cry was raised. The police were brought in and, as was inevitable, the circumstances of his disappearance hit the headlines in the press, and on television and radio, in England. What the accused had done ensured, as he intended, that the news of his death by drowning should be communicated in England to his wife, who he intended should claim the policy moneys, and to the insurance companies, who he intended should pay them over to her.

At his trial the accused was convicted on the five counts of attempting to obtain property by deception. He had discharged his counsel early in the proceedings and no point was taken at the trial that these offences were committed outside the territorial jurisdiction of the English court.

On his appeal to the Court of Appeal, Criminal Division, the accused was represented by counsel who took the territorial jurisdiction point and two other points of law. They were that the acts of the accused at Miami on 20th November 1974 were not sufficiently proximate to the complete offence of obtaining property by deception to be capable in law of constituting an attempt to commit that crime: or, in the alternative, that the question whether they were sufficiently proximate was one of fact for the jury and that the judge had wrongly treated it as one of law and withdrawn that question for them.

The appeal was dismissed, but the Court of Appeal certified that the following point of law of general public importance was involved in the decision to dismiss the appeal against conviction on counts 17 to 21:

Whether the offence of attempting on 20th November 1974 to obtain property in England by deception, the final act alleged to constitute the offence of attempt having occurred outside the jurisdiction of the English courts is triable in an English court, all the remaining acts necessary to constitute the complete offence being intended to take place in England.

. . . I start by considering the territorial element in their jurisdiction to try the complete crime; for on this and on the corresponding offence under s. 32 of the Larcency Act 1916, which has been replaced by s. 15 of the Theft Act 1968, there is long-standing authority to the effect that in a result-crime the English courts have jurisdiction to try the offence if the described consequence of the conduct of the accused which is part of the definition of the crime took place in England.

This was called the 'terminatory theory' of jurisdiction by Professor Glanville Williams in an article, Venue and the Ambit of the Criminal Law where he contrasted it unfavourably with the 'initiatory theory' that the crime is committed where the offender is when he does the acts which constitute the essential physical element of the crime. The terminatory theory has been acted on as a ground of jurisdiction since it was first laid down in R v Ellis [1899] 1 QB 230, a case where the false representations were made in Scotland but the property was obtained in England. As I ventured to point out in Treacy v Director of Public Prosecutions [1971] AC 537, there is no reason in principle why the terminatory theory should have the effect of excluding the initiatory theory as an alternative ground of jurisdiction, though this was held to be so in R v Harden [[1962] 1 All ER 286]; but since in the instant case all the physical acts of the accused himself on which the prosecution rely were done in the United States, your Lordships are not concerned to consider whether R v Harden was rightly decided.

In those reported cases where the false representations have been made abroad but the property has been obtained in England, the property has been obtained by the offender himself and this has in fact involved some physical act in England by the offender or by someone else, not necessarily an accomplice but possibly an innocent agent or bailee accepting possession or control of the property on the offender's behalf. In the instant case if the crime which the accused was charged with attempting to commit had been completed he would have enabled another person, Mrs Stonehouse, to obtain the property, viz the policy moneys, for herself and no further act would have needed to be done in England by the accused himself or anyone acting on his behalf. Should this make any difference? In my opinion it does not. The basis of the jurisdiction under the terminatory theory is not that the accused has done some physical act in England, but that his physical acts, wherever they were done, have caused the obtaining of the property in England from the person to whom it belonged. Whether he has caused it to be obtained for himself through the instrumentality of an innocent agent, such as the Post Office, acting on his behalf, or has caused it to be obtained by an innocent third party cannot in my view make any difference to the jurisdiction of the English court to try the offence.

My Lords, if this be the principle on which the English courts would have had jurisdiction to try the complete offence which the accused was charged with attempting to commit, that principle is broad enough to cover also their jurisdiction to try the inchoate offence of attempting to commit it. The accused had done all the physical acts lying within his power that were needed to comply with the definition of a complete crime justiciable by an English court; and his state of mind at the time he did them also satisfied the definition of that crime. All that was left was for him not to be found out before the intended consequence could occur. Once it is appreciated that territorial jurisdiction over a 'result-crime' does not depend on acts done by the offender in England but on consequences which he causes to occur in England. I see no ground for holding that an attempt to commit a crime which, if the attempt succeeded, would be justiciable in England does not also fall within the jurisdiction of the English courts, not withstanding that the physical acts intended to produce the proscribed consequences in England were all of them done abroad.

Note and question

The jurisdiction over attempts generally depends on the jurisdiction of the court over the substantive offence. For example, murder by a British citizen is indictable in England or Wales wherever commited. However, most offences require acts of the defendant to have some effect within the jurisdiction. What effect would Stonehouse's actions have had in England and Wales?

A   Mens rea

It must be shown that the defendant intended to commit the offence, whether or not intention is the *mens rea* for the completed offence.

R v *Whybrow*
(1951) 35 Cr App R 141
Court of Appeal

LORD GODDARD: . . . The facts of the case, so far as it is necessary to state them, are these: the appellant was living on bad terms with his wife and it was shown that at the time he, a married man with a family, was carrying on a liaison with another young woman. That, of course, was put forward as the motive, and, indeed, it is the oldest motive in the world that is brought up in cases of murder or attempted murder of a wife. It was proved to exist and a letter was produced from the appellant to that young woman's father which could leave no doubt in anybody's mind that the appellant's affections had been transferred to that young woman.

The appellant had had some, but no very great, experience of electrical installations. He had been a labourer in the employ of the electrical department of the Southend Corporation Electricity Works and had no doubt, on occassions, gone round with electricians. He also had had a wireless apparatus and so forth in this house and probably had what may be described as an amateur's knowledge of electricity. On the night of the alleged crime the wife was taking a bath and the appellant was in an adjoining room. He said that he was in the lavatory, but he might equally well have been in the bedroom. The wife was heard to call out, and she complained of having received an electric shock while in the bath. The next day it came to light that an apparatus had been connected with the soap dish, the bath being a porcelain bath and either the soap dish itself or its support being made of metal. An apparatus was found connected with this soap dish which, if prepared intentionally, showed a deliberate, cold-blooded resolve to administer a shock of 230 volts of electricity to a woman in her bath. It is common knowledge, and the appellant admitted that he knew it, that to administer an electric shock to a person in a bath is the most dangerous thing that can be done in that way.

The case lasted two days and the learned Judge's summing-up, so far as the facts were concerned, was meticulouly careful and meticulously accurate, but unfortunately he did, in charging the jury, confuse in his mind for a moment the direction given to a jury in a case of murder with the direction given to a jury in a case of attempted murder. In murder the jury is told – and it has always been the law – that if a person wounds another or attacks another either intending to kill or intending to do grievous bodily harm, and the person attacked dies, that is murder, the reason being that the requisite malice aforethought, which is a term of art, is satisfied if the attacker intends to do grievous bodily harm. . . . But, if the charge is one of attempted murder, the intent becomes the principal ingredient of the crime. It may be said that the law, which is not always logical, is somewhat illogical in saying that, if one attacks a person intending to do grievous bodily harm and death results, that is murder, but that if one attacks a person and only intends to do grievous bodily harm, and death does not result, it is not attempted murder, but wounding with intent to do grievous bodily harm. It is not really illogical because, in that particular case, the intent is the essence of the crime while, where the death of another is caused, the necessity is to prove malice aforethought, which is supplied in law by proving intent to do grievous bodily harm.

R v *O'Toole*
[1987] Crim LR 759
Court of Appeal

On July 31, 1986 the appellant who was a regular customer of a public house in North London was 'barred' from that public house. At closing time, the appellant returned with a can of petrol and splashed it around a vestibule at the entrance of the public house. When he was taxed by the barmaid, he stated that he did not care whether she be burned alive. He had earlier been heard to say that he would smash the public house. When arrested, he told the police that if he did not smash the public house up that night he would do it the following night. In interview he said 'I'll burn the lot of them and you (the police) as well.' The defence case was that the applicant was drunk. He had the can of petrol with him because he was filling the petrol reservoir of his motor car. Whilst doing so he had heard a noise from the public house. He decided to speak with the landlord. Whilst trying to look through a window, he had accidentally spilled petrol into the vestibule.

The appellant was charged with two counts, the first alleging that he attempted to damage by fire the public house intending to damage the same or being reckless as to whether it would be damaged and intending to endanger the life of the barmaid. Count 2 alleged as follows:

On 31st day of July 1986 without lawful excuse attempted to damage by fire the Star Public House, Charlbert Street NW8 belonging to another, intending to damage the said property or being reckless as to whether property would be damaged and being reckless as to whether the life of [the barmaid] would thereby be endangered.

The defendant was convicted by the jury of count 2. In summing up the case to the jury, the learned trial judge defined 'attempt' and 'intent' and 'reckless' in relation to the question of damaging property. The jury having retired to consider their verdicts, sent a note in which they said that they were unanimous in their decision that the defendant was 'not guilty of intent (on both counts)' and asking how significant was 'being reckless.'

The learned trial judge directed them that their note seemed to have disposed of count 1. In relation to count 2 he defined 'attempt' yet again saying that if they were not sure that the appellant intended to damage by fire at all then they should acquit. However he went on to say that if they were satisfied that he attempted to damage, then they must go on to consider whether he intended to damage the property or was reckless as to whether it be damaged by fire.

The Court of Appeal in allowing the appeal and quashing the conviction held that intent is an element inherent in the definition of attempt and is the same at least if not greater than the intent necessary to constitute the full offence. The learned trial judge was in error in relating back to the question of recklessness and intent to damage. There was no room for a reckless damage to property when the offence itself is an attempt because the attempt must have the necessary intent.

It was further held that the difficulty in this case arose from the Indictment. When the offence is an attempt under section 1(1) of the Criminal Attempts Act 1981 it is unnecessary and wrong to include the words 'or being reckless as to whether property would be damaged.' When the substantive offence is charged as opposed to an attempt, the words used are correct. It is only when an attempt to damage property is charged that the words 'being reckless as to whether such property would be damaged' are otiose and wrong.

Notes

1. The requirement that the defendant must intend to commit the offence attempted implicitly requires that the defendant have any intent required for the underlying offence. Thus if a defendant is charged with attempted theft it must be proved that the defendant intended permanently to deprive the victim of her property.

2. The requirement that the defendant must intend to commit the offence also means that if the offence is defined in terms of result (e.g., murder), it must be proved that the defendant intended to bring about the proscribed result. What if, however, the defendant does not desire the result but knows that it is virtually certain to follow from his acts? As we have seen previously (see Chapter 3), such knowledge will satisfy the *mens rea* for murder; but is it sufficient for attempted murder?

R v *Walker and Hayles*
(1990) 90 Cr App R 226
Court of Appeal

LLOYD LJ: On September 9, 1988, these two appellants, Walker and Hayles, were convicted of attempted murder at the Central Criminal Court before the recorder and a jury. They were sentenced to seven years' and five years' imprisonment respectively.

They now appeal against their convictions.

The facts were that Walker's sister, Christine, was having an affair with a man called Royston John, the victim. A week or so before September 20, 1987, there had been a violent quarrel between Christine and John. Christine received two black eyes and a torn fingernail.

On the evening in question (September 20), the two appellants visited Christine's flat. The appellant Hayles was living with another of Walker's sisters. Christine's flat was on the third floor of a block of flats in Battersea Park Road. Royston John was there. He had a key to Christine's flat. He was asked to hand over the key to Christine. He refused. There was then a fight. John ran out onto the balcony, which lead towards the central staircase. The appellants followed him.

According to the prosecution case, the appellants caught him up, lifted him over the balcony, and dropped him horizontally to the ground. Somehow or he other survived, perhaps because he landed on some grass. In the course of the fight the appellants had banged the victim's head against the wall, saying that they were going to kill him. There were bloodstains found on the wall. One of the appellants produced a knife and threatened the victim's throat. Just before they threw the victim over the balcony, he said: 'You deserve to die. I am going to kill you. We don't like you.'
. . .

We turn to the main ground of appeal, namely the direction on intention. Since the charge was attempted murder, the prosecution had to prove an intention to kill. Intention to cause really serious harm would not have been enough. We were told that this is the first case in which this Court has had to consider the correct direction in a case of attempted murder since *R v Moloney* (1985) 81 Cr App R 93, [1985] AC 905. *R v Hancock and Shankland* (1986) 82 Cr App R 264, [1986] AC 455 and *Nedrick* (1986) 83 Cr App R 267, [1986] 3 All ER 1.

We have already said that there could be no criticism of the initial direction at the start of the summing-up, and repeated at the conclusion. The recorder was right to keep it short. 'Trying to kill' was the expression he used as a paraphrase. That was easy for the jury to understand, and could not on any view of the law be regarded as too favourable to the prosecution. 'Trying to kill' is synonymous with purpose. It has never been suggested that a man does not intend what he is trying to achieve. The difficulty only arises when he brings about a result which he is not trying to achieve.

But when the jury returned, the recorder, as we have seen, went further. . . .

We can . . . understand why the recorder went further, since he had only just given a direction in simple terms, which was as clear as could be. Moreover the position is not quite the same in a case of attempted murder as it is in murder. In the great majority of murder cases, as the Court pointed out in *Nedrick (supra)*, the defendant's desire goes hand in hand with his intention. If he desires serious harm, and death results from his action, he is guilty of murder. A simple direction suffices in such cases. The rare and exceptional case is where the defendant does not desire serious harm, or indeed any harm at all. But where a defendant is charged with attempted murder, he may well have desired serious harm, without desiring death. So the desire of serious harm does not provide the answer. It does not go hand in hand with the relevant intention, as it does in the great majority of murder cases, since in attempted murder the relevant intention must be an intention to kill.

Considerations such as these may have led the recorder to give the expanded direction in terms of foresight. But, as we have said, it would have been better if he had not done so. The mere fact that a jury calls for a further direction on intention does not of itself make it a rare and exceptional case requiring a foresight direction. In most cases they will only need to be reminded of the simple direction which they will already have been given, namely that the relevant intention is an intention to kill, and that nothing less will suffice.

[The recorder] may have confused the jury. He may have led them to equate the probability of death and the foresight of death with an intention to kill. That was the very error exposed in *R v Moloney (supra)* and *Nedrick* (1986) 83 Cr App R 267.

[But it] is important to note that the recorder said that the jury would be *entitled* to draw the inference: he was not saying that they must draw the inference. By the use of the word 'entitled,' he was making it sufficiently clear to the jury that the question whether they drew the inference or not was a question for them. This is borne out by the passage which immediately followed in which the recorder said that the jury would be entitled to bear in mind the speed of events on the one hand and the speed at which a man can make up his mind on the other.

So we reject the submission that the recorder was equating foresight with intent, or that he may have given that impression to the jury. He was perfectly properly saying that foresight was something from which the jury could infer intent. He was treating the question as part of the law of evidence, not as part of the substantive law of attempted murder.

Questions
1.   Does the judgment in *Walker and Hayles* resolve the substantive issue, or is it more concerned with a point of evidence?
2.   Where a lesser *mens rea* is required in respect of the circumstances of the offence, is the lesser *mens rea* sufficient for an offence of attempt?

R v Khan
[1990] 2 All ER 783
Court of Appeal

RUSSELL LJ: These appeals raise the short but important point of whether the offence of attempted rape is committed when the defendant is reckless as to the woman's consent to sexual intercourse. The appellants submit that no such offence is known to the law.

Before examining the submissions, we deal briefly with the facts. On 24 June 1987 at the Central Criminal Court before his Honour Judge Rant QC and a jury the appellants Mohammed Iqbal Khan, Mahesh Dhokia, Jaswinder Singh Banga and Navaid Faiz were convicted of the attempted rape of a 16-year-old girl. The case for the Crown was that on 19 March 1986 the girl met and danced with the appellant Dhokia at a daytime discotheque in Uxbridge. Thereafter she accompanied Dhokia and four other youths in a motor car which was driven to an address in Waltham Road, Uxbridge, where the occupants of the car, who included Faiz and Khan as well as Dhokia, were joined by others, including Banga.

Inside the house Dhokia, without success, attempted to have sexual intercourse with the girl. He was followed by others. Three youths succeeded in having sexual intercourse; three others, the remaining appellants, attempted to have sexual intercourse but failed. The girl did not consent to any sexual activity in the house. After her ordeal, she left and travelled to a friend's house, where she made a complaint.

The judge dealt with the offence of rape as follows:
   . . . [W]e have had regard to the observations of Mustill LJ giving the judgment of the Court of Appeal, Criminal Division in *R v Millard and Vernon* [1987] Crim LR 393.

That was a case involving a charge of attempting to damage property the particulars of offence reading:

> Gary Mann Millard and Michael Elliot Vernon, on 11th May 1985, without lawful excuse, attempted to damage a wooden wall at the Leeds Road Football Stand belonging to Huddersfield Town Association Football Club, intending to damage the said wall or being reckless as to whether the said wall would be damaged.

Mustill LJ said (and we read from the transcript):

> The appellants' case is simple. They submit that in ordinary speech the essence of an attempt is a desire to bring about a particular result, coupled with steps towards that end. The essence of recklessness is either indifference to a known risk or (in some circumstances) failure to advert to an obvious risk. The two states of mind cannot co-exist. Section 1(1) of the Criminal Attempts Act 1981 expressly demands that a person shall have an intent to commit an offence if he is to be guilty of an attempt to commit that offence. The word 'intent' may, it is true, have a specialised meaning in some contexts. But even if this can properly be attributed to the word where it is used in s. 1(1) there is no warrant for reading it as embracing recklessness, nor for reading into it whatever lesser degree of mens rea will suffice for the particular substantive offence in question. For an attempt nothing but conscious volition will do. Accordingly, that part of the particulars of offence which referred to recklessness was meaningless, and the parts of the direction which involved a definition of reckless-ness, and an implied invitation to convict if the jury found the appellants to have acted recklessly, were misleading. There was thus, so it was contended, a risk that the jury convicted on the wrong basis and the verdict cannot safely be allowed to stand. At the conclusion of the argument it appeared to us that this argument was logically sound and that it was borne out by the authorities cited to us, especially *R* v *Whybrow* (1951) 35 Cr App R 141, *Cunliffe* v *Goodman* [1950] 1 All ER 720 at 724, [1950] 2 KB 237 at 253 and *R* v *Mohan* [1975] 2 All ER 193, [1976] QB 1, and that it was not inconsistent with anything in *Hyam* v *DPP* [1974] 2 All ER 41, [1975] AC 55. Our attention had, however, been drawn to a difference of opinion between commentators about the relationship between the mens rea in an attempt and the ingredients of the substantive offence, and we therefore reserved judgment so as to consider whether the question was not perhaps more difficult than it seemed. In the event we have come to the conclusion that there does exist a problem in this field, and that it is by no means easy to solve, but also that it need not be solved for the purpose of deciding the present appeal. In our judgment two different situations must be distinguished. The first exists where the substantive offence consists simply of the act which constitutes the actus reus (which for present purposes we shall call the 'result') coupled with some element of volition, which may or may not amount to a full intent. Here the only question is whether the 'intent' to bring about the result called for by s. 1(1) is to be watered down to such a degree, if any, as to make it correspond with the mens rea of the substantive offence. The second situation is more complicated. It exists where the substantive offence does not consist of one result and one mens rea, but rather involves not only the underlying intention to produce the result, but another state of mind directed to some circumstance or act which the prosecution must also establish in addition to providing the result. The problem may be illustrated by reference to the offence of attempted rape. As regards the substantive offence the 'result' takes the shape of sexual intercourse with a woman. But the offence is not established without proof of an additional circumstance (namely that the woman did not consent), and a state of mind relative to that circumstance (namely

that the defendant knew she did not consent, or was reckless as to whether she consented). When one turns to the offence of attempted rape, one thing is obvious, that the result, namely the act of sexual intercourse, must be intended in the full sense. Also obvious is the fact that proof of an intention to have intercourse with a woman, together with an act towards that end, is not enough: the offence must involve proof of something about the woman's consent, and something about the defendant's state of mind in relation to that consent. The problem is to decide precisely what that something is. Must the prosecution prove not only that the defendant intended the act, but also that he intended it to be non-consensual? Or should the jury be directed to consider two different states of mind, intent as to the act and recklessness as to the circumstances? Here the commentators differ: contrast Smith and Hogan *Criminal Law* (5th edn, 1983) p 255 ff with a note on the Act by Professor Griew in *Current Law Statutes 1981*.

We must now grapple with the very problem that Mustill LJ identifies in the last paragraph of the passage cited.

In our judgment an acceptable analysis of the offence of rape is as follows: (1) the intention of the offender is to have sexual intercourse with a woman: (2) the offence is committed if, but only if, the circumstances are that (a) the woman does not consent *and* (b) the defendant knows that she is not consenting or is reckless as to whether she consents.

Precisely the same analysis can be made of the offence of attempted rape: (1) the intention of the offender is to have sexual intercourse with a woman; (2) the offence is committed if, but only if, the circumstances are that (a) the woman does not consent *and* (b) the defendant knows that she is not consenting or is reckless as to whether she consents.

The only difference between the two offences is that in rape sexual intercourse takes place whereas in attempted rape it does not, although there has to be some act which is more than preparatory to sexual intercourse. Considered in that way, the intent of the defendant is precisely the same in rape and in attempted rape and the mens rea is identical, namely an intention to have intercourse plus a knowledge of or recklessness as to the woman's absence of consent. No question of attempting to achieve a reckless state of mind arises; the attempt relates to the physical activity; the mental state of the defendant is the same. A man does not recklessly have sexual intercourse, nor does he recklessly attempt it. Recklessness in rape and attempted rape arises not in relation to the physical act of the accused but only in his state of mind when engaged in the activity of having or attempting to have sexual intercourse.

If this is the true analysis, as we believe it is, the attempt does not require any different intention on the part of the accused from that for the full offence of rape. We believe this to be a desirable result which in the instant case did not require the jury to be burdened with different directions as to the accused's state of mind, dependent on whether the individual achieved or failed to achieve sexual intercourse.

We recognise, of course, that our reasoning cannot apply to all offences and all attempts. Where, for example as in causing death by reckless driving or reckless arson, no state of mind other than recklessness is involved in the offence, there can be no attempt to commit it.

In our judgment, however, the words 'with intent to commit an offence' to be found in s. 1 of the 1981 Act mean, when applied to rape, 'with intent to have sexual intercourse with a woman in circumstances where she does not consent and the defendant knows or could not care less about her absence of consent'. The only 'intent', giving that word its natural and ordinary meaning, of the rapist is to have sexual intercourse. He commits the offence because of the circumstances in which he manifests that intent, i.e. when the woman is not consenting and he either knows it or could not care less about the absence of consent.

Notes and questions
1.   Is the allowance of proof of recklessness as to a circumstance of the crime consistent with the requirement of proof of intention as to the crime itself? Whether *Caldwell* or *Cunningham* recklessness will need to be proved will depend on what type of recklessness must be shown for the underlying offence.
2.   If the defendant has a 'conditional intent', i.e., an intention to commit the offence only if certain factors are found to exist, will he or she be guilty of attempt if acts which are more than merely preparatory are committed but the conditions are then found not to exist? This question proved troublesome until the enactment of the Criminal Attempts Act 1981, which specifically excluded the defence of impossibility. Now if a defendant were charged with attempt to steal items from a handbag and it was shown that he had an intention to steal those items if they were in the bag, he would be guilty of attempting to steal the items even if the bag were empty. (See below, impossibility.)

B   Actus reus

The *actus reus* of attempt is set out in the Criminal Attempts Act 1981, s. 1(1), and consists of the doing of an act 'which is more than merely preparatory to the commission of the offence'. The judge may decide that the threshold requirement of an act beyond mere preparation has not been met and direct the jury to acquit; but in the converse case, where the judge reaches the conclusion that the threshold requirement is met, he must leave it to the jury to decide whether the defendant's acts were more than merely preparatory.

Criminal Attempts Act 1981

4.—(3)   Where, in proceedings against a person for an offence under section 1 above, there is evidence sufficient in law to support a finding that he did an act falling within subsection (1) of that section, the question whether or not his act fell within that subsection is a question of fact.

Question
Does the formula of 'an act which is more than merely preparatory' push the onset of criminal liability too far back in time? Would it have been better to require a 'substantial act' towards completion of the offence? Or the doing of all the acts intended (thus restricting the crime of attempt to those who try but fail to bring about the intended results)?

Note
The statutory formula is rather vague and judges have been tempted to try to refine it in order to elicit some coherent principle. In the following extracts you will find examples of the use of the 'last act necessary' or 'point of no return' approaches, both of which provide an identifiable point for criminalisation.

However, the more recent cases reflect the intention of Parliament that the test should not be further defined but should be applied by the jury as it is set out in the statute on a case to case basis.

R v Widdowson
(1985) 82 Cr App R 314
Court of Appeal

SAVILLE J: At the trial the case for the prosecution was that on July 14, 1984, the appellant had gone to a garage with a view to buying a Ford Escort van on hire purchase. He was said to have told the salesman (a Mr Wilson) that he had looked at the Escort van for sale there, was happy with it and that it would all be subject to finance being arranged. Mr Wilson said that appellant was satisfied that his own van would cover the initial deposit and that if the finance had been cleared by the finance company the vehicle would have been the appellant's. Mr Wilson gave evidence that the appellant then completed a hire purchase form putting the name Steven Pitman and an address, 15 Edinburgh Way, Thetford, as the name and address of the hirer. That address was in fact where a Mr Pitman lived next door to the appellant. Mr Wilson said that had he known that this name and address was not that of the appellant, he would not have taken the matter any further and would not have put it forward to the finance company as he did. He agreed that he did not intend that the form should constitute the actual hire purchase deal, and said it was used so that enquiries could be made whether the person named as hirer was creditworthy. He further agreed that in fact a proposal form rather than a hire purchase form should have been used for this purpose, but explained that the garage had run out of the latter forms at the time in question. It should also be mentioned that the appellant had in fact signed the form at the end in his own name, something which Mr Wilson only discovered later, apparently from the finance company itself. According to evidence from the police, the appellant stated on being interviewed that he had put his own telephone number on the form and explained that he had put the name Steven Pitman on the form because he could not get credit if it was known who he really was. His explanation for signing the form in his own name was simply that he had not been thinking.

According to the defence, the appellant, being himself unable to obtain credit, completed the form solely in order to enquire into the creditworthiness of Pitman. He said he had earlier agreed with Pitman that on being given clearance by the finance company Pitman should thereby obtain the vehicle on his behalf pending the appellant's receipt of funds to pay the outstanding balance of the purchase price. This explanation had not apparently been given to the police on the occasion of his interview.

At the end of the prosecution case counsel for the appellant made three submissions to the learned judge. The first of these (which was not opposed by the Crown) was that there was no sufficient evidence to go to the jury on count 1 of the indictment, which had charged the appellant with an attempt to obtain property, i.e. the vehicle itself, by deception. The learned judge acceded to this submission, saying that he did not think that there was sufficient evidence in law 'that this ever reached the stage of an attempt to obtain the property, in other words to obtain the car.' However, the learned judge rejected a similar submission in relation to count 2 of the indictment (which charged the offence with which we are concerned) stating that: 'It is open to this jury to come to the conclusion that what the defendant did here was not merely preparatory to the obtaining of services in the sense that I have indicated, but had the form produced an affirmative answer that the transaction would go ahead, then the transaction would undoubtedly have gone ahead. It is open to the jury to conclude that the transaction would have gone ahead and what he did was sufficiently close, to use a general expression rather than proximate, to commission of the full offence.'

. . .

There remains the question of attempt. In our judgement there was no evidence of an attempt to commit the crime alleged within the meaning of section 1(1) of the Criminal Attempts Act 1981. It seems to us that at most all the appellant had actually done was to attempt to ascertain whether or not Steven Pitman was creditworthy, in the sense of being acceptable to the finance company as a prospective hire purchaser. It was not suggested that a favourable reply from the finance company could have constituted the obtaining of services within the meaning of the Theft Act 1978, if only because there was no question of payment being made for such a reply. Thus the question is whether this appellant's act in giving the false particulars on the form can reasonably be said to have been more than merely preparatory to the obtaining of hire purchase facilities. In our view this cannot be said. Assuming that the finance company had responded favourably to the proposal, it still remained for the appellant to seek a hire purchase deal from them. To our minds it is that step which would constitute an attempt to obtain the services relied upon in this case. If one asks whether this appellant had carried out every step which it was necessary for him to perform to achieve the consequences alleged to have been attempted, the answer must be that he did not.

Equally, it seems to us, this appellant's acts cannot be described as immediately rather than merely remotely connected with the specific offence alleged to have been attempted. Thus whichever of the tests described in *Ilyas* (1984) 78 Cr App R 17 is applied, what the appellant did cannot reasonably be described as more than merely preparatory.

In the passage we have cited from his ruling in the court below, it would appear that the learned judge was influenced by the suggested inevitability of the transaction going ahead, i.e. that the appellant's intentions would have remained the same. That, with great respect, ignores the fact that dishonest intentions alone do not constitute criminal attempts and that in addition it is necessary to establish, to use the words of Lord Diplock, that the offender has crossed the Rubicon and burned his boats. He had not done so (as the learned judge himself held) in the sense of attempting to obtain the vehicle. In our judgment, he equally had not done so in attempting to obtain the hire purchase of the vehicle.

For the two reasons we have given, therefore, this appeal was allowed and the conviction quashed.

R v *Jones*
[1990] 1 WLR 1057
Court of Appeal

TAYLOR LJ: . . . The appellant, a married man, started an affair with a woman named Lynn Gresley in 1985. She lived with him in Australia during 1986. In September 1987, back in England, she began a relationship with the victim, Michael Foreman. She continued, however, to see the appellant to whom she was still very attached. In November 1987 she decided to break off the relationship with the appellant, but he continued to write to her, begging her to come back to him.

On 12 January 1988 the appellant applied for a shotgun certificate, and three days later bought two guns in company with two companions. He bought two more guns a few days later on his own. On 23 January he shortened the barrel of one of them and test fired it twice the following day.

The appellant told a colleague at work that he would be away on Tuesday, 26 January. On 24 January he phoned Lynn Gresley in a distraught state. The next day he apologised, but she again refused his invitation to resume their relationship. The appellant then told his wife he had packed a bag as he was going to Spain to do some work on their chalet. On 26 January he left home dressed normally for work, saying he would telephone his wife as to whether he was leaving for Spain that evening.

That same morning, the victim, Michael Foreman, took his daughter to school by car as usual. After the child left the car, the appellant appeared, opened the door and jumped into the rear seat. He was wearing overalls, a crash helmet with the visor down, and was carrying a bag. He and the victim had never previously met. He introduced himself, said he wanted to sort things out and asked the victim to drive on. When they stopped on a grass verge, the appellant handed over a letter he had received from Lynn. Whilst the victim read it, the appellant took the sawn-off shotgun from the bag. It was loaded. He pointed it at the victim at a range of some 10 to 12 inches. He said, 'You are not going to like this' or similar words. The victim grabbed the end of the gun and pushed it sideways and upwards. There was a struggle during which the victim managed to throw the gun out of the window. As he tried to get out, he felt a cord over his head pulling him back. He managed to break free and run away, taking the gun with him. From a nearby garage he telephoned the police.

Meanwhile, the appellant drove off in the victim's car. He was arrested jogging away from it carrying his holdall. He said he had done nothing and only wanted to kill himself. His bag contained a hatchet, some cartridges and a length of cord. He also had a sharp kitchen knife which he threw away. In the appellant's car parked near the school was £1,500 sterling together with a quantity of French and Spanish money. The evidence showed that the safety catch of the shotgun had been in the on position. The victim was unclear as to whether the appellant's finger was ever on the trigger. When interviewed, the appellant declined to make any comment.

At the end of the prosecution case, after the above facts had been given in evidence, a submission was made to the judge that the charge of attempted murder should be withdrawn from the jury. It was argued that since the appellant would have had to perform at least three more acts before the full offence could have been completed, i.e., remove the safety catch, put his finger on the trigger and pull it, the evidence was insufficient to support the charge. There was a discussion as to the proper construction of section 1(1) of the Criminal Attempts Act 1981. After hearing full argument, the judge ruled against the submission and allowed the case to proceed on count 1. Thereafter, the appellant gave evidence. In the result, the jury convicted him unanimously of attempted murder. It follows that they found he intended to kill the victim.

The sole ground of appeal is that the judge erred in law in his construction of section 1(1) and ought to have withdrawn the case. . . .

Counsel's second proposition is that section 1(1) of the Act of 1981 has not resolved the question as to which is the appropriate test. Thirdly, he submits that the test deriving from *R* v *Eagleton* (1855) 6 Cox CC 559 should be adopted.

This amounts to an invitation to construe the statutory words by reference to previous conflicting case law. We believe this to be misconceived. The Act of 1981 is a codifying statute. It amends and sets out completely the law relating to attempts and conspiracies. In those circumstances the correct approach is to look first at the natural meaning of the statutory words, not to turn back to earlier case law and seek to fit some previous test to the words of the section. . . .

We do not accept Mr Farrer's contention that section 1(1) of the Act of 1981 in effect embodies the 'last act' test derived from *R* v *Eagleton* [(1855) 6 Cox CC 559]. Had

Parliament intended to adopt that test, a quite different form of words could and would have been used.

It is of interest to note that the Act of 1981 followed a report from the Law Commission on Attempt, and Impossibility in Relation to Attempt, Conspiracy and Incitement (1980) (Law Com. No. 102). At paragraph 2.47 the report states:

> The definition of sufficient proximity must be wide enough to cover two varieties of cases; first, those in which a person has taken all the steps towards the commission of a crime which he believes to be necessary as far as he is concerned for that crime to result, such as firing a gun at another and missing. Normally such cases cause no difficulty. Secondly, however, the definition must cover those instances where a person has to take some further step to complete the crime, assuming that there is evidence of the necessary mental element on his part to commit it; for example, when the defendant has raised the gun to take aim at another but has not yet squeezed the trigger. We have reached the conclusion that, in regard to these cases, it is undesirable to recommend anything more complex than a rationalization of the present law.

In paragraph 2.48 the report states:

> The literal meaning of 'proximate' is 'nearest, next before or after (in place, order, time, connection of thought, causation etc.).' Thus, were this term part of a statutory description of the actus reus of attempt, it would clearly be capable of being interpreted to exclude all but the 'final act'; this would not be in accordance with the policy outlined above.

Clearly, the draftsman of section 1(1) must be taken to have been aware of the two lines of earlier authority and of the Law Commission's report. The words 'an act which is more than merely preparatory to the commission of the offence' would be inapt if they were intended to mean 'the last act which lay in his power towards the commission of the offence.'

[T]he question for the judge in the present case was whether there was evidence from which a reasonable jury, properly directed, could conclude that the appellant had done acts which were more than merely preparatory. Clearly his actions in obtaining the gun, in shortening it, in loading it, in putting on his disguise, and in going to the school could only be regarded as preparatory acts. But, in our judgment, once he had got into the car, taken out the loaded gun and pointed it at the victim with the intention of killing him, there was sufficient evidence for the consideration of the jury on the charge of attempted murder. It was a matter for them to decide whether they were sure those acts were more than merely preparatory. In our judgment, therefore, the judge was right to allow the case to go to the jury, and the appeal against conviction must be dismissed.

R v *Gullefer*
[1987] Crim LR 195
Court of Appeal

The appellant was convicted of attempted theft. During a race at a greyhound racing stadium the appellant had climbed on to the track in front of the dogs and in an attempt to distract them had waved his arms. His efforts were only marginally successful and the stewards decided it was unnecessary to declare 'no race.' Had they done so the bookmakers would have had to repay the amount of his stake to any punter, but would not have been liable to pay any winnings to those punters who would have been successful had the race been valid. The appellant told the police he had attempted to stop the race because the dog on which he had staked £18 was losing. He had hoped for a 'no race' declaration and the recovery of his stake. The appellant's main ground of appeal was that the acts proved to have been carried out by the appellant were not 'sufficiently proximate to the completed offence of theft to be capable of comprising an attempt to commit theft.'

Held, allowing the appeal and quashing the conviction, the appellant was not guilty of attempted theft. The judge's task was to decide whether there was evidence on which a jury could reasonably conclude that the defendant had gone beyond mere preparation and had embarked on the actual commission of the offence. If not, the judge had to withdraw the case from the jury. If there was such evidence, it was then for the jury to decide whether the defendant did in fact go beyond mere preparation. That was how the judge had approached the case and he had ruled there was sufficient evidence. Counsel for the appellant submitted his ruling had been wrong. The Court's first task was to apply the words of the Criminal Attempts Act 1981, s. 1, to the facts. Was the appellant still in the stage of preparation to commit the substantive offence, or was there a basis of fact which would have entitled the jury to say that he had embarked on the theft itself? Might it properly be said that when he jumped onto the track he was trying to steal £18? In the view of the Court it could not be said? that at that stage he was in the process of committing theft. What he was doing was jumping onto the track in an effort to distract the dogs, which in its turn, he hoped, would force the stewards to declare 'no race,' which would in its turn give him the opportunity to demand his £18 stake from the bookmaker. There was insufficient evidence that the appellant had, when he jumped on the track, gone beyond mere preparation.

Questions

1. The court in *Jones* says that the defendant's acts in obtaining the gun, shortening it, loading it, putting on his disguise and going to the school 'could only be regarded as preparatory acts'. Do you agree?

2. What more would Gullefer have had to have done to be guilty of attempt? While it might not make sense to require proof that the defendant did 'the last act necessary', does the converse follow? Where the defendant has done the last act which he intended to do, is there any reason why he should not be guilty of attempt, assuming the other elements of the crime are satisfied? Is this an apt description of *Gullefer*?

C   Impossibility

The statute seems to make clear that factual impossibility is not a defence to a charge of attempt. The House of Lords failed to accept this position in *Anderton* v *Ryan* [1985] AC 560. However, that decision was subsequently overruled.

R v *Shivpuri*
[1987] AC 1
House of Lords

LORD BRIDGE OF HARWICH: . . . The facts plainly to be inferred from the evidence, interpreted in the light of the jury's guilty verdicts, may be shortly

summarised. The appellant, on a visit to India, was approached by a man named Desai, who offered to pay him £1,000 if, on his return to England, he would receive a suitcase which a courier would deliver to him containing packages of drugs which the appellant was then to distribute according to instructions he would receive. The suitcase was duly delivered to him in Cambridge. On 30 November 1982, acting on instructions, the appellant went to Southall station to deliver a package of drugs to a third party. Outside the station he and the man he had met by appointment were arrested. A package containing a powdered substance was found in the appellant's shoulder bag. At the appellant's flat in Cambridge, he produced to customs officers the suitcase from which the lining had been ripped out and the remaining packages of the same powdered substance. In answer to questions by customs officers and in a long written statement the appellant made what amounted to a full confession of having played his part, as described, as recipient and distributor of illegally imported drugs. The appellant believed the drugs to be either heroin or cannabis. In due course the powdered substance in the several packages was scientifically analysed and found not to be a controlled drug but snuff or some similar harmless vegetable matter.
. . .

[T]he first question to be asked is whether the appellant intended to commit the offences of being knowingly concerned in dealing with and harbouring drugs of Class A or Class B with intent to evade the prohibition on their importation. Translated into more homely language the question may be rephrased, without in any way altering its legal significance, in the following terms: did the appellant intend to receive and store (harbour) and in due course pass on to third parties (deal with) packages of heroin or cannabis which he knew had been smuggled into England from India? The answer is plainly yes, he did. Next, did he in relation to each offence, do an act which was more than merely preparatory to the commission of the offence? The act relied on in relation to harbouring was the receipt and retention of the packages found in the lining of the suitcase. The act relied on in relation to dealing was the meeting at Southall station with the intended recipient of one of the packages. In each case the act was clearly more than preparatory to the commission of the *intended* offence; it was not and could not be more than merely preparatory to the commission of the *actual* offence, because the facts were such that the commission of the actual offence was impossible. Here then is the nub of the matter. Does the 'act which is more than merely preparatory to the commission of the offence' in section 1(1) of the Act of 1981 (the actus reus of the statutory offence of attempt) require any more than an act which is more than merely preparatory to the commission of the offence which the defendant intended to commit? Section 1(2) must surely indicate a negative answer; if it were otherwise, whenever the facts were such that the commission of the actual offence was impossible, it would be impossible to prove an act more than merely preparatory to the commission of that offence and subsections (1) and (2) would contradict each other.

This very simple, perhaps over simple, analysis leads me to the provisional conclusion that the appellant was rightly convicted of the two offences of attempt with which he was charged. But can this conclusion stand with *Anderton v Ryan* [1985] AC 560? The appellant in that case was charged with an attempt to handle stolen goods. She bought a video recorder believing it to be stolen. On the facts as they were to be assumed it was not stolen. By a majority the House decided that she was entitled to be acquitted. I have re-examined the case with care. If I could extract from the speech of Lord Roskill or from my own speech a clear and coherent principle distinguishing those cases of attempting the impossible which amount to offences under the statute from those which do not. I should have to consider carefully on which side of the line the instant case fell. But I have to confess that I can find no such principle.

If we fell into error, it is clear that our concern was to avoid convictions in situations which most people, as a matter of common sense, would not regard as involving criminality. In this connection it is to be regretted that we did not take due note of paragraph 2.97 of the Law Commission's report (Criminal Law: Attempt, and Impossiblity in Relation to Attempt, Conspiracy and Incitement (1980) (Law Commission No. 102)) which preceded the enactment of the Act of 1981, which reads:

> If it is right in principle that an attempt should be chargeable even though the crime which it is sought to commit could not possibly be committed, we do not think that we should be deterred by the consideration that such a change in our law would also cover some extreme and exceptional cases in which a prosecution would be theoretically possible. An example would be where a person is offered goods at such a low price that he believes that they are stolen, when in fact they are not; if he actually purchases them, upon the principles which we have discussed he would be liable for an attempt to handle stolen goods. Another case which has been much debated is that raised in argument by Bramwell B. in *R v Collins* (1864) 9 Cox CC 497. If A takes his own umbrella, mistaking it for one belonging to B and intending to steal B's umbrella, is he guilty of attempted theft? Again, on the principles which we have discussed he would in theory be guilty, but in neither case would it be realistic to suppose that a complaint would be made or that a prosecution would ensue.

The prosecution in *Anderton v Ryan* itself falsified the Commission's prognosis in one of the 'extreme and exceptional cases.' It nevertheless probably holds good for other such cases, particularly that of the young man having sexual intercourse with a girl over 16, mistakenly believing her to be under that age, by which both Lord Roskill and I were much troubled.

However that may be, the distinction between acts which are 'objectively innocent' and those which are not is an essential element in the reasoning in *Anderton v Ryan* and the decision, unless it can be supported on some other ground, must stand or fall by the validity of this distinction. I am satisfied on further consideration that the concept of 'objective innocence' is incapable of sensible application in relation to the law of criminal attempts. The reason for this is that any attempt to commit an offence which involves 'an act which is more than merely preparatory to the commission of the offence' but for any reason fails, so that in the event no offence is committed, must ex hypothesi, from the point of view of the criminal law, be 'objectively innocent.' What turns what would otherwise, from the point of view of the criminal law, be an innocent act into a crime is the intent of the actor to commit an offence. I say 'from the point of view of the criminal law' because the law of tort must surely here be quite irrelevant. A puts his hand into B's pocket. Whether or not there is anything in the pocket capable of being stolen, if A intends to steal, his act is a criminal attempt; if he does not so intend, his act is innocent. A plunges a knife into a bolster in a bed. To avoid the complication of an offence of criminal damage, assume it to be A's bolster. If A believes the bolster to be his enemy B and intends to kill him, his act is an attempt to murder B; if he knows the bolster is only a bolster, his act is innocent. These considerations lead me to the conclusion that the distinction sought to be drawn in *Anderton v Ryan* between innocent and guilty acts considered 'objectively' and independently of the state of mind of the actor cannot be sensibly maintained.

Question

Albert intends to rape Jill and has intercourse with her. Unknown to him, however, Jill secretly desired to have intercourse with him and would readily have consented if asked. Albert, however, never asked. Is Albert guilty of attempted rape?

Note
Legal impossibility, where the offence the defendant intends to commit is not a crime, is a valid defence.

D   Abandonment

What if, after the defendant has gone beyond the preparatory stage but before the substantive offence has been completed, the defendant changes his mind and abandons the criminal enterprise? Is he still guilty of attempt? At common law the answer was 'yes', and that answer does not seem to have changed.

R v Becerra
(1975) 62 Cr App R 212
Court of Appeal

For facts and holding, see p. 222.

Notes and questions
1.   Why should voluntary abandonment not be a defence? Is a defendant who abandons his crime dangerous or in need of rehabilitation? Does the answer depend on whether there was a genuine change of heart, or the discovery of circumstances which rendered the completion of the crime more difficult, such as the fact that the bank to be robbed was surrounded by armed guards? Is it possible for the law to discriminate in practice between these types of cases?
2.   Does the failure of the law to recognise abandonment as a defence provide a disincentive to abandonment of a criminal project? (Abandonment might, of course, be taken into account as a mitigating factor in sentencing.)
3.   Similar policy issues arise in respect of a conspirator who attempts to withdraw from the conspiracy. Technically such withdrawal will be ineffective, for the crime of conspiracy is already complete. On a policy level, however, a case can be made to allow withdrawal as a defence to encourage conspirators to withdraw.

V   Double inchoates

(i)   There is an offence of attempting to incite.

(ii)   There is some doubt whether there is an offence of incitement to attempt although such an offence appears in the Draft Criminal Code (clause 47).

(iii) There is an offence of conspiring to incite.

(iv)   The Criminal Law Act 1977, s. 5(7), abolished the offence of incitement to conspire.

(v) *Incitement to incite remains an offence.*

R v Evans
[1986] Crim LR 470
Court of Appeal

The appellant was charged, *inter alia*, with incitement to solicit to murder, the particulars being that she unlawfully incited B to solicit, encourage, persuade, endeavour to persuade and propose to a person or persons unknown, to murder E. The appellant had visited B, a clairvoyant and practitioner in the art of tarot cards. B also had a local reputation as a witch. The appellant told B her husband (E) had put a black magic curse on her. She said to B 'In your business I am sure you can see someone who can put a contract out on him . . . I want him dead.' The appellant offered B £1,000 and gave a description of her husband and his habits and movements. B said she would contact someone but instead went to the police. Later B gave the appellant the telephone number of another astrologer. The appellant telephoned him and they agreed to meet. At that meeting two police officers turned up instead pretending to be 'hit men.' The appellant again gave details and said they could make it appear an accident. The appellant denied the accounts given by B and the officers. She was convicted of incitement to solicit to murder and of soliciting to murder. She appealed against the conviction for incitement on the ground that the Criminal Law Act 1977, s. 5(7) had abolished incitement to conspire and, it was submitted, to incite to solicit murder was in the circumstances the same as to incite to conspire to commit murder. The offence was an attempt to avoid the provisions of section 5(7) and an offence not known to the law.

Held, dismissing the appeal that the validity of that argument depended on whether inciting X to solicit murder was necessarily the same as inciting X to conspire with someone to murder. Was there any distinction between inciting to murder and conspiracy to commit murder? Prima facie there was a distinction between incitement and conspiracy. A person could incite another by threats or pressure as well as by persuasion. And, if as suggested, practically every incitement was a conspiracy to commit the offence incited there would be no need to have an offence for incitement at all. In the present case the facts of the appellant's incitement of B were not actually to enter into an agreement with X or anyone for the commission of a crime. B was being urged to procure an assassin and was not being urged to enter into a conspiracy with anyone, although a conspiracy might have resulted. . . .

(vi) *Incitement to aid, abet, counsel or procure an offence is not an offence.*

R v Bodin and Bodin
[1979] Crim LR 176
Lincoln Crown Court

LB and DB, being annoyed with DB's former husband G, paid to a publican P £50 for P to arrange to have G beaten up. P did not do as arranged and therefore the money was taken back some months later. LB and DB were charged with incitement to assault, contrary to common law. The particulars of the offence alleged that LB and DB on a day unknown between June 1, 1977, and December 31, 1977, unlawfully incited P to assault G. On a submission of no case to answer, the defence argued that to incite X to procure Y to assault Z where X does not actually procure Y is not an offence.

GEOFFREY JONES J: . . . 'I have come to the conclusion, despite the lack of authority, that it is not a crime to incite someone to be an accessory before the fact to a crime. I think it is probable that the reason is quite simple. I think it is this: The procurer, the accessory before the fact commits no crime in the act of procurement. While he is procuring there is no crime he is a party to. Once it is committed there can be a procurement. What I am saying is this: unless the main crime is committed there can be no accessory before the fact. Indeed there is no crime of accessory before the fact until the crime is committed. The Act incited in the evidence is the procurement of a crime and not a crime. The assault is the crime and is not what on the evidence is being incited or procured; it is the procurement of the crime that has been committed.'

(vii)   There is no such offence as an attempt to conspire.
See the Criminal Attempts Act 1981, s. 1(4).

VI   Other inchoate offences

While it has become traditional to think of incitement, conspiracy, and attempt as comprising the totality of inchoate crimes, in fact there are many more offences which could be seen in a similar light. Inchoate crimes share the common theme of punishing criminal behaviour which serves as a prelude to other (usually more serious) criminal behaviour. Viewed in this light, it can be seen that assault, defined as causing another to apprehend the application of immediate, unlawful force, is often an inchoate form of battery, which is the actual application of unlawful force. So too traffic offences, ranging from speeding to driving dangerously, are aimed at preventing vehicular assaults and homicides. Crimes like the unlawful possession of firearms are designed to prevent crimes committed with firearms. This is not to say that the criminalisation of such conduct does not serve other, independent purposes, only that there is an inchoate dimension to all of these offences.

One advantage of focusing on inchoate forms of crime is that it removes the 'fortuity of consequences' (see Chapter 4). Why should a defendant whose gun misfires be guilty of attempted murder, while another whose weapon proves more reliable is convicted of the substantive offence? In recognition of this point the maximum punishment for the inchoate offence is usually the same as or comparable to that for the completed crime. However, the actual sentence imposed in practice may well be less. The practical point is underscored in respect to homicide, where the imposition of a life sentence for murder, but not for attempted murder, is mandatory.

Questions
1.   Should all crimes be written in inchoate form to avoid the fortuity of consequences? What are the arguments for and against?
2.   Should all inchoate crimes be abolished on the theory that society is not harmed until the crime is completed? What are the arguments for and against?

3.   In respect to crimes written in inchoate form, does it make sense to allow a conviction for an attempt to commit such a crime? For example, should there be such an offence as attempted burglary? Is this pushing the point of criminality too far back in time?

8   Defences

I   Introduction

There are three types of defences which a defendant may raise in response to a criminal charge. First is incapacity. The law conclusively presumes that certain persons are incapable of committing a crime. Infants and the insane fall into this category. All that the defendant must establish in order to prevail is that he or she comes within the designated category.

In a second type of defence the defendant seeks to negate an element of the crime. We have already encountered defences of this sort, such as automatism, which can negate either the *actus reus* or the *mens rea* of a crime. Mistake and intoxication provide other examples. It is in fact questionable whether 'defences' is the proper term to be applied in these situations, as the defendant's claim is simply that a reasonable doubt exists as to an element of the offence.

The third category of defences does not relate to any particular element of the crime, but provides a basis for not imposing liability even though all of the elements of the crime have been established. Perhaps it is best to characterise these as *affirmative defences*. The defendant admits the elements of the crime charged but argues that there are other factors to consider. In effect the defendant says 'Yes, . . . but'. Duress, necessity, crime prevention, self-defence and defence of others are defences of this sort.

Sometimes there is an overlap between the second and third categories. A statute may include the term 'unlawful' or 'unlawfully' as part of the definition of the offence. In these instances an affirmative defence may be used to negate the 'unlawfulness' of the accused's conduct.

Whether a defence is an affirmative defence or one that negates an element of the crime can in theory have important ramifications as far as the burden of proof is concerned. The Crown must prove each and every element of a crime by proof beyond a reasonable doubt, and thus must bear the ultimate burden of persuading the jury as to the existence of *all* elements of the crime. A defendant will have the burden of going forward or introducing evidence as to a defence that negates an element, but once there is sufficient evidence to take the issue to the jury, the burden of persuading the jury that the element is not negated or, stated affirmatively, is proved, rests on the Crown by proof beyond a reasonable doubt. See *Woolmington* v *Director of Public Prosecutions* [1935] AC 462.

In theory, the jury's consideration of an affirmative defence should not take place until they have satisfied themselves that the Crown has established each and every element of the crime by proof beyond a reasonable doubt. There is at this point no theoretical objection to shifting to the defendant the burden of persuasion as to a defence that would lift the defendant's conduct out of the realm of the criminal. In effect, the law would say to the defendant: 'The Crown has proved its case; now you show us why you should not be convicted.'

This theoretical analysis notwithstanding, for most affirmative defences, with the primary exception of insanity, the courts have placed the ultimate burden of negating the defence on the prosecution. The defendant, however, bears the initial burden of producing some evidence to establish the defence.

The category of affirmative defences can be subdivided into the subcategories of excuse and justification. When the law says that a defence excuses, it says that under the particular circumstances of the case, it would be unfair to hold the defendant liable for what he did. Involuntary drunkenness is an example of an excuse. Justifications, on the other hand, are said to be implied exceptions to what otherwise would be a crime. A killing of an enemy soldier during wartime is justifiable, although during peacetime that same killing would probably be murder. An excuse concedes the wrongfulness of the defendant's conduct, but says that under the circumstances the defendant should not be convicted of a crime; a claim of justification challenges the wrongfulness of the defendant's conduct. The practical differences between excuse and justification are less significant than the theoretical differences, however, as both will result in an acquittal. See generally J. C. Smith, *Justification and Excuse in the Criminal Law* (1989).

II Incapacity

A Infancy

(i) Rationale
The requirement of *mens rea* presumes that a person is capable of understanding the nature and consequences of his or her actions. It is generally believed that children below a certain age lack this capacity. It follows that they should not be held responsible for acts which if committed by an adult would be criminal. Although the rationale is based on a lack of mental capacity, the exemption extends to crimes of strict liability. Why?

(ii) Age of criminal responsibility
There is an irrebuttable presumption that a child under the age of 10 at the time of the alleged offence lacks the capacity to commit the offence (Children

and Young Persons Act 1933, s. 50). In these circumstances no crime has been committed by the child.

Walters v Lunt
[1951] 2 All ER 645
King's Bench Division

LORD GODDARD CJ: This is a Case stated by justices for the city of Lincoln, before whom the respondents, a husband and wife, were charged under the Larceny Act 1916, s. 33(1), that

> ... they between Aug. 1 and 31, 1950, at the city of Lincoln, jointly feloniously did receive from Richard Norman Lunt (aged seven years) a child's tricycle of the value of £2, the property of Walter Cole, which had theretofore been feloniously stolen, knowing the same to have been so stolen.

There was a similar charge in respect of a child's fairy cycle alleged to have been received by them on Mar. 11, 1951, from Richard Norman Lunt, aged seven years, and we infer from the Case that Richard Norman Lunt is the child of the respondents. The justices refused to convict on the ground that, as the child was under eight years of age, under the Children and Young Persons Act 1933, s. 50, he was incapable of stealing and could not be convicted of the felonious act of larceny, and, therefore, the respondents could not be convicted, under s. 33(1) of the Act of 1916, of receiving stolen property because the property taken by the child was not property 'stolen or obtained ... under circumstances which amount to felony or misdemeanour.'

... In the case now before us the child could not have been found guilty of larceny because he was under eight years of age, and, unless he is eight years old, he is not considered in law capable of forming the intention necessary to support a charge of larceny. Therefore, the justices came to a perfectly proper decision in point of law on the charge of receiving.

Question
While no crime may have been committed by the child who executes the *actus reus*, others may be guilty of committing the offence through an innocent agent. Were the parents in *Walters v Lunt* guilty of theft? As a matter of policy, should parents be held responsible for the crimes of their children? Why?

Note
Boys under the age of 14 are irrebuttably presumed to be incapable of sexual intercourse and thus cannot be convicted of offences (including rape) involving sexual intercourse. See *R v Groombridge* (1835) 7 C & P 582.

Where there is incontrovertible evidence that sexual intercourse has been effected by the defendant, why should the presumption of incapacity prevail?

(iii) Mischievous discretion
Where a child is between the ages of 10 and 14 at the time of the offence, there is a common law presumption that he or she is incapable of committing an offence. This presumption can be rebutted by proof that the child has a 'mischievous discretion'. Proof of 'mischievous discretion' must be established in addition to the elements of the crime.

R v Runeckles
(1984) 79 Cr App R 255
Divisional Court

MANN J: . . . On July 2, 1982 the defendant was aged 13. The circumstances of the offence alleged were as follows. The defendant and another girl had a discussion with the victim in a public open space. After that discussion the victim went home, to which house the defendant and her companion then went. On their arrival at the home, the front door was opened. The victim was hit by the defendant with a milk bottle and was then stabbed by the defendant with the now broken bottle. The defendant and her companion ran off.

The defendant and her companion shortly afterwards were seen in a street by a police officer, whereupon appreciating the sighting, they fled and sought to hide in a garden. They were apprehended.

In those circumstances the justices convicted this defendant and her companion. It is argued before this Court that the defendant's conviction must be quashed because of the operation of the presumption which applies in regard to the acts of children aged between 10 and 14. That presumption is this: at common law a child under 14 is presumed not to have reached the age of discretion and is to be deemed *doli incapax*. The presumption is a rebuttable presumption, and the burden of rebutting it is upon the prosecution. I do not doubt that the prosecution has to discharge that burden by reference to the standard of proof which the prosecution have ordinarily to establish in a criminal case.

Mr Speller for the appellant argued that the prosecution could rebut this presumption only by showing that the child appreciated that that which he or she had done was morally wrong; and that this could not have been done on the facts of this case.

The justices' conclusion was:

We were of the opinion that the presumption of *doli incapax* had been rebutted by the prosecution by strong and pregnant evidence for the following reasons: —

1. The statement under caution made at the dictation of the defendant, in the presence of her mother, 45 minutes after the arrest represented a cogent account, remarkably similar to the victim's, which was signed by the defendant and her mother and bore a caption written in her own hand.

2. Taking into account the content of the statement and the handwriting of the defendant, which in our view was commensurate with the ability of an average 13 year old, we felt justified in coming to the conclusion that the defendant was not a girl with a mental age of less than that age.

3. We then had regard to her actions. After the incident in the park, she and the co-defendant pursued the victim to the victim's home. The defendant knocked on the door and threatened to break in. When the door was opened the defendant, on her own admission, taunted the victim – taunting which led to the fight. The defendant was accompanied, and yet when faced by another 13 year old, on her own admission, threw a milk bottle at the unarmed victim. Again on her own admission, even when the victim was on the floor, having hit her a few more times, she got the then broken milk bottle and stabbed the victim. The defendant and the co-defendant then ran away.

4. Subsequently, upon seeing two police officers, both girls ran away and were later found hiding in a front garden behind a hedge. The defendant immediately admitted to one of the police officers that she thought they were after them.

Our attention has since been drawn to *J. B. H. and J. H. (Minors)* v *O'Connell* [1981] Crim LR 632. However, we would distinguish our case on the basis that we had written admissions from the defendant.

The question which the justices posed for the decision of this Court is whether or not there was evidence on which they could come to the conclusion that the defendant had (what in the old language is called) a mischievous discretion.

The court has been referred to the direction of Salter, J in *Gorrie* (1919) 83 JP 136, where he said:

> The boy was under 14, and the law presumed that he was not responsible criminally; and if the prosecution sought to show that he was responsible although under 14, they must give them (that is, the jury) very clear and complete evidence of what was called mischievous discretion: that meant that they must satisfiy the jury that when the boy did this he knew that he was doing what was wrong – not merely what was wrong, but what was gravely wrong, seriously wrong.

I would respectfully adopt the learned judge's use of the phrase 'seriously wrong'. I regard an act which a child knew to be morally wrong as being but one type of those acts which a child can appreciate to be seriously wrong. I think it is unnecessary to show that the child appreciated that his or her action was morally wrong. It is sufficient that the child appreciated the action was seriously wrong. A court has to look for something beyond mere naughtiness or childish mischief.

In this case the justices had before them the actions of the defendant; that is, a blow with a milk bottle and a stab with a remnant part of that bottle. They had before them her immediate running away. They had before them her hiding when the police were observed. They also had the defendant's statement under caution, a statement which was coherent in content and which contained the caption written in the defendant's handwriting.

In my judgment, taking the matters together, the justices were justified in finding that they were satisfied so as to be sure that the presumption had been rebutted, and that this 13 year old girl (who from her statement seemed of normal intelligence) appreciated that what she did to her victim was a seriously wrong thing to do. For those reasons, I would answer the question in the case by saying there was evidence on which the justices could conclude that the defendant had mischievous discretion.

Appeal dismissed.

Questions
1. On what basis did the court in *Runeckles* find that the presumption of incapacity had been rebutted? What other evidence might be relevant to the determination?
2. Should the seriousness of the crime affect the issue of legal responsibility?

B   Insanity

(i)   Rationale
While the number of cases in which an insanity defence is raised is statistically insignificant, the defence raises some of the most profound issues in criminal law. Why should the insane offender be excused from criminal liability? He

has caused harm to society; often, as in the case of a serial killer, quite grave harm. He is also a danger to society, and, if let loose, may well reoffend. He is clearly in need of restraint and rehabilitation.

There are two considerations which are often said to justify the defence. First, because it is felt that an insane offender is not morally blameworthy. Offender's who, through no fault of their own, do not know what they are doing or that it is wrong lack the 'free will' and rational autonomy which the law envisages, and should not be held responsible for their breaches of the law any more than should a child. Secondly there is little point in imposing criminal punishment for deterrent purposes, as those who are truly insane are unlikely to understand the commands of the law (indeed, this is implicit in the definition of insanity), or be deterred by criminal sanctions.

Insanity is a defence to all crimes, including those which impose strict liability. If a defendant puts into issue his mental state in order to negate the *mens rea* element of a crime, however, the Crown is entitled to show that the defendant is in fact legally insane. See *Bratty* v *Attorney-General for Northern Ireland* [1963] AC 386, at p. 411 per Lord Denning. Thus the defendant may, over his objection, find an insanity claim thrust upon him. His claim of a lack of *mens rea* will go by the board.

(ii)   The M'Naghten test

(a)   *General introduction.* The legal test of insanity was enunciated in *M'Naghten's Case*.

M'Naghten's Case
(1843) 10 Cl & F 200
House of Lords

The prisoner had been indicted for that he, on the 20th day of January 1843, at the parish of Saint Martin in the Fields, in the county of Middlesex, and within the jurisdiction of the Central Criminal Court, in and upon one Edward Drummond, feloniously, wilfully, and of his malice aforethought, did make an assault; and that the said Daniel M'Naghten, a certain pistol of the value of 20s., loaded and charged with gunpowder and a leaden bullet (which pistol he in his right hand had and held), to, against and upon the said Edward Drummond, feloniously, wilfully, and of his malice aforethought, did shoot and discharge; and that the said Daniel M'Naghten, with the leaden bullet aforesaid, out of the pistol aforesaid, by force of the gunpowder, etc., the said Edward Drummond, in and upon the back of him the said Edward Drummond, feloniously, etc. did strike, penetrate and wound, giving to the said Edward Drummond, in and upon the back of the said Edward Drummond, one mortal wound, etc., of which mortal wound the said E. Drummond languished until the 25th of April and then died; and that by the means aforesaid, be the prisoner did kill and murder the said Edward Drummond. The prisoner pleaded Not guilty.

Evidence having been given of the fact of the shooting of Mr Drummond, and of his death in consequence thereof, witnesses were called on the part of the prisoner, to prove that he was not, at the time of committing the act, in a sound state of mind. The medical evidence was in substance this: That persons of otherwise sound mind, might be affected by morbid delusions: that the prisoner was in that condition: that a person so labouring under a morbid delusion, might have a moral perception of right and wrong, but that in the case of the prisoner it was a delusion which carried him away beyond the power of his own control, and left him no such perception; and that he was not capable of exercising any control over acts which had connexion with his delusion: that it was of the nature of the disease with which the prisoner was affected, to go on gradually until it had reached a climax, when it burst forth with irresistible intensity: that a man might go on for years quietly, though at the same time under its influence, but would all at once break out into the most extravagant and violent paroxysms.

. . .

Verdict, Not, guilty, on the ground of insanity.

This verdict, and the question of the nature and extent of the unsoundness of mind which would excuse the commission of a felony of this sort, having been made the subject of debate in the House of Lords (the 6th and 13th March 1843; see Hansard's Debates, vol. 67, pp. 288, 714), it was determined to take the opinion of the Judges on the law governing such cases.

LORD CHIEF JUSTICE TINDAL: . . . The first question proposed by your Lordships is this: 'What is the law respecting alleged crimes committed by persons afflicted with insane delusion in respect of one or more particular subjects or persons: as, for instance, where at the time of the commission of the alleged crime the accused knew he was acting contrary to law, but did the act complained of with a view, under the influence of insane delusion, of redressing or revenging some supposed grievance or injury, or of producing some supposed public benefit?'

In answer to which question, assuming that your Lordships' inquiries are confined to those persons who labour under such partial delusions only, and are not in other respects insane, we are of opinion that, notwithstanding the party accused did the act complained of with a view, under the influence of insane delusion, of redressing or revenging some supposed grievance or injury, or of producing some public benefit, he is nevertheless punishable according to the nature of the crime committed, if he knew at the time of committing such crime that he was acting contrary to law; by which expression we understand your Lordships to mean the law of the land.

Your Lordships are pleased to inquire of us, secondly, 'What are the proper questions to be submitted to the jury, where a person alleged to be afflicted with insane delusion respecting one or more particular subjects or persons, is charged with the commission of a crime (murder, for example), and insanity is set up as a defence?' And, thirdly, 'In what terms ought the question to be left to the jury as to the prisoner's state of mind at the time when the act was committed?' And as these two questions appear to us to be more conveniently answered together, we have to submit our opinion to be that the jurors ought to be told in all cases that every man is to be presumed to be sane, and to possess a sufficient degree of reason to be responsible for his crimes, until the contrary be proved to their satisfaction: and that to establish a defence on the ground of insanity, it must be clearly proved that, at the time of the committing of the act, the party accused was labouring under such a defect of reason from disease of the mind, as not to know the nature and quality of the act he was doing; or if he did know it, that he did not know he was doing what was wrong. The mode of putting the latter part of the question to the jury on these occasions has generally been, whether the accused at the time of doing the act knew the difference between right and wrong: which mode, though rarely, if ever leading to any mistake with the jury, is not, as we conceive, so accurate when put generally and in the abstract, as when put with reference to the party's knowledge of right and wrong in respect to the very act with which he is charged. If the question were to be put as to the knowledge of the accused solely and exclusively with reference to the law of the land, it might tend to confound the jury, by inducing them to believe that an actual knowledge of the law of the land was essential in order to lead to a conviction; whereas the law is administered upon the principle that every one must be taken conclusively to know it, without proof that he does know it. If the accused was conscious that the act was one which he ought not to do, and if that act was at the same time contrary to the law of the land, he is punishable; and the usual course therefore has been to leave the question to the jury, whether the party accused had a sufficient degree of reason to know that he was doing an act that was wrong: and this course we think is correct, accompanied with such observations and explanations as the circumstances of each particular case may require.

The fourth question which your Lordships have proposed to us is this: – 'If a person under an insane delusion as to existing facts, commits an offence in consequence thereof, is he thereby excused?' To which question the answer must of course depend on the nature of the delusion: but, making the same assumption as we did before, namely, that he labours under such partial delusion only, and is not in other respects insane, we think he must be considered in the same situation as to responsibility as if the facts with respect to which the delusion exists were real. For example, if under the influence of his delusion he supposes another man to be in the act of attempting to take away his life, and he kills that man, as he supposes, in self-defence, he would be exempt from punishment. If his delusion was that the deceased had inflicted a serious injury to his character and fortune, and he killed him in revenge for such supposed injury, he would be liable to punishment.

Notes and questions
1.   A defendant is presumed to be sane. Why? How does a defendant go about rebutting this presumption of sanity? Under s. 1(1) of the Criminal Procedure (Insanity and Unfitness to Plead) Act 1991, a defendant may not be acquitted by reason of insanity except on the evidence of at least two registered medical practitioners, one of whom is a specialist approved by the Home Secretary.
2.   The insanity defence is concerned with the defendant's state of mind at the time of commission of the crime, not at the time of trial. One can be sane immediately prior to one's criminal act and immediately afterwards, but if insane at the time of the act the defence is available.
3.   The court in *M'Naghten* said that the defence must be clearly proved – but by whom and by what standard? The rule is that the defence must be proved by the defendant on a balance of probabilities rather than by proof beyond a reasonable doubt. Nonetheless, the allocation to the defendant of this burden of persuasion reverses the prevailing practice in regard to most other defences. What is the justification for this departure from standard practice?

4. Note the difficulty facing the jury. The law is concerned with the defendant's mental state at the time of the crime; but a psychiatric examination of the defendant will probably not be conducted until after arrest. This may be some time after the crime was committed. The jury will have to attempt to reconstruct what the defendant's state of mind was at the time of the crime, based on an after-the-fact psychiatric examination. Nor can the jurors rely on their observations of the defendant at trial, for the defendant's mental state at the time of the trial also may not be the same as at the time of the crime.

5. In the normal case where the jury decide that the defendant has a defence to the crime charged, they return a verdict of 'not guilty'. If the jury find that the defendant was insane, on the other hand, they return a verdict of 'not guilty by reason of insanity'. Why this departure from standard practice?

(b)   'that . . . the . . . accused was labouring under such a defect of reason, from disease of the mind'. In order to establish a defence of insanity, the defendant must be labouring under a defect of reason from disease of the mind. The defect must be more than simply gross stupidity, absent-mindedness or confusion. See *Clarke* [1972] 1 All ER 219. Rather, there must be a total deprivation of the power to reason brought on by a disease of the mind. But what is meant by 'disease of the mind'?

R v Sullivan
[1984] 1 AC 156
House of Lords

LORD DIPLOCK: My Lords, the appellant, Mr Sullivan, a man of blameless reputation, has the misfortune to have been a lifelong sufferer from epilepsy. There was a period when he was subject to major seizures known as grand mal; but, as a result of treatment which he was receiving as an out-patient of the Maudsley Hospital from 1976 onwards, these major seizures had, by the use of drugs, been reduced by 1979 to seizures of less severity known as petit mal, or psychomotor epilepsy, though they continued to occur at a frequency of one or two per week.

One such seizure occurred on May 8, 1981, when Mr Sullivan, then aged 51, was visiting a neighbour, Mrs Killick, an old lady aged 86 for whom he was accustomed to perform regular acts of kindness. He was chatting there to a fellow visitor and friend of his, a Mr Payne aged 80, when the epileptic fit came on. It appears likely from the expert medical evidence about the way in which epileptics behave at the various stages of a petit mal seizure that Mr Payne got up from the chair to help Mr Sullivan. The only evidence of an eyewitness was that of Mrs Killick, who did not see what had happened before she saw Mr Payne lying on the floor and Mr Sullivan kicking him about the head and body, in consequence of which Mr Payne suffered injuries severe enough to require hospital treatment.

As a result of this occurrence Mr Sullivan was indicted upon two counts: the first was of causing grievous bodily harm with intent contrary to section 18 of the Offences against the Person Act 1861; the second of causing grievous bodily harm contrary to section 20 of that Act. At his trial, which took place at the Central Criminal Court before Judge Lymbery and a jury, Mr Sullivan pleaded not guilty to both counts. Mrs

Killick's evidence that he had kicked Mr Payne violently about the head and body was undisputed and Mr Sullivan himself gave evidence of his history of epilepsy and his absence of all recollection of what had occurred at Mrs Killick's flat between the time that he was chatting peacefully to Mr Payne there and his returning to the flat from somewhere else to find that Mr Payne was injured and that an ambulance had been sent for. The prosecution accepted his evidence as true. . . .

The evidence as to the pathology of a seizure due to psychomotor epilepsy can be sufficiently stated for the purposes of this appeal by saying that after the first stage, the prodram, which precedes the fit itself, there is a second stage, the ictus, lasting a few seconds, during which there are electrical discharges into the temporal lobes of the brain of the sufferer. The effect of these discharges is to cause him in the post-ictal stage to make movements which he is not conscious that he is making, including, and this was a characteristic of previous seizures which Mr Sullivan had suffered, automatic movements of resistance to anyone trying to come to his aid. These movements of resistance might, though in practice they very rarely would, involve violence.

. . . , [I]t is submitted the medical evidence in the instant case shows that psychomotor epilepsy is not a disease of the mind, whereas in *Bratty* [1963] AC 386 it was accepted by all the doctors that it was. The only evidential basis for this submission is that Dr Fenwick said that in medical terms to constitute a 'disease of the mind' or 'mental illness,' which he appeared to regard as interchangeable descriptions, a disorder of brain functions (which undoubtedly occurs during a seizure in psychomotor epilepsy) must be prolonged for a period of time usually more than a day; while Dr Taylor would have it that the disorder must continue for a minimum of a month to qualify for the description 'a disease of the mind.'

The nomenclature adopted by the medical profession may change from time to time; Bratty was tried in 1961. But the meaning of the expression 'disease of the mind' as the cause of 'a defect of reason' remains unchanged for the purposes of the application of the M'Naghten Rules. I agree with what was said by Devlin J in *R v Kemp* [1957] 1 QB 399, 407, that 'mind' in the M'Naghten Rules is used in the ordinary sense of the mental faculties of reason, memory and understanding. If the effect of a disease is to impair these faculties so severely as to have either of the consequences referred to in the latter part of the rules, it matters not whether the aetiology of the impairment is organic, as in epilepsy, or functional, or whether the impairment itself is permanent or is transient and intermittent, provided that it subsisted at the time of commission of the act. The purpose of the legislation relating to the defence of insanity, ever since its origin in 1800, has been to protect society against recurrence of the dangerous conduct. The duration of a temporary suspension of the mental faculties of reason, memory and understanding, particularly if, as in Mr Sullivan's case, it is recurrent, cannot on any rational ground be relevant to the application by the courts of the M'Naghten Rules, though it may be relevant to the course adopted by the Secretary of State, to whom the responsibility for how the defendant is to be dealt with passes after the return of the special verdict of 'not guilty by reason of insanity.'

Note

A qualification on 'disease of the mind' has been judicially imposed. It is that the source of the disease must be internal rather than external. We have seen in Chapter 2 that a malfunctioning of the mind caused by an external factor (drugs, insulin, a blow on the head) will give rise to a defence of automatism rather than insanity. Often the distinction is unclear. Compare the following cases:

R v Hennessy
[1989] 1 WLR 287
Court of Appeal

LORD LANE CJ: . . . On Thursday, 28 May 1987, two police constables, Barnes and Grace, were on duty in St Leonards-on-Sea on the Sussex coast, among other things looking for a Ford Granada car which had been stolen. They found the car. It was unattended. They kept it under watch. As they watched they saw the appellant get into the car, switch on the headlights and ignition, start the car and drive off. The appellant at the wheel of the car correctly stopped the car at a set of traffic lights which were showing red against him. Pc Grace then went over to the car as it was stationary, removed the ignition keys from the ignition-lock, but not before the appellant had tried to drive the motor car away and escape from the attention of the policeman. The appellant was put in the police car. On the way to the police station an informal conversation about motor vehicles took place between the appellant and the police officers, in particular about the respective merits of the new Rover motor car and the Ford Sierra. Indeed, the appellant appeared to Pc Barnes not only to be fully in possession of his faculties but to be quite cheerful and intelligent. Indeed he went so far as to say to the police officer that if he had only got the car, which he was in the process of removing, onto the open road, he would have given the policemen a real run for their money.

However after having been at the police station for a time, the appellant was at a later stage escorted by Pc Barnes to hospital. He seemed to be normal when he left the cell block at the police station, but when he arrived at the hospital he appeared to be dazed and confused. He complained to the sister in the casualty ward that he had failed to take his insulin and indeed had had no insulin since the previous Monday when he should have had regular self-injected doses. He was given insulin, with which he injected himself, and the hospital discharged him and he was taken back to the police station.

The appellant gave evidence to the effect that he had been a diabetic for about ten years. He needed, in order to stabilise his metabolism, two insulin injections on a daily basis, morning and afternoon. The amount required would depend on factors such as stress and eating habits. He was on a strict carbohydrate diet. At the time of the offence he said he had been having marital and employment problems. His wife had submitted a divorce petition some time shortly before, and he was very upset. He had not been eating and he had not been taking his insulin. He remembered very few details of the day. He could recall being handcuffed and taken to the chargeroom at the police station. He remembered being given insulin at the hospital and injecting himself and he remembers feeling better when he got back to the police station afterwards. He said he did not recall taking the car.

When cross-examined he agreed that he had understood proceedings at the police station and what had gone on there. Indeed he had given the name and address of his solicitor. That was a considerable time before he had had his insulin at the hospital.

His general practitioner, Dr Higginson, was called to give evidence. He spoke as to the appellant's medical condition. He described in broad outlines the effect of diabetes: it is a deficiency in the system of the production of hormones which should balance the sugar metabolism. The lacking hormone is of course insulin. In the absence of the hormone the blood sugar rises and that results in hyperglycaemia. If the patient does not take his insulin and does not stick to the proper diet, then hyperglycaemia will supervene. If unchecked, the liver will become affected and the increasingly high level of sugar makes the patient drowsy and he will ultimately go into a coma.

If on the other hand the balance tips the other way, if too much insulin is taken, then the blood sugar will fall and hypoglycaemia, that is to say too little sugar in the blood, will supervene.

According to the hospital notes, on the evening in question the appellant's blood sugar had been high at 22 plus millimolecules per litre, the normal being 8 or 9. According to Dr Higginson one would expect to see some physical manifestation of hyperglycaemia at that level. So the doctor was saying in short that eventually hyperglycaemia can result in drowsiness, loss of consciousness and coma, greater or less unresponsiveness to stimuli according to the degree of hyperglycaemia present. He added, I will read a passage from his evidence in a moment, that anxiety or depression can increase the blood sugar level, a person's ability and awareness of what is going on could be impaired if there were 'associated symptoms and he had other conditions and worries at the same time . . .'

. . .

The importance of the [M'Naghten] rules in the present context, namely the context of automatism, is this. If the defendant did not know the nature and quality of his act because of something which *did not* amount to defect of reason from disease of the mind then he will probably be entitled to be acquitted on the basis that the necessary criminal intent which the prosecution has to prove is not proved. But, if, on the other hand, his failure to realise the nature and quality of his act was due to a defect of reason from disease of the mind, then in the eyes of the law he is suffering from insanity, albeit M'Naghten insanity.

. . .

The question in many cases, and this is one such case, is whether the function of the mind was disturbed on the one hand by disease or on the other hand by some external factor. . . .

The point was neatly raised in *R* v *Quick, R* v *Paddison* [1973] 3 All ER 347, [1973] QB 910. also referred to us by counsel for the appellant, in which Lawton LJ reviewed the authorities. It might perhaps help if I read a short passage from the headnote ([1973] QB 910):

> The defendants, Q and P, nurses at a mental hospital, were jointly and severally charged with assaulting a patient occasioning actual bodily harm. Both pleaded not guilty. Q, a diabetic, relied on the defence of automatism. He gave evidence that he had taken insulin as prescribed on the morning of the assault, had drunk a quantity of spirits and eaten little food thereafter and had no recollection of the assault. He called medical evidence to the effect that his condition at the material time was consistent with that of hypoglycaemia. The judge ruled that evidence could only support a defence of insanity, not automatism. Q then pleaded guilty and P was convicted of aiding and abetting Q by encouragement. The defendants appealed against conviction.

I turn to the passage in the judgment where Lawton LJ said ([1973] 3 All ER 347 at 356. [1973] QB 910 at 922–923):

> A malfunctioning of the mind of transitory effect caused by the application to the body of some external factor such as violence, drugs, including anaesthetics, alcohol and hypnotic influences cannot fairly be said to be due to disease. Such malfunctioning, unlike that caused by a defect of reason from disease of the mind, will not always relieve an accused from criminal responsibility . . . In this case Quick's alleged mental condition, if it ever existed, was not caused by his diabetes but by his use of the insulin prescribed by his doctor. Such malfunctioning of his mind as there was, was

caused by an external factor and not by a bodily disorder in the nature of a disease which disturbed the working of his mind. It follows in our judgment that Quick was entitled to have his defence of automatism left to the jury and that Bridge J's ruling as to the effect of the medical evidence called by him was wrong.

Thus in *R v Quick* the fact that his condition was, or may have been, due to the injections of insulin meant that the malfunction was due to an external factor and not to the disease. The drug it was that caused the hypoglycaemia, the low blood sugar. As suggested in another passage of the judgment of Lawton LJ, hyperglycaemia, high blood sugar, caused by an inherent defect and not corrected by insulin is a disease, and if, as the defendant was asserting here, it does cause a malfunction of the mind, then the case may fall within the M'Naghten rules.

The burden of the argument of counsel for the appellant to us is this. It is that the appellant's depression and marital troubles were a sufficiently potent external factor in his condition to override, so to speak, the effect of the diabetic shortage of insulin on him. . . .

In our judgment, stress, anxiety and depression can no doubt be the result of the operation of external factors, but they are not, it seems to us, in themselves separately or together external factors of the kind capable in law of causing or contributing to a state of automatism. . . .

R v T
[1990] Crim LR 256
Snaresbrook Crown Court

T, a young French woman aged 23 and two others (R and B) were arrested and charged with robbery (two cases) and T was further charged with ABH. The Crown alleged a joint enterprise by all three to rob two females whilst armed with a Stanley knife (not recovered) and a pen knife, of their handbags, as the two victims were returning to a car late at night. When first seen, T was leaning on the victims' car and said 'I'm ill, I'm ill.' The three accused then surrounded one of the girls and there was a scuffle. Her bag opened and the contents spilled out, whereupon the two victims ran away. A few minutes later, they met another young woman, dressed in a dark coloured jogging suit, who offered to accompany them to the local police station. En route to the car, T saw the two victims and (allegedly) misidentified the third person as a male. T then followed the three women to the motor vehicle and she was followed by R and B. Near the car, the contents of the first victim's handbag were recovered and she got behind the wheel of the car. The second victim sat in the rear nearside passenger seat and the third woman was standing by the open front nearside passenger's door when they were approached by the three defendants. R went to the driver's side and held a Stanley-type knife to the face of the first victim and demanded her bag, which he was given. T approached the open passenger's door where the third woman was standing. When asked what she was doing and why, T stabbed the third woman in the stomach causing a small puncture wound (no medical treatment required other than a dressing). T then pushed past the third woman, leant into the car and demanded the second victim's handbag, which was given to her. All three defendants remained in the vicinity for about one minute. The third woman realised she had been stabbed and started to scream, whereupon the three defendants decamped. The three victims drove away and pointed out T, R and B to a police officer whereupon R and B decamped. R was seen to discard a pen knife in a rubbish bin and discard the first victim's handbag, both of which were recovered. After a short chase R was arrested and brought back to where the victims were, and the officer also detained T who was standing at the side of the road. On being arrested, T was described as being passive and indifferent to what was happening. During a subsequent interview, T could only recollect some of the events. B was arrested the following day and all three were charged. Seven days later, T was examined by a doctor at H.M. Prison Holloway when it was found that her hymen was ruptured and was bleeding, and that there were injuries posterior to the hymen. T complained that she had been raped three days prior to her arrest but had not told anyone about it. T was later examined on a number of occasions by a psychiatrist who diagnosed that after the rape she was suffering from Post Traumatic Stress Disorder and at the time of the offence she had entered a Dissociative State and the offences had been committed during a psychogenic fugue and she was not acting with a conscious mind or will.

The Defence submitted that the 'defence' of 'non-insane automatism' was open to T on the grounds that the categories of non-insane automatism are not limited to a blow causing concussion, an injection of insulin or anaesthetic or sleep walking (*per* Lord Diplock in *Sullivan* [1983] 3 WLR 123); that rape is the application of an 'external force' (*per* Lawton LJ in *Quick* [1973] 3 WLR 26 at p. 35); that the rape was such an extraordinary external event that might be presumed to affect the average normal person and it contained features of novelty of accident (*per* Lord Lane CJ in *Hennessy* [1989] 1 WLR 287 at p. 294 and Martin J in *Rabey*, 79 Dominion Law Reports 435 (Ontario Court of Appeal); that a proper foundation had been laid for leaving the defence to the jury (*per* Lord Denning in *Bratty* v *Att.-Gen. for Northern Ireland* [1963] AC 368 at p. 413. The Crown argued that the evidence showed the Defendant had some recollection of what happened. Further that the opening of the blade of the pen knife required a controlled and positive action by the Defendant, therefore this was a case where there was 'partial control' (*per Broom* v *Perkins* (1987) 85, Cr App R 321 and *Issit* [1977] RTR 211) and the only 'defence' open to was 'insane automatism' under the M'Naghton [*sic*] Rules.

Held, that there had been no previous case in which an incident of rape had been held to be 'an external factor' causing a malfunctioning of the mind within the definition laid down in *Quick*; that, if what the Defendant says about the rape is true, such an incident could have an appalling effect on any young woman, however well balanced normally, and that could satisfy the requirement; that a condition of Post Traumatic Stress involving a normal person in an act of violence is not itself a disease of the mind, even if there is a delay before a period of dissociation manifests itself; that if the medical evidence is correct this case is distinguishable from *Broom* and *Issit* where there was only a partial loss of control whereas in this case T was acting as though in a 'dream'; that the categories of automatism are not closed and that, on the evidence before the court, a proper foundation had been laid for the matter to go before the jury.

Questions
1.   In *Hennessy*, does the court treat a physical illness as if it were a mental illness? In *T*, does it treat a mental illness as if it were a physical illness? What motivates the courts in these matters?
2.   In *Bratty* v *Attorney-General for Northern Ireland* [1963] AC 386, Lord Denning stated: 'It seems to me that any mental disorder which has manifested itself in violence and is prone to recur is a disease of the mind.' Is Lord Denning correct? Does his statement accord with the internal-external distinction of later cases?

3. Is the requirement of a 'disease of the mind' unnecessary? If a defendant does not know the nature and quality of her act or that it is wrong, and this is due to a defect of reason, why should it matter that the defect of reason is the product of a disease of the mind? In light of the reasons for the insanity defence identified previously, does the source make any difference?

(c) *'as not to know the nature and quality of the act ... or [that it] was wrong'.* The defendant who is suffering from a defect of reason from a disease of the mind can come within the *M'Naghten* rules in either of two ways:

(i) the defendant can show that she did not know the nature and quality of the act she was doing; or
(ii) the defendant can show that she did not know that what she was doing was wrong.

But is the word 'wrong' used in its legal or its moral sense?

R v *Windle*
[1952] 2 QB 826
Court of Appeal

The appellant, Francis Wilfred Windle, was convicted before Devlin J at Birmingham Assizes of the murder of his wife, and sentenced to death. He was a man, 40 years of age, of little resolution and weak character, and was married to a woman 18 years his senior. His married life was very unhappy; his wife was always speaking of committing suicide and the doctors who gave evidence at the trial were of opinion, from the history of the case, that she was certifiably insane. The appellant frequently discussed his home life with his workmates, until, as one of them said, they were sick and tired of hearing about it. Eventually a workmate said to the appellant, 'Give her a dozen aspirins,' and on the following day the appellant gave his wife 100 tablets. He sent for a doctor and told him that he had given his wife so many aspirins. She was taken to hospital, where she died. The appellant informed the police that he had given his wife 100 aspirins, and added: 'I suppose they will hang me for this?' At his trial a defence of insanity was put forward. A doctor was called for him who said that the appellant was suffering from a form of communicated insanity known as *folie à deux*. It was said that if a person was in constant attendance on another of unsound mind, in some way the insanity might be communicated to the attendant, so that, for a time at any rate, the attendant might develop a defect of reason or of mind. Rebutting medical evidence was allowed to be called for the prosecution, and the doctors called on either side expressed the opinion that the appellant, when administering the fatal dose of aspirin to his wife, knew that he was doing an act which the law forbade.

LORD GODDARD CJ: . . . The argument before us has really been on what is the meaning of the word 'wrong.' In this particular case, the only evidence given on the issue of insanity was that of the doctor called by the appellant and of the prison doctor who was allowed to be called by the prosecution to rebut, if indeed it was necessary, any evidence which had been given. It was probably right that the prison doctor should be called as he had had the appellant under constant observation. Both the doctors gave their evidence in a way that commended itself to the judge, and both, without hesitation, expressed the view that the appellant knew, when administering this poison, for such it was, to his wife, that he was doing an act which the law forbade. I need not put it higher than that.

It may well be that, in the misery in which he had been living, with this nagging and tiresome wife who constantly expressed the desire to commit suicide, he thought that she would be better out of this world than in it. He may have thought that it would be a kindly act to release her from what she was suffering from — or thought she was suffering from — but that the law does not permit. In the present case there was some exceedingly vague evidence that the appellant was suffering from a defect of reason. In the opinion of his own doctor, there was a defect of reason which he attributed to communicated insanity. In my opinion, if the only question in this case had been whether the appellant was suffering from a disease of the mind, I should say that that was a question which must have been left to the jury. That, however, is not the question.

. . . A man may be suffering from a defect of reason, but if he knows that what he is doing is 'wrong,' and by 'wrong' is meant contrary to law, he is responsible. Mr Shawcross, in the course of his very careful argument, suggested that the word 'wrong,' as it was used in the M'Naghten rules, did not mean contrary to law but had some kind of qualified meaning, such as morally wrong, and that if a person was in such a state of mind through a defect of reason that, although he knew that what he was doing was wrong in law, he thought that it was beneficial or kind or praiseworthy, that would excuse him.

Courts of law can only distinguish between that which is in accordance with law and that which is contrary to law. . . .

In the opinion of the court there is no doubt that in the M'Naghten rules 'wrong' means contrary to law and not 'wrong' according to the opinion of one man or of a number of people on the question whether a particular act might or might not be justified. In the present case, it could not be challenged that the appellant knew that what he was doing was contrary to law, and that he realized what punishment the law provided for murder. That was the opinion of both the doctors who gave evidence.

Questions
1.   Presumably the court in *Windle* was attempting to narrow the meaning of the term 'wrong'; but could not the decision have the opposite effect? What if an insane individual appreciated that his act was morally wrong but, due to his mental illness, not that it was legally wrong?
2.   Is the requirement that the insane defendant should not know that his act was legally wrong consistent with the general rule that 'ignorance of the law is no excuse'?

(d)   *Partial delusions and irresistible impulses.* There is a second branch of *M'Naghten* relating to partial delusions. The relevant question is set out in the *M'Naghten* extract (above). It is doubtful whether anything is added to the 'core' test by this passage. A person under a delusion is presumably incapable of understanding the nature and quality of his act.

M'Naghten is concerned with cognitive disabilities. The defendant is unable, due to a defect of reason from disease of the mind, to comprehend what he is doing or that it is wrong. What, however, if the defendant is able to comprehend what he is doing, but is unable to stop himself from doing it?

R v Sodeman
[1936] 2 All ER 1138
Privy Council

The petitioner, who was a labourer, took a young girl for a ride on his bicycle, strangled her, tied her hands behind her back, stuffed some of her clothing into her mouth, and left her for dead. The cause of death was suffocation. The petitioner had committed three previous murders in very similar ways. The petitioner's defence was that he was insane at the time. At the trial two government prison doctors and a specialist in mental diseases gave evidence in support of that defence. No expert evidence on that issue was tendered by the Crown.

VISCOUNT HAILSHAM LC: . . . [I]t is suggested by the petitioner that the rules in *M'Naghten's* case (1843) 10 Cl & F 200 are no longer to be treated as an exhaustive statement of the law with regard to insanity, and that there is to be engrafted upon those rules another rule that where a man knows that he is doing what is wrong, none the less he may be held to be insane if he is caused to do the act by an irresistible impulse produced by disease. It is admitted by Mr Pritt that, so far as this country is concerned, the more recent cases, . . . excludes that addition to the law in *M'Naghten's* case, but it is argued that, since there have been earlier decisions which suggest that such a rule exists, this is a good opportunity for establishing the law beyond doubt. Their Lordships do not think that the argument is a sound one. If they are to take a different view of the law from that which prevailed [in recent cases] the effect will be that different standards of law will prevail in England and in the Dominions. The adoption of such a view obviously cannot alter the authorities laid down by the English Court of Criminal Appeal, and their Lordships do not think that the ground suggested is one for granting special leave to appeal in a criminal case. . . .

Questions
Why is there such judicial antipathy to irresistible impulse? Is it because, as is sometimes said, there is no such thing as an irresistible impulse when there is a police officer at one's elbow? Or is it that the more an impulse increases in strength, the greater the legal sanction needed to counteract its effect?

(iii) Procedures
Statistically the insanity defence was not often raised, at least not by defendants (it can be raised by the Crown if defendants place their mental state in issue). See *Bratty v Attorney-General for Northern Ireland* [1963] AC 386.

See generally Mackay, 'Fact and fiction about the insanity defence' [1990] Crim LR 247. The reason was this. In the case of other defences, if the jury accepted the defence, the defendant was released, a free person. Not so in the case of a successful insanity defence. If the defendant's defence of insanity succeeded, and the jury returned a verdict of 'not guilty by reason of insanity', the defendant did not go free but was committed to a mental hospital, to remain at 'Her Majesty's Pleasure', which could be forever. Thus there was little incentive to plead insanity except when the charge was murder, where there existed the possibility of the death penalty. After the death penalty for murder was abolished, and there also became available the plea of diminished responsibility (see Chapter 9) which served to reduce the crime of murder to manslaughter, there was little to be gained by pleading insanity. So the defence lay dormant. At least until 1992.

The Criminal Procedure (Insanity and Unfitness to Plead) Act 1991 attempted to address two troublesome aspects of *M'Naghten*. First was the problem of the accused who may have had a valid defence to the charges other than insanity but who was unable to obtain a trial because his mental state rendered him unfit to plead. Second was the issue of mandatory commitment following a verdict of 'not guilty by reason of insanity', which doubtless deterred many defendants from raising an insanity defence. The Act provides as follows:

Criminal Procedure (Insanity and Unfitness to Plead) Act 1991

2. Findings of unfitness to plead etc.
For section 4 of the Criminal Procedure (Insanity) Act 1964 ('the 1964 Act') there shall be substituted the following sections —

Finding of unfitness to plead
4.—(1) This section applies where on the trial of a person the question arises (at the instance of the defence or otherwise) whether the accused is under a disability, that is to say, under any disability such that apart from this Act it would constitute a bar to his being tried.

(2) If, having regard to the nature of the supposed disability, the court are of opinion that it is expedient to do so and in the interests of the accused, they may postpone consideration of the question of fitness to be tried until any time up to the opening of the case for the defence.

(3) If, before the question of fitness to be tried falls to be determined, the jury return a verdict of acquittal on the count or each of the counts on which the accused is being tried, that question shall not be determined.

(4) Subject to subsections (2) and (3) above, the question of fitness to be tried shall be determined as soon as it arises.

(5) The question of fitness to be tried shall be determined by a jury and —
(a) where it falls to be determined on the arraignment of the accused and the trial proceeds, the accused shall be tried by a jury other than that which determined that question;
(b) where it falls to be determined at any later time, it shall be determined by a separate jury or by the jury by whom the accused is being tried, as the court may direct.

(6)   A jury shall not make a determination under subsection (5) above except on the written or oral evidence of two or more registered medical practitioners at least one of whom is duly approved.

3.   Powers to deal with persons not guilty by reason of insanity or unfit to plead etc.
For section 5 of the 1964 Act there shall be substituted the following section —

Powers to deal with persons not guilty by reason of insanity or unfit to plead etc.
5.—(1)   This section applies where —
    (a)   a special verdict is returned that the accused is not guilty by reason of insanity; or
    (b)   findings are recorded that the accused is under a disability and that he did the act or made the omission charged against him.
    (2)   Subject to subsection (3) below, the court shall either —
    (a)   make an order that the accused be admitted, in accordance with the provisions of Schedule 1 to the Criminal Procedure (Insanity and Unfitness to Plead) Act 1991, to such hospital as may be specified by the Secretary of State; or
    (b)   where they have the power to do so by virtue of section 5 of that Act, make in respect of the accused such one of the following orders as they think most suitable in all the circumstances of the case, namely —
        (i)   a guardianship order within the meaning of the Mental Health Act 1983;
        (ii)   a supervision and treatment order within the meaning of Schedule 2 to the said Act of 1991; and
        (iii)   an order for his absolute discharge.
    (3)   Paragraph (b) of subsection (2) above shall not apply where the offence to which the special verdict or findings relate is an offence the sentence for which is fixed by law.

Note
It is still too early to tell what the long-term effect of this Act will be on the invocation of the insanity defence.

(iv)   Proposals for further reform
The defence of insanity propounded in *M'Naghten* has changed little since its inception in 1843, despite major advances in the understanding and treatment of mental illness. It is a legal rather than a medical test. The judicial extension of the defence to those who suffer from physical illnesses that render them prone to violent episodes may constitute a further departure from the original objective. Indeed, it seems to suggest that the courts have viewed the defence of insanity as a means whereby the law can impose a form of preventive detention on some dangerous individuals who cannot be convicted of a crime. Whether the 1991 Act will bring about a change in this misuse of the defence is unclear.

In any event, basic questions remain. What functions are served by the defence? To whom should the defence be available? Is insanity a medical condition or a legal excuse? Should the mentally ill offender be dealt with within the criminal justice system or within the mental health system? Over the years many of the alternatives to *M'Naghten* which have been proposed have sought to bring insanity closer to a medical model of mental illness. Consider the merits of the Draft Criminal Code's approach (based to a large extent on the recommendations of the Butler Committee (1975)):

Draft Criminal Code Bill 1989

34.   In this Act —
'mental disorder' means —
   (a)   severe mental illness; or
   (b)   a state of arrested or incomplete development of mind; or
   (c)   a state of automatism (not resulting only from intoxication) which is a feature of a disorder, whether organic or functional and whether continuing or recurring, that may cause a similar state on another occasion;
   'return a mental disorder verdict' means —
   (a)   in relation to trial on indictment, return a verdict that the defendant is not guilty on evidence of mental disorder; and
   (b)   in relation to summary trial, dismiss the information on evidence of mental disorder;
   'severe mental illness' means a mental illness which has one or more of the following characteristics —
   (a)   lasting impairment of intellectual functions shown by failure of memory, orientation, comprehension and learning capacity;
   (b)   lasting alteration of mood of such degree as to give rise to delusional appraisal of the defendant's situation, his past or his future, or that of others, or lack of any appraisal;
   (c)   delusional beliefs, persecutory, jealous or grandiose;
   (d)   abnormal perceptions associated with delusional misinterpretation of events;
   (e)   thinking so disordered as to prevent reasonable appraisal of the defendant's situation or reasonable communication with others;
   'severe mental handicap' means a state of arrested or incomplete development of mind which includes severe impairment of intelligence and social functioning.

35.—(1)   A mental disorder verdict shall be returned if the defendant is proved to have committed an offence but it is proved on the balance of probabilities (whether by the prosecution or by the defendant) that he was at the time suffering from severe mental illness or severe mental handicap.
   (2)   Subsection (1) does not apply if the court or jury is satisfied beyond reasonable doubt that the offence was not attributable to the severe mental illness or severe mental handicap.
   (3)   A court or jury shall not, for the purposes of a verdict under subsection (1), find that the defendant was suffering from severe mental illness or severe mental handicap unless two medical practitioners approved for the purposes of section 12 of the Mental Health Act 1983 as having special experience in the diagnosis or treatment of mental disorder have given evidence that he was so suffering.
   (4)   Subsection (1), so far as it relates to severe mental handicap, does not apply to an offence under section 106(1), 107 or 108 (sexual relations with the mentally handicapped).

36.   A mental disorder verdict shall be returned if —
   (a)   the defendant is acquitted of an offence only because, by reason of evidence of mental disorder or a combination of mental disorder and intoxication, it is found that

he acted or may have acted in a state of automatism, or without the fault required for the offence, or believing that an exempting circumstance existed; and

(b)   it is proved on the balance of probabilities (whether by the prosecution or by the defendant) that he was suffering from mental disorder at the time of the act.

37.   A defendant may plead 'not guilty by reason of mental disorder'; and

(a)   if the court directs that the plea be entered the direction shall have the same effect as a mental disorder verdict; and

(b)   if the court does not so direct the defendant shall be treated as having pleaded not guilty.

38.—(1)   Whether evidence is evidence of mental disorder or automatism is a question of law.

(2)   The prosecution shall not adduce evidence of mental disorder, or contend that a mental disorder verdict should be returned, unless the defendant has given or adduced evidence that he acted without the fault required for the offence, or believing that an exempting circumstance existed, or in a state of automatism, or (on a charge of murder) when suffering from mental abnormality as defined in section 57(2).

(3)   The court may give directions as to the stage of the proceedings at which the prosecution may adduce evidence of mental disorder.

39.   Schedule 2 has effect with respect to the orders that may be made upon the return of a mental disorder verdict, to the conditions governing the making of those orders, to the effects of those orders and to related matters.

40.   A defendant shall not, when a mental disorder verdict is returned in respect of an offence and while that verdict subsists, be found guilty of any other offence of which, but for this section, he might on the same occasion be found guilty —

(a)   on the indictment, count or information to which the verdict relates; or

(b)   on any other indictment, count or information founded on the same facts.

Notes and questions

1.   If the definition of insanity is to become more medically orientated, who should determine the defendant's sanity – a judge, a jury, or a panel of mental health experts? One possibility along these lines would be to hold a bifurcated trial – in the first stage the jury consider whether the defendant committed the crime charged; and in the second, assuming a verdict of guilty in the first stage, a panel of mental health experts determines whether the defendant was insane at the time of the crime. A second question would be whether the defendant is still insane, and, if so, what should be the appropriate disposition.

2.   Another alternative (and perhaps the logical import of the suggestion in the preceding paragraph for a bifurcated trial) is to abolish the insanity defence altogether and hold that insanity only becomes relevant at the time of sentencing. A judge should be allowed to sentence a defendant (found 'guilty but insane' by a jury) to an institution in which he can receive appropriate treatment. The length of the sentence, however, would not be affected by the place of confinement. What are the merits of this approach?

3.   If the insanity defence is to be retained and determined by the jury, perhaps a stripped-down, simplified version is needed. Consider the pros and cons of the formula proposed in 1953 by the Royal Commission on Capital Punishment:

[A person is not responsible for his unlawful act if] at the time of the act the accused was suffering from disease of the mind (or mental deficiency) to such a degree that he ought not to be held responsible.

III   Defences which negate an element of the crime

A   Mistake

A mistake made by a defendant may be relevant to criminal liability where it prevents the prosecution from proving an element of the case. For example, the mistake may prevent the defendant from forming the relevant *mens rea*, as when he mistakenly believes a woman is consenting to sexual intercourse. Another situation in which a mistake may be relevant is where it causes the defendant to form a distorted view of the surrounding circumstances of the crime, as when the defendant believes he is being attacked, whereas he is in fact being lawfully arrested. In these circumstances the defendant may have made a mistake as to circumstances which would provide an excuse for his actions if the situation actually was as he believed it to be.

(i)   Mistake negating mens rea
The mistake must be one which will prevent the formation of the relevant *mens rea*. If it does not it is irrelevant.

R v *Ellis, Street and Smith*
(1987) 84 Cr App R 235
Court of Appeal

O'CONNOR LJ: . . . All three appellants accepted that they participated in importing large quantities of cannabis into this country concealed in secret compartments in motor cars. They were indicted in the ordinary form for being knowingly concerned in the fraudulent evasion of the prohibition on the importation of a controlled drug contrary to section 170(2) of the Customs and Excise Management Act 1979. The particulars of offence were that on the relevant dates they were in relation to a class B controlled drug, namely in the case of Ellis and Street 29.3 kilogrammes and in the case of Smith 24.85 kilogrammes of cannabis, 'knowingly concerned in the fraudulent evasion of the prohibition on importation imposed by section 3(1) of the Misuse of Drugs Act 1971.'
    In both cases the defendants as they then were pleaded not guilty and at once asked for a ruling as to whether they had a defence in law if the facts were that they knew that they were participating in the importation of prohibited goods but believed that the goods were pornographic goods which they knew to be subject to a prohibition and which were in fact subject to a prohibition.
    . . . '"[K]nowingly" in the section in question is concerned with knowing that a fraudulent evasion of a prohibition in respect of goods is taking place.' It seems to us that it cannot make any difference whether a particular defendant says: 'I don't know what the goods were; I only know they were prohibited' or a defendant says: 'I didn't know what the goods in fact were. I thought that they were some other prohibited goods' . . .

Questions
1. If Saleem picks up a raincoat on his way out of a restaurant, mistakenly believing the raincoat to be his, is this a relevant mistake? Why? See Chapter 11.
2. If a defendant receives stolen video tapes, believing them to be boxes of soap powder, will he be guilty of handling stolen goods? See *R* v *McCullum* (1973) 57 Cr App R 645.

For many years there was doubt as to whether a mistake in this category needed to be a reasonable mistake before it would negate liability.

Director of Public Prosecutions v *Morgan*
[1976] AC 182
House of Lords

LORD HAILSHAM OF ST MARYLEBONE: . . . The appellant Morgan and his three co-defendants, who were all members of the RAF, spent the evening of August 15, 1973, in one another's company. The appellant Morgan was significantly older than the other three, and considerably senior to them in rank. He was, as I have said, married to the alleged victim, but not, it seems at the time habitually sleeping in the same bed. At this time, Mrs Morgan occupied a single bed in the same room as her younger son aged about 11 years, and by the time the appellants arrived at Morgan's house, Mrs Morgan was already in bed and asleep, until she was awoken by their presence.

According to the version of the facts which she gave in evidence, and which was evidently accepted by the jury, she was aroused from her sleep, frog-marched into another room where there was a double bed, held by each of her limbs, arms and legs apart, by the four appellants, while each of the three young appellants in turn had intercourse with her in the presence of the others, during which time the other two committed various lewd acts upon various parts of her body. When each had finished and had left the room, the appellant Morgan completed the series of incidents by having intercourse with her himself.

According to Mrs Morgan she consented to none of this and made her opposition to what was being done very plain indeed. In her evidence to the court, she said that her husband was the first to seize her and pull her out of bed. She then 'yelled' to the little boy who was sleeping with her to call the police, and later, when the elder boy came out on the landing, she called to him also to get the police, and 'screamed.' Her assailants, however, covered her face and pinched her nose, until she begged them to let her breathe. She was held, wrists and feet, 'dragged' to the neighbouring room, put on the bed where the various incidents occurred. At this stage she was overcome by fear of 'being hit.' There was never a time when her body was free from being held. When it was all over she grabbed her coat, ran out of the house, drove straight to the hospital and immediately complained to the staff of having been raped. This last fact was fully borne out by evidence from the hospital.

In their evidence in court, the appellants made various damaging admissions which certainly amounted to some corroboration of all this. They admitted that some degree of struggle took place in the bedroom, that Mrs Morgan made some noise which was forcibly suppressed, and that she was carried out forcibly into the other bedroom, and that her arms and legs were separately held. In addition to this, Mrs Morgan's evidence was far more fully corroborated by a number of statements (each, of course, admissible

only against the maker) which virtually repeated Mrs Morgan's own story but in far greater and more lurid detail. Of course, the appellants repudiated their statements in the witness box, saying that the words were put into their mouths by the police, even though at least one was written out in the hands of the makers of the statement. I think it likely to the extent of moral certainty that the jury accepted that these statements were made as alleged and contained the truth. But I need not rest my opinion upon this, since the undeniable fact is that the jury accepted, after an impeccable summing up and adequate corroboration, that Mrs Morgan was telling the truth in her evidence. I mention all these details simply to show, that if, as I think plain, the jury accepted Mrs Morgan's statement *in substance* there was no possibility whatever of any of the appellants holding any belief whatever, reasonable or otherwise, in their victim's consent to what was being done.

The primary 'defence' was consent. I use the word 'defence' in inverted commas, because, of course, in establishing the crime of rape, the prosecution must exclude consent in order to establish the essential ingredients of the crime. There is no burden at the outset on the accused to raise the issue. Nevertheless, at the close of the prosecution case the accused had a formidable case to answer, and they answered by going into the witness box and swearing to facts which, if accepted, would have meant, not merely that they reasonably believed that Mrs Morgan had consented, but that, after she entered the bedroom where the acts of intercourse took place, she not merely consented but took an active and enthusiastic part in a sexual orgy which might have excited unfavourable comment in the court of Caligula or Nero.

All four defendants explained in the witness box that they had spent the evening together in Wolverhampton, and by the time of the alleged offences had had a good deal to drink. Their original intention had been to find some women in the town, but when this failed, Morgan made the surprising suggestion to the others that they should all return to his home and have sexual intercourse with his wife. According to the three younger appellants (but not according to Morgan who described this part of their story as 'lying') Morgan told them that they must not be surprised if his wife struggled a bit, since she was 'kinky' and this was the only way in which she could get 'turned on.' However this may be, it is clear that Morgan did invite his three companions home in order that they might have sexual intercourse with his wife, and, no doubt, he may well have led them in one way or another to believe that she would consent to their doing so. This however, would only be matter predisposing them to believe that Mrs Morgan consented, and would not in any way establish that, at the time, they believed she did consent whilst they were having intercourse.

. . .

Once one has accepted, what seems to me abundantly clear, that the prohibited act in rape is non-consensual sexual intercourse, and that the guilty state of mind is an intention to commit it, it seems to me to follow as a matter of inexorable logic that there is no room either for a 'defence' of honest belief or mistake, or of a defence of honest and reasonable belief or mistake. Either the prosecution proves that the accused had the requisite intent, or it does not. In the former case it succeeds, and in the latter it fails. Since honest belief clearly negatives intent, the reasonableness or otherwise of that belief can only be evidence for or against the view that the belief and therefore the intent was actually held, and it matters not whether, to quote Bridge J in the passage cited above, 'the definition of a crime includes no specific element beyond the prohibited act.' If the mental element be primarily an intention and not a state of belief comes within his second proposition and not his third. Any other view as for insertion of the word 'reasonable' can only have the effect of saying that a man intends something which he does not.

R v *Kimber*
[1983] 1 WLR 1118
Court of Appeal

LAWTON LJ: . . . The victim was a female patient in a mental hospital. Her mental
disorder had been diagnosed as schizophrenia. She was aged 56. We will refer to her as
'Betty.' Although she was not a defective within the meaning of sections 7 and 45 of the
Sexual Offences Act 1956, as amended by section 127 of the Mental Health Act 1959,
she was suffering from a severe degree of mental disorder. She had been a patient in the
mental hospital since 1957. Her movements and appearance were odd: she made
strange movements with her face and mouth. She tended to give one word answers to
questions. She was usually quiet and withdrawn but could become manic and
aggressive without provocation. Most days she had to be helped to eat and dress. It
must have been obvious to anyone of sound mind meeting her that she was suffering
from a severe degree of mental disorder. She had never been known to take any erotic
interest in men or to respond to sexual stimuli. The hospital doctor in charge of her said
that it was highly unlikely that she would be capable of giving comprehending consent
to sexual advances, but she might agree without understanding the full implications of
what she was agreeing to. Her condition was such that the prosecution did not call her
as a witness.

On August 1, 1981, she was walking by herself in the hospital gardens near the cricket
ground when she was approached by the appellant. He had come to the hospital to visit
a relative who was a patient. A ward sister said in evidence that she saw the appellant
talking to Betty. He had his hands cupped. There were coins in them and he went
through the motions of counting them out. The appellant then nodded in the direction
of a lane and walked down it. Betty followed a pace or so behind. Ten minutes later the
ward sister saw her again. She was naked from the waist down, her dress having been
rolled up to her waist. She was screaming loudly and was so distressed that she had to
be given a tranquilliser injection and put to bed. Her knickers were found later in the
lane. A hospital porter who had been alerted by the ward sister that something
untoward might have happened saw the appellant in the grounds. He stopped him and
asked him if he had been near the cricket ground with the woman. He said he had not.
This he admitted at his trial was a lie. Later the same day he was interviewed by the
police. At first he denied that he had been involved in any incident. Later, according to
the police witnesses, he admitted trying to have sexual intercourse with Betty but said
he had not succeeded. He told them that she had followed him and 'chucked' her
knickers on the ground and that he had interfered with her in a way which clearly
amounted to an indecent assault if it had been done without her consent. He admitted
to them that he knew she was a patient. He was asked whether she had said anything.
He replied: 'No, she did not. She just started mumbling. I couldn't understand that.
She was mumbling all the time really stupid.' Then came these questions and answers:

(Q) You accept that this woman was mentally subnormal? (A) Well I should think so,
the way she was mumbling and that. (Q) Did you ask her to have intercourse with
you? (A) No, I did not. (Q) Why? (A) Silly thing to do isn't it – ask a woman for
intercourse.

The offence of indecent assault is now statutory: see section 14 of the Sexual Offences
Act 1956. The prosecution had to prove that the appellant made an indecent assault on
Betty. As there are no words in the section to indicate that Parliament intended to

exclude mens rea as an element in this offence, it follows that the prosecution had to prove that the appellant intended to commit it. This could not be done without first proving that the appellant intended to assault Betty. In this context assault clearly includes battery. An assault is an act by which the defendant intentionally or recklessly causes the complainant to apprehend immediate, or to sustain, unlawful personal violence: see *R v Venna* [1976] QB 421, 428–429. In this case the appellant by his own admissions did intentionally lay his hands on Betty. That would not, however, have been enough to prove the charge. There had to be evidence that the appellant had intended to do what he did unlawfully. When there is a charge of indecent assault on a woman, the unlawfulness can be proved, as was sought to be done in *R v Donovan* [1934] 2 KB 498, by evidence that the defendant intended to cause bodily harm. In most cases, however, the prosecution tries to prove that the complainant did not consent to what was done. The burden of proving lack of consent rests upon the prosecution: see *R v May* [1912] 3 KB 572, 575, *per* Lord Alverstone CJ. The consequence is that the prosecution has to prove that the defendant intended to lay hands on his victim without her consent. If he did not intend to do this, he is entitled to be found not guilty; and if he did not so intend because . . . he believed she was consenting, the prosecution will have failed to prove the charge. It is the defendant's belief, not the grounds on which it was based, which goes to negative the intent.

In analysing the issue in this way we have followed what was said by the majority in *R v Morgan* [1976] AC 182: see Lord Hailsham of St Marylebone at p. 214F–H and Lord Fraser of Tullybelton at p. 237E–G. If, as we adjudge, the prohibited act in indecent assault is the use of personal violence to a woman without her consent, then the guilty state of mind is the intent to do it without her consent. Then, as in rape at common law, the inexorable logic, to which Lord Hailsham referred in *R v Morgan*, takes over and there is no room either for a 'defence' of honest belief or mistake, or of a 'defence' of honest and reasonable belief or mistake: [1976] AC 182, 214F–H.

Notes and questions

1. In *R v Tolson* (1889) 23 QBD 168, a prosecution for bigamy, the court seemed to proceed on the assumption that for a mistake to excuse, it had to be both honestly entertained and reasonable. *Tolson* was expressly approved by the House of Lords in *Director of Public Prosecutions v Morgan*. Lord Fraser said 'bigamy does not require any intention except the intention to go through a marriage ceremony'. In respect to *mens rea*, the bigamist, if Lord Fraser is correct, is in no way distinguishable from the ordinary bride/groom. Should then bigamy be a crime?
2. What are the arguments for and against requiring that a mistake be reasonable before it is relevant to criminal liability?
3. Can mistake serve as a defence to a crime of strict liability? To a crime whose *mens rea* is *Caldwell* (objective) recklessness?

The courts have experienced some difficulty in determining precisely what is part of the definition of a crime and what is an excusatory defence. Where the defendant has made a mistake it may be vital to determine this issue. Reasonableness of the mistake needs to be shown where the defendant admits that he has committed the *actus reus* with *mens rea* but nevertheless seeks to be excused (see (ii) below). Where a defendant believes facts which would, if true, justify his behaviour, reasonableness is not an issue.

R v Williams (Gladstone)
(1983) 78 Cr App R 276
Court of Appeal

LORD LANE CJ: The facts were somewhat unusual and were as follows. On the day in question the alleged victim, a man called Mason, saw a black youth seizing the handbag belonging to a woman who was shopping. He caught up with the youth and held him, he said with a view to taking him to a nearby police station, but the youth broke free from his grip. Mason caught the youth again and knocked him to the ground, and he then twisted one of the youth's arms behind his back in order to immobilise him and to enable him, Mason, so he said, once again to take the youth to a police station. The youth was struggling and calling for help at this time, and no one disputed that fact.

Upon the scene then came the appellant who had only seen the latter stages of this incident. According to Mason he told the appellant first of all that he was arresting the youth for mugging the lady and secondly, that he, Mason, was a police officer. That was not true. He was asked for his warrant card, which obviously was not forthcoming, and thereupon something of a struggle ensued between Mason on the one hand and the appellant and others on the other hand. In the course of these events Mason sustained injuries to his face, loosened teeth and bleeding gums.

The appellant put forward the following version of events. He said he was returning from work by bus, when he saw Mason dragging the youth along and striking him again and again. He was so concerned about the matter that he rapidly got off the bus and made his way to the scene and asked Mason what on earth he was doing. In short he said that he punched Mason because he thought if he did so he would save the youth from further beating and what he described as torture.

There was no doubt that none of these *dramatis personae* was known to each other beforehand.
. . .

One starts off with the meaning of the word 'assault.' 'Assault' in the context of this case, that is to say using the word as a convenient abbreviation for assault and battery, is an act by which the defendant, intentionally or recklessly, applies unlawful force to the complainant. There are circumstances in which force may be applied to another lawfully. Taking a few examples: first, where the victim consents, as in lawful sports, the application of force to another will, generally speaking, not be unlawful. Secondly, where the defendant is acting in self-defence: the exercise of any necessary and reasonable force to protect himself from unlawful violence is not unlawful. Thirdly, by virtue of section 3 of the Criminal Law Act 1967, a person may use such force as is reasonable in the circumstances in the prevention of crime or in effecting or assisting in the lawful arrest of an offender or suspected offender or persons unlawfully at large. In each of those cases the defendant will be guilty if the jury are sure that first of all he applied force to the person of another, and secondly that he had the necessary mental element to constitute guilt.

The mental element necessary to constitute guilt is the intent to apply unlawful force to the victim. We do not believe that the mental element can be substantiated by simply showing an intent to apply force and no more.

What then is the situation if the defendant is labouring under a mistake of fact as to the circumstances? What if he believes, but believes mistakenly, that the victim is consenting, or that it is necessary to defend himself, or that a crime is being committed which he intends to prevent? He must then be judged against the mistaken facts as he believes them to be. If judged against those facts or circumstances the prosecution fail to establish his guilt, then he is entitled to be acquitted.

The next question is, does it make any difference if the mistake of the defendant was one which, viewed objectively by a reasonable onlooker, was an unreasonable mistake? In other words should the jury be directed as follows: 'Even if the defendant may have genuinely believed that what he was doing to the victim was either with the victim's consent or in reasonable self-defence or to prevent the commission of crime, as the case may be, nevertheless if you, the jury, come to the conclusion that the mistaken belief was unreasonable, that is to say that the defendant as a reasonable man should have realised his mistake, then you should convict him.'

. . . The reasonableness or unreasonableness of the defendant's belief is material to the question of whether the belief was held by the defendant at all. If the belief was in fact held, its unreasonableness, so far as guilt or innocence is concerned, is neither here nor there. It is irrelevant. Were it otherwise, the defendant would be convicted because he was negligent in failing to recognise that the victim was not consenting or that a crime was not being committed and so on. In other words the jury should be directed first of all that the prosecution have the burden or duty of proving the unlawfulness of the defendant's actions; secondly, if the defendant may have been labouring under a mistake as to the facts, he must be judged according to his mistaken view of the facts; thirdly, that is so whether the mistake was, on an objective view, a reasonable mistake or not.

In a case of self-defence, where self-defence or the prevention of crime is concerned, if the jury came to the conclusion that the defendant believed, or may have believed, that he was being attacked or that a crime was being committed, and that force was necessary to protect himself or to prevent the crime, then the prosecution have not proved their case. If however the defendant's alleged belief was mistaken and if the mistake was an unreasonable one, that may be a powerful reason for coming to the conclusion that the belief was not honestly held and should be rejected.

Even if the jury come to the conclusion that the mistake was an unreasonable one, if the defendant may genuinely have been labouring under it, he is entitled to rely upon it.

(ii)   Mistake as to a defence
Where the defendant puts forward an excuse for his behaviour, any mistake as to the existence of factors making that excuse available will have to be reasonable.

R v Graham
(1982) 74 Cr App R 235
Court of Appeal

LORD LANE CJ: . . . The facts of the case were as follows. The appellant was the victim's husband. He is a practising homosexual. His wife was aware of this and indeed at the material time they were living in a bizarre *ménage à trois* with another homosexual called King. They were living in the flat above two other homosexuals, named Gillis and Minter, with whom the appellant occasionally had sexual relations. The appellant and King were jointly charged with the murder. King pleaded guilty. The appellant admitted playing an active part in the events leading to the killing and admitted seeking to conceal the killing after it had happened.

His defence was twofold. First, that he lacked the necessary intent, and he drew attention particularly to the drink and drugs he had taken; and, secondly, that whatever his intentional actions may have been, they were performed under duress because of his fear of King.

. . . We think that there should be an objective element in the requirements of the defence so that in the final event it will be for the jury to determine whether the threat was one which the defendant in question could not reasonably have been expected to resist. This will allow the jury to take into account the nature of the offence committed, its relationship to the threats which the defendant believed to exist, the threats themselves and the circumstances in which they were made, and the personal characteristics of the defendant. The last consideration is, we feel, a most important one. Threats directed against the weak, immature or disabled person, may well be much more compelling than the same threats directed against a normal healthy person.'

As a matter of public policy, it seems to us essential to limit the defence of duress by means of an objective criterion formulated in terms of reasonableness. Consistency of approach in defences to criminal liability is obviously desirable. Provocation and duress are analogous. In provocation the words or actions of one person break the self-control of another. In duress the words or actions of one person break the will of another. The law requires a defendant to have the self-control reasonably to be expected of the ordinary citizen in his situation. It should likewise require him to have the steadfastness reasonably to be expected of the ordinary citizen in his situation. So too with self-defence, in which the law permits the use of no more force than is reasonable in the circumstances. And, in general, if a mistake is to excuse what would otherwise be criminal, the mistake must be a reasonable one.

Notes and questions
1. In *R* v *Howe* [1987] AC 417, the House of Lords endorsed the view expressed in *Graham* concerning the requirement of reasonableness. The Law Commission in its Draft Criminal Code would remove the requirement of reasonableness. Which do you consider to be the better approach? See also D. W. Elliott, 'Necessity, duress and self-defence' [1989] Crim LR 611.
2. The more reasonable the mistake, the more likely the defendant is to persuade the jury that his mistake was genuine. Are the judges afraid to trust juries with the determination of whether there was a genuine mistake?

(iii)   The relationship between mistake and other defences
Where a mistake is made because of insanity or diminished responsibility, the tests for the availability of those defences will apply. The issue of reasonableness is subsumed by the determination of whether the defendant knew the nature and quality of his act, or whether his mental condition substantially impaired his responsibility for killing (see below, p. 402). In cases where the defendant puts forward an excusatory defence the reasonableness requirement will apply. Therefore a drunken mistake will not avail a defendant as it is by definition unreasonable (see *Graham*, above).

The greatest difficulty has been encountered where the defendant has made a drunken mistake as to facts which would have justified his actions if the facts had been as he believed them to be. Compare the following cases:

R v *O'Grady*
[1987] 3 WLR 321
Court of Appeal

The appellant, who was intoxicated, killed a man and stated to the police, 'If I had not hit him I would be dead myself.' He was tried on a count charging murder. The jury were directed that, if the appellant mistakenly believed he was under attack, he was entitled to defend himself but was not entitled to go beyond what was reasonable.

LORD LANE CJ: . . . How should the jury be invited to approach the problem? One starts with the decision of this court in *R v Williams (Gladstone)* (1983) 78 Cr App R 276, namely, that where the defendant might have been labouring under a mistake as to the facts he must be judged according to that mistaken view, whether the mistake was reasonable or not. It is then for the jury to decide whether the defendant's reaction to the threat, real or imaginary, was a reasonable one. The court was not in that case considering what the situation might be where the mistake was due to voluntary intoxication by alcohol or some other drug.

We have come to the conclusion that where the jury are satisfied that the defendant was mistaken in his belief that any force or the force which he in fact used was necessary to defend himself and are further satisfied that the mistake was caused by voluntarily induced intoxication, the defence must fail. We do not consider that any distinction should be drawn on this aspect of the matter between offences involving what is called specific intent, such as murder, and offences of so called basic intent, such as manslaughter. Quite apart from the problem of directing a jury in a case such as the present where manslaughter is an alternative verdict to murder, the question of mistake can and ought to be considered separately from the question of intent. A sober man who mistakenly believes he is in danger of immediate death at the hands of an attacker is entitled to be acquitted of both murder and manslaughter if his reaction in killing his supposed assailant was a reasonable one. What his intent may have been seems to us to be irrelevant to the problem of self-defence or no.

Jaggard v Dickinson
[1980] 3 All ER 716
Queen's Bench Division

MUSTILL J: . . . The facts set out in the case are short but striking. On the evening of 12th October 1978 the appellant had been drinking. At 10.45 pm she engaged a taxi to take her to 67 Carnach Green, South Ockendon, a house occupied by Mr R F Heyfron, a gentleman with whom she had a relationship such that, in the words of the magistrates, she had his consent at any time to treat his property as if it was her own. Alighting from the taxi, she entered the garden but was asked to leave by a Mrs Raven who was a stranger to her. Persisting, she broke the glass in the hallway of the house. She then went to the back door where she broke another window and gained entry to the house, damaging a net curtain in the process. At some time thereafter, in circumstances not described by the magistrates, it became clear that the house was not 67 Carnach Green but 35 Carnach Green, a house of identical outward appearance, occupied by Mrs Raven. The magistrates have found that the appellant did believe that she was breaking into the property of Mr Heyfron but that this mistake was induced by a state of self-induced intoxication.

. . . If the basis of the decision in *Majewski* [1976] 2 WLR 623 had been that drunkenness does not prevent a person from having an intent or being reckless, then there would be grounds for saying that it should equally be left out of account when deciding on his state of belief. But this is not in our view what *Majewski* decided. The House of Lords did not conclude that intoxication was irrelevant to the fact of the defendant's state of mind, but rather that, whatever might have been his actual state of mind, he should for reasons of policy be precluded from relying on any alteration in that state brought about by self-induced intoxication. The same considerations of policy apply to the intent or recklessness which is the mens rea of the offence created by s. 1(1) [Criminal Damage Act 1971] and that offence is accordingly regarded as one of basic intent (see *R v Stephenson* [1979] 1 QB 695). It is indeed essential that this should be so, for drink so often plays a part in offences of criminal damage, and to admit drunkenness as a potential means of escaping liability would provide much too ready a means of avoiding conviction. But these considerations do not apply to a case where Parliament has specifically required the court to consider the defendant's actual state of belief, not the state of belief which ought to have existed. This seems to us to show that the court is required by s. 5(3) to focus on the existence of the belief, not its intellectual soundness; and a belief can be just as much honestly held if it is induced by intoxication as if it stems from stupidity, forgetfulness or inattention.

It was, however, urged that we could not properly read s. 5(2) in isolation from s. 1(1), which forms the context of the words 'without lawful excuse' partially defined by s. 5(2). Once the words are put in context, so it is maintained, it can be seen that the law must treat drunkenness in the same way in relation to lawful excuse (and hence belief) as it does to intention and recklessness, for they are all part of the mens rea of the offence. To fragment the mens rea, so as to treat one part of it as affected by drunkenness in one way and the remainder as affected in a different way, would make the law impossibly complicated to enforce.

If it had been necessary to decide whether, for all purposes, the mens rea of an offence under s. 1(1) extends as far as an intent (or recklessness) as to the existence of a lawful excuse, I should have wished to consider the observations of James LJ, delivering the judgment of the Court of Appeal in *R v Smith* [1974] 1 All ER 632 at 636, [1974] QB 354 at 360. I do not however find it necessary to reach a conclusion on this matter and will only say that I am not at present convinced that, when these observations are read in the context of the judgment as a whole, they have the meaning which the respondent has sought to put on them. In my view, however, the answer to the argument lies in the fact that any distinctions which have to be drawn as to the relevance of drunkenness to the two subsections arises from the scheme of the 1971 Act itself. No doubt the mens rea is in general indivisible, with no distinction being possible as regards the effect of drunkenness. But Parliament has specifically isolated one subjective element, in the shape of honest belief, and has given it separate treatment and its own special gloss in s. 5(3). This being so, there is nothing objectionable in giving it special treatment as regards drunkenness, in accordance with the natural meaning of its words.

In these circumstances, I would hold that the magistrates were in error when they decided that the defence furnished to the appellant by s. 5(2) was lost because she was drunk at the time. I would therefore allow the appeal.

Questions

1. Is *O'Grady* reconcilable with *Williams* (above)? In *O'Grady*, Lord Lane CJ said that mistake and intent ought to be considered separately. Is this possible?
2. Derek, when drunk, shoots Percy. He is charged with murder. What is the situation if he mistakenly believes (a) that Percy was a bear, (b) that Percy was attacking him violently, (c) that Percy was an alien attacking him?

(iv) Ignorance of law
There is an irrebuttable presumption that a citizen is aware of the provisions of the law.

R v *Bailey*
(1800) Russ & Ry 1
Crown Cases Reserved

It was then insisted that the prisoner could not be found guilty of the offence with which he was charged, because the Act of the 39 Geo. III. c. 37, upon which (together with the statute relating to maliciously shooting (9 Geo. I. c. 22; Black Act) the prisoner was indicted at this Admiralty Sessions, and which Act of the 39 Geo. III. is entitled, 'An Act for amending certain defects in the law respecting offences committed on the high seas,' only received the royal assent on the 10th of May, 1799, and the fact charged in the indictment happened on the 27th of June, in the same year, when the prisoner could not know that any such Act existed (his ship, the 'Langley,' being at that time upon the coast of Africa).

Lord Eldon told the jury that he was of opinion that he was, in strict law, guilty within the statutes, taken together, if the facts laid were proved, though he could not then know that the Act of the 39 Geo. III. c. 37 had passed, and that his ignorance of that fact could in no otherwise affect the case, than that it might be the means of recommending him to a merciful consideration elsewhere should he be found guilty.

Note
Ignorance of the law, it is said, is no excuse. The ignorance referred to relates to the law which the accused is alleged to have violated. A mistake as to a collateral civil law, on the other hand, may serve to negate *mens rea*.

R v *Smith (David)*
[1974] QB 354
Court of Appeal

JAMES LJ: . . . The question of law in this appeal arises in this way. In 1970 the appellant became the tenant of a ground-floor flat at 209, Freemason's Road, E.16. The letting included a conservatory. In the conservatory the appellant and his brother, who lived with him, installed some electric wiring for use with stereo equipment. Also, with the landlord's permission, they put up roofing material and asbestos wall panels and laid floor boards. There is no dispute that the roofing, wall panels and floor boards became part of the house and, in law, the property of the landlord. Then in 1972 the appellant gave notice to quit and asked the landlord to allow the appellant's brother to remain as tenant of the flat. On September 18, 1972, the landlord informed the appellant that his brother could not remain. On the next day the appellant damaged the roofing, wall panels and floorboards he had installed in order – according to the appellant and his brother – to gain access to and remove the wiring. The extent of the damage was £130. When interviewed by the police, the appellant said: 'Look, how can I be done for smashing my own property. I put the flooring and that in, so if I want to pull it down it's a matter for me.'

. . . Section 1 of the Criminal Damage Act 1971 reads:

(1) A person who without lawful excuse destroys or damages any property belonging to another intending to destroy or damage any such property or being reckless as to whether any such property would be destroyed or damaged, shall be guilty of an offence.

. . . Construing the language of section 1(1) we have no doubt that the actus reus is 'destroying or damaging any property belonging to another.' It is not possible to exclude the words 'belonging to another' which describes the 'property.' Applying the ordinary principles of mens rea, the intention and recklessness and the absence of lawful excuse required to constitute the offence have reference to property belonging to another. It follows that in our judgment no offence is committed under this section if a person destroys or causes damage to property belonging to another if he does so in the honest though mistaken belief that the property is his own, and provided that the belief is honestly held it is irrelevant to consider whether or not it is a justifiable belief.

Secretary of State for Trade and Industry v Hart
[1982] 1 WLR 481
Queen's Bench Division

The defendant, who was a director and secretary of one company and a director of another, audited the annual accounts for the companies for the year ending March 31, 1979. Informations were preferred against him alleging that he had acted as an auditor when he knew that he was disqualified from so acting by reason of the offices that he held within the companies, contrary to section 161(2) of the Companies Act 1948 and section 13 of the Companies Act 1976. The magistrate accepted that the defendant was unaware of the offence and dismissed the informations on the ground that knowledge of the disqualification was a necessary ingredient of an offence under section 13(5).
    On appeal by the prosecutor: —
    Held, dismissing the appeal, that, giving the words of section 13(5) and (6) their ordinary meaning, 'knowledge' in subsection (5) had to be construed as knowledge not only of the relevant facts that constituted the offence but that in consequence of those facts a director was disqualified under the subsection from auditing the companies' accounts; that, accordingly, since the defendant had no knowledge of the statutory provisions, he had been properly acquitted of the offence . . ..

Questions
1. In view of the complexity of the law in modern times, is there any longer a place for the presumption that all persons are aware of the criminal law? What functions are served by the general rule?
2. What if before proceeding the defendant consults a solicitor who advises her that the proposed course of action is not illegal? It turns out that the solicitor is mistaken and criminal charges are brought against the defendant. Should the good faith reliance on the advice of the solicitor be a defence? The courts have said not. Why? What more can an ordinary citizen do (be expected to do)?

B   Intoxication

(i)   Rationale
Intoxication, whether the result of alcohol or drugs, can impair a person's judgment, perception and self-control. It can cause persons to commit crimes which they would never have considered committing while sober. In these situations, should the law take the intoxication into account? Should intoxication be a defence? Should it be a factor to be taken into account in sentencing?

Over the years the courts have manifested an ambivalent attitude to intoxication. On the one hand, they recognise that in theory there should be a valid defence available to the defendant whose drunken state prevents him from formulating the *mens rea* of the crime charged. In order to secure a conviction, a prosecutor must establish *mens rea* by proof beyond a reasonable doubt. The drunk defendant may well lack *mens rea*. The reason why he lacked *mens rea* should be irrelevant. On the other hand, reducing oneself to a drunken state is not the type of conduct that the legal system wants to be condoning or encouraging. Drunkenness serves little socially useful purpose, and often leads to significant social harm.

(ii)   Voluntary intoxication
The courts have distinguished between voluntary and involuntary intoxication. Voluntary intoxication is not *per se* a defence. It may, however, be relevant evidence as to whether the defendant had the requisite *mens rea* for the offence. The leading case is *Majewski*.

Director of Public Prosecutions v Majewski
[1976] 2 WLR 623
House of Lords

LORD ELWYN-JONES LC: . . . . In view of the conclusion to which I have come that the appeal should be dismissed and of the questions of law which arise in the case, it is desirable that I should refer in some detail to the facts, which were largely undisputed. During the evening of February 19, 1973, the appellant and his friend, Leonard Stace, who had also taken drugs and drink, went to the Bull public house in Basildon. The appellant obtained a drink and sat down in the lounge bar at a table by the door. Stace became involved in a disturbance. Glasses were broken. The landlord asked Stace to leave and escorted him to the door. As he did so, Stace called to the appellant: 'He's putting me out.' The appellant got up and prevented the landlord from getting Stace out and abused him. The landlord told them both to go. They refused. The appellant butted the landlord in the face and bruised it, and punched a customer. The customers in the bar and the landlord forced the two out through the bar doors. They re-entered by forcing the outer door, a glass panel of which was broken by Stace. The appellant punched the landlord and pulled a piece of broken glass from the frame and started swinging it at the landlord and a customer, cutting the landlord slightly on his arm. The appellant then burst through the inner door of the bar with such force that he fell on the floor. The landlord held him there until the police arrived. The appellant was violent and abusive and spat in the landlord's face. When the police came, a fierce struggle took place to get him out. He shouted at the police: 'You pigs, I'll kill you all, you f. . . . pigs, you bastards,' P.C. Barkway said the appellant looked at him and kicked him deliberately.

P.C. Bird was kicked on the shins. During the struggle to get the appellant into the police car he said to P.C. Barrett: 'You bastard, I'll get you' and then kicked him.

The appellant was placed in the cells of Basildon police station. The next morning Police Inspector Dickinson heard banging and saw the appellant in his cell trying to remove a metal flap under the bed platform. The inspector asked him, what he was doing. According to the inspector he said: 'Come in here and I will stripe you with this.

I'll break your neck.' The inspector and other officers entered the cell. Before he was restrained, he struck the inspector with the handcuffs on his wrists. Dr Mitchell arrived and gave him an injection.

Cross-examined as to the appellant's condition that evening the publican said he seemed to have gone berserk, his eyes were a bit glazed and protruding. A customer said he was 'glarey-eyed,' and went 'berserk' when the publican asked Stace to leave. He was screaming and shouting. A policeman said he was in a fearful temper.

The appellant gave evidence and said than on Saturday, February 17, 1973, he bought, not on prescription, about 40 Dexadrine tablets ('speeds') and early on Sunday morning consumed about half of them. That gave him plenty of energy until he 'started coming down.' He did not sleep throughout Sunday. On Monday evening at about 6 p.m. he acquired a bottle full of sodium nembutal tablets which he said were tranquillisers – 'downers,' 'barbs' and took about eight of them at about 6.30.

He and his friends then went to the Bull. He said he could remember nothing of what took place there save for a flash of recollection of Stace kicking a window. All he recollected of the police cell was asking the police to remove his handcuffs and then being injected.

In cross-examination he admitted he had been taking amphetamines and barbiturates, not on prescription, for two years, in large quantities. On occasions he drank barley wine or Scotch. He had sometimes 'gone paranoid.' This was the first time he had 'completely blanked out.'

Dr Bird called for the defence, said that the appellant had been treated for drug addiction since November 1971. There was no history in his case of psychiatric disorder or diagnosable mental illness, but the appellant had a personality disorder. Dr Bird said that barbiturates and alcohol are known to potentiate each other and to produce rapid intoxication and affect a person's awareness of what was going on. . . .

What then is the mental element required in our law to be established in assault? This question has been most helpfully answered in the speech of Lord Simon of Glaisdale in *R v Morgan* [1976] AC 182, 216:

By 'crimes of basic intent' I mean those crimes whose definition expresses (or, more often, implies) a mens rea which does not go beyond the actus reus. The actus reus generally consists of an act and some consequence. The consequence may be very closely connected with the act or more remotely connected with it: but with a crime of basic intent the mens rea does not extend beyond the act and its consequence, however, remote, as defined in the actus reus. I take assault as an example of a crime of basic intent where the consequence is very closely connected with the act. The actus reus of assault is an act which causes another person to apprehend immediate and unlawful violence. The mens rea corresponds exactly. The prosecution must prove that the accused foresaw that his act would probably cause another person to have apprehension of immediate and unlawful violence, or would possibly have that consequence, such being the purpose of the act, or that he was reckless as to whether or not his act caused such apprehension. This foresight (the term of art is 'intention') or recklessness is the mens rea in assault.

How does the fact of self-induced intoxication fit into that analysis? If a man consciously and deliberately takes alcohol and drugs not on medical prescription, but in order to escape from reality, to go 'on a trip', to become hallucinated, whatever the description may be and thereby disables himself from taking the care he might otherwise take and as a result by his subsequent actions causes injury to another – does our criminal law enable him to say that because he did not know what he was doing he lacked both intention and recklessness and accordingly is entitled to an acquittal?

. . . The authority which for the last half century has been relied upon in this context has been the speech of the Earl of Birkenhead LC in *Director of Public Prosecutions* v *Beard* [1920] AC 479, who stated, at p. 494:

Under the law of England as it prevailed until early in the 19th century voluntary drunkenness was never an excuse for criminal misconduct; and indeed the classic authorities broadly assert that voluntary drunkenness must be considered rather an aggravation than a defence. This view was in terms based upon the principle that a man who by his own voluntary act debauches and destroys his will power shall be no better situated in regard to criminal acts than a sober man.

Lord Birkenhead LC made a historical survey of the way the common law from the 16th century on dealt with the effect of self-induced intoxication upon criminal responsibility. This indicates how, from 1819 on, the judges began to mitigate the severity of the attitude of the common law in such cases as murder and serious violent crime when the penalties of death or transportation applied or where there was likely to be sympathy for the accused, as in attempted suicide. Lord Birkenhead LC concluded, at p. 499, that (except in cases where insanity is pleaded) the decisions he cited

establish that where a specific intent is an essential element in the offence, evidence of a state of drunkenness rendering the accused incapable of forming such an intent should be taken into consideration in order to determine whether he had in fact formed the intent necessary to constitute the particular crime. If he was so drunk that he was incapable of forming the intent required he could not be convicted of a crime which was committed only if the intent was proved. . . . In a charge of murder based upon intention to kill or to do grievous bodily harm, if the jury are satisfied that the accused was, by reason of his drunken condition, incapable of forming the intent to kill or to do grievous bodily harm . . . he cannot be convicted of murder. But nevertheless unlawful homicide has been committed by the accused, and consequently he is guilty of unlawful homicide without malice aforethought, and that is manslaughter: *per* Stephen J in *R* v *Doherty* (1887) 16 Cox CC 306, 307.

He concludes the passage:

the law is plain beyond all question that in cases falling short of insanity a condition of drunkenness at the time of committing an offence causing death can only, when it is available at all, have the effect of reducing the crime from murder to manslaughter.

From this it seemed clear – and this is the interpretation which the judges have placed upon the decision during the ensuing half century – that it is only in the limited class of cases requiring proof of specific intent that drunkenness can exculpate. Otherwise in no case can it exempt completely from criminal liability.
. . .

I do not for my part regard that general principle as either unethical or contrary to the principles of natural justice. If a man of his own volition takes a substance which causes him to cast off the restraints of reason and conscience, no wrong is done to him by holding him answerable criminally for any injury he may do while in that condition. His course of conduct in reducing himself by drugs and drink to that condition in my view supplies the evidence of mens rea, of guilty mind certainly sufficient for crimes of basic intent. It is a reckless course of conduct and recklessness is enough to constitute the necessary mens rea in assault cases; see *R* v *Venna* [1975] 3 WLR 737 *per* James LJ at p. 743. The drunkenness is itself an intrinsic, an integral part of the crime, the other part being the evidence of the unlawful use of force against the victim. Together they add up to criminal recklessness. . . .

Notes and questions

1. What is the difference between specific and basic intent? Is it possible to predict which crimes will be deemed to be ones of basic intent before an authoritative decision is actually handed down?

2. Why does the House of Lords distinguish between basic and specific intent? Is it because self-induced intoxication is itself a reckless act which will satisfy the recklessness requirement of a crime of basic intent? See also *R* v *Caldwell* [1982] AC 341 (Chapter 3). If self-induced intoxication is itself the *mens rea*, it cannot be the basis for arguing that the defendant lacked *mens rea*. Indeed, a defendant would be ill-advised to raise intoxication when charged with a crime of basic intent, for by doing so he in effect concedes *mens rea*.

3. In what sense is it accurate to say that the person who voluntarily becomes intoxicated is reckless? Most persons who get drunk simply wind up making fools of themselves, and eventually passing out. Is such an individual reckless in not foreseeing that he or she would become violent or dangerous, particularly if such a reaction had never occurred previously? Or is the court's point that a *reasonable person* would have appreciated before taking the first drink that there was a risk of becoming drunk and, that while drunk, engaging in antisocial activity of a criminal sort? If so, is the court saying that the recklessness in deciding to drink, which may occur long before the crime charged is committed, will satisfy the *mens rea* for that crime? Are there then not both 'concurrence' and 'transferred intent' issues buried within *DPP* v *Majewski*? Does the court adequately address these issues?

4. Does it make more sense to explain the disallowance of a defence based on voluntary intoxication as simply a policy decision that persons who get drunk take the risk that the alcohol may impair their judgment, lead to a loss of self-control, and cause them to do something which they might not have done if sober; and if that happens, and if what they do would be a crime if *mens rea* could be proved, they will not be allowed to use their intoxication as a defence? Whatever social utility is gained from drinking is not sufficient for the law to excuse the antisocial criminal acts which may follow. If that is the reasoning, as several of the Lords seem to imply at various points in *DPP* v *Majewski*, then does the distinction between crimes of basic and specific intent make any sense? In the Draft Criminal Code Bill 1989, the distinction is abandoned.

5. Note that the fact that intoxication *may* serve as the basis for a defence to a crime of specific intent does not mean that it will so serve. The jury may conclude that, notwithstanding the intoxication, the defendant had the requisite *mens rea*. Moreover, even if the jury conclude that the defendant lacked specific intent because of intoxication, it does not mean that the defendant will escape punishment altogether. If, for example, the defendant is acquitted of murder (a specific intent crime) he may still be found guilty of manslaughter (a basic intent crime).

(iii)   Involuntary intoxication

If the rationale for imposing criminal liability on the person who *voluntarily* becomes intoxicated is in part that he is responsible for his predicament, the same cannot be said of the person who is *involuntarily* intoxicated. Nor can it be maintained that such a person assumed the risks associated with becoming drunk. Involuntary intoxication can occur when someone is given a drink containing alcohol or drugs but not told of that fact. Whether involuntary intoxication is a defence was authoritatively settled in the following case:

R v Kingston
(1993) *The Times*, 10 May 1993
Court of Appeal

The long standing question whether involuntary intoxication was an answer to a criminal charge was answered affirmatively by the Court of Appeal on turning to first principles, including *Hale's Pleas of the Crown* (1685) and *Pearson's Case* ((1835) 2 Lew CC 144), which was extraordinarily the last word on the subject in the reported cases.

Lord Taylor of Gosforth, Lord Chief Justice, so stated in delivering the reserved judgment of the court, allowing an appeal by Barry Kingston, aged 48, of Rottingdean, against conviction at Lewes Crown Court (Mr Justice Potts and a jury) by a majority of 10 to 2 of indecent assault on a male person, for which he was sentenced to five years imprisonment.

. . .

The Lord Chief Justice said that the appellant was a man with admitted paedophiliac homosexual tendencies. A man named Kevin Penn, who evidently had similar tendencies, arranged to blackmail the appellant by photographing and audio-taping him in a compromising situation with a boy.

Penn lured a boy aged 15 to his flat where he gave the boy what seemed an innocuous drink and some cannabis. The boy fell asleep on the bed and remembered nothing until he woke next morning.

While the boy was in that state Penn invited the appellant to come to his flat and after some conversation took him into the bedroom where he invited the appellant to abuse the boy sexually.

The appellant did so and was photographed and taped doing it. His evidence was that he had seen the boy lying on the bed but had no recollection of any other events that night and had woken in his own home the next morning.

When Penn was arrested, two sedative drugs, diazepam (valium) and triazolam, and an empty box which had contained a third type of sedative drug were found in his flat. It was the prosecution's case that Penn had laced the boy's drink with such a drug.

Although the appellant was not able to say for sure in evidence whether he had had anything to drink before going to the bedroom, he sometimes drank coffee at Penn's flat and the tape itself contained a passage in which the appellant had said 'I don't know why, am I falling asleep?' and 'Have you put something in my coffee?'

The two men were indicted jointly for indecent assault on the boy. On re-arraignment Penn pleaded guilty to indecent assault and was convicted of causing a stupefying drug to be taken.

The appellant contested the indecent assault count.

The appellant had committed the *actus reus* of an indecent assault on the boy, even though he had been in some measure entrapped into doing so.

At the outset of the trial, Mr Taylor advanced to the judge the question whether if the jury found the appellant assaulted the boy pursuant to an intent induced by the influence of drugs administered to him secretly by Kevin Penn, it was open to them to find the appellant not guilty.

The judge indicated a provisional view that he would answer 'No' to that question and directed the jury that a drugged intent was still an intent.

By their verdict the jury found that, drugged or not, the appellant had been capable of forming and had formed the necessary intent.

Mr Taylor could succeed on his first ground of appeal only if he could establish that that question should have been answered affirmatively and the jury directed accordingly.

In approaching the question their Lordships accepted that there was evidence from which it was possible to infer that Penn had administered a drug to the appellant without his knowledge.

The classic statement of principle was to be found in *Hale's Pleas of the Crown* (I, 31) contrasting offenders who were demented in conduct or in mind alone and those who were demented by drunkenness and equally deprived of the use of reason.

The common justice of *Hale's* principle appeared briefly and vividly in *Pearson's Case* ((1835) 2 Lew CC 144), tried by Mr Justice Park at Carlisle Assizes, where Pearson's defence to a charge of murdering his wife by beating her to death was that he was drunk. Mr Justice Park was briefly reported as ruling: 'Voluntary drunkenness is no excuse for crime. If a party be made drunk by stratagem, or the fraud of another, he is not responsible.'

From the report it was not apparent whether Pearson was claiming his drunkenness was involuntary or, therefore, whether the second remark was *obiter*. But, extraordinarily, it was effectively the last word on the subject in the reported authorities.

However, the purpose of the criminal law was to inhibit, by proscription and by penal sanction, anti-social acts which individuals might otherwise commit. Its unspoken premise was that people might have tendencies and impulses to do those things which were considered sufficiently objectionable to be forbidden.

Having paedophilic inclinations and desires was not proscribed; putting them into practice was.

If the sole reason why the threshold between the two had been crossed was or might have been removed by the clandestine act of a third party, the purposes of the criminal law were not served by nevertheless holding that the person performing the act was guilty of an offence.

A man was not responsible for a condition produced 'by stratagem or the fraud of another'

If, therefore, drink or a drug surreptitiously administered, caused a person to lose his self-control and for that reason to form an intent which he would not otherwise have formed, it was consistent with principle that the law should exculpate him because the operative fault was not his.

The law permitted a finding that the intent formed was not a criminal intent or, in other words, that the involuntary intoxication negatived the *mens rea*.

There had to be evidence capable of giving rise to the defence of involuntary intoxication before a judge was obliged to leave the issue to the jury. However, once there was an evidential foundation for the defence, the burden was on the Crown to prove that the relevant intent was formed and that, notwithstanding the evidence relied on by the defence, it was a criminal intent.

By answering the first of the questions put to him at the beginning of the trial in the negative, the judge might have inhibited a sufficient ventilation of that issue at a later stage. Further, by summing up as he had, the judge effectively withdrew the issue from the jury.

In their Lordships' judgment that amounted to a material misdirection and their Lordships would not think it appropriate to apply the proviso to section 2 of the Criminal Appeal Act 1968. The conviction had to be quashed.

The appeal was allowed and the appellant discharged.

Questions
1. Does the result in *Kingston* turn on whether the crime involved was one of basic or specific intent? If your answer is, 'no', why does this distinction not matter in the context of involuntary intoxication? Would the result have been the same is the crime charged was one of strict liability?
2. *Kingston* involved a situation where the defendant was unaware that drugs had been administered to him. What if the defendant is aware that he is taking drugs, but is unaware of the effect that the drugs will have?

R v Hardie
[1984] 3 All ER 848
Court of Appeal

PARKER LJ: Shortly after 9.15 p.m. on 2 January 1982 fire broke out in a wardrobe in the bedroom of the ground-floor flat at 55 Bassingham Road, London SW 10. At that time there were in the flat the appellant, Mrs Jeanette Hardie, with whom the appellant had been living at the premises since May 1974 and who had changed her name to Hardie by deed poll in 1976, and her daughter Tonia. The upstairs flat was occupied by a Mrs Young.

Shortly before 2 January the appellant's relationship with Mrs Hardie had broken down and she had insisted that he must leave. He did not wish to do so, but on the morning of 2 January he packed a suitcase. At about lunchtime the appellant found two bottles of tablets in a cabinet. One contained valium which Mrs Hardie had had in 1974 and the other some tablets to assist urination.

The appellant's evidence in regard to this was that he had never taken valium before, that he took one at about 12 noon to calm him down, for he was in a distressed state, that it did not have much effect, that he and Mrs Hardie had then gone shopping, that he had taken two more in front of her and she had said, 'Take as many as you like, they are old stock and will do you no harm', that he had taken two more shortly afterwards, that he may have taken two of the other tablets also, and that shortly thereafter on return to the house he had fallen into a deep sleep and could thereafter remember only periods.

He was in fact collected from the flat by his mother and remained with her until returning to the flat again at 9.15 p.m. It was not disputed that he must have started the fire, for he was alone in the bedroom when it started. Having started it, he emerged, returned to the sitting room where were Mrs Hardie and Tonia and stayed there. Shortly afterwards Mrs Hardie heard sounds from the bedroom, went there and found smoke and flames coming from the wardrobe. There was evidence that before, at the time of and after the fire the appellant was exhibiting signs of intoxication and that such signs might have resulted from the taking of valium some hours earlier.

The defence was that the appellant was so affected by the valium that he could remember nothing about the fire and had not the necessary mens rea to constitute either of the offences charged. On the basis no doubt of *DPP v Majewski* [1976] 2 All ER 142, [1977] AC 443 and *R v Caldwell* [1981] 1 All ER, [1982] AC 341, the judge directed the jury in effect that, as the valium was voluntarily self-administered, it was irrelevant as a defence and its effects could not negative mens rea. The first point taken on appeal was that this was a misdirection.
. . .
In the present instance the defence was that the valium was taken for the purpose of calming the nerves only, that it was old stock and that the appellant was told it would

do him no harm. There was no evidence that it was known to the appellant or even generally known that the taking of valium in the quantity taken would be liable to render a person aggressive or incapable of appreciating risks to others or have other side effects such that its self-administration would itself have an element of recklessness. It is true that valium is a drug and it is true that it was taken deliberately and not taken on medical prescription, but the drug is, in our view, wholly different in kind from drugs which are liable to cause unpredictability or aggressiveness. It may well be that the taking of a sedative or soporific drug will, in certain circumstances, be no answer, for example in a case of reckless driving, but if the effect of a drug is merely soporific or sedative the taking of it, even in some excessive quantity, cannot in the ordinary way raise a *conclusive* presumption against the admission of proof of intoxication for the purpose of disproving mens rea in ordinary crimes, such as would be the case with alcoholic intoxication or incapacity or automatism resulting from the self-administration of dangerous drugs.

In the present case the jury should not, in our judgment, have been directed to disregard any incapacity which resulted or might have resulted from the taking of valium. They should have been directed that if they came to the conclusion that, as a result of the valium, the appellant was, at the time, unable to appreciate the risks to property and persons from his actions they should then consider whether the taking of the valium was itself reckless. We are unable to say what would have been the appropriate direction with regard to the elements of recklessness in this case for we have not seen all the relevant evidence, nor are we able to suggest a model direction, for circumstances will vary infinitely and model directions can sometimes lead to more rather than less confusion. It is sufficient to say that the direction that the effects of valium were necessarily irrelevant was wrong.

Notes and questions
1.   The Court of Appeal is not saying that Hardie should have been acquitted; only that the trial judge had erred in directing the jury that the effects of the valium were irrelevant. The jurors should have been directed that if they concluded that as a result of taking the valium the defendant could not have appreciated the risks to property from his action, they should then have considered whether the taking of the drug was itself a reckless act. Was it?
2.   Compare *Hardie* with the case where a defendant is taking drugs pursuant to medical prescription, and the drugs have an unanticipated, violent side effect. Is this a stronger or a weaker case for allowing the defence? Would it matter if the defendant exceeded the proscribed dosage?

(iv) 'Dutch courage'
What of the defendant who gets drunk in order to summon the courage to commit a crime? Consider the observations of Lord Denning on this issue in *Attorney-General for Northern Ireland* v *Gallagher*.

Attorney-General for Northern Ireland v *Gallagher*
[1963] AC 349
House of Lords

LORD DENNING: My Lords, every direction which a judge gives to a jury in point of law must be considered against the background of facts which have been proved or admitted in the case. In this case the accused man did not give evidence himself. And the facts proved against him were:

He had a grievance against his wife. She had obtained a maintenance order against him and had been instrumental in getting him detained in a mental hospital.

He had made up his mind to kill his wife. He bought a knife for the purpose and a bottle of whisky – either to give himself Dutch courage to do the deed or to drown his conscience after it.

He did in fact carry out his intention. He killed his wife with the knife and drank much of the whisky before or after he killed her.

There were only two defences raised on his behalf: (1) Insanity; (2) Drunkenness.

The Lord Chief Justice directed the jury that the *time* when they had to consider whether he was insane or not (within the M'Naughten Rules) was before he started on the bottle of whisky.' 'You should direct your attention,' he said to them, 'to the state of his mind before he opened the bottle of whisky.' If he was sane at that time, he could not make good the defence of insanity 'with the aid of that bottle of whisky.' Immediately after the jury retired, Mr Kelly took up this point of *time*. He suggested that it was inaccurate and inconsistent with the M'Naughten Rules. But the Lord Chief Justice adhered to his view. He declined to modify his charge to the jury on the matter. 'If I'm wrong,' he said, 'I can be put right.' It was on this view point of *time* that the Court of Criminal Appeal reversed him. His direction was, they said, 'inconsistent with the M'Naughten Rules,' which fix the crucial time as 'the time of the committing of the act,' that is, the time of the killing and not at an earlier time.

The question is whether the direction of the Lord Chief Justice as to the *time* was correct. At least that is how I read the question posed by the Court of Criminal Appeal. It is complicated by the fact that, according to the medical evidence, the accused man was a psychopath. That does not mean that he was insane. But it sharpens the point of the question. He had a disease of the mind. It was quiescent before he started on the whisky. So he was sane then. But the drink may have brought on an explosive outburst in the course of which he killed her. Can he rely on this self-induced defect of reason and put it forward as a defence of insanity'

My Lords, this case differs from all others in the books in that the accused man, whilst sane and sober, before he took to the drink, had already made up his mind to kill his wife. This seems to me to be far worse – and far more deserving of condemnation – than the case of a man who, before getting drunk, has no intention to kill, but afterwards in his cups, whilst drunk, kills another by an act which he would not dream of doing when sober. Yet by the law of England in this latter case his drunkenness is no defence even though it has distorted his reason and his will-power. So why should it be a defence in the present case? And is it made any better by saying that the man is a psychopath?

The answer to the question is, I think, that the case falls to be decided by the general principle of English law that, subject to very limited exceptions, drunkenness is no defence to a criminal charge, nor is a defect of reason produced by drunkenness. . . .

My Lords, I think the law on this point should take a clear stand. If a man, whilst sane and sober, forms an intention to kill and makes preparation for it, knowing it is a wrong thing to do, and then gets himself drunk so as to give himself Dutch courage to do the killing, and whilst drunk carries out his intention, he cannot rely on this self-induced drunkenness as a defence to a charge of murder, nor even as reducing it to manslaughter. He cannot say that he got himself into such a stupid state that he was incapable of an intent to kill. So also when he is a psychopath, he cannot by drinking rely on his self-induced defect of reason as a defence of insanity. The wickedness of his mind before he got drunk is enough to condemn him, coupled with the act which he intended to do and did do. A psychopath who goes out intending to kill, knowing it is wrong, and does kill, cannot escape the consequences by making himself drunk before doing it. That is, I believe, the direction which the Lord Chief Justice gave to the jury and which the Court of Criminal Appeal found to be wrong. I think it was right and for this reason I would allow the appeal.

Notes
1.   The theoretical problem raised by *A-G for Northern Ireland* v *Gallagher* was one of concurrence between *actus reus* and *mens rea*. At the actual moment of committing the crime the defendant's self-induced drunkenness may have prevented him from having the specific intent to kill, even though he may have had this intent at some previous point in time. What counter arguments can the Crown raise?
2.   The 'Dutch courage' cases may provide insight into why the law generally takes a harsh attitude to voluntary intoxication as a defence. Many criminals fortify themselves with drink before embarking on their criminal enterprises. In court this may translate into a defence of lack of *mens rea* based on intoxication. It is clearly not in society's interest to structure its legal rules to encourage such claims.

(v)   Intoxication and mistake
We have seen previously in *DPP* v *Morgan* [1976] AC 182 and *Williams (Gladstone)* (1983) 78 Cr App R 276, that where a defendant proceeds under a mistake of fact which, were he correct, would negate an element of the crime, he is to be judged as if the mistaken version of the facts was the true version. What if, however, the defendant makes a mistake when drunk that he would not have made when sober? Should the drunkenness be taken into account? Compare the following cases:

Jaggard v Dickinson
[1980] 3 All ER 716
Queen's Bench Division

For the facts and holding, see p. 341.

R v O'Grady
[1987] 3 WLR 321
Court of Appeal

For the facts and holding, see pp. 340–1.

Notes and questions
1.   Are *Jaggard* v *Dickinson* and *O'Grady* reconcilable? Are *O'Grady* and *DPP* v *Majewski* reconcilable? Are *O'Grady* and *Williams (Gladstone)* reconcilable? Although *O'Grady* involved a basic intent crime (manslaughter), Lord Lane appeared willing to extend the court's rationale to crimes of specific

intent, such as murder. Has Lord Lane carved out an exception both to *Williams (Gladstone)* regarding mistakes which are to be judged by a subjective standard and to the *DPP* v *Majewski* rule that intoxication is a relevant consideration in crimes of specific intent?

2.   Has Lord Lane in *O'Grady* adopted the policy-based rationale that those who drink must bear the risk that, while drunk, they might commit crimes which they would not commit when sober. See also *O'Connor* [1991] Crim LR 135; *Newell* (1980) 71 Cr App R 331.

3.   Consider the Draft Criminal Code Bill 1989:

Draft Criminal Code Bill 1989

22.—(1)   Where an offence requires a fault element of recklessness (however described), a person who was voluntarily intoxicated shall be treated —

(a)   as having been aware of any risk of which he would have been aware had he been sober;

(b)   as not having believed in the existence of an exempting circumstance (where the existence of such a belief is in issue) if he would not have so believed had he been sober.

(2)   Where an offence requires a fault element of failure to comply with a standard of care, or requires no fault, a person who was voluntarily intoxicated shall be treated as not having believed in the existence of an exempting circumstance (where the existence of such a belief is in issue) if a reasonable sober person would not have so believed.

(3)   Where the definition of a fault element or of a defence refers, or requires reference, to the state of mind or conduct to be expected of a reasonable person, such person shall be understood to be one who is not intoxicated.

(4)   Subsection (1) does not apply —

(a)   to murder (to which section 55 applies); or

(b)   to the case (to which section 36 applies) where a person's unawareness or belief arises from a combination of mental disorder and voluntary intoxication.

(5)   —

(a)   'Intoxicant' means alcohol or any other thing which, when taken into the body, may impair awareness or control.

(b)   'Voluntary intoxication' means the intoxication of a person by an intoxicant which he takes, otherwise than property for a medicinal purpose, knowing that it is or may be an intoxicant.

(c)   For the purposes of this section, a person 'takes' an intoxicant if he permits it to be administered to him.

(6)   An intoxicant, although taken for a medicinal purpose, is not properly so taken if —

(a)   —

(i)   it is not taken on medical advice; or

(ii)   it is taken on medical advice but the taker fails then or thereafter to comply with any condition forming part of the advice; and

(b)   the taker is aware that the taking, or the failure, as the case may be, may result in his doing an act capable of constituting an offence of the kind in question;

and accordingly intoxication resulting from such taking or failure is voluntary intoxication.

(7)   Intoxication shall be taken to have been voluntary unless evidence is given, in the sense stated in section 13(2), that it was involuntary.

Question
If enacted, what would be the effect of this provision on *Jaggard* v *Dickinson* and *O'Grady*?

(vii)   Intoxication and insanity
Prolonged use of alcohol or drugs can sometimes result in brain damage or severe mental impairment. In such cases, should the defendant's proper defence be intoxication or insanity?

R* v *Davis
(1881) 14 Cox CC 563
Newcastle Crown Court

On the 14th day of January, 1881, the prisoner (who had been previously drinking heavily, but was then sober) made an attack upon his sister-in-law, Mrs Davis, threw her down, and attempted to cut her throat with a knife. Ordinarily he was a very mild, quiet, peaceable, well-behaved man, and on friendly terms with her. At the police station he said, 'The man in the moon told me to do it. I will have to commit murder, as I must be hanged.' He was examined by two medical men, who found him suffering from *delirium tremens*, resulting from over-indulgence in drink. According to their evidence he would know what he was doing, but his actions would not be under his control. In their judgment neither fear of punishment nor legal nor moral considerations would have deterred him – nothing short of actual physical restraint would have prevented him acting as he did. He was disordered in his senses, and would not be able to distinguish between moral right and wrong at the time he committed the act. Under proper care and treatment he recovered in a week, and was then perfectly sensible.

For the defence it was submitted that he was of unsound mind at the time of the commission of the act, and was not responsible for his actions.

STEPHEN J to the jury: The prisoner at the bar is charged with having feloniously wounded his sister-in-law, Jane Davis, on the 14th day of January last with intent to murder her. You will have to consider whether he was in such a state of mind as to be thoroughly responsible for his actions. And with regard to that I must explain to you what is the kind or degree of insanity which relieves a man from responsibility. Nobody must suppose – and I hope no one will be led for one moment to suppose – that drunkenness is any kind of excuse for crime. If this man had been raging drunk, and had stabbed his sister-in-law and killed her, he would have stood at the bar guilty of murder beyond all doubt or question. But drunkenness is one thing and the diseases to which drunkenness leads are different things; and if a man by drunkenness brings on a state of disease which causes such a degree of madness, even for a time, which would have relieved him from responsibility if it had been caused in any other way, then he would not be criminally responsible. In my opinion, in such a case the man is a madman, and is to be treated as such, although his madness is only temporary. If you think he was so insane – that if his insanity had been produced by other causes he would not be responsible for his actions – then the mere fact that it was caused by drunkenness will not prevent it having the effect which otherwise it would have had, of excusing him from punishment. Drunkenness is no excuse, but *delirium tremens* caused by drunkenness may be an excuse if you think it produces such a state of mind as would otherwise relieve him from responsibility. . . .

Notes and questions
1. Is *Davis* consistent with *DPP* v *Majewski* and its progeny? In the latter cases, the focus seems to be on the defendant's fault in becoming intoxicated and not on the effects of the intoxication; but in *Davis* the focus is clearly on the effects of the intoxication. Why should this be so?
2. *Davis* was approved by the House of Lords in *Attorney-General for Northern Ireland* v *Gallagher* (above) and in *Director of Public Prosecutions* v *Beard* [1920] AC 479.

(vi) Proposals for reform
It may well be that a defendant is at fault in becoming intoxicated and should be punished for that fault. But should that fault render him liable for any and all subsequent crimes? Typically the law recognises two types of recklessness: subjective recklessness, where a defendant has acted callously in ignoring a known risk; and objective recklessness, where a defendant has acted thoughtlessly in not considering a risk. Is there now a third category of recklessness which consists of becoming intoxicated, and should the penalty for that type of recklessness be the same as that for objective recklessness? Many years ago Glanville Williams wrote: 'If a man is punished for doing something when drunk that he would not have done when sober, is he not in plain truth punished for getting drunk?' (G. Williams, *The General Part* (2d ed. 1961), p. 564). Perhaps punishment is justified, but arguably the amount of punishment should reflect the degree of moral blameworthiness of the defendant. Is there some way that the criminal law might better manifest the culpability in the intoxicated defendant's behaviour? Consider the merits of the following proposals:

(a) Adhering to normal standards of *mens rea*, and allowing a defendant to establish that he lacked the *mens rea* for the crime charged because of intoxication. This is the approach taken in some Australian states. See *O'Connor* [1980] 54 AJLR 349. This approach could be combined with either of the following.

(b) Allowing the jury to return a verdict of 'guilty but intoxicated' on the substantive charge, thereby triggering a reduced scale of punishment for the offence.

(c) Allowing the jury to acquit on the substantive charge but with the option of returning the alternative verdict of 'dangerous drunkenness'. See the recommendations of the Butler Committee (Cmnd 6244 (1975)).

(d) Expanding the range of sentences available for the offence of intoxication so as to allow the sentencing authority to take into account the harm threatened or perpetrated by the intoxicated defendant.

Does every solution have its own problems?

IV Affirmative defences

A Duress and necessity

(i) Rationale

The defences of necessity and duress are close relatives. (Indeed, the Draft Criminal Code Bill 1989 uses the term 'duress of circumstances' to cover both.) Both are affirmative defences in that they do not come into play until the prosecution has established all elements of the offence charged. The situation that both defences are concerned with is one in which the actor is faced with a choice of evils. He or she must either commit a crime or face even more unpleasant consequences. The major difference between the two defences is the source of the evil: in duress, the source is another human being who orders the defendant to commit a crime upon pain of suffering a worse evil; in necessity, nobody orders the defendant to commit a crime but forces of nature or other circumstances create the pressure to do so.

If someone held a knife to your throat and said: 'Your money or your life,' and you chose the former, nobody would be so crass as to assert that your relinquishment of your money was a truly voluntary act. But if that same somebody held a knife to your throat and said 'Help me rob the bank or I will kill you,' and you chose to help rob the bank, can it be said that your participation in the bank robbery was voluntary? Again arguably not, but both of these examples involve a different kind of involuntariness than that which we examined in regard to *actus reus*. When we talked about an involuntary *actus reus*, we were concerned with situations where defendant was physically unable to resist the doing of the act. In duress and necessity cases, the defendant is physically capable of not committing the crime, but judges it imprudent to do so. The defendant has a choice, but an unpalatable one. She or he can choose not to commit the crime, but in so doing may have to suffer an extremely unpleasant consequence.

Yet this distinction between the *physical* inability to resist doing a criminal act and the *normative* inability to resist doing that act is an important one to bear in mind. It accounts in no small measure for the hostility of judges to the defences of duress and necessity. The judges are concerned that these defences will be too often invoked, particularly by members of terrorist organisations, in circumstances where persons with a tougher moral fibre would not have given in to the pressures to commit the offence. The judges want to provide a disincentive in the form of a potential criminal sanction to encourage persons to resist giving in to the pressures to commit crime.

While the defences of necessity and duress cannot be justified on either an involuntary act theory, or, for that matter, a theory that the defendant lacked mental capacity (for the defendant did have the ability to make a rational choice and arguably did make a rational choice), there are two arguments in their favour:

(a) No individual should be punished for doing something that the reasonable man or woman in the same situation would have done. If the reasonable person would not have resisted the pressure to commit the crime, then the unlucky soul who actually found himself in that predicament should not be held criminally liable either. The law should recognise that the deterrent value of criminal sanctions will have little effect on the person faced with loss of life or grievous harm.

(b) Public policy should encourage a defendant to choose the lesser and avoid the greater evil, even if that means that a crime has to be committed. If the harm which will result from compliance with the law is greater than the harm which will result from violation of the law, it would be a strange legal system which required the defendant to choose the greater evil.

Notice that the first rationale is based on pragmatism and is an argument of excuse; while the second rationale, which is based on utilitarian principles (crudely put, the greatest happiness for the greatest number), is an argument of justification.

The burden of introducing some evidence of duress or necessity rests on the defendant. Once that evidence is introduced, however, the burden shifts to the prosecution to negate the defence by proof beyond a reasonable doubt. In other words, the prosecution bears the ultimate burden of persuading the jury that the defence should not succeed.

(ii)   Do the defences exist?
There have been so few cases where the defences of duress and necessity, particularly necessity, have been raised that it is not unfair to ask whether these defences are in fact recognised by the courts. Do they exist? In regard to duress, there is not much dispute. In *Director of Public Prosecutions for Northern Ireland* v *Lynch* [1975] AC 653, the House of Lords traced the history of the defence and clearly accepted its existence.

The defence of necessity is more problematic. Sometimes the defence is specifically recognised by statute. See, e.g., Control of Pollution Act 1974. Even where a statute does not specifically articulate a defence of necessity, the statute might contain words which allow a court to recognise such a defence by implication. Consider, for instance, the following:

Criminal Damage Act 1971

1—(1) A person who without lawful excuse destroys or damages any property belonging to another intending to destroy or damage any such property or being reckless as to whether any such property would be destroyed or damaged shall be guilty of an offence.

Note
The key phrase is 'without lawful excuse'. If one commits damage but in a situation of duress or necessity, is the act with lawful excuse? If, with intent to warn A that his mortal enemy B has set forth to kill him, C breaks a window of D's house in order to use his telephone, it can be argued that the act of criminal

damage in breaking the window is with lawful excuse. A similar argument could be made if X blows up a house with intent to divert a rampaging river which threatens to flood the town.

The preceding analyses seem to proceed on the assumption that necessity is only a defence when permitted either expressly or impliedly by statute. There is a competing thesis which approaches the question from the opposite direction. It maintains that there is a general defence of necessity, which applies to all offences, except where expressly or by implication excluded by statute. In support of this position the following case is often cited:

R v *Bourne*
[1939] 1 KB 687
Central Criminal Court

The evidence called on behalf of the Crown proved that on 14 June 1938, the defendant performed an operation on the girl in question at St Mary's Hospital, and thereby procured her miscarriage. The following facts were also proved: On 27 April 1938, the girl, who was then under the age of 15, had been raped with great violence in circumstances which would have been most terrifying to any woman, let alone a child of fourteen, by a man who was in due course convicted of the crime. In consequence of the rape the girl became pregnant. Her case was brought to the attention of the defendant, who, after examination of the girl, performed the operation with the consent of her parents.

The defence put forward was that, in the circumstances of the case, the operation was not unlawful. The defendant was called as a witness on his own behalf and stated that, after he had made careful examination of the girl and had informed himself of all the relevant facts of the case, he had come to the conclusion that it was his duty to perform the operation. He had satisfied himself that the girl was in fact pregnant in consequence of the rape committed on her. He had also satisfied himself that she had not been infected with venereal disease; if he had found that she was so infected, he would not have performed the operation, since in that case there would have been a risk that the operation would cause a spread of the disease. Nor would he have performed the operation if he had found that the girl was either feeble-minded or had what he called a 'prostitute mind,' since in such cases pregnancy and child-birth would not be likely to affect a girl injuriously. He satisfied himself that she was a normal girl in every respect, though she was somewhat more mature than most girls of her age. In his opinion the continuance of the pregnancy would probably cause serious injury to the girl . . . .

MACNAGHTEN J: . . . The charge against Mr Bourne is made under s. 58 of the Offences Against the Person Act, 1861, that he unlawfully procured the miscarriage of the girl who was the first witness in the case. . . .

Nine years ago Parliament passed an Act called the Infant Life (Preservation) Act, 1929 (19 & 20 Geo. 5, c. 34). Sect. 1, sub-s. 1, of that Act provides that

> any person who, with intent to destroy the life of a child capable of being born alive, by any wilful act causes a child to die before it has an existence independent of its mother, shall be guilty of felony, to wit, of child destruction, and shall be liable on conviction thereof on indictment to penal servitude for life: Provided that no person shall be found guilty of an offence under this section unless it is proved that the act which caused the death of the child was not done in good faith for the purpose only of preserving the life of the mother.

It is true, as Mr Oliver has said, that this enactment provides for the case where a child is killed by a wilful act at the time when it is being delivered in the ordinary course of nature; but in my view the proviso that it is necessary for the Crown to prove that the act was not done in good faith for the purpose only of preserving the life of the mother is in accordance with what has always been the common law of England with regard to the killing of an unborn child. No such proviso is in fact set out in s. 58 of the Offences Against the Person Act, 1861; but the words of that section are that any person who 'unlawfully' uses an instrument with intent to procure miscarriage shall be guilty of felony. In my opinion the word 'unlawfully' is not, in that section, a meaningless word. I think it imports the meaning expressed by the proviso in s. 1, sub-s. 1, of the Infant Life (Preservation) Act, 1929, and that s. 58 of the Offences Against the Person Act, 1861, must be read as if the words making it an offence to use an instrument with intent to procure a miscarriage were qualified by a similar proviso.

In this case, therefore, my direction to you in law is this – that the burden rests on the Crown to satisfy you beyond reasonable doubt that the defendant did not procure the miscarriage of the girl in good faith for the purpose only of preserving her life. If the Crown fails to satisfy you of that, the defendant is entitled by the law of this land to a verdict of acquittal. If, on the other hand, you are satisfied that what the defendant did was not done by him in good faith for the purpose only of preserving the life of the girl, it is your duty to find him guilty. It is said, and I think said rightly, that this is a case of great importance to the public and, more especially, to the medical profession; but you will observe that it has nothing to do with the ordinary case of procuring abortion to which I have already referred. In those cases the operation is performed by a person of no skill, with no medical qualifications, and there is no pretence that it is done for the preservation of the mother's life. Cases of that sort are in no way affected by the consideration of the question which is put before you to-day.

Notes and questions

1. Does *Bourne* turn on the wording of the statute, or on the existence of an implied defence of necessity? See also *In Re F (Mental Patient: Sterilisation)* [1990] 2 AC 1.

2. Many crimes, such as assault and criminal damage, contain the word 'unlawful' in their definition, usually in respect to the *actus reus* of the crime. It might seem that the word 'unlawful' is otiose, since an *actus reus* is by definition unlawful. The argument that gives content to 'unlawful' is that the term should be interpreted to mean 'without excuse or justification'. But arguably this begs the question of what is a legally recognised excuse or justification. Does *Bourne* help answer this question?

(iii) Elements of the defences

The judicial analysis of duress and necessity tends to be similar. A number of important common issues have been addressed which can be broken down into the following five heads:

(a)   the nature and imminence of the harm avoided;
(b)   the nature of the harm caused;
(c)   the relationship between the harm avoided and the harm caused;
(d)   whether the circumstances should be judged from the perspective of the defendant or that of an ordinary person of reasonable firmness;
(e)   the relevance of alternative courses of action.

(a)   *Harm avoided.* It is generally said that to invoke either duress or necessity a defendant must be faced with the threat of death or serious bodily harm. See, e.g., *R v Singh* [1973] 1 All ER 122. The determination of whether such harm is threatened is not always easy.

London Borough of Southwark v *Williams and Another*
[1971] 2 All ER 175
Court of Appeal

LORD DENNING MR: This case arises out of the extreme housing shortage in London. In September 1970 some people who were homeless and others who were living in bad conditions sought the assistance of a squatter's association. They made an orderly entry into some empty houses in the Borough of Southwark which were owned by the council. They squatted there. The council applied to the court under the new procedure which has been brought in to deal with urgent cases of squatting. RSC Ord 113 enables the court to make an order for immediate possession. It is a summary procedure and should be used only when there is no arguable defence. The squatters here admit that they have no title to these houses. They admit that the houses belong to the council. But they seek to justify or excuse their action on the ground that it is the duty of the council to provide temporary accommodation for persons who are in need thereof: and that it was of necessity that they entered the houses.
. . .
Now let me turn to the squatters themselves. Everyone has the greatest sympathy for them.
. . . [These] families occupied empty houses which the council evidently had thought were not worthy of repair and were not fit to be occupied. The evidence shows that there are some hundreds of empty houses in Southwark – 400, we were told, at any rate – and there is some evidence that their actual conversion or development may not take place for some little time. These squatters, in their distress, felt that they were morally justified in entering into occupation. But have they any legal justification?
. . .
I will next consider the defence of 'necessity'. There is authority for saying that in case of great and imminent danger, in order to preserve life, the law will permit of an encroachment on private property. That is shown by *Mouse's Case* (1620) 12 Co Rep 63, where the ferryman at Gravesend took 47 passengers into his barge to carry them to London. A great tempest arose and all were in danger. Mr Mouse was one of the

passengers. He threw a casket belonging to the plaintiff overboard so as to lighten the ship. Other passengers threw other things. It was proved that, if they had not done so, the passengers would have been drowned. It was held by the whole court that 'in any case of necessity, for the safety of the lives of the passengers' it was lawful for Mr Mouse to cast the casket out of the barge. The court said it was like the pulling down of a house, in time of fire, to stop it spreading: which has always been held justified pro bono publico.

The doctrine so enunciated must, however, be carefully circumscribed. Else necessity would open the door to many an excuse. It was for this reason that it was not admitted in *R v Dudley and Stephens* (1884) 14 QBD 273, where the three shipwrecked sailors, in extreme despair, killed the cabin-boy and ate him to save their own lives. They were held guilty of murder. The killing was not justified by necessity. Similarly, when a man who is starving enters a house and takes food in order to keep himself alive. Our English law does not admit the defence of necessity. It holds him guilty of larceny. Lord Hale said that 'if a person, being under necessity for want of victuals or clothes, shall upon that account clandestinely, and *animus furandi*, steal another man's food, it is felony'. The reason is because, if hunger were once allowed to be an excuse for stealing, it would open a way through which all kinds of disorder and lawlessness would pass. So here. If homelessness were once admitted as a defence to trespass, no one's house could be safe. Necessity would open a door which no man could shut. It would not only be those in extreme need who would enter. There would be others who would imagine that they were in need, or would invent a need, so as to gain entry. Each man would say his need was greater than the next man's. The plea would be an excuse for all sorts of wrongdoing. So the courts must, for the sake of law and order, take a firm stand. They must refuse to admit the plea of necessity to the hungry and the homeless; and trust that their distress will be relieved by the charitable and the good. Applying these principles, it seems to me in the circumstances of these squatters are not such as to afford any justification or excuse in law for their entry into these houses. We can sympathise with the plight in which they find themselves. We can recognise the orderly way in which they made their entry. But we can go no further. They must make their appeal for help to others, not to us. They must appeal to the council, who will, I am sure, do all it can. They can go to the Minister, if need be. But, so far as these courts are concerned, we must, in the interest of law and order itself, uphold the title to these properties. We cannot allow any individuals, however great their despair, to take the law into their own hands and enter these premises. The court must exercise its summary jurisdiction and order the defendants to go out.

Notes and questions

1   What is the purpose of requiring that the harm avoided be that of death or serious bodily harm? Were the defendants in *Williams* threatened with death or serious bodily harm? What might they have argued?

2.   Note that this was a civil and not a criminal case. Might the differing burden of proof in the two types of cases (in a criminal case the Crown must show by proof beyond a reasonable doubt that there was no necessity once the defendant has introduced evidence of such) have led to a different result if the defendants had been prosecuted criminally?

3.   The harm avoided need not necessarily be to the defendant; if Eyal drives on to Joseph's property to avoid hitting Susan, the defence of necessity should still be available even though there is no threat to Eyal. In duress, if the threat

is to kill not the person who is under compulsion to participate in the crime, but a close family member (or indeed, any third party), is there any good reason why the defence should not be available? See *Ortiz* (1986) 83 Cr App R 173; *Conway* [1988] 3 All ER 1025.

4. It is often said that the harm threatened must be present and immediate. Doubt as to this requirement was, however, raised in *R v Hudson and Taylor*.

R v Hudson and Taylor
[1971] 2 QB 202
Court of Appeal

LORD PARKER CJ: . . . . These appellants were convicted of perjury at the Manchester Crown Court on May 18, 1970, and each was granted a conditional discharge. They now appeal against their convictions by leave of the single judge.

On April 6, 1969, a fight took place in a Salford public house between one Wright and one Mulligan with the result that Wright was charged with wounding Mulligan. Each of the present appellants gave statements to the police and they were the principal prosecution witnesses at Wright's trial. Elaine Taylor is 19, and Linda Hudson is 17.

Wright's trial took place on August 4, 1969, but when called to give evidence the appellants failed to identify Wright as Mulligan's assailant. Taylor said that she knew no one called Jimmy Wright, and Hudson said that the only Wright she knew was not the man in the dock. Wright was accordingly acquitted and, in due course, the appellants were charged with perjury. At their trial they admitted that the evidence which they had given was false but set up the defence of duress. The basis of the defence was that, shortly after the fight between Wright and Mulligan, Hudson had been approached by a group of men including one Farrell who had a reputation for violence and was warned that if she 'told on Wright in court' they would get her and cut her up. Hudson passed this warning to Taylor who said that she had also been warned by other girls to be careful or she would be hurt. The appellants said in evidence that, in consequence of these threats, they were frightened and decided to tell lies in court in order to avoid the consequences which might follow if they testified against Wright. This resolve was strengthened when they arrived at court for Wright's trial and saw that Farrell was in the gallery.
. . .

This appeal raises two main questions; first, as to the nature of the necessary threat and, in particular, whether it must be 'present and immediate'; secondly, as to the extent to which a right to plead duress may be lost if the accused has failed to take steps to remove the threat as, for example, by seeking police protection.

It is essential to the defence of duress that the threat shall be effective at the moment when the crime is committed. The threat must be a 'present' threat in the sense that it is effective to neutralise the will of the accused at that time. Hence an accused who joins a rebellion under the compulsion of threats cannot plead duress if he remains with the rebels after the threats have lost their effect and his own will has had a chance to re-assert itself: *R v M'Growther* (1746) Fost 13; *Attorney-General v Whelan* [1934] IR 518. Similarly a threat of future violence may be so remote as to be insufficient to overpower the will at that moment when the offence was committed, or the accused may have elected to commit the offence in order to rid himself of a threat hanging over him and not because he was driven to act by immediate and unavoidable pressure. In none of these cases is the defence of duress available because a person cannot justify the commission of a crime merely to secure his own peace of mind.

When, however, there is no opportunity for delaying tactics, and the person threatened must make up his mind whether he is to commit the criminal act or not, the existence at that moment of threats sufficient to destroy his will ought to provide him with a defence even though the threatened injury may not follow instantly, but after an interval. This principle is illustrated by *Subramaniam* v *Public Prosecutor* [1956] 1 WLR 965, when the appellant was charged in Malaya with unlawful possession of ammunition and was held by the Privy Council to have a defence of duress fit to go to the jury, on his plea that he had been compelled by terrorists to accept the ammunition and feared for his safety if the terrorists returned.

In the present case the threats of Farrell were likely to be no less compelling, because their execution could not be effected in the court room, if they could be carried out in the streets of Salford the same night. In so far, therefore, as the recorder ruled as a matter of law that the threats were not sufficiently present and immediate to support the defence of duress we think that he was in error. He should have left the jury to decide whether the threats had overborne the will of the appellants at the time when they gave the false evidence.

Questions

1.   What purpose does an immediacy requirement serve? Did the court in *Hudson and Taylor* abandon the requirement, modify it, or reinterpret it? Or none of the above?

2.   Mary is kidnapped. Her kidnappers give her parents one month to raise the ransom money and tell them that if the ransom is not paid, Mary will be killed. They inform Mary that they are serious. Two weeks before the ransom is due, while her kidnappers are in another room, Mary finds a pair of scissors. She attacks her kidnappers with the scissors and kills them. Will her defence fail because no immediate harm was threatened?

(b)   *Harm caused.* It is generally agreed that duress and necessity can be defences to crimes short of murder and possibly treason. The more controversial question is whether one can ever kill an innocent human being in the name of duress or necessity. This is the issue in one of the most famous criminal cases of all time.

R v *Dudley and Stephens*
(1884) 14 QBD 273
Queen's Bench Division

At the trial of an indictment for murder it appeared, upon a special verdict, that the prisoners D and S, seamen, and the deceased, a boy between seventeen and eighteen, were cast away in a storm on the high seas, and compelled to put into an open boat; that the boat was drifting on the ocean, and was probably more than 1,000 miles from land; that on the eighteenth day, when they had been seven days without food and five without water, D proposed to S that lots should be cast who should be put to death to save the rest, and that they afterwards thought it would be better to kill the boy that their lives should be saved; that on the twentieth day D, with the assent of

S, killed the boy, and both D and S fed on his flesh for four days; that at the time of the act there was no sail in sight nor any reasonable prospect of relief; that under these circumstances there appeared to the prisoners every probability that unless they then or very soon fed upon the boy, or one of themselves, they would die of starvation.

LORD COLERIDGE CJ: . . . From these facts, stated with the cold precision of a special verdict, it appears sufficiently that the prisoners were subject to terrible temptation, to sufferings which might break down the bodily power of the strongest man, and try the conscience of the best. Other details yet more harrowing, facts still more loathsome and appalling, were presented to the jury, and are to be found recorded in my learned Brother's notes. But nevertheless this is clear, that the prisoners put to death a weak and unoffending boy upon the chance of preserving their own lives by feeding, upon his flesh and blood after he was killed, and with the certainty of depriving, *him* of any possible chance of survival. The verdict finds in terms that 'if the men had not fed upon the body of the boy they would *probably* not have survived,' and that 'the boy being in a much weaker condition was *likely* to have died before them.' They might possibly not have been picked up next day by a passing ship; they might possibly not have been picked up at all; in either case it is obvious that the killing of the boy would have been an unecessary and profitless act. It is found by the verdict that the boy was incapable of resistance, and, in fact, made none; and it is not even suggested that his death was due to any violence on his part attempted against, or even so much as feared by, those who killed him. . . .

Now, except for the purpose of testing how far the conservation of a man's own life is in all cases and under all circumstances, an absolute, unqualified, and paramount duty, we exclude from our consideration all the incidents of war. We are dealing with a case of private homicide, not one imposed upon men in the service of their Sovereign and in the defence of their country. Now it is admitted that the deliberate killing of this unoffending and unresisting boy was clearly murder, unless the killing can be justified by some well-recognised excuse admitted by the law. It is further admitted that there was in this case no such excuse, unless the killing was justified by what has been called 'necessity.' But the temptation to the act which existed here was not what the law has ever called necessity. Nor is this to be regretted. Though law and morality are not the same, and many things may be immoral which are not necessarily illegal, yet the absolute divorce of law from morality would be of fatal consequence; and divorce would follow if the temptation to murder in this case were to be held by law an absolute defence of it. It is not so. To preserve one's life is generally speaking a duty, but it may be the plainest and the highest duty to sacrifice it. War is full of instances in which it is a man's duty not to live, but to die. The duty in case of shipwreck, of a captain to his crew, of the crew to the passengers, of soldiers to women and children, as in the noble case of the *Birkenhead*; these duties impose on men the moral necessity, not of the preservation, but of the sacrifice of their lives for others, from which in no country, least of all, it is to be hoped, in England, will men ever shrink, as indeed, they have not shrunk. It is not correct, therefore, to say that there is any absolute or unqualified necessity to preserve one's life.

. . . It is not needful to point out the awful danger of admitting the principle which has been contended for. Who is to be the judge of this sort of necessity? By what measure is the comparative value of lives to be measured? Is it to be strength, or intellect, or what? It is plain that the principle leaves to him who is to profit by it to determine the necessity which will justify him in deliberately taking another's life to save own. In this case the youngest, the most unresisting, was chosen. Was it more necessary to kill him than one of the grown men? The answer must be 'No' –

> So spake the Fiend, and with necessity,
> The tyrant's plea, excused his delivish deeds.

It is not suggested that in this particular case the deeds were 'devilish,' but it is quite plain that such a principle once admitted might be made the legal cloak for unbridled passion and atrocious crime. There is no safe path for judges to tread but to ascertain the law to the best of their ability and to declare it according to their judgment; and if in any case the law appears to be too severe on individuals, to leave it to the Sovereign to exercise that prerogative of mercy which the Constitution has intrusted to the hands fittest to dispense it.

It must not be supposed that in refusing to admit temptation to be an excuse for crime it is forgotten how terrible the temptation was; how awful the suffering; how hard in such trials to keep the judgment straight and the conduct pure. We are often compelled to set up standards we cannot reach ourselves, and to lay down rules which we could not ourselves satisfy. But a man has no right to declare temptation to be an excuse, though he might himself have yielded to it, nor allow compassion for the criminal to change or weaken in any manner the legal definition of the crime. It is therefore our duty to declare that the prisoners' act in this case was wilful murder, that the facts as stated in the verdict are no legal justification of the homicide; and to say that in our unanimous opinion the prisoners are upon this special verdict guilty of murder.

The Court then proceeded to pass sentence of death upon the prisoners. This sentence was afterwards commuted by the Crown to six months' imprisonment.

Questions
1.   The court in *Dudley and Stephens* said: 'We are often compelled to set up standards we cannot reach ourselves, and to lay down rules which we could not ourselves satisfy.' Do you agree? Can this statement be reconciled with the concept of *Caldwell* recklessness (see Chapter 3), which seeks to hold defendants to the standards of the reasonable person?
2.   To what extent may the court in *Dudley and Stephens* have been influenced by the method of selecting the victim? Might the court have been more sympathetic if the victim had been chosen by lot, as occurred in the American counterpart to *Dudley and Stephens, United States* v *Holmes*, 26 F Cas 360 (No. 15,383) (CCED 1842)? If the randomness of the selection process in *Holmes* offends, is there a rational method of choosing the victim?
3.   Do numbers matter? Consider the following science fiction(?) scenario: A mad scientist has affixed a bomb to an innocent victim. If the bomb explodes, thousands will be killed or seriously injured. The bomb can be dismantled only by first killing the innocent person to whom it is attached. Would such a killing be justified?

Note
Duress or necessity are all or nothing defences, i.e., they do not, like provocation or diminished responsibility, serve to reduce the seriousness of a crime from, say, murder to manslaughter. Rather, if successful, they lead to a

verdict of not guilty. However, even if a defence of duress or necessity does not succeed, the circumstances may be such as to give rise to either a subsequent pardon or commutation of sentence by the Crown, as in fact occurred in *Dudley and Stephens*, or form the basis for a reduced sentence or probation. In some cases necessity or duress may lead the Crown to decide not to pursue a criminal prosecution.

The issue of whether one can raise a claim of *duress* when an innocent victim has been killed arose in a trilogy of cases beginning with *Director of Public Prosecutions for Northern Ireland* v *Lynch* [1975] AC 653. The defendant was the driver on an IRA terrorist expedition in the course of which a police officer was killed. He was charged with aiding and abetting a murder. His defence was that he believed that he would be shot if he did not cooperate. In a three to two decision the House of Lords held that the defence of duress was available to one charged with aiding and abetting a murder. Two years later, however, in *Abbott* v *R* [1977] AC 755, the Lords, sitting as the Judicial Committee of the Privy Council, held that the defence of duress was not available to one charged as a principal to murder. There was an obvious tension between *Lynch* and *Abbott*, which the Lords had to resolve:

R v *Howe and Others*
[1987] 1 AC 417
House of Lords

LORD HAILSHAM OF ST MARYLEBONE: . . .

Count 1: murder of Elgar. The first victim was a 17-year old youth called Elgar. He was offered a job as a driver by Murray. On the evening of 10 October 1983 all five men were driven by Murray up into the hills between Stockport and Buxton, eventually stopping at some public lavatories at a remote spot called Goytsclough. Murray at some stage told both appellants in effect that Elgar was a 'grass,' and that they were going to kill him. Bannister was threatened with violence if he did not give Elgar 'a bit of a battering.' From thenceforwards Elgar, who was naked, sobbing and begging for mercy, was tortured, compelled to undergo appalling sexual perversions and indignities, he was kicked and punched. Bannister and Howe were doing the kicking and punching. The coup de grace was executed by Bailey who strangled Elgar with a headlock. It is unnecessary to go into further details of the attack on Elgar which are positively nauseating. In brief the two appellants asserted that they had only acted as they did through fear of Murray, believing that they would be treated in the same way as Elgar had been treated if they did not comply with Murray's directions. The prosecution were content to assent to the proposition that death had been caused by Bailey strangling the victim, although the kicks and punches would have resulted in death moments later even in the absence of the strangulation. The body was hidden by the appellants and the other two men. On this basis the appellants were in the position of what would have earlier been principals in the second degree and duress was left to the jury as an issue on this count.
Count 2: murder of Pollitt. Very much the same course of conduct took place as with Elgar. On 11 October 1983 the men picked up Pollitt, a 19-year-old labourer, and

took him to the same place where all four men kicked and punched the youth. Murray told Howe and Bannister to kill Pollitt, which they did by strangling him with Bannister's shoe lace. As the appellants were in the position of principals in the first degree, the judge did not leave duress to the jury on this count.

Count 3: conspiracy to murder Redfern. The third intended victim was a 21-year old man. The same procedure was followed, but Redfern suspected that something was afoot and managed with some skill to escape on his motorcycle from what would otherwise have inevitably been another horrible murder. The judge left the defence of duress to the jury on this charge of conspiracy to murder. The grounds of appeal, which are the same in respect of each of these appellants, are as follows. That the judge erred in directing the jury (1) in respect of count 2, that the defence of duress was not available to a principal in the first degree to the actual killing; (2) in respect of counts 1 and 3, that the test as to whether the appellants were acting under duress contains an 'objective' element; that is to say, if the prosecution prove that a reasonable man in the position of the defendant would not have felt himself forced to comply with the threats, the defence fails.

. . .

In general, I must say that I do not at all accept in relation to the defence of murder it is either good morals, good policy or good law to suggest, as did the majority in *Lynch* [1975] AC 653 and the minority in *Abbott* [1977] AC 755 that the ordinary man of reasonable fortitude is not to be supposed to be capable of heroism if he is asked to take an innocent life rather than sacrifice his own. Doubtless in actual practice many will succumb to temptation, as they did in *Dudley and Stephens*. But many will not, and I do not believe that as a 'concession to human frailty' the former should be exempt from liability to criminal sanctions if they do. I have known in my own lifetime of too many acts of heroism by ordinary human beings of no more than ordinary fortitude to regard a law as either 'just or humane' which withdraws the protection of the criminal law from the innocent victim and casts the cloak of its protection upon the coward and the poltroon in the name of a 'concession to human frailty.'

. . .

LORD GRIFFITHS: . . . [A]re there any present circumstances that should impel your Lordships to alter the law that has stood for so long and to extend the defence of duress to the actual killer? My Lords, I can think of none. It appears to me that all present indications point in the opposite direction. We face a rising tide of violence and terrorism against which the law must stand firm recognising that its highest duty is to protect the freedom and lives of those that live under it. The sanctity of human life lies at the root of this ideal and I would do nothing to undermine it, be it ever so slight.

. . . If the defence is not available to the killer what justification can there be for extending it to others who have played their part in the murder. I can, of course, see that as a matter of commonsense one participant in a murder may be considered less morally at fault than another. The youth who hero-worships the gangleader and acts as lookout man whilst the gang enter a jeweller's that shop and kill the owner in order to steal is an obvious example. In the eyes of the law they are all guilty of murder, but justice will be served by requiring those who did the killing to serve a longer period in prison before being released on licence than the youth who acted as lookout. However, it is not difficult to give examples where more moral fault may be thought to attach to a participant in murder who was not the actual killer; I have already mentioned the example of a contract killing, when the murder would never have taken place if a contract had not been placed to take the life of the victim. Another example would be an intelligent man goading a weakminded individual into a killing he would not otherwise commit.

It is therefore neither rational nor fair to make the defence dependent upon whether the accused is the actual killer or took some other part in the murder.

Questions
1. Is the decision in *Howe* based on legal principle or social policy?
2. What if the defendant's efforts to kill prove unsuccessful, and the charge is attempted murder. Should duress be a defence? Given that an innocent life has not been taken, does the logic of *Abbott* apply? See *R* v *Gotts* [1992] 2 WLR 284.

(c)   *The relationship between the harm avoided and the harm caused.* We have separately examined the nature of the harm avoided and the nature of the harm caused, and have seen that the courts have tended to place absolute limitations on each of these elements. Is this in fact the best way to approach duress and necessity? Where the defendant, through no fault of his own, is faced with a choice of evils, would it not make more sense to weigh the harm avoided against the harm caused and to allow the defence when the former was greater than the latter? In other words, if the defendant chose the lesser of the two evils, the defence should succeed; if not, then the defence should fail. Why do you think the law has not taken this approach?

If the controlling question were to be whether the defendant chose the lesser of two evils, many of the limitations which have developed would arguably make little sense. Why should the defence be available only when one is threatened with death or grievous bodily harm? Why should not a homeless derelict who seeks shelter from the cold in an unoccupied building have a defence of necessity to a charge of trespass? Why should duress or necessity not be available in cases of murder where the killing of the victim is justified by the need to save the lives of many?

There are some decisions which indicate a more flexible approach on the part of the courts:

R v *Willer*
[1987] RTR 22
Court of Appeal

WATKINS LJ: The appellant is 19 years of age. He is of excellent character. He appeals against his conviction for reckless driving.

What happened to bring him to conviction was that at about 9.30 p.m. on 24 April 1984 he and two school friends, Martin and Richard Jordan, were driving around the town of Hemel Hempstead in the appellant's Vauxhall Cavalier car. They heard a broadcast on the car's, what is known as, Citizen Band radio. From what they heard, the appellant was persuaded to drive to a shopping precinct at Leverstock Green. There they expected to meet another enthusiast of Citizen Band radio. At one stage of the journey the appellant had to drive up a very narrow turning off a road called Green Lane in order to keep his assignment with the other enthusiast mentioned. As he made his way up what is called Leaside, which is, as we see from the photographs, an alleyway, he was suddenly confronted with a gang of shouting and bawling youths, 20 to 30 strong. He heard one of them shouting: 'I'll kill you Willer' – and – 'I'll kill you Jordan'. He stopped and tried to turn the car round. These youths surrounded him. They banged on the car. A youth called Smallpiece opened the rear door of the car and dived upon Richard Jordan who was sitting in the back of it. Martin Jordan, his brother, got out of the front seat to help. The appellant realised that the only conceivable way he could somehow escape from this formidable gang of youths, who were obviously bent upon doing further violence, was to mount the pavement on the right-hand side of Leaside and on the pavement to drive through a small gap into the front of the shopping precinct. That he did quite slowly, it was accepted, at about 10 mph.

Having gained the security, if that was what it could be called, of the front of the shopping precinct and moved somewhere in the vicinity of a car park which was there, he realised that he had lost one of his companions. So he turned the car round and drove very slowly, at five mph, back towards the gap and through it. He had to make a couple of turns in his search for his missing companion. All this time Smallpiece was in the back of the car fighting with Richard Jordan. With that going on the appellant drove to the local police station and reported the matter. For his pains he was prosecuted – a very surprising turn of events indeed.

He was charged with reckless driving. Very properly, so it seems to us, he chose trial by jury. He appeared at the Crown Court of St Albans on 16 April 1985. The trial was presided over by Mr Curwen, an assistant recorder. During the course of the trial an argument developed between the assistant recorder and counsel over the question whether or not the defence of necessity was available to the appellant. The assistant recorder ruled that it was not. . . .

. . . The appellant in fact said: 'I could do no other in the face of this hostility than to take the right turn as I did, to mount the pavement and to drive through the gap out of further harm's way – harm to person and harm to my property'. Thus the defence of duress, it seems to us, arose but was not pursued. What ought to have happened here, therefore, was that the assistant recorder on those facts should have directed that he would leave to the jury the question whether or not on the outward or the return journey, or both, the appellant was wholly driven by force of circumstances into doing what he did and did not drive the car otherwise than under that form of compulsion.

Note

Willer is neither a situation where the defendant was threatened by a third person nor one where natural forces caused him to commit the crime. It involved what might be referred to as duress of circumstances. The defendant took it upon himself to violate the law because of his perceived fear that to do otherwise would have resulted in serious bodily harm. See also *Conway* [1988] 3 All ER 1025.

Question

Is one justified in speeding on a deserted road in order not to be late to an important appointment? Does it matter how 'important' the appointment is? Why one is late? See *Martin* [1989] 1 All ER 652.

(d) *From whose perspective?* In determining whether circumstances of duress or necessity exist, should the law adopt an objective or a subjective perspective? What if a defendant believes, albeit unreasonably, that unless he takes a certain course of criminal action his life will be in danger? Conversely, what if a defendant does not believe his life to be in danger, although a reasonable person would so believe?

There are, in fact, both subjective and objective limitations on duress and necessity. Subjectively, a defendant both must believe that serious bodily injury or worse is threatened unless he takes criminal action *and* the defendant must act with the intent to avoid that harm. Another subjective feature is that a defence of duress or necessity may not be available to a defendant who voluntarily or recklessly places himself in a position where he would be subjected to harm:

R v Sharp
[1987] QB 833
Court of Appeal

The appellant, who joined a gang of robbers, knew that they used firearms and he participated in a robbery during which the gang leader shot and killed the victim. The appellant was tried on a count charging murder. He submitted that the defence of duress was available to him since he had wished to pull out of the robbery but had participated in fear because a gun had been pointed at his head by the gang leader with a threat to blow it off if the appellant did not participate. The submission was rejected by the trial judge and the appellant was convicted of manslaughter.

LORD LANE CJ: . . . [Counsel] agrees that everything in this appeal depends upon whether the judge was correct or not in ruling that a defendant who has voluntarily joined a gang such as this cannot subsequently rely upon the defence of duress.
. . .
No one could question that if a person can avoid the effects of duress by escaping from the threats, without damage to himself, he must do so. In other words if there is a moment at which he is able to escape, so to speak, from the gun being held at his head by Hussey, or the equivalent of Hussey, he must do so. It seems to us to be part of the same argument, or at least to be so close to the same argument as to be practically indistinguishable from it, to say that a man must not voluntarily put himself in a position where he is likely to be subjected to such compulsion.

[I]n our judgment, where a person has voluntarily, and with knowledge of its nature, joined a criminal organisation or gang which he knew might bring pressure on him to commit an offence and was an active member when he was put under such pressure, he cannot avail himself of the defence of duress. . . .

Questions
1. Consider the following variant of *Sharp*. An advocacy group is formed whose objective is to get across its message through peaceful picketing. The picketing is ignored by both the public and the media. The leaders of the group decide to escalate their activities to include destruction of governmental property. At this point a minority of members seek to withdraw, but are threatened by the majority with violence if they do not participate. What result

under *Sharp* if the minority reluctantly go along with the majority? See *R* v *Shepherd* (1988) 86 Cr App R 47.

2. Assume that a defendant subjectively believes that in order to avoid threatened harm, it is necessary to commit a crime. Will the defendant lose the defence of duress or necessity if a reasonable person would have reached a different conclusion as to the need to commit the crime?

R v *Graham*
(1982) 74 Cr App R 235
Court of Appeal

For the facts and holding, see p. 339.

Questions
1. Is *Graham* reconcilable with *Williams (Gladstone)* above, which uses a 'pure' subjective test in determining whether a defendant who was operating under a mistake of fact used 'unlawful' force in the defence of another? In what ways are the cases distinguishable?
2. What characteristics of the defendant should be deemed relevant under *Graham*? Youth? Mental ability? Intoxication? An unduly cowardly character? Other?

Note
Graham was affirmed in *Howe* [1987] 1 AC 417.

(e) *The relevance of alternative courses of action.* Related to the issue of whether a reasonable person of ordinary firmness would have resisted committing a crime is the question of alternative courses of action. If a defendant has a legal means to avoid the threatened harm, must he take that avenue, even if it entails some risks?

R v *Gill*
[1963] 2 All ER 688
Court of Criminal Appeal

EDMUND DAVIES J: . . . The appellant was charged at Bedford County Sessions and convicted of (i) conspiring with James Lockett and other persons unknown to steal a lorry and its load, and (ii) with larceny pursuant to that conspiracy. Against those convictions he now appeals by leave of the full court. The appellant, who was employed as a lorry-driver by A. E. Meeks, Ltd., himself testified that he was approached by a group of men (of whom his co-accused Lockett was not one) who suggested that he should steal a valuable load from his employers and hand it over to them in return for a payment of £1,000, and that he agreed to do this. It was arranged that he would leave the loaded lorry in a car-park in Bristol, that during his absence it would be driven away, and that he would then falsely report to the police that it had been stolen without his knowledge. On this evidence, the learned deputy-chairman rightly told the jury that the conspiracy charge was clearly established on the appellant's own testimony, and (subject to two matters later to be mentioned) no question now arises as to the correctness of that direction or of the conviction on that count. According to the appellant, however, although the lorry and its load were in fact later stolen by his fellow-conspirators, this was done not pursuant to the conspiracy to which he had been a party, but wholly against his will. He testified that he repented of the conspiracy the day after he entered into it, and that, when 'Reg' (one of his fellow-conspirators) and three others arrived at his home by arrangement to collect him for the purpose of the theft being effected, he told them that he was not going through with it. They thereupon threatened physical violence both to him and to his wife, one of them flourishing a crowbar and another showing him a bottle of petrol, and, in great fear for the safety of his wife and himself, he obeyed their orders to accompany them to his employers' premises. They dropped him outside, he went into the yard and then, still in fear, collected his lorry and drove it to a point on the M.1 near St. Albans, where he was forced by threats to leave the lorry. It was then promptly driven away and has never since been recovered. When later seen by the police, however, the appellant signed two statements in which he confessed that he had been a party to the larceny and made no mention of having been subjected to duress.

. . .

The third and most interesting point taken relates only to the larceny count, it being submitted that the learned deputy-chairman wrongly directed the jury that it was for the appellant to establish that he was acting under duress. The account given by the appellant himself makes it very doubtful whether such a defence was strictly open to him, inasmuch as there was a time after the alleged threats when, having been left outside his employers' yard and having then entered it, he could presumably have raised the alarm and so wrecked the whole criminal enterprise. In *M'Growther's Case* (1746) Fost 13, Lee LCJ, directed the jury that, to establish a plea of duress, the defendant must have resisted or fled from the wrongdoer if that were possible. Seemingly, the position under American law is the same, as appears from the statement in *Professor Rollin Perkins Criminal Law* that, 'The excuse (of compulsion) is not available to someone who had an obviously safe avenue of escape before committing the prohibited act.'

The issue of duress was, nevertheless, left to the jury in the present case, and that may well have been the prudent course. Having been left, did the burden rest on the Crown conclusively to destroy this defence, in the same way as it is required to destroy such other defences as provocation or self-defence? Or was the appellant required to establish it, on the balance of probabilities? . . . The Crown are not called on to anticipate such a defence and destroy it in advance. The accused, either by the cross-examination of the prosecution witnesses or by evidence called on his behalf, or by a combination of the two, must place before the court such material as makes duress a live issue fit and proper to be left to the jury. But, once he has succeeded in doing this, it is then for the Crown to destroy that defence in such a manner as to leave in the jury's minds no reasonable doubt that the accused cannot be absolved on the grounds of the alleged compulsion. . . .

R v Hudson and Taylor
[1971] 2 QB 202
Court of Appeal

(For the facts, see p. 364.)

LORD PARKER CJ: . . . Mr Franks, however contends that the recorder's ruling can be supported on another ground, namely, that the appellants should have taken steps to neutralise the threats by seeking police protection either when they came to court to give evidence, or beforehand. He submits on grounds of public policy that an accused should not be able to plead duress if he had the opportunity to ask for protection from the police before committing the offence and failed to do so. The argument does not distinguish cases in which the police would be able to provide effective protection, from those when they would not, and it would, in effect, restrict the defence of duress to cases where the person threatened had been kept in custody by the maker of the threats, or where the time interval between the making of the threats and the commission of the offence had made recourse to the police impossible. We recognise the need to keep the defence of duress within reasonable bounds but cannot accept so severe a restriction upon it. The duty, of the person threatened, to take steps to remove the threat does not seem to have arisen in an English case but, in a full review of the defence of duress in the Supreme Court of Victoria (*R v Hurley and Murray* [1967] VR. 526), a condition of raising the defence was said to be that the accused 'had no means, with safety to himself, of preventing the execution of the threat.'

In the opinion of this court it is always open to the Crown to prove that the accused failed to avail himself of some opportunity which was reasonably open to him to render the threat ineffective, and that upon this being established the threat in question can no longer be relied upon by the defence. In deciding whether such an opportunity was reasonably open to the accused the jury should have regard to his age and circumstances, and to any risks to him which may be involved in the course of action relied upon. . . .

Notes and questions
1. Are *Gill* and *Hudson and Taylor* reconcilable?
2. The alternative course of action most often suggested is for the defendant to notify the police. If one under duress fails to do so when presented with the opportunity, then the defence may be lost. The problem is that the police often will not intervene until a crime has been committed or is about to be committed. Nor is notification of the police seen as an attractive alternative when the person threatened is a close relative. Why? Should the courts treat this case differently?

B   Private defence and prevention of crime

(i)   Duress and necessity compared
As a practical matter, one who is forcefully attacked by another will instinctively resort to self-defensive actions. The law gives recognition to this reaction by allowing the defender in such circumstances a defence to criminal charges.

So too if one acts not from selfish but from altruistic motives and goes to the aid of another in trouble. Many believe that the law should encourage citizens to help one another. To deny a defence in this situation would be a positive discouragement. A further point is that the fact that the law is prepared to allow force in response to an attack may deter would-be attackers. Nonetheless, the law proceeds cautiously, not wanting to appear to give licence to vigilantes.

Self-defence and defence of another are similar to necessity and duress in many respects. All are affirmative defences which do not come into play until the prosecution have established the elements of the crime. None of the defences is aimed at negating *mens rea* or any other element of the crime (although there are some theorists who argue that absence of excuse or justification is part of *actus reus*). All are all-or-nothing defences in the sense that they either succeed or fail, but do not serve as a basis for reducing the seriousness of the crime, as does provocation. The defendant pleading one of these defences, like the defendant pleading duress or necessity, has been caught in a choice of evils situation. Either the person must commit a crime, most often assault or homicide, or submit to a harm being inflicted upon himself or another.

Self-defence and defence of another are, on the other hand, distinguishable from duress and necessity in that they are deemed to justify the defendant's actions, not simply to excuse them. Partly for this reason some of the limitations which have evolved in respect of duress and necessity have not been extended to self-defence and defence of another. Unlike in respect of duress and necessity, one can raise self-defence or defence of another as a defence to a crime, including murder. Nor does one have to be defending against death or serious bodily harm to invoke these defences.

While the scope of self-defence and defence of another can thus be broader than that of necessity and duress, it also can be narrower. The object of the defendant's force must be the assailant, or the person thought to be the assailant. One cannot commit a crime against an innocent third party, as is often the case in situations involving duress and necessity.

(ii)   Crime prevention
Force used in self-defence or defence of another is usually directed against an assailant who is attempting an unlawful attack. This suggests that these defences will often overlap with two others – prevention of crime and the making of a lawful arrest. Interestingly, while defence of another and self-defence have not been statutorily codified, and continue to have their development shaped by common law principles, the common law rules regarding lawful arrest and crime prevention have been replaced by statute.

Criminal Law Act 1967

3.—(1)   A person may use such force as is reasonable in the circumstances in the prevention of crime, or in effecting or assisting in the lawful arrest of offenders or suspected offenders or of persons unlawfully at large.

(2)   Subsection (1) above shall replace the rules of the common law on the question when force used for a purpose mentioned in the subsection is justified by that purpose.

Question
Which defence controls in those situations where the defendant uses force both in self-defence and to prevent the commission of a crime? Can a

defendant plead both, or must the defendant choose? See *R* v *Cousins* [1982] QB 526.

Note
In cases where the assailant has not in fact committed a crime, the defendant will be restricted to claiming self-defence or defence of another. This is not necessarily fatal, however, as these defences may be available even though the attack which the defendant sought to repel was not unlawful. See, *Williams (Gladstone)*, above.

(iii) Elements of the defences
The critical words in s. 3(1) of the Criminal Law Act 1967, and the core concepts around which revolve the defences of self-defence and defence of another, are force that is 'reasonable in the circumstances'. This is a question of fact for the jury.

Reasonable force may be used in self-defence, defence of another, crime prevention and lawful arrest. But it is reasonable force *in the circumstances* – force which is reasonable in preventing a serious crime may be unreasonable in preventing a less serious crime. While one threatened with death may be justified in using deadly force to repel the attack, that same force could not be used against a thief who was threatening to steal one's property.

What does it mean to say that a defendant acted reasonably in the circumstances? Reasonableness is a two pronged concept:

(a) Was it reasonable for the defendant to believe that any force was necessary under the circumstances – the necessity prong?

(b) Was the amount of force used reasonable in the circumstances – the proportionality prong?

Proportionality is concerned with the amount of force used; necessity with whether or not there was any need to use force at all. Both questions are for the jury to decide.

(a) *The necessity prong.* By definition, reasonableness implies an objective standard – what a reasonable person would consider was warranted under the circumstances. The perception of circumstances, however, may be a subjective matter.

Consider the case where X uses force against Y although he had no reason to believe that Y was committing a crime. Will X escape liability if he uses reasonable force in effecting the arrest, and then is pleasantly surprised to discover that Y was in fact committing a crime which, had X known, would have justified his use of force? Or what of the converse case, where X uses force against Y thinking that he is committing an arrestable offence but it turns out that Y was engaged in lawful activity? These examples present opposite sides of a common coin, and similar answers were given to the questions presented in cases decided more than a century apart.

R v Dadson
(1881) 3 Car & Kerr 148
Kent Assizes

A, a constable employed to guard a copse from which wood had been stolen, saw B come from it, who, on being called to stop, ran away, and A, having no other means of apprehending B fired at and wounded him. B had just before committed a felony in the copse, but A did not know it. A was convicted of having feloniously wounded B.

ERLE J: It appeared that the prisoner, being a constable, was employed to guard a copse from which wood had been stolen, and for this purpose carried a loaded gun. From this copse he saw the prosecutor come out, carrying wood, which he was stealing, and called him to stop. The prosecutor ran away, and the prisoner having no other means of bringing him to justice fired, and wounded him in the leg. These were the facts on which the prisoner acted, but it was alleged in addition that Waters was actually committing a felony, he having been before convicted repeatedly of stealing wood; but these convictions were unknown to the prisoner, nor was there any reason for supposing that he knew the difference between the rules of law relating to felony and those relating to less offences.

I told the jury that this shooting by the prisoner with intent to do grievous bodily harm amounted to the felony charged, unless from other facts there was a justification, and that neither the belief of the prisoner that it was his duty to fire if he could not otherwise apprehend the prosecutor, nor the alleged felony, it being unknown to him, constituted such justification.

The jury found the prisoner guilty of the felony.

R v Williams (Gladstone)
(1983) 78 Cr App R 276
Court of Appeal

For the facts and holding, see p. 255.

Notes and questions
1.   Why should unknown circumstances of justification not be a defence? The *Dadson* rule has been heavily criticised in the literature. Nonetheless, it was implicitly affirmed in *Chapman* v *DPP* [1988] Crim LR 843.
2.   Why should the law allow an accused a defence when he is incorrect in his assumptions about the need for force? Will this not encourage intervention without adequate investigation of the circumstances? In both *Dadson* and *Williams (Gladstone)*, the views of the reasonable person were seemingly disregarded. Why?
3.   The standard relating to the necessity for the use of force in self-defence and defence of others is subjective in another sense – the defendant must have honestly believed that the force was necessary. If a would-be assailant approaches his victims with a replica gun, but the victim is a seller of replica guns and is aware of the gun's true nature, he cannot use the opportunity to kill the assailant, claiming that he was in fear for his life. The fact that a reasonable person would have thought that his life was in danger is irrelevant.

Williams (Gladstone) is concerned with the converse situation. Say that our victim is threatened by an assailant carrying a toy pistol which is a poor replica of a real gun. A reasonable person would realise the gun was not real but the victim does not. According to the decision in *Williams (Gladstone)*, the victim will be judged in accordance with what he believed. Of course, if the victim's belief was wholly unreasonable, a jury might not believe him.

Should it matter why the victim was mistaken? What if he was of subnormal intelligence (as in *Elliot v C (a minor)* [1983] 1 WLR 939, discussed in Chapter 3)? What if he was drunk?

If an attack is not threatened until some future time, can it be said that any force is necessary beforehand? The use of a preemptive strike is obviously more difficult to justify than force used during an actual attack. Indeed, it is often said that one who acts in self-defence or defence of another must be faced with an immediate or imminent threat of harm. But is an absolutist approach appropriate? Desirable? Consider the following case:

Devlin v Armstrong
[1971] NI 13
Court of Appeal

After serious disturbances in the City of Londonderry the appellant was charged with and convicted of four offences of riotous behaviour and incitement to riotous behaviour in Londonderry on 13 August 1969, and she was sentenced to six months' imprisonment. The facts found by the resident magistrate showed that on different occasions on 13 August the appellant had exhorted a crowd of people who had been stoning the police to build a barricade to keep the police out of an area known as the Bogside, to man the barricades and to fight the police with petrol bombs, and that the appellant had herself thrown a stone towards the police. The defence was one of justification, it being submitted that the appellant did the acts complained of because she honestly and reasonably believed that the police were about to behave unlawfully in assaulting people and damaging property in the Bogside, though it was not suggested that there had in fact been any unlawful conduct on the part of any of the police.

Held by the Court of Appeal that, if it be assumed that the appellant did honestly and reasonably believe that the police were about to behave unlawfully in the ways mentioned, such belief did not afford a defence to the charges against her in that: (i) it was one of the common purposes of the appellant and the persons incited to exclude the police from the Bogside by force; (ii) the danger which the appellant was alleged to have anticipated was not sufficiently specific or imminent to justify her actions; and since the police were at the time engaged in containing a riot in the course of their duty, the interventions of the appellant were too aggressive and premature to rank as justifiable efforts to prevent the prospective danger of the police getting out of hand and behaving unlawfully; (iii) the force used by the appellant, assuming it to have been in the exercise of a right of self-defence or of a statutory right to prevent crime, was so excessive as to be unwarrantable; (iv) as regards the charges of incitement, there was no evidence or finding to show that those who were exhorted by the appellant to riot were actuated by an honest and reasonable apprehension of unlawful violence on behalf of the police such as the appellant is assumed to have had. Her incitements were therefore directed to encourage others to do what for them was prima facie unlawful. (v) while it might be that in a case of extreme necessity where the forces of law are absent or have ceased to act as such, individuals could be justified in doing acts which would otherwise be unlawful, the right to do such acts could not justify action directed against a lawfully constituted constabulary while acting as such in the exercise of its proper functions; (vi) there was no sufficient relationship between the appellant and the people of the Bogside to justify her acting in their defence or exercising a right of self-defence on their behalf; (vii) the common law duty imposed on all citizens to help in the suppression of riots and assist the constabulary in so doing made it impossible for the appellant to justify her conduct in encouraging the rioters as she did.

Notes and questions

1. In *Beckford* v *R* [1988] 1 AC 130, a case decided by the Privy Council, Lord Griffiths, speaking for their lordships, said *obiter* (at p. 144): '[A] man about to be attacked does not have to wait for his assailant to strike the first blow or fire the first shot; circumstances may justify a pre-emptive strike.' How close should an attack have to be before one should be allowed to engage in a preemptive strike?

2. The argument against preemptive action is that when the attack is not threatened until the future, there is time to take other action, such as notifying the police. The police, however, may not be able to provide effective protection. Reconsider in this context *Hudson and Taylor*, above.

3. If a preemptive strike is permitted, does it follow that one can justify reasonable but illegal preparatory actions, such as arming oneself, in anticipation of the expected attack, if these preparatory actions would otherwise themselves be criminal? See *Attorney-General's Reference (No. 2 of 1983)* [1984] QB 456.

Another troublesome issue relating to the necessity prong is whether any force is necessary when one who is attacked can, by retreating, avoid the need for force. Should there be a duty to retreat, when retreat can be safely accomplished, before resort to force? The issue had become clouded by considerations of honour. Does the law make cowards of us all, or simply demand that we behave in a prudent manner?

R v *Bird*
[1985] 1 WLR 816
Court of Appeal

LORD LANE CJ: . . . On 24 January 1985 in the Crown Court at Chelmsford, the appellant, as she now is, this court having given her leave to appeal against conviction, was convicted after a re-trial of unlawful wounding under section 20 of the Offences against the Person Act 1861, and she was sentenced to nine months' youth custody.

The facts of the case are these. On 10 March 1984 the appellant, Debbie Bird, was celebrating her seventeenth birthday. There was a party at a house in Harlow. Unhappily it was at that party that the events occurred which ended with her being sent to youth custody. There was a guest at the party called Darren Marder, who was to be the victim of the events which occurred thereafter. He and the appellant had been friendly and had been going out together between about January and the middle of

1983. That close friendship had come to an end, but Marder arrived at the party with his new girl friend and; for reasons which it is not necessary to explore, an argument broke out. After a great deal of bad language and shouting, the appellant told Marder to leave, and leave he did. A little later he unwisely came back and a second argument took place together with a second exchange of obscenities between the two of them. What happened thereafter was the subject of dispute between the parties, though not so much dispute as often arises in these sudden events. The appellant poured a glassful of Pernod over Marder, and he retaliated by slapping her around the face. Further incidents of physical force took place between them. The appellant said that the time came when she was being held and held up against a wall, at which point she lunged at Marder with her hand, which was the hand, unhappily, which held the Pernod glass. The glass hit him in the face, broke, and his eye as a result was lost. It was a horrible event in the upshot, but of course she would not realise the extent to which she was going to cause injury to this young man.

The prosecution case was this, that Marder only slapped the appellant once and that was in order to calm her down, the commonly believed remedy for hysterics. The jury were accordingly invited to infer from that that she could not possibly have been acting in reasonable self-defence when she retaliated against that slap with a weapon as grave as a glass. Secondly, there was evidence of Marder, and also a Miss Bryant, who was his new girl friend, that so far from showing remorse after the event, the appellant said that she would do it again if the same situation arose. Thirdly, there was the evidence of Mrs Sharpe, who was the owner of the house where the party was taking place, who said that after the incident the appellant had admitted to her, Mrs Sharpe, that she had slashed Marder in the face with a glass after he had punched her.

The appellant herself was interviewed by the police. She said that it was only afterwards that she realised that a glass was in her hand, the hand with which she struck the appellant. The appellant gave evidence. She insisted that she had been acting in self-defence. She was being pushed. Marder had said to her that he would hit her if she did not shut up. He slapped her in the face, she was being held by him and thought the only thing for her to do was to strike back to defend herself. In the agony of the moment, so to speak, she did not realise that she was holding the glass. These are the comparatively simple facts of the case.

The grounds of appeal are these. First of all, the judge was in error in directing the jury that before the appellant could rely upon a plea of self-defence, it was necessary that she should have demonstrated by her action that she did not want to fight. That really is the essence of the appellant's case put forward by Mr Pavry to this court in what, if we may say so, was a most helpful argument.

The relevant passages in the summing up are these – first, towards the beginning of the direction to the jury:

> You cannot wrap up an attack in the cloak of self-defence and it is necessary that a person claiming to exercise a right of self-defence should demonstrate by her action that she does not want to fight. At one time it was thought that in order to demonstrate that, that the person seeking to raise a question of self-defence had to retreat. That is not so any longer at all, but there is an obligation to see whether the person claiming to exercise the right of self-defence should have demonstrated that she does not want to fight at all.

Towards the end of the summing up the judge used these words:

> You will have to consider whether in the circumstances of this case self-defence has any application at all. Does it look to you that this lady, who was behaving in this

fashion, had demonstrated that she did not want to fight, was the use of the glass with a hard blow which broke it, reasonable in the circumstances? All these are matters for you and not for me.

The court in *R v Julien* [1969] 1 WLR 839 was anxious to make it clear that there was no duty, despite earlier authorities to the contrary, actually to turn round or walk away from the scene. But reading the words which were used in that judgement, it now seems to us that they placed too great an obligation upon a defendant in circumstances such as those in the instant case, an obligation which is not reflected in the speeches in *Palmer* v *The Queen* [1971] AC 814.

The matter is dealt with accurately and helpfully in *Smith and Hogan Criminal Law*, 5th ed. (1983), p. 327:

> There were formerly technical rules about the duty to retreat before using force, or at least fatal force. This is now simply a factor to be taken into account in deciding whether it was necessary to use force, and whether the force was reasonable. If the only reasonable course is to retreat, then it would appear that to stand and fight must be to use unreasonable force. There is, however, no rule of law that a person attacked is bound to run away if he can but it has been said that – '. . . what is necessary is that he should demonstrate by his actions that he does not want to fight. He must demonstrate that he is prepared to temporise and disengage and perhaps to make some physical withdrawal.' [*R v Julien* [1969] 1 WLR 839, 842]. It is submitted that it goes too far to say that action of this kind is *necessary*. It is scarcely consistent with the rule that it is permissible to use force, not merely to counter an actual attack, but to ward off an attack honestly and reasonably believed to be imminent. A demonstration by [the defendant] at the time that he did not want to fight is, no doubt, the best evidence that he was acting reasonably and in good faith in self-defence; but it is no more than that. A person may in some circumstances so act without temporising, disengaging or withdrawing; and he should have a good defence.

We respectfully agree with that passage. If the defendant is proved to have been attacking or retaliating or revenging himself, then he was not truly acting in self-defence. Evidence that the defendant tried to retreat or tried to call off the fight may be a cast-iron method of casting doubt on the suggestion that he was the attacker or retaliator or the person trying to revenge himself. But it is not by any means the only method of doing that.

It seems to us therefore that in this case the judge – we hasten to add through no fault of his own – by using the word 'necessary' as he did in the passages in the summing up to which we have referred, put too high an obligation upon the appellant.

Notes and questions

1. What are the pros and cons of a retreat rule?

2. Is part of the reluctance to impose a retreat rule the difficulty of making a defendant who is faced with an attack guess at his peril whether as a matter of law he has to retreat? Is it 'reasonable' to expect one who is attacked to make such a calculation? United States Supreme Court Justice Oliver Wendell Holmes poignantly observed: 'Detached reflection cannot be demanded in the face of an uplifted knife.'

3. Even if there is no formal duty to retreat, it behoves one contemplating using force in self-defence to make clear that he is willing to cease and desist,

if for no other reason than to lay the groundwork for a subsequent defence. To the extent that the announcement of a willingness to desist is a relevant evidentiary consideration, then arguably its importance increases with the amount of force that is contemplated being used. If deadly force is contemplated, it is arguable that a fairly clear indication of willingness to desist should be made before resort to such force. Presumably a communication that one is prepared to desist is unnecessary, however, when it would clearly be useless; even more so when it would be dangerous to take the time to make such a communication.

4. Is an offer to retreat, as maintained by the court, in fact the best evidence that the defendant was acting in a reasonable manner?

Consider the distinction drawn in the following case:

R v *Shannon*
(1980) 71 Cr App R 192
Divisional Court

The appellant, with no history of violence or aggression, was attacked by an older and heavier man than himself who had convictions for violence. He stabbed that heavier man three times with a pair of scissors and the latter died. The appellant was charged with his murder. The prosecution case, if accepted by the jury, was that the appellant had gone over to the offensive and stabbed his victim by way of revenge, punishment, retaliation or pure aggression. The appellant pleaded self-defence and an absence of intent to inflict serious bodily injury. His evidence, if accepted by the jury, was that the stabbing was essentially defensive in character. The jury were directed that they might conclude that the appellant had not formed the necessary intent but on the issue of self-defence that the matter to be decided was whether he had used more force than was necessary in the circumstances. The jury acquitted the appellant of murder but convicted him of manslaughter. On appeal,

Held, that the real issue on self-defence was whether the stabbing was within the conception of necessary self-defence judged by the standards of common sense, bearing in mind the position of the appellant at the moment of the stabbing, or whether it was a case of angry retaliation or pure aggression on his part; since the jury by acquitting him of murder must have concluded that he had not intended to cause really serious bodily harm but in returning a verdict of manslaughter had seemingly excluded his state of mind in considering self-defence, the verdict of manslaughter was unsafe and unsatisfactory and the appeal would be allowed and the conviction quashed.

Questions
1. Is the defensive/retaliatory distinction drawn by the court helpful? Is it likely to be an easy distinction for a jury to apply in practice?
2. In asking the jury to consider why the defendant used force, is not the court in *Shannon* inviting the jury to look at the defendant's motive? Motive, as we have seen in Chapter 3, is generally said to be irrelevant to criminal law. Is it relevant in the private defence context?

(b) *The proportionality prong.* In respect of the amount of force used, the generally stated position is that the force used in defence must be proportional to the force used in attack. One may use less force or an equal amount of force in repelling an attack, but one cannot use greater force. The issue that presents itself is whether a defendant should be allowed to use that amount of force which he considered to be proportional under the circumstances. *Williams (Gladstone)* would seem to suggest an affirmative answer, but the courts have not extended that decision to the proportionality issue. On the other hand, they do not seem committed to a pure objective standard either.

Palmer v *R*
[1971] AC 814
Privy Council

LORD MORRIS OF BORTH-Y-GEST: . . . In their Lordships' view the defence of self-defence is one which can be and will be readily understood by any jury. It is a straightforward conception. It involves no abstruse legal thought. It requires no set words by way of explanation. No formula need be employed in reference to it. Only common sense is needed for its understanding. It is both good law and good sense that a man who is attacked may defend himself. It is both good law and good sense that he may do, but may only do, what is reasonably necessary. But everything will depend upon the particular facts and circumstances. Of these a jury can decide. It may in some cases be only sensible and clearly possible to take some simple avoiding action. Some attacks may be serious and dangerous. Others may not be. If there is some relatively minor attack it would not be common sense to permit some action of retaliation which was wholly out of proportion to the necessities of the situation. If an attack is serious so that it puts someone in immediate peril then immediate defensive action may be necessary. If the moment is one of crisis for someone in imminent danger he may have to avert the danger by some instant reaction. If the attack is all over and no sort of peril remains then the employment of force may be by way of revenge or punishment or by way of paying off an old score or may be pure aggression. There may no longer be any link with a necessity of defence. Of all these matters the good sense of a jury will be the arbiter. There are no prescribed words which must be employed in or adopted in a summing up. All that is needed is a clear exposition, in relation to the particular facts of the case, of the conception of necessary self-defence. If there has been no attack then clearly there will have been no need for defence. If there has been attack so that defence is reasonably necessary it will be recognised that a person defending himself cannot weigh to a nicety the exact measure of his necessary defensive action. If a jury thought that in a moment of unexpected anguish a person attacked had only done what he honestly and instinctively thought was necessary that would be most potent evidence that only reasonable defensive action had been taken. A jury will be told that the defence of self-defence, where the evidence makes its raising possible, will only fail if the prosecution show beyond doubt that what the accused did was not by way of self-defence. But their Lordships consider that if the prosecution have shown that what was done was not done in self-defence then that issue is eliminated from the case. If the jury consider that an accused acted in self-defence or if the jury are in doubt as to this then they will acquit. The defence of self-defence either succeeds so as to result in an acquittal or it is disproved in which case as a defence it is rejected. . . .

Notes and questions
1.   If a defendant honestly thought that the amount of force he used was reasonable, why, given *Williams (Gladstone)*, should the defence be denied?

Why should not the same subjective standard apply in respect of the amount of force as applies in respect of the need for force?

2. Lord Morris states in *Palmer* that what an attacked individual 'honestly and instinctively thought was necessary . . . would be most potent evidence that only reasonable defensive action had been taken'. Lecturer believes that deadly force is necessary to prevent Student from stealing her notes, and kills Student. Is Lecturer's belief really the 'most potent evidence that only reasonable defensive action had been taken'?

3. A distinction is often drawn between the use of force and the threat to use force. One may be able to threaten to use more force than one in fact would be legally privileged to use. Why?

The question with the most far-reaching consequences is 'When may one use deadly force?'. The leading case follows:

Attorney-General for Northern Ireland's Reference (No. 1 of 1975)
[1975] QB 773
House of Lords

The accused was a soldier serving with the armed forces of the Crown. His unit was engaged in the suppression of terrorist activities in Northern Ireland. The accused was a member of an army patrol on foot in an area where terrorists were believed to be active. During the course of the patrol the accused saw the deceased, who was on his own, and ordered him to halt. The deceased ran off and thereupon the accused shot and killed him. The accused was charged with murder and was tried by a judge sitting alone under s. 2 of the Northern Ireland (Emergency Provisions) Act 1972. The accused was acquitted. The judge gave a judgment stating his reasons for finding the accused not guilty and set out his findings of fact in considerable detail. In particular the judge stated that he was not satisfied that it had been accused's intention to kill or seriously wound the deceased. Following the acquittal the Attorney-General, acting under s. 48A of the Criminal Appeal (Northern Ireland) 1968 and the Criminal Appeal (References of Points of Law) (Northern Ireland) Rules 1973, referred, inter alia, the following point of law to the Court of Criminal Appeal in Northern Ireland: 'Whether a soldier commits a crime when, in the circumstances set out in [the reference], he fires to kill or seriously wound an unarmed person because he honestly and reasonably believes that that person is a member of a proscribed organisation (in this case the Provisional IRA) who is seeking to run away, and the soldier's shot kills that person.' Paragraph 2 of the reference, in accordance with r. 3(1) of the 1973 rules, set out the 'facts of the case [which were] necessary for the proper consideration of the point of law'. Those facts, which were taken from the judgment of the trial judge, included expressions of opinion as to the likelihood of attack on the patrol and as to the accused's state of mind at the time when he fired the shot. The Court of Criminal Appeal gave its opinion on the point of law and, on the application of the Attorney-General, referred the point to the House of Lords under s. 48A(3) of the 1968 Act.

LORD DIPLOCK: ... My Lords, to kill or seriously wound another person by shooting is prima facie unlawful. There may be circumstances, however, which render the act of shooting and any killing which results from it lawful; and an honest and reasonable belief by the accused in the existence of facts which if true would have rendered his act lawful is a defence to any charge based on the shooting. So for the purposes of the present reference one must ignore the fact that the deceased was an entirely innocent person and must deal with the case as if he were a member of the Provisional IRA and a potentially dangerous terrorist, as the accused honestly and reasonably believed him to be.

The facts to be assumed for the purposes of the reference are not capable in law of giving rise to a possible defence of 'self-defence'. The deceased was in fact, and appeared to the accused to be, unarmed. He was not attacking the accused; he was running away. So if the act of the accused in shooting the deceased was lawful it must have been on the ground that it was done in the performance of his duty to prevent crime or in the exercise of his right to stop and question the deceased under s. 16 or to arrest him under s. 12 of the Northern Ireland (Emergency Provisions) Act 1973.

There is little authority in English law concerning the rights and duties of a member of the armed forces of the Crown when acting in aid of the civil power; and what little authority there is relates almost entirely to the duties of soldiers when troops are called on to assist in controlling a riotous assembly. Where used for such temporary purposes it may not be inaccurate to describe the legal rights and duties of a soldier as being no more than those of an ordinary citizen in uniform. But such a description is in my view misleading in the circumstances in which the army is currently employed in aid of the civil power in Northern Ireland. In some parts of the province there has existed for some years now a state of armed and clandestinely organised insurrection against the lawful government of Her Majesty by persons seeking to gain political ends by violent means, that is by committing murder and other crimes of violence against persons and property. Due to the efforts of the army and police to suppress it the insurrection has been sporadic in its manifestations but, as events have repeatedly shown, if vigilance is relaxed the violence erupts again. In theory it may be the duty of every citizen when an arrestable offence is about to be committed in his presence to take whatever reasonable measures are available to him to prevent the commission of the crime; but the duty is one of imperfect obligation and does not place him under any obligation to do anything by which he would expose himself to risk of personal injury, nor is he under any duty to search for criminals or seek out crime. In contrast to this a soldier who is employed in aid of the civil power in Northern Ireland is under a duty, enforceable under military law, to search for criminals if so ordered by his superior officer and to risk his own life should this be necessary in preventing terrorist acts. For the performance of this duty he is armed with a firearm, a self-loading rifle, from which a bullet, if it hits the human body, is almost certain to cause serious injury if not death.

The use of force in the prevention of crime or in effecting the lawful arrest of suspected offenders is now regulated by s. 3 of the Criminal Law (Northern Ireland) Act 1967 as follows:

(1)   A person may use such force as is reasonable in the circumstances in the prevention of crime, or in effecting or assisting in the lawful arrest of offenders or suspected offenders or of persons unlawfully at large.

(2)   Subsection (1) shall replace the rules of the common law as to the matters dealt with by that subsection.

That section states the law applicable to the defence raised by the accused at the trial of his case.

In the instant reference the relevant purpose for which it is to be assumed that force was used by the accused is the prevention of crime. That is the purpose for which the power to stop and question is conferred on soldiers by s. 16 of the Northern Ireland (Emergency Provisions) Act 1973; and it has not been suggested that shooting to kill or seriously wound would be justified in attempting to effect the arrest under s. 12 of a person who, though he was suspected of belonging to a proscribed organisation (which constitutes an offence under s. 19), was not also believed on reasonable grounds to be likely to commit actual crimes of violence, if he succeeded in avoiding arrest.

What amount of force is 'reasonable in the circumstances' for the purpose of preventing crime is, in my view, always a question for the jury in a jury trial, never a 'point of law' for the judge.

The form in which the jury would have to ask themselves the question in a trial for an offence against the person in which this defence was raised by the accused, would be: are we satisfied that no reasonable man (a) with knowledge of such facts as were known to the accused or reasonably believed by him to exist (b) in the circumstances and time available to him for reflection (c) could be of opinion that the prevention of the risk of harm to which others might be exposed if the suspect were allowed to escape, justified exposing the suspect to the risk of harm to him that might result from the kind of force that the accused contemplated using?

To answer this the jury would have first to decide what were the facts that did exist and were known to the accused to do so and what were mistakenly believed by the accused to be facts. In respect of the latter the jury would have had to decide whether any reasonable man on the material available to the accused could have shared that belief. To select, as is done in para. 2(13) of the reference, two specific inferences of fact as to which it is said that the accused had no belief is merely to exclude them from the jury's consideration as being facts mistakenly believed by the accused to exist; but this does not preclude the jury from considering what inferences of fact a reasonable man would draw from the primary facts known to the accused.

The jury would have also to consider how the circumstances in which the accused had to make his decision whether or not to use force, and the shortness of the time available to him for reflection, might affect the judgment of a reasonable man. In the facts that are to be assumed for the purposes of the reference there is material on which a jury might take the view that the accused had reasonable grounds for apprehension of imminent danger to himself and other members of the patrol if the deceased were allowed to get away and join armed fellow members of the Provisional IRA who might be lurking in the neighbourhood, and that the time available to the accused to make up his mind what to do was so short that even a reasonable man could only act intuitively. This being so, the jury in approaching the final part of the question should remind themselves that the postulated balancing of risk against risk, harm against harm, by the reasonable man is not undertaken in the calm analytical atmosphere of the court room after counsel with the benefit of hindsight have expounded at length the reasons for and against the kind and degree of force that was used by the accused; but in the brief second or two which the accused had to decide whether to shoot or not and under all the stresses to which he was exposed.

In many cases where force is used in the prevention of crime or in effecting an arrest there is a choice as to the degree of force to use. On the facts that are to be assumed for the purposes of the reference the only options open to the accused were either to let the deceased escape or to shoot at him with a service rifle. A reasonable man would know that a bullet from a self-loading rifle if it hit a human being, at any rate at the range at which the accused fired, would be likely to kill him or to injure him seriously. So in one scale of the balance the harm to which the deceased would be exposed if the accused aimed to hit him was predictable and grave and the risk of its occurrence high. In the other scale of the balance it would be open to the jury to take the view that it would not be unreasonable to assess the kind of harm to be averted by preventing the deceased's escape was even graver – the killing or wounding of members of the patrol by terrorists in ambush, and the effect of this success by members of the Provisional IRA in encouraging the continuance of the armed insurrection and all the misery and destruction of life and property that terrorist activity in Northern Ireland has entailed. The jury would have to consider too what was the highest degree at which a reasonable man could have assessed the likelihood that such consequences might follow the escape of the deceased if the facts had been as the accused knew or believed them reasonably to be.

My Lords, the facts as they have been stated for the purpose of the reference are much less detailed than those that were proved at the trial of the accused before MacDermott J without a jury. As stated they are so scanty and couched in such general terms (e.g. there was 'a real threat') that for my part I should not find it possible as a judge of fact to say that in the circumstances as stated the force used by the accused was not reasonable.

In the result I do not think that this House can give to the first question in the reference any more specific answer than that which was given by the majority of the Court of Criminal Appeal in Northern Ireland:

> Point (i) The facts and circumstances set out in the reference are sufficient to raise an issue for the tribunal of fact as to whether the Crown had established beyond reasonable doubt that the respondent's act of shooting constituted, in the circumstances, unreasonable force.

Notes and questions

1.   In respect of the necessity prong, and in light of the subsequent decision in *Williams (Gladstone)*, it would seem that the reasonableness of a belief in the need for force is no longer necessary so long as the defendant's belief was honest. Is *Attorney-General's Reference* to this extent modified or should a different rule apply when deadly force is contemplated?

2.   In *Attorney-General's Reference*, was the defendant himself under threat of immediate attack? Was anybody? Was the threat, if it did exist, real or conjectural? If the defendant believed that at some future point in time the escaped individual would expose another to harm, would that have been sufficient to justify the use of deadly force under Lord Diplock's test? Would it matter if that point in time was the following week? The following month? The following year? Ten years hence?

3.   The burden of persuading the jury that deadly force was not reasonable under the circumstances rests on the prosecution. Once the defendant has introduced some relevant evidence, the prosecution must negate the claim by proof beyond a reasonable doubt.

9 HOMICIDE

I Introduction: Homicide

Homicide for the purposes of the criminal law consists of an *unlawful* killing of a human being. Particular problems are encountered with the limits of this offence because all human beings eventually die. What does it mean to say that a defendant 'caused' what is an inevitable event? Properly defined, 'killing' in the context of homicide refers to any acceleration of the time of death.

The unjustified killing of another human being has traditionally been regarded as the most serious offence known to the law. For this reason the most severe sentences authorised by the law are reserved for this crime. Because murder and manslaughter were and are severely punished, the borderline between a killing which falls into these categories and other justifiable or excusable killings has been the subject of numerous closely reasoned decisions.

Save for constructive manslaughter, the offences of murder and manslaughter have a common *actus reus* which is the unlawful killing of another human being. The following discussion of the *actus reus* of murder will therefore be equally pertinent when the offence of manslaughter is under consideration.

II Murder

It is interesting to note that murder is a common law offence. There is no statutory definition of the crime. The usual starting place for consideration of the elements of murder is the definition put forward by Coke:

> Murder is when a man of sound memory, and of the age of discretion, unlawfully killeth within any county of the realm any reasonable creature *in rerum natura* under the king's peace, with malice aforethought, either expressed by the party or implied by law, so as the party wounded, or hurt etc. die of the wound or hurt, etc. within a year and a day after the same. (3 Inst 47)

At common law the sentence for murder was death, the extreme example of retributive theory in practice. The death penalty has now been abolished, but the judge is constrained to impose a mandatory sentence of life imprisonment. (This does not mean that the prisoner will necessarily serve a life sentence; he may be released on licence by the Home Secretary on the advice of the Parole Board and Lord Chief Justice.) The mandatory life sentence leaves no room for consideration by the sentencing judge of mitigating circumstances. As a consequence, there have been created several 'defences' which will reduce murder to manslaughter. The most important of these defences are diminished responsibility and provocation. Although the maximum penalty for manslaughter is also life imprisonment, a judge has the discretion to impose a lesser sentence – anything from life imprisonment to absolute discharge may be the result.

A   The killer and the victim

The term 'man' in Coke's definition is not to be taken literally. Any person may be guilty of murder, provided that he or she satisfies the general principles of criminal responsibility.

Any human being can be the victim of murder. The two problems that can be encountered relate to when life begins for the purposes of being a victim and when life ends such that one can no longer be a victim. The courts have taken a very conservative view of the commencement of life:

R v *Poulton*
(1832) 5 C & P 329
Central Criminal Court

The prisoner was indicted for wilful murder. The indictment stated, in substance, that the prisoner, on a certain day, was delivered of a female bastard child, which was born alive; and that she afterwards, to wit, on the same day, a certain string of no value, around the neck of the said female bastard child, did bind, tie, and fasten, and by such binding, etc., the said child feloniously and wilfully, of her malice aforethought, did choke and strangle, etc.

LITTLEDALE J: . . . With respect to the birth, the being born must mean that the whole body is brought into the world; and it is not sufficient that the child respires in the progress of the birth. Whether the child was born alive or not depends mainly upon the evidence of the medical men. None of them say that the child was born alive; they only say that it had breathed: and if there is all this uncertainty among these medical men, perhaps you would think it too much for you to say that you are satisfied that the child was born alive.

R v *Brain*
(1834) 6 C & P 350
Oxford Assizes

The prisoner was indicted for the murder of her male bastard child. It appeared that the prisoner had been delivered of a child at Sandford Ferry;

and that the body of the child was afterwards found in the water, about fifteen feet from the lock gate, near the ferry-house; but it was proved by two surgeons, Mr Box and Mr Hester, that the child had never breathed.

PARK J: A child must be actually wholly in the world in a living state to be the subject of a charge of murder; but if it has been wholly born, and is alive, it is not essential that it should have breathed at the time it was killed; as many children are born alive, and yet do not breathe for some time after their birth. But you must be satisfied that the child was wholly born into the world at the time it was killed, or you ought not to find the prisoner guilty of murder. This is not only my opinion, but the law was so laid down in a case as strong as this, by a very learned Judge (Mr Justice Littledale) at the Old Bailey. (His Lordship read the case of *R* v *Poulton*.)

Verdict – Not guilty of murder, but guilty of concealment.

Note

The child must be born alive in order for it to be a victim of murder but the act which caused the death can take place before the birth:

R v *Senior*
(1832) 1 Mood CC 346
King's Bench Division

The prisoner practised midwifery in the town of Stockport, and was called in, at about five in the morning of the 24th of March, to attend Alice Hewitt, who was taken in labour. At about seven in the evening of that day the head of the child became visible; and the prisoner, being grossly ignorant of the art which he professed, and unable to deliver the woman with safety to herself and the child, as might have been done by a person of ordinary skill, broke and compressed the skull of the infant, and thereby occasioned its death immediately after it was born.

It was submitted to the learned Judge by the counsel for the prisoner that the indictment was misconceived, though the facts would warrant an indictment in another form; and that the child being *in ventre sa mere* at the time the wound was given, the prisoner could not be guilty of manslaughter; and quoted 1 Russ. 424.

The learned Judge did not consider the objections valid; and sentenced the prisoner to imprisonment for one year.

Coke, 3 Inst. 50.

All the Judges (except Lord Lyndhurst CB and Taunton J) considered this case at a meeting in Easter term, 1832; and held unanimously that the conviction was right.

Notes

1. The position is the same even if birth has not commenced so that the child is entirely inside the mother at the time the injury was inflicted (see *R* v *West* (1848) 2 Car & Kir 784).

2. The point at which a human entity is capable of being killed is an issue with both legal and moral dimensions. Some people believe that human life begins at conception, and that therefore abortion is murder. English law does not accept this view, although under appropriate circumstances both abortion and the destruction of a child capable of being born alive can be criminal.

3. The killing of an infant under 12 months old by its mother may constitute the crime of infanticide rather than murder (Infanticide Act 1938) if the mother establishes that her mind was disturbed by virtue of her not having fully recovered from the effect of giving birth or by reason of lactation consequent on the birth. The medical underpinnings of this defence are no longer regarded as valid.

Problems have also been encountered with identifying when life ends. For example, consider the case of a victim of a serious assault who is placed on a life support system. Such systems are capable of supporting breathing and heart function after a patient has no functioning of the central nervous system and is so-called 'brain dead'. Is it open to the perpetrator of the assault to argue that the doctors who turn off the life support system of a victim deemed to be 'brain dead' are the cause of the victim's death?

R v *Malcherek and Steel*
[1981] 1 WLR 690
Court of Appeal

LORD LANE CJ: . . . This is not the occasion for any decision as to what constitutes death. Modern techniques have undoubtedly resulted in the blurring of many of the conventional and traditional concepts of death. A person's heart can now be removed altogether without death supervening; machines can keep the blood circulating through the vessels of the body until a new heart can be implanted in the patient, and even though a person is no longer able to breathe spontaneously a ventilating machine can, so to speak, do his breathing for him, as is demonstrated in the two cases before us. There is, it seems, a body of opinion in the medical profession that there is only one true test of death and that is the irreversible death of the brain stem, which controls the basic functions of the body such as breathing. When that occurs it is said the body has died, even though by mechanical means the lungs are being caused to operate and some circulation of blood is taking place.

Airedale NHS Trust v *Bland*
[1993] 2 WLR 316
House of Lords

The patient, then aged 17, was very seriously injured in the disaster which occurred at the Hillsboroough football ground on 15 April 1989. His lungs were crushed and punctured and the supply of oxygen to the brain was interrupted. As a result, he sustained catastrophic and irreversible damage to the higher centres of the brain, which had left him since April 1989 in a condition known as a persistent vegetative state (P.V.S.). The medical opinion of all who had been consulted about his case was unanimous in the diagnosis, and also all were agreed on the prognosis that there was no hope of any improvement in his condition or recovery. At no time before the disaster had the patient indicated his wishes if he should find himself in such a condition. But his father, in evidence, was of the opinion that his son would not 'want to be left like that'. With the concurrence of the patient's family and the consultant in charge of his case and the support of independent physicians, the authority responsible for the hospital where he was being treated, as plaintiffs in the action, sought declarations that they might (i) lawfully discontinue all life-sustaining treatment and medical support measures designed to keep the patient alive in his existing persistent vegetative state including the termination of ventilation, nutrition and hydration by artificial means; and (ii) lawfully discontinue and thereafter need not furnish medical treatment to the patient except for the sole purpose of enabling the patient to end his life and die peacefully with the greatest dignity and the least of pain, suffering and distress. Sir Stephen Brown P granted the declarations sought. On appeal by the Official Solicitor the Court of Appeal upheld the President's order.

On appeal by the Official Solicitor:—

Held, dismissing the appeal, that the object of medical treatment and care was to benefit the patient, but since a large body of informed and responsible medical opinion was of the view that existence in the persistent vegetative state was not a benefit to the patient, the principle of the sanctity of life, which was not absolute, was not violated by ceasing to give medical treatment and care involving invasive manipulation of the patient's body, to which he had not consented and which conferred no benefit upon him, to a P.V.S. patient who had been in that state for over three years; that the doctors responsible for the patient's treatment were neither under a duty, nor (*per* Lord Browne-Wilkinson) entitled, to continue such medical care; that since the time had come when the patient had no further interest in being kept alive, the necessity to do so, created by his inability to make a choice, and the justification for the invasive care and treatment had gone; and that, accordingly, the omission to perform what had previously been a duty would no longer be unlawful . . .

Note

Since 1976, the medical profession has accepted the brain death test for determining when a patient is dead. Is this the correct standard for the law to adopt? You might recall in this regard that in other areas of the law, such as in respect of the legal definition of insanity, legal doctrine does not accord with medical doctrine.

B   Causation

(i)   Death within a year and a day

In the case of both murder and manslaughter, death must occur within a year and a day of the infliction of injury. The original rationale for this rule lay in the difficulty in proving a causal connection between old injuries and a subsequent death. Although such a connection might be easier now because of the more advanced state of medical science, the rule persists, although it is not often in issue before the courts.

R v Dyson
[1908] 2 KB 454
Court of Appeal

LORD ALVERSTONE CJ: The prisoner was indicted for the manslaughter of his child, who died on March 5, 1908. There was evidence that the prisoner had inflicted injuries upon the child in November, 1906, and certain further injuries in December, 1907. The jury convicted the prisoner, who appeals against that conviction upon the ground that the judge misdirected the jury in that he left it to them to find the prisoner guilty if they considered the death to have been caused by the injuries inflicted in 1906. That was clearly not a proper direction, for, whatever one may think of the merits of such a rule of law, it is still undoubtedly the law of the land that no person can be convicted of manslaughter where the death does not occur within a year and a day after the injury was inflicted, for in that event it must be attributed to some other cause.

The conviction was quashed.

Questions
1.   Does the year and a day rule serve any useful function in this medically advanced age?
2.   Jack, the victim of a serious assault by Jill, is rushed to hospital and placed on a life support system. The attendant doctor reaches the conclusion that Jack is in a persistent vegetative state and will never recover consciousness. Jack's parents petition the court to have the support system turned off so that Jack may be allowed to die. Jill argues that the system should be maintained for at least one year and a day from the attack. What should the court decide? Why?
3.   Xavier, knowing that he is HIV positive, has sexual intercourse with Norma. Two years later Norma develops AIDS and dies. Is Xavier guilty of murder?

(ii)   Contributing causes
A further point considered in *R* v *Dyson* (above) was the fact that the child victim was suffering from meningitis and would have died shortly anyway. The acts of the defendant accelerated what was an imminent event in that case and is an inevitable event in all cases. It is problematic, however, whether an acceleration of death from benign motives should be regarded as murder. When, for example, pain relieving drugs are given to patients who are near death it is often the case that death will be accelerated. The general view of the criminal law is that the motive of the defendant is irrelevant (see Chapter 3). Is the doctor who knows that he is accelerating death guilty of murder? (See the extract from the trial of Dr Adams in Chapter 4.)

Questions
1.   Is the position of the courts best understood in terms of logic or humanitarianism? Would a relative administering a pain killing injection be in the same position as a doctor?
2.   Is this an area best left to the medical profession to regulate?

Causation, as we have seen previously, does not rely solely on a test that asks whether 'but for' the defendant's conduct the victim would be dead. The 'reductio ad absurdem' of the pure 'but for' test could lead to the prosecution of the killer's parents. If they had never met and had sexual intercourse the killer would not exist, so, 'but for' their acts, the killing could not have taken place. In the context of homicide the courts ask whether the defendant's acts were the legal or proximate cause, often expressed in the cases as the 'substantial and operating' cause, of the death. In the following cases we can see how this rule operates when the defendant's act is combined with other factors to cause the death of the victim. Troublesome are the cases where death would not have occurred except for the negligence or deliberate acts of others (including the victim) and where the act of the defendant was so insubstantial as to be negligible (where, for example, a person is bleeding rapidly to death because of a cut throat and the defendant accelerates the death by adding a pin prick – this may provide an alternative explanation of R v *Adams*, referred to above). Another difficult case is where there is a cause of death which occurs after the defendant's acts – when should it displace the defendant's acts so as to relieve him of liability?

(a) *Acts of the victim* The victim's contribution to his own death is generally deemed to be irrelevant.

R v Benge
(1865) 4 F & F 504
Maidstone Crown Court

The prosecution arose out of a fatal railway accident, which occurred on the South Eastern Railway at a place called Staplehurst, where there was a bridge, about two miles in the direction towards London from a station called Headcorn. . . .

Piggott, B, said, that assuming culpable negligence on the part of the prisoner which materially contributed to the accident, it would not be material that others also by their negligence contributed to cause it. Therefore he must leave it to the jury whether there was negligence of the prisoner which had been the substantial cause of the accident. In summing up the case to the jury, he said, their verdict must depend upon whether the death was mainly caused by the culpable negligence of the prisoner. Was the accident mainly caused by the taking up of the rails at a time when an express train was about to arrive, was that the act of the prisoner, and was it owing to culpable negligence on his part? His counsel had urged that it was not so, because the flagman and engine-driver had been guilty of negligence, which had contributed to cause the catastrophe; but they, in their turn, might make the same excuse, and so, if it was valid, no one could be criminally responsible at all. This would be an absurd and unreasonable conclusion, and showed that the contention of the prisoner's counsel could not be sound. Such was not the right view of the law – that of the negligence of several persons at different times and places contributed to cause an accident, any one of them could set up that his was not the sole cause of it. It was enough against any one of them that his negligence was the substantial cause of it. Now, here the primary cause was certainly the taking up of the rails at a time when the train was about to arrive, and when it would be impossible to replace them in time to avoid the accident. And this the prisoner admitted was owing to his own mistake. Was that mistake culpable negligence, and did it mainly or substantially cause the accident? The book was clearly and plainly printed, and must have been read carelessly to admit of such a mistake. Was it not the duty of the prisoner who knew the fearful consequences of a mistake to take reasonable care to be correct? And had he taken such care? Then as to its being the main cause of the accident, it was true that the company had provided other precautions to avoid any impending catastrophe, and that these were not observed upon this occasion; but was it not owing to the prisoner's culpable negligence that the accident was impending, and, if so, did his negligence the less cause it, because if other persons had not been negligent it might possibly have been avoided?

Verdict – Guilty.

R v *Swindall and Osborne*
(1846) 2 Car & Kir 230
Nisi Prius

Manslaughter. – The prisoners were indicted for the manslaughter of one James Durose. The second count of the indictment charged the prisoners with inciting each other to drive their carts and horses at a furious and dangerous rate along a public road, and with driving their carts and horses over the deceased at such furious and dangerous rate, and thereby killing him.

. . .

Pollock, CB (in summing up). – The prisoners are charged with contributing to the death of the deceased, by their negligence and improper conduct, and, if they did so, it matters not whether he was deaf, or drunk, or negligent, or in part contributed to his own death . . .

Note

1. As we have seen in Chapter 4 on causation, courts generally take the view that one must take one's victim as one finds him. Normally the rule applies to physical frailties such as the haemophilia or eggshell skull of the victim but the rule may be more far-reaching.

R v *Blaue*
[1975] 3 All ER 446
Court of Appeal

For facts and holding, see p. 159.

Questions

For what proposition does *Blaue* stand? That one must take one's victim as one finds her, even if she is not a reasonable person? That the victim, a Jehovah's Witness, was not unreasonable in her refusal to accept a blood transfusion, even though it would cost her her life? That whether or not the victim's refusal was unreasonable, it did not 'break the chain of causation' so that the death would no longer be attributable to the acts of the defendant? That the contributory acts of a victim are not (or rarely) relevant to issues of causation? That events intervening between the defendant's act and the victim's death must be of earth-shattering significance before they will remove the defendant's responsibility?

The rule that the actions of the victim do not break the chain of causation extends to two other situations:

(a)   Where the cause of the death is pressure exerted by threats.

R v Hayward
(1908) 21 Cox CC 692
Maidstone Autumn Assizes

It appeared from the evidence of neighbours that on the night in question the prisoner came home before his wife. He was in a condition of violent excitement, and was overheard to express a determination of 'giving his wife something' when she came in. When the woman did come home there were at once sounds of an altercation, and shortly afterwards the woman was seen by several witnesses to rush from the house into the road closely pursued by the prisoner, who was at the same time using violent threats towards her. She was then seen to fall into the roadway, and lying there she was kicked on the left forearm by the prisoner. When picked up she was found to be dead.

The medical evidence showed that the bruise on her arm, due to the kick, could not have been the cause of death. The post-mortem examination showed that the deceased, whose organs were otherwise in a perfectly healthy condition, was suffering from a persistent thymus gland, two inches wide and weighing one and three-quarter ounces, lying at the base of the heart. Such a state of affairs was proved to be quite abnormal at the deceased's age – 22. The cause of death was given as cardiac inhibition, and the medical evidence was to the effect that in a person the subject of persistent thymus gland, such as the deceased, any combination of physical exertion and fright or strong emotion might occasion death in such a fashion.

. . .

Ridley, J, in summing up, directed the jury that if they believed the witnesses there was a sufficient chain of evidence to support a conviction of manslaughter. He pointed out that no proof of actual physical violence was necessary, but that death from fright alone, caused by an illegal act, such as threats of violence, would be sufficient. The abnormal state of the deceased's health did not affect the question whether the prisoner knew or did not know of it if it were proved to the satisfaction of the jury that the death was accelerated by the prisoner's illegal act.

The prisoner was convicted and sentenced to three months' imprisonment with hard labour.

(b)   Where the victim is frightened into taking his own life.

R v Halliday
(1889) 61 LT 701
Court of Appeal

LORD COLERIDGE CJ: . . . Here the woman came by her mischief by getting out of the window – I use a vague word on purpose – and in her fall broke her leg. Now that might have been caused by an act which was done accidentally or deliberately, in which case the prisoner would not have been guilty. It appears from the case, however, that the prisoner had threatened his wife more than once, and that on this occasion he came home drunk, and used words which amounted to a threat against her life saying, 'I'll make you so that you can't go to bed;' that she rushing to the window got half out of the window when she was restrained by her daughter. The prisoner threatened the daughter, who let go, and her mother fell. It is suggested to me by my learned brother that, supposing the prisoner had struck his daughter's arm without hurting her but sufficiently to cause her to let go and she had let her mother fall, could anyone doubt but that that would be the same thing as if he had pushed her out himself? If a man creates in another man's mind an immediate sense of danger which causes such person to try to escape, and in so doing he injures himself, the person who creates such a state of mind is responsible for the injuries which result. I think that in this case there was abundant evidence that there was a sense of immediate danger in the mind of the woman caused by the acts of the prisoner, and that her injuries resulted from what such sense of danger caused her to do. I am therefore of opinion that the prisoner was rightly convicted, and that this conviction must be affirmed.

Note

A defendant who has the *mens rea* for murder or manslaughter but does not cause death cannot be liable for the substantive crime (although there could be liability for attempted murder).

R v White
[1910] 2 KB 124
Court of Appeal

BRAY J: In this case the appellant was indicted for the murder of his mother and was convicted of an attempt to murder her and sentenced to penal servitude for life. He appeals from this conviction on several grounds, which we will deal with one by one. First it is said that there was no reasonable evidence on which he could be convicted, or, as it is put in s. 4 of the Criminal Appeal Act, that the verdict cannot be supported having regard to the evidence.

The evidence put shortly was this. On January 9 last the mother was found dead in a sitting posture on a sofa in a sitting-room in her house. There was a round table standing two feet from the sofa, on the further side of which was a wine glass three parts filled with a liquid made up of a drink called nectar and, as was afterwards shewn, containing two grains of cyanide of potassium. There were also on the table a nectar bottle, two lumps of sugar, and a spoon. There was no evidence to shew that she had taken any of this liquid, and the result of the post-mortem examination and of the analysis of the contents of the stomach and of the contents of the wine glass was to shew that she had not died from poisoning by cyanide of potassium, but that death was most probably caused by syncope or heart failure, due to fright or some other external cause.

Appeal dismissed.

R v Dalloway
(1847) 2 Cox CC 273
Stafford Crown Court

The prisoner was indicted for the manslaughter of one Henry Clarke, by reason of his negligence as driver of a cart.

It appeared that the prisoner was standing up in a spring-cart, and having the conduct of it along a public thoroughfare. The cart was drawn by one horse. The reins were not in the hands of the prisoner, but loose on the horse's back. While the cart was so proceeding down the slope of a hill, the horse trotting at the time, the deceased child, who was about three years of age, ran across the road before the horse, at the distance of a few yards, and one of the wheels of the cart knocking it down and passing over it, caused its death. It did not appear that the prisoner saw the child in the road before the accident.

Erle, J, in summing up to the jury, directed them that a party neglecting ordinary caution, and, by reason of that neglect, causing the death of another, is guilty of manslaughter; that if the prisoner had reins, and by using the reins could have saved the child, he was guilty of manslaughter; but that if they thought he could not have saved the child by pulling the reins, or otherwise by their assistance, they must acquit him.

The jury acquitted the prisoner.

Questions
1.   In *White*, was the death caused by the victim's heart attack or by the defendant's action? What if it could be shown that the victim realised that the glass contained poison and, distraught that her child would contemplate killing her, suffered a fatal heart attack?
2.   Dalloway clearly caused the death of the child. Why, then, did he escape criminal liability?

(b)   *Acts of third parties*. The action or inaction of third parties is often claimed to be the cause of death, rather than the acts of the defendant. Many of the cases involve medical treatment:

R v Jordan
(1956) 40 Cr App R 152
Court of Appeal

For the facts and holdings, see p. 161.

R v Smith
[1959] 2 QB 35
Courts-Martial Appeal Court

For the facts and holdings, see p. 163.

Questions
Are *Smith* and *Jordan* reconcilable? Are there policy reasons for not ruling that a doctor who treats the victim of an assault causes the victim's death, even if that doctor is negligent? These and related issues are also explored in Chapter 4 (Causation and Concurrence).

The 'human shield' cases have also caused problems:

R v Pagett
(1983) 76 Cr App R 279
Court of Appeal

For the facts and holdings, see p. 166.

Where the death occurs in the manner intended, the unwitting intervention of a third party is generally deemed to be irrelevant.

R v *Michael*
(1840) 9 C & P 356
Central Criminal Court

It appeared that the deceased was a child between nine and ten months old, and that the prisoner was its mother, and was a single woman living in service as wet nurse at Mrs Kelly's, in Hunter Street, Brunswick Square. The child was taken care of by a woman named Stevens, living at Paddington, who received five shillings a week from the prisoner for its support. A few days before its death the prisoner told Mrs Stevens that she had an old frock for the child, and a bottle of medicine, which she gave her, telling her it would do the baby's bowels good. Mrs Stevens said the baby was very well, and did not want medicine; but the prisoner said it had done her mistress's baby good, and it would do her baby good, and desired Mrs Stevens to give it one tea-spoonful every night. Mrs Stevens did not open the bottle, or give the child any of its contents, but put the bottle on the mantel-piece, where it remained till Tuesday, the 31st of March, on which day, about half-past four in the afternoon, Mrs Stevens went out, leaving the prisoner's child playing on the floor with her children, one of whom, about five years of age, during the absence for about ten minutes of his elder sister, gave the prisoner's child about half the contents of the bottle, which made it extremely ill, and in the course of a few hours it died. The bottle was found to contain laudanum.

Alderson B, in his summing up, told the jury, that if the prisoner delivered the laudanum to Sarah Stevens with the intention that she should administer it to the child, and thereby produce its death, and the quantity so directed to be administered was sufficient to cause death, and while the prisoner's original intention continued, the laudanum was administered by an unconscious agent, the death of the child, under such circumstances, would sustain the charge of murder against the prisoner. His Lordship added, that if the tea-spoonful of laudanum was sufficient to produce death, the administration by the little boy of a much larger quantity would make no difference.

The jury found the prisoner guilty. . . .

At a subsequent Session, Mr Baron Alderson, in passing sentence upon the prisoner, said, that the Judges were of opinion that the administering of the poison by the child of Mrs Stevens, was, under the circumstances of the case, as much, in point of law, an administering by the prisoner as if the prisoner had actually administered it with her own hand. They therefore held that she was rightly convicted.

C   *Jurisdiction*

The normal territorial jurisdiction of the English courts has been extended for the offences of murder and manslaughter:

(a)   A killing by a British citizen can found a conviction for murder or manslaughter whether the killing takes place in England or Wales or abroad (i.e. outside the normal territorial limits of the court's jurisdiction) (Offences Against the Person Act 1861, s. 9 and British Nationality Act 1948, s. 3). The defendant may also be subject to the jurisdiction of the courts in the territory where the killing takes place.

(b)   Murder or manslaughter committed on a British ship or aircraft is triable in England or Wales whether the killing is committed by a British citizen or not.

(c)   Murder *of* a British citizen committed abroad is *not* triable in England or Wales merely because of the nationality of the victim.

Where the crime is committed outside the jurisdiction of the courts of the United Kingdom and the offender is arrested where the crime is committed, it will be necessary to extradite the defendant if he or she is to stand trial in the United Kingdom. Although most countries will allow extradition for murder or manslaughter, it is not automatic. If the courts of the foreign jurisdiction conclude that the defendant will not receive a fair trial in the United Kingdom, they may refuse to order extradition.

D   Mens rea

Under Coke's definition of murder (see p. 389 above), the prosecution must establish *malice aforethought*. The meaning of this concept must be gleaned from judicial pronouncements in decided cases as there is no statutory definition of the term. The courts have now settled that malice aforethought means an intention to kill any person or an intention to cause grievous bodily harm to any person.

'Intention' has the meaning examined above in Chapter 3 (*Mens rea*).

R v Hancock and Shankland
[1986] 1 AC 455
House of Lords

For the facts and holdings, see p. 101.

Notes
1.   In most cases the presence of an intention to kill will be clear. The probability of death or serious injury resulting from the actions of the defendant are not relevant where the defendant desires the death (see *Michael*, above).
2.   Where the intention to kill or cause serious harm is not so clear the courts have held that the defendant's foresight of death or serious harm as a consequence of his actions is evidence of his intention to cause those consequences. The less likely he believes such an outcome to be, the weaker the inference of an intent to kill. See *Hancock and Shankland* (above).

The alternative *mens rea* which will justify a conviction for murder is an intent to cause 'grievous bodily harm'. This is the 'implied malice' referred to in Coke's definition. See *Cunningham* [1982] AC 566. In *Director of Public Prosecutions* v *Smith* [1961] AC 290, 'grievous bodily harm' was explained as 'really serious harm'. Whether this clarification adds much to our understanding of the concept is debatable. The basic policy question presented is whether one who does not have the intent to kill should be subject to a conviction for murder. What is the justification for convicting in these circumstances? What are the arguments against? It should be recalled that in order to convict a defendant for attempted murder, the Crown must prove an intent to kill; an intent to commit grievous bodily harm is not sufficient.

For a discussion by one of the current Law Lords of some of the issues involved in *mens rea* in murder, see Goff, 'The mental element in the crime of murder' (1988) 104 LQR 30.

III Manslaughter

There are two categories of manslaughter, voluntary and involuntary. A killing which would otherwise be murder may be reduced to *voluntary manslaughter* if the jury consider that the defendant is entitled to rely on one of three statutory defences specific to murder. *Involuntary manslaughter* consists of all other killings which do not amount to murder, but for which a defendant is criminally liable. Unlike for murder, there is no mandatory sentence of life imprisonment for manslaughter.

A   Voluntary manslaughter

The Homicide Act 1957 establishes three murder-specific defences which will reduce murder to manslaughter. These are provocation, diminished responsibility, and suicide pact. The general defences discussed in Chapter 8 are also available to a defendant charged with murder, but if they succeed the defendant will be acquitted. In contrast, a successful defence of provocation, diminished responsibility or suicide pact will not lead to an acquittal, but only to a reduction in charge from murder to manslaughter.

(i)   Diminished responsibility
The defence of diminished responsibility was established in the Homicide Act 1957, s. 2:

Homicide Act 1957

2.—(1)   Where a person kills or is a party to the killing of another, he shall not be convicted of murder if he was suffering from such abnormality of mind (whether arising from a condition of arrested or retarded development or any inherent causes or induced by disease or injury) as substantially impaired his mental responsibility for his acts and omissions in doing or being a party to the killing.

(2)   On a charge of murder, it shall be for the defence to prove that the person charged is by virtue of this section not liable to be convicted of murder.

(3)   A person who but for this section would be liable, whether as principal or as accessory, to be convicted of murder shall be liable instead to be convicted of manslaughter.

(4)   The fact that one party to a killing is by virtue of this section not liable to be convicted of murder shall not affect the question whether the killing amounted to murder in the case of any other party to it.

Note
The burden of proving the defence rests on the defendant. The standard of proof required is a balance of probabilities (*Dunbar* [1958] 1 QB 1). Unlike in the case of insanity, the issue of diminished responsibility may not be raised by the prosecution; and, indeed, the judge cannot instruct the jury on the issue without the defendant's consent. See *Campbell* (1986) 84 Cr App R 255. The defence must be supported by medical or other scientific evidence.

R v Dix
(1981) 74 Cr App R 306
Court of Appeal

SHAW LJ: . . . [Counsel] pointed out that there have been cases in which medical evidence was tendered by both defence and prosecution supporting a plea of diminished responsibility, but the jury rejected that evidence and convicted of murder. The history and circumstances of the offence were treated by the jury as having greater significance than the scientific evidence. If, so Mr Hamilton contended, a jury was entitled to act in that way and to convict of murder, why are they not entitled to come to a conclusion, one way or the other, as to diminished responsibility when there is no medical evidence at all?

The logic of this argument might be stronger if there was no onus on the defence to prove diminished responsibility. Having regard to that onus the argument must fail. In any case, it is inseparable from the proposition that the part of section 2(1) in parenthesis is descriptive of all forms of abnormality of the mind so that no proof is required that an accused's asserted abnormality of mind falls within the categories described within the brackets. Mr Hamilton's argument to this effect was cogent and almost persuasive but the judgment of the Court of Criminal Appeal in *Byrne* (1960) 44 Cr App R 246; [1960] 2 QB 396 is conclusive against his proposition. Giving the judgment of the Court, Lord Parker CJ said at p. 252 and p. 402 respectively: 'It is against that background of the existing law that section 2(1) of the Homicide Act 1957 falls to be construed. To satisfy the requirements of the subsection the accused must show: (a) that he was suffering from an abnormality of mind; and (b) that such abnormality of mind (i) arose from a condition of arrested or retarded development of mind or any inherent causes or was induced by disease or injury; and (ii) was such as substantially impaired his mental responsibility for his acts in doing or being a party to the killing.'

This analysis of the subsection has not been doubted or criticised. Notwithstanding Mr Hamilton's attractive argument, this Court sees no reason to qualify it in any way whatsoever. What emerges from Lord Parker's statement is that scientific evidence of a medical kind is essential to establish what is referred to in (b)(i) and (b)(ii). Thus while the subsection does not in terms require that medical evidence be adduced in support of a defence of diminished responsibility, it makes it a practical necessity if that defence is to begin to run at all. In the result, Griffith J's ruling was in substance a correct one. The appeal accordingly fails and is dismissed.

Questions
Why should the law require medical or other scientific evidence? Why should not the testimony of ordinary persons who observed the defendant at the time of the killing suffice?

Note
One problem encountered here is the same as we observed in respect to determining whether a defendant was insane at the time of the crime, and that is that a medical examination may not occur until after arrest, which may be some time after the killing. The examining doctor must make an informed guess at the defendant's mental state at a previous point in time based on this later examination. A further complicating factor is that the killing itself may

have had an effect on the defendant's mental state. Guilt about the killing may have exacerbated the defendant's condition, or conversely, the killing may have relieved the mental stress which gave rise to the urge to kill. In either case the doctor will not see the same person that he or she would have seen had the examination taken place prior to the killing.

Three major problems have been encountered in the use of the defence of diminished responsibility. The first is the definition of *abnormality of mind*; the second the relationship between the abnormality and the defendant's responsibility for the killing; and the third the relationship between diminished responsibility and other defences.

(a) *Abnormality of mind*. What constitutes 'abnormality of mind'? The leading case interpreting this phrase is *Byrne*.

R v Byrne
[1960] 2 QB 396
Court of Appeal

LORD PARKER CJ: . . . The appellant was convicted of murder before Stable J at Birmingham Assizes and sentenced to imprisonment for life. The victim was a young woman whom he strangled in the YWCA hostel, and after her death he committed horrifying mutilations upon her dead body. The facts as to the killing were not disputed, and were admitted in a long statement made by the accused. The only defence was that in killing his victim the accused was suffering from diminished responsibility as defined by section 2 of the Homicide Act, 1957, and was, accordingly, guilty not of murder but of manslaughter.

Three medical witnesses were called by the defence, the senior medical officer at Birmingham Prison and two specialists in psychological medicine. Their uncontradicted evidence was that the accused was a sexual psychopath, that he suffered from abnormality of mind, as indeed was abundantly clear from the other evidence in the case, and that such abnormality of mind arose from a condition of arrested or retarded development of mind or inherent causes. The nature of the abnormality of mind of a sexual psychopath, according to the medical evidence, is that he suffers from violent perverted sexual desires which he finds it difficult or impossible to control. Save when under the influence of his perverted sexual desires he may be normal. All three doctors were of opinion that the killing was done under the influence of his perverted sexual desires, and although all three were of opinion that he was not insane in the technical sense of insanity laid down in the M'Naughten Rules it was their view that his sexual psychopathy could properly be described as partial insanity.
. . .

'Abnormality of mind,' which has to be contrasted with the time-honoured expression in the M'Naughten Rules 'defect of reason,' means a state of mind so different from that of ordinary human beings that the reasonable man would term it abnormal. It appears to us to be wide enough to cover the mind's activities in all its aspects, not only the perception of physical acts and matters, and the ability to form a rational judgment as to whether an act is right or wrong, but also the ability to exercise will power to control physical acts in accordance with that rational judgment. The expression 'mental responsibility for his acts' points to a consideration of the extent to which the accused's mind is answerable for his physical acts which must include a consideration of the extent of his ability to exercise will power to control his physical acts.

Whether the accused was at the time of the killing suffering from any 'abnormality of mind' in the broad sense which we have indicated above is a question for the jury. On this question medical evidence is no doubt of importance, but the jury are entitled to take into consideration all the evidence, including the acts or statements of the accused and his demeanour. They are not bound to accept the medical evidence if there is other material before them which, in their good judgment, conflicts with it and outweighs it.

The aetiology of the abnormality of mind (namely, whether it arose from a condition of arrested or retarded development of mind or any inherent causes, or was induced by disease or injury) does, however, seem to be a matter to be determined on expert evidence.

Assuming that the jury are satisfied on the balance of probabilities that the accused was suffering from 'abnormality of mind' from one of the causes specified in the parenthesis of the subsection, the crucial question nevertheless arises: was the abnormality such as substantially impaired his mental responsibility for his acts in doing or being a party to the killing? This is a question of degree and essentially one for the jury. Medical evidence is, of course, relevant, but the question involves a decision not merely as to whether there was some impairment of the mental responsibility of the accused for his acts but whether such impairment can properly be called 'substantial,' a matter upon which juries may quite legitimately differ from doctors.

Furthermore, in a case where the abnormality of mind is one which affects the accused's self-control the step between 'he did not resist his impulse' and 'he could not resist his impulse' is, as the evidence in this case shows, one which is incapable of scientific proof. A fortiori there is no scientific measurement of the degree of difficulty which an abnormal person finds in controlling his impulses. These problem which in the present state of medical knowledge are scientifically insoluble, the jury can only approach in a broad, common-sense way. This court has repeatedly approved directions to the jury which have followed directions given in Scots cases where the doctrine of diminished responsibility forms part of the common law. We need not repeat them. They indicate that such abnormality as 'substantially impairs his mental responsibility' involves a mental state which in popular language (not that of the M'Naughten Rules) a jury would regard as amounting to partial insanity or being on the border-line of insanity.

Notes and questions
1.   Is the test of the *Byrne* court – that an abnormality of mind is 'a state of mind so different from that of ordinary human beings that the reasonable man would term it abnormal' – at all helpful? How could more in the way of guidance be provided to the jury?
2.   Does the source of the abnormality of mind matter? A bracketed clause after the phrase 'abnormality of mind' in s. 2(1) states '(whether arising from a condition of arrested or retarded development of mind or any inherent causes or induced by disease or injury)'. What does this mean? Are a lay jury likely to understand? This leads to the question of whether and when a jury should be allowed to reject the medical testimony of abnormality of mind. Would it make more sense to allow this specific issue to be decided by a panel of medical experts?

3. The test of partial insanity referred to in *Byrne* should be approached with caution; it is not appropriate in all cases. See *Seers* (1984) 79 Cr App R 261.

(b) *Impaired responsibility for the killing.* Mere proof of abnormality of mind is not enough to establish the defence. The abnormality of mind must *substantially impair* the defendant's mental responsibility for his acts and omissions in doing or being a party to the killing. The problem with this formula is that it confuses two concepts: that of reduced capacity to control one's actions and that of moral culpability. The jury are asked to decide whether an abnormality has reduced the defendant's control over his actions and omissions and whether, as a consequence, his moral responsibility for the killing is reduced. Because of this difficulty and difficulties defining 'abnormality of mind' the defence has attracted much criticism. See, e.g., Griew, E., 'The future of diminished responsibility' [1988] Crim LR 75.

Rather than risk a problematic prosecution for murder in which the defendant is likely to raise the defence of diminished responsibility, the Crown is often inclined to accept a plea to a lesser charge.

Notes and questions
1. The Butler Committee, examining the defence of diminished responsibility, found evidence that there was a tendency for the legal and medical professions to stretch the terms of s. 2 out of motives of humanity (see Cmnd 6244, 1975, para. 19.5).
2. As a practical matter, defendants charged with murder have historically been reluctant to raise a defence of insanity, as an acquittal on the grounds of insanity led to automatic committal to a mental institution for an indefinite period, potentially for life. It was partly in recognition of this fact that the defence of diminished responsibility was created. The Criminal Procedure (Insanity and Unfitness to Plead) Act 1991 (discussed in Chapters 2 and 8) does away with automatic commitment. In the light of this development, is there any point in retaining the defence of diminished responsibility? To what extent do the two defences overlap?

(c) *Relationship with other defences.* In addition to any overlap between diminished responsibility and insanity (see above), the question often arises as to the relationship between diminished responsibility and other defences. What happens when there are multiple causes of the defendant's abnormal behaviour, one of which is outside those listed in the Homicide Act 1957, s. 2? The most common example is intoxication. This would seem to be excluded by the words in brackets in that section '(whether arising from a condition of arrested or retarded development of mind or any inherent causes or induced by disease or injury)'. However, alcoholism may give rise to an admissible abnormality if proof of brain damage is forthcoming.

In circumstances where the defendant is suffering from two causes of abnormality, one within the section and the other not, the usual approach adopted by the courts is to ask the jury to ignore the cause of abnormality outside the section and to try to assess the effects of the admissible abnormality. Clearly this is a difficult, if not near impossible, task.

R v Atkinson
[1985] Crim LR 314
Court of Appeal

The appellant, aged 18, together with other youths stole spirits which they drank and later burgled a house occupied by a 77 year old woman, who disturbed them and shouted for help. The appellant threatened to kill her if she did not stop shouting, punched her in the back of the head and then beat her including stamping on her face and she died of a fractured skull. In February 1984 he was tried on a charge of murder. He did not give evidence and a defence of diminished responsibility was advanced. Medical evidence was that he had grossly arrested or retarded development of mind and that alcohol had played a part in the events. The jury were directed to pose themselves the questions, first, whether they thought it more probable than not at the time of the killing his responsibility was substantially impaired by the fact that he was suffering from arrested or retarded development; and, if they thought that drink had something to do with it, secondly, whether that was the substantial cause, the root cause, of his inability to control himself at the time of the killing. He was convicted of murder. He appealed on the ground of misdirection on diminished responsibility.

Held, dismissing the appeal, that at the trial in February the trial judge had, so to speak, to anticipate what the Court of Appeal would say in *R v Gittens* [1984] QB 698. *Gittens* was reported and commented on by Professor J. C. Smith at [1984] Crim LR 553-554, where he stated that the two questions for the jury, in logical sequence, would seem to be: 'Have the defence satisfied you on the balance of probabilities – that if the defendant had not taken drink – (i) he would have killed as he in fact did? And (ii) he would have been under diminished responsibility when he did so?' The Court would like respectfully and gratefully to agree with Professor Smith's analysis, which put the matter clearly and in a way which could be understood by all. In the direction to the jury the judge was, in effect, posing the questions posed by Professor Smith in his commentary, although the other way round. The question for the jury was: if the appellant had not taken drink would he have killed as in fact he did? The jury were entitled to answer the question as they had. The direction of the authorities was to be drawn to the medical reports, which were ordered to be appended to the transcript.

Notes and questions

1. The Criminal Law Revision Committee in its 'Fourteenth Report: Offences Against the Person' (Cmnd 7844) recommended a revision of the defence of diminished responsibility. The Law Commission in its Draft Criminal Code Bill 1989 largely adopted the suggested revisions. Clause 56 of the Draft Code provides:

56. (1) A person who, but for this section, would be guilty of murder is not guilty of murder if, at the time of his act, he is suffering from such mental abnormality as is a substantial enough reason to reduce his offence to manslaughter.

(2)   In this section 'mental abnormality' means mental illness, arrested or incomplete development of mind, psychopathic disorder, and any other disorder or disability of mind, except intoxication.

(3)   Where a person suffering from mental abnormality is also intoxicated, this section applies only where it would apply if he were not intoxicated.

The proposed formulation has the advantage of:

(a)   requiring the defendant only to raise evidence of diminished responsibility rather than prove it on a balance of probabilities as at present;

(b)   providing a clearer definition of the states of mind covered, using terms more readily understood by the medical profession;

(c)   disentangling the medical issue as to whether the defendant is suffering from abnormality (which will remain a matter for medical testimony) and the moral issue of the effect of that abnormality on the defendant's moral responsibility. The latter is a matter clearly put within the jury's domain by cl. 56(1).

There are, unfortunately, no moves at present to implement the proposed reform.

2.   To a large extent the defence of diminished responsibility owes its existence to the fact that the mandatory sentence for murder is life imprisonment. If the defence did not exist, a judge in sentencing could not take into account extenuating cirumstances such as the defendant's mental state at the time of the crime. Would the Butler Committee's suggestion of abolition of the mandatory life sentence be an acceptable alternative solution to the problems encountered in this area?

(ii) Provocation

Provocation was a defence at common law, but was modified by the Homicide Act 1957, s. 3:

Homicide Act 1957

3.   Where on a charge of murder there is evidence on which the jury can find that the person charged was provoked (whether by things done or by things said or by both together) to lose his self-control, the question whether the provocation was enough to make a reasonable man do as he did shall be left to be determined by the jury; and in determining that question the jury shall take into account everything both done and said according to the effect which, in their opinion, it would have on a reasonable man.

Note

Like diminished responsibility, the defence of provocation is *only* a partial defence and *only* a defence to a charge of murder. Provocation is not a defence to lesser crimes, even attempted murder. However, provoked killings have long been thought to be qualitatively different and less reprehensible than other killings. The effect of successfully pleading provocation is to reduce one's crime from murder to manslaughter. Unlike in diminished responsibility, the defendant needs only introduce some evidence of provocation to force the prosecution to prove beyond reasonable doubt that the defendant was not provoked.

R v *Cascoe*
[1970] 2 All ER 833
Court of Appeal

SALMON LJ: . . . At about 5.00 am on 19th January 1969 a party was still going on at a dance hall somewhere in north London. At that late or early hour a man called 'Manny' Francis, with three or four other guests, arrived at the party. The appellant had been there for some time. Very shortly after Mr Francis arrived, there was a good deal of evidence that the appellant shot Mr Francis. He was seen with a smoking pistol in his hand. The evidence showed conclusively that he shot Mr Francis no fewer than seven times and that as a result Mr Francis died.

According to the case for the prosecution, the appellant had come to that dance hall armed with the pistol. Evidence had been called of persons who had seen him with the pistol prior to 19th January 1969. The appellant, however, when he gave evidence, said that it was entirely untrue to say that he had ever possessed that pistol or any other. His case was that shortly after he arrived at the dance hall he saw Mr Francis, whom he had known for some two years and with whom he was on very bad terms owing to an association which the appellant had previously formed with Mr Francis's stepdaughter. Indeed, on one occasion Mr Francis had attacked him with a knife. According to the appellant, Mr Francis came up to him, put his hand in his pocket as if to produce a pistol and then half drew a pistol from his pocket. The appellant, who said that he was a karate expert, acted very promptly. He administered what is called a karate chop just above Mr Francis's right wrist which caused him to drop the pistol on the floor. The appellant then picked up the pistol. As he did so, so he said, he saw four or five of Mr Francis's cronies advancing towards him. According to the appellant, he knew that they were all violent men and carried knives, whereupon in order to defend himself and to dissuade Mr Francis's cronies from attacking him with their knives, he fired at Mr Francis and hit him with all seven shots. There was no suggestion by the appellant that he fired at Mr Francis other than with the intention of hitting him.

The defence that was run at the trial was based on three grounds: first of all, that the appellant was suffering from diminished responsibility; secondly, that he was acting in self-defence; thirdly, that if the actions which he took exceeded what could reasonably be done by way of self-defence, the jury would be entitled to find the appellant guilty of manslaughter.
. . .

I now turn to the only real point made on behalf of the appellant on this appeal, and it concerns provocation. It should be noted that this was never run by the defence at the trial. Nevertheless, it is quite plain that although the defence is not run at the trial, the judge, if he considers that there is evidence on which a jury might reasonably, and I repeat the word 'might', find provocation, has a duty to leave that issue to the jury. The learned recorder clearly thought that there was some evidence on which a jury might reasonably find provocation which would reduce the appellant's crime from murder to manslaughter.

The complaint that is made of the recorder's direction on provocation is as follows. Counsel for the appellant says that when the recorder came to deal with provocation, he explained the law in relation to provocation with complete accuracy except in one important respect. He failed to tell the jury, as he had done when he dealt with self-defence, that from beginning to end the onus lay on the Crown, that it was not for the appellant to prove provocation, but that if, at the end of the day, the jury were left in any reasonable doubt by the evidence whether the appellant had been provoked, then they should acquit him of murder and find him guilty of manslaughter.
. . .

It seems to this court that the evidence of provocation was extremely tenuous. On the other hand, we consider it impossible to say that there was no evidence of provocation. All matters of fact were for the jury to decide.

. . . It seems to this court that a jury might have come to the conclusion that acts done by Mr Francis in those circumstances so frightened and angered the appellant that he lost all control of himself and took up the gun, and in a passion fired it at Mr Francis. We are far from saying that it is probable that the jury would have taken that view. All that we conclude is that there was evidence on which they could have taken that view. If they could have taken that view, then the question whether the provocation was enough to make a reasonable man do as the appellant did had to be left to be determined by the jury. It was left, and no one in all the circumstances here can criticise the learned recorder for leaving that question to the jury. Having left it to the jury, it was essential that they should have been given a correct direction on where the burden of proof lay so far as provocation was concerned.

. . . Whether the issue is raised at the trial or not, if there is evidence which might lead the jury to find provocation, then it is the duty of the court to leave that issue to the jury. The evidence in this case was very thin indeed. The very experienced recorder, however, considered that there was some evidence or he would not have left that issue to the jury. We cannot disagree with him in the view which he took on that point. It follows from what has been said that since there was the oversight in the summing-up to which reference has been made, the appeal must be allowed and a verdict of manslaughter substituted for the verdict of murder.

Notes and questions

1.   Note that defendants who raise the issue of provocation are not saying that they did not have an intent to kill or cause grievous bodily harm. Rather they are saying that they did so in a situation where they were provoked to the point that they lost self-control.

2.   Why should not the burden of persuading the jury of the defence of provocation be on the defendant, as it is with diminished responsibility?

3.   *Cascoe* underlines the fact that the issue of provocation must be left to the jury even when the defence does not put forward evidence of provocation as such. This situation may arise when the main plank of the defence is self-defence rather than provocation:

R v Johnson
[1989] 1 WLR 740
Court of Appeal

WATKINS LJ: . . . The deceased died during the night of 18/19 May 1987 in a night club in Sheffield when the appellant stabbed him in the chest with a knife. The blade of the knife, 3.8 inches long, penetrated the chest to the heart. The wound, there was but one, travelled from the deceased's left to right parallel with the ground. There were no defensive wounds on the deceased.

During the evening both the appellant and the deceased had been drinking at the night club. The appellant was carrying a knife. It was a flick or 'swish' knife. The deceased was unarmed. A tense atmosphere developed in the club when the appellant started to behave in an unpleasant way. Threats of violence were made by him to a female friend of the deceased and then to the deceased himself. This woman and the deceased became extremely annoyed. A struggle developed between the two men during the course of which the stabbing occurred.

. . .

It was accepted before us by counsel for the Crown that the evidence before the jury included the following. Before the stabbing incident the appellant had been taunted by a woman who called him a 'white nigger'. Apparently, although a white man himself, he affected at times a West Indian accent. He reacted to that abuse. It upset him. It made him angry. There were high words between him and others, the deceased included. Seemingly to leave the club or that part of it, the appellant walked away towards the exit. The deceased however followed him and poured beer over him. The deceased then removed his jacket. The appellant did not. The deceased by placing his arm across the appellant's chest or throat seized hold of the appellant and pinned him against a wall. While he was thus pinned against the wall the woman, who had described him as a 'white nigger,' attacked him by punching his head and pulling his hair. There were shouts from some of the others present that the deceased should drop the glass which he held in his hand. He did so. Until this moment the appellant had not retaliated. But his attitude to being held captive suddenly changed. He somehow bent down and produced the knife and lunged at the deceased with it. He lunged again, so it was said, but failed to make contact. He was restrained by one of his friends. His explanation for his conduct was, as has been stated, a fear of being 'glassed'. He did not, as has also been stated, claim that he had lost his self-control.

Nevertheless, if the jury rejected, as they did, his account that he was acting in self-defence they might, in our judgement, very well have inferred from all that evidence that there had indeed been a sudden loss of self-control.

That evidence may not have been powerfully suggestive of provocation. But it was, in our view, rather more than tenuous. It is easily conceivable, we think, that the jury, if directed on the issue, would have come to the conclusion that the appellant was so provoked as to reduce murder to manslaughter. Therefore, subject only to the question of self-induced provocation referred to by the judge, in our judgment this defence should have been left to the jury.

. . . In view of the express wording of section 3, as interpreted in *R v Camplin* [1978] AC 705 which was decided after *Edwards* v *The Queen* [1973] AC 648, we find it impossible to accept that the mere fact that a defendant caused a reaction in others, which in turn led him to lose his self-control, should result in the issue of provocation being kept outside a jury's consideration. Section 3 clearly provides that the question is whether things done or said or both provoked the defendant to lose his self-control. If there is any evidence that it may have done, the issue must be left to the jury. The jury would then have to consider all the circumstances of the incident, including all the relevant behaviour of the defendant, in deciding (a) whether he was in fact provoked and (b) whether the provocation was enough to make a reasonable man do what the defendant did.

Accordingly, whether or not there were elements in the appellant's conduct which justified the conclusion that he had started the trouble and induced others, including the deceased, to react in the way they did, we are firmly of the view that the defence of provocation should have been left to the jury.

Since it is not possible for us to infer from their verdict that the jury inevitably would have concluded that provocation as well as self-defence had been disproved the verdict of murder will be set aside. A conviction for manslaughter on the basis of provocation will be substituted.

Note
See also *Hopper* [1915] 2 KB 431, per Lord Reading at p. 435, *Newell* [1989] Crim LR 906.

The defence of provocation contains a subjective and an objective component. To succeed the defendant must produce some evidence that:

(a)   he was provoked to lose his self-control;
and
(b)   the provocation was enough to make a reasonable man lose self-control and, having lost self-control, to do as the defendant did.

The subjective element should not be overlooked. If a reasonable man would have been driven wild with rage by the provoking act, but the defendant was not in fact provoked, the defence will not succeed. Why should this be so?

The objective element presents the jury with a conundrum. Section 3 speaks in terms of the provocation being 'enough to make a reasonable man do as he [the defendant] did'. But arguably, reasonable men do not kill; and if reasonable men do kill, why should the defendant be punished for doing only what other reasonable men would do in his place? Yet the fact remains that provocation is not a complete defence.

What is clear is that s. 3 modified the common law by laying greater emphasis on the role of the jury. Prior to passage of the section it was possible for a judge to withdraw the defence from jury consideration if the judge formed the opinion that there was no evidence that a reasonable man would have been provoked in the circumstances. This led to some curious case law on the reactions of the reasonable man (see, e.g., *Mancini* v *Director of Public Prosecutions* [1942] AC 1). Section 3 specifically provides that where there is evidence that the defendant himself was provoked, the question as to the reaction of the reasonable man must be left to the jury.

(a)   *What constitutes provocation?* Prior to passage of the Homicide Act 1957, the judges developed narrow and fairly rigid categories of provocation. The Act opted in favour of a more flexible approach. Section 3 refers to provocation by 'things done or by things said or by both together'. Any words or action *may* thus constitute provocation, even a lawful act by an innocent party. In *Doughty* (1986) Cr App R 319, the alleged provocation was the crying and restlessness of the defendant's 17-day-old baby. The defendant gave evidence that this behaviour had caused him to lose his self-control and kill the child. The judge refused to leave the issue of provocation to the jury. The Court of Appeal quashed the resultant conviction for murder on the grounds that the issue should have been left to the jury.

It is now clear that any person's (and not just the victim's) actions or words may constitute provocation. It is therefore incorrect for a judge to instruct the jury to consider only the victim's behaviour.

R v Davies
(1975) 1 QB 691
Court of Appeal

LORD WIDGERY CJ: . . . The defendant killed his wife by shooting her in the presence of her lover. The only issue in the court below was whether the charge should have been reduced to manslaughter on account of provocation. The contention of the defendant is that in directing the jury as to provocation the judge excluded provocation from any source other than from the victim, that is to say, other than the wife. The question is whether that exclusion was justified or not.

. . . [I]t seems quite clear to us that we should construe section 3 as providing a new test, and on that test that we should give the wide words of section 3 their ordinary wide meaning. Thus we come to the conclusion that whatever the position at common law, the situation since 1957 has been that acts or words otherwise to be treated as provocative for present purposes are not excluded from such consideration merely because they emanate from someone other than the victim.

Notes and questions
1. While 'any person's' acts or behaviour may constitute provocation, what of natural events? Marion returns home to find her house has been struck by lightning and has burned to the ground. In her rage at this development she throws her child to the ground with fatal results. Has there been provocation that the law will recognise? Should the law recognise this type of provocation?
2. What if in the preceding example the house had been destroyed by a terrorist bomb? Again an out-of-control Marion throws her child to the ground with fatal results. Will her defence of provocation succeed, or is there (should there be) a requirement that the *actus reus* be directed at the provoker?

(b) *The subjective prong.* The leading authority on the subjective prong of manslaughter is *Duffy*.

R v Duffy
[1949] 1 All ER 932
Court of Appeal

The appellant, who was convicted on 16 March 1949, before Devlin J, at Manchester Assizes, of the murder of her husband, had been subjected to brutal treatment by him. On the night of the offence, there had been quarrels and blows had been struck. The appellant had wished to take their child away and the husband had prevented her. The appellant left the room for a short while and changed her clothes, and eventually, when her husband was in bed, she returned with a hatchet and a hammer, with both of which she struck him. For the defence it was pleaded that the appellant had acted under provocation, but the jury, having been directed by the judge as to what constituted provocation sufficient to reduce murder to manslaughter, found the appellant guilty of murder. The Court of Criminal Appeal now dismissed the appeal.

LORD GODDARD: . . . The only possible defence that could be set up was that the appellant acted under such provocation as to reduce the crime to manslaughter, and on this point the summing-up of the learned judge, in the opinion of this court, was impeccable. I am going to read a passage from his summing-up because I think it deserves to be remembered as clear and accurate a charge to a jury when provocation is pleaded as can well be made. He said:

Provocation is some act, or series of acts, done by the dead man to the accused which would cause in any reasonable person, and actually causes in the accused, a sudden and temporary loss of self-control, rendering the accused so subject to passion as to make him or her for the moment not master of his mind. Let me distinguish for you some of the things which provocation in law is not. Circumstances which merely predispose to a violent act are not enough. Severe nervous exasperation or a long course of conduct causing suffering and anxiety are not by themselves sufficient to constitute provocation in law. Indeed, the further removed an incident is from the crime, the less it counts. A long course of cruel conduct may be more blameworthy than a sudden act provoking retaliation, but you are not concerned with blame here – the blame attaching to the dead man. You are not standing in judgment on him. He has not been heard in this court. He cannot now ever be heard. He has no defender here to argue for him. It does not matter how cruel he was, how much or how little he was to blame, except in so far as it resulted in the final act of the appellant. What matters is whether this girl had the time to say: 'Whatever I have suffered, whatever I have endured, I know that Thou shalt not kill.' That is what matters. Similarly, as counsel for the prosecution has told you, circumstances which induce a desire for revenge, or a sudden passion of anger, are not enough. Indeed, circumstances which induce a desire for revenge are inconsistent with provocation, since the conscious formulation of a desire for revenge means that a person has had time to think, to reflect, and that would negate a sudden temporary loss of self-control which is of the essence of provocation . . . Provocation being, therefore, as I have defined it, there are two things, in considering it, to which the law attaches great importance. The first of them is whether there was what is sometimes called time for cooling, that is, for passion to cool and for reason to regain dominion over the mind. That is why most acts of provocation are cases of sudden quarrels, sudden blows inflicted with an implement already in the hand, perhaps being used, or being picked up, where there has been no time for reflection. Secondly, in considering whether provocation has or has not been made out, you must consider the retaliation in provocation – that is to say, whether the mode of resentment bears some proper and reasonable relationship to the sort of provocation that has been given. Fists might be answered with fists, but not with a deadly weapon, and that is a factor you have to bear in mind when you are considering the question of provocation.

That is as good a definition of the doctrine of provocation as it has ever been my lot to read.

Notes
1. The *Duffy* court's approach to the subjective limb of provocation was affirmed in *Ibrams and Gregory* (1981) 74 Cr App 154, where the Court of Appeal approved of the decision of the trial judge to withdraw the issue of provocation from the jury because the defendant's attack on the victim took place five days after the last incident of provocation had occurred.
2. The *Duffy* test has been criticised as discriminating against women. It is argued that a sudden violent response to provocation is behaviour much more typical of males than it is of females. Women may suffer provocation over many years, but their response may be akin to a 'slow fuse' which may not lead to an immediate attack. Indeed, a sudden response in the face of the provocation may be wholly impracticable since the provoker is likely to be more powerful than the defendant. The ultimate homicide may nevertheless be a direct response to the provoking behaviour. See generally Edwards, 'Battered women who kill' (1990) 141 NLJ 1380; Wasik 'Cumulative provocation and domestic killing' [1982] Crim LR 29.

Questions
1. Consider the description of the defence of provocation in the light of the above criticism. Is the language male-orientated?
2. The pyschological assumption behind the *Duffy* test is that time cools passions. Is this true? Does not reflection on past wrongs sometimes exacerbate one's sense of anger and frustration?

(c) *The objective prong.* As noted previously, the objective requirement for provocation presents the jury with the idea that the reasonable man can be a killer. The charge of murder is to be reduced to manslaughter where there is evidence that the provocation would have made a reasonable man act in the same way as the defendant (Homicide Act 1957, s. 3). Arguably the more accurate interpretation of the section is that the provocation must be such to cause the reasonable man to lose self-control.

The major difficulty that has arisen in this area lies in determining the relevant characteristics of the reasonable man. At common law the reasonable man was 'Mr Average' as envisaged by the judiciary (*Bedder* v *Director of Public Prosecutions* [1954] 1 WLR 1119). He had no particuar idiosyncracies or disabilities. In many circumstances this severely limited the scope of the defence. Often, provoking behaviour is directed at a peculiar weakness or disadvantage of the defendant about which he is particularly sensitive. For example, in *Bedder*, the victim mocked the defendant's impotency. The 'reasonable man', however, is not impotent. Indeed, an 'old style' reasonable man would not be provoked by insulting words, and Bedder's defence was duly rejected.

Following passage of the 1957 Act the courts adopted a more flexible approach, holding that the reasonable man should be imbued with the relevant characteristics of the defendant. The problem now is to determine which of the defendant's characteristics should be attributed to the reasonable man in any particular case:

Director of Public Prosecutions v *Camplin*
[1978] AC 705
House of Lords

LORD DIPLOCK: My Lords, for the purpose of answering the question of law upon which this appeal will turn only a brief account is needed of the facts that have given rise to it. The respondent, Camplin, who was 15 years of age, killed a middle-aged Pakistani, Mohammed Lal Khan, by splitting his skull with a chapati pan, a heavy kitchen utensil like a rimless frying pan. At the time, the two of them were alone together in Khan's flat. At Camplin's trial for murder before Boreham J his only defence was that of provocation so as to reduce the offence to manslaughter. According to the story that he told in the witness box but which differed materially from that which he had told to the police, Khan had buggered him in spite of his resistance and had then laughed at him. Whereupon Camplin had lost his self-control and attacked Khan fatally with the chapati pan.

In his address to the jury on the defence of provocation Mr Baker, who was counsel for Camplin, had suggested to them that when they addressed their minds to the question whether the provocation relied on was enough to make a reasonable man do as Camplin had done, what they ought to consider was not the reaction of a reasonable adult but the reaction of a reasonable boy of Camplin's age. The judge thought that this was wrong in law. So in his summing up he took pains to instruct the jury that they must consider whether:

> . . . the provocation was sufficient to make a reasonable man in like circumstances act as the defendant did. Not a reasonable boy, as Mr Baker would have it, or a reasonable lad; it is an objective test – a reasonable man.

The jury found Camplin guilty of murder. On appeal the Court of Appeal (Criminal Division) allowed the appeal and substituted a conviction for manslaughter upon the ground that the passage I have cited from the summing up was a misdirection. The court held that

> . . . the proper direction to the jury is to invite the jury to consider whether the provocation was enough to have made a reasonable person of the same age as the defendant in the same circumstances do as he did.

The point of law of general public importance involved in the case has been certified as being:

> Whether on the prosecution for murder of a boy of 15, where the issue of provocation arises, the jury should be directed to consider the question under section 3 of the Homicide Act 1957 whether the provocation was enough to make a reasonable man do as he did by reference to a 'reasonable adult' or by reference to a 'reasonable boy of 15.'

. . . [F]or the purposes of the law of provocation the 'reasonable man' has never been confined to the adult male. It means an ordinary person of either sex, not exceptionally excitable or pugnacious, but possessed of such powers of self-control as everyone is entitled to expect that his fellow citizens will exercise in society as it is today. . . . now that the law has been changed so as to permit of words being treated as provocation even though unaccompanied by any other acts, the gravity of verbal provocation may well depend upon the particular characteristics or circumstances of the person to whom a

taunt or insult is addressed. To taunt a person because of his race, his physical infirmities or some shameful incident in his past may well be considered by the jury to be more offensive to the person addressed, however equable his temperament, if the facts on which the taunt is founded are true than it would be if they were not. It would stultify much of the mitigation of the previous harshness of the common law in ruling out verbal provocation as capable of reducing muder to manslaughter if the jury could not take into consideration all those factors which in their opinion would affect the gravity of taunts or insults when applied to the person whom they are addressed.
. . .

That he was only 15 years of age at the time of the killing is the relevant characteristic of the accused in the instant case. It is a characteristic which may have its effects on temperament as well as physique. If the jury think that the same power of self-control is not to be expected in an ordinary, average or normal boy of 15 as in an older person, are they to treat the lesser powers of self-control possessed by an ordinary, average or normal boy of 15 as the standard of self-control with which the conduct of the accused is to be compared?
. . .

In my opinion a proper direction to a jury on the question left to their exclusive determination by section 3 of the Act of 1957 would be on the following lines. The judge should state what the question is using the very terms of the section. He should then explain to them that the reasonable man referred to in the question is a person having the power of self-control to be expected of an ordinary person of the sex and age of the accused, but in other respects sharing such of the accused's characteristics as they think would affect the gravity of the provocation to him; and that the question is not merely whether such a person would in like circumstances be provoked to lose his self-control but also whether he would react to the provocation as the accused did.

I accordingly agree with the Court of Appeal that the judge ought not to have instructed the jury to pay no account to the age of the accused even though they themselves might be of opinion that the degree of self-control to be expected in a boy of that age was less than in an adult. So to direct them was to impose a fetter on the right and duty of the jury which the Act accords to them to act upon their own opinion on the matter.

I would dismiss this appeal.

Question

As a juror in Camplin's case, what other characteristics would you like to know about? What if Camplin were phobic about his possible homosexuality? What if he was extremely hot-tempered, even for his age? What if Camplin were female – would (should) this factor affect the analysis?

Note

The characteristic to be attributed to the reasonable man must be relevant to the provocation; taunting a one-armed man about his lack of a sense of humour would not be regarded as provoking behaviour. As the reasonable man is deemed to be sober, the defendant's voluntary intoxication will also be ignored.

A further limitation is that the relevant characteristic must have a degree of permanence:

R v *Newell*
(1980) 71 Cr App R 331
Court of Appeal

The appellant, a chronic alcoholic of 10 years standing, lived for some time with a young woman. She left him and he was distressed and attempted to commit suicide. A few days later the appellant was drinking heavily with a friend who made disparaging remarks about the young woman and suggested that he forget her and come to bed with him. Thereupon the appellant picked up a heavy ashtray and struck the friend over the head with it some 20 times, causing the latter's death. He was charged with murder and sought to raise the defence of provocation under section 3 of the Homicide Act 1957. Medical evidence at his trial was that he was an unstable drunkard, very distressed by the young woman's defection, and was in a highly emotional state and a state of toxic confusion, so that the alcohol that he had consumed removed his inhibitions so that his friend's offensive remarks had made the appellant over-react causing him to lose his self-control. The trial judge read section 3 of the Act of 1957 to the jury and told them that they had to assume that the friend's drunken observations were made to a sober man, and they were asked whether any of them individually or collectively would have so behaved on the provocation offered. The appellant was convicted of murder and appealed contending that the jury had been misdirected on the defence of provocation and the reasonable man under section 3 aforesaid.

THE LORD CHIEF JUSTICE: . . . It seems to us that to ascertain the meaning of the speeches in *DPP* v *Camplin* (*supra*) it is necessary to consider the meaning of the word 'characteristics' as used in those speeches. To do so we find it helpful to refer, as we were invited to do by Mr Crespi, to *McGregor* [1962] NZLR 1069, referred to by Lord Simon of Glaisdale. First, we would read the material parts of section 169 of the New Zealand Crimes Act 1961:

(1) Culpable homicide that would otherwise be murder may be reduced to manslaughter if the person who caused the death did so under provocation. (2) Anything done or said may be provocation if – (a) In the circumstances of the case it was sufficient to deprive a person having the power of self-control of an ordinary person, but otherwise having the characteristics of the offender, of the power of self-control; and (b) It did in fact deprive the offender of the power of self-control and thereby induced him to commit the act of homicide. (3) Whether there is any evidence of provocation is a question of law. (4) Whether, if there is evidence of provocation, the provocation was sufficient as aforesaid, and whether it did in fact deprive the offender of the power of self-control and thereby induced him to commit the act of homicide, are questions of fact.

In *McGregor* (*supra*) the judgment of the court was delivered by North J, and contains the following passage which appears to us to be entirely apt to the situation in the instant case:

The Legislature has given us no guide as to what limitations might be imposed, but perforce there must be adopted a construction which will ensure regard being had to the characteristics of the offender without wholly extinguishing the ordinary man.

The offender must be presumed to possess in general the power of self-control of the ordinary man, save in so far as his power of self-control is weakened because of some particular characteristic possessed by him. It is not every trait or disposition of the offender that can be invoked to modify the concept of the ordinary man. The characteristic must be something definite and of sufficient significance to make the offender a different person from the ordinary run of mankind, and have also a sufficient degree of permanence to warrant its being regarded as something constituting part of the individual's character or personality. A disposition to be unduly suspicious or to lose one's temper readily will not suffice, nor will a temporary or transitory state of mind such as a mood of depression, excitability or irascibility. These matters are either not of sufficient significance or not of sufficient permanency to be regarded as 'characteristics' which would enable the offender to be distinguished from the ordinary man. The 'unusually excitable or pugnacious individual' spoken of in *Lesbini* (1914) 11 Cr App R 11; [1914] 3 KB 1116 is no more entitled to special consideration under the new section than he was when that case was decided. Still less can a self-induced transitory state be relied upon, as where it arises from the consumption of liquor. The word 'characteristics' in the context of this section is wide enough to apply not only to physical qualities but also to mental qualities and such more indeterminate attributes as colour, race and creed. It is to be emphasised that of whatever nature the characteristic may be, it must be such that it can fairly be said that the offender is thereby marked off or distinguished from the ordinary man of the community. Moreover, it is to be equally emphasised that there must be some real connection between the nature of the provocation and the particular characteristic of the offender by which it is sought to modify the ordinary man test. The words of conduct must have been exclusively or particularly provocative to the individual because, and only because, of the characteristic. In short, there must be some direct connection between the provocative words or conduct and the characteristic sought to be invoked as warranting some departure from the ordinary man test . . ..

That passage, and the reasoning therein contained, seem to us to be impeccable. It is not only expressed in plain, easily comprehended language; it represents also, we think, the law of this country as well as that of New Zealand. In the present case the only matter which could remotely be described as a characteristic was the appellant's condition of chronic alcoholism. Assuming that that was truly a characteristic (and we expressly make no determination as to that), nevertheless it had nothing to do with the words by which it is said that he was provoked. There was no connection between the derogatory reference to the appellant's girl friend and the suggestion of a possible homosexual act and his chronic alcoholism. It had nothing at all to do with the words by which it is said that he was provoked.

If the test set out in *McGregor (supra)* is applied, the learned judge in the instant case was right in not inviting the jury to take chronic alcoholism into account on the question of provocation.

Notes and questions
1. If Newell was in fact provoked, and if a reasonable man with his characteristics *at the time* would also have been provoked, what should it matter that the characteristic is not permanent? Consider the case of a wife who watches a drunk driver run over her husband. Distraught with grief and rage, she strangles the driver to death. Should the mere fact that her grief and rage will subside in time preclude her from arguing provocation?

2.   Taking the argument one step further, if the defendant is in fact provoked, why should it even matter whether a reasonable person would also have been provoked? Why add an objective test at all if the provocation defence is designed to recognise human frailty in the face of provoking circumstances?
3.   What about cases of 'imperfect' self-defence, i.e., defendant's claim of self-defence (which would lead to an acquittal) fails for some reason, such as that he used excessive force – should the defendant be able to have a fall-back position of provocation? In the final section of this chapter the proposals of the Criminal Law Revision Committee contained in the Draft Criminal Code Bill are presented. Note how the drafters address this issue.

Having determined that the reasonable man would have been provoked, the jury must consider whether the reasonable man would have reacted as the defendant did. The relationship between provocation and reaction was considered in *Brown* [1972] 2 QB 229, and by the Privy Council in *Phillips* [1969] 2 AC 130.

R v Brown
[1972] 2 QB 229
Court of Appeal

TALBOT J: . . . In the view of this court, when considering whether the provocation was enough to make a reasonable man do as the accused did it is relevant for a jury to compare the words or acts or both of these things which are put forward as provocation with the nature of the act committed by the accused. It may be for instance that a jury might find that the accused's act was so disproportionate to the provocation alleged that no reasonable man would have so acted. We think therefore that a jury should be instructed to consider the relationship of the accused's acts to the provocation when asking themselves the question 'Was it enough to make a reasonable man do as he did?' . . .

R v Phillips
[1969] 2 AC 130
Privy Council

LORD DIPLOCK: . . . Before their Lordships, counsel for the appellant contended, not as a matter of construction but as one of logic, that once a reasonable man had lost his self-control his actions ceased to be those of a reasonable man and that accordingly he was no longer fully responsible in law for them whatever he did. This argument is based on the premise that loss of self-control is not a matter of degree but is absolute; there is no intermediate stage between icy detachment and going berserk. This premise, unless the argument is purely semantic, must be based upon human experience and is, in their Lordships' view, false. The average man reacts to provocation according to its degree with angry words, with a blow of the hand, possibly if the provocation is gross and there is a dangerous weapon to hand, with that weapon. It is not insignificant that the appellant himself described his own instantaneous reaction to the victim's provocation in spitting on his mother as 'I spin around quickly was to punch her with my hand.'

In that part of his direction which the Court of Appeal held to be objectionable, the learned judge followed closely the actual words of the section and made it clear to the jury that it was their responsibility, not his, to decide whether a reasonable man would have reacted to the provocation in the way that the appellant did. In their Lordships' view this was an impeccable direction.

Question
The cases seem to suggest that there are degrees of loss of self-control. Are there? Even if there are, should the jury be called upon to make such fine discriminations? To what end?

(d)   *Self-induced provocation.* In *Edwards* [1973] AC 648, the Privy Council stated that ordinarily a blackmailer could not rely on the predictable hostile reaction to his blackmail attempt as constituting provocation sufficient to reduce murder to manslaughter. This position was disapproved in *Johnson.*

R v *Johnson*
[1989] 1 WLR 740
Court of Appeal

For the facts of this case, see p. 410 above.

WATKINS LJ: . . . That evidence may not have been powerfully suggestive of provocation. But it was, in our view, rather more than tenuous. It is easily conceivable, we think, that the jury, if directed on the issue, would have come to the conclusion that the appellant was so provoked as to reduce murder to manslaughter. Therefore, subject only to the question of self-induced provocation referred to by the judge, in our judgment this defence should have been left to the jury.
   There was undoubtedly evidence to suggest that, if the appellant had lost his self-control, it was his own behaviour which caused others to react towards him in the way we have described.
   We were referred to the decision of the Privy Council in *Edwards* v *The Queen* [1973] AC 648. In that case the trial judge had directed the jury, at p. 658:

   In my view the defence of provocation cannot be of any avail to the accused in this case . . . it ill befits the accused in this case, having gone there with the deliberate purpose of blackmailing this man – you may well think it ill befits him to say out of his own mouth that he was provoked by any attack. In my view the defence of provocation is not one which you need consider in this case.

The full court in Hong Kong held that this direction was erroneous. The Privy Council agreed with the full court. On the particular facts of the case Lord Pearson, giving the judgment of the Board, said, at p. 658:

   On principle it seems reasonable to say that – (1) a blackmailer cannot rely on the predictable results of his own blackmailing conduct as constituting provocation . . . and the predictable results may include a considerable degree of hostile reaction by the person sought to be blackmailed . . . (2) but if the hostile reaction by the person sought to be blackmailed goes to extreme lengths it might constitute sufficient provocation even for the blackmailer; (3) there would in many cases be a question of degree to be decided by the jury.

Those words cannot, we think, be understood to mean, as was suggested to us, that provocation which is 'self-induced' ceases to be provocation for the purposes of section 3.

The relevant statutory provision being considered by the Privy Council was in similar terms to section 3. In view of the express wording of section 3, as interpreted in *R v Camplin* [1978] AC 705 which was decided after *Edwards* v *The Queen* [1973] AC 648, we find it impossible to accept that the mere fact that a defendant caused a reaction in others, which in turn led him to lose his self-control, should result in the issue of provocation being kept outside a jury's consideration. Section 3 clearly provides that the question is whether things done or said or both provoked the defendant to lose his self-control. If there is any evidence that it may have done, the issue must be left to the jury. The jury would then have to consider all the circumstances of the incident, including all the relevant behaviour of the defendant, in deciding (a) whether he was in fact provoked and (b) whether the provocation was enough to make a reasonable man do what the defendant did.

Accordingly, whether or not there were elements in the appellant's conduct which justified the conclusion that he had started the trouble and induced others, including the deceased, to react in the way they did, we are firmly of the view that the defence of provocation should have been left to the jury.

Since it is not possible for us to infer from their verdict that the jury inevitably would have concluded that provocation as well as self-defence had been disproved the verdict of murder will be set aside. A conviction for manslaughter on the basis of provocation will be substituted.

(iii)   Suicide pact

Homicide Act 1957

4.—(1)   It shall be manslaughter, and shall not be murder, for a person acting in pursuance of a suicide pact between him and another to kill the other or be a party to the other killing himself or being killed by a third person.

(2)   Where it is shown that a person charged with the murder of another killed the other or was a party to his killing himself or being killed, it shall be for the defence to prove that the person charged was acting in pursuance of a suicide pact between him and the other.

(3)   For the purposes of this section 'suicide pact' means a common agreement between two or more persons having for its object the death of all of them, whether or not each is to take his own life, but nothing done by a person who enters into a suicide pact shall be treated as done by him in pursuance of the pact unless it is done while he has the settled intention of dying in pursuance of the pact.

Notes and questions
1.   The burden of proving the defence to the balance of probabilities standard is on the defendant.
2.   At common law suicide was a crime. Although the individual who was successful could obviously not be tried, his estate was forfeited to the Crown. Today, suicide is no longer a crime. Should the killing of a partner in the course of a suicide pact therefore also cease to attract criminal sanctions? Is the issue of consent to one's own death a relevant consideration here?

3. In addition to cases involving suicide pacts, should special allowance be made for cases of mercy killing? The present English law does not formally do so. See Dr Adams' case (chapter 4).

B   Involuntary manslaughter

This category of homicide includes all killings which are regarded as criminally unlawful but where the defendant does not have the *mens rea* of murder. The term 'involuntary manslaughter' is, however, a misnomer, for the killings involved are not involuntary as that term has traditionally been used in the context of *actus reus*. It is used only to distinguish this class of homicide from murder and voluntary manslaughter. In struggling to define the boundaries of involuntary manslaughter the courts have encountered considerable difficulties and the resulting muddle is not a credit to English jurisprudence. There are probably three categories, but it must be noted that some killings could fit into more than one of them. The three categories are:

(a)   constructive manslaughter;
(b)   reckless manslaughter;
(c)   gross negligence manslaughter.

(i)   Constructive manslaughter
It is manslaughter when the defendant performs an unlawful and dangerous act likely to cause physical harm and death results. This is an offence which is 'built upon' another, i.e. the death is an incidental result of the unlawful act. For that reason there has been some confusion as to whether the usual causation rules apply. The issue has appeared in the case law as a question as to whether the defendant's act must be 'aimed or directed' at the victim (see extracts below).

(a)   An *unlawful act*. Taken literally, the term 'unlawful act' would include a tort, and, indeed, that was the position at early common law. It is now settled that more is required for purposes of convicting a defendant of manslaughter. Not even all criminal offences may qualify as unlawful acts.

Andrews v *Director of Public Prosecutions*
[1937] AC 576
House of Lords

LORD ATKIN: . . . There is an obvious difference in the law of manslaughter between doing an unlawful act and doing a lawful act with a degree of carelessness which the Legislature makes criminal. If it were otherwise a man who killed another while driving without due care and attention would ex necessitate commit manslaughter. . . .

Notes
1.   An act is not 'unlawful' if it is justifiable, as it might be if the defendant struck a fatal blow to the victim in self-defence.

2.   Whether the defendant has committed an unlawful act is a jury question and the court may not decide the issue on its own authority. See *R* v *Jennings* [1990] Crim LR 588.

Both the *mens rea* and the *actus reus* of the unlawful act must be proved:

R v *Lamb*
[1967] 2 QB 981
Court of Appeal

SACHS LJ: ... The defendant, Terence Walter Lamb, aged 25, had become possessed of a Smith & Wesson revolver. It was a revolver in the literal old-fashioned sense, having a five-chambered cylinder which rotated clockwise each time the trigger was pulled. The defendant, in jest, with no intention to do any harm pointed the revolver at the deceased, his best friend, when it had two bullets in the chambers, but neither bullet was in the chamber opposite the barrel. His friend was similarly treating the incident as a joke. The defendant then pulled the trigger and thus killed his friend, still having no intention to fire the revolver. The reason why the pulling of the trigger produced that fatal result was that its pulling rotated the cylinder and so placed a bullet opposite the barrel so that it was struck by the striking pin or hammer.

The defendant's defence was that, as neither bullet was opposite the barrel, he thought they were in such chambers that the striking pin could not hit them; that he was unaware that the pulling of the trigger would bring one bullet into the firing position opposite the barrel; and that the killing was thus an accident. There was not only no dispute that that was what he in fact thought, but the mistake he made was one which three experts agreed was natural for somebody who was not aware of the way the revolver mechanism worked. ... The trial judge took the view that the pointing of the revolver and the pulling of the trigger was something which could of itself be unlawful even if there was no attempt to alarm or intent to injure. ...

[Prosecution counsel] had at all times put forward the correct view that for the act to be unlawful it must constitute at least what he then termed 'a technical assault.' In this court moreover he rightly conceded that there was no evidence to go to the jury of any assault of any kind. Nor did he feel able to submit that the acts of the defendant were on any other ground unlawful in the criminal sense of that word. Indeed no such submission could in law be made: if, for instance, the pulling of the trigger had had no effect because the striking mechanism or the ammunition had been defective no offence would have been committed by the defendant.

Another way of putting it is that *mens rea*, being now an essential ingredient in manslaughter ... that could not in the present case be established in relation to the first ground except by proving that element of intent without which there can be no assault.

Question
Is the decision in *Lamb* based on the fact that the victim was not put in fear (a requirement of the crime of assault), or the fact that there was no assault because the defendant lacked the *mens rea* of the crime?

Note
In *Director of Public Prosecutions* v *Newbury* [1976] 2 All ER 365, the House of Lords indicated that it was sufficient that the defendants, who had pushed a

paving stone from a railway bridge on to a passing train, killing a guard, had 'basic intent'. This was defined as an 'intention to do the acts which constitute the crime'. As we have noted previously, this adds little to the requirement of a voluntary *actus reus*.

(b) A *dangerous* act. Can any unlawful act support a conviction for manslaughter?

R v Church
[1965] 2 All ER 72
Court of Criminal Appeal

EDMUND DAVIES J: . . . The facts may be shortly stated. On Sunday, May 31, 1964, the dead body of Mrs Nott was found in the River Ouse within a few yards of the appellant's van which stood near the bank. The corpse bore the marks of grave injuries. The face had been battered, the hyoid bone had been broken and there had been some degree of manual strangulation. These injuries were likely to have caused unconsciousness and eventually death, but they were inflicted a half-hour or an hour before death supervened and did not in fact cause it. According to the medical evidence, her injuries were inflicted not long before Mrs Nott was thrown into the river, but she was alive when that was done, she continued to breathe for an appreciable time afterwards, and the eventual cause of death was drowning. When the appellant was first interviewed about the matter he lied, but ultimately signed a statement admitting complicity in the death. He then said that he had taken Mrs Nott to his van for sexual purposes, that he was unable to satisfy her and she then reproached him and slapped his face; that they then had a fight during which he knocked her out and thereafter she only moaned. The statement continued:

> 'I was shaking her to wake her for about half-an-hour, but she didn't wake up, so I panicked and dragged her out of the van and put her in the river.'

He repeated this account at his trial and then said for the first time, 'I thought she was dead'.

. . .

(c) *An unlawful act causing death*. Two passages in the summing up are here material. They are these: (i)—

> If, by an unlawful act of violence done deliberately to the person of another, that other is killed, the killing is manslaughter even though the accused never intended either death or grievous bodily harm to result. If [the deceased] was alive, as she was, when he threw her in the river, what he did was a deliberate act of throwing a living body into the river. That is an unlawful killing and it does not matter whether he believed she was dead, or not, and that is my direction to you.

and (ii)—

> I would suggest to you, though, of course, it is for you to approach your task as you think fit, that a convenient way of approaching it would be to say: What do we think about this defence that he honestly believed the [deceased] to be dead? If you think that it is true, why then, as I have told you, your proper verdict would be one of manslaughter, not murder.

Such a direction is not lacking in authority . . . Nevertheless, in the judgment of this court [that] was a misdirection. It amounted to telling the jury that, whenever any unlawful act is committed in relation to a human being which resulted in death there must be, at least, a conviction for manslaughter. This might at one time have been regarded as good law. It appears to this court, however, that the passage of years has achieved a transformation in this branch of the law and, even in relation to manslaughter, a degree of mens rea has become recognised as essential. To define it is a difficult task, and in *Andrews v Director of Public Prosecutions* [1937] AC 576 Lord Atkin spoke of 'the element of "unlawfulness" which is the elusive factor'. Stressing that we are here leaving entirely out of account those ingredients of homicide which might justify a verdict of manslaughter on the grounds of (a) criminal negligence, or (b) provocation or (c) diminished responsibility, the conclusion of this court is that an unlawful act causing the death of another cannot, simply because it is an unlawful act, render a manslaughter verdict inevitable. For such a verdict inexorably to follow, the unlawful act must be such as all sober and reasonable people would inevitably recognise must subject the other person to, at least, the risk of some harm resulting therefrom, albeit not serious harm. See, for example, *R v Franklin* (1883) 15 Cox CC 163, *R v Senior* [1899] 1 QB 283.

If such be the test, as we adjudge it to be, then it follows that, in our view, it was a misdirection to tell the jury simpliciter that it mattered nothing for manslaughter whether or not the appellant believed Mrs Nott to be dead when he threw her into the river. . . .

Notes and questions

1.   According to the court, the unlawful act has to be such that 'all sober and reasonable people would inevitably recognise [it as an act which] must subject the other person to, at least, the risk of some harm resulting therefrom, albeit not serious harm'. The test is an objective one; actual foresight by the defendant of danger to others is not required; what is critical is the perception of the reasonable man. If so, why did the court deem it a misdirection for the trial judge to have told the jury that the defendant's belief as to whether the victim was dead at the time that he threw her into the river mattered nothing?
2.   What if it could be shown that the defendant was not a reasonable man; that, for example, he was mentally retarded? Is it just to hold a defendant to the standard of the reasonable man if the defendant is incapable through no fault of his own of achieving such a standard? Similar issues were raised by *Elliot v C (A minor)* [1983] 1 WLR 939, discussed in Chapter 3.

The harm which the reasonable person must be able to foresee is physical harm, but shock which produces physical injury will suffice if the other elements of the offence are present.

R v Dawson
(1985) 81 Cr App R 150
Court of Appeal

After midnight one night two masked men, one carrying a pickaxe handle and another armed with a replica gun, while a third kept watch, demanded money from a 60 year old petrol filling station attendant who, unknown to them, suffered from heart disease. The attendant pressed the alarm button and the three men fled. Shortly after the police arrived, the attendant collapsed and died from a heart attack.

WATKINS LJ: ... It has, in our experience, been generally understood that the harm referred to in the second element of the offence of manslaughter, namely, the unlawful act, must be one that all sober and reasonable people would realise was likely to cause some, albeit not serious, harm, means physical harm. ...

However, there seems to us to be no sensible reason why shock produced by fright should not come within the definition of harm in this context. From time to time one hears the expression 'frightened to death' without thinking that the possibility of such event occurring would be an affront to reason or medical knowledge. Shock can produce devastating and lasting effects, for instance upon the nervous system. That is surely harm, i.e. injury to the person. Why not harm in this context?

... [The judge] directed the jury that a definition of harm was 'emotional disturbance which is detrimental produced by terror'. He had, as we have seen from a transcript of discussion between him and counsel, intended to direct the jury that a definition of harm for present purposes was emotional *and* physical disturbance produced by terror. We think it was unfortunate that the judge, probably through inadvertence, used the disjunctive 'or.' As it was, the jury were left with a choice. Which they chose and acted upon we cannot tell. If they acted upon the basis that emotional disturbance was enough to constitute harm then, in our judgment, they would have done so upon a misdirection. Emotional disturbance does not occur to us as sensibly descriptive of injury or harm to the person through the operation of shock produced by terror or fright; morever, we do not think the word 'deterimental' assists to clarify whatever the expression 'emotional disturbance' is meant to convey. The further phrase used, namely, 'some such disturbancce which would be bad for him' is likewise not helpful.

In his endeavours to give the jury appropriate guidance upon the meaning of harm within the facts of this case the judge was sailing uncharted seas. We have every sympathy with him. Unfortunately we think that what he said, other than the use of the phrase 'physical disturbance which is detrimental' (this was, we think, by itself, though easier to understand, inadequate) could have led the jury to contemplate merely a disturbance of the emotions as harm sufficient for the purpose of the second element when clearly, in our view, it is not.

In our judgment, a proper direction would have been that the requisite harm is caused if the unlawful act so shocks the victim to cause him physical injury.

Note
The reasonable person is taken to know facts known to the defendant or which would be evident to the reasonable bystander. Watkins LJ continued:

We look finally at the direction, 'That is to say all reasonable people who knew the facts that you know.' What the jury knew included, of course, the undisputed fact that the deceased had a very bad heart which at any moment could have ceased to function. It may be the judge did not intend that this fact should be included in the phrase 'the facts that you know.' If that was so, it is regrettable that he did not make it clear. By saying as he did, it is argued 'including the fact that the gun was a replica' and so on, the jury must have taken him to be telling them that all facts known to them, including the heart condition, should be taken into account in performing what is undoubtedly an objective test. We think there was a grave danger of that.

Homicide

This test can only be undertaken upon the basis of the knowledge gained by a sober and reasonable man as though he were present at the scene of and watched the unlawful act being performed and who knows that, as in the present case, an unloaded replica gun was in use, but that the victim may have thought it was a loaded gun in working order. In other words, he has the same knowledge as the man attempting to rob and no more. It was never suggested that any of these appellants knew that their victim had a bad heart. They knew nothing about him.

A jury must be informed by the judge when trying the offence of manslaughter what facts they may and those which they may not use for the purpose of performing the test in the second element of this offence. . . .

Question
Is there tension between the decision in *Dawson* and the general rule of causation that maintains that one must take one's victim as one finds her?

Note
In *R* v *Watson* [1989] 2 All ER 865, the Court of Appeal indicated that the jury could take into account facts acquired by a defendant during the course of the crime. In *Watson* the defendants, two burglars, discovered that the resident of the house which they were burgling was an old and frail lady. An hour and a half after the crime she died of a heart attack. The Court of Appeal held that the defendants should be credited with knowledge of the victim's condition, even though they became aware of it only after the break-in.

(c)   An *unlawful and dangerous act*. Should the requirement of an unlawful *act* be taken literally? A strange (and probably unjustified) distinction between acts and omissions in this context was made in *Lowe*.

<h3 style="text-align:center">R v Lowe</h3>
[1973] 1 QB 702
Court of Appeal

The defendant, who was of low average intelligence, knew that his infant child was sick but did not call a doctor. The child died from dehydration and gross emaciation. The defendant was indicted on counts of manslaughter of the child and of wilfully neglecting it so as to cause unnecessary suffering or injury to health, contrary to s. 1(1) of the Children and Young Persons Act 1933. The jury, in convicting the defendant on both counts, negatived reckless behaviour by him as being the cause of death and emphasised that the conviction of manslaughter was solely due to the direction of the judge that a finding of manslaughter must follow a conviction of wilful neglect if that neglect was the cause of death.

PHILLIMORE LJ: . . . Now in the present case the jury negatived recklessness. How then can mere neglect, albeit wilful, amount to manslaughter? This court feels that there is something inherently unattractive in a theory of constructive manslaughter. It seems strange that an omission which is wilful solely in the sense that it is not inadvertent and the consequences of which are not in fact foreseen by the person who is neglectful should, if death results, automatically give rise to an indeterminate sentence instead of the maximum of two years which would otherwise be the limit imposed.

We think that there is a clear distinction between an act of omission and an act of commission likely to cause harm. Whatever may be the position with regard to the latter it does not follow that the same is true of the former. In other words, if I strike a child in a manner likely to cause harm it is right that, if the child dies, I may be charged with manslaughter. If, however, I omit to do something with the result that it suffers injury to health which results in its death, we think that a charge of manslaughter should not be an inevitable consequence, even if the omission is deliberate.

Appeal against conviction of manslaughter allowed.

Note
It is submitted that the reference to a 'deliberate' omission in *Lowe* should be understood in relation to the particular facts of the case. It is clear that the defendant neglected the child 'deliberately' in the sense that he decided not to call the doctor. However, the defendant was not aware of the probable consequences of his failure. It is therefore likely that the problems which commentators have with regard to the concept of 'deliberate' neglect are unfounded as the word was used in a rather curious fashion in the case. If that is so, however, the distinction between omissions and actions becomes wholly unnecessary, as all the court needed to decide in order to quash the defendant's conviction for manslaughter was that he was carrying out a lawful act (looking after a child) in a negligent way and that this did not amount to an unlawful act under the doctrine in *Andrews* v *DPP*.

(d)   *The effect of intoxication.* Where intoxication would not prevent a conviction of the defendant for the alleged unlawful act, it follows that he may be convicted of manslaughter if death results.

R v Lipman
[1970] 1 QB 152
Court of Appeal

WIDGERY LJ: . . . Both the defendant and the victim were addicted to drugs, and on the evening of September 16, 1967, both took a quantity of a drug known as LSD. Early on the morning of September 18, the defendant, who is a United States citizen, hurriedly booked out of his hotel and left the country. On the following day, September 19, the victim's landlord found her dead in her room. She had suffered two blows on the head causing haemorrhage of the brain, but she had died of asphyxia as a result of some eight inches of sheet having been crammed into her mouth.

The defendant was returned to this country by extradition proceedings, and at the trial he gave evidence of having gone with the victim to her room and there experienced what he described as an LSD 'trip'. He explained how he had the illusion of descending to the centre of the earth and being attacked by snakes, with which he had fought. It was not seriously disputed that he had killed the victim in the course of this experience, but he said he had no knowledge of what he was doing and no intention to harm her. He was charged with murder, but the jury evidently accepted that he lacked the necessary intention to kill or to do grievous bodily harm.

. . .

It was pointed out in this court that [in *R v Lamb* [1967] 2 QB 981] no unlawful act on the part of the prisoner had been proved in the absence of the necessary intent to constitute an assault. But this is intention of a different kind. Even if intent has to be proved to constitute the unlawful act, no specific further intent is required to turn that act into manslaughter. Manslaughter remains a most difficult offence to define because it arises in so many different ways and, as the mental element (if any) required to establish it varies so widely, any general reference to mens rea is apt to mislead.

We can dispose of the present application by reiterating that when the killing results from an unlawful act of the prisoner no specific intent has to be proved to convict of manslaughter, and self-induced intoxication is accordingly no defence. Since in the present case the acts complained of were obviously likely to cause harm to the victim (and did, in fact, kill her) no acquittal was possible and the verdict of manslaughter, at the least, was inevitable.

If and so far as this matter raises a point of law on which the defendant was entitled to appeal without leave, such appeal is dismissed.

Question

What was the unlawful act in *Lipman*? What was the *mens rea* of that crime? How is this case distinguishable from *Lamb*? See also *O'Driscoll* (1977) 65 Cr App R 50.

Note

Another case in which the unlawful act doctrine may have been stretched is *Cato* [1976] All ER 260. The Court of Appeal upheld a manslaughter verdict where the defendant had injected the victim with heroin, fatally as it transpired, supplied by the victim for that purpose. The defendant had also been convicted of administering a noxious thing with intent to endanger life contrary to s. 23 of the Offences Against the Person Act 1861. The Court of Appeal stated that even if they had not upheld the conviction for the s. 23 offence, they still would have confirmed the conviction for manslaughter. It is difficult to see what would have constituted the unlawful act in those circumstances, however, as the injection would not have been in violation of the Misuse of Drugs Act 1971.

(e)   *Causation — must the act be directed at the victim?* Because constructive manslaughter requires proof of the *mens rea* and *actus reus* of the 'unlawful act', it might be thought that if death follows from the unlawful act, however tenuous the causal link, then the offence would be made out. However, the courts have been reluctant to abandon all principles in respect to the causation issue.

R v Goodfellow
(1986) 83 Cr App R 23
Court of Appeal

LORD LANE CJ: . . . On August 14, 1984 in the early hours of the morning, the appellant set light to the council house he occupied at 24 Cossock Terrace, Pallion. He poured petrol over the sideboard, chair and walls of the downstairs living room, and then set the house on fire by igniting the petrol. In the ensuing blaze three people died: his wife Sarah aged 22, another young woman named Jillian Stuart with whom the appellant was having a liaison, who was in the house that night, and the appellant's two year old son Darren.

. . .

It is submitted by Mr Stewart on behalf of the appellant that this was not a case of 'unlawful act' manslaughter, because the actions of the appellant were not directed at the victim. The authority for that proposition is said to be *Dalby* (1982) 74 Cr App R 348.

. . .

It was held that since the act of supplying the scheduled drug was not an act which caused direct harm and since the unlawful act of supply of the dangerous drug by Dalby *per se* did not constitute the *actus reus* of the offence of manslaughter, the conviction had to be quashed. Waller LJ at page 352, said: ' . . . where the charge of manslaughter is based on an unlawful and dangerous act, it must be an act directed at the victim and likely to cause immediate injury, however slight.'

However we do not think that he was suggesting that there must be an intention on the part of the defendant to harm or frighten or a realisation that his acts were likely to harm or frighten. . . . What he was, we believe, intending to say was that there must be no fresh intervening cause between the act and the death. Indeed at p. 351 he said this: ' . . . the supply of drugs would itself have caused no harm unless the deceased had subsequently used the drugs in a form and quantity which was dangerous.'

Notes and questions
1. In *Ball* [1989] Crim LR 730, the Court of Appeal used the *Dalby* formula, saying that the assault in that case was directed at the victim. However, this was a clear case where there was no intervening cause and it is probable that the interpretation of *Dalby* in *Goodfellow* is the correct one.
2. Is the whole idea of constructive manslaughter misconceived? What justifies convicting a defendant of a homicide offence when the defendant did not intend to kill and was not even reckless as to endangering life? Often the death is due to a fortuity. Would it not make more sense to convict the defendant of the underlying crime, taking into account where appropriate at sentencing the fact that a death resulted? See J. Gobert 'The Fortuity of Consequences' [1993] 4 Crim Law Forum 1.

(ii)   Reckless manslaughter
The second category of involuntary manslaughter is that of reckless manslaughter. The concept of 'recklessness' in the criminal law has proved troublesome generally (see discussion in Chapter 3), and in particular in the context of manslaughter. There are two major issues:

(a)   Does recklessness require foresight by the defendant of the relevant risk?
(b)   What is the relevant risk?

(a)   *The definition of recklessness.* It is now clear that reckless manslaughter can be committed:

(i)   where the defendant himself recognises that the relevant risk exists but nevertheless goes on to take it; or

(ii)   where the defendant takes the relevant risk without having given any thought to the possibility of there being any such risk but a reasonable man would have appreciated the risk.

R v Lawrence
[1982] AC 510
House of Lords

For the facts and holding, see p. 119.

Notes

1.   *Lawrence* was followed in *R v Reid* [1992] 1 WLR 793. In that case the House of Lords held that 'recklessness' included heedlessness of the presence of a risk. Lord Ackner quoted the following definition of 'heedlessness' from *Austin's Jurisprudence*. A person who is heedless:

> does an act from which he was bound to forbear, because he adverts not to certain of its probable consequences. Absence of thought which one's duty would naturally suggest, is the main ingredient in each of the complex notions which are styled 'negligence and heedlessness' . . . the party who is guilty of heedlessness, thinks not of the probable mischief.

2.   *Lawrence* involved the (now abolished) offence of causing death by reckless driving. However, in *R v Seymour* (below), the direction in *Lawrence* was applied to manslaughter generally, with no modification regarding the degree of foresight of the risk. It may therefore be accepted that *Lawrence* and *Reid* (which was another case of causing death by reckless driving) incorporate an objective definition of recklessness into the offence of manslaughter. See also *Kong Cheuk Kwan* v *R* (1985), a case involving a fatal collision between two passenger hydrofoils, in which *Seymour* was applied.

(b)   *The relevant risk.*

R v Seymour
[1983] 2 AC 493
House of Lords

LORD FRASER OF TULLYBELTON: . . . With regard to the certified question in this appeal, Mr Connell's submission that the direction suggested in *R v Lawrence (Stephen)* [1982] AC 510, should not be given in its entirety where the charge is one of manslaughter, is not, in my opinion, well founded. If any modification of the '*Lawrence* direction' is appropriate in a case where manslaughter alone is charged, it would be to add a warning to the jury that before convicting of manslaughter they must be satisfied that the risk of death being caused by the manner of the accused's driving was very high. Such a direction will, of course, always be necessary where the common law crime and the statutory offence are charged alternatively, but where, as in this case, the common law crime is charged alone, it may be unnecessary and inappropriate. In the present case I think it was unnecessary.

I would dismiss the appeal.

(iii) Gross negligence manslaughter

The classic definition of this category of manslaughter is to be found in *Bateman*:

R v Bateman
(1925) 19 Cr App R 8
Court of Criminal Appeal

LORD HEWART LCJ: . . . In explaining to juries the test which they should apply to determine whether the negligence, in the particular case, amounted or did not amount to a crime, judges have used many epithets, such as 'culpable,' 'criminal,' 'gross,' 'wicked,' 'clear,' 'complete.' But, whatever epithet be used and whether an epithet be used or not, in order to establish criminal liability the facts must be such that, in the opinion of the jury, the negligence of the accused went beyond a mere matter of compensation between subjects and showed such disregard for the life and safety of others as to amount to a crime against the State and conduct deserving punishment.

Note

This passage has been much criticised on the ground that it leaves the question of the threshold of liability (which should be a legal question) to the jury.

What of the defendant who considered the risk of death but who incorrectly concluded that the risk did not exist or was negligible? Lord Goff addressed the point in *Reid*:

R v Reid
[1992] 1 WLR 793
House of Lords

LORD GOFF OF CHIEVELEY: . . . It follows that, in cases of driving recklessly (with which your Lordships are here concerned), I find myself to be in respectful agreement with the conclusion of Lord Diplock, that recklessness cannot sensibly be restricted to the so-called subjective test, but must be extended to embrace cases where the defendant has failed to give any thought to the possibility of risk. At the very least his view is, in my opinion, perfectly tenable; and in these circumstances it would not be an appropriate exercise of the power under *Practice Statement (Judicial Precedent)* [1966] 1 WLR 1234 to depart from the decision in *Lawrence* [1982] AC 510.

I recognise that it has been suggested that, if this is right, driving recklessly cannot be so sharply differentiated from careless driving, i.e. driving without due care and attention, as it would be if the purely subjective test were to be adopted as the sole criterion of recklessness, in which case a clear distinction could be drawn between cases where the defendant was aware of the risk and nevertheless disregarded it, and cases where the defendant failed to advert to the relevant risk. But the answer to this criticism is, I believe, as follows. First, as I have already said, we have to recognise that there are cases where, although the defendant is unaware of the risk, his conduct coupled with his state of mind is such that, in ordinary speech, he can properly be described as driving recklessly. Second, these cases can be differentiated from mere careless driving, because they are cases in which the defendant's driving would be described as dangerous in the sense that he was driving in such a manner as to create a serious risk of causing physical injury to other people or substantial damage to other people's property, and yet he did not even address his mind to the possibility of there being any such risk. This is different from a case where, for example, momentary inadvertence happens incidentally to create a risk: for the recklessness arises from the combination of the dangerous character of the driving coupled with failure by the driver even to address his mind to the possibility of risk. I for my part see no real difficulty, in practice, in perceiving a sufficiently clear differentiation between cases of this kind and cases of driving without due care and attention, which we see happening so often on the roads and of which many of us may, I fear, be guilty from time to time. Take the simple case of a man driving his car on the motorway in a group of other cars, all travelling at say 60 mph, and he fails for a moment or so to keep his eye on the car in front – perhaps his attention is caught by a pretty girl in the car alongside – with the result that he does not notice that the car in front has had to brake suddenly and he drives straight into it causing it damage. This is a classic case of careless driving: I do not think that on these simple facts anybody would say that he was driving recklessly. This is not a case of a man driving dangerously (in the sense described by Lord Diplock) and nevertheless failing to address his mind to the possibility of risk: it is a case of a man who failed to drive with due care and attention, and no more.

It has been pointed out that, although Lord Diplock's two categories of recklessness taken together have the effect that, in most cases where the defendant is driving dangerously in the sense I have described, he will in fact be driving recklessly, nevertheless there are cases in which this is not so. This may occur where the defendant considers the possibility of risk but nevertheless concludes that there is none. But we have to remember that, ex hypothesi, the defendant is driving dangerously in the sense I have described: and in practice his evidence that in such circumstances he thought that there was no risk is only likely to carry weight if he can point to some specific fact as to which he was mistaken and which, if true, would have excluded the possibility of risk – which might occur if, for example, as my noble and learned friend, Lord Ackner, has pointed out, he misunderstood in good faith some direction or instruction, or if he drove the wrong way down a one-way street at a normal speed in the mistaken belief that it was a two-way street. If that was indeed the case, his driving might well not be described as reckless, though such cases are likely to be rare. It has been suggested that there is therefore a 'loophole' or 'lacuna' in Lord Diplock's definition of recklessness. I feel bound to say that I myself regard these expressions as misleading. The simple fact is that Lord Diplock was concerned to define driving recklessly, not dangerous driving; and it is not in every case where the defendant is in fact driving dangerously that he should be held to be driving recklessly, although in most cases the two will coincide. Another example where they may not coincide could occur where a driver who, while driving, is afflicted by illness or shock which impairs his capacity to address his mind to the possibility of risk: it may well not be right to describe him as driving recklessly in such circumstances. Likewise (as my noble and learned friend has pointed out) if a driver takes evasive action in an emergency, his action may involve the taking of a risk which is regarded as justified in the special circumstances, so that he cannot be described as driving recklessly. Such cases, which again are likely to be rare, can be dealt with if and when they arise. It is however unnecessary to consider any such case on the present appeal.

Note
There was some question of whether the category of gross negligence manslaughter survived following the Privy Council's failure to advert to it in *Kong Cheuk Kwan* v *R* (1985) 82 Cr App R 18. This was a case of a fatal collision between two passenger hydrofoils. The Privy Council referred only to the *Lawrence* test. The gross negligence test was, however, apparently ignored rather than overruled. It was subsequently referred to without disapproval in *Goodfellow* (above), where Lord Lane LCJ said that the question in *Kong Cheuk Kwan* was whether the defendant had been guilty of recklessness or gross negligence, and in *R* v *Ball* [1989] Crim LR 730. These lukewarm endorsements of support did little to lift the cloud which hung over gross negligence manslaughter, or to dispel the argument that the category was to a large extent redundant in light of the developing law of reckless homicide. When reaffirmation finally came, however, it was emphatic and, indeed, it was the category of reckless manslaughter, and not that of gross negligence manslaughter, that was severely restricted.

R v *Sulman*
(1993) *The Times*, 21 May 1993
Court of Appeal

For facts and opinion, see chapter 3, p. 130.

Question
Should either reckless manslaughter or gross negligence manslaughter, one or the other, be abolished? Will the continued existence of both serve only to trap the unwary prosecutor who must charge the defendant who is responsible for another's death but who has not acted intentionally?

IV Reform of the law

The law of homicide seems almost a quaint oddity in modern times. In an era where the definitions of virtually all crimes can be found in statute, it is anomalous that one must search ancient tomes to find the definition of the most serious crime known to the law (murder). Other doctrines in both the law of murder and manslaughter also cry out for clarification. This task of providing guidance was undertaken by the Criminal Law Revision Committee in its Fourteenth Report. The fruits of its efforts are reflected in the Draft Criminal Code Bill 1989:

Draft Criminal Code Bill 1989

53. For the purposes of this Chapter—
(a) 'another' means a person who has been born and has an existence independent of his mother and, unless the context otherwise requires, 'death' and 'personal harm' mean the death of, or personal harm to, such a person;

(b)   a person does not cause death unless the death occurs within a year after the day on which any act causing it was done by that person or on which any fatal injury resulting from such an act was sustained, or (where the fatal injury was done to an unborn child) within a year after the day on which he was born and had an independent existence.

Homicide

54.—(1)   A person is guilty of murder if he causes the death of another—
(a)   intending to cause death; or
(b)   intending to cause serious personal harm and being aware that he may cause death,
unless section 56, 58, 59, 62 or 64 applies.

(2)   A person convicted of murder shall be sentenced to life imprisonment, except that, where he appears to the court to have been under the age of eighteen years at the time the offence was committed, he shall be sentenced to detention in such place and for such period and subject to such conditions as to release as the Secretary of State may determine.

55.   A person is guilty of manslaughter if—
(a)   he is not guilty of murder by reason only of the fact that a defence provided by section 56 (diminished responsibility), 58 (provocation) or 59 (use of excessive force) applies; or
(b)   he is not guilty of murder by reason only of the fact that, because of voluntary intoxication, he is not aware that death may be caused or believes that an exempting circumstance exists; or
(c)   he causes the death of another—
(i)   intending to cause serious personal harm; or
(ii)   being reckless whether death or serious personal harm will be caused.

56.—(1)   A person who, but for this section, would be guilty of murder is not guilty of murder if, at the time of his act, he is suffering from such mental abnormality as is a substantial enough reason to reduce his offence to manslaughter.

(2)   In this section 'mental abnormality' means mental illness, arrested or incomplete development of mind, psychopathic disorder, and any other disorder or disability of mind, except intoxication.

(3)   Where a person suffering from mental abnormality is also intoxicated, this section applies only where it would apply if he were not intoxicated.

57.—(1)   Whether evidence is evidence of mental abnormality is a question of law.

(2)   Where on a charge of murder or attempted murder the defendant has given or adduced evidence of mental disorder, severe mental handicap or automatism, the prosecution may adduce evidence of mental abnormality; but the court may give directions as to the stage of the proceedings at which it may do so.

(3)   Where a person is charged with murder (or attempted murder) the prosecution may, with his consent, adduce evidence of mental abnormality at the committal proceedings, whereupon the magistrates' court may commit him for trial for manslaughter (or attempted manslaughter).

(4)   Where the defendant has been committed for trial for murder (or attempted murder) the prosecution may, with the consent of the defendant, serve notice in accordance with Rules of Court of evidence of mental abnormality and indict him for manslaughter (or attempted manslaughter).

58. A person who, but for this section, would be guilty of murder is not guilty of murder if—

(a)   he acts when provoked (whether by things done or by things said or by both and whether by the deceased person or by another) to lose his self-control; and

(b)   the provocation is, in all the circumstances (including any of his personal characteristics that affect its gravity), sufficient ground for the loss of self-control.

59. A person who, but for this section, would be guilty of murder is not guilty of murder if, at the time of his act, he believes the use of the force which causes death to be necessary and reasonable to effect a purpose referred to in section 44 (use of force in public or private defence), but the force exceeds that which is necessary and reasonable in the circumstances which exist or (where there is a difference) in those which he believes to exist.

60. A person is guilty of murder or manslaughter (where section 54 or 55 applies) if—

(a)   he causes a fatal injury to another to occur within the ordinary limits of criminal jurisdiction, whether his act is done within or outside and whether the death occurs within or outside those limits;

(b)   he causes the death of another anywhere in the world by an act done within the ordinary limits of criminal jurisdiction; or

(c)   being a British citizen, he causes the death of another anywhere in the world by an act done anywhere in the world.

61. A person who attempts to cause the death of another, where section 56, 58 or 59 would apply if death were caused, is not guilty of attempted murder but is guilty of attempted manslaughter.

62.—(1)   A person who, but for this section, would be guilty of murder is not guilty of murder but is guilty of suicide pact killing if his act is done in pursuance of a suicide pact between himself and the person killed.

(2)   'Suicide pact' means an agreement between two or more persons having for its object the death of all of them, whether or not each is to take his own life, but nothing done by a person who enters into a suicide pact shall be treated as done by him in pursuance of the pact unless it is done while he has the settled intention of dying in pursuance of the pact.

(3)   A person acting in pursuance of a suicide pact between himself and another is not guilty of attempted murder but is guilty of attempted suicide pact killing if he attempts to cause the death of the other.

63. A person is guilty of an offence if he procures, assists or encourages suicide or attempted suicide committed by another.

Notes and questions
1.   In what ways would the Draft Criminal Code change the existing law?
2.   A more radical reform would be to do away with murder and manslaughter, crimes which turn on result, and substitute for them crimes of endangering life. Should a defendant who commits an assault be guilty of a homicide offence punishable by life imprisonment if the victim happens to die, but only be guilty of what may be a summary offence punishable by a maximum of six months' imprisonment if the victim is fortunate enough to live? Consider in this regard the proposed (but yet to be enacted) New Zealand endangering statute, extracted in Chapter 4. Many of the issues raised by the proposals are explored in the final section of that chapter.

10 NON FATAL OFFENCES AGAINST THE PERSON

I Introduction

This chapter deals with attacks on the personal integrity of a victim. The criminal law in this area is very muddled. The basic offences, of common law origin, are supplemented by a number of statutory offences. The statute (Offences Against the Person Act 1861) itself dates from the mid-nineteenth century and contains many anachronisms. It covers several aggravated offences which require proof of a common law assault as a prerequisite to conviction of a more serious, aggravated offence under the statute.

It would require a separate book to examine all the offences contained in the 1861 Act, and many of them are rarely charged. However, a student would be well advised to look at the whole statute in order to acquire the flavour of the legislation. In this chapter only the common law offences and the main aggravated assaults are examined.

Anyone studying the topic of assault needs to be sensitive to the value judgments which have to be made; for instance, the age at which people may consent to various activities or the purposes for which consent may be given. The answer to such questions may vary as society's attitudes change over time.

II Assault

Confusion is often caused by the court's use of the term 'assault' to cover two distinct offences —
 (a) assault; and
 (b) battery.
This is perhaps because typically a defendant commits both offences at the same time. However, the two offences are not identical and each will be examined separately.

An assault (or 'common assault', as it is sometimes called) is committed when the accused intentionally or recklessly causes the victim to apprehend the application of immediate and unlawful physical force to his or her person. The essence of the offence is the inducing of fear and no touching is necessary.

A   Actus reus

The victim must anticipate the immediate unlawful application of force to his or her person. No force need actually be applied (if it is, the defendant is guilty of battery). The victim has only to be in fear of a battery which 'need not necessarily be hostile, rude or aggressive . . . ' according to Lord Lane in *Faulkner* v *Talbot* [1981] 3 All ER 468, at p. 471.

It should be noted that the force which must be apprehended is *unlawful* force. If there is evidence that the victim consented or that the force was in any other way lawful (see defences, below) it will be for the prosecution to establish beyond reasonable doubt that the force was unlawful. If the victim did not apprehend the application of force no offence is committed, even if the victim was tragically wrong:

R v Lamb
[1967] 2 QB 981
Court of Appeal

For facts and holding, see p. 424.

Note
The victim must apprehend the *immediate* application of force:

Smith v *Chief Superintendant of Woking Police Station*
(1983) 76 Cr App R 234
Divisional Court

KERR LJ: . . . The justices found the following facts. On the evening of September 8, 1982, the defendant entered the grounds of Milford House and looked through the windows of Miss Mooney's bed-sitting room, and that the grounds form part of an enclosed garden. Then they found that Miss Mooney saw the defendant through the windows and recognised him and, 'she was absolutely terrified, to the extent that she was very nervous and jumpy for a few days afterwards.' Finally, they found that the defendant intended to frighten the person in that room.

In view of the question of law I must also refer shortly to the evidence on the basis of which the justices convicted. The incident happened at about 11 p.m., when Miss Mooney was in her room wearing a pink, knee-length nightie. There was a bay window and a side window. The curtains were drawn but they left a gap. She saw the defendant peering in and stated that he was right up against the window. She said: 'I instantly recognised him. I was very scared, very shocked. He was there about three or four seconds. I walked backwards and could no longer see him. I turned and he was at the other window, again right against the glass. I just stood and stared at him, didn't know what to do. He was just standing there, didn't seem he was going to go away. I jumped

across the bed towards the window and screamed. I was terrified, absolutely terrified. He must have seen me look at him. He moved away when I went across the bed. I looked at him for about 20 seconds at the side window. . . .'
. . .

Ultimately, as it seems to me, the only point taken by Mr Denny which requires some consideration is whether there was a sufficient apprehension, within the definition which I have read, of immediate and unlawful violence. He takes the point that there is no finding here that what Miss Mooney was terrified of was some violence, and indeed some violence which can be described as immediate. However, as it seems to me, Mr Greenbourne is right when he submits, really in the form of a question: 'What else, other than some form of immediate violence, could Miss Mooney have been terrified about?'

When one is in a state of terror one is very often unable to analyse precisely what one is frightened of as likely to happen next. When I say that, I am speaking of a situation such as the present, where the person who causes one to be terrified is immediately adjacent, albeit on the other side of a window. Mr Denny relied on a sentence in Smith and Hogan's *Criminal Law* (4th ed.), p. 351, where an illustration is given as follows: 'There can be no assault if it is obvious to P' – the complainant – 'that D' – the defendant – 'is unable to carry out his threat, as where D shakes his fist at P who is safely locked inside his car.' That may be so, but those are not the facts of the present case.

In the present case the defendant intended to frighten Miss Mooney and Miss Mooney was frightened. As it seems to me, there is no need for a finding that what she was frightened of, which she probably could not analyse at that moment, was some innominate terror of some potential violence. It was clearly a situation where the basis of the fear which was instilled in her was that she did not know what the defendant was going to do next, but that, whatever he might be going to do next, and sufficiently immediately for the purposes of the offence, was something of a violent nature. In effect, as it seems to me, it was wholly open to the justices to infer that her state of mind was not only that of terror, which they did find, but terror of some immediate violence. In those circumstances, it seems to me that they were perfectly entitled to convict the defendant who had gone there, as they found, with the intention of frightening her and causing her to fear some act of immediate violence, and therefore with the intention of committing an assault upon her. Accordingly, I would dismiss this appeal.

Notes and questions

1.   In *Smith*, how realistic were the victim's fears? Would the result have been different if there had been bars over the windows? Must the apprehension be reasonable? Should one have to take one's victim as one finds her?

2.   In the course of his opinion Kerr LJ cites the example of a victim inside a locked car. He thought it would not be an assault if such a person was threatened from outside the car. Was the threat in *Smith* more immediate than the one in Kerr's hypothetical?

3.   Given the well-developed law of attempt, is there any continuing need for the crime of assault? Is there a difference between an assault and an attempted battery? Should the law protect against pyschological, as opposed to physical, harm?

There is a question as to whether words alone can be sufficient for an assault. It appears that words can *prevent* actions from being an assault where otherwise they would have been considered sufficient for the offence:

Turberville v *Savage*
(1669) 1 Mod Rep 3
King's Bench Division

Action of *assault, battery,* and *wounding.* The evidence to prove a provocation was, that the plaintiff put his hand upon his sword and said, '*If it were not assize-time, I would not take such language from you.*' – The question was, If that were an assault? – The Court agreed that it was not; for the declaration of the plaintiff was, that he would not assault him, the Judges being in town; and *the intention* as well as *the act* makes an assault. Therefore if one strike another upon the hand, or arm, or breast in discourse, it is no assault, there being no *intention* to assault; but if one, intending to assault, strike *at* another and miss him, this is an assault: so if he hold up his hand against another in a threatening manner and say nothing, it is an assault. – In the principal case the plaintiff had judgment.

Can words alone constitute an assault? In *Meade and Belt* (1823) 1 Lew CC 184, Holroyd J stated that 'No words or singing are equivalent to an assault'. However, the court in *Wilson* threw doubt on that proposition, although the point was not necessary for the decision.

R v *Wilson*
[1955] 1 All ER 744
Court of Appeal

LORD GODDARD CJ: . . . No doubt what the court thought was the serious part of this case, as I think the jury must have thought too, was that the man threatened to get out knives. He called out 'Get out knives', which itself would be an assault, in addition to kicking the gamekeeper. . . .

Note
Giving the victim the choice between an assault and an unpleasant alternative will not prevent threatening behaviour from amounting to an assault. In *Ansell* v *Thomas* [1974] Crim LR 31, it was held that a verbal threat forcibly to eject the victim from a meeting if he did not leave voluntarily was an assault. This was a civil case, but civil and criminal assault have generally been considered to have the same ingredients. *Ansell* v *Thomas* probably falls into a category of cases where threats are sufficient to constitute an assault when the victim's safety depends on his compliance with the wishes of the defendant. In *Read* v *Coker* (1853) 13 CB 850, the defendant threatened to break the neck of the victim if he did not leave the premises. This was held to be an assault.

Question
An unseen person from outside a locked ground floor flat says 'I have a large knife and I'm going to carve you up'. Has the speaker committed an assault on the frightened man inside the flat? If instilling fear in a victim is the essence of the offence, why should not words constitute an assault if they have this effect?

There is also a question as to whether an omission can constitute an assault.

Fagan v *Metropolitan Police Commissioner*
[1969] 1 QB 439
Queen's Bench Division

JAMES J: . . . On August 31, 1967, the appellant was reversing a motor car in Fortunegate Road, London, N.W.10, when Police Constable Morris directed him to drive the car forwards to the kerbside and standing in front of the car pointed out a suitable place in which to park. At first the appellant stopped the car too far from the kerb for the officer's liking. Morris asked him to park closer and indicated a precise spot. The appellant drove forward towards him and stopped it with the offside wheel on Morris's left foot. 'Get off, you are on my foot,' said the officer. 'Fuck you, you can wait,' said the appellant. The engine of the car stopped running. Morris repeated several times 'Get off my foot.' The appellant said reluctantly 'Okay man, okay,' and then slowly turned on the ignition of the vehicle and reversed it off the officer's foot. The appellant had either turned the ignition off to stop the engine or turned it off after the engine had stopped running.

. . . An assault is any act which intentionally – or possibly recklessly – causes another person to apprehend immediate and unlawful personal violence. Although 'assault' is an independent crime and is to be treated as such, for practical purposes today 'assault' is generally synonymous with the term 'battery' and is a term used to mean the actual intended use of unlawful force to another person without his consent. On the facts of the present case the 'assault' alleged involved a 'battery'. Where an assault involves a battery, it matters not, in our judgement, whether the battery is inflicted directly by the body of the offender or through the medium of some weapon or instrument controlled by the action of the offender. An assault may be committed by the laying of a hand upon another, and the action does not cease to be an assault if it is a stick held in the hand and not the hand itself which is laid on the person of the victim. So for our part we see no difference in principle between the action of stepping on to a person's toe and maintaining that position and the action of driving a car on to a person's foot and sitting in the car whilst its position on the foot is maintained. . .

To constitute the offence of assault some intentional act must have been performed: a mere omission to act cannot amount to an assault. . . .

Appeal dismissed.

Notes and questions

1.   James J in his opinion in *Fagan v MPC* stated that 'a *mere* omission to act cannot amount to an assault'. Does the thrust of the opinion contradict this observation?

2.   *Fagan v MPC* was decided prior to *Miller* and the court's reasoning was based on the series of events constituting a single transaction. *Miller* would now provide an alternative rationale for reaching the same result.

3.   In *Director of Public Prosecutions v K* [1990] 1 All ER 331, a 15-year-old schoolboy took a test tube of sulphuric acid to the boys' toilet. Panicking at the sound of footsteps, he deposited the acid in an electric hand drier. He intended subsequently to remove the acid, but before he had the opportunity to do so, another student used the drier. The acid squirted on the student's face, causing scarring. The Queen's Bench Division held that the defendant was guilty of occasioning bodily harm. What was the *actus reus* of the offence?

B   Mens rea

The *mens rea* of assault was rendered uncertain by a number of incompatible judicial opinions over the past decade. In *R v Savage* and *Director of Public Prosecutions* v *Parmenter* the House of Lords had to choose between conflicting decisions of the Court of Appeal.

R v *Savage, Director of Public Prosecutions* v *Parmenter*
[1991] 3 WLR 914
House of Lords

LORD ACKNER: My Lords, these two appeals have been heard together, because they each raise the issue of the mental element which the prosecution have to establish in relation to offences under two sections of the Offences against the Person Act 1861, viz. section 20, unlawfully and maliciously wounding or inflicting grievous bodily harm and section 47, assault occasioning actual bodily harm.

It will be observed that some of the certified questions in *Parmenter* overlap with those in *Savage*.

My Lords, I will now seek to deal with the issues raised by these appeals seriatim.
. . .

2.   *Can a verdict of assault occasioning actual bodily harm be returned upon proof of an assault together with proof of the fact that actual bodily harm was occasioned by the assault, or must the prosecution also prove that the defendant intended to cause some actual bodily harm or was reckless as to whether such harm would be caused?*

Your Lordships are concerned with the mental element of a particular kind of assault, an assault 'occasioning actual bodily harm'. It is common ground that the mental element of assault is an intention to cause the victim to apprehend immediate and unlawful violence or recklessness whether such apprehension be caused: see *R v Venna* [1976] QB 421. It is of course common ground that Mrs Savage committed an assault upon Miss Beal when she threw the contents of her glass of beer over her. It is also common ground that however the glass came to be broken and Miss Beal's wrist thereby cut, it was, on the finding of the jury, Mrs Savage's handling of the glass which caused Miss Beal 'actual bodily harm.' Was the offence thus established or is there a further mental state that has to be established in relation to the bodily harm element of the offence? Clearly the section, by its terms, expressly imposes no such a requirement. Does it do so by necessary implication? It neither uses the word 'intentionally' or 'maliciously'. The words 'occasioning actual bodily harm' are descriptive of the word 'assault', by reference to a particular kind of consequence.

In neither *Savage*, nor *Spratt*, nor in *Parmenter* was the court's attention invited to the decision of the Court of Appeal in *R v Roberts* (1971) 56 Cr App R 95. [In that case the Court of Appeal used the following test:]

Was it [the action of the victim which resulted in actual bodily harm] the natural result of what the alleged assailant said and did, in the sense that it was something that could reasonably have been foreseen as the consequence of what he was saying or doing? As it was put in one of the old cases, it had got to be shown to be his act, and if of course the victim does something so 'daft', in the words of the appellant in this case, or so unexpected, not that this particular assailant did not actually foresee it but that no reasonable man could be expected to foresee it, then it is only in a very

remote and unreal sense a consequence of his assault, it is really occasioned by a
voluntary act on the part of the victim which could not reasonably be foreseen and
which breaks the chain of causation between the assault and the harm or injury.

Accordingly no fault was found in the following direction of the chairman to the jury,
at p. 103:

> if you accept the evidence of the girl in preference to that of the man, that means that
> there was an assault occasioning actual bodily harm, that means that she did jump out
> as a direct result of what he was threatening her with, and what he was doing to her,
> holding her coat, telling her he had beaten up girls who had refused his advances, and
> that means that through his acts he was in law and in fact responsible for the injuries
> which were caused to her by her decision, if it can be called that, to get away from his
> violence, his threats, by jumping out of the car.

Thus once the assault was established, the only remaining question was whether the
victim's conduct was the natural consequence of that assault. The words 'occasioning'
raised solely a question of causation, an objective question which does not involve
inquiring into the accused's state of mind. . . . The decision in *Roberts* case, 56 Cr App
R 95 was correct. The verdict of assault occasioning actual bodily harm may be
returned upon proof of an assault together with proof of the fact that actual bodily harm
was occasioned by the assault. The prosecution are not obliged to prove that the
defendant intended to cause some actual bodily harm or was reckless as to whether such
harm would be caused.

3. *In order to establish an offence under section 20 of the Act, must the prosecution prove
that the defendant actually foresaw that his act would cause harm, or is it sufficient to prove
that he ought so to have foreseen?*
    . . . [I]n order to establish an offence under section 20 the prosecution must prove
either the defendant intended or that he actually foresaw that his act would cause harm.

4. *In order to establish an offence under section 20 is it sufficient to prove that the
defendant intended or foresaw the risk of some physical harm or must he intend or foresee
either wounding or grievous bodily harm?*
    . . . Professor Glanville Williams and . . . Professor J. C. Smith in their text books and
in articles [and] commentaries . . . argue that a person should not be criminally liable
for consequences of his conduct unless he foresaw a consequence falling into the same
legal category as that set out in the indictment.

Such a general principle runs contrary to the decision in *Roberts'* case, 56 Cr App R
95 which I have already stated to be, in my opinion, correct. The contention is
apparently based on the proposition that as the actus reus of a section 20 offence is the
wounding or the infliction of grievous bodily harm, the mens rea must consist of
foreseeing such wounding or grievous bodily harm. But there is no such hard and fast
principle. To take but two examples, the actus reus of murder is the killing of the
victim, but foresight of grievous bodily harm is sufficient and indeed, such bodily harm,
need not be such as to be dangerous to life. Again, in the case of manslaughter, death is
frequently the unforeseen consequence of the violence used.

The argument that as section 20 and section 47 have both the same penalty, this
somehow supports the proposition that the foreseen consequences must coincide with
the harm actually done, overlooks the oft repeated statement that this is the irrational
result of this piece-meal legislation.

If section 20 was to be limited to cases where the accused does not desire but does
foresee wounding or grievous bodily harm, it would have a very limited scope. The

mens rea in a section 20 crime is comprised in the word 'maliciously'. As was pointed out by Lord Lane CJ, giving the judgment of the Court of Appeal in *R v Sullivan* on 27 October 1980 (unreported save in [1981] Crim LR 46) the 'particular kind of harm' in the citation from Professor Kenny was directed to 'harm to the person' as opposed to 'harm to property.' Thus it was not concerned with the degree of the harm foreseen. It is accordingly in my judgment wrong to look upon the decision in *Mowatt* [1968] 1 QB 421 as being in any way inconsistent with the decision in *Cunningham* [1957] 2 QB 396.

My Lords, I am satisfied that the decision in *Mowatt* was correct and that it is quite unnecessary that the accused should either have intended or have foreseen that his unlawful act might cause physical harm of the gravity described in section 20, i.e. a wound or serious physical injury. It is enough that he should have foreseen that some physical harm to some person, albeit of a minor character, might result.

Question
What is the *mens rea* of assault? Is the test objective or subjective? Does the House of Lords resolve the issue in *Savage*?

II Battery

A Actus reus

The *actus reus* of battery is the application of unlawful physical force against the person of the victim. An assault is not necessary – there need be no apprehension of an attack by the victim. Thus, if the victim is struck from behind, unaware of the presence of her assailant, that will be a battery, although it will not have been preceded by an assault.

(i) When is an application of force unlawful?
The problems of analysis are compounded by the fact that a battery may consist of anything from a slight touching to a severe beating. Is it possible for the law to recognise the types of distinctions that ordinary people make in their everyday lives?

Collins v Wilcock
[1984] 3 All ER 374
Queen's Bench Division

ROBERT GOFF LJ: There is before the court an appeal by way of a case stated by a metropolitan stipendiary magistrate sitting at Marylebone, under which the appellant, Alexis Collins, appeals against her conviction on 20 January 1983, of assaulting the respondent, Tracey Wilcock, a constable of the Metropolitan Police Force, in the execution of her duty at Craven Road, London W2, on 22 July 1982, contrary to s. 51(1) of the Police Act 1964.

The magistrate found the following facts. (a) On 22 July 1982 the respondent and Police Sgt Benjamen were on duty in a police vehicle and saw two women walking along the street; one of the two was a known prostitute, the other was the appellant. (b) The officers observed the two women, both of whom appeared to them to be soliciting men in the street. (c) The officers, without alighting from their vehicle, asked the two women to get into the police car so that they could have a word with them. One woman got into the car, the appellant refused to do so. (d) The officers repeated their request to the appellant, who again refused and walked away, followed by the police car which then pulled up alongside her. She again walked away. (e) The respondent, got out of the car and followed the appellant on foot, asking her why she didn't want to talk to the police, and also for her name and address. The appellant again started to walk away. The respondent told her that she had not finished talking to her and the appellant replied, 'Fuck off', and started to walk away yet again. (f) The respondent took hold of the appellant by the left arm to restrain her and the appellant shouted, 'Just fuck off, Copper' and scratched the respondent's right forearm with her fingernails. (g) The appellant was then arrested for assaulting a police officer in the execution of her duty.

Before the magistrate, the contentions of the parties were as follows. For the appellant, it was contended that the respondent was not acting in the execution of her duty at the time when the assault (if any) took place, having gone beyond the scope of her duty in detaining the appellant in circumstances short of arresting her. It was contended by the respondent, on the other hand, that there was on the evidence good ground for her to make inquiries and administer a caution under the Street Offences Act 1959, and that she was therefore acting in the execution of her duty at the time when the assault took place.

. . . [W]e think it right to consider whether, on the facts found in the case, the magistrate could properly hold that the respondent was acting in the execution of her duty. In order to consider this question, it is desirable that we should expose the underlying principles.

The law draws a distinction, in terms more easily understood by philologists than by ordinary citizens, between an assault and a battery. An assault is an act which causes another person to apprehend the infliction of immediate, unlawful, force on his person; a battery is the actual infliction of unlawful force on another person. Both assault and battery are forms of trespass to the person.

. . .

We are here concerned primarily with battery. The fundamental principle, plain and incontestable, is that every person's body is inviolate. It has long been established that any touching of another person, however slight, may amount to a battery. So Holt CJ held in 1704 that 'the least touching of another in anger is a battery': see *Cole* v *Turner* (1704) 6 Mod Rep 149, 90 ER 958. The breadth of the principle reflects the fundamental nature of the interest so protected; as Blackstone wrote in his Commentaries, 'the law cannot draw the line between different degrees of violence, and therefore totally prohibits the first and lowest stage of it; every man's person being sacred, and no other having a right to meddle with it, in any the slightest manner' (see 3 Bl Com 120). The effect is that everybody is protected not only against physical injury but against any form of physical molestation.

But so widely drawn a principle must inevitably be subject to exceptions. For example, children may be subjected to reasonable punishment; people may be subjected to the lawful exercise of the power of arrest; and reasonable force may be used in self-defence or for the prevention of crime. But, apart from these special instances where the control or constraint is lawful, a broader exception has been created to allow for the exigencies of everyday life. Generally speaking, consent is a defence to battery; and most of the physical contacts of ordinary life are not actionable because they are impliedly consented to by all who move in society and so expose themselves to the risk of bodily contact. So nobody can complain of the jostling which is inevitable from his presence in, for example, a supermarket, an underground station or a busy street; nor can a person who attends a party complain if his hand is seized in friendship, or even if his back is (within reason) slapped (see *Tuberville* v *Savage* (1669) 1 Mod Rep 3, 86 ER 684). Although such cases are regarded as examples of implied consent, it is more common nowadays to treat them as falling within a general exception embracing all physical contact which is generally acceptable in the ordinary conduct of daily life. We observe that, although in the past it has sometimes been stated that a battery is only committed where the action is 'angry, or revengeful, or rude, or insolent' (see 1 Hawk PC c. 62, s. 2), we think that nowadays it is more realistic, and indeed more accurate, to state the broad underlying principle, subject to the broad exception.

Among such forms of conduct, long held to be acceptable, is touching a person for the purpose of engaging his attention, though of course using no greater degree of physical contact than is reasonably necessary in the circumstances for that purpose. So, for example, it was held by the Court of Common Pleas in 1807 that a touch by a constable's staff on the shoulder of a man who had climbed on a gentleman's railing to gain a better view of a mad ox, the touch being only to engage the man's attention, did not amount to a battery (see *Wiffin* v *Kincard* (1807) 2 Bos & PNR 471, 127 ER 713; for another example, see *Coward* v *Baddeley* (1859) 4 H & N 478, 157 ER 927). But a distinction is drawn between a touch to draw a man's attention, which is generally acceptable, and a physical restraint, which is not. So we find Parke B observing in *Rawlings* v *Till* (1837) 3 M & W 28 at 29, 150 ER 1042, with reference to *Wiffin* v *Kincard*, that 'There the touch was merely to engage a man's attention, not to put a restraint on his person.' Furthermore, persistent touching to gain attention in the face of obvious disregard may transcend the norms of acceptable behaviour, and so be outside the exception. We do not say that more than one touch is never permitted; for example, the lost or distressed may surely be permitted a second touch, or possibly even more, on a reluctant or impervious sleeve or shoulder, as may a person who is acting reasonably in the exercise of a duty. In each case, the test must be whether the physical contact so persisted in has in the circumstances gone beyond generally acceptable standards of conduct; and the answer to that question will depend on the facts of the particular case.

The distinction drawn by Parke B in *Rawlings* v *Till* is of importance in the case of police officers. Of course, a police officer may subject another to restraint when he lawfully exercises his power of arrest; and he has other statutory powers, for example, his power to stop, search and detain persons under s. 66 of the Metropolitan Police Act 1839, with which we are not concerned. But, putting such cases aside, police officers have for present purposes no greater rights than ordinary citizens. It follows that, subject to such cases, physical contact by a police officer with another person may be unlawful as a battery, just as it might be if he was an ordinary member of the public. But a police officer has his rights as a citizen, as well as his duties as a policeman. A police officer may wish to engage a man's attention, for example if he wishes to question him. If he lays his hand on the man's sleeve or taps his shoulder for that purpose, he commits no wrong. He may even do so more than once; for he is under a duty to prevent and investigate crime, and so his seeking further, in the exercise of that duty, to engage a man's attention in order to speak to him may in the circumstances be regarded as acceptable (see *Donnelly* v *Jackman* [1970] 1 All ER 987, [1970] 1 WLR 562). But if, taking into account the nature of his duty, his use of physical contact in the face of non-co-operation persists beyond generally acceptable standards of conduct, his action will become unlawful; and if a police officer restrains a man, for example by gripping his arm or his shoulder, then his action will also be unlawful, unless he is lawfully exercising his power of arrest. A police officer has no power to require a man to answer him, though he has the advantage of authority, enhanced as it is by the uniform which the state provides and requires him to wear, in seeking a response to his inquiry. What is not permitted, however, is the unlawful use of force or the unlawful threat (actual or implicit) to use force; and, excepting the lawful exercise of his power of arrest, the lawfulness of a police officer's conduct is judged by the same criteria as are applied to the conduct of any ordinary citizen of this country.

. . . The fact is that the respondent took hold of the appellant by the left arm to restrain her. In so acting, she was not proceeding to arrest the appellant; and since her action went beyond the generally acceptable conduct of touching a person to engage his or her attention, it must follow, in our judgement, that her action constituted a battery on the appellant, and was therefore unlawful. It follows that the appellant's appeal must be allowed, and her conviction quashed.

Questions
1.   What should the officer have done? Was she required to permit the defendant to walk away?
2.   The court creates an exception for 'all' physical contact which is generally acceptable in the ordinary conduct of daily life. Who decides? Is this (should this be) a question of law or fact? If in a given community it is customary to punch a friend in the ribs as a greeting, would this be a battery elsewhere?

(ii)   Must the touching be hostile?

Wilson v *Pringle*
[1986] 2 All ER 440
Court of Appeal

The plaintiff and the defendant were two schoolboys involved in an incident in a school corridor as the result of which the plaintiff fell and suffered injuries. The plaintiff issued a writ claiming damages and alleging that the defendant had committed a trespass to the person of the plaintiff. In his defence the defendant admitted that he had indulged in horseplay with the plaintiff.

CROOM-JOHNSON LJ: . . . Nevertheless, it still remains to indicate what is to be proved by a plaintiff who brings an action for battery. Robert Goff LJ's judgment [in *Collins* v *Wilcock* [1984] 3 All ER 374] is illustrative of the considerations which underlie such an action, but it is not practicable to define a battery as 'physical contact which is not generally acceptable in the ordinary conduct of daily life'.

In our view, the authorities lead one to the conclusion that in a battery there must be an intentional touching or contact in one form or another of the plaintiff by the defendant. That touching must be proved to be a hostile touching. That still leaves unanswered the question, when is a touching to be called hostile? Hostility cannot be equated with ill-will or malevolence. It cannot be governed by the obvious intention shown in acts like punching, stabbing or shooting. It cannot be solely governed by an expressed intention, although that may be strong evidence. But the element of hostility, in the sense in which it is now to be considered, must be a question of fact for the tribunal of fact. It may be imported from the circumstances. Take the example of the police officer in *Collins* v *Wilcock*. She touched the woman deliberately, but without an intention to do more than restrain her temporarily. Nevertheless, she was acting unlawfully and in that way was acting with hostility. She was acting contrary to the woman's legal right not to be physically restrained. . . .

Questions
1.   Is 'hostility' as defined in *Wilson* v *Pringle* a helpful concept? What does it add to the notion of unlawfulness as defined in *Collins* v *Wilcock?*
2.   Can an action be hostile but not unlawful? Unlawful but not hostile?

Note
In *F* v *West Berkshire Health Authority* [1989] 2 All ER 545, at pp. 563–64, Lord Goff doubted the correctness of a requirement that the touching be hostile.

(iii)   Can a battery be committed by an omission to act?
It is generally assumed that a battery requires a positive action on the part of the defendant (see *Innes* v *Wylie* (1844) 1 Car & Kir 257), although it may be seen that an accidental application of force followed by a refusal to desist may be a battery (see *Fagan* v *MPC* above). The court held that there was a continuing act, not a mere omission. Further, the principle in *Miller* (above) would apply in a situation where the defendant creates a dangerous situation and then fails to rectify it. In *DPP* v *K* [1990] 1 All ER 331 (discussed above), Parker LJ stated (at pp. 333–34) that he had no doubt that if the defendant in the case had placed acid in a hand drier, which ejected onto the next user, an assault or battery would have been committed.

Can the force be applied indirectly?

R v Martin
(1881) 8 QBD 54
Divisional Court

Shortly before the conclusion of a performance at a theatre, M, with the intention and with the result of causing terror in the minds of persons leaving the theatre, put out the gaslights on a staircase which a large number of such persons had to descend in order to leave the theatre, and he also, with the intention and with the result of obstructing the exit, placed an iron bar across a doorway through which they had in leaving to pass.
   Upon the lights being thus extinguished a panic seized a large portion of the audience, and they rushed in fright down the staircase forcing those in front against the iron bar. By reason of the pressure and struggling of the crowd thus created on the staircase, several of the audience were thrown down or otherwise severely injured, and amongst them A and B.
   On proof of these facts the jury convicted M of unlawfully and maliciously inflicting grievous bodily harm upon A and B:—
   Held, by the Court (Lord Coleridge, CJ, Field, Hawkins, Stephen, and Cave, JJ), that M was rightly convicted.

Question
Jane slaps a horse on which Calvin is seated, the horse bolts and Calvin is
thrown to the ground. Has Jane committed a battery against Calvin?

B   Mens rea

The *mens rea* of battery is an intention to apply unlawful force, or subjective
recklessness as to whether such force will be applied (see *R* v *Savage* and *DPP
v Parmenter*, above).

III   Defences to assault and battery

A   In general

The defences which may defeat a charge of assault and/or battery are also
relevant to the more serious (aggravated) assaults discussed later in this
chapter. This is because some of the latter require proof of an assault or battery
before a conviction for the more serious offence can be made out.

Any of the general defences discussed in Chapter 8 may be relevant,
although self-defence is the most commonly pleaded. It must be noted that
provocation is not a defence to either assault or battery; it is a defence only in
the sense that it will reduce a charge of murder to manslaughter. Provocation
may be relevant to reduce the sentence of the court following a conviction, but
it will not prevent the defendant from being convicted in the first place.

B   Consent

A defence which often arises in cases of assault and battery and which may
prevent conviction is that of consent. We have already examined that aspect of
consent which operates to prevent a conviction for battery when a touching is
'generally acceptable in the ordinary conduct of daily life' (*Collins* v *Wilcock*,
above). Ordinary citizens are deemed to have given an implied consent to such
touching. More delicate issues arise when a decision has to be taken as to what
conduct can be the subject of consent. Is it permissible, for example, for two
people to batter each other in a contest which carries a high risk of brain
damage and some risk of immediate death? The law so far has permitted this
in the context of boxing. There are many intractable issues in this area, not
least the meaning of consent itself and the age and/or mental capacity which is
necessary before a 'real' consent can be given. Further, where the behaviour
carries a hidden risk (such as a risk of AIDS), can a true consent be given if the
victim is unaware of the hidden risk?

The issues raised may be broken down into the following questions,
although they overlap to a degree:

(a)   What limits will the State place on the ability of a victim to consent to
conduct which would be criminal in the absence of consent?
(b)   When will the State imply or impose consent on a victim?

(c)   What constitutes valid consent?

(i)   State limitations on effective consent

Consent is not a defence to a charge of murder or manslaughter. This is the case even if a victim begs to be killed because he or she is in intolerable pain.

Further down the 'harm' table, the courts seek to balance the benefit that the behaviour may bring, either to the public or to the individual, against the degree of harm that is inflicted upon the victim. Thus, even quite serious injury may be consented to where the perception of a useful outcome is high. This is the case in consent to surgery. Conversely, where the harm inflicted is slight but there is no benefit, the courts are less willing to recognise consent as a defence. As a general proposition, the more serious the harm inflicted, the less likely consent is to be effective, even where the behaviour takes place in private and the only persons directly affected are the participants. The factors to consider are:

(a)   the possible benefits to individuals or to the public;
(b)   the degree of harm inflicted on the victim;
(c)   the extent to which the law is prepared to interfere with private behaviour.

The delicate balancing required will often result in decisions which are controversial.

R v Brown
[1993] 2 WLR 556
House of Lords

The appellants, a group of sado-masochistics, willingly and enthusiastically participated in the commission of acts of violence against each other for the sexual pleasure it engendered in the giving and receiving of pain. They pleaded guilty on arraignment to counts charging various offences under ss. 20 and 47 of the Offences against the Person Act 1861, relating to the infliction of wounds or actual bodily harm on genital and other areas of the body of the consenting victim. On a ruling by the trial judge that, in the particular circumstances, the prosecution did not have to prove lack of consent by the victim, the appellants were re-arraigned, pleaded guilty, some to offences under s. 20 and all to offences under s. 47 and they were convicted. They appealed against conviction on the ground that the judge had erred in his rulings, in that the willing and enthusiastic consent of the victim to the acts on him prevented the prosecution from proving an essential element of the offence, whether charged under s. 20 or s. 47.

LORD TEMPLEMAN: . . . In some circumstances violence is not punishable under the criminal law. When no actual bodily harm is caused, the consent of the person affected precludes him from complaining. There can be no conviction for the summary offence of common assault if the victim has consented to the assault. Even when violence is intentionally inflicted and results in actual bodily harm, wounding or serious bodily harm the acused is entitled to be acquitted if the injury was a foreseeable incident of a lawful activity in which the person injured was participating. Surgery involves intentional violence resulting in actual or sometimes serious bodily harm but surgery is a lawful activity. Other activities carried on with consent by or on behalf of the injured person have been accepted as lawful notwithstanding that they involve actual bodily harm or may cause serious bodily harm. Ritual circumcision, tattooing, ear-piercing and violent sports including boxing are lawful activites.

In earlier days some other forms of violence were lawful and when they ceased to be lawful they were tolerated until well into the 19th century. Duelling and fighting were at first lawful and then tolerated provided the protagonists were voluntary participants. But where the results of these activities was the maiming of one of the participants, the defence of consent never availed the aggressor; see *Hawkins' Pleas of the Crown*, 8th ed. (1824), vol. 1, ch. 15. A maim was bodily harm whereby a man was deprived of the use of any member of his body which he needed to use in order to fight but a bodily injury was not a maim merely because it was a disfigurement. The act of maim was unlawful because the King was deprived of the services of an able-bodied citizen for the defence of the realm. Violence which maimed was unlawful despite consent to the activity which produced the maiming. In these days there is no difference between maiming on the one hand and wounding or causing grievous bodily harm on the other hand except with regard to sentence.

When duelling became unlawful, juries remained unwilling to convict but the judges insisted that persons guilty of causing death or bodily injury should be convicted despite the consent of the victim.

Similarly, in the old days, fighting was lawful provided the protagonists consented because it was thought that fighting inculcated bravery and skill and physical fitness. The brutality of knuckle fighting however caused the courts to declare that such fights were unlawful even if the protagonists consented. Rightly or wrongly the courts accepted that boxing is a lawful activity.

. . .

The question whether the defence of consent should be extended to the consequences of sado-masochistic encounters can only be decided by consideration of policy and public interest. Parliament can call on the advice of doctors, psychiatrists, criminologists, sociologists and other experts and can also sound and take into account public opinion. But the question must at this stage be decided by this House in its judicial capacity in order to determine whether the convictions of the appellants should be upheld or quashed.

Counsel for some of the appellants argued that the defence of consent should be extended to the offence of occasioning actual bodily harm under section 47 of the Act of 1861 but should not be available to charges of serious wounding and the infliction of serious bodily harm under section 20. I do not consider that this solution is practicable. Sado-masochistic participants have no way of foretelling the degree of bodily harm which will result from their encounters. The differences between actual bodily harm and serious bodily harm cannot be satisfactorily applied by a jury in order to determine acquittal or conviction.

Counsel for the appellants argued that consent should provide a defence to charges under both section 20 and section 47 because, it was said, every person has a right to deal with his body as he pleases. I do not consider that this slogan provides a sufficient guide to the policy decision which must now be made. It is an offence for a person to abuse his own body and mind by taking drugs. Although the law is often broken, the criminal law restrains a practice which is regarded as dangerous and injurious to individuals and which if allowed and extended is harmful to society generally. In any event the appellants in this case did not mutilate their own bodies. They inflicted bodily harm on willing victims. Suicide is no longer an offence but a person who assists another to commit suicide is guilty of murder or manslaughter.

The assertion was made on behalf of the appellants that the sexual appetites of sadists and masochists can only be satisfied by the infliction of bodily harm and that the law should not punish the consensual achievement of sexual satisfaction. There was no evidence to support the assertion that sado-masochist activities are essential to the happiness of the appellants or any other participants but the argument would be acceptable if sado-masochism were only concerned with sex, as the appellants contend. In my opinion sado-masochism is not only concerned with sex. Sado-masochism is also concerned with violence. The evidence discloses that the practices of the appellants were unpredictably dangerous and degrading to body and mind and were developed with increasing barbarity and taught to persons whose consents were dubious or worthless.

A sadist draws pleasure from inflicting or watching cruelty. A masochist derives pleasure from his own pain or humiliation. The appellants are middle-aged men. The victims were youths some of whom were introduced to sado-masochism before they attained the age of 21. In his judgment in the Court of Appeal, Lord Lane CJ said that two members of the group of which the appellants formed part, namely one Cadman and the appellant Laskey:

> were responsible in part for the corruption of a youth K . . . It is some comfort at least to be told, as we were, that K has now it seems settled into a normal heterosexual relationship. Cadman had befriended K when the boy was 15 years old. He met him in a cafeteria and, so he says, found out that the boy was interested in homosexual activities. He introduced and encouraged K in 'bondage affairs'. He was interested in viewing and recording on videotape K and other teenage boys in homosexual scenes . . . One cannot overlook the danger that the gravity of the assaults and injuries in this type of case may escalate to even more unacceptable heights.

The evidence disclosed that drink and drugs were employed to obtain consent and increase enthusiasm. The victim was usually manacled so that the sadist could enjoy the thrill of power and the victim could enjoy the thrill of helplessness. The victim had no control over the harm which the sadist, also stimulated by drink and drugs might inflict. In one case a victim was branded twice on the thigh and there was some doubt as to whether he consented to or protested against the second branding. The dangers involved in administering violence must have been appreciated by the appellants because, so it was said by their counsel, each victim was given a code word which he could pronounce when excessive harm or pain was caused. The efficiency of this precaution, when taken, depends on the circumstances and on the personalities involved. No one can feel the pain of another. The charges against the appellants were based on gential torture and violence to the buttocks, anus, penis, testicles and nipples. The victims were degraded and humiliated sometimes beaten, sometimes wounded with instruments and sometimes branded. Bloodletting and the smearing of human blood produced excitement. There were obvious dangers of serious personal injury and blood infection. Prosecuting counsel informed the trial judge against the protests of defence counsel, that although the appellants had not contracted Aids, two members of the group had died from Aids and one other had contracted an H.I.V. infection although not necessarily from the practices of the group. Some activities involved excrement. The assertion that the instruments employed by the sadists were clean and sterilised could not have removed the danger of infection, and the assertion that care was taken demonstrates the possibility of infection. Cruelty to human beings was on occasions supplemented by cruelty to animals in the form of bestiality. It is fortunate that there were no permanent injuries to a victim though no one knows the extent of harm inflicted in other cases. It is not surprising that a victim does not complain to the police when the complaint would involve him in giving details of acts in which he participated. Doctors of course are subject to a code of confidentiality.

In principle there is a difference between violence which is incidental and violence which is inflicted for the indulgence of cruelty. The violence of sado-masochistic encounters involves the indulgence of cruelty by sadists and the degradation of victims. Such violence is injurious to the participants and unpredictably dangerous. I am not prepared to invent a defence of consent for sado-masochistic enounters which breed and glorify cruelty and result in offences under sections 47 and 20 of the Act of 1861.

Society is entitled and bound to protect itself against a cult of violence. Pleasure derived from the infliction of pain is an evil thing. Cruelty is uncivilised. I would answer the certified question in the negative and dismiss the appeals of the appellants against conviction.

Lord Mustill (dissenting) . . .

I   *The decided cases*

Throughout the argument of the appeal I was attracted by an analysis on the following lines. First, one would construct a continuous spectrum of the infliction of bodily harm, with killing at one end and a trifling touch at the other. Next, with the help of reported cases one would identify the point on this spectrum at which consent ordinarily ceases to be an answer to a prosecution for inflicting harm. This could be called 'the critical level'. It would soon become plain however that this analysis is too simple and that there are certain types of special situation to which the general rule does not apply. Thus, for example, surgical treatment which requires a degree of bodily invasion well on the upper side of the critical level will nevertheless be legitimate if performed in accordance with good medical practice and with the consent of the patient. Conversely, there will be cases in which even a moderate degree of harm cannot be legitimated by consent. Accordingly, the next stage in the analysis will be to identify those situations which have been identified as special by the decided cases, and to examine them to see whether the instant case either falls within one of them or is sufficiently close for an analogy to be valid. If the answer is negative, then the court will have to decide whether simply to apply the general law simply by deciding whether the bodily harm in the case under review is above or below the critical level, or to break new ground by recognising a new special situation to which the general law does not apply.

For all the intellectual neatness of this method I must recognise that it will not do, for it imposes on the reported cases and on the diversities of human life an order which they do not possess. Thus, when one comes to map out the spectrum of ordinary consensual physical harm, to which the special situations form exceptions, it is found that the task is almost impossible, since people do not ordinarily consent to the infliction of harm. In effect, either all or almost all the instances of the consensual infliction of violence are special. They have been in the past, and will continue to be in the future, the subject of special treatment by the law.

There are other objections to a general theory of consent and violence. Thus, for example, it is too simple to speak only of consent, for it comes in various sorts. Of these, four spring immediately to mind. First, there is an express agreement to the infliction of the injury which was in the event inflicted. Next, there is express agreement to the infliction of some harm, but not to that harm which in the event was actually caused. These two categories are matched by two more, in which the recipient expressly consents not to the infliction of harm, but to engagement in an activity which creates a risk of harm; again, either the harm which actually results, or to something less. These examples do not exhaust the categories, for corresponding with each are situations of frequent occurrence in practice where the consent is not express but implied. These numerous categories are not the fruit of academic over-elaboration, but are a reflection of real life. Yet they are scarcely touched on in the cases, which just do not bear the weight of any general theory of violence and consent.

... 'Contact' sports

Some sports, such as the various codes of football, have deliberate bodily contact as an essential element. They lie at a mid-point between fighting, where the participant knows that his opponent will try to harm him, and the milder sports where there is at most an acknowledgement that someone may be accidentally hurt. In the contact sports each player knows and by taking part agrees that an opponent may from time to time inflict upon his body (for example by a rugby tackle) what would otherwise be a painful battery. By taking part he also assumes the risk that the deliberate contact may have unintended effects, conceivably of sufficient severity to amount to grievous bodily harm. But he does not agree that this more serious kind of injury may be inflicted deliberately. This simple analysis conceals a number of difficult problems, which are discussed in a series of Canadian decisions, culminating in *R v Ciccarelli* (1989) 54 CCC (3d) 121, on the subject of ice hockey, a sport in which an ethos of physical contact is deeply entrenched. The courts appear to have started with the proposition that some level of violence is lawful if the recipient agrees to it, and have dealt with the question of excessive violence by enquiring whether the recipient could really have tacitly accepted a risk of violence at the level which actually occurred. These decisions do not help us in the present appeal, where the consent of the recipients was express, and where it is known that they gladly agreed, not simply to some degree of harm but to everything that was done. What we need to know is whether, notwithstanding the recipient's implied consent, there comes a point at which it is too severe for the law to tolerate. Whilst common sense suggests that this must be so, and that the law will not license brutality under the name of sport, one of the very few reported indications of the point at which tolerable harm becomes intolerable violence is in the direction to the jury given by Bramwell LJ in *R v Bradshaw* (1878) 14 Cox CC 83 that the act (in this case a charge at football) would be unlawful if intended to cause 'serious hurt'. This accords with my own instinct, but I must recognise that a direction at nisi prius, even by a great judge, cannot be given the same weight as a judgment on appeal, consequent upon full argument and reflection. The same comment may be made about *R v Moore* (1898) 14 TLR 229.

5. Surgery

Many of the acts done by surgeons would be very serious crimes if done by anyone else, and yet the surgeons incur no liability. Actual consent, or the substitute for consent deemed by the law to exist where an emergency creates a need for action, is an essential element in this immunity; but it cannot be a direct explanation for it, since much of the bodily invasion involved in surgery lies well above any point at which consent could even arguably be regarded as furnishing a defence. Why is this so? The answer must in my opinion be that proper medical treatment, for which actual or deemed consent is a prerequisite, is in a category of its own.

6. Lawful correction

It is probably still the position at common law, as distinct from statute, that a parent or someone to whom the parent has delegated authority may inflict physical hurt on his or her child, provided that it does not go too far and is for the purpose of correction and not the gratification of passion or rage: see *R v Conner* (1836) 7 C & P 438; *R v Cheeseman* (1836) 7 C & P 455; *R v Hopley* (1860) 2 F & F 202; *R v Griffin* (1869) 11 Cox CC 402. These cases have nothing to do with consent, and are useful only as another demonstration that specially exempt situations can exist and that they can involve an upper limit of tolerable harm.

. . . I ask myself, not whether as a result of the decision in this appeal, activities such as those of the appellants should *cease* to be criminal, but rather whether the Act of 1861 (a statute which I venture to repeat once again was clearly intended to penalise conduct of a quite different nature) should in this new situation be interpreted so as to *make* it criminal. Why should this step be taken? Leaving aside repugnance and moral objection, both of which are entirely natural but neither of which are in my opinion grounds upon which the court could properly create a new crime, I can visualise only the following reasons. (1) Some of the practices obviously created a risk of genito-urinary infection, and others of septicaemia. these might indeed have been grave in former times, but the risk of serious harm must surely have been greatly reduced by modern medical science.

(2) The possibility that matters might get out of hand, with grave results. It has been acknowedged throughout the present proceedings that the appellants' activities were performed as a pre-arranged ritual, which at the same time enhanced their excitement and minimised the risk that the infliction of injury would go too far. Of course things might go wrong and really serious injury or death might ensue. If this happened, those responsible would be punished according to the ordinary law, in the same way as those who kill or injure in the course of more ordinary sexual activities are regularly punished. But to penalise the appellants' conduct even if the extreme consequences do not ensue, just because they might have done so would require an assessment of the degree of risk, and the balancing of this risk against the interests of individual freedom. Such a balancing is in my opinion for Parliament, not the courts; and even if your Lordships' House were to embark upon it the attempt must in my opinion fail at the outset for there is no evidence at all of the seriousness of the hazards to which sado-masochistic conduct of this kind gives rise. this is not surprising, since the impressive argument of Mr Purnell for the respondents did not seek to persuade your Lordships' to bring the matter within the Act of 1861 on the ground of special risks, but rather to establish that the appellants are liable *under the general law* because the level of harm exceeded the critical level marking off criminal from non-criminal consensual violence which he invited your Lordships to endorse.

(3) I would give the same answer to the suggestion that these activities involved a risk of accelerating the spread of auto-immune deficiency syndrome, and that they should be brought within the Act of 1861 in the interests of public health. The consequence would be strange, since what is currently the principal cause for the transmission of this scourge, namely consenting buggery between males, is now legal. Nevertheless, I would have been compelled to give this proposition the most anxious consideration if there had been any evidence to support it. But there is none, since the case for the respondent was advanced on an entirely different ground.

(4) There remains an argument to which I have given much greater weight. As the evidence in the present case has shown, there is a risk that strangers (and especially young strangers) may be drawn into these activities at an early age and will then become

established in them for life. This is indeed a disturbing prospect, but I have come to the conclusion that it is not a sufficient ground for declaring these activities to be criminal under the Act of 1861. The element of the corruption of youth is already catered for by the existing legislation; and if there is a gap in it which needs to be filled the remedy surely lies in the hands of Parliament, not in the application of a statute which is aimed at other forms of wrongdoing. As regards proselytisation for adult sado-masochism the argument appears to me circular. For if the activity is not itself so much against the public interest that it ought to be declared criminal under the Act of 1861 then the risk that others will be induced to join in cannot be a ground for making it criminal.

Leaving aside the logic of this answer, which seems to me impregnable, plain humanity demands that a court addressing the criminality of conduct such as that of the present should recognise and respond to the profound dismay which all members of the community share about the apparent increase of cruel and senseless crimes against the defenceless. Whilst doing so I must repeat for the last time that in the answer which I propose I do not advocate the decriminalisation of conduct which has hitherto been a crime; nor do I rebut a submission that a new crime should be created, penalising this conduct, for Mr Purnell has rightly not invited the House to take this course. The only question is whether these consensual private acts are offences against the existing law of violence. To this question I return a negative response.

Appeal dismissed.

Notes and questions
1.   Why should competent, rational adults free from duress or coercion be prevented from consenting to activities which give them pleasure, particularly if those activities are conducted in private? Is there a *human right* of liberty and autonomy which requires that such choices be respected?
2.   Does the court in *Brown* assume an unduly paternalistic role? Does the State and/or the judiciary have an obligation to enforce the prevailing moral values of the community? How does one determine what those values are?
3.   Is there a *qualitative* distinction between permitting a person to consent to his own death and permitting a person to consent to lesser harms? Is the concern in the former that unscrupulous individuals may be able to talk gullible victims into consenting to their death? With the victim dead, the task of proving or disproving consent is likely to be extremely difficult. Or is the critical factor that death is qualitatively different from all other forms of harm?
4.   How does *Brown* differ from a permitted boxing match? Does the difference have anything to do with consent? Even in the context of professional and amateur sport, the possibility of a prosecution for battery has been recognised where the force exceeds the legitimate parameters of the rules of the game. See, e.g., *Lloyd* [1989] Crim LR 513.
5.   May a person consent to cosmetic surgery? Who does it benefit? Why does Lord Mustill reject a distinction based on the seriousness of the harm caused and then place surgery in a category of its own because of the degree of harm caused?

(ii)   When will the State imply or impose consent on a victim?
We have already seen that the law implies consent to physical contact which is generally acceptable in the ordinary conduct of daily life (*Collins* v *Wilcock*,

above). Similarly, the courts will not allow the absence of formal consent by an unconscious patient to convert a beneficial medical procedure into a battery. Thus, if a paramedic comes upon an unconscious victim of a car accident and gives a blood transfusion it will not amount to a battery, even though the recipient is a Jehovah's Witness who would have refused such treatment on religious grounds had she been conscious. Parents too are allowed to use reasonable force for the purpose of corporal punishment, although whether it is strictly accurate to say that the child 'consents' to such force is questionable.

The law formerly implied consent to sexual intercourse between a married couple even where they were estranged. This is no longer the case [see *R* v *R* [1991] 4 All ER 481], although it took the courts a long time to come around to this position. The history of this development provides an instructive illustration of the difficulty that the law has in changing with social attitudes.

(iii) *What constitutes valid consent?*
If a victim is unable to comprehend the nature of the act to which he or she apparently consented, the consent will be invalid.

Burrell v *Harmer*
[1965] 3 All ER 684
Divisional Court

The defendant tattooed devices on the arms of two boys aged respectively 12 and 13. The marks subsequently became inflamed and he was charged with, and convicted of, causing the boys actual bodily harm.

Held, dismissing his appeal, that if a child of the age of understanding was unable to appreciate the nature of an act, apparent consent to it was no consent at all.

Questions
Is the court's position that the boys did not appreciate what it meant to be tattooed; or that even if they did know, they were not legally capable of giving consent? Would the result have been different if the boys had been 15? 18?

Notes
1. Note that the court's ruling may lead to the conviction of a defendant who had not only an honest but also a reasonable belief in the consent of the victim. This appears to be in direct contravention of *Director of Public Prosecutions* v *Morgan* [1976] AC 182 and the similar decision in *R* v *Kimber* [1983] 1 WLR 1118, where it was held by the Court of Appeal that an honest belief in the consent of a mentally retarded woman would have been sufficient to negative a charge of indecent assault. Both *Morgan* and *Kimber* are examined in Chapter 8.
2. In the case of a very young child, absence of consent will be implied from the child's age. See, e.g. *R* v *Howard* [1965] 3 All ER 684 (child of six unable to comprehend sexual intercourse and so unable to consent). In other cases the jury must decide whether there was a valid consent:

R v *D*
[1984] 1 AC 778
House of Lords

LORD BRANDON OF OAKBROOK: . . . I must now deal with two matters to which I said that I would return later. One of those matters is whether the doctrine laid down by the Irish Supreme Court in *Edge's* case [1943] IR 115 that the person the absence of whose consent is an essential ingredient of the common law offence of kidnapping is that of the child if it has reached an age of discretion fixed by law, but that of its father or other guardian if it has not, applies also under English law.

In my opinion, to accept that doctrine as applicable under English law would not be consistent with the formulation of the third ingredient of the common law offence of kidnapping which I made earlier on the basis of the wide body of authority to which your Lordships were referred. That third ingredient, as I formulated it earlier, consists of the absence of consent on the part of the person taken or carried away. I see no good reason why, in relation to the kidnapping of a child, it should not in all cases be the absence of the child's consent which is material, whatever its age may be. In the case of a very young child, it would not have the understanding or the intelligence to give its consent, so that absence of consent would be a necessary inference from its age. In the case of an older child, however, it must, I think be a question of fact for a jury whether the child concerned has sufficient understanding and intelligence to give its consent; if, but only if, the jury considers that a child has these qualities, it must then go on to consider whether it has been proved that the child did not give its consent. While the matter will always be for the jury alone to decide, I should not expect a jury to find at all frequently that a child under 14 had sufficient understanding and intelligence to give its consent.

Note
An apparent consent which is the product of duress or fear will not be valid. What then of consent induced by fraud?

Bolduc and Bird v *R*
(1967) 63 DLR (2d) 82
Supreme Court of Canada

A physician, about to conduct a vaginal examination and, if necessary, perform a medical procedure in the area to be examined, falsely introduced a lay friend of his to the patient as a medical intern and asked if the friend, who, in fact, was present for his own gratification, might observe the examination. The patient consented to the friend's presence and the physician proceeded with the examination during which he touched the patient's private parts and inserted an instrument therein for the purposes of the examination while the friend looked on but at no time touched the patient. Both the physician and his friend were convicted of indecent assault on the patient and their conviction was affirmed by the Court of Appeal but on their further appeal from conviction, *held*, Spence, J, dissenting, the appeals should be allowed and the convictions quashed.

Per Hall, J, Cartwright, Fauteux and Ritchie, JJ, concurring: It cannot be said that the fraud practised on the patient vitiated her consent to what the physician was supposed to do and to what, in fact, he did do and, accordingly, the consent of the patient was not obtained by false and fraudulent representations as to the nature and quality of the act. The fraud related rather to the friend's identity as a medical intern and his presence, having regard for the fact that he did not touch the patient, was not an assault.

Per Spence, J, dissenting: Under s. 230 of the *Criminal Code*, the application of force, however slight, is an assault when it is 'without the consent of another person or with consent, where it is obtained by fraud.' The patient's consent to the touching of her person by the physician was a consent to such touching in the presence of a doctor and not a mere layman. The indecent assault upon her was not, then, the act to which she consented and, hence, even without recourse to the provisions of s. 141(2), the accused physician's conduct amounted to the offence of indecent assault to which the co-accused was a party by virtue of the provisions of s. 21 of the *Code*.

Notes and questions
1.   What is the rationale of the decision? Is it at all relevant whether the woman would have consented to the examination if she had known the true state of affairs?
2.   What if a doctor indicates that he intends only to perform a vaginal examination. The patient consents and the doctor proceeds (in a highly unprofessional manner) to engage in conduct which in law would amount to an indecent assault. Would consent be a defence to the ensuing charge? How does this case differ from *Bolduc and Bird*? See *R* v *Williams* [1980] Crim LR 589.
3.   In *R* v *Clarence* (1888) 22 QBD 23, the defendant had intercourse with the victim, who was not aware that he had a venereal disease. It was held that his concealment of his condition was *not* a sufficient fraud as to the nature and quality of the act so as to prevent the victim's consent from being a valid consent. Would the same result be reached today if the concealed condition were AIDS?

IV   Aggravated assaults

The Offences Against the Person Act 1861 and other statutes contain many offences which are regarded as more serious than assault and battery because of aggravating factors. The most commonly charged are examined here. In most of these offences the *actus reus* and *mens rea* of assault or battery must be proved as well as the aggravating factor.

A   Assault occasioning actual bodily harm

Offences Against the Person Act 1861

47.   Whosoever shall be convicted upon an indictment of any assault occasioning actual bodily harm shall be liable . . . to be kept in penal servitude . . . ; and whosoever shall be convicted upon an indictment for a common assault shall be liable, at the discretion of the court, to be imprisoned for any term not exceeding one year, with or without hard labour.

Note
'Actual bodily harm' was defined in the following case:

R v Miller
[1954] 2 QB 282
Queen's Bench Division

LYNSKEY J: ... The point has been taken that there is no evidence of bodily harm. The bodily harm alleged is said to be the result of the prisoner's actions, and that is, if the jury accept the evidence, that he threw the wife down three times. There is evidence that afterwards she was in a hysterical and nervous condition, but it is said by counsel that that is not actual bodily harm. Actual bodily harm, according to Archbold, 32nd ed., p. 959, includes 'any hurt or injury calculated to interfere with the health or comfort of the prosecutor.' There was a time when shock was not regarded as bodily hurt, but the day has gone by when that could be said. It seems to me now that if a person is caused hurt or injury resulting, not in any physical injury, but in an injury to her state of mind for the time being, that is within the definition of actual bodily harm, and on that point I would leave the case to the jury.

Note
There was some doubt as to the *mens rea* for this offence, in particular the extent to which the defendant must foresee the degree of harm which would result. This controversy has now been settled by the opinion of the House of Lords in *R* v *Savage* and *DPP* v *Parmenter* [1991] 3 WLR 914, discussed at p. 443.

Question
Naomi hits Jacob intentionally, not foreseeing any actual bodily harm, but he (reasonably foreseeably) trips, falls and fractures his skull. Is Naomi guilty of a s. 47 offence? What would be the position if Jacob died?

B   Wounding and inflicting grievous bodily harm

Offences Against the Person Act 1861

18.   Whosoever shall unlawfully and maliciously by any means whatsoever wound or cause any grievous bodily harm to any person, or shoot at any person, or, by drawing a trigger or in any other manner attempt to discharge any kind of loaded arms at any person, with intent, in any of the cases aforesaid, to maim, disfigure, or disable any person, or with intent to resist or prevent the lawful apprehension or detainer of any person, shall be guilty of felony, and being convicted thereof shall be liable . . . to be kept in penal servitude for life . . .

20.   Whosoever shall unlawfully and maliciously wound or inflict any grievous bodily harm upon any other person, either with or without any weapon or instrument, shall be guilty of a misdemeanour, and being convicted thereof shall be liable . . . to be kept in penal servitude . . .

(i)   Actus reus
The *actus reus* of a s. 20 offence is an unlawful wounding *or* the unlawful infliction of grievous bodily harm. In contrast, a s. 18 offence requires proof of an unlawful wounding or the causing of grievous bodily harm. The courts have

drawn a distinction between infliction and causing which is discussed below. There is also a difference in the *mens rea* requirements for the two sections. This is also explored below.

The reasons for treating wounding and infliction of GBH as equivalent are historical, since when the Act was passed even a small breaking of the skin was liable to lead to infection and death.

A wound is a breaking of the skin:

Moriarty v *Brooks*
(1834) 6 C & P 684
Court of Appeal

LORD LYNDHURST CB: The definition of a wound in criminal cases is an injury to the person, by which the skin is broken. If the skin is broken, and there was a bleeding, that is a wound.

His Lordship (in summing up) said – If the violence which occurred took place in an endeavour by the defendant to turn the plaintiff out of the house, the third plea is proved. However, this plea does not profess to justify any wounding; therefore, if there was a wound, the plaintiff is entitled to recover for that. It is proved that the plaintiff was cut under the eye, and that it bled; and I am of opinion that that is a wound. . . .

R v *McLoughlin*
(1838) 8 C & P 635
Central Criminal Court

A surgeon, named Hore, was called as a witness, and said, – 'About eleven o'clock on the night of the 14th of July, I was called on to attend the prosecutor; I examined his head and found an abrasion of the skin, with blood issuing from it; he had received a violent blow on the left temple, there was great tumefaction; I could not ascertain at the time whether the bone was fractured; he lost the sight of his left eye, and it rendered him deaf on the left ear; he had great difficulty of speech; he could scarcely answer questions put to him, not being able to articulate; and on moving the bandage off his head, he shortly became insensible; I have seen the fragments of the bottle; it was such a wound as might have been inflicted with a bottle; I have attended him ever since, frequently twice a-day; I considered him in a dangerous state for several weeks; he is not yet recovered.' On his cross-examination, *inter alia*, he said – 'The skin was broken on the left temple, that would not be visible now, nor the cicatrix, from its having healed; I never said the skin was not broken; I have said it was a sort of injury which a medical man would hardly consider a wound, but it was in the eye of the law a wound; there were signs of it visible four days after.'

COLERIDGE J: . . . It is essential for you to be quite clear that a wound was inflicted. I am inclined to understand, and my learned brothers are of the same opinion, that, if it is necessary to constitute a wound, that the skin should be broken, it must be the whole skin, and it is not sufficient to shew a separation of the cuticle only. You will, therefore, have to say on the first three counts, whether there was a wounding in the sense in which I have stated it, viz. was there a wound – a separation of the whole skin? If you think there was not, you will find the prisoner not guilty upon these counts. Then, as to the fourth count, which charges an intent to murder, you will, perhaps, think, that under all the circumstances of this case, there is not sufficient evidence of that malice aforethought which is necessary to constitute such an intent. But you may on either of the counts find the prisoner guilty of an assault.

C (a minor) v *Eisenhower*
[1984] 1 QB 331
Queen's Bench Division

The defendant, aged 15, was involved in an incident in which C was hit by an air gun pellet near his eye. The defendant was charged with unlawfully and maliciously wounding C, contrary to section 20 of the Offences against the Person Act 1861. The justices held that the abnormal presence of red blood cells in the fluid of the eye, indicating at least the rupture of one or more internal blood vessels, was sufficient to constitute a wound for the purposes of section 20.

On appeal by the defendant:—

Held, allowing the appeal, that on the authorities, the word 'wound' meant a break in the continuity of the whole skin; that, accordingly, the rupture of internal blood vessels was not sufficient to constitute a wound for the purposes of section 20 of the Act of 1861; and that, therefore, the defendant had not committed an offence under the section . . .

Note

'Grievous bodily harm' was rather unhelpfully redefined as 'really serious harm' in *Director of Public Prosecutions* v *Smith* [1961] AC 290.

(ii) 'Inflict' and 'wound'

In respect of *actus reus*, what are the differences between the aggravated offences? The precise differences have been the subject of some confusion in the case law, but basically:

(a)   s. 47 requires an assault or a battery;
(b)   s. 20 requires *infliction* of GBH or a *'wounding'*;
(c)   s. 18 requires the *causing* of GBH.

In a series of cases it was held that 'inflict' and 'wound' required proof of an assault. See *R* v *Taylor* (1869) LR 1 CCR 194, *R* v *Clarence* (1888) 22 QBD 23. However, in a poorly reasoned judgment the House of Lords held that the word 'inflict' did not necessarily imply an assault.

R v *Wilson*
[1984] AC 242
House of Lords

LORD ROSKILL: . . . The two respondents, Edward and Ronald Jenkins, were father and son. They faced a single count of burglary at Canterbury Crown Court before Mr

Recorder Michael Lewis QC and a jury. That charge was laid under section 9(1)(b) of the Theft Act 1968, the particulars being that they had entered a building at Westgate 'as trespassers' and there 'inflicted grievous bodily harm' upon a man named Wilson. If one omits the references to entering the building 'as trespassers,' the particulars apart from the omission of the word 'maliciously' were identical with those in *Wilson*. I shall refer to this case as '*Jenkins*'. The learned recorder, after lengthy legal arguments – he himself had first raised the question – gave the same direction to the jury as had been given in *Wilson* regarding the possibility, in the event of acquittal on the burglary count, of convicting these respondents of assault occasioning actual bodily harm.

These rulings and directions were founded upon section 6(3) of the Act of 1967. All the respondents, upon their respective convictions, appealed. *Wilson* was heard by the Court of Appeal (Criminal Division) (Watkins LJ and Cantley and Hirst JJ) judgment being given on 28 January 1983 by Cantley J. *Jenkins* was heard by a differently constituted Court of Appeal (Criminal Division) (Purchas LJ and Talbot and Staughton JJ) judgment being given on 18 February 1983 by Purchas LJ. The convictions in both cases were quashed. The reasons were substantially the same with the additional reason in *Jenkins* that that court was bound by the earlier decision in *Wilson*. Stated briefly, the reason was that the decision of the Court of Appeal (Criminal Division) in *R v Springfield* (1969) 53 Cr App R 608 made it impossible to justify a conviction for assault occasioning actual bodily harm, contrary to section 47 of the Offences against the Person Act 1861, by virtue of section 6(3) of the Act of 1967, since the offence charged of '*inflicting* grievous bodily harm' did not, upon the authorities, *necessarily* include the offence of *assault* occasioning actual bodily harm. The emphasis added to these three words is mine.

My Lords, it would be convenient to preface discussion of the problems to which section 6(3) of the Act of 1967 gives rise by first setting out the several statutory provisions which fall for consideration in this appeal. Section 6(3) itself reads:

> (3)   Where, on a person's trial on indictment for any offence except treason or murder, the jury find him not guilty of the offence specifically charged in the indictment, but the allegations in the indictment amount to or include (expressly or by implication) an allegation of another offence falling within the jurisdiction of the court of trial, the jury may find him guilty of that other offence or of an offence of which he could be found guilty on an indictment specifically charging that other offence.

What, then, are the allegations expressly or impliedly included in a charge of 'inflicting grievous bodily harm.' Plainly that allegation must, so far as physical injuries are concerned, at least impliedly if not indeed expressly, include the infliction of 'actual bodily harm' because infliction of the more serious injuries must include the infliction of the less serious injuries. But does the allegation of 'inflicting' include an allegation of 'assault'? The problem arises by reason of the fact that the relevant English case law has proceeded along two different paths. In one group it has, as has already been pointed out, been held that a verdict of assault was a possible alternative verdict on a charge of inflicting grievous bodily harm contrary to section 20. In the other group grievous bodily harm was said to have been inflicted without any assault having taken place, unless of course the offence of assault were to be given a much wider significance than is usually attached to it. This problem has been the subject of recent detailed analysis in the Supreme Court of Victoria in *R v Salisbury* [1976] VR 452. In a most valuable judgment – I most gratefully acknowledge the assistance I have derived from that judgment in preparing this speech – the full court drew attention, in relation to comparable legislation in Victoria, to the problems which arose from this divergence in the main stream of English authority. The problem with which your Lordships' House is now faced arose in *Salisbury* in a different way from the present appeals. There, the appellant was convicted of an offence against the Victorian equivalent of section 20. He appealed on the ground that the trial judge had refused to leave to the jury the possibility of convicting him on that single charge of assault occasioning actual bodily harm or of common assault. The full court dismissed the appeal on the ground that at common law these latter offences were not 'necessarily included' in the offence of 'inflicting grievous bodily harm.' The reasoning leading to this conclusion is plain:

> It may be that the somewhat different wording of section 20 of the English Act has played a part in bringing about the existence of the two lines of authority in England, but, be that as it may, we have come to the conclusion that, although the word 'inflicts' . . . does not have as wide a meaning as the word 'causes' . . . the word 'inflicts' does have a wider meaning than it would have if it were construed so that inflicting grievous bodily harm always involved assaulting the victim. In our opinion, grievous bodily harm may be inflicted . . . either where the accused has directly and violently 'inflicted' it by assaulting the victim, or where the accused has 'inflicted' it by doing something, intentionally, which, though it is not itself a direct application of force to the body of the victim, does directly result in force being applied violently to the body of the victim, so that he suffers grievous bodily harm. Hence, the lesser misdemeanours of assault occasioning actual bodily harm and common assault . . . are not necessarily included in the misdemeanour of inflicting grievous bodily harm . . .
> . . .
> . . . I am content to accept, as did the full court, that there can be an infliction of grievous bodily harm contrary to section 20 without an assault being committed. . . .

Notes and questions
1.   The effect of *Wilson* is that where a defendant is charged with a s. 20 offence and the harm suffered was not 'grievous' but was 'actual' he can only be convicted of the s. 47 offence if the facts were sufficient to prove an assault. This can only be determined on examination of the facts of each particular case at the time of trial. Thus prior to trial there may be some doubts as to the charges of which the defendant is accused. Is this unfair to the defendant?
2.   The House in *Wilson* also took the view that there is no assault unless force is directly applied to the victim and that 'cause' was wider than 'inflict'. This has the effect that the more serious the offence, the wider the definition of the *actus reus*. Is such a policy desirable?

The House of Lords in *Wilson* did not deal with whether 'wound' implied an assault, but in *R* v *Savage* [1991] 3 WLR 418, Glidewell LJ was of the opinion that wounding did require an assault. This question was dealt with on appeal to the House of Lords in *R* v *Savage* and *DPP* v *Parmenter*:

R v *Savage, Director of Public Prosecutions* v *Parmenter*
[1991] 3 WLR 914
House of Lords

LORD ACKNER: . . .

1.   *Is a verdict of guilty of assault occasioning actual bodily harm a permissible alternative verdict on a count alleging unlawful wounding contrary to section 20 of the Act?*

... The allegation of inflicting grievous bodily harm or for that matter wounding, as was observed by Glidewell LJ, giving the judgment of the court in the *Savage* case [1991] 2 WLR 418, 421, inevitably imports or includes an allegation of assault, unless there are some quite extraordinary facts.

The critical question remained – do the allegations in a section 20 charge 'include either expressly or by implication' allegations of assault occasioning actual bodily harm. As to this, Lord Roskill concluded [1984] AC 247, 261:

> If 'inflicting' can, as the cases show, include 'inflicting by assault', then even though such a charge may not necessarily do so, I do not for myself see why on a fair reading of section 6(3) these allegations do not at least impliedly *include* 'inflicting by assault.' That is sufficient for present purposes though I also regard it as also a possible view that those former allegations *expressly* include the other allegations.

I respectfully agree with this reasoning and accordingly reject the submission that *R* v *Wilson* was wrongly decided. I would therefore answer the first of the certified questions in the *Savage* case in the affirmative. A verdict of guilty of assault occasioning actual bodily harm is a permissible alternative verdict on a count alleging unlawful wounding contrary to section 20 of the Offences against the Persons Act 1861.

Question
If a defendant rigs a booby trap which falls onto the victim's head, causing a small cut, for what offences will she be liable?

(iii)   Mens rea
The wounding or infliction of GBH must be done 'maliciously'. Must the defendant actually foresee the possibility of harm, and, if so, what degree of harm must be foreseen?

R v *Mowatt*
[1968] 1 QB 421
Court of Appeal

DIPLOCK LJ: ... In the offence under section 20, and in the alternative verdict which may be given on a charge under section 18, for neither of which is any specific intent required, the word 'maliciously' does import upon the part of the person who unlawfully inflicts the wound or other grievous bodily harm an awareness that his act may have the consequence of causing some physical harm to some other person. That is what is meant by 'the particular kind of harm' in the citation from Professor Kenny. It is quite unnecessary that the accused should have foreseen that his unlawful act might cause physical harm of the gravity described in the section, i.e., a wound or serious physical injury. It is enough that he should have foreseen that some physical harm to some person, albeit of a minor character, might result.

Note
Mowatt was affired in *DPP* v *Parmenter* (above).

An intention to frighten is not enough:

R v Sullivan
[1981] Crim LR 46
Court of Appeal

The victim's evidence was that the appellant and a companion were undoubtedly drunk and, while the victim was in a street only eight feet wide with a narrow pavement, the appellant drove his car through the street at 25 to 30 miles per hour, mounted the pavement and injured the victim. The appellant, who had made a written statement to the police denying that he was the driver, did not give evidence and, in an unsworn statement from the dock, said that he could add nothing to the written statement he had given to the police. The sole defence was that the appellant was not driving, but during counsel's closing speech for the defence he suggested that all that the appellant had been intending to do was to frighten the victim and no more and that was insufficient mens rea.

Held . . . [M]ere intention to frighten without more was insufficient; the person charged must be proved to have been aware that probable consequences of his voluntary act would be to cause some injury to the victim, but not necessarily grievous bodily harm.

C   Wounding or causing grievous bodily harm with intent

Offences Against the Person Act 1861

18.   Whosoever shall unlawfully and maliciously by any means whatsoever wound or cause any grievous bodily harm to any person, or shoot at any person, or, by drawing a trigger or in any other manner attempt to discharge any kind of loaded arms at any person, with intent, in any of the cases aforesaid, to maim, disfigure, or disable any person, or to do some other grievous bodily harm to any person, or with intent to resist or prevent the lawful apprehension or detainer of any person, shall be guilty of felony, and being convicted thereof shall be liable . . . to be kept in penal servitude for life . . .

Note and question
The offence in question requires proof of one of the ulterior intentions specified, i.e. an intent to wound, an intent to do GBH, or an intent to prevent lawful apprehension or detention of any person. It is necessary that intention as to the relevant consequence be proved. Recklessness is not enough. Why should this be so?

V   Reform of the law

The Law Commission has proposed the following provisions to replace the existing hodgepodge of laws:

Draft Criminal Code Bill 1989

70.—(1)   A person is guilty of an offence if he intentionally causes serious personal harm to another.
  (2)   A person may be guilty of an offence under subsection (1) if either—
    (a)   the act causing serious personal harm is done; or

(b) the serious personal harm occurs, within the ordinary limits of criminal jurisdiction.

71. A person is guilty of an offence if he recklessly causes serious personal harm to another.

72. A person is guilty of an offence if he intentionally or recklessly causes personal harm to another.

73.—(1) A person is guilty of an offence if he administers to, or causes to be taken by, another without his consent any substance which he knows to be capable of interfering substantially with the other's bodily functions.

(2) For the purposes of this section a substance capable of inducing unconsciousness or sleep is capable of interfering substantially with bodily functions.

75. A person is guilty of assault if he intentionally or recklessly —
    (a) applies force to or causes an impact on the body of another; or
    (b) causes another to believe that any such force or impact is imminent,
without the consent of the other or, where the act is likely or intended to cause personal harm, with or without his consent.

76. A person is guilty of an offence if he assaults a constable acting in the execution of his duty, or anyone assisting a constable so acting, knowing that, or being reckless whether the person assaulted or the person being assisted is a constable, whether or not he is aware that the constable is or may be acting in the execution of his duty.

77. A person is guilty of an offence if he assaults another, intending to resist, prevent or terminat the lawful arrest of himself of a third person.

78. A person is guilty of an offence if he assaults another, intending to rob him or a third person.

Questions
1. In what ways does the Draft Criminal Code change the law? Is it an improvement? What problems in interpretation are likely to arise?
2. Is it wise to attempt to grade the various categories of assault and battery? If so, which of the following factors should be taken into account in the rational grading of these offences?

    (a) the amount of force threatened or inflicted;
    (b) the amount of harm (both physical and psychological) experienced by the victim;
    (c) any provocation by the victim;
    (d) the mental state of the defendant;
    (e) the particular characteristics of the victim;
    (f) a sexual dimension to the offence;
    (g) other.

11 THEFT

I Introduction

The law of theft reinforces society's view of the extent to which property rights ought to be protected. The legislature has made a choice in bringing these matters within the scope of the criminal law, because most of the matters we shall discuss in this chapter and those immediately following may also be the subject to a civil action by the victim. A number of factors prompt the criminalisation of the law relating to the ownership of property. One is the view (which may or may not be accurate) that making theft subject to criminal penalties is a powerful deterrent which will prevent widespread indulgence in such behaviour. Another consideration is that civil remedies may not be of value to the victim because the villain has no means of repaying money or goods taken.

The laws promoting the security of property in this country take little account of disparities in wealth. The concentration on protection of the status quo as far as wealth is concerned reveals an inherent tension when such laws are applied in a capitalist society. It is extremely difficult to draw the line between acceptable, thrusting entrepreneurial activity which is normally regarded as useful to society and immoral greed which should be subject to criminal sanctions. In some of the instances we will discuss you may feel that the courts have drawn the line in the wrong place.

When the Theft Act 1968 was drafted, the aim was to use simple terminology so far as was possible. Because the protection of property must to some extent depend on complicated rules concerning ownership of property, the rules are not always as simple as the legislators would have wished.

In some instances, too, the courts have created their own difficulties, or have had such difficulties thrust upon them by prosecutors choosing to charge the defendant with the wrong offence (see *Director of Public Prosecutions* v *Gomez* [1992] 3 WLR 1067, *Lawrence* v *Metropolitan Police Commissioner* [1972] AC 626). In a number of instances the courts have perceived the moral wickedness of the defendant and been tempted to stretch the words of the statute in order to secure a conviction. This results in a distortion of the overall scheme intended by the legislators.

The Theft Act 1968 can be usefully approached by thinking in terms of three 'tiers'. At the first tier is the definition of the crime. The definition of 'theft' is set out in s. 1 of the 1968 Act. From this definition one can extract all of the elements of the crime. At the second tier, also to be found in the statute, is either a qualification or a more detailed description of one of the elements to be found in the definition section. Thus s. 3 of the Act defines 'appropriation' and identifies whether there is an appropriation in certain areas that had previously proved troublesome, and s. 5 discusses what it means to 'belong to another'. Despite the guidance provided in the statute, cases will arise that require the courts to interpret and apply specific provisions of the statute. The third tier consists of the judgments of the courts interpreting and applying the statutory provisions.

Theft Act 1968

1.—(1)   A person is guilty of theft if he dishonestly appropriates property belonging to another with the intention of permanently depriving the other of it; and 'thief' and 'steal' shall be construed accordingly.

Note
Section 1 can be broken down into the following elements:

(a)   *actus reus*

(i)   an appropriation,
(ii)   of property,
(iii)   which belongs to another;

(b)   *mens rea*

(i)   dishonesty, and
(ii)   an intent permanently to deprive the person to whom the property belongs of that property.

II   *Actus reus*

As indicated above, the *actus reus* of theft is made up of three component elements: (i) an appropriation (ii) of property (iii) which belongs to another. These elements are themselves explained by other sections of the Theft Act 1968 and the case law.

A   *Appropriation*

What is an appropriation? As will be seen, it may range from an outright taking of property to a relatively trivial interference with property. Indeed, it may occur without any physical contact with the property on the part of the defendant. Section 3 of the Theft Act 1968 defines appropriation as 'any assumption . . . of the rights of an owner'. The section goes on to address three specific problem areas. These are:

(a)   where property was acquired innocently but there has been subsequent dishonesty in relation to that property;
(b)   where an innocent buyer exercises rights over the property to which he believes he is entitled because of his purchase; and
(c)   where the alleged appropriation is an act which has been consented to by the owner.

In the cases raising the issue of appropriation, one can identify six areas which have proved particularly troublesome:

(a)   Where the defendant is innocently in possession of the goods at the outset, but then forms a dishonest intent.
(b)   Where the defendant assumes the rights of an owner without being in possession of the goods.
(c)   Where the defendant's acts are consented to by the owner, especially if the owner's consent is obtained by deception.
(d)   Where not all the rights of the owner are assumed by the defendant.
(e)   Where title to the goods passes immediately before or at the time of the appropriation.
(f)   Where the defendant was a bona fide purchaser of the property but subsequently discovers that he has no title to the goods.

(i)   Original innocent possession

Theft Act 1968

3.—(1) Any assumption by a person of the rights of an owner amounts to an appropriation, and this includes, where he has come by the property (innocently or not) without stealing it, any later assumption of a right to it by keeping or dealing with it as an owner.

Note
The operation of s. 3(1) is illustrated by *Pilgram* v *Rice-Smith* [1977] 1 WLR 671, where the defendant was a shop assistant who supplied her friend with cold meat at a reduced price. She was dishonest in respect of the transaction. The Court of Appeal found it perfectly proper to convict the shop assistant of theft. The whole of the corned beef and bacon had been stolen by her despite the fact that when the defendant was honestly doing her job she was innocently in possession of all the articles at her counter.

(ii)   Assumption of the rights of an onwer while not in possession of the goods

R v Pitham and Hehl
(1976) 65 Cr App Rep 45
Court of Appeal

One M, who knew an acquaintance X was in prison, decided to take advantage of X's incarceration to steal his furniture and sell it. M offered the furniture to the appellants for sale and they both went individually to X's house to look at the furniture and agreed to buy it, paying M a sum which they knew to be considerably under the true value. M and the appellants were later seen to enter X's house after arriving there in a furniture van. M was arrested, but the appellants escaped, but both were later interviewed by the police. They insisted that 'they had not screwed the place'. All three were charged on counts of burglary, the appellants additionally each on an individual count of handling stolen goods. M was convicted on two counts of burglary and the appellants only on the individual handling counts.

Note
The appellants argued that they could not be convicted of handling stolen goods because they were 'in the course of stealing' the goods. This would have exempted them from liability under s. 22 of the Theft Act 1968, but the exemption applies only to the 'first thief'. The court concluded that M was the first thief and had appropriated the contents of the house when he took the appellants to X's house and showed them the furniture, inviting them to buy what they wanted. The appellants were therefore rightly convicted of handling as M had committed the 'first theft'. Appropriation in *Pitham and Hehl* did not require a 'taking', but consider the following case.

R v Gallasso
[1993] Crim LR 459
Court of Appeal

G, a nurse, was a house leader of a home for severely mentally handicapped adults and was (*inter alia*) in charge of the patients' finances. Each of the patients had a trust account at a building society into which various benefits were paid; G was the sole signatory and drew out money to pay for patients' day-to-day needs. A very severely handicapped patient, J, had accrued benefits which G paid into his trust account. Later a further cheque for £4,000 arrived for J; G opened a second account for him (count 1) and later transferred £3,000 from the second to the first account. She then withdrew the remaining £1,000 which she paid into her own account (count 2). A few months later she paid another cheque, for £1,800, into a new cash card account for J at the same branch as the first account (count 3). The judge rejected a submission of no case to answer on count 3 (and count 1) made on the basis that the cheques were properly paid in by G, J being unable to pay them in himself, and that there was no evidence of appropriation on G's part. G was convicted of two counts of theft: count 2 – the payment of £1,000 into her own account – and count 3 – the payment of the cheque for £1,800 into the new account for J. (The jury acquitted her of count 1: theft of the cheque for £4,000, count 2 being an alternative.) She appealed against conviction on count 3 only – the theft of the cheque for £1,800 – submitting that the judge wrongly rejected the submission of no case to answer.

Held, allowing the appeal and quashing the conviction on count 3, it was now clear that a taking of property with the owner's consent could amount to appropriation. . . . The Crown had based its argument on G dealing in the cheque in a way which was not to J's advantage, and that there was no need for the second account to have been opened, except to assist G to make unauthorised withdrawals. However, the court accepted G's argument that a dishonest motive or a breach of employers' rules (which was in any case not proved) could not turn into an appropriation something which was not; and it was significant that the jury had acquitted G on count 1 which alleged theft of a cheque paid into a different account in J's name. Paying the cheque into J's account could not be regarded as appropriation since it was evidence of G affirming J's rights rather than assuming them for herself.

Questions
1. Would the decision in *Pitham and Hehl* have been the same if the purchasers had offered to buy the goods before the defendants had offered to sell them? Did M steal *all* the contents of the house, or only those items which he eventually sold?
2. In the light of *Gallasso*, is *Pitham and Hehl* still good law, or does appropriation require an actual taking?
3. If Kevin offers to sell Tower Bridge to an unsuspecting American tourist, has he stolen it? How is an intention permanently to deprive established in such a case? Consider s. 6(1) below.

(iii)   Is it an appropriation where the defendant's acts are consented to by the owner?
Whether or not an appropriation takes place in these circumstances has been a matter of considerable controversy. The issue has been settled for the time being by the House of Lords:

R v Gomez
[1992] 3 WLR 1067
House of Lords

LORD KEITH OF KINKEL: . . . . The facts of this case are that the defendant, Edwin Gomez, was employed as an assistant manager at a shop trading by retail in electrical goods. In September 1987 he was asked by an acquaintance called Jit Ballay to supply goods from the shop and to accept payment by two stolen building society cheques, one for £7,950 and the other for £9,250, which were undated and bore no payee's name. The defendant agreed, and prepared a list of goods to the value of £7,950 which he submitted to the manager, Mr Gilberd, saying that it represented a genuine order by one Johal and asking him to authorise the supply of the goods in return for a building society cheque in that sum. Mr Gilberd instructed the defendant to confirm with the bank that the cheque was acceptable, and the defendant later told him that he had done so and that such a cheque was 'as good as cash'. Mr Gilberd agreed to the transaction, the defendant paid the cheque into the bank, and a few days later Ballay took possession of the goods, the defendant helping him to load them into his vehicle. Shortly afterwards a further consignment of goods to the value of £9,250 was ordered and supplied in similar fashion (apart from one item valued at £1,002.99 which was not delivered), against the second stolen building society cheque. Mr Gilberd agreed to this transaction without further inquiry. Later the two cheques were returned by the bank marked 'Orders not to pay. Stolen cheque.'

The defendant, Ballay and another employee of the shop, named Rai, were arrested and later tried on an indictment the fourth and fifth counts in which charged all three with theft contrary to section 1(1) of the Theft Act 1968 in respect of the two transactions. After evidence had been led for the prosecution counsel for the defendant submitted that there was no case to answer on the theft charges because the manager of the shop had authorised the transactions, so that there had been no appropriation within the meaning of section 1(1) of the Act. . . .

In my opinion Lord Roskill was undoubtedly right when he said in [Morris [1983] QB 587] that the assumption by the defendant of any of the rights of an owner could amount to an appropriation within the meaning of section 3(1), and that the removal of an article from the shelf and the changing of the price label on it constituted the assumption of one of the rights of the owner and hence an appropriation within the meaning of the subsection. But there are observations in the passage which, with the greatest possible respect to my noble and learned friend Lord Roskill, I must regard as unnecessary for the decision of the case and as being incorrect. In the first place, it seems to me that the switching of price labels on the article is in itself an assumption of one of the rights of the owner, whether or not it is accompanied by some other act such as removing the article from the shelf and placing it in a basket or trolley. No one but the owner has the right to remove a price label from an article or to place a price label upon it. If anyone else does so, he does an act, as Lord Roskill puts it, by way of adverse interference with or usurpation of that right. This is no less so in the case of the practical joker figured by Lord Roskill than in the case of one who makes the switch with dishonest intent. The practical joker, of course, is not guilty of theft because he has not acted dishonestly and does not intend to deprive the owner permanently of the article. So the label switching in itself constitutes an appropriation and so to have held would have been sufficient for the dismissal of both appeals. On the facts of the two cases it was unnecessary to decide whether, as argued by Mr Jeffreys, the mere taking of the article from the shelf and putting it in a trolley or other receptacle amounted to the assumption of one of the rights of the owner, and hence an appropriation. There was much to be said in favour of the view that it did, in respect that doing so gave the shopper control of the article and the capacity to exclude any other shopper from taking it. However, Lord Roskill expressed the opinion, at p. 332, that it did not, on the ground that the concept of appropriation in the context of section 3(1)

> involves not an act expressly or impliedly authorised by the owner but an act by way of adverse interference with or usurpation of those rights.

While it is correct to say that appropriation for purposes of section 3(1) includes the latter sort of act, it does not necessarily follow that no other act can amount to an appropriation and in particular that no act expressly or impliedly authorised by the owner can in any circumstances do so. Indeed, R v Lawrence [1972] AC 626 is a clear decision to the contrary since it laid down unequivocally that an act may be an appropriation notwithstanding that it is done with the consent of the owner. It does not appear to me that any sensible distinction can be made in this context between consent and authorisation.

. . . Lawrence makes it clear that consent to or authorisation by the owner of the taking by the rogue is irrelevant. The taking amounted to an appropriation within the meaning of secton 1(1) of the Act of 1968. *Lawrence* also makes it clear that it is no less irrelevant that what happened may also have constituted the offence of obtaining property by deception under section 15(1) of the Act.

In my opinion it serves no useful purpose at the present time to seek to construe the relevant provisions of the Theft Act by reference to the report which preceded it, namely the Eighth Report of the Criminal Law Revision Committee on Theft and Related Offences (1966) (Cmnd. 2977). The decision in *Lawrence* was a clear decision of this House upon the construction of the word 'appropriate' in section 1(1) of the Act, which had stood for 12 years when doubt was thrown upon it by obiter dicta in *Morris*. *Lawrence* must be regarded as authoritative and correct, and there is no question of it now being right to depart from it.

. . .

LORD LOWRY (dissenting): . . . The certified question in this appeal is:

> When theft is alleged and that which is alleged to be stolen passes to the defendant with the consent of the owner, but that consent has been obtained by a false representation, has, (a) an appropriation within the meaning of section 1(1) of the Theft Act 1968 taken place, or, (b) must such a passing of property necessarily involve an element of adverse interference with or usurpation of some right of the owner?

I can say now that I would answer (a) 'No', and (b) 'No, because such a passing of property does not involve an appropriation.'

. . .

To be guilty of theft the offender, as I shall call him, must act dishonestly and must have the intention of permanently depriving the owner of property. Section 1(3) shows that in order to interpret the word 'appropriates' (and thereby to define theft), sections 1 to 6 must be read together. The ordinary and natural meaning of 'appropriate' is to take for oneself, or to treat as one's own, property which belongs to someone else. The primary dictionary meaning is 'take possession of, take to oneself, especially without authority,' and that is in my opinion the meaning which the word bears in section 1(1). The act of appropriating property is a one-sided act, done without the consent or authority of the owner. And, if the owner consents to transfer property to the offender or to a third party, the offender does not appropriate the property, even if the owner's consent has been obtained by fraud.

. . . I turn, for such guidance as it may afford, to the Eighth Report of the Criminal Law Revision Committee on Theft and Related Offences.

While the report may not completely resolve the question for your Lordships, it provides in the first place a very useful summary of the state of the law in 1966. It also discusses in some detail the shortcomings of the law in regard to theft and kindred offences, as they appeared to the committee, and it proposes remedies. A reading of the Act of 1968, which was based on the draft Bill annexed to the report, leads me to the conclusion that, when using the very words of the draft, Parliament intended to implement the committee's thinking. Of course, if the words of the Act clearly achieve a different result from that which seemed to be intended by the committee, it is the words which must prevail and strained constructions must not be adopted in order to give effect to the report.

. . .

The committee's proposed remedies for the defects of the law as they found it appear clearly from the foregoing paragraphs. 'Fraudulent conversion' is accepted as the starting point for the new and comprehensive definition of theft and 'dishonest appropriation' is chosen as a synonym. Both expressions embody the notion of an adverse unilateral act done to the prejudice of the owner and without his authority; indeed, fraudulent conversion can have no other meaning. . . .

Before going on to consider the cases and some of the observations which the academic writers have made on section 1, I should like to say something more about section 15. According to the Crown's argument, this provision seems to be unnecessary and must have been included in the Act (and presumably also in the draft Bill) as a mere matter of convenience. A possible alternative theory is that the committee, the responsible government department and the parliamentary draftsmen all thought that section 15 (clause 12) was needed, which turns out to be a mistaken view when section 1 is properly understood. I call this an alternative theory because it seems obvious to me that the committee *did* think that clause 12 was necessary – and I am not simply referring to the definition of 'deception'. The Crown say that section 15 merely describes a particular type of theft and that all stealing by means of deception can be prosecuted under section 1 just as well as under section 15. I would point out that section 15 covers what were formerly two offences, obtaining by false pretences (where the ownership of the property is transferred by the deceived victim) and theft (or larceny) by a trick (where the possession of the property passes, but not the ownership). In the former case, according to the interpretation which I prefer, the offender does not *appropriate* the property, because the ownership (in colloquial terms, the property) is transferred with the owner's consent, albeit obtained by deception. In the latter case the offender does appropriate the property because, although the owner has handed over *possession* by consent (which was obtained by deception), he has not transferred the property (that is, the ownership) and the offender, intending to deprive the owner permanently of his property, appropriates it, not by taking possession, but by the unilateral act, adverse to the owner, of treating as his own and taking to himself property of which he was merely given *possession*. Thus, the kind of obtaining by deception which amounts to larceny by a trick and involves appropriation *could* be successfully prosecuted under section 1, but the old false pretences type of obtaining by deception could not. Of course, unless the facts were absolutely clear, it would be foolish to prosecute under section 1 an offence of obtaining by deception, since something which at first looked like larceny by a trick might turn out to have involved a transfer of the ownership, in which case only section 15 would meet the prosecution's needs, if I am right. Some theft cases can be prosecuted under section 15, but it is fallacious, having regard to what I perceive as the true meaning of appropriation, to say that *all* cases of obtaining by deception can be prosecuted under section 1.
. . .

My Lords, I think I have in passing taken account of most of the points made in the pro-*Lawrence* academic contributions to the debate. I feel no qualms about taking sides against these contributions, nearly all of which seem to me to disregard the Criminal Law Revision Committee Report and to neglect to analyse the meaning in its context of the word 'appropriate.' Morever, they choose to disregard the ordinary law governing the transfer of title, calling it the civil law, as if to contrast it with the criminal law and thus render it surplus to requirements. At least, Bingham LJ refused to fall in with this idea, saying in *Dobson v General Accident Fire and Life Assurance Corporation Plc* [1990] 1 QB 274, 289:

But whether, in the ordinary case to which section 5 of the Theft Act 1968 does not apply, goods are to be regarded as belonging to another is a question to which the criminal law offers no answer and which can only be answered by reference to civil law principles.

Accordingly, it is both proper and rational to rely on such cases as *Phillips* v *Brooks Ltd* [1919] 2 KB 243 and *Lewis* v *Averay* [1972] 1 QB 198, 207G.
. . .

In my opinion, any attempt to reconcile the statements of principle in *Lawrence* and *Morris* is a complete waste of time. And certainly reconciliation cannot be achieved by the unattractive solution of varying the meaning of 'appropriation' in different provisions of the Act of 1968. It is clear that, whether they succeeded or not, both the Criminal Law Revision Committee and the draftsman must have intended to give the word one meaning, which would be the same in the Act as in the committee's report.

To simplify the law, where possible, is a worthy objective but, my Lords, I maintain that the law, as envisaged in the report, is simple enough: there is no problem (and there would have been none in *Lawrence*, *Morris* and the present case) if one prosecutes under section 15 all offences involving obtaining by deception and prosecutes theft in general under section 1. In that way some thefts will come under section 15, but no 'false pretences' will come under section 1.
. . .

LORD BROWNE-WILKINSON: . . . For myself, . . . I regard the word 'appropriation' in isolation as being an objective description of the act done irrespective of the mental state of either the owner or the accused. It is impossible to reconcile the decision in *Lawrence* (that the question of consent is irrelevant in considering whether there has been an appropriation) with the views expressed in *Morris*, which latter views in my judgment were incorrect.

It is suggested that this conclusion renders section 15 of the Act of 1968 otiose since a person who, by deception, persuades the owner to consent to part with his property will necessarily be guilty of theft within section 1. This may be so though I venture to doubt it. Take for example a man who obtains land by deception. Save as otherwise expressly provided, the definitions in sections 4 and 5 of the Act apply only for the purposes of interpreting section 1 of the Act: see section 1(3). Section 34(1) applies subsection (1) of section 4 and subsection (1) of section 5 generally for the purposes of the Act. Accordingly the other subsections of section 4 and section 5 do not apply to section 15. Suppose that a fraudster has persuaded a victim to part with his house: the fraudster is not guilty of theft of the land since section 4(2) provides that you cannot steal land. The charge could only be laid under section 15 which contains no provisions excluding land from the definition of property. Therefore, although there is a substantial overlap between section 1 and section 15, section 15 is not otiose.

Notes and questions
1. Should their Lordships have considered the Eighth Report of the Criminal Law Revision Committee? Reconsider the material on statutory interpretation in Chapter 1.
2. After *Gomez*, is there any distinction between obtaining property by deception under s. 15 of the Theft Act 1968 and s. 1 theft? Is this what Parliament intended?
3. In his commentary on *Gomez*, Professor Smith writes ([1993] Crim LR, p. 306):

Anyone doing anything whatever to property belonging to another, with or without the authority or consent of the owner, appropriates it: and, if he does so dishonestly and with intent, by that act or any subsequent act, permanently to deprive, he commits theft.

Is Professor Smith correct? If he is, is *Gallasso* (above) correctly decided? At what point in time must the property belong to another? (See discussion of 'belonging to another', below.)

4. As a result of *Gomez*, 'appropriation' should no longer be viewed as a pejorative term. Rather, it is a neutral term. One effect of neutering 'appropriation' is to shift the focus even more than is ordinarily the case onto the *mens rea* elements of the crime in order to determine a defendant's culpability.

(iv)   Do all the rights of the owner need to be assumed?

Ownership confers many rights; for example, one can sell one's own property, give it away, move it, destroy it, etc. In *Morris*, the House of Lords held that it was not necessary to appropriate *all* of the rights of an owner to be guilty of theft; an appropriation of *any* of them would be sufficient.

R v Morris
[1983] 3 WLR 697
House of Lords

LORD ROSKILL: Mr Denison submitted that the phrase in section 3(1) 'any assumption by a person of *the rights*' (my emphasis) 'of an owner amounts to an appropriation' must mean any assumption of '*all* the rights of an owner.' Since neither respondent had at the time of the removal of the goods from the shelves and of the label switching assumed *all* the rights of the owner, there was no appropriation and therefore no theft. Mr Jeffreys for the prosecution, on the other hand, contended that *the* rights in this context only meant *any* of the rights. An owner of goods has many rights – they have been described as 'a bundle or package of rights.' Mr Jeffreys contended that on a fair reading of the subsection it cannot have been the intention that every one of an owner's rights had to be assumed by the alleged thief before an appropriation was proved and that essential ingredient of the offence of theft established.

My Lords, if one reads the words 'the rights' at the opening of section 3(1) literally and in isolation from the rest of the section, Mr Denison's submission undoubtedly has force. But the later words 'any later assumption of a right' in subsection (1) and the words in subsection (2) 'no later assumption by him of rights' seem to me to militate strongly against the correctness of the submission. Moreover the provisions of section 2(1)(a) also seem to point in the same direction. It follows therefore that it is enough for the prosecution if they have proved in these cases the assumption by the respondents of *any* of the rights of the owner of the goods in question, that is to say, the supermarket concerned. . . .

Question

Is *Morris* consistent with the words of the statute? When read together with *Gomez*, does it virtually eliminate the need for the Crown to prove wrongful conduct by the defendant or harm to the victim?

Note

This aspect of *Morris* was affirmed in *Gomez*.

(v) Must the property belong to another at the time of the appropriation?
The usual concurrence rule requires that the *actus reus* and *mens rea* should coincide. This rule seems to require that the property should belong to another at the time of the appropriation. Indeed the House of Lords has so stated:

Lawrence v *Metropolitan Police Commissioner*
[1972] AC 626
House of Lords

LORD DONOVAN: . . . I now turn to the third element 'property belonging to another.' Mr Back QC, for the appellant, contended that if Mr Occhi consented to the appellant taking the £6, he consented to the property in the money passing from him to the appellant and that the appellant had not, therefore, appropriated property belonging to another. He argued that the old distinction between the offence of false pretences and larceny had been preserved. I am unable to agree with this. The new offence of obtaining property by deception created by section 15(1) of the Theft Act also contains the words 'belonging to another.' 'A person who by any deception dishonestly obtains property belonging to another, with the intention of permanently depriving the other of it' commits that offence. 'Belonging to another' in section 1(1) and in section 15(1) in my view signifies no more than that, at the time of the appropriation or the obtaining, the property belonged to another, with the words 'belonging to another' having the extended meaning given by section 5. The short answer to this contention on behalf of the appellant is that the money in the wallet which he appropriated belonged to another, to Mr Occhi.

Note
Both *Lawrence* and *Gomez* were cases where the defendant obtained property by trickery. In terms of contract law, the ownership of the property would pass to the defendant but the contract would be voidable for fraud. The contract would be valid unless the victim subsequently took steps to avoid the sale. Seen in this light, it is arguable that the defendants in *Lawrence* and *Gomez* appropriated their own property. If so, the cases run counter to the usual concurrence rule and seem to require only that at some time in the past the property must have belonged to another. Consider whether the following case would be decided in the same way following *Gomez*:

Edwards v *Ddin*
[1976] 1 WLR 942
Queen's Bench Division

CROOM-JOHNSON J: This is an appeal by way of case stated from the magistrates' court sitting at Amersham in which the defendant had an information preferred against him that he stole three gallons of petrol and two pints of oil together of the value of £1.77, the property of Mamos Garage at Amersham, contrary to section 1 of the Theft Act 1968.

On the facts as found by the justices the following things happened. The defendant arrived with a motor car and he asked for some petrol and oil to be placed in his car. Petrol and oil to the value as stated, £1.77, was placed into the car at his request by the garage attendant. When he ordered the petrol and oil the defendant impliedly made to the attendant the ordinary representation of an ordinary customer that he had the means and the intention of paying for it before he left. He was not in fact asked to pay and he did not in fact pay, but the moment when the garage attendant was doing something else he simply drove away. The justices also found, as one would think was perfectly obvious, that whilst the petrol and oil had been placed in the car, either in the tank or in the sump, it could not reasonably be recovered by the garage in default of payment.

The questions therefore which have to be resolved in order to satisfy section 1 of the Act were two in number. First of all, was the defendant dishonest? It appears that the justices must have considered that that was so. Secondly, had he appropriated property belonging to another with the intention of permanently depriving the other of it? Upon that point the defence submitted successfully that at the time when the car was driven away the petrol and oil which had got into the tank or sump were in fact not the property of the garage any more but were the property of the defendant. On that basis the justices said that that particular essential ingredient of theft under section 1 of the Act had not been fulfilled and dismissed the information.

The whole question therefore was: whose petrol and oil was it when the defendant drove away? Property passes under a contract of sale when it is intended to pass. In such transactions as the sale of petrol at a garage forecourt ordinary common sense would say that the garage and the motorist intended the property in the petrol to pass when it is poured into the tank and irretrievably mixed with the other petrol that is in it, and I think that is what the justices decided.

But the prosecutor has appealed and has based his appeal on a consideration of the Sale of Goods Act 1893 and the provisions of that Act, and seeks a ruling that transfer of the petrol was conditional only and that therefore until payment the petrol remained the property of the garage.

But if one considers the provisions of the Sale of Goods Act 1893 one comes out at the same answer as common sense would dictate.

The prosecution argument went this way, that when the motorist arrives at the garage and says 'will you fill me up, please?' or 'will you give me two gallons?', then there is a contract for the sale of unascertained goods by description. In such circumstances when does the property in the petrol pass? Nothing will have been said between the motorist and the pump attendant about that, so one is thrown back on section 18 of the Sale of Goods Act 1893 and rules made under it in order to ascertain the intention of the parties.

By pouring the petrol into the tank the goods have been appropriated to the contract with the assent of both parties. If that is done unconditionally, then the property in the petrol passes to the motorist: rule 5(1). The prosecution argument then goes on that, however, there is a condition which is waiting to be fulfilled, namely, payment and says that under section 19 of the Sale of Goods Act 1893 the garage reserves the right of disposal of the petrol until the payment has been made and that therefore the property has not passed under rule 5(1).

It is at this point that the argument breaks down. The garage owner does not reserve the right to dispose of the petrol once it is in the tank, nor is it possible to see how effect could be given to any such condition wherever the petrol has been put in and is all mixed up with what other petrol is already there. Consequently one passes back to rule 5(2) of section 18, which says that where a seller delivers the goods to the buyer and does not reserve the right to dispose of them, he is deemed to have unconditionally appropriated the goods to the contract and in those circumstances the property has passed to the buyer in accordance with rule 5(1).

Questions
1.   If the appropriation and the fact that the property must belong to another need no longer occur at the same point in time, is the same true for the dishonesty and the appropriation? Consider again Professor Smith's comment on *Gomez* (above, p. 477).
2.   Carol obtains a ring from a jeweller's shop by giving the shop a forged note. John, the manager of the shop, discovers the forgery but decides to do nothing because he feels his reputation will suffer if it is known that he has been tricked. Is Carol, who now owns the ring, guilty of theft?

(vi)   The bona fide purchaser
The problem of the bona fide purchaser is specifically dealt with by s. 3(2) of the Theft Act 1968:

Theft Act 1968

3.—(2)   Where property or a right or interest in property is or purports to be transferred for value to a person acting in good faith, no later assumption by him of rights which he believed himself to be acquiring shall, by reason of any defect in the transferor's title, amount to theft of the property.

Note
The effect of this section is that a person who pays for stolen goods is not guilty of theft if he or she was not aware of the stolen character of the goods at the time of purchase. Nor does the purchaser become a thief if he or she subsequently discovers that the goods were stolen. (Whether or not he or she can keep the goods if sued by the original owner is an altogether different question and is a matter for the civil law.) However, having discovered the true state of affairs, if the purchaser later re-sells the goods, claiming to have good title, he or she will be guilty of obtaining property by deception under the Theft Act 1968, s. 15.

B   Property

Section 4 of the 1968 Act excludes real property (land and rights to do with land) from the definition of property for the purposes of s. 1 of the Act unless the exceptions set out in the section are satisfied. Section 4 also makes clear that wild flowers are not property within s. 1 unless the defendant has a commercial purpose when picking them. Similarly, wild animals are not property unless another person has or is about to get possession.

Theft Act 1968

4.—(1)   'Property' includes money and all other property, real or personal, including things in action and other intangible property.

Notes
1.   'Money' refers only to current coins and banknotes.
2.   'Real property' includes land and houses.

3. 'Personal property' includes all moveable things which can be owned.

4. 'Things in action' are rights of action which are protected by law but cannot be seen. Examples are copyrights, trade marks and contractual rights. The last includes the right to sue the bank which arises between a customer and his bank when a current bank account is in credit. If a defendant dishonestly pays his debts with money from another's account (e.g. by using a forged cheque) he steals not only the cheque but also part of the debt (the thing in action) owed by the bank to the other.

5. 'Other intangible property' includes patents which, by the Patents Act 1977, s. 30, are not things in action but are personal property. Information is not included:

Oxford v Moss
[1979] Crim LR 119
Queen's Bench Division

In 1976, M was an engineering student at Liverpool University. He acquired the proof of an examination paper for a Civil Engineering examination at the University: An information was preferred against him by O, alleging that he stole certain intangible property, i.e. confidential information, being property of the Senate of the University. It was agreed that he never intended to permanently deprive the owner of the piece of paper on which the questions were printed.

Held, by the stipendiary at Liverpool: on the facts of the case, confidential information is not a form of intangible property as opposed to property in the paper itself, and that confidence consisted in the right to control the publication of the proof paper and was a right over property other than a form of intangible property. The owner had not been permanently deprived of any intangible property. The charge was dismissed.

On appeal by the prosecutor, as to whether confidential information can amount to property within the meaning of section 4 of the Theft Act 1968.

Held: there was no property in the information capable of being the subject of a charge of theft, i.e. it was not intangible property within the meaning of section 4.

Notes and questions

1. The court in *Oxford* v *Moss* was faced with a question to which the statute provided no clear answer. In certain circumstances confidential information is treated by the civil law as the property of a company (see *Island Export Finance* v *Umunna* [1986] BCLC 460 and *Industrial Developments* v *Cooley* [1972] 2 All ER 162). Further, the Patents Act 1977 treats an invention for which no patent has been granted or applied for as intangible property. Allen, in his *Textbook of Criminal Law* (2nd ed.), p. 294, argues that this latter situation is similar to the facts in *Oxford* v *Moss*. Do you agree?

2. It has also been argued that confidential information cannot be appropriated. (Griew, *The Theft Acts 1968 and 1978*, 6th ed.). Is this right? If not, what acts constitute the appropriation? See generally, R. Hammond, 'Theft of information' (1984) 100 LQR 252.

3. Export quotas were held by the Privy Council to be intangible property in *Attorney-General of Hong Kong* v *Nai-Keung* (1987) 86 Cr App R 174. In what way do they differ from the information in *Oxford* v *Moss*?

Electricity is also not included in the definition of property. The Theft Act 1968, s. 13 creates a specific offence to cover misuse of electricity.

A human corpse is also outside the definition of property for the purposes of s. 1:

R v Sharpe
(1857) Dears & B 160
Court of Criminal Appeal

The indictment in the first count charged that the defendant a certain burial ground belonging to a certain meeting house of a congregation of Protestants, dissenting from the Church of England, unlawfully and wilfully did break and enter; a certain grave there, in which the body of one Louisa Sharpe had before then been interred, with force and arms unlawfully, wilfully, and indecently did dig open, and the said body of the said Louisa Sharpe out of the same grave unlawfully, wilfully, and indecently did take and carry away.

ERLE J: We are of opinion that the conviction ought to be affirmed. The defendant was wrongfully in the burial ground, and wrongfully opened the grave, and took out several corpses, and carried away one. We say he did this wrong fully, that is to say, by trespass; for the licence which he obtained to enter and open, from the person who had the care of the place, was not given or intended for the purpose to which he applied it, and was, as to that purpose, no licence at all. The evidence for the prosecution proved the misdemeanor, unless there was a defence. We have considered the grounds relied on in that behalf, and, although we are fully sensible of the estimable motives on which the defendant acted, namely, filial affection and religious duty, still neither authority nor principle would justify the position that the wrongful removal of a corpse was no misdemeanor if the motive for the act deserved approbation. A purpose of anatomical science would fall within that category. Neither does our law recognise the right of any one child to the corpse of its parent as claimed by the defendant. Our law recognises no property in a corpse, and the protection of the grave at common law, as contradistinguished from ecclesiastical protection to consecrated ground, depends upon this form of indictment; and there is no authority for saying that relationship will justify the taking a corpse away from the grave where it has been buried.

Note
That fluids taken from a living body can be stolen was confirmed in *Rothery*:

R v Rothery
[1976] RTR 550
Court of Appeal

By s. 9(3) of the Road Traffic Act 1972, 'A person who, without reasonable excuse, fails to supply a specimen for a laboratory test in pursuance of a requirement imposed under this section shall be guilty of an offence.'

A motorist who has complied with the provisions of ss. 8 and 9 of the Road Traffic Act 1972 and provides s specimen of blood when requested to do so by a constable at a police station and later steals the police part specimen, though guilty of the theft, is not guilty of the statutory offence under s. 9(3) of the Act of 1972, for the theft was a subsequent and distinct event from the provision of the specimen.

(i)   Real property

Theft Act 1968

4.—(2)   A person cannot steal land, or things forming part of land and severed from it by him or by his directions, except in the following cases, that is to say—

(a)   when he is a trustee or personal representative, or is authorised by power of attorney, or as liquidator of a company, or otherwise, to sell or dispose of land belonging to another, and he appropriates the land or anything forming part of it by dealing with it in breach of the confidence reposed in him; or

(b)   when he is not in possession of the land and he appropriates anything forming part of the land by severing it or causing it to be severed, or after it has been severed; or

(c)   when, being in possession of the land under a tenancy, he appropriates the whole or part of any fixture or structure let to be used with the land.

For purposes of this subsection 'land' does not include incorporeal hereditaments; 'tenancy' means a tenancy for years or any less period and includes an agreement for such a tenancy, but a person who after the end of a tenancy remains in possession under the tenancy, and 'let' shall be construed accordingly.

Notes

1.   A distinction is made between property which is 'on' the land and other property which 'forms part of the land'. The latter can only be stolen in the circumstances specified in s. 4(a), (b) and (c).

2.   The same distinction was made in the Larceny Act 1916. It was explained in *Billing* v *Pill*:

Billing v *Pill*
[1954] 1 QB 70
Queen's Bench Division

An army hut, which was constructed in seven sections, rested on a concrete foundation, the floor of the hut being secured to the foundation by bolts let into the concrete. The hut was one of a number erected by the War Office during the war on land used as a gun emplacement. In 1946 the army vacated the huts, and in 1947 the local authority was instructed to demolish them. In 1951 the appellant, without lawful authority, dismantled the hut in question, removed it from the site and re-erected it on his own land. He was convicted by justices of stealing the hut. . . .

LORD GODDARD CJ: Can anybody doubt that the hut in question was erected for a temporary purpose? It can be removed without doing any damage to the freehold at all. It rests upon a concrete bed which is let into the land. I should say that there is no question but that the concrete bed has become part of the land, but the hut which stands upon it has not become part of the land merely because some bolts have been put through the floor of the hut to stabilise or steady it. It was erected merely for a temporary purpose so that the Army personnel who were going to the site for a presumed temporary purpose, to man a gun emplacement during the war, would have somewhere to sleep.

In my opinion, it would be quite wrong to hold that this hut was attached to or formed part of the realty. It was not so attached any more than if one takes a garden seat out into one's garden and, because the seat may be in an exposed position and liable to be blown over, one drives a spike through it to hold it to the ground. In one sense that is an attachment, but it is not an attachment sufficient to make it part of the realty. It is simply a spike put in to hold the chattel firm. In my opinion, this hut was a chattel, remained a chattel and is capable of larceny. . . .

Note
The more difficult a 'thing' is to remove from the ground, the more likely it is that it will be regarded as 'land' or a 'thing forming part of the land'.

Question
What would be the position of a telegraph pole? A coffin which had been buried?

Section 4 sets out the only three instances in which 'land' or 'things forming part of land' can be stolen. The following is a summary of the effects of that section:

(a)   If the defendant is in a position of trust then, according to s. 4(2)(a), he can steal land (or things forming part of it) to which his position of trust relates.

(b)   When the defendant is not in possession of land he can steal anything forming part of the land (but not the land itself) (s. 4(2)(b)).

(c)   When the defendant is in possession of the land under a tenancy he can steal a fixture or structure (e.g. a bath or a greenhouse – if a greenhouse is a structure – it is not a fixture: *Dean* v *Andrews and another* (1985) *The Times*, 25 May 1985).

None of the subsections specifically cover a person who has permission to be on the land but who has no lease. It is not clear whether such a person would be considered to be 'in possession' of the land. If he were, the curious situation would be that he would be in a better position than a person in possession of land under a tenancy.

Incorporeal hereditaments can be stolen. Examples would be rights of way and rent charges. These could be stolen by conveying the benefit of the right dishonestly. The occasions on which this type of theft will occur will be very rare.

'Tenancy' includes a statutory tenancy. A statutory tenancy arises most frequently when an ordinary lease comes to an end and yet the tenant remains in possession and continues to pay rent to the landlord.

(ii)   Mushrooms, flowers, etc.

Theft Act 1968

4.—(3) A person who picks mushrooms growing wild on any land, or who picks flowers, fruit or foliage from a plant growing wild on any land, does not (although not in possession of the land) steal what he picks, unless he does it for reward or for sale or other commercial purpose.

For purposes of this subsection 'mushroom' includes any fungus, and 'plant' includes any shrub or tree.

Notes and questions
1.   What is the borderline between s. 4(2) and s. 4(3)? What is the difference between 'severance' of a plant growing wild and 'picking' part of that plant? If Jill cuts off a branch of an oak tree with a chain saw, is that picking or severance?
2.   Taking a whole plant will probably be theft (if the *mens rea* is present). This will be the case because there was severance of a 'thing forming part of land' (s. 4(2)), and because the defendant's action could not be described as 'picking from' a plant within s. 4(3).
3.   It will be theft if all other elements of s. 1 theft are present and the picking is done 'for sale or other commercial purpose'. When must the commercial purpose be formed? If Dora picks blackberries growing wild and later decides to make jam to sell at the local church bazaar, will this be theft?

(iii)   Wild creatures

Theft Act 1968

4.—(4) Wild creatures, tamed or untamed, shall be regarded as property; but a person cannot steal a wild creature not tamed nor ordinarily kept in captivity, or the carcase of any such creature, unless either it has been reduced into possession by or on behalf of another person and possession of it has not since been lost or abandoned, or another person is in course of reducing it into possession.

Note
'Wild' refers to the way of life of the creature rather than its disposition:

R v *Howlett*
[1968] Crim LR 222
Court of Appeal

H was convicted of stealing, in 1965, mussels from a mussel bed on the foreshore. The foreshore was alleged to belong to S who had granted to L the exclusive right of taking shellfish from it. L had tended the bed in order to try to preserve and improve it but it remained subject to the action of the sea. H appealed on the grounds, *inter alia*, that the mussels were not capable of being stolen since they adhered to the realty, alternatively they were animals *ferae naturae* and not capable of being stolen until reduced into possession.

Held, allowing the appeal, it was not necessary to decide the first question because there was not sufficient evidence that the mussels had been reduced into possession. The most that could be said to have been done was that the bed was tended with a view to improving the growth and edible qualities of the mussels until they were removed from the bed. The mere act of raking over an existing natural bed, and occasionally moving some mussels from a place where they were growing too thickly to a place where they were growing too thinly, and where they would again come to rest and adhere to the soil, did not amount to the reduction into possession of the mussels, particularly since in 1966 the majority of the mussels had disappeared as the result of the action of the sea.

Notes and questions

1.   Although *Howlett* was a decision under the Larceny Act 1916, there seems to be no reason why the position should be any different under the 1968 Act. Thus a wild creature can only be stolen if:

(a)   it is tamed or ordinarily kept in captivity;
(b)   it is in the course of being reduced into another's possession or has been reduced into and remains in another's possession.

2.   Land and wild creatures not reduced into possession are outside the law of theft under s. 1 but can theoretically be obtained by deception under s. 15 of the Theft Act 1968. Following *Gomez*, is this the only area where the two offences do not overlap?

3.   If Emma shot a pheasant and her gun dog is on its way to fetch it, can it be stolen from her? At what point in time has it been reduced into possession?

C   Belonging to another

Section 5 of the 1968 Act expands the scope of theft to protect not only those who own property, but also those who possess or control property. For the purposes of the Theft Act 1968, property 'belongs to another' when that other person has ownership, or possession or control. Section 5(3) extends the concept of property to cover the situation where, although ownership of the property has passed to the defendant, the defendant is under an obligation to deal with that property in a particular way. Section 5(4) also extends the notion of property belonging to another to the situation where the defendant has received the relevant item only because of a mistake made by another person. Where the defendant is under an obligation to return the property, the law regards ownership as being retained by the person making the mistake.

Theft Act 1968

5.—(1)   Property shall be regarded as belonging to any person having possession or control of it, or having in it any proprietary right or interest (not being an equitable interest arising only from an agreement to transfer or grant an interest).

Notes and question
Equitable interests arising from an agreement to transfer or grant an interest
will arise in at least two situations. Where there is a contract to sell land or to
sell shares, the transaction is in two stages. The conclusion of an agreement to
sell gives the buyer a right to have the sale completed. This right is the
equitable right referred to in s. 5(1). It is excluded from the rights protected
by the Theft Act 1968. Why should this be so?

Several issues arise under the provision of the statute:

(i)   What is a proprietary right or interest?
Subject to the implications of *Gomez* (above), the property appropriated must
belong to another at the time of appropriation. The term 'belong to another' is
not restricted to the owner of the property, but includes those in rightful
possession or control of the property.
    An owner of land owns the things on the land if he intends to exclude
trespassers from the land.

R v *Woodman*
[1974] QB 758
Court of Appeal

The defendant was charged with the theft of scrap metal remnants from a disused
factory site. The occupier of the site had no knowledge of the existence of the scrap,
although a barbed-wire fence had been erected around the site to exclude trespassers.
The defendant submitted that there was no case to answer on the ground that the scrap
did not belong to another within the meaning of s. 5(1) of the Theft Act 1968. The
recorder allowed the case to go to the jury on the question whether the occupier was in
control of the scrap, and the defendant was convicted.
    On appeal against conviction:—
    Held, dismissing the appeal, that a person in control of a site, by excluding others
from it, was prima facie also in control of articles on that site within the meaning of s.
5(1) of the Theft Act 1968, it being immaterial that he was unconcious [sic] of their
existence; and accordingly the case had been rightly allowed to go to the jury.
    Per curiam. If articles of serious criminal consequence, such as explosives or drugs,
were placed within the barbed-wire fence by some third person in circumstances in
which the occupier had no means of knowledge, it might produce a different result from
that which arose under the general presumption. . . .

Questions
1.   Why does the court say that the victim's awareness of the existence of the
items taken is irrelevant? Abandoned property belongs to nobody and cannot
be the subject of theft. Was the property taken in *Woodman* abandoned?
2.   Why did the court adopt one test for the objects in *Woodman* and suggest
the possibility of another test for objects of 'serious consequence'? What
should the test be in the latter case?

Property can 'belong' to more than one person. In the case of a partnership each partner has an interest in the partnership property and can steal it from the other partners:

R v Bonner
[1970] 1 WLR 838
Court of Appeal

EDMUND DAVIES LJ: The facts which gave rise to this complicated trial were that on May 16, 1969, Bonner and the other three appellants called at the house of a Mr Webb. Putting it quite neutrally for the moment, Bonner and Webb were business associates. The defence was, in fact, that they were partners and, therefore, co-owners of all the property with which the trial was concerned. Having called with a van at Webb's house in the afternoon at a time when Webb was out, they broke the lock of a garage and splintered the door and, having gained access that way, they loaded some metal from inside the garage on to the van and Anthony Town and Michael Town claimed that they were moving it for Bonner, who they thought had a right to do what he had asked them to do. Bonner's defence was that he honestly thought he had a right to take the lead as it was partnership property owned by himself and Webb, and, in any event, he did not intend to deprive Webb of it permanently.

Webb's case at first was that there was no partnership at all, and then that it was not what he called 'a true partnership'. During his evidence he specifically denied that he had ever applied for registration in the Business Names Register of himself and Bonner as partners. But this court has been furnished with a document, which unhappily was not before the lower court. It is a certified copy of an application made on March 8, 1966, for registration by a firm, and the business name is 'J. Webb, Excavation & Demolition Co.,' the partners are described as 'Joseph Webb' and 'George Andrew Bonner,' and it was signed by each of them.

I said a little earlier that the object of the Theft Act, 1968, was to get rid of the subtleties and, indeed, in many cases the absurd anomalies of the pre-existing law. The view of this court is that in relation to partnership property the provisions in the Theft Act, 1968, have the following result: provided there is the basic ingredient of dishonesty, provided there be no question of there being a claim of right made in good faith, provided there be an intent permanently to deprive, one partner can commit theft of partnership property just as much as one person can commit the theft of the property of another to whom he is a complete stranger.

Early though these days are, this matter has not gone without comment by learned writers. Professor Smith in his valuable work on the Theft Act, 1968, expresses his own view quite clearly in paragraph 80 under the heading 'Co-owners and partners' in this way:

D and P are co-owners of a car. D sells the car without P's consent. Since P has a proprietary right in the car, it belongs to him under s. 5(1). The position is precisely the same where a partner appropriates the partnership property.

In the joint work of Professor Smith and Professor Hogan, the matter is thus dealt with (*Smith and Hogan's 'Criminal Law'*, 2nd ed. (1969), p. 361):

... D and P . . . may . . . be joint owners of property. Obviously, there is no reason in principle why D should not be treated as a thief if he dishonestly appropriate's P's share, and he is so treated under the Theft Act.

We thus have no doubt that there may be an 'appropriation' by a partner within the meaning of the Act, and that in a proper case there is nothing in law to prevent his being convicted of the theft of partnership property.

(ii)   Theft of the defendant's own property by the defendant
This may occur where another person has a right to possess or control the property which the owner violates. A typical case might involve a lease or bailment. Gerald rents his car to Neil for a week. Mid-week he finds himself in desperate need of an automobile and, using his spare key to the car, takes it without asking Neil's permission. Gerald in fact is guilty of stealing his own car. The situation where a second individual has an interest in an owner's property such that the owner can commit theft of his own property can arise in other situations as well:

R v *Turner (No 2)*
[1971] 1 WLR 901
Court of Appeal

The defendant took the car of which he was the registered owner to a garage to have it repaired. Those repairs having been practically completed, the car was left in the road outside the garage. The defendant called at the garage and told the proprietor that he would return the following day, pay him and take the car: instead, he took the car away several hours later without paying for the repairs.

He was charged on indictment with theft of the car contrary to s. 1 of the Theft Act 1968. The defendant submitted that the car did not 'belong' to the proprietor within the meaning of s. 5(1) of the Theft Act 1968 and that the appropriation was not dishonest within the meaning of s. 2(1)(a) of the Act.

LORD PARKER CJ: This court is quite satisfied that there is no ground whatever for qualifying the words 'possession or control' in any way. It is sufficient if it is found that the person from whom the property is taken, or to use the words of the Act, appropriated, was at the time in fact in possession or control. At the trial there was a long argument as to whether that possession or control must be lawful, it being said that by reason of the fact that this car was subject to a hire purchase agreement, Mr Brown could never even as against the defendant obtain lawful possession or control. As I have said, this court is quite satisfied that the judge was quite correct in telling the jury they need not bother about lien, and that they need not bother about hire purchase agreements. The only question was whether Mr Brown was in fact in possession or control.

Notes and questions
1.   In *Turner* the garage almost certainly had a better right to possession of the car than the owner at the time it was taken by him. This is because the garage would have had a repairer's lien on the car – a right to keep the car until the bill was paid. However, the judge told the jury that they were not concerned with liens and the Court of Appeal upheld this direction. What if the bill for repairs was greater than originally agreed by the parties, the owner had paid the amount originally agreed and then taken the car – would this be theft?

2. Suppose a book is stolen from Mary, who later finds it among the possessions of the thief. If Mary believes it is against the law to take the book back, is she guilty of theft if she takes it?

3. Can a mother steal property belonging to her son of three months? Three years? Ten years? Can a wife steal her husband's property? (See the Theft Act 1968, s. 30.)

(iii)   Where the defendant gets ownership by fraud

The House of Lords in *Gomez* established that where property is obtained with the consent of the owner but that consent is induced by fraud, the defendant can be convicted of theft. The implications of the case have been examined previously (see above pp. 477–8).

(iv)   To whom does trust property belong?

Theft Act 1968

5.—(1)   Property shall be regarded as belonging to any person having possession or control of it, or having in it any proprietary right or interest (not being an equitable interest arising only from an agreement to transfer or grant an interest).

Note

There is doubt about the ambit of this section in relation to 'constructive trusts'. An ordinary trust is set up when persons are appointed as trustees to look after property on behalf of others. Both the trustees and the beneficiaries have interests in the property that are defined by law. A constructive trust occurs when a court believes that the imposition of a trust-like framework will do justice in particular circumstances. The court will impose such a trust where, for example, a company director joins with others in the misuse of company property (*Selangor United Rubber Estates Ltd v Cradock (No. 3)* [1968] 1 WLR 1555. In *Attorney-General's Reference (No. 1 of 1985)* [1986] QB 491, the court excluded interests arising under constructive trusts from the ambit of the Theft Act. However, the seemingly opposite conclusion was reached in *Shadrokh-Cigari*, a decision which also has implications for the interpretation of s. 5(4) (see below).

R v Shadrokh-Cigari
[1988] Crim LR 465
Court of Appeal

The appellant was convicted of four counts of theft. He acted as guardian to his nephew whose father in Iran arranged for money to be paid to the child's bank account from the USA. Through an error by the United States bank $286,000 was credited to the account instead of $286. At the appellant's suggestion the child signed an authority for the issue of four banker's drafts drawn in favour of the appellant for sums of £51,300, £64,000, £53,000 and £29,000. The appellant paid two into his own bank account and used the others to open other accounts to his name. By the time of his arrest some three weeks later only £21,000 remained. He appealed against conviction on the ground that the judge should have directed the jury that they had to be satisfied that the drafts belonged to the Bank and that had he done so the jury would have been bound to have concluded that the drafts did not belong to the bank but were the property of the appellant and so there was no question of him appropriating property belonging to another.

Held, dismissing the appeal, the submission erred in assuming that the entire proprietary interest in the drafts existed and vested in the appellant leaving the bank with no rights at all. The mistake of the United States bank totally undermined the basic assumption upon which the English bank issued the drafts, namely that the funds which had been received could properly be dealt with as directed by the account holder. As between the English bank and the appellant, the transaction fell fairly and squarely within the principles of the law relating to the mistake – *Kelly* v *Solari* [1941] (9) M & W 547. The mistake must be fundamental or basic, one in respect of the underlying assumption of the contract or transaction – *Norwich Union* v *Price* [1934] [AC] 455. That was so here. If the mistake must be one of fact rather than law, that condition was satisfied in the present case. Thus the appellant was under an obligation to make restoration of the instruments on the basis that the English bank retained an equitable proprietary interest in the drafts as a result of the mistake. The fact that the choses in action created by the drafts could not be owned by the bank, since they were debts due from the bank was irrelevant. The bank created the drafts and before delivery they owned them, although as promissory notes they were inchoate and incomplete. Upon delivery under the mistake, the bank retained an equitable interest in those instruments. Such an equitable interest amounted to property within s. 5(1) of the Theft Act 1968. That conclusion was not only supported by s. 5(4) of the 1968 Act, but could be reached by another route through the application of that sub-section. Even if it could not be said that the property belonged to another in the sense of that other having proprietary rights over the property itself, nevertheless (other things being equal) the property was to be regarded for the purposes of theft as belonging to that other even if the person getting it was only under an obligation to restore the proceeds of the property or its value as opposed to the property itself. The appellant was obliged to restore the proceeds or value of the instruments.

Notes and questions
1.   In *Shadrokh-Cigari* the court held that an equitable proprietary interest arising from the imposition of a constructive trust *did* amount to property within s. 5(1). As we shall see, where there is an obligation to make restoration of property obtained because of a mistake, s. 5(4) creates fictional ownership in the original owner for the purpose of the statute. In the light of s. 5(4), why was it necessary for the court to decide on the extended meaning of s. 5(1)?
2.   In the light of *Gomez*, is an extended definition of either s. 5(1) or s. 5(4) necessary at all?

Theft Act 1968

5.—(2)   Where property is subject to a trust, the persons to whom it belongs shall be regarded as including any person having a right to enforce the trust, and an intention to defeat the trust shall be regarded accordingly as an intention to deprive of the property any person having that right.

Note
Any beneficiary of a trust has a right to enforce a trust. A charitable trust, which may or may ot have particular individuals as beneficiaries, is enforceable by the Attorney-General so that property which is the subject to such a trust would be regarded as belonging to him. Any non-charitable trust without human beneficiaries would be regarded as belonging to the person entitled to the residue. This subsection makes it impossible for anyone dishonestly taking trust funds to argue that the funds belonged to no one.

(v)   When does an obligation arise to retain and deal with another's property?

Theft Act 1968

5.—(3)   Where a person receives property from or on account of another, and is under an obligation to the other to retain and deal with that property or its proceeds in a particular way, the property or proceeds shall be regarded (as against him) as belonging to the other.

Question
When does an obligation envisaged by the section arise, and to what property does it attach?

R v *Hall*
[1973] 1 QB 126
Court of Appeal

The defendant, who carried on the business of a travel agent, received money as deposits and payments for air trips to America. No flights were provided for the defendant's clients and no money was refunded. He was charged with seven counts of theft, contrary to s. 1 of the Theft Act 1968. The defendant claimed that the money received had become his property which he had applied in the conduct of the firm's business and that he had not been guilty of theft merely because the firm had failed and no money remained. He was convicted.

The defendant appealed on the ground, *inter alia*, that the moneys belonged to him and not to his clients as he was under no obligation, under s. 5(3) of the Theft Act 1968, to retain and deal with the money or its proceedings in a particular way.

EDMUND DAVIES LJ: Point (1) turns on the application of s. 5(3) of the Theft Act 1968, which provides that:

Where a person receives property from or on account of another, and is under an obligation to the other to retain and deal with that property or its proceeds in a particular way, the property or proceeds shall be regarded (as against him) as belonging to the other.

Mr Jolly submitted that in the circumstances arising in [previous] cases there arose no such 'obligation' upon the defendant. He referred us to a passage in the eighth report the Criminal Law Revision Committee (1966) (Cmnd. 2977), at p. 127, which reads:

Subsection (3) provides for the special case where property is transferred to a person to retain and deal with for a particular person and he misapplies it or its proceeds. An example would be the treasurer of a holiday fund. The person in question is in law the owner of the property; but the subsection treats the property, as against him, as belonging to the persons to whom he owes the duty to retain and deal with the property as agreed. He will therefore be guilty of stealing from them if he misapplies the property or its proceeds.

Mr Jolly submitted that the example there given is, for all practical purposes, identical with the actual facts in *R* v *Pulham* (unreported) June 15, 1971, where, incidentally, s. 5(3) was not discussed, the convictions there being quashed, as we have already indicated, owing to the lack of a proper direction as to the accused's state of mind at the time he appropriated. But he submits that the position of a treasurer of a solitary fund is quite different from that of a person like the defendant, who was in general, and genuine, business as a travel agent, and to whom people pay money in order to achieve a certain object – in the present cases, to obtain charter flights to America. It is true, he concedes, that thereby the travel agent undertakes a contractual obligation in relation to arranging flights and at the proper time paying the air line and any other expenses. Indeed, the defendant throughout acknowledged that this was so, though contending that in some of the seven cases it was the other party who was in breach. But what Mr Jolly resists is that in such circumstances the travel agent 'is under an obligation' to the client 'to retain and deal with . . . in a particular way' sums paid to him in such circumstances.

What cannot of itself be decisive of the matter is the fact that the defendant paid the money into the firm's general trading account. As Widgery J said in *R* v *Yule* [1964] 1 QB 5, decided under s. 20(1)(iv) of the Larceny Act 1916, at p. 10:

The fact that a particular sum is paid into a particular banking account . . . does not affect the right of persons interested in that sum or any duty of the solicitor either towards his client or towards third parties with regard to disposal of that sum.

Nevertheless, when a client goes to a firm carrying on the business of travel agents and pays them money, he expects that in return he will, in due course, receive the tickets and other documents necessary for him to accomplish the trip for which he is paying, and the firm are 'under an obligation' to perform their part to fulfil his expectation and are liable to pay him damages if they do not. But, in our judgment, what was not here established was that these clients expected them 'to retain and deal with that property or its proceeds in a particular way,' and that an 'obligation' to do this was undertaken by the defendant.

We must make clear, however, that each case turns on its own facts. Cases could, we suppose, conceivably arise where by some special arrangement (preferably evidenced by documents), the client could impose upon the travel agent an 'obligation' falling within s. 5(3). But no such special arrangement was made in any of the seven cases here being considered. It is true that in some of them documents were signed by the parties; thus, in respect of the counts 1 and 3 incidents there was a clause to the effect that the 'People to People' organisation did not guarantee to refund deposits if withdrawals were made later than a certain date; and in respect of counts 6, 7 and 8 the defendant wrote promising 'a full refund' after the flights paid for failed to materialise. But neither in those nor in the remaining two cases (in relation to which there was no documentary evidence of any kind) was there, in our judgment, such a special arrangement as would give rise to an 'obligation' within s. 5(3).

It follows from this that, despite what on any view must be condemned as scandalous conduct by the defendant, in our judgment upon this ground alone this appeal must be allowed and the conviction quashed.

R v Hayes
(1977) 64 Cr App Rep 82
Court of Appeal

The appellant started trading with another man as estate agents. He received money from clients as deposits on account of sales or purchase of houses. He was charged, *inter alia*, on 11 counts alleging theft contrary to s. 1 of the Theft Act 1968. In summing-up the judge, *inter alia*, failed to invite the jury to consider whether there was an obligation on the appellant to deal with the clients' money within s. 5(3) of the Act of 1968; nor did he direct them that there was an obligation on the prosecution to prove that at the time when the misappropriation took place there was already an intention to be dishonest. The appellant was convicted, *inter alia*, of theft. . . .

THE LORD CHIEF JUSTICE: The case really revolved around s. 5(3) because, as will be understood from the brief extracts I have already given of the facts, the real issue which arose between the prosecution and the defence was whether the appellant was appropriating and therefore stealing property of another which would amount to an offence under the Theft Act 1968, or whether the true position was that he was apparently appropriating or stealing money which had become his because it had become his property according to this argument when the payment was made.

The circumstances which gave rise to count 1 form a useful illustration of the working of those principles. In the transaction on October 23, 1970 the appellant through Blake gave a receipt to a Mr Newman for £300, which was described as being a deposit and part-payment of a dwelling house at Sheppart Street, Stoke, the purchase price being £600. That money was paid over in cash. It was not paid into the bank, the bank at that time having only a credit balance of £13 in it. It was entered in a book kept by the appellant which was intended to disclose cash in hand, and it was entered in that book at a time in Occtober 1970 when, according to the book, there was cash in hand to the tune of £6,480. The prosecution sought, not without some success, to show that this record of cash in hand was itself bogus and that the money referred to as being in hand never was in hand. But conclusions of that sort were not necessarily obtained on the directions which were given to the jury in this case, and I cite those facts merely to disclose the oddities of the transaction upon which count 1 is based, the other counts being based on similar oddities.

It is important, we think, to compare the situation in *Hall* [[1973] 1 QB 126] with the situation in our present case. In *Hall* (*supra*) the argument on the one side was that the ticket agent receiving the money for the tickets was obliged to use that money in a particular way and to go and buy tickets with it. On the other side it was argued that he was not bound to use the particular money in a particular way. All that happened on his receiving the money was that he incurred a civil responsibility to carry out his side of the bargain. Edmund Davies LJ is taking the point there that in the absence of some special term in the contract the second view is the right one.

Convictions quashed.

Davidge v Bunnett
[1984] Crim LR 296
Queen's Bench Division

In July 1982 D shared a flat with two other young women, C and McF. In September 1982 they were joined by H. There was an oral agreement to share the costs of gas, electricity and telephone. The gas account was in C's name. In October 1982 C received a gas bill for £159.75. D, C and McF each agreed to pay £50, and H the balance of £9.75. D did not have a bank account. The others all did, and gave D cheques in the appropriate sums, made payable to P, D's employer. They thought that D would either encash the cheques with P, add her own £50 and pay the gas bill, or that P would write out a cheque for the Gas Board on receipt of funds totalling £159.75. They did not expect D to apply any actual banknotes received from P to the discharge of the bill. On November 18, 1982, £59.75 was paid to the Gas Board. The balance of £100 was carried over to the next account in December. In January 1983 C received a final demand. C asked D to look into the matter, to which D agreed. D then left the flat without giving notice or leaving a forwarding address. C and McF later discovered that their cheques for £50 had been cashed on November 1, 1982. When interviewed by the police, D admitted 'I spent the £100 on Christmas presents but intended to pay it back.' The magistrates convicted D of theft, finding that D was under a legal obligation to apply the proceeds of C and McF's cheques to the payment of the gas bill. They also found that the proceeds of the cheques were property belonging to another within the meaning of the Theft Act 1968, and that there was evidence of an appropriation of two sums of £50, notwithstanding the payment of £59.75.

Held, dismissing the appeal, that the position was simple. D was under an obligation to use the cheques or their proceeds in whatever way she saw fit to long as they were applied *pro tanto* to the discharge of the gas bill. This could have been achieved by one cheque from her employer, or a banker's draft, or her own cheque had so opened her own bank account, or by endorsing the other cheques. Hence the magistrates' finding that she was not obliged to use the actual banknotes. Using the proceeds of the cheques on presents amounted to a very negation of her obligation to discharge the bill. She was under an obligation to deal with the proceeds in a particular way. As against D, the proceeds of the cheques were property belonging to another within s. 5(3) of the Act.

Lewis v Lethbridge
[1987] Crim LR 59
Queen's Bench Division

The appellant was convicted of theft from a charity. He obtained sponsorship for a colleague who had entered the London Marathon. He also completed sponsorship forms in false names. He received £54 which he did not hand over to the charity. The justices found that although there was no rule of the charity requiring the appellant to hand over the notes and coins actually collected so long as a sum equal to the amount collected was handed over, the appellant had dishonestly appropriated the proceeds of the money received. The appellant appealed by way of case stated.

Held, allowing the appeal and quashing the conviction, the justices erred in finding that the debt owed by the appellant could be described as proceeds of the property received. In any event he could not be said to have appropriated a debt which he himself owed simply by not paying it. The Court approved of the summary set out by Professor J. C. Smith in *The Law of Theft* (5th ed.): 'the obligation is to deal with that property or its proceeds in a particular way.' The words 'or its proceeds' make it clear that D need not be under an obligation to retain particular monies. It is sufficient that he is under an obligation to keep in existence a fund equivalent to that which he has received. If the arrangement permits D to do what he likes with the money, his only obligation being to account in due course for an equivalent sum, s. 5(3) does not apply.

Questions
1.   Do the above cases turn on the obligation of the holder of the funds or the expectations of those whose moneys comprise the funds? Must the obligation attach to particular property?
2.   Will s. 5(3) be of use only where the relationship between the victim and the defendant is contractual? If a wife gives her husband housekeeping money and he spends it on flowers for her, has he stolen it?
3.   Will the obligation in s. 5(3) arise only when a contractual relationship obliges the defendant to keep in existence a fund sufficient to fulfil the purpose for which the money was given within a reasonable time?
4.   Carla is given money by Abdul, her uncle. He tells her that he money is to pay for pet food for his dog. As she leaves to go shopping, the window cleaner arrives, demanding payment, so she uses the money to pay him. Has Carla committed theft? Would it make a difference if the window cleaner was Carla's lover and the money was later used to buy Carla a present?

Must the 'obligation' be legally enforceable?

R v Mainwaring
(1982) 74 Cr App R 99
Court of Appeal

LAWTON LJ: The prosecution case was that when Mainwaring and Madders received money from prospective purchasers they did so knowing that it was in part payment of villas purchased from Frenchmen or Spaniards, that they were under an obligation to hand that money over to the developers in France or Spain, as the case might be, and that it would have been, and in fact was, dishonest of them to appropriate the money there and then for their own purposes.

   Clearly there was some confusion in the mind of the learned judge about the operation of s. 5(3) of the Theft Act 1968.

   We think that it may help judges if we make this comment about that section of the Act. Whether or not an obligation arises is a matter of law, because an obligation must be a legal obligation. But a legal obligation arises only in certain circumstances, and in many cases the circumstances cannot be known until the facts have been established. It is for the jury, not the judge, to establish the facts, if they are in dispute.

   What, in our judgment, a judge ought to do is this: if the facts relied upon by the prosecution are in dispute he should direct the jury to make their findings on the facts, and then say to them: 'If you find the facts to be such-and-such, then I direct you as a matter of law that a legal obligation arose to which s. 5(3) applies.'

R v Meech
[1974] QB 549
Court of Appeal

ROSKILL LJ: . . . A man named McCord had obtained a cheque for £1,450 from a hire-purchase finance company by means of a forged instrument. The cheque itself was a perfectly valid document. McCord, who was an undischarged bankrupt, feared that were he to cash this cheque himself his crime would be more likely to be discovered than if he persuaded a friend to cash it for him. McCord, therefore, asked Meech (to whom McCord owed £40) to cash the cheque for him and Meech agreed so to do. At the time he agreed so to do Meech was wholly unaware of the dishonest means whereby McCord had become possessed of the cheque. Meech paid the cheque into his own account at a branch of Lloyds Bank Ltd. at High Wycombe on September 11, 1972. The bank was seemingly unwilling to allow him to cash the cheque until it had been cleared. On September 13, 1972, Meech drew his own cheque for £1,410 on his own account at that branch and that cheque was duly cashed by the bank on that day. The difference between the two sums was represented by McCord's £40 debt to Meech. By the time this cheque was cashed, the original cheque had been cleared. Between the paying in of the original cheque on September 11 and the obtaining of the cash on September 13, Meech became aware that McCord had acquired the original cheque dishonestly.

We were told by counsel that Meech, following legal argument at the end of the evidence, was allowed by the judge to be re-called. Meech then told the jury that not only did he find out about McCord's dishonesty but that he then honestly believed that if he cashed the cheque he would commit an offence. In view of the direction given by the judge to which we refer later, we think it clear that the jury must be taken to have rejected this story of honest belief on Meech's part.

Before the cheque was cashed but after Meech discovered its dishonest origin, Meech agreed with Parslow and Jolliffe that after the cheque was cashed Meech would take the money to a prearranged destination. The two other men were to join him there. A fake robbery, with Meech as the victim, was to be staged and indeed was staged, the purpose clearly being to provide some explanation to McCord of Meech's inability to hand over the money to McCord.

This was done; Parslow and Jolliffe between them removed the money after leaving Meech as the apparent victim. The bogus robbery was reported to the police, who being less credulous than the three men imagined McCord might be, investigated the matter and soon became convinced that the robbery story was bogus, as indeed it was soon shown to be. It is clear that Meech was influenced by the thought that even if the bogus nature of the robbery were suspected by McCord, McCord would never dare to go to the police and complain for that would involve revealing his own dishonesty.

Counsel for all the defendants relied strongly on the series of recent decisions that 'obligation' means 'legal obligation'. The judge so directed the jury. In giving this direction he no doubt had in mind the successive decisions of this court in R v Hall [1973] QB 126; R v Gilks [1972] 1 WLR 1341 and R v Pearce (unreported), November 21, 1972 (both the court and counsel were supplied with copies of the judgment). Reliance was also placed on paragraph 76 of Professor Smith's The Law of Theft, 2nd ed. (1972) – a passage written just before the decisions referred to. Since the judge so directed the jury, we do not find it necessary further to consider those decisions beyond observing that the facts of those cases were vastly different from those of the present case.

Starting from this premise – that 'obligation' means 'legal obligation' – it was argued that even at the time when Meech was ignorant of the dishonest origin of the cheque, as he was at the time when he agreed to cash the cheque and hand the proceeds less the £40 to McCord, McCord could never have enforced that obligation because McCord had acquired the cheque illegally. In our view this submission is unsound in principle. The question has to be looked at from Meech's point of view, not McCord's.

Meech plainly assumed an 'obligation' to McCord which, on the facts then known to him, he remained obliged to fulfil and, on the facts as found, he must be taken at that time honestly to have intended to fulfil. The fact that on the true facts if known McCord might not and indeed would not subsequently have been permitted to enforce that obligation in a civil court does not prevent that 'obligation' on Meech having arisen. The argument confuses the creation of the obligation with the subsequent discharge of that obligation either by performance or otherwise. That the obligation might have become impossible of performance by Meech or of enforcement by McCord on grounds of illegality or for reasons of public policy is irrelevant. The opening words of s. 5(3) clearly look to the time of the creation of or the acceptance of the obligation by the bailee and not to the time of performance by him of the obligation so created and accepted by him.

Notes and questions
1.   Lord Roskill's judgment in *Meech* looks not at whether the obligation was legally enforceable, but at whether the defendant believed the obligation to be enforceable. In fact no legally enforceable obligation ever arose between Meech and McCord. It seems strange that if the defendant believes such an obligation to exist, this should cause s. 5(3) to operate. The subsection refers to a situation where the defendant *is* 'under an obligation', not where he believes himself to be so.

A possible way out of the difficulty would be to hold that a legal obligation did arise but it was not such a one as could be enforced by the dishonest McCord. This raises the whole question of whether there is such a thing as an 'unenforceable obligation'. Such a thing would, of course, be quite useless to its owner.
2.   Whether s. 5(3) operates where no legally enforceable obligation has in fact arisen but the defendant believes himself to be under such an obligation must remain doubtful. Where the section does operate, ownership of the property concerned, by a fiction, remains with the person who has given the property to the defendant. The property therefore 'belongs to another' within the definition of theft in s. 1 of the 1968 Act. In view of the discussion of *Gomez* (above), is s. 5(3) necessary?
3.   In deciding *Meech*, was the court unduly influenced by the evident dishonesty of the defendants?

(vi)   When does an obligation arise to restore property got by another's mistake?

Theft Act 1968

5.—(4)   Where a person gets property by another's mistake, and is under an obligation to make restoration (in whole or in part) of the property or its proceeds or of the value thereof, then to the extent of that obligation the property or proceeds shall be regarded (as against him) as belonging to the person entitled to restoration, and an intention not to make restoration shall be regarded accordingly as an intention to deprive that person of the property or proceeds.

Note
The subsection was designed to alter the pre-Act law as represented by the following case:

Moynes v *Coopper*
[1956] 1 QB 439
Queen's Bench Division

A wages clerk, by mistake, put £6 19s. 6½d. more money than was in fact due to an employee into a pay packet which he handed to the employee, thinking that the whole amount was due to him and intending that the employee should receive the whole of the contents. At the time when he received the pay packet the employee did not know that it contained more than was due to him, and he first discovered what it contained when he opened it later the same day at his home. When he opened the packet the employee knew that he had been overpaid £6 19s. 6½d. by mistake and dishonestly decided to, and did, appropriate to his own use the whole of the contents of the packet. The employee was charged with stealing £6 19s. 6½d., the property of his employers, contrary to s. 2 of the Larceny Act, 1916:—

Held, (Stable J dissenting), that the definition of 'takes' in s. 2(i)(c) of the Larceny Act 1916, affirmed the common law that to constitute the offence of larceny the taker must have animus furandi at the time when he took the property and that, since at the time when he took the packet the employee did not know of the mistake on the part of the wages clerk, the taking was not animo furandi and, therefore, was not a taking within the section. Accordingly, although the employee had been guilty of grave dishonesty, he was not guilty of larceny or of any criminal offence.

Note
The 1968 Act was applied in the following cases:

Attorney-General's Reference (No. 1 of 1983)
[1985] QB 182
Court of Appeal

LORD LANE CJ: This is a reference under s. 36 of the Criminal Justice Act 1972 by the Attorney-General. It arises by virtue of the following facts. The respondent is a woman police officer and she received her pay from the Receiver of the Metropolitan Police. Owing to an error in the receiver's department she was credited, in a way which will have to be described in more detail in a moment, with the sum of £74.74 for wages and overtime in respect of a day when she was not at work at all. That amount, together with other sums which were properly due to her, was paid into her bank by direct debit by the receiver's bank. She knew nothing of the error until later, though it was not proved precisely when. There was some evidence before the jury that she had decided to say nothing about this unsolicited windfall which had come her way, and had decided to take no action about it after she discovered the error. No demand for payment of the sum was made by the Receiver of the Metropolitan Police or anyone else.
. . .

First of all, what is the legal position with regard to the payment of money by one bank to another for the credit of a customer's account? The position was described in clear language by Lord Goddard CJ in *R v Davenport* [1954] 1 WLR 569. He said [1954] 1 All ER 602, 603:

> although we talk about people having money in a bank, the only person who has money in a bank is a banker. If I pay money into my bank, either by paying cash or a cheque, that money at once becomes the money of the banker. The relationship between banker and customer is that of debtor and creditor. He does not hold my money as an agent or trustee. The leading case of *Foley v Hill* (1848) 2 HL Cas 28 exploded that idea. When the banker is paying out, whether in cash over the counter or whether by crediting the bank account of somebody else, he is paying out of his own money, not my money, but he is debiting me in my account with him. I have a chose in action, that is to say, I have a right to expect that the banker will honour my cheque, but he does it out of his own money.

From that exposition of the true relationship between bank and client, it follows that what the respondent in the present case got was simply the debt due to her from her own bank. That is so unless her account was overdrawn or overdrawn beyond any overdraft limit, in which case she did not even get that right to money. That point is made in a decision of this court in *R v Kohn* (1979) 69 Cr App R 395. There was no evidence in the present case as to whether the respondent's bank balance was in credit, overdrawn or anything about overdraft limits imposed by the manager of the bank. It was assumed on all hands that the account was in credit.

That brings us to the question of the basic definition of theft, which is to be found in s. 1(1) of the Theft Act 1968, which provides: 'A person is guilty of theft if he dishonestly appropriates property belonging to another with the intention of permanently depriving the other of it; and 'thief' and 'steal' shall be construed accordingly.'

The property in the present case was the debt owed by the bank to the respondent and in order to show that that can be property one turns to s. 4(1) of the Act of 1968 which reads: 'Property includes money and all other property, real or personal, including things in action and other intangible property.' The debt here was a thing in action, therefore the property was capable of being stolen.

It will be apparent that, at first blush, that debt did not belong to anyone except the respondent herself. She was the only person who had the right to go to her bank and demand the handing over of that £74.74. Had there been no statutory provision which altered that particular situation that would have been the end of the case, but if one turns to s. 5(4) of the Act, one finds these words:

> Where a person gets property by another's mistake, and is under an obligation to make restoration (in whole or in part) of the property or its proceeds or of the value thereof, then to the extent of that obligation the property or proceeds shall be regarded (as against him) as belonging to the person entitled to restoration, and an intention not to make restoration shall be regarded accordingly as an intention to deprive that person of the property or proceeds.

In order to determine the effect of that subsection upon this case one has to take it piece by piece to see what the result is read against the circumstances of this particular prosecution. First of all: 'Did the respondent get property?' The word 'get' is about as wide a word as could possibly have been adopted by the draftsman of the Act. The answer is 'Yes,' the respondent in this case did get her chose in action, that is, her right to sue the bank for the debt which they owed her – money which they held in their hands to which she was entitled by virtue of the contract beween bank and customer.

Secondly: 'Did she get it by another's mistake?' The answer to that is plainly: 'Yes.' The Receiver of the Metropolitan Police made the mistake of thinking she was entitled to £74.74 when she was not entitled to that at all.

'Was she under an obligation to make restoration of either the property or its proceeds or its value?' We take each of those in turn. 'Was she under an obligation to make restoration of the property?' – the chose in action. The answer to that is 'No.' It was something which could not be restored in the ordinary meaning of the word. 'Was she under an obligation to make restoration of its proceeds?' The answer to that is 'No.' There were no proceeds of the chose in action to restore. 'Was she under an obligation to make restoration of the value thereof?' – the value of the chose in action. The answer to that seems to us to be 'Yes.'

As a result of the provisions of s. 5(4) the debt of £74.74 due from the respondent's bank to the respondent notionally belonged to the Receiver of the Metropolitan Police; therefore the prosecution, up to this point, have succeeded in proving – remarkable though it may seem – that the 'property' in this case belonged to another within the meaning of s. 1 in the Theft Act 1968 from the moment when the respondent became aware that this mistake had been made and that her account had been credited with the £74.74 and she consequently became obliged to restore the value. Furthermore, by the final words of s. 5(4), once the prosecution succeed in proving that the respondent intended not to make restoration, that is notionally to be regarded as an intention to deprive the receiver of that property which notionally belongs to him.

. . .

Before parting with the case we would like to say that it should often be possible to resolve this type of situation without resorting to the criminal law. We do, however, accept that there may be occasions – of which this may have been one — where a prosecution is necessary. We do not feel it possible to answer the question posed to us in any more specific form than the form in which this opinion has been delivered and that is our answer to the question posed to us.

R v *Davis*
(1988) 88 Cr App R 347
Court of Appeal

The appellant was convicted of six counts of theft. The counts charged theft of specified amounts of money belonging to the London Borough of Richmond. The appellant was eligible for housing benefit from the local authority. By mistake the authority's computer generated duplicate issues of a number of payments, sending the appellant two cheques. When he ceased to be eligible for the benefit only one of the computer entries was deleted and the remaining entry continued to generate cheques. The appellant admitted to police that he had 'cashed' the cheques he had received. The evidence before the jury was that he had either endorsed the cheque over to a shopkeeper in return for cash or had endorsed it to his landlord for accommodation etc. He denied receiving some cheques and was acquitted of counts relating to those cheques. The appellant appealed against conviction.

Held, allowing the appeal in part and quashing two of the convictions, there was not sufficient evidence in relation to the cheques endorsed to the landlord that the appellant had received cash in exchange for the cheques. As to the remaining counts, the language of the first part of s. 5(4) of the Theft Act 1968 was framed to cater for the ordinary tangible article and to recognise that by the time the defendant comes to commit his dishonest appropriation, the article may be in one of three conditions: it may still exist, so that it can and should be returned: it may have been exchanged for money or goods, in which case the defendant may be under an obligation to account for the fruits of the exchange, at least if they are traceable; and it may have ceased to exist altogether or to have gone out of reach of recovery, in which event the defendant may be obliged to 'restore' the value. In those cases where the defendant is indeed under a duty to 'make restoration' the second part of the subsection will put him in peril of conviction for stealing the article or its proceeds, although not its value, since there is no reference to value in this part of the subsection. The deceptively plain words of s. 5(4) give rise to problems, e.g. when is the defendant obliged to 'make restoration'; where the property received by the defendant by mistake is exchanged for something else? The Court did not need to answer those questions in the circumstances of the present case. It was plain that if an article is sold for cash, the sum represents the 'proceeds' of the article; there is no reason why this should be any the less so where the transaction involves not simply the piece of paper but also the rights which it conveys. On the assumption that the appellant was paid cash for the cheque, the offences were made out subject to the proof of dishonesty.

Questions
1.   In *Davis*, could the same result have been reached by the application of the reasoning used in *Shadrokh-Cigari* (above)? In the light of the latter case and/or *Gomez*, is s. 5(4) necessary?
2.   In the *Attorney-General's Reference* (above), the court stated that such situations might be resolved without resort to the criminal law. Why did they say this? Do you agree?
3.   If a student reeives an overpayment in her grant cheque, tells the relevant authorities of the overpayment and they do nothing, may she spend the money? Will she be guilty of theft if she does so? How does the situation change if the student fails to inform the authorities of the overpayment?

Must the 'obligation' be a legal one?

R v Gilks
[1972] 3 All ER 280
Court of Appeal

CAIRNS LJ: . . . An alternative ground on which the deputy chairman held that the money should be regarded as belonging to Ladbrokes was that 'obligation' in s. 5(4) meant an obligation whether a legal one or not. In the opinion of this court that was an incorrect ruling. In a criminal statute, where a person's criminal liability is made dependent on his having an obligation, it would be quite wrong to construe that word so as to cover a moral or social obligation as distinct from a legal one.

(vii)   Who owns the property of a vacant corporation sole?
For the sake of completeness the provisions of s. 5(5) should be noted:

Theft Act 1968

5.—(5) Property of a corporation sole shall be regarded as belonging to the corporation notwithstanding a vacancy in the corporation.

III Mens rea

Theft Act 1968

1.—(1) A person is guilty of theft if he dishonestly appropriates property belonging to another with the intention of permanently depriving the other of it: and 'thief' and 'steal' shall be construed accordingly.

The two elements in the *mens rea* of theft are:

(a) Dishonesty.
(b) Intent permanently to deprive.

A Dishonesty

(i) The application of s. 2
The Theft Act 1968, s. 2, while not providing a test of dishonesty, identifies three situations where a defendant will not be deemed to have acted dishonestly.

Theft Act 1968

2.—(1) A person's appropriation of property belonging to another is not to be regarded as dishonest—
(a) if he appropriates property in the belief that he has in law the right to deprive the other of it, on behalf of himself or of a third person; or
(b) if he appropriates the property in the belief that he would have the other's consent if the other knew of the appropriation and the circumstances of it; or
(c) (except where the property came to him as trustee or personal representative) if he appropriates the property in the belief that the person to whom the property belongs cannot be discovered by taking reasonable steps.
(2) A person's appropriation of property belonging to another may be dishonest notwithstanding that he is willing to pay for the property.

Notes
1. The belief referred to in all three situations identified in s. 2(1) is an honest belief, i.e. one actually held by the defendant. There is no requirement that the belief should be reasonable (*R* v *Kell* [1985] Crim LR 239, *R* v *Holden* [1991] Crim LR 478).
2. Notice that under s. 2(2) a willingness to pay for the items taken will not prevent a finding that the defendant acted dishonestly.

(ii) The test of dishonesty
In most cases the dishonesty of the defendant will be obvious if the facts alleged by the prosecution are proved. Normally, therefore, the jury need not be directed as to the legal meaning of 'dishonesty' (see *R* v *Squire* [1990] Crim LR 341). Where there is some doubt, the jury must be directed in accordance with the model direction set out in *Ghosh* (below). This case achieves a

reconciliation between two conflicting lines of authority. One of these sought to impose a subjective test of dishonesty (i.e. did the defendant believe that he had been acting dishonestly?) (See, e.g. *R v Gilks* [1972] 3 All ER 280). The other line of authority put forward a wholly objective test (i.e. would the jury consider such behaviour dishonest?) (see, e.g., *R v Greenstein* [1976] 1 All ER 1).

R v Ghosh
[1982] 1 QB 1053
Court of Appeal

The appellant, while a surgeon acting as a locum tenens consultant at a hospital, claimed fees for carrying out operations or fees payable for an anaesthetist in circumstances where either another surgeon had performed the operation or the operation had been carried out under the National Health Service. He was tried on an indictment containing one count alleging that he had attempted to procure the execution of a valuable security by deception, contrary to s. 20(2) of the Theft Act 1968, and three counts alleging that he had obtained or attempted to obtain money by deception, contrary to s. 15(1) of the Act. The appellant denied that he had been dishonest and stated that the sums were legitimately payable to him for consultation fees. The judge directed the jury that it was for them to decide whether the appellant had been dishonest by applying contemporary standards of honesty and dishonesty in the context of all that they had heard in the case. The jury found the appellant guilty on all four counts.

LORD LANE CJ: . . . Is 'dishonesty' in s. 1 of the Theft Act 1968 intended to characterise a course of conduct? Or is it intended to describe a state of mind? If the former, then we can well understand that it could be established independently of the knowledge or belief of the accused. But if, as we think, it is the latter, then the knowledge and belief of the accused are at the root of the problem.

Take for example a man who comes from a country where public transport is free. On his first day here he travels on a bus. He gets off without paying. He never had an intention of paying. His mind is clearly honest; but his conduct, judged objectively by what he has done, is dishonest. It seems to us that in using the word 'dishonestly' in the Theft Act 1968, Parliament cannot have intended to catch dishonest conduct in that sense, that is to say conduct to which no moral obloquy could possibly attach. This is sufficiently established by the partial definition in section 2 of the Theft Act itself. All the matters covered by section 2(1) relate to the belief of the accused. Section 2(2) relates to his willingness to pay. A man's belief and his willingness to pay are things which can only be established subjectively. It is difficult to see how a partially subjective definition can be made to work in harness with the test which in all other respects is wholly objective.

If we are right that dishonesty is something in the mind of the accused (what Professor Glanville Williams calls 'a special mental state'), then if the mind of the accused is honest, it cannot be deemed dishonest merely because members of the jury would have regarded it as dishonest to embark on that course of conduct.

So we would reject the simple uncomplicated approach that the test is purely objective, however attractive from the practical point of view that solution may be.

There remains the objection that to adopt a subjective test is to abandon all standards but that of the accused himself, and to bring about a state of affairs in which 'Robin Hood would be no robber': *R v Greenstein* [1975] 1 WLR 1353. this objection misunderstands the nature of the subjective test. It is no defence for a man to say 'I knew that what I was doing is generally regarded as dishonest; but I do not regard it as dishonest myself. Therefore I am not guilty.' What he is however entitled to say is 'I did not know that anybody would regard what I was doing as dishonest.' He may not be believed: just as he may not be believed if he sets up 'a claim of right' under section 2(1) of the Theft Act 1968, or asserts that he believed in the truth of a misrepresentation under section 15 of the Act of 1968. But if he *is* believed, or raises a real doubt about the matter, the jury cannot be sure that he was dishonest.

In determining whether the prosecution has proved that the defendant was acting dishonestly, a jury must first of all decide whether according to the ordinary standards of reasonable and honest people what was done was dishonest. If it was not dishonest by those standards, that is the end of the matter and the prosecution fails.

If it was dishonest by those standards, then the jury must consider whether the defendant himself must have realised that what he was doing was by those standards dishonest. In most cases, where the actions are obviously dishonest by ordinary standards, there will be no doubt about it. It will be obvious that the defendant himself knew that he was acting dishonestly. It is dishonest for a defendant to act in a way which he knows ordinary people consider to be dishonest, even if he asserts or genuinely believes that he is morally justified in acting as he did. For example, Robin Hood or those ardent anti-vivisectionists who remove animals from vivisection laboratories are acting dishonestly, even though they may consider themselves to be morally justified in doing what they do, because they know that ordinary people would consider these actions to be dishonest.

Notes and questions

1.   M. Allen, *Textbook of Criminal Law* (2nd ed.), p. 323 argues that the Court of Appeal in *Ghosh* based their view on a misconception. Taking the example of a man who comes from a country where public transport is free and who fails to pay a fare on public transport in England where it is not, Allen argues that such conduct would be objectively honest as the conduct was based on a mistake of fact. Thus there was no need to introduce the subjective part of the *Ghosh* test. The same result could be reached by telling the jury that they should judge the defendant's behaviour objectively, but in doing so they must put themselves into the position of someone who is only as aware of the facts surrounding the situation as the defendant was. If this is done, the defendant in the example was objectively honest. It is only if he takes a free ride knowing that it should have been paid for that he would be dishonest. Is Allen correct? Would the same criticism of the subjective element of *Ghosh* apply where a man takes a loaf of bread to feed his starving child, believing no one would begrudge him it? Or if a woman stranded on a cross-Channel ferry breaks into a canteen to take biscuits for her sister who is about to go into a diabetic coma because of lack of sugar? Does the subjective element in *Ghosh* import a defence of necessity?

2.   J. C. Smith, *Law of Theft* (6th ed.) suggests that the test of dishonesty should be 'knowing that the appropriation will or may be detrimental to the interests of the owner in a significantly practical way'. Do you agree?

3. Will the *Ghosh* test inevitably lead to different results in similar cases? See Griew, 'Dishonesty: The Objections to *Feely* and *Ghosh*' [1985] Crim LR 341.
4. The *Ghosh* test may prove particularly troublesome in the context of business crime, where the standards of the marketplace and the standards of ordinary people may well clash, most ordinary people not being conversant with what is acceptable in the world of businesses. Should this matter? See generally Chapter 6.

B   *Intent permanently to deprive*

The intention of the defendant must be to deprive the loser of the whole of his interest. If this is a limited interest, then, so long as an intention to deprive him of all of that interest can be shown, the requisite intent will be present.

Three main issues arise in determining when there is an intent permanently to deprive:

(a)   Is there an intent permanently to deprive if the defendant intends to return the goods but puts himself into a position where he may not be able to do so?
(b)   In what circumstances can an intended borrowing amount to an intention permanently to deprive?
(c)   Can a 'conditional intention' be sufficient *mens rea?*

(i)   Intention to return goods but possible inability to do so

Theft Act 1968

6.—(2)   Without prejudice to the generality of subsection (1) above, where a person, having possession or control (lawfully or not) of property belonging to another, parts with the property under a condition as to its return which he may not be able to perform, this (if done for purposes of his own and without the other's authority) amounts to treating the property as his own to dispose of regardless of the other's rights.

Note
Section 6(2) was specifically designed to cover the case where the defendant pawns another's property without authority. The condition 'which he may not be able to perform' in those circumstances is the condition imposed by the pawnbroker that the property will not be returned unless repayment of the loan with interest is first forthcoming. However, the subsection is not confined to pawning situations and there may well be other cases falling within its ambit.

(ii)   When can an intended borrowing amount to an intention permanently to deprive?

Theft Act 1968

6.—(1)   A person appropriating property belonging to another without meaning the other permanently to lose the thing itself is nevertheless to be regarded as having the intention of permanently depriving the other of it if his intention is to treat the thing as his own to dispose of regardless of the other's rights; and a borrowing or lending of it may amount to so treating it if, but only if, the borrowing or lending is for a period and in circumstances making it equivalent to an outright taking or disposal.

R v Duru
[1973] 3 All ER 715
Court of Appeal

The accused, D, A and K, collaborated together to assist certain prospective house buyers to obtain mortgages from the Greater London Council. D was at the time employed by the council in the department which dealt with such applications. The applications in question, to the knowledge of each of the accused, contained false information about the applicants' income and employment. On the basis of that information, the applications, which were dealt with by D on behalf of the council, were granted. The council's cheques representing the mortgage loans were sent to solicitors who acted both for the council and for the respective applicants. those cheques were in due course cashed and on completion of the house purchases the moneys represented by them were paid as mortgage moneys to the persons who thereupon became mortgagors. The accused were convicted of obtaining property, i.e. the cheques, 'with the intention of permanently depriving' the council of them, contrary to s. 15(1) of the Theft Act 1968. D and A appealed against their convictions contending (i) that they had no intention of depriving the council permanently either of the cheques, since the cheques themselves would ultimately, after they had been paid by the council's bank on presentation, go back to the council, or of the moneys represented by the cheques, since the mortgage transactions involved a loan of the moneys which would in due course be repaid; and (ii) that, even if the accused had such an intention, they had not themselves 'obtained' the property in question, nor had they enabled another to obtain or retain it, within s. 15(2) of the 1968 Act, because the cheques went into the hands of solicitors who were acting for both the council and the applicants with the result that neither ownership, possession nor control of the property had passed to anybody for whom it had been obtained.

MEGAW LJ: . . . In the view of this court there can be no doubt that the intention of both of these appellants, as would necessarily have been found by the jury if the matter had been left to the jury on a proper direction of law (a direction which would no doubt have been given if the pleas of guilty had not been entered), was permanently to deprive the Greater London Council of that thing in action, that cheque; that piece of paper, in the sense of a piece of paper carrying with it the right to receive payment of the sum of £6,002.60, which is the amount concerned in count 3.

So far as the cheque itself is concerned, true it is a piece of paper. But it is a piece of paper which changes its character completely once it is paid, because then it receives a rubber stamp on it saying it has been paid and it ceases to be a thing in action, or at any rate it ceases to be, in its substance, the same thing as it was before: that is, an instrument on which payment falls to be made. It was the intention of the appellants, dishonestly and by deception, not only that the cheques should be made out and handed over, but also that they should be presented and paid, thereby permanently depriving the Greater London Council of the cheque in substance as their things in action. The fact that the mortgagors were under an obligation to repay the mortgage loans does not affect the appellants' intention permanently to deprive the council of these cheques.

If it were necessary to look to s. 6(1) of the Theft Act 1968, this court would have no hesitation in saying that that subsection, brought in by the terms of s. 15(3), would also be relevant, since it is plain that the appellants each had the intention of causing the cheque to be treated as the property of the person by whom it was to be obtained, to dispose of, regardless of the rights of the true owner.

For those reasons the grounds of appeal which have been put forward in respect of conviction are unsound and the appeals of Duru and Asghar in respect of conviction are both dismissed.

R v *Johnstone, Comerford and Jalil*
[1982] Crim LR 454
Newcastle-Upon-Tyne Crown Court

D1 and D2 were employed by a bottling company as draymen to deliver supplies of bottled soft drinks, cider and beer to, and to collect the empties and crates from, retail outlets. They were required to note down on a separate delivery sheet for each outlet the amount of empties collected so that the retailer could be credited with the deposit upon them on D1 and D2's return to the bottling company. Evidence was adduced by the prosecution that on the day in question D1 and D2 collected 28 more bottles and crates than they credited to the outlets, thereby creating a surplus of empties upon the lorry. Instead of delivering the surplus directly to their employers they dishonestly delivered it to D3, a retailer who was also a customer of the employers, with the intention of receiving a part of the deposit which D3 would himself dishonestly obtain. The Recorder accepted that this scheme only made sense if the surplus bottles were returned to the bottling company either directly or via a bottle exchange with only a short delay, since it was only in such circumstances that D3 would be able to obtain credit for the deposit. It was thus intended by D1 and D2 that the bottling company would receive their bottles back and would have to pay no more than one deposit, albeit to the wrong person.

D1 and D2 were charged with theft of the surplus bottles from the bottling company (it not being possible for the prosecution to prove from which individual retail outlet(s) the surplus had been obtained). D3 was charged with handling the surplus.

On a submission at the end of the prosecution case of no case to answer upon the argument that D1 and D2 did not intend permanently to deprive their employers of the surplus bottles the prosecution sought to rely upon the provisions of section 6(1) of the Theft Act upon the basis that D1 and D2 had treated the bottles as their own to dispose of regardless of the others rights:

Held: That since on the above facts D1 and D2 contemplated and intended that the bottles should be returned to the true owners, albeit with some delay and since the object of the scheme was merely to manipulate the bottles in order to obtain the deposit, it could not be said that D1 and D2 were treating the bottles as their own to dispose of. A disposal which negates an intention permanently to deprive cannot be capable of providing what an be regarded as an intent permanently to deprive under section 6(1) of the Theft Act.

Notes and questions
1.   In *Duru*, the 'thing' which was returned to the owner was so different in nature as to have lost all its value so far as the owner was concerned. Would the same argument apply to a season ticket which has almost expired? Jane has a season ticket to watch Sheffield Wednesday football club. The ticket is valid for 13 matches. David takes the season ticket after Jane has been to three matches and returns it in time for her to attend the last match. Has David stolen the ticket?
2.   In *Johnstone, Comerford and Jalil*, the court reasoned that the defendants always treated the bottles as belonging to the bottling company, and that an intention to return the bottles and collect the deposits was not consistent with any other intention. The bottling company would not, in any event, be entitled to the return of the bottles unless they paid the deposits. It was not, therefore, a case of taking the company's property intending to sell it back to them. The defendants were diverting the money rather than claiming extra money from the company. Is this reasoning persuasive? See also *Chan Man Sin* v *Attorney-General for Hong Kong* [1988] 1 All ER 1.
3.   If the defendants did not commit a crime against the bottling company, did they commit a crime against anybody?
4.   Could the law be simplified by eliminating the requirement of proof of an intent permanently to deprive someone of his property? Why should not unauthorised borrowing constitute theft, even if there is not an intent permanently to deprive? See G. Williams, 'Temporary appropriation should be theft' [1981] Crim LR 129. The all too prevalent problem of joyriding (where there is usually no intent to deprive the owner of her car) is specifically addressed in the Theft Act 1968, s. 12, and, more recently, the Aggravated Vehicle Taking Act 1992.

(iii)   Can a 'conditional intention' be sufficient mens rea?
This problem arises where the defendant only intends permanently to keep anything which he finds to be valuable after he has examined the property. In *Easom* [1971] 2 QB 315, such an intention was held not to be sufficient for theft. Whether the defendant is guilty of attempted theft used to turn on the way in which the indictment was framed. According to the court in *Re Attorney-General's References (Nos 1 & 2 of 1979)* [1980] QB 180, the defendant in *Easom* could have been convicted if he had been charged with 'attempting to steal some or all of the contents of the handbag'. The problem has now been solved by the Criminal Attempts Act 1981 (impossibility no defence). See Chapter 7.

IV   Robbery

Theft Act 1968

8.—(1)   A person is guilty of robbery if he steals, and immediately before or at the time of doing so, and in order to do so, he uses force on any person or puts or seeks to put any person in fear of being then and there subjected to force.

(2) A person guilty of robbery, or of an assault with intent to rob, shall on conviction on indictment be liable to imprisonment for life.

A   Theft

Robbery is essentially an aggravated form of stealing. It follows that if a defendant is not guilty of theft he cannot be guilty of robbery. The offence of robbery is complete when the theft is complete:

R v Robinson
[1977] Crim LR 173
Court of Appeal

R ran a clothing club. He was charged (with others) with robbing and assaulting I, who, with his wife, was a contributor to the club. I's wife owed £7. It was the prosecution case that R and two others had approached him in the street late at night, R brandishing a knife, and that a fight ensued during the course of which a £5 note fell from I's pocket. R had snatched the note and asked if I had any more money as he was still owed £2. R's defence to robbery, reduced by the jury to theft, was that I gave him the money and he had received it willingly as repayment of the debt and that it was not dishonestly appropriated. R appealed on the ground of misdirection to the jury that an honest belief by the defendant that he was entitled in law to get his money in a particular way was necessary before he could avail himself of the defence under s. 2(1)(a) of the Theft Act 1968.

Held, allowing the appeal, that the law as laid down in *Skivington* [1968] 1 QB 166 had not been altered by s. 2(1)(a) of the Theft Act 1968, and that it was unnecessary for a defendant to show that he had an honest belief not only that he was entitled to take the money but also that he was entitled to take it in the way that he did.

Corcoran v Anderton
[1980] Crim LR 385
Queen's Bench Division

Two youths, the defendant and his co-accused, saw a woman in the street, and agreed together to steal her handbag. The co-accused hit her in the back and tugged at her bag to release it, while the defendant participated. She released her bag, screamed, and fell to the ground. The two youths ran away empty-handed, and the woman recovered her bag, neither youth having had sole control of the bag at any time. The defendant was later convicted of robbery under s. 8 of the Theft Act 1968; which provided that a person was guilty of robbery if he stole, using force.

The defendant appealed against conviction on the ground that neither he nor the co-accused had sole control of the boy at any time.

Held, dismissing the appeal, that an appropriation took place at the moment when the youths, acting with an intention to deprive the woman of the bag, snatched it from her grasp so that she no longer had physical control of it. In doing so each accused was trying to exclude the woman from her exclusive claim to the bag, and was trying to treat the bag as his. Such an action was an unlawful assumption of the rights of the owner and accordingly the defendant was properly convicted by the justices.

Questions
1.   Robinson was not guilty of robbery because no theft could be proved. Could he have been found guilty of blackmail?
2.   Would the definition of appropriation adopted by the House of Lords in *Gomez* affect the result in *Corocan* v *Anderton*?

B   *Force or threat of force*

Section 8 is satisfied only if the defendant is found to have used 'force on any person' or to have sought 'to put any person in fear of being then and there subjected to force'. What amounts to force is a matter for each individual jury.

R v Dawson
[1976] Crim LR 692
Court of Appeal

D was convicted of robbery. He and two others approached a man in the street and two of them stood either side of him and the third behind him. One of them nudged the man so that he lost his balance and whilst he was thus unbalanced another stole his wallet. It was submitted that what D and his accomplices did could not amount to the use of force, relying on cases prior to the Theft Act 1968.

Held, dismissing the appeal, what counted now was the words of the Act, the object of which was to get rid of the old technicalities. The choice of the word force was not without interest because the Larceny Act 1916 used violence. Whether there was any difference between the words was not relevant to the case. Force was a word in ordinary use which juries understood. The judge left it to the jury to decide whether jostling to an extent which caused a person to have difficulty in keeping his balance amounted to the use of force. In deference to the submissions he said that the force must be substantial. It was not necessary to consider whether he was right to apply an adjective to the word of the Act. It was a matter for the jury and it could not be said that they were wrong. It had also been canvassed whether the force had been used for distracting the victim's attention or for overcoming resistance. That sort of refinement might have been relevant under the old law: the sole question under the new was whether force had been used in order to steal.

Question
Must the force be used to overcome resistance to the theft, or is force used to gain possession of an article enough?

R v Clouden
[1987] Crim LR 56
Court of Appeal

The appellant was seen to follow a woman who was carrying a shopping basket in her left hand. He approached her from behind and wrenched the basket down and out of her grasp with both hands and ran off with it. He was charged in two counts with robbery and theft respectively and convicted on the first count of robbery. He appealed on the grounds (i) that there was insufficient evidence of resistance to the snatching of the bag to constitute force on the person under s. 8 of the Theft Act 1968; and (ii) that the learned judge's direction to the jury on the requirement of force on the person was inadequate and confused.

Held, dismissing the appeal, the old cases distinguished between force on the actual person and force on the property which in fact causes force on the person but, following *Dawson and James* (1976) 64 Cr App R 170, the court should direct attention to the words of the statute without referring to the old authorities. The old distinctions have gone. Whether the defendant used force on any person in order to steal is an issue that should be left to the jury. The judge's direction to the jury was adequate. He told the jury quite clearly at the outset what the statutory definition was, though thereafter he merely used the word 'force' and did not use the expression 'on the person'.

Note and questions

The Criminal Law Revision Committee which was responsible for drafting the Theft Act 1968 said (Cmnd 2977, para. 65) that they 'would not regard mere snatching of property, such as a handbag, from an unresisting owner as using force for the purpose of the definition'. Does *Clouden* reflect this opinion? Which view more accurately reflects the wording of the statute?

C   Before or at the time of the theft

When must the force or threat of force occur? It seems that (as with burglary) an appropriation can be a continuing act for the purposes of robbery:

R v Hale
(1978) 68 Cr App R 415
Court of Appeal

The appellant was charged with robbery. The prosecution case was that he and one M, both wearing stocking masks, had forced their way into the house of a Mrs C who had answered the door to their knock. The appellant had then put his hand over Mrs C's mouth to stop her screaming while M went upstairs and returned carrying a jewellery box and had asked Mrs C 'where the rest was.' A neighbour who had heard Mrs C's scream had then rung up to ask if she was all right. Under threats from the appellant and M she replied that she was. They again asked Mrs C where she kept her money and before leaving the house tied her up and threatened what would happen to her young boy if she informed the police within five minutes of their leaving.

The trial judge read the definition of robbery in s. 8 of the Theft Act 1968 to the jury and the meaning of 'steal' in s. 1 of that Act. He directed them that the question they had to decide was whether they felt sure that the appellant by use of force or putting Mrs C in fear got hold of her property without her consent and without believing that he had her consent and intending to appropriate that property to himself without giving it back to her afterwards. The jury convicted. On appeal that the jury had been misdirected in that the judge's direction could indicate to the jury that if an accused used force in order to effect his escape with the stolen goods that would be sufficient to constitute robbery and that on the facts of the present case it was submitted that the theft was completed as soon as the jewellery box was seized.

EVELEIGH LJ: . . . In so far as the facts of the present case are concerned, counsel submitted that the theft was completed when the jewellery box was first seized and any force thereafter could not have been 'immediately before or at the time of stealing' and certainly not 'in order to steal.' The essence of the submission was that the theft was completed as soon as the jewellery box was seized.

Secction 8 of the Theft Act 1968 begins: 'A person is guilty of robbery if he steals . . .' He steals when he acts in accordance with the basic definition of theft in s. 1 of the Theft Act; that is to say when he dishonestly appropriates property belonging to another with the intention of permanently depriving the other of it. It thus becomes necessary to consider what is 'appropriation' or, according to s. 3, 'any assumption by a person of the rights of an owner.' An assumption of the rights of an owner describes the conduct of a person towards a particular article. It is conduct which usurps the rights of the owner. To say that the conduct is over and done with as soon as he lays hands upon the property, or when he first manifests an intention to deal with it as his, is contrary to common-sense and to the natural meaning of words. A thief who steals a motor car first opens the door. It is to be said that the act of starting up the motor is no more a part of the theft?

In the present case there can be little doubt that if the appellant had been interrupted after the seizure of the jewellery box the jury would have been entitled to find that the appellant and his accomplice were assuming the rights of an owner at the time when the jewellery box was seized. However, the act of appropriation does not suddenly cease. It is a continuous act and it is a matter for the jury to decide whether or not the act of appropriation has finished. Moreover, it is quite clear that the intention to deprive the owner permanently, which accompanied the assumption of the owner's rights was a continuing one at all material times. This Court therefore rejects the contention that the theft had ceased by the time the lady was tied up. As a matter of common-sense the appellant was in the course of committing theft; he was stealing.

There remains the question whether there was robbery. Quite clearly the jury were at liberty to find the appellant guilty of robbery relying upon the force used when he put his hand over Mrs Carrett's mouth to restrain her from calling for help. We also think that they were also entitled to rely upon the act of tying her up provided they were satisfied (and it is difficult to see how they could not be satisfied) that the force so used was to enable them to steal. If they were still engaged in the act of stealing the force was clearly used to enable them to continue to assume the rights of the owner and permanently to deprive Mrs Carrett of her box, which is what they began to do when they first seized it.

D   In order to steal

The force must be used 'in order to steal':

R v *Shendley*
[1970] Crim LR 49
Court of Appeal

S was convicted of robbery, contrary to s. 8 of the Theft Act 1968. The complainant said that S attacked him, took some of his property and forced him to sign receipts purporting to show that S had brought the property from him. S said that he had purchased the property. The judge directed the jury: 'robbery is stealing property in the presence of the owner . . . the allegation is that immediately before taking the property, or at the time of taking it, or immediately after, force was used towards [the complainant] to put him in fear . . . if you came to the conclusion that the violence was unconnected with the stealing but you were satisfied there was a stealing it does not mean that is an acquittal because it would be open to you to find [him] guilty of robbery, that is, robbery without violence.'

Held: the directions were wrong. The judge must have had in mind s. 23 of the Larceny Act 1916 and overlooked the fact that the definition of robbery in the Theft Act is different. There is no such thing as robbery without violence. What the judge no doubt intended to say was that if the jury were satisfied that S stole the property but not satisfied that he used violence for the purpose of stealing they should find him not guilty of robbery but guilty of theft (the court substituted a conviction for theft).

Questions
1.   George rapes Vera. He runs off taking her handbag. Has he committed robbery as well as rape?
2.   John and David were involved in a heated argument. John lost his temper and hit David who was knocked unconscious. John took David's wallet from him and ran off. Is John a robber?

12 OFFENCES OF DECEPTION

I Introduction: Common elements

The critical element which sets deception offences apart from theft is that the owner of the property voluntarily parts with it, albeit as a result of the deceit of the defendant. After *Gomez* (p. 473), the line between the offences has been blurred if not eliminated. Now most cases involving deception can be prosecuted as theft, although the opposite is not true.

The Theft Acts contain a number of offences which prohibit a defendant from obtaining various advantages by deception. They are:

(a) Obtaining property (Theft Act 1968, s. 15);

(b) Obtaining a pecuniary advantage (Theft Act 1968, s. 16);

(c) Procuring the execution of a valuable security (Theft Act 1968, s. 20(2));

(d) Obtaining services (Theft Act, 1978, s. 1);

(e) Securing the remission of a liability (Theft Act 1978, s. 2(1)(a));

(f) Inducing a creditor to wait for or to forgo payment (Theft Act 1978, s. 2(1)(b));

(g) Obtaining an exemption from or an abatement of liability (Theft Act 1978, s. 2(1)(c)).

The deception offences have certain elements in common and it is convenient to deal with these first, reserving the particular difficulties special to each offence for separate consideration.

The common elements can be set out as follows:

(a) There must be a causal link between the deception and the prohibited result.

    (i) The deception must be operative.

(ii)   Where cheque or credit cards are involved the deception will be presumed to be operative in certain circumstances.

(iii)   A human mind must be deceived.

(iv)   The deception must not be too remote from the prohibited result.

(b)   There must be a deception, that is, an untrue 'statement'.

(i)   The statement must actually be false.

(ii)   The defendant must be deliberate or reckless as to the falsity of the statement.

(iii)   The statement must be by words or conduct (including implied statements).

(c)   The defendant must be dishonest.

A   Causation

There must be a deception, and the deception must be operative. But what does this mean?

A. T. H. Smith: 'The Idea of Criminal Deception'
[1982] Crim LR 721

Deception defined

Deception could have been explained by the legislators in the Theft Act, but it was not. The Act confines itself to the somewhat unhelpful observation that ' "deception" means any deception', the remainder of the section being devoted to reversing certain of the old common law rules surrounding the former 'false pretences'. To some extent this left the courts free to apply their own gloss to the word as the need to do so arose. But 'deception' already had, by the time the Theft Act became law in 1968, acquired a reasonably settled meaning, classically that stated by Buckley J in *Re London and Globe Finance Corporation* [1903] 1 Ch 728. 'To deceive is, I apprehend, to induce a man to believe that a thing is true which is false . . . to deceive is by falsehood to induce a state of mind.' The Criminal Law Revision Committee explained its use of 'deception' by saying:

> The substitution of 'deception' for 'false pretence' is chiefly a matter of language. The word 'deception' seems to us (as to the framers of the American Law Institute's Model Penal Code) to have the advantage of directing attention to the effect that the offender deliberately produced on the mind of the person deceived, whereas 'false pretence' makes one think of what exactly the offender did in order to deceive. 'Deception' seems also more apt in relation to deception by conduct.

This reinforces the suggestion in Buckley J's definition that it is essential that the representation must operate on the conscious mind of the victim and cause him to believe that the facts are otherwise than they really are.

Apart from being inherent in the very notion of deception, there is an additional reason why the motivation of the victim must be examined in deception cases. It must be shown by the prosecution that the obtaining was *caused* by the deception, since in all the deception offences it must be established that the obtaining was effected 'by' the deception. As Professor Williams puts it, 'an obvious consequence of the rule [as to causation] is that the deception must affect the victim's mind. Otherwise, there will be at most an attempted deception.' This analysis shows that, as classically understood, there are at least two links in the causal chain. It must be shown that the victim was induced into a certain affirmative belief, and that as a result of his belief, he behaved in a certain way, as a further result of which property (or a service or other protected interest) was obtained.

Question
Who is it that must be deceived? Is it the person to whom the deception is addressed, or the person who was induced to part with the property?

Smith v *Koumourou*
[1979] Crim LR 116
Queen's Bench Division

In March 1976 a constable took possession of the defendant's car excise licence, which was due to expire in September 1976, and gave the defendant a police memorandum to display on his windscreen instead. The memorandum was undated. In October 1977 another constable found the undated memorandum still displayed on the defendant's windscreen and was misled into thinking that it was in substitution for a current excise licence. The defendant was charged with obtaining a pecuniary advantage by deception under s. 16 of the Theft Act 1968. The justices acceded to a submission of no case, being of the view that the person deceived should be the creditor. The prosecutor appealed by case stated.

Held, allowing the appeal, that there was no such requirement that the person deceived should be the creditor.

Note
It should be proved, if possible by direct evidence, that the deception affected the conduct of the person to whom it was addressed:

R v *Laverty*
[1970] 3 All ER 432
Court of Appeal

LORD PARKER CJ: . . . The facts are in a very short compass. The car bearing number plates DUV 111C, a Hillman Imp, was bought by a Mr Bedborough from the appellant, and a cheque was given as part of the price. In fact the car bearing those number plates was a car originally bearing number plates JPA 945C which had been stolen. According to the appellant when he got the car, and there was no question of his having stolen it, it was in a bad condition, he repaired it and he put on to it the chassis and rear number plates of DUV 111C, those plates having been obtained from another source relating of course to another car.

The charge made in the indictment in count 3 took the form of alleging a false representation which here was by conduct. It was not a false representation that the appellant was the owner and had a good title to sell but the false representation was by purporting that a Hillman Imp motor car which the appellant sold to Roy Clinton Bedborough was the original Hillman Imp motor car, index number DUV 111C.

Although it was contested at the trial, it was conceded in this court that there was a representation by conduct that the car being sold to Mr Bedborough was the original Hillman Imp to which the chassis plate and rear plate which it bore had been assigned. It is conceded that such a representation was made by conduct; it is clear that that was false, and false to the knowledge of the appellant. The sole question was whether this false representation operated on Mr Bedborough's mind so as to cause him to hand over his cheque.

As sometimes happens, in this case Mr Bedborough did not give the answers which were helpful to the prosecution, and no leading questions could be put. The nearest answer was 'I bought this because I thought the appellant was the owner'. In other words Mr Bedborough was saying: 'What induced me to part with my money was the representation by conduct that the appellant had a title to sell.' It was in those circumstances that at the end of the prosecution's case a submission was made that there was no case to answer. The deputy chairman did not accede to that submission. The trial proceeded, and when he came to sum up to the jury, the deputy chairman said:

> There is no evidence at all that anything was said by [the appellant] to that effect, but the prosecution is entitled to say that that representation can be made by conduct, and it is a matter for you whether you feel, in the circumstances of this case, a representation was made by conduct that the motor car in question was the original Hillman Imp, bearing in mind that there had been put upon it number plates with the registration number DUV 111C, one of which indeed had come off the original car, and that in due course a log book was produced: but it does not appear in the evidence that the log book was seen or relied on by Mr Bedborough at the time when he handed over the cash and the cheque.
>
> What is meant by 'the original Hillman Imp' in this case? You may think that that means the car which was originally so registered, and it is a matter for you whether or not it is a necessary inference that a car offered for sale with the registration number upon it is the car for which that number was originally issued; if you think the answer to that is 'yes' then you will have to consider: Is that an inference which must have been in the mind of the purchaser: is it something that must have operated on the mind of Mr Bedborough and played its part in inducing him to hand over the cash and the cheque?

The jury apparently were satisfied that that was the true inference and convicted the appellant.

The point really is whether there was any evidence here which enabled the jury to draw that inference. It is axiomatic that it is for the prosecution to prove that the false representation acted on the mind of the purchaser; and in the ordinary way, and the court emphasises this, the matter should be proved by direct evidence. However, it was said in *R v Sullivan* that the inducement need not be proved by direct evidence, and I quote from the headnote:

> If the facts are such that the alleged false pretence is the only reason that could be suggested as having been the operative inducement.

And in the special facts of that case it was held that the prosecution had given sufficient proof, although it was made very clear that the proper way and the ordinary way of proving the matter was by direct evidence.

Counsel for the Crown submits that when the court in *R v Sullivan* referred to the only reason that could be suggested, it was not emphasising that it was the only reason but that it was the only inference that could be drawn. He is saying here that the only inference in this case is that the false representation did operate on Mr Bedborough's mind and the jury were fully entitled to come to the conclusion which they did.

This court is very anxious not to extend the principle in *R* v *Sullivan* more than is necessary. The proper way of proving these matters is through the mouth of the person to whom the false representation is conveyed, and further it seems to the court in the present case that no jury could say that the only inference here was that Mr Bedborough parted with his money by reason of this false representation. Mr Bedborough may well have been of the mind as he stated he was, namely that what operated on his mind was the belief that the appellant was the owner. Provided that the [sic] appellant was the owner it may well be that Mr Bedborough did not mind that the car did not bear its original number plates. At any rate as it seems to the court it cannot be said that the only possible inference here is that it actuated on Mr Bedborough's mind.

In those circumstances, although with some reluctance, this court feels that the proper course here is to allow the appeal and quash the conviction.

Notes and questions

1.   Is the conviction in *Laverty* quashed simply because the victim was a poor witness, or is the court making a more substantive point?

2.   The court indicates that it might well have been that factors other than the false licence plate may have influenced the victim. What kinds of factors did the court have in mind?

3.   If the deception does not occur until after the property is obtained, as a matter of logic it cannot have caused the victim to part with the property.

The courts seem to have become increasingly likely to assume that a misrepresentation operated on someone without any evidence that such as indeed the case. This tendency reaches extremes where cheque cards or credit cards are in question, but a similar trend can be seen in other situations:

Director of Public Prosecutions v *Ray*
[1974] AC 370
House of Lords

The defendant and four friends went to a Chinese restaurant intending to have a meal there and pay for it. After eating the main course they decided not to pay for it but they remained until the waiter went out of the room and then they ran from the restaurant. The defendant was convicted by the justices of dishonestly obtaining a pecuniary advantage by deception contrary to section 16(1) of the Theft Act 1968. The Divisional Court of the Queen's Bench Division quashed the conviction.

LORD MacDERMOTT: . . . Was the respondent's evasion of the debt obtained by that deception?

I think the material before the justices was enough to show that it was. The obvious effect of the deception was that the respondent and his associates were treated as they had been previously, that is to say as ordinary, honest customers whose conduct did not excite suspicion or call for precautions. In consequence the waiter was off his guard and vanished into the kitchen. That gave the respondent the opportunity of running out without hindrance and he took it. I would therefore answer this second question in the affirmative.

I would, accordingly, allow the appeal and restore the conviction.

LORD MORRIS OF BORTH-Y-GEST: The final question which arises is whether, if there was deception and if there was pecuniary advantage, it was by the deception that the respondent obtained the pecuniary advantage. In my view, this must be a question of fact and the magistrates have found that it was by his deception that the respondent dishonestly evaded payment. It would seem to be clear that if the waiter had thought that if he left the restaurant to go to the kitchen the respondent would at once run out, he (the waiter) would not have left the restaurant and would have taken suitable action. The waiter proceeded on the basis that the implied representation made to him (i.e. of an honest intention to pay) was effective. The waiter was caused to refrain from taking certain courses of action which but for the representation he would have taken. In my view, the respondent during the whole time that he was in the restaurant made and by his continuing conduct continued to make a representation of his intention to pay before leaving. When in place of his original intention he substituted the dishonest intention of running away as soon as the waiter's back was turned, he was continuing to lead the waiter to believe that he intended to pay. He practised a deception on the waiter and by so doing he obtained for himself the pecuniary advantage of evading his obligation to pay before leaving. That he did so dishonestly was found by the magistrates who, in my opinion, rightly convicted him.

I would allow the appeal.

Questions
1.   When did the deception occur – at the time of ordering the meal, during the meal, or when the bill was presented? Does it matter?
2.   Were the defendants in *DPP* v *Ray* guilty of obtaining property by deception? Of what other crimes might they now be convicted? The difficulties encountered in this case provides part of the reason for enactment of s. 3 of the Theft Act 1978 (making off without payment)?

The indictment against the defendant must indicate the precise deception alleged. This is often quite difficult. What was the deception which was allegedly practised by each of the defendants in the following cases?

R v Doukas
[1978] 1 All ER 1061
Court of Appeal

The applicant was employed as a casual wine waiter at a hotel. He was discovered on the hotel premises with six bottles of wine in his coat pockets. He told the police that if a guest in the restaurant ordered a carafe wine he would substitute his own wine, make out a separate bill and keep the money. He was charged with the offence under s. 25(1) of the Theft Act 1968 of going equipped to 'cheat', which, by ss. 25(5) and 15 of the 1968 Act, meant obtaining property by deception. He was convicted and applied for leave to appeal on the ground, *inter alia*, that the prosecution evidence did not prove the necessary causal connection between the intended deception and the obtaining of money from the customer.

Held: It had to be assumed that the hypothetical customer against whom the intended deception was to be practised was reasonably honest as well as being reasonably intelligent. It could not be supposed that such a customer to whom the true situation had been made clear would have willingly made himself a party to what would obviously have been a fraud by the waiter on his employers. It was therefore open to the jury to find that the obtaining of money from the customer would have been caused by the deception practised on him. The application would therefore be dismissed. . . .

R v King
[1987] 1 All ER 547
Court of Appeal

NEILL LJ: . . . On 5 March 1985 the appellants went to the house of Mrs Mitchell, in New Milton. Mrs Mitchell, who had lived in the house all her life, was a widow of 68 years of age. The appellants told her that they were from Streets, a firm of tree surgeons. She knew of the firm, and in answer to her question one of the appellants claimed to be Mr Street. They told her that a sycamore tree in her garden was likely to cause damage. They purported to carry out a test, with a plastic strip placed against the tree, and one of the appellants then said that the tree was dangerous.

They told her that the roots of the tree were growing into the gas main and could cause thousands of pounds in damage. They told her that it would cost £150 to fell the tree, which Mrs Mitchell agreed to pay. They then looked at other trees and told her that another sycamore was dangerous as well as one of her conifers. In addition they told her that the roots of her bay tree were causing damage to the foundations of the house. Mrs Mitchell asked the appellants about the cost of doing all the work, and they told her that to remove the four trees including the bay tree would cost about £500. When Mrs Mitchell told them that she was going to telephone her brother, one of the appellants informed her that they would do the work for £470 if paid in cash. . . .

. . . [C]ounsel for the appellants argued . . . that if the appellants had received £470 for cutting down the trees they would have been paid by reason of the work they had done, and not by reason of any representation they had made to secure the work . . .
. . .

We have given careful consideration to the argument based on causation or remoteness, and have taken account of the fact that some support for the argument may be provided by the writings of a number of distinguished academic lawyers. Nevertheless, we have come to the conclusion that on the facts of the present case the argument is fallacious.

In our view, the question in each case is: was the deception an operative cause of the obtaining of the property? This question falls to be answered as a question of fact by the jury applying their common sense.

Note

An excessively high charge for work done *may* amount to obtaining money by deception where a situation of mutual trust has arisen over the years. This was suggested by the Court of Appeal in *R v Silverman* [1987] Crim LR 574, where the defendant had charged grossly excessive prices for work done to the property of two elderly sisters.

Where cheque or credit cards are involved the deception will often be presumed to be operative.

Metropolitan Police Commissioner v *Charles*
[1977] AC 177
House of Lords

The defendant was granted an overdraft of £100 by his bank and given a cheque book and a cheque card on which was printed an undertaking by the bank to honour any cheque up to £30 on certain stated conditions. Between December 18 and 31, 1972, he used the card to back 18 cheques for £30 each. On January 2, 1973, four of them were presented for payment so that his account was overdrawn to an amount exceeding £100. On the same day the manager of the bank told him that he should not cash more than one cheque for £30 a day at a bank but gave him no further instructions as to the use of the card. He allowed another book of 25 cheques to be issued to him. That night the defendant used the card to back all 25 cheques for £30 each at a gambling club.

In relation to two of the cheques he was convicted of obtaining a pecuniary advantage by deception contrary to secton 16 of the Theft Act 1962 [sic]. The Court of Appeal (Criminal Division) upheld the conviction.

LORD EDMUND-DAVIES: . . . There remains to be considered the vitally important question of whether it was established that it was as a result of such dishonest deception that the club's staff were induced to give chips for cheques and so, in due course, caused the accused's bank account to become improperly overdrawn. This point exercised the Court of Appeal, though they were not troubled by the fact that, whereas the deception alleged was said to have induced the club servants to accept the cheques, the pecuniary advantage was obtained from and damnified only the bank. In that they were, in my judgment, right, for *R* v *Kovacks* [1941] 1 WLR 370 correctly decided (as, indeed, appellant's counsel accepted) that, in the words of Lawton LJ, at p. 373:

> Section 16(1) does not provide either expressly or by implication that the person deceived must suffer any loss arising from the deception. What does have to be proved is that the accused by deception obtained for himself or another a pecuniary advantage. What there must be is a causal connection between the deception used and the pecuniary advantage obtained.

What had troubled the Court of Appeal, however, was the question of inducement, and this after hearing Mr Tabachnik, learned counsel for the accused, submit that in a cheque card case there is no such implied representation as that conveniently labelled 'Page (2)':

> for the simple reason that the payee is not, in the slightest degree, concerned with the question of the drawer's credit-worthiness. The state of the drawer's account at the bank, the state of the contractual relationship between the bank and the drawer is . . . a matter of complete indifference to the payee of the cheque; it is a matter to which he never needs to apply his mind . . . where the recipient of the cheque has the bank's express undertaking held out in the form of a cheque card to rely on, there is no necessity, in order to give business efficacy to the transaction, that there should be any collateral representation implied on the part of the drawer of the cheque as to the state of his account with the bank or the state of his authority to draw on that account.

Still less is there any basis for an inference that any such representation operates on the mind of the recipient of the cheque as an inducement persuading him to accept it. He relies, . . . and relies exclusively, on the bank's undertaking embodied in the cheque card. (*per* Bridge LJ [1976] 1 WLR 248, 255C–F).

Whether a party was induced to act as he did because of the deception to which he was dishonestly subjected is a question of fact to be decided on the evidence adduced in each case. In the present case the Court of Appeal were apparently led to reject – with some reluctance – the foregoing trenchant submissions on behalf of the accused because in what the court regarded as the virtually indistinguishable case of *R* v *Kovacks* [1974] 1 WLR 370, 373 Lawton LJ had said:

> The railway booking clerk and the pet shop owner had been deceived because the appellant in presenting the cheque card with her cheque had represented that she was entitled to be in possession of it and to use it . . . The next question is: how did she obtain this pecuniary advantage? On the facts the answer is clear, namely, by inducing the railway booking clerk and the pet shop owner to believe that she was entitled to use the cheque card when she was not.

Then is there room for coming to a different conclusion on the similar, though not identical, facts of the present case? In my judgment, it again emerges clearly from the evidence of Mr Cersell that there is not. He accepted that

> with a cheque card, so long as the conditions on the back are met, the bank will honour that card irrespective of the state of the drawer's account or the authority, or lack of it, which he has in drawing on the account,

and that 'All those matters, in fact, once there is a cheque card, are totally irrelevant.' But in this context it has again to be borne in mind that the witness made clear that the accused's cheques were accepted *only* because he produced a cheque card, and he repeatedly stressed that, had he been aware that the accused was using his cheque book and cheque card 'in a way in which he was not allowed or entitled to use [them]' no cheque would have been accepted. The evidence of that witness, taken as a whole, points irresistibly to the conclusions (a) that by this dishonest conduct the accused deceived Mr Cersell in the manner averred in the particulars of the charges and (b) that Mr Cersell was thereby induced to accept the cheques because of his belief that the representations as to both cheque and card were true. These and all other relevant matters were fully and fairly dealt with in the admirable summing up of His Honour Judge Finestein QC, the jury showed by their verdicts that they were fully alive to the nature of the issues involved, and in my judgment there was ample evidence to entitle them to arrive at their 'guilty' verdicts on the two charges with which we are concerned in this appeal. I would therefore dismiss it.

Something finally needs to be said about the point of law of public importance certified as fit to be considered by this House. It was expressed in this way [1976] 1 WLR 248, 259:

> When the holder of a cheque card presents a cheque in accordance with the conditions of the card which is acccepted in exchange for goods, services or cash, does this transaction provide evidence of itself from which it can or should be inferred (a) that the drawer represented that he then had authority, as between himself and the bank, to draw a cheque for that amount, and (b) that the recipient of the cheque was induced by that representation to accept the cheque?

I have to say that (b) is not a point of law at all. It raises a question of pure fact. As such, it is unanswerable in general terms (which is the object of certifying points for consideration by this House), for whether people were induced must depend on all the circumstances and, above all, upon what the recipient of cheques in those circumstances has to say. In the vast majority of cases the recipient will be a witness, and it becomes a question for the jury who have seen and heard him to determine whether inducement has been established.

Questions

If a person presents a cheque guarantee card and writes a cheque within the credit limits indicated on the card, it will be honoured by the bank and the recipient of the cheque will receive the appropriate amount. This is what happened in *MPC* v *Charles*. What, then, was the deception? Who was deceived? Who was the victim of the crime? Who suffered loss? Who committed a crime against whom?

It seems that whether the deception was operative is a matter for the jury to decide. However, it also appears that the jury may infer that the deception was operative where there is little or no evidence to that effect:

R v *Lambie*
[1981] Crim LR 712
House of Lords

The defendant possessed a Barclaycard. She had substantially exceeded her credit limit and been asked to return the card, but at the material time had not done so. She selected some items in a shop and tendered the card. The assistant checked her signature on the voucher against that on the card and ascertained that the total purchase was within the shop's 'floor limit' and that the card was not on the current 'stop list.' She then allowed the defendant to take the goods. The defendant was subsequently charged with, *inter alia*, obtaining a pecuniary advantage by deception, contrary to s. 16(1) of the Theft Act 1968 and was convicted. She appealed against conviction, contending, *inter alia*, that the evidence had not shown that any deception had been operative, and the Court of Appeal (Criminal Division) allowed the appeal. The Crown appealed by leave of the House of Lords.

Held, allowing the appeal, that the representation arising from the presentation of the credit card had nothing to do with the defendant's credit standing at the bank but was a representation of actual authority to make the contract with, in the present case, the shop on the bank's behalf that the bank would honour the voucher on presentation: *Charles* [1977] AC 177. On that view, the existence and terms of the agreement between the bank and the shop were irrelevant, as was the fact that the shop, because of that agreement would look to the bank for payment. As to whether the shop assistant had been induced by the defendant's representation to complete the transaction and allow the defendant's representation to complete the transaction and allow the defendant to take away the goods, had she been asked whether, if she had known that the defendant was acting dishonestly and had no authority from the bank to use the card in that way, she would have completed the transaction, only one answer was possible: 'no.' Although that question had not been put to her at the trial, where, as in the present case, no one could reasonably be expected to remember a particular transaction in detail, and the inference of inducement might well be in all the circumstances quite irresistible, there was no reason in principle why it should not be left to the jury to decide, on the evidence as a whole, whether that inference was in truth irresistible, as it was in the present case . . .

Questions
1.   The shop assistant in *Lambie* was presumably only concerned to see that the shop in which she was employed received payment. The court speculates as to whether the employee would have entered the transaction if she had asked whether the defendant had the authority to use the card and had received a negative answer. But why would any merchant ask such a question? Is not one of the primary purposes of having cheque guarantee cards to obviate the need for such prying enquiries?
2.   Should the law infer that a deception is operative in the absence of positive evidence of the deception acting on the mind of the person allegedly deceived?
3.   Is it appropriate for the criminal law to become involved in matters relating to the misuse of credit cards? Should not credit institutions bear the burden of protecting themselves and collecting their own debts without the assistance of the criminal law? Persons who exceed their overdraft or credit limit are already subjected to financial penalties by the credit institutions – should they be subjected to criminal charges as well?
4.   Do *Lambie* and *MPC* v *Charles* distort the law of causation in order to convict persons of whose conduct the judges personally disapprove?

It follows from the definition of 'deception' used by the court in *Re London and Globe Finance Corporation* [1903] 1 Ch 728, at p. 732 that a human mind must be deceived. Buckley J stated: 'to deceive is, I apprehend, to induce a man to believe that a thing is true which is false . . . To deceive is by falsehood to induce a state of mind.' The implication of Buckley J's statement creates difficulties in our more technological advanced age. Will false information fed into a computer, or a false card inserted into a pay phone constitute a deception? Neither computers nor phone cards were around in 1903 when Buckley J gave his opinion. Is deceiving a machine any less culpable than deceiving a human being?

Note
The deception must not be too remote from the prohibited result:

R v Button
[1900] 2 QB 597
Queen's Bench Division

On the trial of an indictment for attempting to obtain property by false pretences the following facts were proved.
   Entries for two handicaps were sent to the secretary of an athletic meeting, in the name of Sims, containing statements as to the recent performances of Sims, which were very moderate, and in consequence Sims was given long starts. The entries were not written by either Sims or the prisoner. At the meeting the prisoner, who was a good

runner, personated Sims, who was absent, and came in first in both races. After the first race the handicapper asked the prisoner whether he was really Sims, whether the performance given in the entry form was really his, and whether he had never won a race, as stated in the entry. He answered these questions, falsely, in the affirmative.

On a case stated:–

Held: that the attempt to obtain the prizes was not too remote from the pretence, that the case was rightly left to the jury, and the prisoner was properly convicted.

R v *Clucas*
[1949] 2 KB 226
King's Bench Division

On the trial of an indictment for conspiring to obtain, attempting to obtain and obtaining, money by false pretences the following facts were proved:

The appellant and another man, induced bookmakers to bet with them by representing that they were commission agents acting on behalf of a large number of workmen who were placing small bets on various races, whereas in fact they were making bets in considerable sums of money for themselves alone. Payment was made by the bookmaker on the horse winning.

LORD GODDARD CJ: . . . In the opinion of the court it is impossible to say that there was an obtaining of the money by the false pretences which were alleged, because the money was obtained not by reason of the fact that the people falsely pretended that they were somebody else or acting in some capacity which they were not; it was obtained because they backed a winning horse and the bookmaker paid because the horse had won. No doubt the bookmaker might never have opened an account with these men if he had known the true facts, but we must distinguish in this case between one contributing cause and the effective cause which led the bookmaker to pay the money.

The effective cause which led the bookmaker to pay the money was the fact that these men had backed a winning horse.

Questions
In what respect does *Clucas* differ from *Charles* (above)? In light of *Clucas*, if Charles had won his bets, would the criminal case have been sustainable?

A deception that follows the obtaining in point of time cannot have caused the obtaining. Another way of looking at the issue is to say the deception is too remote.

R v *Collis-Smith*
[1971] Crim LR 716
Court of Appeal

C was convicted of obtaining property by deception contrary to s. 15(1) of the Theft Act 1968 in that he obtained petrol by a false oral representation that he was authorised to draw petrol for his private motor-car on the account of his employer. He drove his car to a petrol station and asked for petrol which the attendant put in the tank of his car. The attendant then asked if he were paying for it and he said it was to be booked to his firm as he had the use of the car for business, and it was so booked. C appealed on the ground that the conviction was wrong since no false representation was made until after the petrol had been obtained.

Held, allowing the appeal, it appeared from the wording of s. 15 (1) that if a conviction were to be obtained the order of events must be that there should be a deception which operated on the mind of the person to whom it was directed and that by reason of that deception the obtaining took place.

Question

Was Collis-Smith guilty of theft? Could he have been convicted of obtaining by deception if different deception had been alleged?

B   Deception

Theft Act 1968

15.—(4)   For purposes of this section 'deception' means any deception (whether deliberate or reckless) by words or conduct as to fact or as to law, including a deception as to the present intentions of the person using the deception or any other person.

Note

The statement must actually be false and the falsity of the statement is for the jury to determine.

R v *Mandry and Wooster*
[1973] 3 All ER 996
Court of Appeal

M and W were street traders who worked in partnership. Acting in concert they offered bottles of scent for sale in a street in Romford. M told a crowd of by-standers that they could go down the road to the big stores and buy the scent for two guineas whereas he was offering it to them for £1. He also displayed magazines which contained advertisements offering the scent for sale at 42s a bottle. M and W were charged, *inter alia* with going equipped to cheat, contrary to s. 25 of the Theft Act 1968 (count 1), and attempting to obtain £1 by deception (count 2). Evidence was given for the prosecution by a constable that he had visited four shops in the area and that the scent was not sold at any of them. In cross-examination he was asked if he had visited a well-known London Department store and he replied that he had not. The fact that the advertisement in the magazines were spurious was not denied by the defence. The judge directed the jury that the police could not be expected to visit every shop in London in order to prove that the scent was not being sold for 42s in any shop; on the contrary, the onus was on the defence to prove something that was within their personal knowledge. M and W were convicted and appealed on the ground that the judge had misdirected the jury that the onus was on the accused to prove that the scent was sold in the shops at 42s a bottle.

Held: The onus was on the Crown to prove the falsity of M's statement. The fact that the constable had been unable to find any of the scent in the shops he visited was positive evidence, when taken in conjunction with the evidence of the false magazine advertisement and in the absence of any other evidence, that what M had said was false. Furthermore the constable's negative answer in cross-examination about the department store was not evidence to put in the scales against the positive evidence given by him. Accordingly, the criticism of the direction was unfounded and the appeal would be dismissed.

R v *Banaster*
[1979] RTR 113
Court of Appeal

The appellant, a minicab driver operating from Heathrow airport, was approached there by a young foreign visitor newly arrived for the first time in the United Kingdom, who asked whether the vehicle was a taxi. The appellant replied 'Yes, I am an airport taxi'. Thereupon the visitor entered and gave an address in Ealing where the appellant drove him and told him that the correct fare was £27.50, which he paid. The appellant was charged with obtaining property by deception, contrary to s. 15 of the Theft Act 1968. The jury were directed that they might think that the appellant's reference to an airport taxi and the correct fare implied that 'it was all official', thereby encouraging the visitor to think that the appellant was a man of substance so as to be relied on, and that they had to find both deception and dishonesty if they were to convict.

The appellant was convicted.

On his appeal against conviction on the ground that there was no such thing in fact or law as an 'airport taxi' so that he could not be said to have been guilty of deception within s. 15(4):

LORD WIDGERY CJ: The main submission made by Mr Lyon in respect of this case is that there is no such thing in fact or in law in this country as an 'airport taxi'.

It is just an animal which does not exist. Accordingly, so it is argued, if A represents that his car is an airport taxi, he cannot be responsible for any consequences which might flow because he cannot be said to have told a falsity. If there is not an airport taxi as such in existence at all, then to say you are hired as an airport taxi cannot be a deception, or so I understand the argument to go.

The judge was fully apprised of the difficulties in this case such as they were, and he put it to the jury – indeed he left it all to the jury, which was very sensible of him – that they might think that the reference to 'an airport taxi' and 'the correct fare' implied, in the judge's words, that 'it was all official'. In other words, he left it to the jury to decide whether when those words were spoken they encouraged the complainant to think that the appellant was not a fly-by-night but a man of substance, and as such he could be relied upon.

Appeal dismissed.

Questions
1. Were the potential purchasers in *Mandry and Wooster* deceived? What does one expect from a street vendor? What is it reasonable to expect? If a buyer felt that the price was unreasonable, could she not have checked the seller's claim at the 'big stores'?
2. In *Banaster*, would it be at all relevant that the mini-cab driver charged the customer a reasonable fee?

3.   In the two cases is the criminal law being used to protect victims from deceit, or more established and entrenched economic interests from competitors? Is this an appropriate use of the criminal law?

The defendant must be deliberate or reckless as to the falsity of the statement. See s. 15(4) above.

R v Staines
(1974) 60 Cr App R 160
Court of Appeal

JAMES LJ: . . . Two points are argued before us as a basis upon which the conviction should be quashed. The first point relates to the meaning of deception for the purposes of section 15(1) of the Theft Act 1968 and in particular the construction that has to be placed upon the wording of subsection (4) of that section. Subsection (4) reads as follows: 'For purposes of this section "deception" means any deception (whether deliberate or reckless) by words or conduct as to fact or as to law, including a deception as to the present intentions of the person using the deception or any other person.'

The important words for present purposes are 'any deception (whether deliberate or reckless).' There is no dispute between the appellant and the Crown through their counsel that the word 'reckless' in that subsection should be given the construction of meaning 'without caring,' being something more than carelessness or negligence.

In support of his argument that that is the proper construction to be placed on the statute Mr Forbes has referred us to the old authority in civil law of *Derry* v *Peek* (1889) 14 App Cas 337, and also invited our attention to Professor Smith's current book on the Theft Act and the law of theft in which he deals with that particular statutory provision. This Court accepts the contention put forward that in this section 'reckless' does mean more than being careless, does mean more than being negligent, and does involve an indifference to or disregard of the feature of whether a statement be true or false.

Questions

1.   Would it be possible to apply *Caldwell* recklessness in this context? Can someone be at the same time dishonest and merely careless as to the falsity of the statement?

2.   A builder does work on a house, basing his price on the amount of money he believes the houseowner will be prepared to pay rather than the price of labour and materials. Is the builder guilty of deception? What if the builder is an amateur and he simply mentions the first figure that comes into his head (it is in fact well above the market rate)?

The statement must be by words or conduct (including implied statements). A difficulty here is to determine how positive the behaviour of the defendant must be. It seems that an omission to tell the truth will amount to a deception where that omission gives a manifestly false impression of the true state of affairs.

R v Kylsant
[1932] 1 KB 442
King's Bench Division

By the Larceny Act 1861, s. 84, a director of a body corporate or public company is guilty of a misdemeanour if he makes, circulates or publishes any written statement or account which he shall know to be false in any material particular with intent to induce any person to intrust or advance property to the company.

A prospectus for the issue of debenture stock issued by a company of which the appellant was chairman was composed of statements which in themselves were perfectly true, but it omitted information about the company's affairs, with the result that the prospectus, taken as a whole, gave a false impression of the position of the company. On the trial of the appellant for an offence under s. 84 of the Larceny Act 1861, the judge directed the jury that a written statement might be false within the meaning of the section not only because of what it stated, but also because of what it concealed, or omitted, or implied:—

Held: that this was a correct statement of the effect of the section, and that the appellant was rightly convicted of an offence under it.

Director of Public Prosecutions v Ray
[1974] AC 370
House of Lords

LORD MORRIS OF BORTH-Y-GEST: . . . By ordering his meal and by his conduct in assuming the role of an ordinary customer the respondent had previously shown that it was his intention to pay. By continuing in the same role and behaving just as before he was representing that this previous intention continued. That was a deception because his intention, unknown to the waiter, had become quite otherwise. The dishonest change of intention was not likely to produce the result that the waiter would be told of it. The essence of the deception was that the waiter should not know of it or be given any sort of clue that it (the change of intention) had come about. Had the waiter suspected that by a change of intention a secret exodus was being planned, it is obvious that he would have taken action to prevent its being achieved.

It was said in the Divisional Court that a deception under section 16 should not be found unless an accused has actively made a representation by words or conduct which representation is found to be false. But if there was an original representation (as, in my view, there was when the meal was ordered) it was a representation that was intended to be and was a continuing representation. It continued to operate on the mind of the waiter. It became false and it became a deliberate deception. The prosecution do not say that the deception consisted in not informing the waiter of the change of mind; they say that the deception consisted in continuing to represent to the waiter that there was an intention to pay before leaving.

R v Firth
[1990] Crim LR 326
Court of Appeal

The appellant, a consultant obstetrician/gynaecologist, was head of an NHS department and also ran a private practice from home. At all stages of pregnancy, ante-natal, confinement and post-natal, treatment could be either free under the NHS or paid for privately. Payment for cytological tests at the ante-natal stage would be paid for by the health authority in the case of NHS patients, but by the patient herself in the case of private patients. However, the consultant could agree with the Authority, and did so here, that he would pay for the tests and recoup the expenses from his private patients. For accommodation during confinement, private patients had to pay the hospital direct, not via the consultant. The appellant was accused of abusing the system either for his own or his private patients' benefit. Counts 4 and 5 related to the ante-natal period and alleged evasion of liability by deception by false representations that named patients were being treated by him on the NHS and that no charge should be raised for cytology tests done by the Pathology Department thus dishonestly obtaining from the Authority exemption from liability to pay for the tests. Counts 6 and 7 related to the confinement stage, alleging false representations that named patients were being treated on the NHS rather than privately, thus dishonestly obtaining exemption from liability to pay for the in-patient treatment which they had received. The Crown alleged that by failing dishonestly to inform the hospital of the private-patient status of the women he had caused either himself or them not be billed for services which should have been charged. The appellant had admitted that the women in counts 6 and 7 had been admitted as NHS patients but said that it was part of his 'package deal' which involved private ante-natal care, free confinement and private post-natal treatment. The Crown suggested that that was an elaborate scheme to enable him to have his private patients hospitalised for delivery without paying for the privilege of the bed. The defences to counts 4 and 5 included a claim that there was no need for him to indicate which requests related to private patients because most of his patients were private so the hospital should have billed him for them all; the recipients of the requests for tests should have known which were private because of the days on which the requests were delivered; there was an agreement between the appellant and the health authority whereby he would pay a lump sum for tests obviating a need for him to indicate which tests related to private patients and which to NHS.

Section 2(1) of the Theft Act 1978 provides:

Subject to subsection (2) below, where a person by any deception – (a) dishonestly secures the remission of . . . any existing liability . . . (b) with intent to make permanent default . . . on any existing liability to make a payment . . . or (c) dishonestly obtains any exemption from or abatement of liability to make a payment; he shall be guilty of an offence. (2) . . . 'liability' means legally enforceable liability; and subsection (1) shall not apply in relation to a liability that has not been accepted or established to pay compensation for a wrongful act or omission . . . (4) . . . 'obtains' includes obtaining for another or enabling another to obtain.

Following conviction, he appealed on the grounds, *inter alia*, that the Recorder had erred in not acceding to the submission that counts 4–7 were wrongly laid because s. 2(1)(c) required proof that the dishonest obtaining was achieved by acts of commission, whereas the evidence showed only acts of omission. Further, the words 'legally enforceable' in subsection (2) meant that the prosecution had to establish an existing liability at the time of the alleged deception. If the appellant had requested the performance of a service, his liability would only arise when that service had been performed. Consequently, liability must first be established before consideration of whether a deception had been practised. If the deception was practised before the liability to pay had come into existence, no offence was committed.

Held, dismissing the appeal, if, as was alleged, it was incumbent upon the appellant to give the relevant information to the hospital, and if he deliberately and dishonestly refrained from so doing, with the result that no charge was levied either upon himself or his patients, the section was satisfied. It mattered not whether it was an act of commission or omission. As to the time of liability, the submission overlooked not only the wording of s. 2(1)(c) but also of paragraphs (a) and (b) which contained the words 'existing liability.' It was noteworthy that the word 'existing' was omitted from paragraph (c) which was indicative of what the Parliamentary draftsman meant.

Appellate counsel's submission might have had something to commend it if 'existing' had been present in s. 2(1)(c) but the omission seemed to have been purposeful rather than by chance. The words as they stood were apt to cover an expected or future liability, even if the alleged deception was not in truth a continuing one.

Questions
In what way is *Firth* distinguishable from *DPP* v *Ray* and *Kylsant*? What was the deception practised by each defendant? To what extent should the law impose a positive duty to tell the truth?

Note
In all the above cases a failure to reveal the whole truth was held to amount to a deception. That was the case in *Kylsant*, even though the statements made were literally true. It was confirmed in *R* v *King* [1979] Crim LR 122, that literally true statements could amount to deception.

Another difficulty is to determine precisely what representations are being made when they are being made by conduct alone. In *DPP* v *Ray* (above), Lord Morris of Borth-y-Gest discussed the representations made by a person who orders a meal in a restaurant. The following cases give other examples of representations the defendant is said to make when he pursues a particular course of conduct:

Metropolitan Police Commissioner v *Charles*
[1977] AC 177
House of Lords

For facts, see p. 523.

LORD EDMUND-DAVIES: . . . What representation, if any, did the accused make when he cashed each of those cheques? It was against the background of his knowledge of his limited overdraft facilities that he drew each for £30 in favour of Mr Cersell, the club manager, and on each occasion produced his cheque card so that its number could be endorsed on the back of each cheque. The essence of the defence consists in Mr Comyn's submissions that by such conduct the only representation made was that 'This cheque, backed by the card, will be honoured without question'; that such representation was true; that there was accordingly no deception of the club staff; and that therefore no offence was committed even though as a result of the accused's account became overdrawn substantially beyond the permitted limit in consequence of his bank doing precisely what he had represented they would do on presentation of each of the cheques.

Both in the Court of Appeal and before your Lordships there was considerable discussion as to what representation is to be implied by the simple act of drawing a cheque. Reference was made to *R* v *Page (Note)* [1971] 2 QB 330, where the Court of Appeal (Criminal Division) adopted with apparent approval the following passage which (citing *R* v *Hazelton* (1874) LR 2 CCR 134 in support) has appeared in *Kenny, Outlines of Criminal Law* ever since the 1st edition appeared in 1902, see pp. 246–247:

Similarly the familiar act of drawing a cheque – a document which on the face of it is only a command of a future act – is held to imply at least three statements about the present: (1) That the drawer has an account with that bank; (2) That he has authority to draw on it for that amount; (3) that the cheque, as drawn, is a valid order for the payment of that amount (i.e. that the present state of affairs is such that, in the ordinary course of events, the cheque will on its future presentment be duly honoured). It may be well to point out, however, that it does not imply any representation that the drawer now has money in this bank to the amount drawn for; inasmuch as he may well have authority to overdraw, or may intend to pay in (before the cheque can be presented) sufficient money to meet it.

My noble and learned friend, Lord Fraser of Tullybelton, rightly pointed out that representations (1) and (2) were supererogatory in the light of representation (3), which embraced both of them. My noble and learned friend, Lord Diplock, also criticised representation (2) on the ground that the representation made by the simple act of drawing a cheque does not relate to or rest upon 'authority' but is rather a representation that the drawer has contracted with his bank to honour his cheques. Notwithstanding the antiquity of the quoted passage, it acccordingly appears right to restrict the representation made by the act of drawing and handing over a cheque to that which has been conveniently labelled 'Page (3).' The legal position created by such an act was even more laconically described by Pollock B in *R* v *Hazelton*, LR 2 CCR 134, 140 in this way:

> I think the real representation made is that the cheque will be paid. It may be said that that is a representation as to a future event. But that is not really so. It means that the existing state of facts is such that in ordinary course the cheque will be met.

With understandable enthusiasm, Mr Comyn submitted that this was correct and that such representation was manifestly true when made, as was demonstrated by the later honouring of all the accused's cheques. But it has to be remembered that we are presently concerned to inquire what was the *totality* of the representations; with whether they were true or false to the accused's knowledge; whether they deceived; and whether they induced the party to whom they were addressed to act in such a manner as led to the accused obtaining 'increased borrowing by way of overdraft.' What of the production and use of the cheque card when each of the 25 cheques in the new cheque book was drawn on the night of January 2–3, 1973? Is Mr Comyn right in submitting that the only representation made by its productionn was the perfectly correct one that, 'This cheque, backed by this card, will be honoured without question?' In my judgment, he is not. The accused knew perfectly well that he would not be able to get more chips at the club simply by drawing a cheque. The cheque alone would not have been accepted; it had to be backed by a cheque card. The card played a vital part, for (as my noble and learned friend, Lord Diplock, put it during counsel's submission) in order to make the bank liable to the payee there must be knowledge on the payee's part that the drawer has the bank's authority to bind it, for in the absence of such knowledge the all-important contract between payee and bank is not created; and it is the representation by the drawer's production of the card that he has that authority that creates such contractual relationship and estops the bank from refusing to honour the cheque. By drawing the cheque the accused represented that it would be met, and by producing the card so that the number thereon could be endorsed on the cheque he in effect represented, 'I am authorised by the bank to show this to you and so create a direct contractual relationship between the bank and you that they will honour this cheque.'

R v *Gilmartin*
[1983] Crim LR 330
Court of Appeal

The defendant was charged with three counts of obtaining property by deception and one count of obtaining a pecuniary advantage by deception, contrary to ss. 15 and 16 of the Theft Act 1968, after using post-dated cheques to pay for goods, which were dishonoured upon presentation. He maintained at the trial that the cheques were not intended to be presented, but that the three cheques, the subject-matter of the first three counts, would be bought back for cash and that the cheque the subject-matter of the pecuniary advantage count would be handed over for bookkeeping purposes. He was convicted on all four counts and appealed on the ground that a drawer of a post-dated cheque impliedly represented no more than the fact that he was a customer of the bank on which the cheque was drawn, and since he did have such an account, there was no case for him to answer.

Held, dismissing the appeal, that following the decision of the House of Lords in *Commissioner of Police for the Metropolis* v *Charles* [1977] AC 177, the often quoted passage in *Kenny's Outlines of Criminal Law* as to the relevant representation implied by the giving of a cheque could no longer be regarded as accurate. Of the three elements in the definition, the second element, that the drawer had authority to draw on his account for the amount specified on the cheque, had to be rejected and the first element was logically covered by the third. The third element had been expressed by Kenny in two different ways; a statement that the cheque as drawn was a valid order for the payment of the amount of the cheque and a statement that the present state of affairs was such that in the ordinary course of events the cheque would on its future presentment be duly honoured. Alhough [sic] the first statement could be read as referring to the future, it was only relevant to have regard to a representation as to existing facts. The second statement should properly be regarded as an authoritative statement of the law. Was the position any different in the case of a post-dated cheque? *Maytum-White* (1958) 42 Cr App R 165 provided no authority for the proposition in *Archbold* that the only representation about the present that could properly be said to be implied in the drawing of a post-dated cheque was that the drawer was a customer of the bank concerned. The court could see no reason why in the case of a post-dated cheque the drawer did not impliedly represent that the existing facts at the date when he gave the cheque to the payee were such that in the ordinary course of events the cheque would on presentation be met on or after the date specified in the cheque. In a case like the present, when a post-dated cheque was issued when the account was heavily overdrawn and there was, as the drawer well knew, no prospect of future funds being paid in or of the bank providing other overdraft facilities, the drawer was as much guilty of deception as he would have been in the case of a cheque not post-dated. Indeed, where a drawer gave a cheque which was not post-dated, his account may have been overdrawn but he may have had in his pocket another cheque payable to him which he intended to pay into his account immediately and which would allow the cheque he had drawn to be paid on presentation; if so it was difficult to see that he had made any representation. Accordingly there was no relevant distinction between the case of a cheque which had not been post-dated and one which had.

Question
Does not a post-dated cheque imply the present lack of funds in the bank to cover the cheque? Should not this fact put one who is about to accept a post dated cheque on notice of the danger involved therein; and, if so, can he said to be deceived?

R v Williams
[1980] Crim LR 589
Court of Appeal

The appellant, a school boy aged 17, who bought some Jugoslavian dinar banknotes, which he knew were obsolete, at Stanley Gibbons, took them to the bureau de change at a department store and said to a cashier either 'Will you change these notes?' or 'Can I cash these in?' For notes totalling 1,100 dinars, which cost him £1.80 he received £27.39 and, two days later, for notes whih cost him £5.20 he received £79.20. He went again the following day and was detained and seen by the police. He agreed that he knew the notes were obsolete and said that he thought to exchange them 'for a laugh' and then could not resist trying it again because it was 'so easy'. He was arraigned on four pairs of counts charging obtaining property by deception and, alternatively, theft. At the close of evidence for the prosecution the appellant, who admitted dishonesty, submitted that he had made no representation and the recorder ruled that there was no evidence on which a jury could safely find that the appellant had made any of the false representations alleged against him in the indictment. However, he ruled that there was a case to answer on theft. Thereupon the appellant pleaded guilty to two counts of theft and was conditionally discharged for two years and ordered to pay compensation of £107.09 – see [1979] Crim LR 736. He appealed against conviction contending that there was no evidencce of guilt of theft since there had been no appropriation of money belonging to another, for the cashiers had handed over the money voluntarily and, at that moment, it was the property not of the store but the appellant.

Held, dismissing the appeal, that when a person went to the foreign exchange counter of such a concern, as opposed to the numismatic or curio counter, and proffered a banknote for exchange using words such as those used by the appellant, it was open to a jury to find that he was representing the notes to be genuine and valid as currency in the country of origin. The principle was, perhaps, slightly distinguishable from that laid down in *Charles* [1976] 1 WLR 248. The person proffering the note was, in effect, saying to the cashier 'This is currency. I believe it to be valid currency in Jugoslavia. Will you please exchange it on that basis into English money.' Dishonestly being admitted, an offence under section 15 of the Theft Act 1968 had been made out.

Question
In deciding on whether a deception has occurred, do the courts take into account the characteristics of the victim? Should they? For example, should it matter in *Williams* that the victim was a bureau de change as opposed to a kindly neighbour who knows nothing about currency exchanges?

C   Dishonesty

Is there (should there be) a distinction between dishonesty in theft cases and dishonesty in deception cases, or should the rule in *Ghosh* (see Chapter 11) apply in both?

R v Woolven
[1983] Crim LR 632
Court of Appeal

The appellant was tried on a charge of attempting to obtain property by deception. He had opened a bank account in a false name and knew that money would be transferred to it from an account belonging to his former employer, who gave evidence for the prosecution; the appellant understood that the employer could not withdraw the money in the ordinary way because, if he did so, the bank would claim it to discharge or reduce his overdraft. The appellant had a letter, false to his knowledge, purporting to establish his identity in the false name in order to induce the bank, which had refused to pay without evidence of identity, [to cash] a cheque for £16,200. He conceded that ordinary people would, on his own version, have found his behaviour to be dishonest but maintained that he at the time had not thought it to be dishonest since he thought that the money belonged to the employer. The jury were directed in accordance with *Ghosh* [1982] QB 1053 and the issue of dishonesty was left to them. The appellant was convicted. He appealed on the ground that, while s. 1(3) of the Theft Act 1968 prevented the application to section 15 of the 'claim of right' defence under s. 2(1)(a), nevertheless its effect was to be read into the definition of obtaining by deception, so that the direction should have been to the effect that the jury should acquit if they concluded that the appellant might have attempted to obtain money from the bank in the belief that he had in law the right to deprive them of it on behalf of the employer, whom the appellant understood to be its owner.

Held, dismissing the appeal, that *Williams* (1836) 7 C & P 354; *Hamilton* (1845) 1 Cox 244; *Parker* (1910) 74 JP 208 and *Bernhard* [1938] 2 KB 264 constituted no decisive authority against the appellant's argument. The question arising for decision was whether the direction as to the element of dishonesty was adequate to do justice in the instant case. Any direction based on the concept of claim of right as set out in s. 2(1)(a), or otherwise, would have added nothing to what the judge had said. A direction based on *Ghosh* seemed likely to cover all occasions when a s. 2(1)(a) type direction might otherwise have been desirable. The direction was to be contrasted with that in *Falconer-Atlee* (1973) 58 Cr App R 349. In the present case the jury inevitably disbelieved the appellant's proposition that he had not thought his behaviour dishonest at the time, even if they believed his account otherwise. The conviction was not unsafe or unsatisfactory.

II Deception offences

A Obtaining property by deception

Theft Act 1968

15.—(1) A person who by any deception dishonestly obtains property belonging to another, with the intention of permanently depriving the other of it, shall on conviction on indictment be liable to imprisonment for a term not exceeding ten years.

(2) For purposes of this section a person is to be treated as obtaining property if he obtains ownership, possession or control of it, and 'obtain' includes obtaining for another or enabling another to obtain or retain.

(3) Section 6 above shall apply for the purposes of this section, with the necessary adaptation of the reference to appropriating, as it applies for purposes of section 1.

(4) For purposes of this section 'deception' means any deception (whether deliberate or reckless) by words or conduct as to fact or as to law, including a deception as to the present intentions of the person using the deception or any other person.

(i) Actus reus
The following is a summary of the elements of the *actus reus* of this offence. Detailed consideration of the definition of those elements is to be found in the preceding section of this chapter.

(a)   Obtaining. There must be a causal link between the deception and the obtaining (see above, p. 518 et seq.).

(b)   Property. The defendant must obtain property – as defined in s. 4(1) (above, pp. 484–7). The limitations in s. 4(2) (land, etc.) do not apply.

(c)   Belonging to another. Section 5(1) applies (see above, p. 487 et seq.). Property belongs to anyone having ownership, possession, control or a proprietary right in it.

(d)   Deception. There must be a false representation which has an effect on someone and which causes the obtaining.

(ii)   Mens rea
This consists of four elements:

(a)   dishonesty (see above, p. 504);

(b)   intention permanently to deprive (s. 6 applies, see above, p. 507);

(c)   deliberation or recklessness in making the deception (see above, p. 530);

(d)   an intention to obtain property (s. 15(1)).

B   Obtaining a pecuniary advantage

The Theft Act 1968, s. 16(2)(a) *has been repealed.* The only situations in which a s. 16 offence can be committed are set out below:

Theft Act 1968

16.—(1)   A person who by any deception dishonestly obtains for himself or another any pecuniary advantage shall on conviction on indictment be liable to imprisonment for a term not exceeding five years.

(2)   The cases in which a pecuniary advantage within the meaning of this section is to be regarded as obtained for a person are cases where—

(a)   [Repealed].

(b)   he is allowed to borrow by way of overdraft, or to take out any policy of insurance or annuity contract, or obtains an improvement of the terms on which he is allowed to do so; or

(c)   he is given the opportunity to earn remuneration or greater remuneration in an office or employment, or to win money by betting.

(3)   For purposes of this section 'deception' has the same meaning as in section 15 of this Act.

Note
The general principles of deception offences apply to s. 16 as they do to s. 15. These matters are discussed in detail in the preceding section of this chapter. Particular points to note about s. 16 are:

(a)   Only one offence is created by the section although an indictment should specify the exact allegation against the defendant (*Bale* v *Rosier* [1977] 2 All ER 160).

(b)   A person is 'allowed' to borrow by way of overdraft despite the fact that the bank has expressly forbidden him to do so (*MPC* v *Charles* above, pp. 523–33).

(c)   Under s. 16(2)(b), it appears to be irrelevant that the 'contract' of insurance is invalid (*Alexander (John)* [1981] Crim LR 182).

(d)   The pecuniary advantage may be obtained 'for himself or another'.

C   *Procuring the execution of a valuable security*

Theft Act 1968

20.—(2)   A person who dishonestly, with a view to gain for himself or another or with intent to cause loss to another, by any deception procures the execution of a valuable security shall on conviction on indictment be liable to imprisonment for a term not exceeding seven years; and this subsection shall apply in relation to the making, acceptance, indorsement, alteration, cancellation or destruction in whole or in part of a valuable security, and in relation to the signing or sealing of any paper or other material in order that it may be made or converted into, or used or dealt with as, a valuable security, as if that were the execution of a valuable security.

(3)   For purposes of this section 'deception' has the same meaning as in section 15 of this Act, and 'valuable security' means any document creating, transferring, surrendering or releasing any right to, in or over property, or authorising the payment of money or delivery of any property, or evidencing the creation, transfer, surrender or release of any such right, or the payment of money or delivery of any property, or the satisfaction of any obligation.

Note
For the general principles relevant to the construction of this section, see the previous section of this chapter. The use of the phrase 'by any deception procures' instead of the more familiar 'by any deception . . . obtains' (found in ss. 15 and 16) makes no difference to the necessity to prove a causal connection between the deception and the bringing about of the *actus reus* of the offence.

D   *Obtaining services*

Theft Act 1978

1.—(1)   A person who by any deception dishonestly obtains services from another shall be guilty of an offence.

(2)   It is an obtaining of services where the other is induced to confer a benefit by doing some act, or causing or permitting some act to be done, on the understanding that the benefit has been or will be paid for.

Note
This section raises four issues apart from those general to all deception offences which are discussed in the preceding section. The particular issues are:

(a) The deception must *induce* the 'other' to confer the benefit. There must be a direct link between the deception and the act which causes the defendant or 'another' to receive the benefit. A secret entry to, e.g., a football stadium would not be an offence under this section as no one would have been deceived.

(b) There must be an understanding that the benefit has been or will be paid for. This has the curious result that the better the 'hard luck story' the less likely the defendant is to have committed an offence under this section. If he can persuade his victim to provide the service free he will not be liable to conviction under s. 1. However, if this proviso were not there the section would be very wide indeed and could cover favours done by members of a family or by relatives unless those requesting the favours were meticulously precise in their requests for help.

(c) Services must be obtained. By s. 1(2) an omission is not sufficient. What constitutes services, however, was rendered somewhat uncertain after the surprising decision that a mortgage advance is not a service:

R v *Halai*
[1983] Crim LR 624
Court of Appeal

At a time when he had £28 in his bank account H applied for a mortgage through C, the agent of a building society. He said that he had held his current job for 18 months when in fact he had held it for two months. He drew a post-dated cheque for £40 to pay for a survey by the society and opened a savings account with a post-dated cheque for £500. He was issued with a passbook showing a credit of £500 and went to a branch of the society where he dealt with R. He handed over a cheque for £250 and his account was credited with that sum. At the same time he withdrew £100 from the account, saying that the £500 had been paid in cash (it was a society rule that withdrawals could not be made against cheque credits until seven days had elapsed). All three cheques were dishonoured, as he knew they would be. He was convicted on four counts contrary to section 1 of the Theft Act 1978 and one count contrary to section 15 of the Theft Act 1968 as follows: (1) obtaining from C a service, the preparation of a surveyor's report and valuation, by representing that the cheque was good and would be honoured; (2) obtaining from C a service, the opening of a savings account, by a like representation; (3) attempting to obtain from the society a service, a mortgage advance, by representing that he had been employed for 18 months; (4) obtaining from R a service, the increase of the apparent credit balance on a savings account, by representing that the cheque was good and would be honoured; (5) obtaining from R £100 by representing that the savings account had been credited with and contained £500.

Held: count 1 (on which it was submitted that H received no benefit since the survey was for the purposes of the society, and it was not a service provided by C even as agent for the society) was made out. There was a false representation, it being immaterial that the cheque was post-dated, there was a benefit from the survey to H because it was an essential step in obtaining a mortgage and C, as agent for the society, caused it to be prepared. Counts 2, 3 and 4 were bad because no service was obtained. No benefit was conferred by a building society, or a bank, on a customer when he paid money into an account. Nor was any payment made, or expected, for making entries in the passbook or the associated office work. A mortgage advance was not a service: it was the lending of money for property. Count 5 was properly laid. He represented that the account contained £500 when he said that £500 in cash had been paid in. In fact it contained nothing despite what appeared in the passbook.

Questions
Do people open bank accounts for their own benefit or for the benefit of the bank? How is the service paid for? Is a mortgage advance a benefit which will be paid for?

Note
Halai was distinguished in *Widdowson* (1985) 82 Crim App R 314.

(d)   There must be a benefit conferred. Where the alleged 'benefit' is itself a criminal offence it is unlikely to be regarded as a benefit under s. 1 if either:

(i)   the object of the statute making the 'benefit' illegal is to protect persons in the category to which the defendant charged with the offence belongs; or
(ii)   it is an act (such as grievous bodily harm) to which the victim may not give a consent effective to prevent a criminal offence being committed.

The position with regard to acts which are immoral but not illegal (such as sexual intercourse in the course of prostitution) is more debatable.

E   *Offences under the Theft Act 1978, s. 2*

Theft Act 1978

2.—(1)   Subject to subsection (2) below, where a person by any deception —
(a)   dishonestly secures the remission of the whole or part of any existing liability to make a payment, whether his own liability or another's; or
(b)   with intent to make permanent default in whole or in part on any existing liability to make a payment, or with intent to let another do so, dishonestly induces the creditor or any person claiming payment on behalf of the creditor to wait for payment (whether or not the due date for payment is deferred) or to forgo payment; or
(c)   dishonestly obtains any exemption from or abatement of liability to make a payment;
he shall be guilty of an offence.
(2)   For purposes of this section 'liability' means legally enforceable liability; and subsection (1) shall not apply in relation to a liability that has not been acccepted or established to pay compensation for a wrongful act or omission.
(3)   For purposes of subsection (1)(b) a person induced to take in payment a cheque for other security for money by way of conditional satisfaction of a pre-existing liability is to be treated not as being paid but as being induced to wait for payment.
(4)   For purposes of subsection (1)(c) 'obtains' includes obtaining for another or enabling another to obtain.

Note
The major problem of interpretation raised by s. 2 is to determine the degree of overlap between the three subsections. This can most conveniently be dealt

with by examining the possible scope of each subsection. It should first be noted that, as with the other deception offences, the prohibited result must be obtained by reason of the operation of the defendant's deception:

R v *Andrews and Hedges*
[1981] Crim LR 106
Central Criminal Court

Defendants were charged with inducing creditors to wait for payment by deception contrary to s. 2(1)(b) of the Theft Act 1978. The creditors had in the course of dealing supplied large quantities of meat to the defendants on credit terms of up to three weeks for which payments were duly made by cheques which were met. The dishonesty relied upon by the prosecution was that thereafter having obtained meat from suppliers in a later period the defendants issued cheques unsupported by funds in their bank account which were not met on presentation, and induced the creditors to wait for payment. The deception relied on in each case was the false representation that the cheque in question was a good and valid order and that in the ordinary course, the cheque would be met.

Held: there was no inducement to wait for payment where the parties had traded together previously and where credit terms had been allowed and where payment by cheque was accepted in the ordinary course of dealing between the parties; for s. 2 (1)(b) only applied where a creditor is induced to accept a cheque instead of cash, and only then did s. 2(3) operate as a matter of law to treat the creditor as having been induced to wait for payment. There was no evidence that the creditors had asked for cash and no evidence that they had been induced to accept cheques or to wait for payment. Accordingly, there was no case to answer.

Note
The deception may be by omission; see *Firth* (above, p. 531).

(i)   Securing the remission of a liability
This requires the remission of an existing liability. As with the other subsections, s. 2(1)(a) may be widely construed, in which case it overlaps very substantially with the rest of s. 2, or 'remission' may be held to mean that the creditor must actually alter the legal liability in question, i.e., after the operation of the deception the debtor's liability would actually be less. One problem with this interpretation is that it would be very narrow. This is because a mere agreement by a creditor to accept less money in full satisfaction of a debt is not binding in the absence of new consideration. The Criminal Law Revision Committee thought that the section would have a wider sphere of operation than that narrow interpretation. In their 13th Report (para. 13, Cmnd 6733) they gave the following example of the way in which they expected s. 2 to operate:

An example would be where a man borrows £100 from a neighbour and when repayment is due, tells a false story of some family tragedy which makes it impossible for him to find the money; this deception persuades the neighbours to tell him that he need never repay.

Note
The neighbour would not be legally bound by his agreement to forget the debt.

(ii) Inducing a creditor to wait for or to forgo payment
Section 2(1)(b) is the only one of the three constituent subsections of s. 2 to require an intent to make permanent default. It may be that this supports the narrow construction of 'remission' which is suggested above. If remission requires that the debtor's legal liablity is altered it would be superfluous to add to s. 2(1)(a) a requirement that there must be an intent to make permanent default; the debtor's liability has in any event been permanently altered by the remission.

It seems likely that s. 2(1)(b) is, of the three, the subsection most likely to be contravened. It will cover all situations where the deception is directed at inducing the creditor not to demand what is legally due to him at the due date. This type of deception may well be more common than deceptions aimed at reducing the legal liability of the debtor. If s. 2(1)(a) does not require the alteration of the debtor's liability the two subsections almost wholly overlap. The existing case law on the subject is not very illuminating:

R v *Holt and Lee*
[1981] Crim LR 499
Court of Appeal

The appellants ate meals costing £3.65 in a restaurant. An off-duty police officer overheard them planning to evade payment by pretending that a wiatress had removed a £5 note which had been placed on the table. When presented with their bill they advanced this deception and declined payment. They were arrested and charged with attempting to evade liability by deception. They were convicted and appealed on the ground, *inter alia* that on the facts the offence should have been charged under s. 2 (1)(a) of the Theft Act 1978 as an attempt to secure the remission of the debt instead of under s. 2(1)(b) as an attempt to induce the forgoing of payment with intent to make permanent default.

Held, dismissing the appeals, that the differences betwen paragraphs (a), (b) and (c) of s. 2(1) of the Theft Act 1978 related principally to the different situations in which the debtor-creditor relationship had arisen. Although there were substantial differences in the elements of the offences there defined they showed common features: (i) the use of deception to a creditor in relation to a liability; (ii) dishonesty in the use of deception; (iii) the use of deception to gain some advantage in time or money. The element unique to s. 2(1)(b) was the intention to make permanent default on the whole or part of an existing liability. The jury concluded that the appellants' conduct was motivated by the intent to make permanent default on their supper bill. The appellants were rightly convicted as charged.

R v *Jackson*
[1983] Crim LR 617
Court of Appeal

A stolen Access credit card was presented by occupants of the appellant's car at petrol stations and accepted in satisfaction of payment for petrol and other goods. The appellant was charged, *inter alia* with handling stolen goods (count 3) and evading liability by deception by dishonestly securing the remission of an existing liability, contrary to s. 2(1)(a) of the Theft Act 1978 (counts 5 and 8). At the close of the prosecution evidence the defence submitted that counts 5 and 8 should have been charged under s. 2(1)(b), and should be withdrawn from the jury. The trial judge ruled that the case should proceed as charged. The appellant was convicted and appealed on the ground, *inter alia*, that the judge had failed properly to rule on the defence submission.

Held, dismissing the appeal, that although in *Holt* [1981] 1 WLR 1000 it was held that the element under s. 2(1)(b) of an intent to make permanent default on the whole or part of an existing liability was unique to sub-paragraph (b), that judgment was not authority for the proposition that the elements in sub-paragraphs (a), (b) and (c) of s. 2(1) were mutually exclusive. The transaction of tendering a stolen credit card and having it accepted by a trader who forthwith would look to the authority issuing the card for payment and not to the person tendering the card, meant that that person had dishonestly secured the remission of an existing liability. It was not necessary to consider whether a charge in respect of that transaction could be brought under s. 2(1)(b). In the circumstances the matter was not wrongly charged under s. 2(1)(a).

(iii)   Obtaining an exemption from or abatement of liability
Section 2(1)(c) is the only one of the three subsections not requiring proof of an existing legal liability. It is suggested that this section should only cover the situation where the deception is directed at making the victim believe that no or less money is due from a potential or an actual debtor. If the following case is correctly decided the subsection has a wider reach:

R v *Sibartie*
[1983] Crim LR 470
Court of Appeal

The appellant, a law student who lived in Acton and attended college in Hendon, bought two season tickets on the Underground, one ticket covering the beginning of his journey on one line for two stations and the other ticket covering the end of his journey on another line for two stations; in between were 14 change stations including an interchange station between the two lines. At the interchange station, on passing a ticket inspector, the appellant held aloft a wallet containing the season ticket – according to the inspector, 'flashing it' so that she could not see what was on it – and on being challenged said that he was going to the first of the two stations at the end of his journey. The appellant's version was that he was going out at the interchange station and was intending to pay. He was charged on counts 1 and 2 with evasion of a liability by deception, contrary to s. 2(1)(c) of the Theft Act 1978 and on count 3 of an attempted evasion of a liability by deception. The jury acquitted him on counts 1 and 2 but convicted on count 3. He appealed against conviction.

Held, dismissing the appeal, that the correct method of approach was to ask whether, taking the words of s. 2(1)(c) in their ordinary meaning, one would say that what the appellant was attempting to do fell within the ambit of the words. The jury by their verdict must have been satisfied that the appellant dishonestly used his season tickets, which did not in fact cover the journey he was making, in an attempt to persuade the ticket inspector that they did cover the journey. Did that amount to an attempt to obtain exemption from liability to make a payment for the journey he was making or had made? He was saying, albeit tacitly, by waving the supposed season ticket in the air that he was the holder of a ticket authorising him to be making the journey without further payment and consequently he was not under any liability to pay any more. In the ordinary meaning of words that was dishonestly obtaining an exemption from the liability to pay the excess which, had he been honest, he would have had to pay. There might be a degree of overlap between s. 2(1)(a), (b) and (c), and the fact that what the appellant did might also have been an attempt to commit an offence under s. 2(1)(b) was neither here nor there.

Notes and questions
1.   Was a more appropriate charge to cover the behaviour of the defendant in *Sibartie* one of attempt to commit any of the offences in s. 2? Theft?
2.   Section 2(1)(c) does clearly include (but is not confined to) the situation where a contract is *made* at a better rate than it would otherwise have been. An example (not covered by the other two subsections) would occur where the defendant pretends to be an old age pensioner in order to get cheap or free entry into a museum.
3.   It should be noted that offences under all three subsections can be committed in respect of the defendant's liability or the liability of another.
4.   When s. 16(2)(a) was repealed, should it have been replaced at all? Is the criminal law too much invoked in matters which should be settled in civil court?

13 FURTHER OFFENCES AGAINST PROPERTY

I Making off without payment

Section 3 of the Theft Act 1978 was designed to fill a gap in the law of theft which was created when s. 16(2)(a) of the 1968 Act was repealed. It proscribes making off without payment.

Theft Act 1978

3.—(1) Subject to subsection (3) below, a person who, knowing that payment on the spot for any goods supplied or service done is required or expected from him, dishonestly makes off without having paid as required or expected and with intent to avoid payment of the amount due shall be guilty of an offence.

(2) For purposes of this section 'payment on the spot' includes payment at the time of collecting goods on which work has been done or in respect of which service has been provided.

(3) Subsection (1) above shall not apply where the supply of the goods or the doing of the service is contrary to law, or where the service done is such that payment is not legally enforceable.

A Actus reus

There are three component elements to the *actus reus*:

(a) The defendant must 'make off'.

(b) The defendant must make off 'from the spot' where payment is required or expected.

(c) There must be an enforceable debt which the defendant is avoiding.

The statute requires that the defendant must make off without payment. It may follow that if the defendant is sufficiently clever at trickery to gain the victim's consent to the departure, there will be no offence:

R v *Hammond*
[1982] Crim LR 611
Lincoln Crown Court

Philip Hammond was charged under s. 2(1)(b) and 3 of the Theft Act 1978. Hammond admitted to the police that he had, between May and August 1980, gone to various garages to have repairs done to his car which he needed for his business. On each occasion when he collected the car he had offered and in fact tendered a cheque drawn on his account at the Yorkshire Bank in payment. He admitted to the police that he knew at the time of giving the cheques that he had no money in the account to meet them, but he hoped that money would be forthcoming in the future.

At the close of the prosecution the defence were invited by the judge to submit as to whether the action of the defendant amounted to an offence of making off without payment under s. 3 or only to an offence of evasion of liability by deception under s. 2(1)(b). The prosecution conceded that the principal reason for including the count under s. 3 was because of the difficulty of proving an intention never to pay which was required under s. 2(1)(b).

Held: there were two questions in issue. First was the tendering of a cheque, which the defendant knew would not be met in the ordinary course of banking, payment for the purposes of s. 3 and, second did s. 3 apply to the stalling debtor?

As to the 'payment' the offer of a cheque was not the same as offering counterfeit money. A cheque without a banker's card is always taken at risk by the recipient. The defendant gave the worthless cheque and departed with the consent of the recipient and could not therefore be said to be 'making off'. This consent was not vitiated simply by the fact that the payee did not at that time know that the drawer had insufficient funds to his credit in his account to meet payment.

In any event it was unrealistic to look at s. 3 in isolation. Sections 2 and 3 appeared in identical terms as cll. 2 and 3 of the Thirteenth Report of the Criminal Law Revision Committee in which cl. 2(1)(b) is expressed to be concerned with the stalling debtor (*Archbold*, para. 1599(a)), namely one 'who intends to make permanent default in whole or in part of his liability to pay. . . . We recognise that the practical difficulties of proving an intention never to pay will have the consequence that there will be few prosecutions under this head, but this is consistent with our view that the criminal law should not apply to the debtor who is merely trying to delay the making of payment. . . . '

If then s. 2(1)(b) does not apply to a debtor who is delaying payment, why should s. 3 cover it since the Committee clearly wished to exclude the criminal law from cases where a debtor is merely trying to delay the making of payment?

The offence committed by the defendant, if any, was an offence under s. 2(1)(b) and the jury were directed to acquit of the charges under s. 3.

Question
In *Hammond*, did the creditor consent to the defendant leaving the 'spot' where payment was required, or was the creditor 'paid' by the worthlesss cheque?

Note
Section 3 was introduced to assist the prosecution to gain convictions where some difficulty would be experienced in proving an intention permanently to deprive. Consider whether a charge under s. 15 of the Theft Act 1968 would

have succeeded, despite the requirement to prove an intent permanently to deprive.

The defendant must make off from 'the spot' where payment is required or expected.

R v McDavitt
[1981] Crim LR 843
Croydon Crown Court

The defendant had a meal with three friends in a restaurant. At the end of the meal his friends left the restaurant and the defendant remained at the table where they had all been sitting. The bill was brought on a saucer to his table and an argument ensued between the defendant and the owner of the restaurant which ended with the defendant refusing to pay any of the bill. He went towards the door whereupon someone standing by the door advised him not to leave as the police were being called. The defendant then went to the toilet in the restaurant where he remained until the police arrived. He was arrested and taken to a police station where he later made a statement under caution in which he admitted the above facts saying that it was his intention to leave without paying for the meal but that he decided to stay on being told about the police being summoned. He was subsequently indicted under s. 3 of the Theft Act 1978 with making off from the restaurant without paying for the food and wine which had been consumed. On a submission of no case to answer:

Held: 'Makes off' refers to making off from the spot where payment is required or expected. What is the spot depends on the circumstances of each case. In this case the spot was the restaurant. The jury would be directed that it was not open to them to find the defendant guilty of the offence on the indictment but that it was open to them to find him guilty of an attempt to commit the offence.

Notes and questions
1.   There must be an enforceable debt which the defendant is avoiding. This requirement is specifically imposed by the language of s. 3(3): 'Subsection (1) ... shall not apply where the supply of the goods or the doing of the service is contrary to law, or where the service done is such that payment is not legally enforceable.'
2.   Alice, dissatisfied with the quality of the food served, disputes the amount of a restaurant bill. The owner refuses to take anything less than the full amount. Unable to reach a compromise, Alice leaves the restaurant. Has she violated s. 3? Must the answer await the outcome of a civil suit between Alice and the restaurant?

B   Mens rea

Here again there are three elements:

(a)   The defendant must act dishonestly at the time of making off without payment.
(b)   The defendant must know that payment on the spot is required or expected.

(c)   There must be an intent permanently to avoid payment.

The requirement of 'dishonesty' presumably imports the test in *Ghosh* (above, Chapter 11). The dishonesty must be present at the time of the making off. See *Brooks and Brooks* (1982) 76 Cr App R 66. Moreover, the defendant must know that payment on the spot is required or expected. This latter requirement is expressly provided for by s. 3(1).

Unlike in respect of theft (see Chapter 11), there is no express requirement in s. 3 that the defendant should have an intention to make permanent default. If this omission were significant, a dishonest intention to avoid payment temporarily would be sufficient. However, despite this apparently clear statutory language, the House of Lords has held that the intent must be to avoid payment permanently.

R v Allen
[1985] AC 1029
House of Lords

LORD HAILSHAM OF ST MARYLEBONE: . . . The facts, which are not disputed, and which I draw from the case for the appellant, were as follows. The respondent, Christopher Allen, booked a room at a hotel for ten nights from 15 January 1983. He stayed on thereafter and finally left on 11 February 1983 without paying his bill in the sum of £1,286.94. He telephoned two days later to explain that he was in financial difficulties because of some business transactions and arranged to return to the hotel on 18 February 1983 to remove his belongings and leave his Australian passport as security for the debt. He was arrested on his return and said that he genuinely hoped to be able to pay the bill and denied he was acting dishonestly. On 3 March 1983 he was still unable to pay the bill and provided an explanation to the police of his financial difficulties.

The respondent's defence was that he had acted honestly and had genuinely expected to pay the bill from the proceeds of various business ventures. . . .

[Boreham J said:]

Finally, we can see no reason why, if the intention of Parliament was to provide, in effect, that an intention to delay or defer payment might suffice, Parliament should not have said so in explicit terms. This *might* have been achieved by the insertion of the word 'such' before payment in the phrase in question. It *would* have been achieved by a grammatical reconstruction of the material part of s. 3(1) thus, 'dishonestly makes off without having paid and with intent to avoid payment of the amount due as required or expected'. To accede to the Crown's submission would be to read the section as if it were constructed in that way. That we cannot do. Had it been intended to relate the intention to avoid 'payment' to 'payment as required or expected' it would have been easy to say so. The section does not say so. At the very least it contains an equivocation which should be resolved in favour of [the respondent].

There is really no escape from this argument. There may well be something to be said for the creation of a criminal offence designed to protect, for instance, cab drivers and restaurant keepers against persons who dishonestly abscond without paying on the spot and without any need for the prosecution to exclude an intention to pay later, so long as the original act of 'making off' could be described as dishonest. Unlike that in the present section, such an offence might very well as with the railway ticket offence, be triable summarily, and counsel for the Crown was able to call in aid the remarks of Cumming-Bruce LJ in *Corbyn v Saunders* [1978] 2 All ER 697 at 699, [1978] 1 WLR 400 at 403 which go a long way to support such a view. But, as the Court of Appeal remarked, that decision was under a different statute and a differently worded section which did not contain both the reference to 'dishonestly' and the specific intention 'to avoid payment' as two separate elements in the mens rea of the offence. In order to give the section now under consideration the effect required the section would have to be remodelled in the way suggested by Boreham J in the passage quoted above, or the word 'and' in the ultimate phrase would have to be read as if it meant 'that is to say' so that the required intent would be equated with 'dishonestly' in the early part of the subsection.

Questions

1. How does a prosecutor prove an intent permanently to deprive in this context, where the arrest will usually have to be made immediately if there is to be any chance of apprehending the offender?

2. Jennifer and Marilyn have dinner at a restaurant. At the conclusion of the meal, Jennifer offers to pay but realises that she has not enough money with her to do so. She tells the manager that she will get some money from a cash machine on the other side of the street while Marilyn waits for her in the restaurant. The manager agrees. On reaching the cashpoint Jennifer finds that it is out of order. She then decides to go home without paying the restaurant bill. Has Jennifer or Marilyn committed any offence?

II Burglary

The Theft Act 1968, s. 9, makes burglary a criminal offence. The section creates two quite distinct offences.

Theft Act 1968

9.—(1) A person is guilty of burglary if—

(a) he enters any building or part of a building as a trespasser and with intent to commit any such offence as is mentioned in subsection (2) below; or

(b) having entered any building or part of a building as a trespasser he steals or attempts to steal anything in the building or that part of it or inflicts or attempts to inflict on any person therein any grievous bodily harm.

(2) The offences referred to in subsection (1)(a) above are offences of stealing anything in the building or part of a building in question, of inflicting on any person therein any grievous bodily harm or raping any woman therein, and of doing unlawful damage to the building or anything therein.

(3) A person guilty of burglary shall on conviction on indictment be liable to imprisonment for a term not exceeding—

(a) where the offence was committed in respect of a building or part of a building which is a dwelling, fourteen years;

(b) in any other case ten years.

(4)   References in subsections (1) and (2) above to a building, and the reference to in subsection (3) above to a building which is a dwelling, shall also apply to an inhabited vehicle or vessel, and shall apply to any such vehicle or vessel at times when the person having a habitation in it is not there as well as at times when he is.

A   Actus reus

Both parts of s. 9(1) require proof that the defendant entered as a trespasser. If the requisite intent is present, a s. 9(1)(a) offence is committed at the moment of entry, whereas a s. 9 (1)(b) offence is committed at the time that the ulterior offence is complete.

The *actus reus* of burglary presents a number of questions:

(a)   What constitutes sufficient entry?
(b)   When is a defendant trespassing?
(c)   How are 'building' and 'part of a building' defined?
(d)   For s. 9(1)(b) only, when can the ulterior offence be considered to have been committed?

(i)   Entry

Many of the problems encountered in proving burglary were discussed in the following case:

R v Collins
[1972] 2 All ER 1105
Court of Appeal

EDMUND DAVIES LJ: . . . This is about as extraordinary a case as my brethren and I have ever heard either on the Bench or while at the Bar. Stephen William George Collins was convicted on 29th October 1971 at Essex Assizes of burglary with intent to commit rape and he was sentenced to 21 months' imprisonment. He is a 19 year old youth, and he appeals against that conviction by the certificate of the trial judge. The terms in which that certificate is expressed reveals that the judge was clearly troubled about the case and the conviction.

Let me relate the facts. Were they put into a novel or portrayed on the stage, they would be regarded as being so improbable as to be unworthy of serious consideration and as verging at times on farce. At about two o'clock in the early morning of Saturday, 24th July 1971, a young lady of 18 went to bed at her mother's home in Colchester. She had spent the evening with her boyfriend. She had taken a certain amount of drink, and it may be that this fact affords some explanation of her inability to answer satisfactorily certain crucial questions put to her. She has the habit of sleeping without wearing night apparel in a bed which is very near the lattice-type window of her room. At one stage of her evidence she seemed to be saying that the bed was close up against the window which, in accordance with her practice, was wide open. In the photographs which we have before us, however, there appears to be a gap of some sort between the two, but the bed was clearly quite near the window. At about 3.30 or 4.00 a.m. she awoke and she then saw in the moonlight a vague form crouched in the open window. She was unable to remember, and this is important, whether the form was on the outside of the window sill or on the part of the sill which was inside the room, and for reasons which will later become clear, that seemingly narrow point is of crucial importance. The young lady then realised several things: first of all that the form in the window was that of a male; secondly that he was a naked male; and thirdly that he was a naked male with an erect penis. She also saw in the moonlight that his hair was blond. She thereupon leapt to the conclusion that her boyfriend, with whom for some time she had been on terms of regular and frequent sexual intimacy, was paying her an ardent nocturnal visit. She promptly sat up in bed, and the man descended from the sill and joined her in bed and they had full sexual intercourse. But there was something about him which made her think that things were not as they usually were between her and her boyfriend. The length of his hair, his voice as they had exchanged what was described as 'love talk', and other features led her to the conclusion that somehow there was something different. So she turned on the bed-side light, saw that her companion was not her boyfriend and slapped the face of the intruder, who was none other than the appellant. He said to her, 'give me a good time tonight', and got hold of her arm, but she bit him and told him to go. She then went into the bathroom and he promptly vanished.

The complainant said that she would not have agreed to intercourse if she had known that the person entering her room was not her boyfriend. But there was no suggestion of any force having been used on her, and the intercourse which took place was undoubtedly effected with no resistance on her part.

The appellant was seen by the police at about 10.30 a.m. later that same morning. According to the police, the conversation which took place then elicited these points: He was very lustful the previous night. He had taken a lot of drink, and we may here note that drink (which to him is a very real problem) had brought this young man into trouble several times before, but never for an offence of this kind. He went on to say that he knew the complainant because he had worked around her house. On this occasion, desiring sexual intercourse – and according to the police evidence he had added that he was determined to have a girl, by force if necessary, although that part of the police evidence he challenged – he went on to say that he walked around the house, saw a light in an upstairs bedroom, and he knew that this was the girl's bedroom. He found a step ladder, leaned it against the wall and climbed up and looked into the bedroom. What he could see inside through the wide open window was a girl who was naked and asleep. So he descended the ladder and stripped off all his clothes, with the exception of his socks, because apparently he took the view that if the girl's mother entered the bedroom it would be easier to effect a rapid escape if he had his socks on than if he was in his bare feet. That is a matter about which we are not called on to express any view, and would in any event find ourselves unable to express one. Having undressed, he then climbed the ladder and pulled himself up on to the window sill. His version of the matter is that he was pulling himself in when she awoke. She then got up and knelt on the bed, she put her arms around his neck and body, and she seemed to pull him into the bed. He went on:

> ... I was rather dazed, because I didn't think she would want to know me. We kissed and cuddled for about ten or fifteen minutes and then I had it away with her but found it hard because I had had so much to drink.

The police officer said to the appellant:

> It appears that it was your intention to have intercourse with this girl by force if necessary and it was only pure coincidence that this girl was under the impression that you were her boyfriend and apparently that is why she consented to allowing you to have sexual intercourse with her.

It was alleged that he then said:

Yes, I feel awful about this. It is the worst day of my life, but I know it could have been worse.

Thereupon the officer said to him – and the appellant challenges this – 'What do you mean, you know it could have been worse?' to which he is alleged to have replied:

Well, my trouble is drink and I got very frustrated. As I've told you I only wanted to have it away with a girl and I'm only glad I haven't really hurt her.'

Then he made a statement under caution, in the course of which he said:

When I stripped off and got up the ladder I made my mind up that I was going to try and have it away with this girl. I feel terrible about this now, but I had too much to drink. I am sorry for what I have done.

In the course of his testimony, the appellant said that he would not have gone into the room if the girl had not knelt on the bed and beckoned him into the room. He said that if she had objected immediately to his being there or to his having intercourse he would not have persisted. While he was keen on having sexual intercourse that night, it was only if he could find someone who was willing. He strongly denied having told the police that he would, if necessary, have pushed over some girl for the purpose of having intercourse.

There was a submission of no case to answer on the ground that the evidence did not support the charge, particularly that ingredient of it which had reference to entry into the house 'as a trespasser'. But the submission was overruled, and as we have already related, he gave evidence.

Now, one feature of the case which remained at the conclusion of the evidence in great obscurity is where exactly the appellant was at the moment when according to him, the girl manifested that she was welcoming him. Was he kneeling on the sill outside the window or was he already inside the room, having climbed through the window frame, and kneeling on the inner sill? It was a crucial matter, for there were certainly three ingredients that it was incumbent on the Crown to establish. Under s. 9 of the Theft Act 1968, which renders a person guilty of burglary if he enters any building or part of a building as a trespasser and with the intention of committing rape, the entry of the appellant into the building must first be proved. Well, there is no doubt about that, for it is common ground that he did enter this girl's bedroom. Secondly, it must be proved that he entered as a trespasser. We will develop that point a little later. Thirdly it must be proved that he entered as a trespasser with intent at the time of entry to commit rape therein.

. . . Unless the jury were entirely satisfied that the appellant made an effective and substantial entry into the bedroom without the complainant doing or saying anything to cause him to believe that she was consenting to his entering it, he ought not to be convicted of the offence charged. The point is a narrow one, as narrow maybe as the window sill which is crucial to this case. But this is a criminal charge of gravity and, even though one may suspect that his *intention* was to commit the offence charged, unless the facts show with clarity that he in fact committed it he ought not to remain convicted.

Notes and questions

1. The court speaks of an 'effective entry'. What is the difference between that and an ordinary entry? What if only part of Collins's body had entered into the room? Whether there has been an effective entry is a question of fact for the jury.

2.   Permission to enter premises may be either express or implied. There is, for example, implied permission to enter a public building.

The entry must be 'effective and substantial'. This formula was applied in the following case:

R v Brown
[1985] Crim LR 611
Court of Appeal

Lord Justice Watkins said that the appellant had been seen by a witness to be half inside a broken shop window, as though he were rummaging inside it. He was later arrested and charged with burglary.
    He appealed on the ground that a person could not be said to have 'entered' a building if only part of his body had been in it.
    The requirement in *R v Collins* ([1973] QB 100) that entry be 'substantial' and 'effective' did not support the appellant's case. Although it was right that a jury should be directed that entry must be 'effective', the direction in the present case was perfectly adequate. It seemed an astounding proposition that a person could break a shop window, put in his hand and steal and not be held as having entered as a trespasser.

(ii)   Trespass

In *Collins* the Court of Appeal made it clear that not all the technicalities of the tort of trespass will be used to define the concept of trespass as an ingredient of the offence of burglary. Three issues are raised by the decision:

(a)   Does the defendant need to know he is trespassing?
(b)   Is it trespass when the defendant is invited into premises but, unknown to the person issuing the invitation, he has a secret unlawful intent?
(c)   Will the doctrine of *trespass ab initio* apply?

(a)   *Does the defendant need to know that he is trespassing? What are the limits of an invitation?*

R v Collins
[1972] 2 All ER 1105
Court of Appeal

For the facts, see p. 551.

EDMUND DAVIES LJ: . . . The second ingredient of the offence – the entry must be as a trespasser – is one which has not, to the best of our knowledge, been previously canvassed in the courts. Views as to its ambit have naturally been canvassed by the textbook writers, and it is perhaps not wholly irrelevant to recall that those who were advising the Home Secretary before the Theft Bill was presented to Parliament had it in mind to get rid of some of the frequently absurd technical rules which had been built up in relation to the old requirement in burglary of a 'breaking and entering'. The cases are legion as to what this did or did not amount to, and happily it is not now necessary for us to consider them. But it was in order to get rid of those technical rules that a new test was introduced, namely that the entry must be as a 'trespasser'.

. . . In the judgment of this court, there cannot be a conviction for entering premises 'as a trespasser' within the meaning of s. 9 of the Theft Act 1968 unless the person entering does so knowing that he is a trespasser and nevertheless deliberately enters, or, at the very least, is reckless whether or not he is entering the premises of another without the other party's consent.

R v Smith and Jones
[1976] 3 All ER 54
Court of Appeal

JAMES LJ: . . . Christopher Smith's father, Alfred Smith, lived at 72 Chapel Lane, Farnborough. He was in the course of negotiating a move from the house to other premises. At the material time, in May 1975, in that house were two television sets; one owned by Mr Alfred Smith, the other owned by another person but lawfully in possession of Mr Alfred Smith. Christopher Smith lived with his own family at Aberfield. The appellant Jones lived in the opposite direction from Chapel Lane, Farnborough to Aberfield, namely in Lakeside Road, Ashvale.

In the early hours of 10 May, 1975, a police officer in Ashvale saw a motor car with the two appellants inside and a television set protruding from the boot of the car. Having regard to that which he saw and the time of the morning he followed the car which turned into a side road where eventually it was stopped by a gate being in its way. The officer called for further officers to attend and when another officer went to the car he saw the appellant Jones sitting on the back seat with a second television set behind him. In the front of the car was Smith. They were told that the police believed that the television sets were stolen and that they were being arrested. Smith responded with the questions: 'Are they bent?' and Jones made the observation: 'You cannot arrest me for just having a ride in a car.'

At the trial both of the appellants gave evidence. It was the case for Smith that he had permission from his father to go into the house of his father. With that permission was a general licence to go there at any time he wanted to. It was the case for Jones at the trial that, contrary to what he had said to the police, he had gone into the house, he had gone purely as a passenger with Smith and gone in in the belief, honestly held, that Smith had permission to take the television sets from his father and that in taking them Smith was not stealing them or acting in any dishonest way. He himself, in so far as he was concerned with the matter, was not acting in any dishonest way.

Mr Rose argues that a person who had a general permission to enter premises of another person cannot be a trespasser. His submission is as short and as simple as that. Related to this case he says that a son to whom a father thas given permission generally to enter the father's house cannot be a trespasser if he enters it even though he had decided in his mind before making the entry to commit a criminal offence of theft against the father once he had got into the house and had entered the house solely for the purpose of committing that theft. It is a bold submission. Mr Rose frankly accepts that there has been no decision of the Court since this statute was passed which governs particularly this point. He has reminded us of the decision in *Byrne v Kinematograph Renters Society Ltd* [1958] 2 All ER 579, which he prays in aid of his argument. In that case persons had entered a cinema by producing tickets not for the purpose of seeing the show, but for an ulterior purpose. It was held in the action, which sought to show that they entered as trespassers pursuant to a conspiracy to trespass, that in fact they were not trespassers. The important words in the judgment of Harman J at p. 593D are 'They did nothing that they were not invited to do, . . .' That provides a distinction between that case and what we consider the position to be in this case.

Mr Rose has also referred us to one of the trickery cases, a case of *Boyle* (1954) 38 Cr App R 111; [1954] 2 QB 293, and in particular the passage on pp. 112–113, 295 of the respective reports. He accepts that the trickery cases can be distinguished from such a case as the present because in the trickery cases it can be said that that which would otherwise have been consent to enter was negatived by the fact that consents was obtained by a trick.' We do not gain any help in the particular case from that decision.

We are also referred to *Collins* (1972) 56 Cr App R 554; [1973] QB 100 and in particular to the long passage of Edmund Davies LJ, as he then was, commencing at pp. 559 and 104 of the respective reports where the learned Lord Justice commenced the consideration of what is involved by the words '. . . the entry must be "as a trespasser".' At p. 561 and pp. 104–105 – again it is unnecessary to cite the long passage in full, suffice it to say that this Court on that occasion expressly approved the view expressed in Professor Smith's book on the *Law of Theft* (1968) (1st ed.) para. 462, and also the view of Professor Griew in his book on the *Theft Act* (1968) (1st ed.) para. 4–05 upon this aspect of what is involved in being a trespasser.

In our view the passage there referred to is consonant with the passage in the well known case of *Hillen and Pettigrew* v *I.C.I. (Alkali) Ltd* [1936] AC 65 where, in the speech of Lord Atkin these words appear at p. 69:

> My Lords, in my opinion this duty to an invitee only extends so long as and so far as the invitee is making what can reasonably be contemplated as an ordinary and reasonable use of the premises by the invitee for the purpose for which he has been invited. He is not invited to use any part of the premises for purposes which he knows are wrongfully dangerous and constitute an improper use. As Scrutton LJ has pointedly said [in *The Calgarth* [1926] P 93 at p. 110] 'When you invite a person into your house to use the staircase you do not invite him to slide down the banisters'.

That case of course was a civil case in which it was sought to make the defendant liable for a tort.

The decision in *Collins (supra)* in this Court, a decision upon the criminal law, added to the concept of trespass as a civil wrong only the mental element of *mens rea*, which is essential to the criminal offence. Taking the law as expressed in *Hillen and Pettigrew* v *I.C.I. Ltd (supra)* and in the case of *Collins (supra)* it is our view that a person is a trespasser for the purpose of section 9(1)(b) of the Theft Act 1968, if he enters premises of another knowing that he is entering in excess of the permission that has been given to him, or being reckless as to whether he is entering in excess of the permission that has been given to him to enter, providing the facts are known to the accused which enable him to realise that he is acting in excess of the permission given or that he is acting recklessly as to whether he exceeds that permission, then that is sufficient for the jury to decide that he is in fact a trespasser.

In this particular case it was a matter for the jury to consider whether, on all the facts, it was shown by the prosecution that the appellants entered with the knowledge that entry was being effected against the consent or in excess of the consent that had been given by Mr Smith senior to his son Christopher. The jury were, by their verdict satisfied of that . . ..

Questions
1. Do *Collins* and *Smith and Jones* take the same approach to what constitutes a trespass? If not, are the positions reconcilable?
2. Is it trespass when the defendant is invited into premises but, unknown to the person issuing the invitation, he has a secret unlawful intent? Does the rationale of *Smith and Jones* convert all instances of shoplifting into burglary?
3. Would it have made more sense to prosecute Smith and Jones for theft? Part of the justification for the higher maximum penalty for burglary as compared to theft is the concern to protect the residents of a dwelling from uninvited intruders.
4. If Collins knew that the parents of the girl would not have approved of his presence, did he know he was trespassing? Can a lodger invite guests into a house to a party contrary to the wishes of a landlord? What if the guests stay for a week?

(b)   *Will the doctrine of trespass ab initio apply?* The doctrine of *trespass ab initio* holds that even if one is on premises lawfully as an invitee, one can become a trespasser by exceeding the limits of the invitation.

R v Collins
[1972] 2 All ER 1105
Court of Appeal

For the facts, see p. 551.

EDMUND DAVIES LJ: . . . Some question arose whether or not the appellant can be regarded as a trespasser *ab initio*. But we are entirely in agreement with the view expressed in *Archbold* that the common law doctrine of trespass *ab initio* has no application to burglary under the Theft Act 1968. One further matter that was canvassed ought perhaps to be mentioned. The point was raised that, the complainant not being the tenant or occupier of the dwelling-house and her mother being apparently in occupation, this girl herself could not in any event have extended an effective invitation to enter, so that even if she had expressly and with full knowledge of all material facts invited the appellant in, he would nevertheless be a trespasser. Whatever be the position in the law of tort, to regard such a proposition as acceptable in the criminal law would be unthinkable.

Questions
Why should not the doctrine of *trespass ab initio* apply in the context of criminal law? Would it convert all thieves into burglars?

Note
Part of the need for the doctrine is obviated by the language in s. 9(1) referring to 'building or part of a building.' See the discussion below.

(iii)   Building/part of a building

The Act speaks in terms of a 'building' or 'part of a building'. 'Part of a building' includes any part into which the defendant has no authority to go.

There need be no physical barrier between the 'part' into which the defendant is invited and the 'part' in which he is trespassing:

R v *Walkington*
(1979) 68 Cr App Rep 427
Court of Appeal

At 5.40 pm one evening the appellant entered a department store at a time when the assistants were 'cashing-up' their tills, the store closing at 6 pm. A store detective and two colleagues noticed that the appellant only appeared to be interested in the tills in the menswear department; but he was seen to ascend an escalator to the first floor to the dress display part where there was an unattached till in the centre of a three-sided counter, the till being left partially open and, unknown to the appellant but appreciated by the staff, empty. That drawer was located at least four yards inside the private area of the store restricted to the sales staff. The appellant moved into the opening of that counter, looked around him, and bent down and opened the drawer of the partially open till. After looking inside it, he slammed it shut and left the store when he was detained for questioning and later charged with burglary contrary to s. 9(1)(a) and (2) of the Theft Act 1968. The particulars of the offence alleged that he had entered the store in question as a trespasser with intent to steal therein. At the end of the prosecution case the appellant submitted that he had no case to answer in that there had been no trespass. The trial judge overruled that submission and directed that jury to consider first, so far as the store was concerned, whether the area where the half-opened till was situated was a prohibited area; secondly, if so, did the appellant realise when he crossed the limit that that area was prohibited; thirdly, at the time when he crossed that limit, the first two questions being decided against the appellant, did he have the intention to steal? The jury convicted. On appeal it was contended that the judge had erred in refusing to withdraw the case from the jury in that it was wrong to divide the store artificially and the appellant could not be said to have trespassed behind the counter . . .

GEOFFREY LANE LJ (approving the judge's summing-up which he quoted):

. . . The first question really arising out of this, which you have to consider is the use of the words 'part of a building.' The case for the prosecution is that the defendant formed an intent to steal while within this Debenhams, but before he entered the cash desk area, so that the prosecution are alleging that when he entered that area he was entering part of a building. Now, it is for you to decide whether on this section of the Theft Act that area was part of a building. Now, if you take the case of an ordinary shop, at the ordinary shop, which comprises a room with one part of it separated off by a counter, you might find little difficulty in deciding that the part of the room behind the counter was a separate part of the building from the shop area, and one which the public were not allowed to enter unless invited to do so. On the other hand, if you have the case of a large store, such as Debenhams, and there is a till placed on a table situated in the middle of the shop area, you might find it difficult, or even impossible, to say that any particular area, definable area, round that table was a separate part of the building. So that in approaching the problem you are entitled, of course, to use your own experience. You have been round shops, so you know the sort of layout you find in shops, so you may find it helpful to ask yourselves whether a shopper coming into a store and seeing the area with which you are concerned in this case would realise that that is an area to which the public were not entitled to go, and separate from the rest of the shopping area where they were entitled to go. It is a matter for you to decide. It is for you to decide whether that is the case. Coming back to the question of the definition of trespass, that is to say, of entering any part of a building as a trespasser, you now have to consider the next part of the definition, that is to say, 'with intent to steal.' Now in order to convict under this part of the section, section 9 of the Theft Act, the intent to steal must have been formed before the defendant entered that part of the area which was a separate part of the building. . . .

Note
When considering the definition of 'building', the extended definition in s. 9(4) should be noted:

Theft Act 1968

9.—(4) References in subsection (1) and (2) above to a building, and the reference in subsection (3) above to a building which is a dwelling, shall also apply to an inhabited vehicle or vessel, and shall apply to any such vehicle or vessel at times when the person having a habitation in it is not there as well as at times when he is.

Question
When is a vehicle or vessel 'inhabited'? Is a caravan 'inhabited' during the week if it is kept ready to be used, but only used, at weekends? What about a yacht, fitted out but not yet launched?

While s. 9(1)(a) requires only an intent to commit an offence within the building, s. 9(1)(b) requires that the defendant steal or attempt to steal something that is in the building, or inflict or attempt to inflict grievous bodily harm on a person in the building. Thus in construing the statute one must refer back to the substantive law of theft (see Chapter 11) and that of attempt (see Chapter 7). However, for the purposes of s. 9(1)(b) the infliction of grievous bodily harm on any person need not amount to an offence under ss. 18 or 20 of the Offences Against Persons Act 1861. See *R v Jenkins* [1983] Crim LR 386. *Jenkins* was reversed by the House of Lords ([1983] 3 All ER 448) on other grounds. The House of Lords decision does not affect the Court of Appeal ruling that the infliction of grievous bodily harm for purposes of s. 9(1)(b) need not amount to an offence.

Question
Nigel enters Buckingham Palace to see how the Queen lives. He wanders around undetected for several hours before being discovered and apprehended by security guards. Has he committed any offence? If he had picked up a vase

intending to smash it on the pavement outside, would he have committed burglary? When would the burglary have taken place?

B Mens rea

There are different *mens rea* which may have to be proved, depending on which part of the statute is charged:

(a) An intention to commit one of the ulterior offences is required for a s. 9(1)(a) burglary.

(b) For a s. 9(1)(b) burglary, the *mens rea* of the ulterior offence must be proved.

Recall also that in respect to both s. 9(1)(a) and s. 9(1)(b), the defendant must know that he is entering as a trespasser.

The s. 9(1)(a) *mens rea* must be present at the time of entering the building; the s. 9(1)(b) *mens rea* need not be present at the time of entry, only at the time of the commission of the ulterior offence.

The ulterior offences relevant to s. 9(1)(a) are contained in s. 9(2):

Theft Act 1968

9.—(2) The offences referred to in subsection (1)(a) above are offences of stealing anything in the building or part of a building in question, of inflicting on any person therein any grievous bodily harm or raping any woman therein, and of doing unlawful damage to the building or anything therein.

The ulterior offences relevant to s. 9(1)(b) are contained in the subsection itself. They are stealing or attempting to steal anything in the building or that part of it, or inflicting or attempting to inflict on any person therein any grievous bodily harm.

What if the defendant's intention is conditional?

Attorney-General's References (Nos. 1 & 2 of 1979)
[1980] QB 180
Court of Appeal

In the first reference a grocer who lived above his shop heard the backdoor open and close late one night and intercepted the defendant who was ascending the stairs. The police were called and arrested the defendant. They asked him why he had entered the house and he replied 'To rob £2,000' and on being asked why he thought there was £2,000 there he said 'I don't know, I was just going to take something.' The indictment before the Crown Court averred that he had entered the grocer's premises as a trespasser 'with intent to steal therein'. The trial judge withdrew the case from the jury at the close of the prosecution case and directed an acquittal. The Attorney-General referred to the court for opinion the question whether a man who had entered a house as a trespasser with the intention of stealing money therein was entitled to be acquitted of an offence against s. 9(1)(a) of the Theft Act 1968 on the ground that his intention to steal was conditional upon his finding money in the house.

In the second reference a householder heard a sound at the French windows at the rear of her house. She called the police who went to the rear of the house and found the defendant holding and turning the handle of the French windows and inserting a long thin stick between the door and the doorframe. Later at the police station the defendant made a written statement in which he said 'I wasn't going to do any damage in the house, only see if there was anything lying around.' The indictment averred that the defendant had attempted to enter the dwelling house concerned 'with intent to steal therein'. At the close of the prosecution case the judge directed the jury to return a verdict of not guilty upon the ground that the evidence did not disclose a present intention to steal but merely a conditional intention. The Attorney-General referred to the court for opinion the question whether a man who was attempting to enter a house as a trespasser with the intention of stealing anything of value which he might find therein was entitled to be acquitted of the offence of attempted burglary on the ground that at the time of the attempt his intention was insufficient to amount to 'the intention of stealing anything' necessary for conviction under s. 9 of the Theft Act 1968.

On the hearing of both references:—

Held: (1) that, under s. 9(1)(a) of the Theft Act 1968, the offence of burglary was committed if a person entered a building as a trespasser with an intention to steal; that, where a person was charged with burglary, it was no defence to show that he did not intend to steal any specific objects, and, accordingly, the fact that the intention to steal was conditional on finding money in the house did not entitle a person to be acquitted on a charge of entering premises as a trespasser with intent to steal therein; and that the question asked in the first reference was to be answered in the negative.

Note and question

The issue of conditional intent is in a sense a red herring for the defendant can be convicted of a crime of attempted burglary, where impossibility will not be a defence. This observation suggests a more fundamental question about burglary: Why is there a need for the offence at all? Why is it not sufficient to charge the defendant with either the ulterior offence committed, or, where the ulterior offence is not completed, an attempt to commit the ulterior offence?

III   Aggravated burglary

The Theft Act 1968, s. 10 creates an aggravated form of burglary:

Theft Act 1968

10.—(1)   A person is guilty of aggravated burglary if he commits any burglary and at the time has with him any firearm or imitation firearm, any weapon of offence, or any explosive; and for this purpose—

(a) 'firearm' includes an airgun or air pistol, and 'imitation firearm' means anything which has the appearance of being a firearm, whether capable of being discharged or not; and

(b) 'weapon of offence' means any article made or adapted for use for causing injury to or incapacitating a person, or intended by the person having it with him for such use; and

(c) 'explosive' means any article manufactured for the purpose of producing a practical effect by explosion, or intended by the person having it with him for that purpose.

(2) A person guilty of aggravated burglary shall on conviction on indictment be liable to imprisonment for life.

Note

Two main questions are raised by the section:

(a) What is a weapon of offence?
(b) When is 'at the time of burglary'?

R v Williamson
(1977) 67 Cr App R 35
Court of Appeal

GEOFFREY LANE LJ: In section 1(4) [of the Prevention of Crime Act 1953] the following words appear: ' "offensive weapon" means any article made or adapted for use for causing injury to the person, or intended by the person having it with him for such use by him.'

As has been pointed out in numerous cases, that provides three categories of weapons. The first category is the weapon which is made for causing injury to the person. The second type of weapon is one not made for the purpose but adapted for it, such as, as counsel pointed out in this case, a potato with a razor blade inserted into it. The third type of weapon is one neither made nor adapted but is one which is intended by the person having it with him for the purpose of causing personal injury to someone. That sort of thing could be any object that one can think of.

But what is sometimes lost sight of is this. It is for the jury to decide these matters. It is for the jury to decide whether a weapon held by the defendant was an offensive weapon, bearing in mind the definition in the section which I have just read. Consequently whether the object in the possession of the defendant in any case can properly be described as an offensive weapon is a matter not for the judge but for the jury to decide. The jury must determine whether they feel sure that the object was made or adapted for use in causing injury to the person or was intended by the person having it with him for such use by him. . . .

Notes

1. The term 'weapon of offence' in s. 10 is wider than 'offensive weapon' in s. 1(4) of the Prevention of Crime Act 1953. Section 10 includes articles made for incapacitating a person and articles adapted for incapacitating a person. These categories do not appear in the Prevention of Crime Act 1953.

2. Whether or not some article is an offensive weapon is a matter for the jury to decide unless the thing in question was made for the purpose of injuring another.

When is 'at the time of the burglary'?

R v Francis and Another
[1982] Crim LR 363
Court of Appeal

The defendants, armed with sticks, demanded entry to a dwelling house by banging and kicking the door. As a result of the banging and kicking, the occupant, with whom the defendants were acquainted, allowed them to enter. Either just before entering the house, or soon after entering the house, the defendants discarded their sticks. They subsequently stole items from the house and committed other offences against the occupant. The defendants were charged, *inter alia* with aggravated burglary, contrary to s. 10(1) of the Theft Act 1968. At their trial on indictment the judge directed the jury that the prosecution had to prove that the defendants entered the house as trespassers; that having entered they stole; and that when they entered they were armed with weapons of offence. The jury returned a verdict of guilty and the defendants appealed against conviction.

Held, allowing the appeal and substituting convictions for burglary, that having regard to the provisions of ss. 9 and 10 of the Theft Act 1968 it was clear that if a person entered a building as a trespasser with intent to steal, he was guilty of burglary under s. 9(1)(a) and if at the time of entry he had with him a weapon of offence, he was guilty of aggravated burglary; and that if a person entered a building as a trespasser and stole under s. 9(1)(b) he committed burglary at the moment when he stole and he committed aggravated burglary only if he had with him a weapon of offence at the time when he stole; that, accordingly, the judge misdirected the jury that all the prosecution were required to prove was that the defendants were armed when they entered the house as trespassers.

R v O'Leary
(1986) 82 Cr App R 341
Court of Appeal

LORD LANE CJ: The facts of the case, which are not in dispute, were these. In the early hours of January 31, 1985 the appellant entered a house in South East London, almost certainly in search of money and valuables, though such an intent, namely the intent at the time of entry to steal, was not alleged against him. At the time of that entry he was unarmed. He looked round the house downstairs. It seems he found nothing there which interested him, except a kitchen knife with which he armed himself.

He then went upstairs. The occupants of the house, husband and wife, were disturbed. A struggle ensued in the course of which all three, husband, wife and the appellant, received injuries. The appellant demanded and was given, he at that point being armed still with the kitchen knife, some cash and a bracelet.

Counsel for the appellant submitted to the judge that in those circumstances, where the appellant at the time of entering the house, probably aiming to steal, was not equipped with a knife, he could not be guilty of aggravated burglary under section 10(1) of the Theft Act 1968. That submission was rejected by the learned Judge. Hence the re-arraignment of the appellant and hence his plea of guilty as already indicated.

There are, as already indicated in section 9(1)(a) and (b) two means by which the prosecution can make out a charge of burglary: first of all by proving that the defendant entered as a trespasser with intent to steal, and secondly, by proving that the defendant having entered as a trespasser, actually stole. In order to discover whether aggravated burglary had been committed or not, it is necessary to determine which of those two limbs is the one which applies in the instant case.

In order to find that out, one has to look at the indictment. Count 2 of the indictment reads as follows: 'Statement of Offence: Aggravated Burglary contrary to section 10(1) of the Theft Act 1968. Particulars of Offence: Michael O'Leary on the 31st day of January 1985 entered as a trespasser a building known as 104 Lyndhurst Grove, London, S.E.15, and stole therein a sum of money, a bracelet, a number of keys and a cash card belonging to John Marsh, and at the time of committing the said burglary had with him a weapon of offence, namely a knife.'

If he had been charged under subsection (1)(a), the offence of burglary would be completed and committed when he entered and it would be at that point that one would have to consider whether or not he was armed. But in the case of subsection (1)(b), which is the one under which he was charged, the offence is complete when, and not until, the stealing is committed, provided again of course that he has trespassed in the first place. The prosecution did not have to prove an intent to steal at the time of entry as the charge is laid here. Indeed such an intent is irrelevant to the charge as laid.

It follows that under this particular charge, the time at which the defendant must be proved to have had with him a weapon of offence to make him guilty of aggravated burglary was the time at which he actually stole. As already indicated at that moment, when he confronted the householders and demanded their cash and jewellery, which was the theft, he still had the kitchen knife in his hand. No one alleged that he entered with the intent to steal, and that would not have been, had this matter proceeded to trial before a jury, a matter for the jury to consider at all. Indeed such evidence would, strictly speaking, be inadmissible and irrelevant.

The judge ruled, as this Court has indicated he should have ruled, namely that the material time in this charge for the possession of the weapon was the time when he confronted the householders and stole.

Appeal dismissed.

Questions
1.   Identify the time of the burglary in the above two cases. Does the relevant time differ according to whether the charge is under s. 9(1)(a) or s. 9(1)(b). Why?
2.   Jim, Kevin and Steve decide to steal statues from the gardens of large houses in Essex. While taking the statue of a large frog, Steve realises that there are no lights on in the house. He urges the others to come inside with him to see what they can steal. Kevin states that it is too risky but offers to watch outside. Before the others can break into the house, Kevin becomes interested in something else and rushes off. Jim and Steve break into the garage of the house where they find a shiny red car. Entranced by this, Jim immediately drives off in it. Steve picks up a spanner 'in case of trouble' and enters the house through a door from the garage. Inside he finds a housekeeper whom he threatens with the spanner. The housekeeper tells him where the valuables are kept and Steve takes them. What offences have been committed?
3.   Why is there an offence of aggravated burglary? Why not just take into account aggravating circumstances in sentencing for the basic crime?

IV   Handling stolen goods

Without a means of disposing stolen property, there would arguably be less incentive to commit theft. It is partly for this reason that s. 22 of the Theft Act 1968 makes handling of stolen goods a crime. But the offence goes beyond the professional fence to include others who help the thief dispose of the stolen goods.

Theft Act 1968

22.—(1)   A person handles stolen goods if (otherwise than in the course of the stealing) knowing or believing them to be stolen goods he dishonestly receives the goods, or dishonestly undertakes or assists in their retention, removal, disposal or realisation by or for the benefit of another person, or if he arranges to do so.

(2)   A person guilty of handling stolen goods shall on conviction on indictment be liable to imprisonment for a term not exceeding fourteen years.

A   Actus reus

The *actus reus* of handling presents seven particular problems:

(i)   When are goods 'stolen goods'?
The term 'stolen goods' has two components: 'stolen' and 'goods'. What is meant by 'goods', and what constitutes 'stealing' so that goods become 'stolen'?

Theft Act 1968

24.—(1)   The provisions of this Act relating to goods which have been stolen shall apply whether the stealing occurred in England or Wales or elsewhere, and whether it occurred before or after the commencement of this Act, provided that the stealing (if not an offence under this Act) amounted to an offence where and at the time when the goods were stolen; and references to stolen goods shall be construed accordingly.
. . .
(4)   For purposes of the provisions of this Act relating to goods which have been stolen (including subsections (1) to (3) above) goods obtained in England and Wales or elsewhere either by blackmail or in the circumstances described in section 15(1) of this Act shall be regarded as stolen; and 'steal', 'theft' and 'thief' shall be construed accordingly.

34.—(2)   . . .
(b)   'Goods', except in so far as the context otherwise requires, includes money and every other description of property except land, and includes things severed from the land by stealing.

Notes and questions
1.   As well as goods obtained by theft contrary to s. 1 of the Theft Act 1968 and by deception contrary to s. 15 of the Theft Act 1968. Goods are also 'stolen' for the purposes of s. 22 if they have been obtained by blackmail or if they have been obtained by an act done in a foreign country which (a) was a crime by the law of that country and which (b) had the act been done in England or Wales would have been theft, blackmail or obtaining by deception as defined by the Theft Act 1968. Is this too wide a definition? What policies lie behind the rules extending to acts done in foreign countries?
2.   Note that while the basic theft crimes require an appropriation, handling does not.

Is the defendant's belief that the goods are stolen sufficient to make them 'stolen goods'?

R v *Porter*
[1976] Crim LR 58
Middlesex Crown Court

Porter was charged with dishonestly handling stolen goods. He was questioned by two police officers who told him that they were investigating the theft of oil from a nearby refinery. Porter admitted that he had bought oil and that he believed it to have been stolen. There was no other evidence before the court.

It was argued for Porter that the prosecution had failed to adduce any evidence of theft or of any circumstances from which the jury could infer that.

For the Crown it was argued that the state of the defendant's mind at the time of the handling of the goods was a circumstance of such handling. Accordingly *Fuschillo* (1940) 27 Cr App R 193 should be applied and the jury invited to infer theft from the circumstances.

Held, upholding the defence submission that there was no case to answer, that the belief of the defendant that the oil had been stolen was not a circumstance from which that inference could be drawn. *Fuschillo* should not be extended so that a defendant's belief that goods were stolen became evidence of the theft of those goods. A defendant might be mistaken in his belief that the goods which he received were stolen.

Question
Although Porter could not be convicted of handling stolen goods, could he be convicted of an attempt to handle? Would his belief that the goods were stolen be relevant? See *R* v *Shivpuri* [1987] 1 AC 1 (Chapter 7) and the discussion of impossibility as a defence to an attempt charge in Chapter 7.

(ii)   When do goods cease to be 'stolen goods'?

Theft Act 1968

24.—(3) But no goods shall be regarded as having continued to be stolen goods after they have been restored to the person from whom they were stolen or to other lawful possession or custody, or after that person and any other person claiming through him have otherwise ceased as regards those goods to have any right to restitution in respect of the theft.

Note and question
The 'right to restitution' referred to in s. 24(3) of the 1968 Act probably includes a potential right to restitution of goods where title passes to the defendant under a contract voidable for fraud. The Criminal Law Revision Committee explained s. 24(3) in their Eighth Report (Cmnd 2977, para. 139):

> ... this is because, if the person who owned the goods when they were stolen no longer has any title to them, there will be no reason why the goods should continue to have the taint of being stolen goods. For example, the offence of handling stolen goods will . . . apply also to goods obtained by criminal deception under [s. 15]. If the owner of the goods who has been deceived chooses on discovering the deception to ratify his disposal of the goods he will cease to have any title to them.

To what extent is this approach consistent with the decision of the House of Lords in *Gomez* (Chapter 11)?

Whether the goods have been reduced into lawful possession or custody is a matter for the jury to decide:

Attorney-General's Reference (No. 1 of 1974)
[1974] 1 QB 744
Court of Appeal

A police officer found an unlocked and unattended car containing packages of new clothing which he suspected had been stolen, as was subsequently proved to be the case. He immobilised the car and kept observation. The respondent appeared and attempted to start the car. When questioned by the officer he gave an implausible explanation and was arrested.

LORD WIDGERY CJ: . . . [D]id the conduct of the police officer, as already briefly recounted, amount to a taking of possession of the woollen goods in the back seat of the motor car? What he did, to repeat the essential facts, was: that seeing these goods in the car and being suspicious of them because they were brand new goods and in an unlikely position, he removed the rotor arm and stood by in cover to interrogate any driver of the car who might subsequently appear. Did that amount to a taking possession of the goods in the back of the car? In our judgment it depended primarily on the intentions of the police officer. If the police officer seeing these goods in the back of the car had made up his mind that he would take them into custody, that he would reduce them into his possession or control, take charge of them so that they could not be removed and so that he would have the disposal of them, then it would be a perfectly proper conclusion to say that he had taken possession of the goods. On the other hand, if the truth of the matter is that he was of an entirely open mind at that stage as to whether the goods were to be seized or not and was of an entirely open mind as to whether he should take possession of them or not, but merely stood by so that when the driver of the car appeared he could ask certain questions of that driver as to the nature of the goods and why they were there, then there is no reason whatever to suggest that he had taken the goods into his possession or control. It may be of course, that he had both objects in mind. It is possible in a case like this that the police officer may have intended by removing the rotor arm both to prevent the car from being driven away and to enable him to assert control over the woollen goods as such. But if the jury came to the conclusion that the proper explanation of what had happened was that the police officer had not intended at that stage to reduce the goods into his possession or to assume the control of them, and at that stage was merely concerned to ensure that the driver, if he appeared, could not get away without answering questions, then in that case the proper conclusion of the jury would have been to the effect that the goods had not been reduced into the possession of the police and therefore a defence under section 24(3) of the Theft Act 1968 would not be of use to this particular defendant.

In the light of those considerations it has become quite obvious that the trial judge was wrong in withdrawing the issue from the jury. As a matter of law he was not entitled to conclude from the facts which I have set out more than once that these goods were reduced into the possession of the police officer. What he should have done in our opinion would have been to have left that issue to the jury for decision, directing the jury that they should find that the prosecution case was without substance if they thought that the police officer had assumed control of the goods as such and reduced them into his possession. Whereas on the other hand, they should have found the case proved, assuming that they were satisfied about its other elements, if they were of the opinion that the police officer in removing the rotor arm and standing by and watching was doing no more than ensure that the driver should not get away without interrogation and was not at that stage seeking to assume possession of the goods as such at all. That is our opinion.

Question
Does *A-G's Reference* create a trap for the unwary police officer? A potential windfall for the lucky defendant?

(iii)   When are goods representing stolen goods considered to be 'stolen goods'?

Theft Act 1968

24.—(2) For purposes of those provisions references to stolen goods shall include, in addition to the goods originally stolen and parts of them (whether in their original state or not),—
(a) any other goods which directly or indirectly represent or have at any time represented the stolen goods in the hands of the thief as being the proceeds of any disposal or realisation of the whole or part of the goods stolen or of goods so representing the stolen goods; and
(b) any other goods which directly or indirectly represent or have at any time represented the stolen goods in the hands of a handler of the stolen goods or any part of them as being the proceeds of any disposal or realisation of the whole or part of the stolen goods handled by him or of goods so representing them.

Question
A steals a painting from B. She sells it to C, who knows that it is stolen. C gives the money to her friend D, who is aware of its source. D uses the money to purchase a motorcycle from E, who is sublimely ignorant of the preceding events. Who is guilty of handling?

(iv)   In what ways can 'handling' be committed?
The Theft Act 1968, s. 22 creates one offence which may be committed in a number of different ways. It was held in *Nicklin* [1977] 2 All ER 444 that, although s. 22 creates only one offence, the alleged mode of commission should be particularised in the indictment, although an indictment containing two allegations, one of handling by receiving and another of handling by undertaking or assisting in the retention, etc. of goods, would be accceptable. Such an indictment would cover virtually all possible modes of committing the offence. However, if only one mode was alleged and not proved, it would not be possible to secure the conviction of the defendant.
The ways in which an offence of handling can be committed are by:

(a) receiving the goods;

(b)   undertaking the retention, removal, disposal or realisation of the goods for the benefit of another person;
(c)   assisting in the retention, removal, disposal or realisation of the goods by another person;
(d)   arranging to do (a), (b) or (c).

Only receiving or arranging to receive can be committed without the acts being done 'by or for the benefit of another person' (see *Bloxham*, below).

(v)   Can handling be committed by omission?

R v Brown
[1970] 1 QB 105
Court of Appeal

The defendant was tried on an indictment containing three counts charging him (1) with burglary, (2) with handling stolen goods contrary to s. 22(1) of the Theft Act 1968, in that he dishonestly received them, and (3) in that he dishonestly assisted in their retention. In January 1969, a cafe was broken into and food and cigarettes were stolen. A quantity of the stolen food was found at the defendant's flat. The defendant denied any knowledge of the theft and told the police to 'Get lost.' Subsequently the cigarettes were found in the flat. At the trial, evidence was given by the prosecution that the defendant knew that the stolen goods were in the flat before the police arrived. The chairman directed the jury that 'the matter for you to consider is whether, assuming that you are satisfied that [the defendant] knew that the stolen cigarettes were in the wardrobe . . . he was dishonestly assisting in their retention by not telling the constable they were there.' The defendant was acquitted on the first two counts and convicted on count 3. On appeal against conviction on the ground that the chairman had misdirected the jury in that mere failure to reveal the presence of stolen property was incapable of amounting to assistance in their retention within the meaning of s. 22(1) of the Theft Act, 1968:

LORD PARKER CJ: . . . It is urged here that the mere failure to reveal the presence of the cigarettes, with or without the addition of the spoken words 'Get lost,' was incapable in itself of amounting to an assisting in the retention of the goods within the meaning of section 22 (1). The court has come to the conclusion that that is right. It does not seem to this court that the mere failure to tell the police, coupled if you like with the words 'Get lost,' amounts in itself to an assisting in their retention. On the other hand, those matters did accord strong evidence of what was the real basis of the charge here, namely that, knowing that they had been stolen, he permitted them to remain there or, as it has been put, provided accommodation for these stolen goods in order to assist Holden to retain them. To that extent, it seems to this court, that the direction was incomplete. The chairman should have gone on to say:

But the fact that he did not tell the constable that they were there and said 'Get lost' is evidence from which you can infer if you think right that this man was permitting the goods to remain in his flat, and to that extent assisting in their retention by Holden.

It may be thought to be a matter of words, but in the opinion of the court some further direction was needed. On the other hand it is a plain case in which the proviso should be applied. It seems to the court that the only possible inference in these circumstances, once Holden was believed, is that the defendant was assisting in their retention by housing the goods and providing accommodation for them, by permitting them to remain there. In those circumstances the court is satisfied that the appeal fails and should be dismissed.

R v *Pitchley*
(1972) Cr App R 30
Court of Appeal

The appellant's son handed the appellant £150 and the appellant paid the amount into his post office savings bank book.

Held: that the appellant was properly convicted under s. 22 of the Theft Act 1968, as he had assisted in the retention of the money for the benefit of his son. 'Retain' in the section means 'keep possession of, not lose, continue to have.'

CAIRNS LJ: . . . The main point that has been taken by Mr Kalisher, who is appearing for the appellant in this Court, is that, assuming that the jury were not satisfied that the appellant received the money knowing it to have been stolen, and that is an assumption which clearly it is right to make, then there was no evidence after that, that from the time when the money was put into the savings bank, that the appellant had done any act in relation to it. His evidence was, and there is no reason to suppose that the jury did not believe it, that at the time when he put the money into the savings bank he still did not know or believe that the money had been stolen – it was only at a later stage that he did. That was on the Saturday according to his evidence, and the position was that the money had simply remained in the savings bank from the Saturday, to the Wednesday when the police approached the appellant.

In this present case there was no question on the evidence of the appellant himself, that he was permitting the money to remain under his control in his savings bank book, and it is clear that this Court in the case of *Brown* [[1970] 1 QB 105] regarded such permitting as sufficient to constitute retention within the meaning of retention. . . .

In the course of the argument, Nield J cited the dictionary meaning of the word 'retain' – keep possession of, not lose, continue to have. In view of this Court, that is the meaning of the word 'retain' in this section. It was submitted by Mr Kalisher that, at any rate, it was ultimately for the jury to decide whether there was retention or not and that even assuming that what the appellant did was of such a character that it could constitute retention, the jury ought to have been directed that it was for them to determine as a matter of fact, whether that was so or not. The Court cannot agree with that submission. The meaning of the word 'retention' in the section is a matter of law in so far as the construction of the word is necessary. It is hardly a difficult question of construction because it is an ordinary English word and in the view of this Court, it was no more necessary for the Deputy Chairman to leave to the jury the question of whether or not what was done amounted to retention, than it would be necessary for a judge in a case where goods had been handed to a person who knew that they had been stolen for him to direct the jury it was for them to decide whether or not that constituted receiving.

R v Sanders
(1982) 75 Cr App R 84
Court of Appeal

A garage was burgled and a fan heater and a battery charger stolen. The fan heater was found by the police in a garage owned by the appellant's father, where he, the appellant, was employed. The battery charger was found in a nearby garage. When interviewed by the police the appellant admitted using both stolen items while working in his father's garage.

The father was charged with dishonestly handling stolen goods by receiving them and the appellant with assisting in their retention. In respect of the appellant the jury were directed that if they were satisfied that the appellant had used the goods, knowing or believing them to be stolen, then he would be guilty of the offence charged because the goods were in his control or possession. The jury convicted both the appellant and his father. . . .

DUNN LJ: . . . It is accepted in this Court that the question whether or not the goods are in the control or possession of the accused, though relevant to a charge of handling by receiving, is not relevant to a charge of handling by assisting in their retention for the benefit of another. The deputy judge left the case to the jury simply on the basis that if they were satisfied that the appellant had used the goods, knowing or believing them to be stolen, then he would be guilty of the offence as charged. . . .

The mere use of the goods knowing them to be stolen is not enough. It must be proved that in some way the accused was assisting in the retention of the goods by concealing them, or making them more difficult to identify, or by holding them pending their ultimate disposal, or by some other act that was part of the chain of the dishonest handling. As Mr Pearse Wheatley said, this criminal transaction was complete when the father received the goods. All that the appellant did was to use them thereafter. In the view of this Court the judge was wrong in the particular circumstances of this case to direct the jury that if they were satisfied of that, then the appellant was guilty. Accordingly this appeal must be allowed and the conviction quashed.

R v Kanwar
[1982] Crim LR 532
Court of Appeal

The police searched the appellant's house in her absence and found property which had been brought there by her husband and which was later identified as the proceeds of burglaries. During a second police search the appellant entered the house, said that there was no stolen property there, and when questioned about specific articles told lies to persuade the police that they were lawfully hers. She was charged with handling stolen goods contrary to s. 22(1) of the Theft Act 1968 by dishonestly assisting in their retention for the benefit of her husband. On conviction she appealed on the ground that the verdict was unsafe and unsatisfactory.

Held, dismissing the appeal, that verbal representations, whether oral or in writing, made to conceal the identity of stolen goods, if made dishonestly and for another's benefit, might amount to handling stolen goods by assisting in their retention within the meaning of s. 22 of the Theft Act 1968. It was not enough merely to use stolen goods in the possession of another. Something must be done intentionally, dishonestly, knowing or believing the goods to be stolen, for the purpose of enabling the goods to be retained for the benefit of another. There was no reason, however, why that assistance should be restricted to physical acts, nor need it be successful in its object. The appellant lied to protect her husband, but nonetheless she was dishonestly assisting in the retention of the stolen property.

R v *Coleman*
[1986] Crim LR 56
Court of Appeal

The appellant was convicted of handling by assisting in the disposal of money stolen by his wife from her employers. (He was acquitted of several other counts of handling.) It was undisputed that the appellant knew his wife was stealing large sums of cash and was disposing of the money on goods and their living expenses. The count on which he was convicted concerned £650 his wife had paid in solicitors fees in relation to the purchase of a flat in their joint names. There was no evidence as to who had instructed the solicitors. The appellant told the police his wife had paid in cash with stolen money. He agreed that as the mortgage was in joint names the bill had been for them both.

There was no other evidence. The appellant did not give evidence. The judge directed the jury that if the prosecution had proved the appellant was acting dishonestly, knowing or believing the money was stolen, and he was playing his part, assisting (perhaps by visiting the solicitors) and getting the benefit because the flat was in joint names then he would be guilty. The appellant appealed against his conviction.

Held, allowing the appeal and quashing the conviction, that the judge's directions had been wrong and not in accordance with the evidence. The *actus reus* of the offence was assisting in the disposal of the money, not getting the benefit and the fact that the appellant benefited from what his wife did was not proof that he had assisted her. Assisting meant helping or encouraging amongst other things. There had to be either affirmative or circumstantial evidence of helping or encouraging. In the instant case the evidence was circumstantial. From the evidence the jury could have inferred that the appellant and his wife had agreed to buy a flat, that he must have signed the contract of purchase and the mortgage, and that he knew the legal fees would be paid out of stolen money. The jury could also have properly inferred that there had been a discussion regarding payment of the fees and that the appellant had told his wife to use the stolen money or agreed that she should do so. The jury should have been told that those inferences could properly be drawn. The evidence was slight. Had the jury been adequately directed it was impossible to say they would inevitably have convicted. They might have inferred that his wife made the decisions without assistance. The proviso could not be applied.

Questions
1.   How active must the defendant be? Can an omission to act ever amount to 'receiving', 'undertaking' or 'arranging'? Can assistance be given by inactivity?
2.   Are the courts consistent in their treatment of this problem? How can it be that permitting goods to remain in one's house may be an offence, whereas using the goods may not?

3. Are these cases consistent with the principle that liability for omissions to act should only arise where the defendant is under a clear duty to act (see Chapter 2)?

(vi) When is an act considered to be 'otherwise than in the course of the stealing'?

R v Pitham and Hehl
(1976) 65 Cr App R 45
Court of Appeal

For the facts, see p. 472.

LAWTON LJ: . . . What was the appropriation in this case? The jury found that the two appellants had handled the property *after* Millman had stolen it. That is clear from their acquittal of these two appellants on count 3 of the indictment which had charged them jointly with Millman. What had Millman done? He had assumed the rights of the owner. He had done that when he took the two appellants to 20 Parry Road, showed them the property and invited them to buy what they wanted. He was then acting as the owner. He was then, in the words of the statute, 'assuming the rights of the owner.' The moment he did that he appropriated McGregor's goods to himself. The appropriation was complete. After this appropriation had been completed there was no question of these two appellants taking part, in the words of section 22, in dealing with the goods 'in the course of the stealing.'

R v Sainthouse
[1980] Crim LR 506
Court of Appeal

The appellant was present while another man stole from the boot of an unattended car a box full of tools, a can of petrol and a brief-case. The appellant, who was admittedly dishonest, sold the box and tools, forced open the brief-case and took some part in putting the petrol from the can into the vehicle used by him and the other man. Later on the same day the appellant put the brief-case inside a suitcase stolen by the other man, which the appellant knew was to be thrown away. The appellant was arraigned at the Crown Court on two counts of theft of the property, contrary to s. 1(1) of the Theft Act 1968. He offered to plead guilty as charged. The recorder questioned the appellant when giving evidence in chief and then ruled that, on the appellant's own account in the witness box, he was guilty; the jury were directed to return verdicts of guilty, which they did. He appealed on the grounds, *inter alia*, that the recorder was wrong in ruling that the appellant could be said to have appropriated the property at a time when the property had already been appropriated by the other man and the legislature could not have intended to provide that a person might (subject to the exception in s. 22) be guilty of both stealing and handling goods by the same actions.

Held, allowing the appeal, that the legislature's intention was to be sought from the words used in the statute. There was no need to go further than s. 1(1) and s. 3(1), from which it followed that, when the actions of the handler amounted to a dishonest assumption by him of the rights of an owner with the intent permanently to deprive, the handler would also be guilty of theft. e.g. *Stapylton* v *O'Callaghan* [1973] 2 All ER 782, DC. Nothing in s. 22, apart from the words in parenthesis ('otherwise than in the course of the stealing') indicated that handling was to be treated as an offence separate and apart from theft. Difficult questions might arise as to what was or was not done 'in the course of stealing' e.g. *Pitham and Hehl* (1976) 65 Cr App R 45, but they were irrelevant, for the use of 'the' made clear that the reference was to the previous stealing, namely, the theft by the other man. The recorder was technically correct in deciding that the appellant's handling actions were capable of amounting to the dishonest appropriation necessary for establishing theft; it would have been better to have left the matter to the jury. However, he had taken too active a part in the prosecution of the case, the convictions were unsatisfactory and they had to be quashed.

R v Dolan
(1976) 62 Cr App R 36
Court of Appeal

LORD SCARMAN: A defendant may be convicted both of theft and of handling the same goods, if the evidence warrants such a conclusion. If the handling of the goods occurred only in the course of the theft, he cannot be found guilty of handling, by reason of section 22(1) of the Theft Act 1968, but if he handles the goods later than the occasion of the theft, he may be convicted both of theft and handling.

Note
It is now settled that the prosecution do not have a positive duty to prove that the handling is 'otherwise than in the course of the stealing'.

(vii)   When is the handling 'by or for the benefit of another person'?

R v Bloxham
[1982] 1 All ER 582
House of Lords

LORD BRIDGE OF HARWICH: . . . The judge ruled that the purchaser derived a benefit from the transaction, in that, although he got no title, he had the use of the car; that there was no reason to give any restricted construction to the words 'another person' in the subsection; that, accordingly, on the undisputed facts, the appellant had undertaken the disposal or realisation of the car for the benefit of another person within the meaning of section 22(1). In face of this ruling the appellant entered a plea of guilty, thereby, it may be noted, confessing both his guilty knowledge and his dishonesty in relation to the December transaction.

On appeal against conviction to the Court of Appeal, the court affirmed the trial judge's ruling and dismissed the appeal. The court certified the following point of law of general public importance as involved in their decision:

Does a bona fide purchaser for value commit an offence of dishonestly undertaking the disposal or realisation of stolen property for the benefit of another if when he sells the goods on he knows or believes them to be stolen.

The crucial words to be construed are 'undertakes . . . their . . . disposal or realisation . . . for the benefit of another person.' Considering these words first in isolation, it seems to me that, if A sells his own goods to B it is a somewhat strained use of language to describe this as a disposal or realisation of the goods for the benefit of B. True it is that

B obtains a benefit from the transaction, but it is surely more natural to say that the disposal or realisation is for A's benefit than for B's. It is the purchase, not the sale, that is for the benefit of B. It is only when A in selling as agent for a third party C that it would be entirely natural to describe the sale as a disposal or realisation for the benefit of another person.

But the words cannot, of course, be construed in isolation. They must be construed in their context, bearing in mind, as I have pointed out, that the second half of the subsection creates a single offence which can be committed in various ways. I can ignore for present purposes the concluding words 'or if he arranges to do so,' which throw no light on the point at issue. The preceding words contemplate four activities (retention, removal, disposal, realisation). The offence can be committed in relation to any one of these activities in one or other of two ways. First, the offender may himself undertake the activity *for the benefit of* another person. Secondly, the activity may be undertaken *by* another person and the offender may assist him. Of course, if the thief or an original receiver and his friend act together in, say, removing the stolen goods, the friend may be committing the offence in both ways. But this does not invalidate the analysis and if the analysis holds good, it must follow, I think, that the category of other persons contemplated by the subsection is subject to the same limitations in whichever way the offence is committed. Accordingly, a purchaser, as such, of stolen goods, cannot, in my opinion, be 'another person' within the subsection, since his act of purchase could not sensibly be described as disposal or realisation of the stolen goods *by* him. Equally, therefore, even if the sale to him could be described as a disposal or realisation for his benefit, the transaction is not, in my view, within the ambit of the subsection.

B   Mens rea

Handling requires proof of two mental elements:

(a)   dishonesty; and
(b)   knowledge or belief that the goods are stolen goods.

(i)   Dishonesty

An intention to return the goods to the true owner or to hand them over to the police would prevent an offence being committed, even if the goods had been received in the knowledge that they were stolen. The determination of the defendant's honesty will be a matter for the jury, applying the test in *Ghosh* (see above, Chapter 11).

(ii)   Knowledge or belief that the goods are stolen goods

To determine whether or not the defendant knew or believed the goods were stolen a subjective test is applied. The fact that any reasonable man would have known that the goods were stolen goods is only evidence to show the likelihood that the defendant himself believed that they were stolen. See *Stagg* [1978] Crim LR 227. Belief, however, is not to be equated with suspicion.

R v *Reader*
(1978) 66 Cr App R 33
Court of Appeal

WALLER LJ: . . . We are clearly of opinion that to have in mind that it is more likely that they are stolen than that they are not, which is the test which the judge told the jury to apply, is not sufficient to comply with the terms of the section. To believe that the goods are probably stolen is not to believe that the goods are stolen, and in our view this was a misdirection by the learned judge and one which was not a misdirection which was in favour of the appellant but which was against him. The jury were being told to accept a lower state of guilty mind than the section actually requires.

Our attention was drawn to two cases, *Grainge* (1973) 59 Cr App R 3; [1974] 1 WLR 619, and *Griffiths* (1974) 60 Cr App R 14, where two other directions about suspicion were considered by this Court. In the case of *Grainge* (*supra*) in giving the judgment of the Court, Eveleigh J pointed out that where there are simple words it is undesirable for the judge to try to explain what those words mean, and we entirely agree with that. If the learned judge had left the word 'belief' entirely alone and left the jury to decide what is belief, that is something which everybody is concerned with almost every day of their lives and they would have been able to come to a proper conclusion without any explanation being given. In his mistaken attempt to give an explanation he erred. He erred in a sense in two ways, not only by putting the degree of belief wrong, but also in confusing the jury in our view by adding balance of probabilities into the concept which they had to be satisfied about. Accordingly there was in our view a material misdirection in this case.

R v Belleni
[1980] Crim LR 437
Court of Appeal

The defendant was a partner in a firm which owned two hardware and do-it-yourself shops. One of the shops was run by a manager, but the defendant visited it regularly. He and his manager were indicted in three counts of handling stolen screws and hinges. The issue for the jury was whether the defendant knew that the goods were stolen. The trial judge, when directing the jury as to the constitutents of handling, said ' . . . a man must not turn a blind eye to things which would have told him – had he given the matter ordinary attention – that he was in fact taking possession of stolen property,' and ' . . . a man must not shut – as it were – a convenient blind eye to things which would have undoubtedly indicated to him that he ought to be on his inquiry about that property.' the defendant appealed on the ground that the judge had misdirected the jury.

Held, allowing the appeal, that knowledge or belief was the essence of the offence of handling. Suspicion was not enough, unless it amounted to belief, and that was the vice of a 'blind eye' direction. Proof that a man should have been put on inquiry was not proof that he knew or believed the goods to have been stolen. If a jury were satisfied that an accused man's eyes were blind, they would have to go on to consider whether this blindness resulted from the fact that he already knew or believed that the goods were stolen, or merely from the fact that he was gullible, stupid or inattentive. In the present case the jury had been misdirected, and the conviction must be quashed.

R v Hall
(1985) 81 Cr App R 260
Court of Appeal

BOREHAM J: . . . Mr Owen's second submission . . . is that the learned judge did not make clear to the jury what state of mind had to be proved if they were to convict of this offence, namely that the defendant either knew or believed that the goods were stolen. In particular, he contends that no clear distinction was drawn between belief and suspicion. He has reminded us, if reminder was necessary, that this has been a recurrent problem in this Court as a number of comparatively recent decisions of the Court demonstrate. With his encouragement we have concluded that the time has come for us to give some guidelines on this subject to those who have to direct juries upon it.

We think that a jury should be directed along these lines. A man may be said to know that goods are stolen when he is told by someone with first hand knowledge (someone such as the thief or the burglar) that such is the case. Belief, of course, is something short of knowledge. It may be said to be the state of mind of a person who says to himself: 'I cannot say I know for certain that these goods are stolen, but there can be no other reasonable conclusion in the light of all the circumstances, in the light of all that I have heard and seen'. Either of those two states of mind is enough to satisfy the words of the statute. The second is enough (that is, belief) even if the defendant says to himself: 'Despite all that I have seen and all that I have heard, I refuse to believe what my brain tells me is obvious.' What is not enough, of course, is mere suspicion. 'I suspect that these goods may be stolen, but it may be on the other hand that they are not.' That state of mind, of course, does not fall within the words 'knowing or believing'. As I understand it, Mr Owen accepts those propositions.

The question remains whether the learned judge has, in substance, directed the jury in those terms. He commences this part of his summing-up . . . thus:

> It is 'knowing or believing', not knowing and believing, 'knowing *or* believing'. If you were to come to the conclusion in this case that the thieves made it perfectly plain to this Defendant that they had been out stealing that night and that they told him so, that is knowing, is it not, because he has been told so by the thieves themselves, so he knows and that would be an end of the case. But, members of the jury, the law has spread the net wider in pursuit of those who are dishonest with other people's property, it is knowing or believing. You cannot shut your eyes to the obvious. You know what believing means because we all believe things every day. We look at all the circumstances and we make up our minds about something, we come to a belief about them having looked at all the circumstances of the case and we say yes, everything points in that direction and I believe that such and such is the fact. We do it all the time and, members of the jury, it means exactly the same in this charge.

In our judgment, that is an impeccable direction to the jury so far as both knowledge and belief is concerned.

Questions
1. Why does the offence require 'knowledge or belief'? Are they two different things? See J. C. Smith's commentary to *Belleni* [1980] Crim LR 437, and the preceding cases.
2. Can you articulate the point at which suspicion crosses the line into wilful blindness? When wilful blindness becomes 'knowledge or belief'?

V Criminal damage

Like theft offences, the law of criminal damage seeks to protect property interests; but whereas theft protects the owner from having his property appropriated, the present offence protects against damage to or destruction of property. The controlling statute is the Criminal Damage Act 1971. There are also aggravated forms of the offence.

In almost all the circumstances envisaged by the statute, the victim will also have a right to seek compensation in the civil courts (although, of course, the defendant may not have sufficient funds to pay). In many circumstances the loss may also be covered by insurance.

Question
What are the arguments for and against using the criminal law to protect property from damage? Are they the same as for protecting property from theft?

A   Damaging or destroying property belonging to another

The basic offence is set out in s. 1 of the Criminal Damage Act 1971:

Criminal Damage Act 1971

1.—(1) A person who without lawful excuse destroys or damages any property belonging to another intending to destroy or damage any such property or being reckless as to whether any such property would be destroyed or damaged shall be guilty of an offence.

. . .

(8) An offence committed under this section by destroying or damaging property by fire shall be charged as arson.

Note
The maximum punishment for a violation of s. 1(1) following a trial on indictment is 10 years' imprisonment (s. 4(2)). Where the offence is committed by fire it will be charged as arson and the maximum sentence is then life imprisonment (s. 1(3) and s. 4(1)).

(i)   Actus reus
Three main problems arise:

    (a)   What is damage?
    (b)   What is property?
    (c)   When can property be regarded as belonging to another?

(a) *Damage.* Whether property is damaged is a question of fact. What constitutes damage is not defined in the Act, but it appears to involve a reduction in the value or usefulness of the property.

Cox v Riley
(1986) 83 Cr App R 54
Queen's Bench Division

STEPHEN BROWN LJ: This is an appeal by way of case stated from the decision of the justices for the petty sessional division of Tamworth in the county of Stafford on April 1, 1985. On that day the defendant was charged on 'an information which alleged that on July 30, 1984 at Tamworth without lawful excuse he damaged the plastic circuit card of a G.S.C. computerised saw to the value of £620, belonging to High-Tech Profiles Ltd., intending to damage such property or being reckless as to whether such property would be damaged, contrary to section 1(1) of the Criminal Damage Act, 1971.

The justices in the case state that they found the following facts: (i) the defendant was employed by Hi-Tech Profiles Limited to work on a computerised saw owned by that company; (ii) that the computerised saw relied for its operation on a printed circuit card being inserted into it, containing programs which enabled the saw to be operated so that it could cut window frame profiles of different designs; (iii) that the printed circuit card was of no use to the company unless it contained programs which enabled it to cause the saw to operate as (ii) above; (iv) that on July 30, 1984 the defendant blanked the computerised saw of all its 16 programs thereby erasing the said programs from the printed circuit card by operating the program cancellation facility, contained within the computerised saw, once for each individual program removed; (v) that the defendant's action rendered the computerised saw inoperable, save for limited manual operation, which would cause production to be slowed dramatically.

The damage alleged was the removing of the program and really, it seems to me, the only possible argument which Mr Orme could put forward is that there was no damage within the meaning of the Act.

The question of damage has been considered by the Court of Appeal, Criminal Division, on November 29, 1984 in the unreported case of *Henderson & Battley*. The Court was presided over by Lawton CJ and he was sitting with Cantley J and Sir John Thompson. Cantley J gave the judgment of the Court.

In that case the facts were different, but it is relevant on the meaning of damage. In that case the charge was one of damaging a development land site, intending to damage that property or being reckless as to whether it would be damaged. The facts concerned a development site in the Isle of Dogs which had been cleared for development. It was flat except for a pile of crushed concrete which was kept there intentionally so that it could be used eventually in the laying of temporary roads whilst the development was carried on.

On the occasion in question 30 lorry loads of soil and rubble and mud were tipped on to the site. The appellants in that case, pretending to act with authority, had been operating the site, as Cantley J said, impudently as a public tip and charging their customers for the rubbish which was tipped. There was a submission before the trial judge which was repeated before the Court of Appeal that what they had done could not be said to have damaged the land, bearing in mind that this was a site cleared for building development. The argument was that the land was not damaged because the land beneath the piles of rubbish which had been tipped upon it was in the same condition as it was before the rubbish was tipped upon it. It was argued that there must be a distinction between the cost of putting something right and actual damage.

Cantley J said in the course of his judgment at p. 3B of the transcript:

There is of course such a distinction, but if as here there is evidence that the owner of the land reasonably found it necessary to spend about £2,000 to remove the results of the appellants' operations it is not irrelevant to the question of whether this land, as a building site, was damaged. Ultimately whether damage was done to this land was a question of fact and degree for the jury. Damage can be of various kinds. In the *Concise Oxford Dictionary* 'damage' is defined as 'injury impairing value or usefulness'. That is a definition which would fit in very well with doing something to a cleared building site which at any rate for the time being impairs its usefulness as such. In addition, as it necessitates work and the expenditure of a large sum of money to restore it to its former state, it reduces its present value as a building site. This land was a perfectly good building site which did not need £2,000 spending on it in order to sell or use it as such until the appellants began their operations.

Cantley J continued:

It was held as long ago as 1865 in the case of *Fisher* (LR 1 CCR 7) that an obstruction temporarily rendering a machine useless for the purpose for which it was intended to be used can be damage. In that case the facts were briefly these. A disgruntled employee who had been employed to operate an agricultural steam-engine had parted from his employer and it had seemed to him to be a good idea to put the steam-engine out of action. He screwed it up fairly tightly and he put a piece of stick up the water feed, and did other things of that kind. It is not necessary to enumerate them all: it is sufficient if I say that it took two hours, but no more, and no materials, to restore the machine to proper working order.

Some 'ancestor' of counsel in that case said Cantley J

argued that in all the cases decided on the statute charging his client with malicious damage a certain portion of the machinery had been removed, and some absolute damage had been done to prevent the machine from working, and that there must be some 'lesion', as he put it, to the machine. Pigott B said there was damage because labour was required to reinstate the machine; not money, be it noted, but just two hours labour. Delivering a very short judgment of the Court for Crown Cases Reserved Pollock CB said: 'We are all of opinion that the conviction is good. It is like the case of spiking a gun, where there is no actual damage done to the gun, although it is rendered useless.'

It seems to me that the principle as explained by Cantley J applies in full measure to the present case. Undoubtedly, as in the old case of *Fisher (supra)*, the defendant in this instance for some reason, perhaps a grudge, wished to put out of action, albeit temporarily, the computerised saw, and he was able to do that by operating the computer blanking mechanism in order to erase from the printed circuit card the relevant programs. That made it necessary for time and labour and money to be expended in order to replace the relevant programs on the printed circuit card.

Note
The misconduct at issue in *Cox* v *Riley* would now probably be covered by the Computer Misuse Act 1990.

Question
Is there a '*de minimis*' principle (*de minimis non curat lex*) in respect of damage? Compare the following two cases:

R v *A*
[1978] Crim LR 689
Kent Crown Court

A was convicted by the Brentford Juvenile Court of an offence of criminal damage and remitted to Folkestone Juvenile Court for sentence. He appealed against conviction. He was one of a number of football supporters who were being escorted to an 'away' football ground 'crocodile fashion' by several police officers. The evidence given for the prosecution was that a police constable walking beside the 'crocodile' saw the appellant spit once at the back of a uniformed police sergeant. The police constable saw spittle land upon the sergeant's raincoat which was already covered with similar spittle, and arrested A. The sergeant continued on duty unaware of what had happened. When later informed of the state of his raincoat, he attempted to remove the spittle with a paper tissue, so as to present a less embarrassing spectacle.

On his return to the police station, the sergeant heard of the arrest of the appellant for the offence of criminal damage to his coat and so no further attempts were made to clean the raincoat. At the hearing, the raincoat was produced and a faint mark could be seen upon it, in the general vicinity of where the constable said he saw the spittle land. The prosecution contended that the raincoat required dry-cleaning, and must, therefore, have been 'damaged'.

It was contended on behalf of A that there was no case to answer because the prosecution had failed to prove any damage. The court was referred to a definition of 'damage' as 'rendering imperfect or inoperative.'

Held, allowing the appeal, that when interpreting the word 'damage,' the court must consider the use of an ordinary English word. Spitting at a garment could be an act capable of causing damage. However, one must consider the specific garment which has been allegedly damaged. If someone spat upon a satin wedding dress, for example, any attempt to remove the spittle might in itself leave a mark or stain. The court would find no difficulty in saying that an article had been rendered 'imperfect' if, after a reasonable attempt at cleaning it, a stain remained. An article might also have been rendered 'inoperative' if, as a result of what happened, it had been taken to dry cleaners.

However, in the present case, no attempt had been made, even with soap and water, to clean the rainccoat, which was a service raincoat designed to resist the elements. Consequently, there was no likelihood that if wiped with a damp cloth, the first obvious remedy, there would be any trace or mark remaining on the raincoat requiring further cleaning. Furthermore, the raincoat was not rendered 'inoperative' at the time; if it was 'inoperative,' it was solely on account of being kept as an exhibit.

Thus, in the view of the court, nothing occurred which could properly be described as damage. An offence of assault might well have been appropriate but this was not a point which the court had to decide.

Hardman and Others v The Chief Constable of Avon and Somerset Constabulary
[1986] Crim LR 330

The appellants were convicted by the Justices of causing criminal damage to a pavement. They appealed.

They were members of the Campaign for Nuclear Disarmament. On 6 August, 1985 (which was the fortieth anniversary of the Hiroshima bombing) they painted human silhouettes on an asphalt pavement to represent vaporised human remains. The 'paint' was a fat free unstable whitewash, which was soluble in water. It was specially mixed in the expectation that rainwater would wash away the markings. The evidence suggested that this was correct and that rainwater and pedestrian traffic would *eventually* eradicate the markings. However, the Local Authority had acted before this happened and a 'Graffiti Squad' was employed to clean the pavement using high pressure water jets. It was contended by the appellants that following *'A' (a Juvenile)* v *The Queen* (1978) Crim LR 689 there was no 'damage' within the meaning of s. 1 of the Criminal Damage Act 1971.

Held: Notwithstanding the fact that the markings could be washed away there had nonetheless been damage, which had caused expense and inconvenience to the Local Authority. An unduly narrow definition of damage was not appropriate. The approach of Walters J in *Samuels* v *Stubbs*, 4 SASR 200 was approved when he said at p. 203:

> It seems to me that it is difficult to lay down any very general and, at the same time, precise and absolute rule as to what constitutes 'damage'. One must be guided in a great degree by the circumstances of each case, the nature of the article, and the mode in which it is affected or treated. Moreover, the meaning of the word 'damage' must as I have already said, be controlled by its context. The word may be used in the sense of 'mischief done to property.'. . .

Notes and questions

1.   Are *Hardman* and *R* v *A* reconcilable? How much damage must be done to give rise to a charge of criminal damage? Is it critical whether the damage requires the expenditure of money to repair?

2.   Damage to a machine can be caused by dismantling it, even if the individual components are not themselves damaged. However, if damage by dismantling is alleged it must be charged as damage to the machine and not to the individual parts. In *Morphitis* v *Salmon* [1990] Crim LR 48, the defendant dismantled a barrier across the road. He was charged with damage to the bar component of the barrier and acquitted. If he had been charged with damage to the barrier as a whole he could have been convicted. The court also made the point that a scratch on the bar of the barrier would not have constituted sufficient damage for a conviction as it could not have impaired its value or usefulness as scaffolding components get scratched in the normal course of events.

3.   Would a charge of battery have been successful in *A (a Juvenile)*?

4.   The s. 1(1) offence speaks in terms of either damage to or destruction of property. Is the reference to destruction of property otiose? Can one destroy property without damaging it? Does the destruction of another's property constitute theft?

(b)   *Property*.

Criminal Damage Act 1971

10.—(1)   In this Act 'property' means property of a tangible nature, whether real or personal, including money and—

(a)   including wild creatures which have been tamed or are ordinarily kept in captivity, and any other wild creatures or their carcases if, but only if, they have been reduced into possession which has not been lost or abandoned or are in the course of being reduced into possession; but

(b)   not including mushrooms growing wild on any land or flowers, fruit or foliage of a plant growing wild on any land.

For the purposes of this subsection 'mushrooms' includes any fungus and 'plant' includes any shrub or tree.

Question
What are the differences between this definition of property and that contained in s. 4 of the Theft Act 1968? Why are the definitions different?

(c)   *Belonging to another.*

Criminal Damage Act 1971

10.—(2)   Property shall be treated for the purposes of this act as belonging to any person—
  (a)   having the custody or control of it;
  (b)   having in it any proprietary right or interest (not being an equitable interest arising only from an agreement to transfer or grant an interest); or
  (c)   having a charge on it.
  (3)   Where property is subject to a trust, the persons to whom it belongs shall be so treated as including any person having a right to enforce the trust.
  (4)   Property of a corporation sole shall be so treated as belonging to the corporation notwithstanding a vacancy in the corporation.

Questions
1.   The Theft Act 1968 s. 5 uses the concepts of 'possession or control'. Is the Criminal Damage Act's term 'custody or control' clearer? See *Warner* v *MPC* [1969] 2 AC 256.
2.   Is it possible to be guilty of criminal damage to property which you own? If you lend your property to another and then destroy it, have you committed criminal damage? If you destroy your own property in order to collect the insurance money, have you committed criminal damage? Any other criminal offence?

(ii)   Mens rea
The defendant must intend or be reckless in respect of causing the damage. The requisite intent is lacking if the defendant believes the property is his own. This latter requirement overlaps to some extent with the statutory defence set out in s. 5(2).

R v *Smith (David)*
[1974] 1 QB 354
Court of Appeal

For the facts and holdings, see p. 343.

Note
Recklessness in this context means *Caldwell* recklessness (see Chapter 3). Indeed, *Caldwell* involved an interpretation of the Criminal Damage Act. What this means is that the defendant is guilty if his or her acts create an obvious risk of damage to property and (i) he or she recognises that there is some risk but nevertheless goes on to take it; or (ii) gives no thought to the possiblity of there being such a risk. The defendant is reckless even if

incapable of recognising the risk because of an incapacity (see *Elliott* v *C* [1983] 2 All ER 1005, discussed in Chapter 3). The defendant can also be convicted even if the risk of damage foreseen is slight and the defendant takes what he or she sees as adequate precautions to avoid the risk (see *Shimmen* (1986) 84 Cr App R 7).

(iii) '*Without lawful excuse*'
The Criminal Damage Act 1971, s. 1(1) contains the phrase 'without lawful excuse'. This phrase is defined in s. 5:

Criminal Damage Act 1971

5. 'Without lawful excuse'
    (1)   This section applies to any offence under section 1(1) above and any offence under section 2 or 3 above other than one involving a threat by the person charged to destroy or damage property in a way which he knows is likely to endanger the life of another or involving an intent by the person charged to use or cause or permit the use of something in his custody or under his control so to destroy or damage property.
    (2)   A person charged with an offence to which this section applies shall whether or not he would be treated for the purposes of this Act as having a lawful excuse apart from this subsection, be treated for those purposes as having a lawful excuse—
        (a)   if at the time of the act or acts alleged to constitute the offence he believed that the person or persons whom he believed to be entitled to consent to the destruction of or damage to the property in question had so consented, or would have so consented to it if he or they had known of the destruction or damage and its circumstances; or
        (b)   if he destroyed or damaged or threatened to destroy or damage the property in question or, in the cause of a charge of an offence under section 3 above, intended to use or cause or permit the use of something to destroy or damage it, in order to protect property belonging to himself or another or a right or interest in property which was or which he believed to be vested in himself or another, and at the time of the act or acts alleged to constitute the offence he believed—
        (i)   that the property, right or interest was in immediate need of protection; and
        (ii)   that the means of protection adopted or proposed to be adopted were or would be reasonable having regard to all the circumstances.
    (3)   For the purposes of this section it is immaterial whether a belief is justified or not if it is honestly held.
    (4)   For the purposes of subsection (2) above a right or interest in property includes any right or privilege in or over land, whether created by grant, licence or otherwise.
    (5)   This section shall not be construed as casting doubt on any defence recognised by law as a defence to criminal charges.

Question
What if the defendant makes a mistake about the ownership of property because she is drunk?

Jaggard v *Dickinson*
[1980] 3 All ER 716
Court of Appeal

For the facts and holdings, see p. 341.

Question
Drunkenness is not usually a defence to a charge where the *mens rea* is *Caldwell* recklessness. Why should it afford a defence under s. 5(2)? Is *Jaggard* v *Dickinson* consistent with *DPP* v *Majewski* (Chapter 8)?

If the belief in permission to damage the property is honest, the reason for the action is not relevant, even if fraud is involved.

R v *Denton*
[1982] 1 All ER 65
Court of Appeal

LORD LANE CJ: . . . The facts of the case were somewhat unusual. There is no dispute that on 3 January 1980 the defendant set light to some machinery in the cotton mill. The machinery was very badly damaged, and as a result of that conflagration damage was also done, to a much lesser degree it is true, to the building itself. The total damage to stock and building was said to be some £40,000.

On Monday, 17 March 1980 the defendant presented himself at the police station and told the police that he had in fact started that fire. He described how he had done it, and he then made a statement under caution, in which he gave his reason for having started the fire: that it was for the benefit of the business, because the business was in difficulties, and, although he was going to get no direct benefit from it himself, he thought he would be doing a good turn to the financial status of the company if he were to set light to the premises and goods as he did. Hence the charge against him.

When it came to the trial he gave evidence that his employer, to whom we will refer to as 'T' for obvious reasons, had asked him to put the machines out of action and he had agreed to set light to it. The reason given to him by the employer for that request was because the company was in difficulties; the way that T put it was: 'There is nothing like a good fire for improving the financial circumstances of a business.'

. . . The fact that somebody may have had a dishonest intent which in the end he was going to carry out, namely to claim from the insurance company, cannot turn what was not originally a crime into a crime. There is no unlawfulness under the 1971 Act in burning a house. It does not become unlawful because there may be an inchoate attempt to commit fraud contained in it; that is to say it does not become a crime under the 1971 Act, whatever may be the situation outside of the Act.

Consequently it is apparent to us that the judge, in his ruling in this respect, was wrong. Indeed it seems to us, if it is necessary to go as far as this, that it was probably unnecessary for the defendant to invoke s. 5 of the 1971 Act at all, because he probably had a lawful excuse without it, in that T was lawfully entitled to burn the premises down. The defendant believed it. He believed that he was acting under the directions of T and that on its own, it seems to us, may well have provided him with a lawful excuse without having resort to s. 5.

Notes and questions
1.   Of what offence, if any, could Denton be convicted? His employer?
2.   Is there an inconsistency in the 'subjective' approach taken in *Denton* and the 'objective' approach taken in respect to *mens rea* (see *Caldwell*, Chapter 3)?
3.   Under s. 5(2) the question of whether or not a particular act was done in order to protect property is answered by applying an objective test. See *Hunt*

(1978) 66 Cr App R 105; *Hill* [1989] Crim LR 136. Is this inconsistent with *Denton*?

B   *Destroying or damaging property with intent to endanger life*

Criminal Damage Act 1971

1.—(2) A person who without lawful excuse destroys or damages any property, whether belonging to himself or another—

(a) intending to destroy or damage any property or being reckless as to whether any property would be destroyed or damaged; and

(b) intending by the destruction or damage to endanger the life of another or being reckless as to whether the life of another would be thereby endangered; shall be guilty of an offence.

(3) An offence committed under this section by destroying or damaging property by fire shall be charged as arson.

Note

The maximum punishment for this aggravated offence is life imprisonment (s. 4(1)). In many cases the defendant may also be subject to a charge of attempted murder. However, while the criminal damage offence requires proof of damage to property, it is wider than attempted murder because it is sufficient that the defendant is reckless as to whether life is endangered. Attempted murder will require proof of an attempt to kill.

(i)   Actus reus

The terms 'damage', 'destroy' and 'property' are defined as for s. 1(1), above. However, here there is no need to prove that the property belonged to another. Why this difference? Is it because the gist of the offence is against persons rather than against property?

(ii)   Mens rea

The defendant must:

(a)   intend or be reckless as to damaging or destroying property; and
(b)   intend or be reckless that by that damage will endanger life.

R v *Steer*
[1987] 2 All ER 833
House of Lords

The defendant went to the house of his former business partner, against whom he had a grudge, and fired several shots at the house with an automatic rifle. No injuries were caused to the partner or his wife inside the house and there was no suggestions that any of the shots had been aimed at either of them. The defendant was charged with and convicted of, *inter alia*, damaging property being reckless whether the life of another would be endangered thereby, contrary to s. 1(2) of the Criminal Damage Act 1971. He appealed, contending that s. 1(2) only applied if property was damaged and the damage in turn caused danger to life, whereas any danger to the defendant's partner and his wife had been directly caused by the bullets fired by the defendant and not by the damaged property. The Crown contended that 'intending by the destruction or damage' in s. 1(2)(b) referred to the act which caused the destruction of or damage to property was the cause of the danger to life. The Court of Appeal allowed the defendant's appeal and quashed the conviction, holding that a person could only be convicted under s. 1(2) of recklessly endangering the life of another by damaging or destroying property if it was proved that the danger to life resulted from the destruction of or damage to property. The Crown appealed to the House of Lords.

Held: For a person to be guilty of the offence under s. 1(2) of the 1971 Act of destroying or damaging any property with intent to endanger the life of another by the destruction or damage or being reckless whether the life of another would be thereby endangered the prosecution had to prove that the danger to life resulted from the destruction of or damage to the property and it was not sufficient for the prosecution to prove that the danger to life resulted from the act which caused the destruction or damage. It followed therefore that the defendant was not guilty of the offence charged and the appeal would accordingly be dismissed . . .

Note
The fact that lives are not endangered is not relevant if the requisite intention can be proved:

R v Dudley
[1989] Crim LR 57
Court of Appeal

D who had a grievance against the J family, consumed drink and drugs, went to their house and, using an accelerant, threw a fire bomb at the house, causing a high sheet of flame outside the glass door. The fire was extinguished by the J family and only trivial damage was caused. He was charged with arson under s. 1(1) and (2) of the Criminal Damage Act 1971; he pleaded guilty to simple arson and a trial proceeded on the counts laid under s. 1(2). At the close of the prosecution case D's counsel submitted that there was no case to answer because the jury could not properly find that the actual damage caused was intended to endanger life or was likely to do so, and he relied on *R v Steer* [1988] AC 111. The trial judge rejected the submission and D thereupon changed his plea to guilty to the count of arson being reckless as whether life would be endangered. He appealed against conviction, submitting that the judge's ruling was wrong in law.

Held, the appeal would be dismissed. The words 'destruction or damage' in s. 1(2)(b) of the Act (endangering life) referred back to destruction or damage intended, or as to which there was recklessness, in s. 1(2)(a) (damaging property). The words did not refer to the destruction or damage actually caused . . .

R v Sangha
[1988] 2 All ER 385
Court of Appeal

During a visit to squatters who occupied a council-owned flat the appellant set fire to a mattress. Later that afternoon the appellant returned to the flat and set fire to two armchairs in it, with the result that the premises were burnt out. The appellant was charged with, *inter alia*, arson in that he damaged the flat by fire, being reckless whether the life of another would be thereby endangered, contrary to s. 1(2)(b) of the Criminal Damage Act 1971. At the time the fire was started there was no one in the flat and because of its construction there was no danger of the fire spreading to adjoining properties. At his trial the appellant submitted that there was no case to answer because if when starting the fire he had known that no one was in the flat or if in fact there was no one there his act could not be said to have created a risk of danger to the life of another and he could not have been reckless whether life was endangered. The judge rejected that submission and the appellant was convicted. He appealed to the Court of Appeal.

TUCKER J: ... In our judgment, when consideration is given whether an act of setting fire to something creates an obvious and serious risk of damaging property and thereby endangering the life of another, the test to be applied is this: is it proved that an ordinary prudent bystander would have perceived an obvious risk that property would be damaged and that life would thereby be endangered? The ordinary prudent bystander is not deemed to be invested with expert knowledge relating to the construction of the property, nor to have the benefit of hindsight. The time at which his perception is material is the time when the fire is started.

Section 1(2) of the 1971 Act uses the word 'would' in the context of recklessness whether property would be destroyed or damaged, and whether the life of another would be thereby endangered. We interpret this word 'would' as going to the expectations of the normal prudent bystander.

Applying this test to the facts of the case before us, it is clear that in setting fire to these armchairs as the jury found the appellant did, he created a risk which was obvious and serious that property would be damaged and that the life of another would thereby be endangered. The fact that there were special features here which prevented that risk from materialising is irrelevant.

Question
How satisfactory is the 'ordinary prudent bystander' test? What if the defendant has less knowledge than the ordinary prudent bystander? More knowledge?

Note
Without lawful excuse does not have the same meaning in s. 1(2) as in s. 1(1). Section 5 specifically states that it does not apply to s. 1(2). Lawful excuse in the context of s. 1(2) is therefore confined to situations where the defendant acts in self-defence, defence of another, or in prevention of crime, or to apprehend an offender.

INDEX